LEST WE FORGET

THE PARISH OF
CANISBAY

*A miscellany of memories written by parishioners
and friends so that future generations can know
what made Canisbay a very special place.*

Edited by Anne L. Houston

Sold in aid of Canisbay Parish Church Fabric Fund.

Typeset by the Book Division of North of Scotland Newspapers,
42 Union Street, Wick, Caithness, Scotland.

Printed by Highland News Group Ltd,
Henderson Road, Inverness, Scotland.

Published by the Congregational Board of Canisbay Parish Church.

ISBN 0 9529167 0 3

Front Cover – Designed by Rognvald Brown, Swartigill, John O'Groats,
using a map of the parish from John Thomson's Atlas of Scotland 1822.

Back Cover – The ferthie "Emulate" in the Firth drawn by Alex Ross,
White Broo, Canisbay.

Cover – Graphics and compilation – Thierry Oquidam,
27 rue de Maubeuge, Paris.

CONTENTS

The articles are set more or less in the areas listed – most span boundaries, many span oceans. They have "landed" with the ebb and flow. . . "Counting out" and skipping rhymes, weather lore and sayings which are going out of use are included as page enders.

These and other line drawings by Janice Stark (née Rosie).
For the church she used a photograph (c.1880) which was too faded to reproduce.

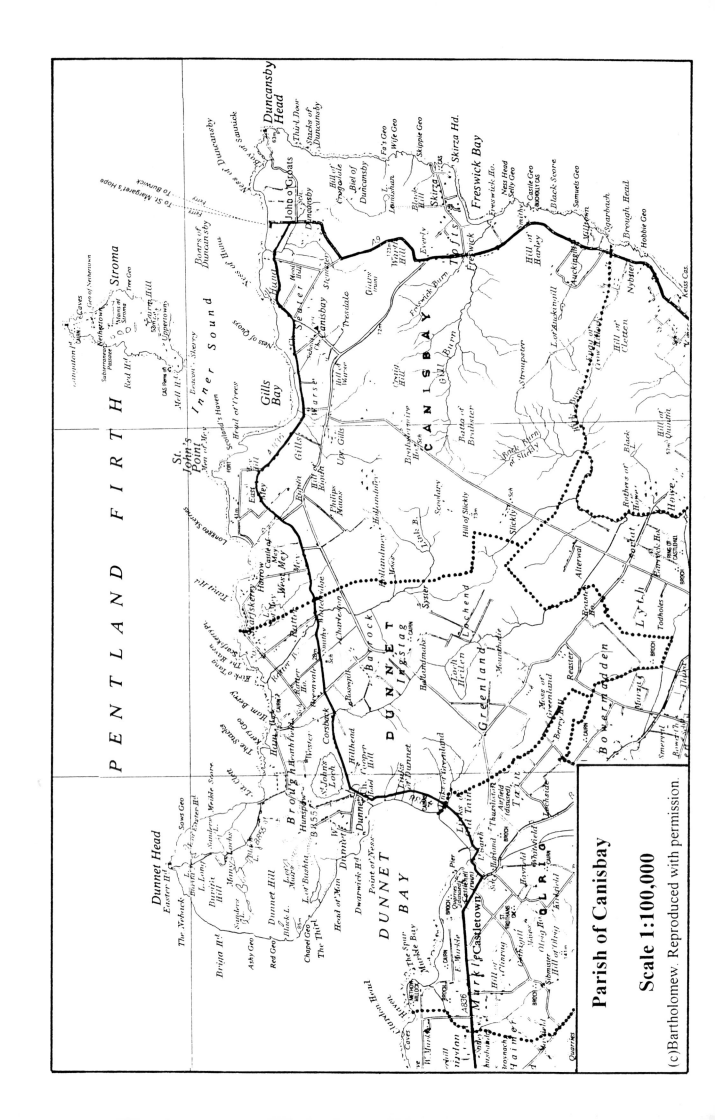

Parish of Canisbay

Scale 1:100,000

(c)Bartholomew. Reproduced with permission.

ROYAL MESSAGE

Queen Elizabeth, the Queen Mother, has sent her good wishes in the following terms,
"Queen Elizabeth sends you her best wishes for the success of your history,
'Canisbay, Lest We Forget'.

*Queen Elizabeth, the
Queen Mother and the
Rev. Alex Robertson leaving
Canisbay Parish Church
1994.*

*Photo courtesy, J. McDonald,
Shore Lane, Wick*

FOREWORD

What constitutes the beauty and character of any area? It cannot simply lie in the beauty of the coast and hinterland alone, nor in the characteristics of the people alone, but surely in a combination of them both.

Such we see in this book which is devoted to indicating the strength of character of those of this particular area; their faith, their own brand of humour, their concern for tradition, their interests, their wealth of wisdom and wit and a readiness to adapt where it is necessary.

It is hoped that as you read this book that you will be able to catch a glimpse of the people who made and still make this area what it was and still is, and discover something of what made and still makes them "tick".

Deep appreciation is expressed to those who have made any kind of contribution to this publication, by way of story and photograph and to the painstaking work of its editor.

May the reading of this book prove both a source of knowledge and give a feeling of identification with this part of Caithness.

Rev. Alex Robertson, Canisbay Manse, Canisbay.

v

ACKNOWLEDGEMENTS

Appreciative thanks to all the photographers, both professional and amateur. The credits are given to the photographers if they are known, otherwise to the lenders. All the school photos appear courtesy of H. Tempest Ltd, St Ives, Cornwall and they deserve extraordinary thanks for this fine record. [George Tempest took the earliest John O'Groat School photo, his son Horace followed and now almost one hundred years on we are glad that Mrs Shearer, Head Teacher, Canisbay is holding with tradition and getting Tempests to take group photographs.]

Warm thanks to George J. Green for letting us use the 1901 Freswick Estate Map which belonged to his grandfather George Green, The Breck, John O'Groats and is now on loan to the Wick Library.

The publication of this book has been made possible in part by support from:

Grampian Television P.L.C.
Bank of Scotland
Clydesdale Bank of Scotland
Caithness Glass
Calor Gas Scotland
Royal Bank of Scotland
Scottish Co-op
Scottish Hydro Electric
S. & J.D. Robertson Group

J.O'G. Saddle

J.O'G. Nightcap

INTRODUCTION

It is so often said, "things should be written down" and that is just what has been done to make this book. It is essentially about people, for the people and by the people so that future generations with Canisbay roots can look back and learn about the richness of our heritage and traditions.

The individual authors have written about life, work, events, people and places which they want known and remembered. We are fortunate to have previously unpublished first hand accounts, by Donald Banks and Simon Bremner, of the way things were in days gone by. The number and variety of contributions, including the finest of old photographs, make this volume unique and shows clearly the long inherited love and pride of our own folk in our own parish handed down through the generations.

Words cannot express the privilege and pleasure it has been to put together this priceless collection. I have been overwhelmed by the enthusiastic support and help from old and new friends and want to thank most warmly and sincerely all who have contributed to and assisted with the publication of this book.

Special thanks are due to Laurence for correcting my writings, Bet for unstinting help and accuracy of research, and for the constant encouragement and support of my brother Magnus who has been a tower of strength and the moving power behind this book.

All of us have done our very best and request you gently scan. . . . . . have we made a "Kirk or a Mill" of it?

Anne L. Houston, St Magnus, John O'Groats.

LIFE AND WORK IN THE PARISH

PEOPLE OF THE PARISH

Yowlies of Auckengill, Tammy Fuds of Freswick, Mutton Eaters of John O'Groats, Warrie Bugs of Huna, Persians of Canisbay, Green Runners of Gills, Hoggs of Brabster, Shortcoats of Slickly, Baggy Airses of Mey and Codling Heids of Stroma!

Well, yes!! – but who exactly are or were these odd sounding folk?

We can begin by having a look at some very old records – those of Baptisms and Marriages in Canisbay Parish for the years 1652 - 1660. The surname occurring most frequently is Mowat (46 entries) then Groat (42), Lyall (35), Dunnet (29), Rosie (29), Bain (26), McBeath (21), Harrold (18) and Steven (17). (All these names appear with various spelling forms.) Sinclairs are there too, but only twelve of them and most are the "Landed Gentry".

Next let us jump forward a couple of centuries. Compulsory registration of births, deaths and marriages commenced in Scotland in 1855 and if we study the births recorded in our Parish between then and 1864 we find Dunnet(t)s in the lead now, appearing 77 times, well ahead of Mowats with 44 entries. Then come Mansons, Beggs, Smiths, Kennedys, Bremners, Mathiesons and Banks. I think it was about the early 19th century that someone wrote "there is a Dunnet in every house in Huna and Seater". Interestingly, the name Groat only turns up three times in this sample.

Lastly – to the present-day score. A careful perusal of the 1991 Register of Electors of Caithness North-East Division (of which Canisbay Parish comprises a large part) reveals the following names: – Dunnets and Dunnetts 24, Shearers 22, Cormacks and Banks 20 each, and Sinclairs 16. They are closely followed by Greens, Mansons, Mowats, Rosies and Stevens – and there are no Groats at all!

Of course one cannot really compare these different sources of information but they do indicate some significant trends. The Dunnet(t)s have always been numerous in this Parish, and the Mowats too, though they haven't done quite so well in the present-day stakes! Sinclairs, once the "lairds", are more plentiful now than in the past, though still not in the forefront. However the name "Groat", so well known to tourists who visit us, has completely disappeared from this corner of Caithness.

Some of the 17th Century names seem strange until we realise that they are really old ways of spelling ones we know well, such as Liell for Lyall, Moresone (Morrison), Rossay (Rosie) and Steivin (Steven) to mention but a few. But what about "Youthheid" and "Mendtheplay"? It has been suggested that they could be offspring of "tourists" of those days – namely Cromwell's soldiers!

Another interesting line of thought might point to the origin of frequently occurring names – for instance some, such as Dunnet, Ham, Swannay (Swona) and Wares are also place-names. Research in that direction, however, has really been covered most comprehensively by the late John Mowat in his "Place Names of Canisbay".

Addresses in the Canisbay Baptismal Marriage records starting 1652 and in the Registers of Births, Deaths and Marriages as late as the 1920s only state the area. (One wonders how the post in Huna coped?)

The spelling given C.1660 –

Okingill	Stromah	Slicklie
Friswick	Carmucks	Skullery
Skirserie	Cannasbey	Gills
Dungasbey	Warrs	Holomey
Huna	Braibster	Mey

A Naturalised "Mutton Eater"

CANISBAY PARISH

Far to the North it lies,
Washed by the sea,
Spread under spacious skies,
Our parish Canisbay.

Peatland and fertile field,
Flagstone dykes for lea,
Havens with boat and creel,
Our parish Canisbay.

Dusk merges with the dawn,
O'er South Ronaldsay,
Winds are still, and seas are calm,
Our parish Canisbay.

Sands where no footprints lie,
Empty and free,
Far horizons meet the eye,
Our parish Canisbay.

Surging seas of spume and spray,
Tides of treachery,
Stern cliffs stand amid the fray,
Our parish Canisbay.

Searching winds and blinding rain,
Storm force gales there be,
Here I am, and here remain,
Our parish Canisbay.

Ancestry and heritage,
Home and history,
Tales of old from book and page,
Our parish Canisbay.

Warm hearts and loyal friends,
Kindred, fidelity,
Open doors, and hands extend,
Our parish Canisbay.

Elsie Cowe, The Ha, John O'Groats.

Canisbay War Memorial
Unveiled by Lord Horne 14th September 1921

Photo: John Dunnet, Seater.
John R. Forbes first right and James Russell third right at memorial. (John and Alex Ross built the wall around the memorial.)

Grateful remembrance of the men from Canisbay Parish who at the call of King and Country left all that was dear to them, endured hardness, faced danger, and finally passed out of the sight of men by the path of duty and self sacrifice giving up their own lives that others might live in freedom.

Canisbay Roll of Honour 1914-1919

Seaforth Highlanders
Lieut. Robert M. Stalker, RFC, Auckengill.
Corpl. John Mackay, M.M., Croix de Guerre, John O'Groats.
Corpl. David Miller.
L. Corpl. David Banks, John O'Groats.
Pte. Alexander Baikie, East Canisbay.
Pte. George Banks, Mey.
Pte. Alexander Campbell, John O'Groats.
Pte. George Dunnet, Mill of Mey.
Pte. Alexander Innes, Gills.
Pte. William J. L. Manson, John O'Groats.
Pte. John Sinclair, Stroma.
Pte. Joseph Matheson, John O'Groats.
Pte. John G. Matheson, John O'Groats.

Canadians
Sergt. Donald Henderson, Freswick.
Corpl. George B. Manson, Auckengill.
Pte. James Dunnet, Mey.
Pte. David Sinclair, Canisbay.

Gordon Highlanders
Pte. John W. Banks, Upper Gills.
Pte. Charles Innes, Freswick.

Scottish Rifles
Pte. Charles Dunnet, Brabster.

Royal Inniskillen Fusiliers
Pte. Andrew Henderson, Freswick.

Royal Naval Reserve
Seaman Gunner William Bain, John O'Groats.
Seaman Gunner David K. Dunnet, Mill of Mey.
Seaman Gunner Alexander G. Manson, John O'Groats.
Leading Seaman George Ross, John O'Groats.
Seaman William Sinclair, Stroma.
Seaman Walter Steven, John O'Groats.
Seaman David Manson, Stroma.

Cameron Highlanders
Sgt. George Geddes, Mill of Mey.

Lovat Scouts
L. Corpl. John Bain, Slickly.

Army Service Corps
Driver James McLeod, Gills.

Australians
Signlr. Robert Campbell, Canisbay.

A. and S.M.
Charles McPhee.

Canisbay Roll of Honour 1939-1945

Seaforth Highlanders
Pte. John G.C. Gunn, Seater.
Pte. James Harris, Mill of Mey.
Pte. Lachlan S. Sinclair, Mey.

Royal Engineers
Sapper James Forrester, Canisbay.
Sapper Alexander Gunn, Brabster.

Royal Regiment of Artillery
Bdr. David Spence, Canisbay.

Merchant Navy
Capt. Walter J. Steven, East Mey.
Fst R. Off. Andrew Miller, Malligoe.
Sec. Off. Cecil T. Dundas, Stroma.
Seaman Thomas Dunnett, Mill of Mey.

Auckengill Roll of Honour 1914-1919

In undying memory of our warriors.

*Greater love hath no man than this, that a man
lay down his life for his friends (St. John XV.13).*

James McKenzie, Mid Auckengill.
Henry McKenzie, Mid Auckengill.
Robert Stalker, School House.
Malcolm Manson, Nybster.
Maurice Dunnet, Auckengill.
George Manson, Nybster.
David Nicolson, Roadside.
Andrew MacKay, Quarries Nybster.
George Begg, Milton Auckengill.
Peter Miller, North Keiss.

Second World War

William Miller, Nybster.
John Matheson, Auckengill.
*(John Nicolson used a six-inch nail to carve out
the names.)*

Stroma Roll of Honour 1914-1919

*To the Glory of God and in memory of the men of this
island who gave their lives in the first Great War
1914-18.*

Alex Campbell, Seaforths.
James Falconer, Seaforths.
William McAdie, Seaforths.
John Sinclair, Seaforths.
David Manson, R.N.R.
William Sinclair, R.N.R.

And the Second Great War 1939 - 1945

Cecil Dundas, M.N.
Donald Smith, M.N.
Malcolm Robertson, R.M.
David Sinclair, R.N.F.R.
Nicol Smith, R.N.
William Smith, Paratrooper.

Dedication of War Memorial – Stroma

Photo courtesy Northern Studios, Wick.
*From left:– David Steven, Donald Mellor, Peter Simpson, Rev. Dungavel, James Sinclair, William MacDonald, Donald
Mackay, Sandy Webster, Reg Hatton, Bob Lyall, Charles Tait, Andrew Moir, Sandy Grant.*

The committee of the Canisbay Branch of the Royal British Legion Scotland decided to build a memorial in Stroma to the fallen of World Wars I and II. The memorial is built close to the church on the foundations of the old Co-op shop. The cross on the memorial was made by Peter Simpson, a native of Stroma who served with the Boom Defence in Scapa and with the Royal Navy in World War I and who was a member of Glasgow Police during World War II (third from left).

THE FISHING

Down the ages and at least for a century or more the north-east corner of Caithness has had a strong association with the fishing industry.

The fish caught in this area were usually lined such as cod or caught in creels such as lobsters or crabs, but "The Fishing" was really the herring fishing with its centres first at Staxigoe and later at Wick itself. It was to Wick then, that the crofters who owned boats, set sail each May to begin the summer fishing which lasted until the middle of August. Those who did not share or own a boat or nets, would hire themselves out for the fishing, sometimes on local boats, but often aboard boats whose skippers were mainly Wickers (Weekers).

Like all forms of fishing the herring catch varied greatly from year to year. Before the First World War when the herring industry was at its peak, a hired man who came home with £50 in his pocket for the 14 or so weeks he had been away would consider himself lucky indeed and this ensured that the winter could be faced with a smile for this was money to buy food and above all money to pay the rent. Another important investment made by father or brother coming home from the "Fishing" would be the bringing of a half-barrel, or if the family was large, a whole barrel of herring ready cured and ready for the pot. This was the staple diet of the crofting families in the parish, and along with mealy tatties and a drink of milk here was a dinner worth the eating. However, like all good things the shine does wear off after a while, and when the pig was killed towards the festive season, the skirl of the frying pan brought a welcome relief, as well as a change.

Now who would turn up their nose at fresh pork, cut in fine thick slices with a gulley and fried to a nicety on the embers of a good peat fire? But there were restrictions, because at these times people were not selfish – neighbours and relatives had to be treated to a share – and much of the animal had to be turned into ham, for winter lasts long, and fresh pork does not.

I have allowed myself to drift somewhat away from the fishing, and to continue I should point out that the herring boat was a "Fifie" perhaps 50 to 60 ft in length and 15 or 16 ft abeam, and carried an enormous fore sail which was its main means of propulsion. These boats did not lie all winter in Wick Harbour, because that meant dues, in other words, more money, which usually being in short supply had to be looked after. Consequently the boats were brought round to the pier at John O'Groats where Allan's (Mey) steam Charlie (engine) would be waiting to haul them up, one after the other onto the sandy beach – there was indeed a fine stretch of beautiful white sand in those days. Though I was not around, I have been told that the event was indeed an occasion. This would happen in late August or early September and very often the harvest in those days would still be several weeks away, and so the man of the house would now turn his attentions to his second love, namely the hand line.

It is in this type of fishing that the yawl was used, usually of the Stroma build, although some of the crofters here preferred the Orkney Yawl, because it was lighter in build and somewhat easier to handle on the beach – in those days boats had to be hauled and launched daily. It should be noted that we live on the shores of the Pentland Firth where the tide runs by at quite a rate, and fishing for cod with a hand line requires a situation where a boat is reasonably still so that the line can be kept reasonably plumb. Not so easy when the tide is rushing along, therefore hand lining in the Firth had to be plied with the neap tide, only in fair weather, although a breeze for sailing to and fro was certainly welcome. Without the wind the oars came into use and that was jolly hard work, for the fishing ground could be anywhere from Dunnet Head in the west to off Freswick Bay in the south. It should be noted too, that even with the neap tide, time was at a premium, because the tide only remains slack or quiet for about one to two hours just before the change from each ebb to flow and vice versa. It was on the passage to and from the hand line that the yawl was really put to the test. The full rig of the yawl was Jib, Foresail and Mainsail in that order from forward to aft, and the sight of the boats sailing home laden with well grown, firm and full cod was an occasion for great expectation. A tide of cod was really the catch, and it was interesting to watch a responsible and experienced crew member share out the catch – it was essential to have fair shares and as the lines of cod were allocated to each crewman, this was done by one man standing blind while the sharer called out whose was whose. If the tide of fish (catch) was too great for the back, then carts were called for and here grand-father, now too old to fish, would appear with the horse and cart to carry home the welcome cargo. From there on in, mother came into play, for it was her task to gut and split the cod and get ready (except for the ones eaten fresh) for the salting and later the drying.

This process required huge quantities of clean fresh water, and it was the task of the younger members of the family to carry the water from the well in pails or buckets. Sometimes if the tide was late in the day it would be the small hours of the morning before the entire catch was stored away in tubs or barrels, well salted and now carefully covered. Several days later the fish would reappear (if the day was dry and better still if it was sunny) placed carefully on slate roofs or on stretched netting to begin the drying process. This was repeated day after day until the fish were ready to be hung up in the kitchen roof to be finished – after which they were stowed away in a dry cupboard ready for use. The fish in a properly dried state would remain edible and acceptable for months.

Finally the shell fish industry, which was of little account when cod and herring were the front runners, is today the only type of fishing left around our particular coast. Up to the end of the

Second World War shellfishing, mainly lobsters and crabs, was regarded as seasonal and was therefore pursued by the crofters to augment the croft income. Crofter-fishermen took their creels ashore when the harvest drew near and they remained ashore until the following spring or early summer, and in this way the stocks of shellfish were conserved, but since the end of the war bigger boats have replaced the traditional yawl and the fishing was prosecuted on an all year round basis. The nearer and more accessible fishing grounds were first to suffer and as the years go by shellfishermen are finding the going getting harder and harder and the fishing grounds are getting into deeper and deeper water. Also, the huge numbers of creels employed to catch the lobsters and crabs are continually increasing as more and more gear is required to reap the same return.

Years ago the creel (lobster pot) was hand made by the crofter during the dark evenings of winter – a replacement for the mending of herring nets. Nowadays, the demand for creels is so great that small factories have sprung up specialising in creel design and manufacture. There is such a factory in Wick, established and run by two brothers from John O'Groats, and has turned out to be a real success story.

Now the marketing of the shellfish has also changed greatly over the years. Firstly, and up to the First World War the only shellfish worth marketing from this area was the lobster and lobsters travelled all the way south to Billingsgate Fish Market in London. So little was the return on crabs that it was uneconomical to send them, in other words the return on crabs would not pay the carriage. Lobsters happen to be easy creatures to keep alive, and once their toes are tied or bound with an elastic band which prevents them crushing each other, they will live on in a floating box or keep creel for as long as required. Consequently lobsters were forwarded to Billingsgate weekly by passenger train which was the speediest way of getting them to market in days gone by.

After the First World War, crabs however came more to the fore and were in greater demand in the restaurants and hotels of the south, so crabs were also sent to Billingsgate from then on, and a combination of lobster and crab going regularly to market was an enormous help to the income of the crofter fisherman.

In recent years there has come to the fore a vigorous market for the velvet crab in the cities of Europe, especially Spain, and as technology has provided the means of transporting shellfish in salt water tanks placed in huge trucks, marketing of shellfish has undergone a revolution. Instead of packing lobsters and crabs in boxes and barrels which were despatched by rail, the truck now collects the shellfish (lobsters, crabs and velvets) at the pier head, then heads for the next little harbour. When full, that is when the tanks are full, the truck heads for a Channel port, is ferried across the Channel, and soon after our shellfish from the far north of Scotland is being enjoyed by a Spanish family out for a seafood meal in Vigo or Madrid or elsewhere in Spain.

It should be noted that until quite recently, the velvet crab was regarded by creelmen as perhaps nuisance number one in the creels. They destroyed the bait in the creel, and were sometimes so numerous that it was common practice to open the door of the creel and simply dump the entire contents back into the sea. Times do change, and one wonders which other frequenters of the creel, not saleable at the moment, will next become a delicacy for someone, somewhere. The velvet crab like the brown crab is now an important element in the income from the creels, and goes some way to compensate for the scarcity of lobsters and brown crabs.

Finally, before leaving the subject of shellfish, one should remember that whelks (wilks locally) were picked from the rocks, boiled and the contents removed with a pin, needle or small pick and eaten greedily by the local people. Even limpets, which were often used for bait on the large hooks of the cod line, were also sometimes boiled and eaten, but were not so popular as the wilk.

And in all, we were in the past, great devourers of fish of one kind or another and it is rather sad that today there is so little of it about – and the different ways of cooking fish to give a little variety in the diet, is going to be lost for all time.

It would not be fair, however, not to make mentions of the cudding and the sellag. As a matter of fact it should be the other way round because the sellag grows into a cudding (coal fish) much used for baiting creels, but also eaten fresh. My favourite way of enjoying a cudding was absolutely fresh, gutted and thoroughly cleaned, rolled in salted oatmeal and roasted on the brander. The gaps between the bars of the brander allowed surplus oils to run away into the fire, and though frying was also popular for a cudding it was less popular than roasting with many people.

The nearest piece of cooking apparatus to a brander is, of course, the grill and with the high cost of cod and haddock – well – who knows grilled cudding might soon be a worthwhile feed. The sellag on the other hand was sometimes boiled fresh, but it was more common to dry these little fishes on a spit or rod – the rod going through the gills and head and hung out like the cod in dry weather until they were quite hard, then boiled and eaten with fat and tatties. The fat was necessary to prevent choking when trying to swallow dried sellag and mealy tatties.

Ben Green, Roadside, John O'Groats.

Leeped Bait – *For Line Fishing*

Scald limpets with boiling water and leave for a minute or two. Pour out of pail and pick up the bait and leave the shells.

George Gunn, The Bungalow, John O'Groats.

Filling a Herring Basket

Herring shovelled in simultaneously from each side. The herrings then leant up against each other and it took less to fill the basket. Woe betide the man who knocked the basket and the herrings flattened out!

Robbie Dundas, Swona View, Huna.

GREAT-GRANDAD

Now listen folks you must all agree
That times are not what they used to be
The price of food has risen sare
And the tax man's oot for his annual share
So – we'll turn a page of history
And I'll get ye all tae come wi' me
In fancy's flight I'll take ye a'
Back tae the days of your Great Grand Pa.

Great Grandad in the days gaen by
Cut his crop with a hame made scye
He never knew hoo a back cood nag
That hid been wracked wi' liftan slag
He never heard o' a "Power Drive"
A David Broon or a "thirty five"
He grew enough for his humble needs
He soed no wild white clover seeds.

Great Grandad hed a crewsy lamp
He niver heard o' a watt or amp
He lichted up an he thanked 'e Lord
He hed no rows wi' 'e Hydro Board,
Wae broose and tatties, kale and pork
He aye kept fit for his daily work
He bocht no beef fae 'e butcher's van
So Great Grandad was a wealthy man.

Great Grandad hed his annual trip
To 'e Loch of Mey for his usual dip
Hid left him clean and hid left him cool
He saw nae need for a sweeming pool

His woo came straight fae the auld grey yow
An he lit his pipe wi' a heather tow
An 'e only "Power Plug" he knew
Wis 'e cork in a bottle o' good Home Brew.

When Great Grandad went down wi' flu
He did what a prudent man should do
He went tae bed and he put his life
In the skilful hands o' his loving wife
Wi' a doze o' salts and a toddy drink
She brought him back fae the very brink
Great Grandad knew he wad be cured
Because *his* life was *not* insured.

Great Grandad was an active soul
Never wance did he draw the dole
An' his pocket book wis always full
He lost no cash on a football pool
Wi' hob-nail boots he took the road
He never studied the Highway Code
For he had no car wi' a rattlin noise
To need repairs fae the Garage Boys.

So why! oh why! should you feel dismayed
When your TV set or yir phone goes dead
An yer sewer chocks and yir tractor knocks
An' 'e Hydro Board has given ye shocks
There's a quarry hol ootside iss haal
An' its beeg enough to hoad them all
So dump them there an' enjoy a glad
An happy life, like yer Great Grandad.

George Corrigall, Ballarat, Harray.
Thanks to his sister Mrs Mowat, Scorne, Birsay and to Peter Davidson, Skaill, Sandwick.

Ibbie Ronald's Great-Grandad

Photo: Margaret Cormack, Kirkstyle.
First left: George Grant (Grandfather of Margaret) with neighbours cutting a fine crop of hay.

CROFTING

The other half of the way of life in north east Caithness was of course, the croft. It was perhaps possible to scrape a living from the combination of the two, provided the family circle was not too large. But truth to tell the family was often quite large and all sorts of ways of making a pound had to be explored to add to the meagre income. I shall, a little later, go into the other ways, but first of all let us have a look at the croft. The size and fertility or productivity of a croft depended on where it was situated. Near the hillside the soil was usually mossy and thin and produced little. Nearer the sea and along the banks of a burn the soil was deeper and heavier and much more productive.

One very important crop on the croft was "tatties" for if the tatties were a failure then more bread was required to satisfy the pangs of hunger of a growing son or daughter.

One of the features of the croft was the absolute necessity of keeping one and very often a pair of horses, for the land work and carting peat etc. Now working horses, and especially the big Clydesdale breed (popular for land and carting work), had huge frames and consequently required a lot of food. Because of this the number of cows and sheep on the crofts had to be kept at a level which was much below the numbers that are now kept with the crofts being cultivated (if cultivated at all) by tractor power.

Before the First World War many of the crofts were worked on a five year rotation. New grass was kept for hay, an essential crop especially for feeding the horses, with the residue going to feed stirks which went to the mart in spring.

The grasses before the 1930s were poor, and grass seed was mostly of the rye variety so that after a second year the land would be ploughed up and sown with oats. Then a second crop of oats would follow after which the root crops (turnips and potatoes) would follow that.

Root crops are excellent for cleaning the land (freeing it of weeds) and then the ground after the root crops (clean land) would be sown out to oats or bere (similar to barley) along with a fresh grass crop producing the new grass again after five years. However, in the late 20s there came on the scene the famous wild white clover which literally transformed grazing on the crofts. Grass could now easily be retained for three years then ploughed up and sown out to oats. The increase in the cereal crop was equally conspicuous after the three year period and as a consequence the stock on the croft could be somewhat increased adding a little to the general income.

The crofts too lacked adequate fencing and much of the land, especially marginal land, lacked drainage. In the late 20s the Board of Agriculture provided a grant large enough to allow crofters to purchase tiles for draining, and for those who were willing to do the laborious work themselves (i.e. the digging by hand) the land was greatly improved and produced more. A high percentage of crofters did take advantage of this grant and it was noticeable that as a result of the drainage there was much less surface water lying in the fields in winter.

Fencing was a different story and no grants for this purpose came available until after the creation of the Crofters Commission in the middle 50s, so it was common practice to tether cattle and even sheep on the pasture of the crofts. Tethering meant a length of rope and an iron or wooden stop to allow the animal a limited freedom. This practice was essential also to ration the pasture, and the stop (or backie) was driven into the ground, very often with a stone or hammer when the dry season came. Animals on tether had to be shifted two or three times a day and this in itself involved a great deal of strenuous work. It was also a time when cows in milk were milked by hand. At one time cows were milked three times a day, literally at morning, noon and night. The young calves were fed the milk from a pail, and calves were not allowed out on tether until they had reached a certain age and size. Young calves behaved very badly on tether to begin with, and it was regarded as a bit of a game to introduce a calf to a tether. A rope halter was normally used to attach the cow or calf to the rope, but the short horn cattle (usually red in the skin) were often fastened by a running loop around their horns (this was known as a "horn tow").

The short horn cows were then crossed with an Aberdeen-Angus bull and the result was a very satisfactory beef stirk which was very popular with the butchers.

Going back to the milking. As already mentioned hand milking was the order of the day and this task usually fell to the women – mother or daughter or both would do the milking. Only rarely would you see a man involved in what was regarded strictly as a woman's job. A man found to be doing the milking was very likely to be a widower or a bachelor living with an aged mother. About half the milk produced was fed to the calves from a pail (no suckling in those days) and the remainder was poured into large tin dishes and left on the shelves of the milk house or large cupboard until the cream was well and truly on the top.

The cream was then skimmed off with a saucer or skimmer, put into a jar, and when the cream was sufficient in quantity, it was put into the churn and made into butter. The residue left when the butter formed was butter milk, and the butter milk was a popular drink on a warm day in summer.

Butter was served up either fresh from the churn which lasted only a day or so, or it was salted for later, and where the housewife could manage it, she would store some of it away in a large earthenware jar and place it in a cool niche which was a feature of many a croft house. The niche would be deliberately designed when the house was built, usually in the cool passage-way leading to the front door.

This was the fridge of former days. Also as I recall there were two types of churns. The revolving churn with a handle on the side or the up and down churn with a wooden cross on the end of a pole – the cross had holes in it to allow the butter to come through while the formation took place. The local joiner or a handyman crofter were the suppliers of the churns.

The work on the croft varied from season to season but you may be sure it was neverending. In the winter the time was spent on feeding cattle, horses and sheep. The cattle and horses were housed in the winter and they had to be regularly fed and watered – mucked as well and always bedded down for the night. The feed for the cattle was usually oat straw, turnips and, if the cereal was plentiful, a little bruised oats or bere. This went on three times a day, and while the cattle were usually watered from buckets in their stalls, the horses were taken out to the nearby pond for this purpose, as it was reckoned that horses required exercise as well. Great care was taken to look after the health of the horses, for yoked to a cart or a plough they were the hauliers of the time. Frankly, the loss of a healthy horse created a financial crisis that few crofters could face without much anxiety. In those days the sheep were the cinderella animals of the croft. The history of sheep rearing is somewhat different to that of cattle and horses. Before and up to a few years after the turn of the century there was a breed of sheep locally known as the "Rockies" – they were community owned and in one big herd they grazed along the cliff tops and faces from the boundary fence of the now common grazing to Skirza Head.

They were little nimble sheep and horned. At shearing and at the time for taking away the males for mutton (females remained for breeding), representatives from every family in the district gathered and herded the flock down the winding path at Shinscliff. Along the boulder strewn beach they were driven south to the "Bocht" – a goe half way between Shinscliff and Fasgoe and the furthest point possible when the tide is well flowed up.

Here the business of shearing and sharing took place and each family claimed a share to be taken home and salted down for winter food. I have been told that the "Rockies" were themselves on the way out before being replaced with other breeds, because of in-breeding and various diseases common to sheep in general.

However, about the time the "Rocky" venture was coming to an end, the Duncansby Head grazing became available to the crofters and from then on the rearing of sheep began to improve. The first breed to be tried out on the new found grazing was the Border Leicester not crossed. In this pure bred state they proved to be difficult to rear, but soon the practice of crossing the Border Leicester with the North Country Cheviot was adopted and remains to this day a most satisfactory pairing. Sheep rearing, though popular before World War II became doubly so after the Second World War, and though in recent years half-bred lambs have taken a serious knock price-wise, yet the crofters are for the present continuing with it in the hope that things will improve. Look across the district today and a glance at the fields will make you realise the importance of sheep in the croft economy.

I have mentioned earlier some of the winter chores on the croft and as winter changed to spring so did the work – the feeding and mucking of the cattle remained until the grass came, but the horses now came into their own. Freshly shod with their hooves neatly trimmed at the Sutherland's Smiddy at Huna, the horses stepped out to the long haul of the ploughing. Day after day the ploughing proceeded with monotonous regularity until a good part of the croft now looked black instead of a dingy green, and as April approached with longer days and sometimes drier weather, seed time had arrived. The bags of oats, specially dressed at Allan's Steam Mill, would be laid out intermittently for sowing – the grass field which would have been ploughed up first would now receive the first seed and the neat little cradle V shaped between the furrows would receive the oat seed. The horses would now get a different drag – the harrows would appear on the ploughed turf to fill in the V shapes and flatten the top and so cover the seed. At a later date the stone roller would appear to crush up the lumps missed by the harrows, and so leave the field flat and tidy for the next crop to thrive in.

The roller was usually a one horse yoke whereas the plough and harrows required a pair. This process was repeated with the stubble which had produced a crop of oats the year before, but the stubble field which had already produced two crops of oats was now the one dressed and prepared for the "tatties" and neeps. Again the horses would have a change of yoke and to break up the furrows a three or five pawed implement known as a grubber came into use. In fact, if the weather had been very wet and lots of weeds abounded, it would be necessary to plough this field a second time. A second ploughing was always very helpful to bring the weeds to the surface and also to break up large lumps of soil and clay. It was important to get rid of weeds, as weeds grow up quickly and choke the turnip seed and even spoil the growth of the "tatties". When I first remember, the neeps and tatties involved a great deal of work, for once the land was sufficiently well dressed so that it would heap up into drills, then drilling commenced and whereas a drill plough was sometimes used, not every crofter could afford such an extra and most crofters just used an ordinary plough for drilling. Once the drilling was done then the horses were back in the carts, and at the horse midden where the muck had collected all winter _ the carts were loaded with horse dung and down the drills the cart was taken while the horseman was aboard the cart with a "greep" in hand, distributing the dung at regular intervals into the drill and keeping the horse moving on at the same time – this was known as "sparting" dung. The little heaps in the drills were then spread out by someone else, along the drill, and a bed of dung was laid. Then the seed potatoes, which had already been picked and sometimes cut, were laid on the dung bed about 14ins apart. Then on went a quantity of artificial manure such as bone meal. Then it was back to the horses and the plough – to close the drills as we used to say. That is, the plough went down the middle of the heaped drill pushing one half over onto the planted tatties thus making a fresh drill. This task had to be completed before the end of the day, and the poor horseman would sometimes finally "lowse" at 10 p.m. or later.

The tatties planted, it was off to the hill, and before the First World War the man of the house would probably be off to the "fishing". The hill, though hard work, was sometimes quite enjoyable if the weather was good, especially if a squad (a number of people) were on the job. There would be banter and half-yokings (a small picnic of thermos flask tea or even a glass of lemonade if funds could face it – pork sandwiches, flour bread and home made rhubarb jam and pancakes to boot.) There were several processes involved in peat production. The garden spade was used to take off the turf (tirvins locally) then a shiel or tusker spade was used to take out the moss. After cutting came the spreading (scaling locally) and then it was back to the land, for the scaled out peats would need three weeks of reasonably dry weather before setting up into heaps (roos locally).

Back to the land it was, for the neeps had to be put down (planted). The tattie planting would have been completed by the 10th of May – a week or 10 days in the peats and then the neeps. Getting the area of land allocated for neeps ready would take some time, but the first neeps were usually sown about term, 28th May. The swedes were first followed by the yellow neeps – a poorer quality product but easier to grow. The neeps were sown into drills just like that made for the tatties and there were machines (horse drawn – one type of machine sowed a single drill, more sophisticated machines would sow two at a time). The neeps were dunged and manured just like the tatties so one can imagine the labour involved.

A day or two respite perhaps and it was back to the hill for the setting up of the peats and when that was completed the first sown neeps would be ready for thinning (singling). Out came the hoes and the thinning had begun. Now, I must confess that of all the chores in the croft, I disliked, even hated, thinning neeps above all. To me it was totally soul destroying and as a boy I was quite lucky to be able to escape sometimes, for I was one of the characters who sold strings of homemade beads (i.e. to frock beads interspersed with "groatie buckies") to the tourists who by the 1930s were coming in considerable numbers in the now popular motor car.

This sideline gave me great joy and satisfaction for a number of reasons. Along with postcards, an energetic young salesman could gross on a good day up to £2 which really was fantastic in the 1930s. The summer holidays would now be approaching and they couldn't come too soon so that we young lads could get to the business of selling our wares to the tourists. A good deal of money could be made and saved by this means during the summer, and when the summer holidays were coming to an end, mother would expect you to hand over your summer hoarding, so that she might go to Wick to buy new clothes for those who had to return to school.

The summer was, however, just great – no shortage of pocket money to purchase apple juice, ice cream, pies, sweets and above all cigarettes. The long summer vacation came to an end all too soon – the money earned in summer was gone, and back to the screeching slate pencil took a little time to get used to. Recover we did, and autumn or the back end was soon with us. The oats and bere had grown their full height and were now turning to the golden shade of harvest. More hard work lay ahead for the corn had to be cut, hand bound from the Back Delivery – so called because it landed enough corn at each cut from the back to make up a sheaf. There was a binder or two about in my youth but the main cutting implements on the croft were the scythe and the back delivery – a machine requiring two horses, one on each side of a pole to drag it along. The more sophisticated binder usually had a three-horse yoke. The binder had the great labour saving of binding the sheaves mechanically. I should tell you that for the harvest of 1936, father finally managed to purchase from W. and A. Geddes, Wick, an new Ideal Deering No.3 – a Canadian model and as fine a going machine as one would wish for. It was indeed, a huge step forward. However, whether hand bound or machine bound the sheaves still required to be set up into stooks to allow them to dry out in readiness for stacking. There's an art for you now – building or stacking corn into the screws was not everyone's cup of tea, for if the heart of the screw or stack was not properly built then the screw would draw water in the winter, and a green growth would appear.

It was not funny to have screws of corn in this state and it was much sneered at by the connoisseurs of corn stacking. The carting in of the corn and the stacking of it, was not the final chore to be faced, for another and an important one lay around the corner, namely the lifting and pitting of the tatties. There were few, if any, mechanical tattie diggers in my youth, although they appeared on the scene later. The method used in my young days was to run the plough through the middle of the tattie drill and some of the tatties were exposed, although a great deal of groping with hands was needed to seek out the precious tatties. The picked tatties were placed in the waiting cart and taken home at the end of the day to be pitted. The load of tatties would be emptied and then manoeuvred into a neat pit shape covered by divids cut from the moor, the heather going next to the tatties to keep the frost out. A layer of earth would be placed on top of the divid at a later date just to be sure that frost would not penetrate. By the time this chore was completed, the month of December would be close and the long nights of winter with us again.

Some way back I confess to having lost my way somewhat, as I have omitted to mention the hay-making, another important croft chore.

Cutting of the hay took place in early July after the neep thinning and the carting home of peats were completed. An important feature of the hay was most certainly the weather. A dry spell for the hay was something every crofter dreamed of and the reason was simply labour. There were few high speed power-driven mowers around in the 30s and the hay was cut by the same back delivery machine as that used for cutting oats and bere, except that the revolving flies and the back rake were removed leaving only the bar through which the triangular bladed knife went to and fro to cut down the long grass. The crank movement of the cutting knives in those days was comparatively slow, thus much sticking during cutting could not be avoided. A thick lump of close growing grass would often jam the knife and cause problems for horses and man.

However, after much cutting, sticking and shunting, the rich green grass would then be lying in long strips exposed to sun and wind for several days. Then the turning process would follow and this process was undertaken by using a fork. Some used the handle end of the fork for this process and if young and fit, a person could fairly slip up and down the strips of grass turning the mown grass up to wind and sun. However, very often the rain would intervene and the turning process would have to be tackled all over again, and again, and again as required by weather conditions. The hay finally would be ready for colan (building into small hand made stacks called coles), and this involved gathering the hay into much larger strips. The implement used for gathering the hay strips was known as a tilter made from a 12 to 15ft plank with long teeth bolted to it to hold quantities of hay. The teeth naturally had to be close to the ground to collect the hay cleanly. Again it was horse drawn and the yoke required long ropes attached to the end of the plank of the tilter.

Long ropes, because as its name suggests, the implement when fully loaded was tilted forward and the long yoke was required so that the implement when tilted forwards to empty, did not hit the horse's heels. Colan completed with the coles tightly secured with a simmon twisted from the hay, stretched over the top of the cole and tied at the other side, the coles or little stacks remained on the field until it was considered the hay was finally cured. Then with a rope or chain carefully placed as close as possible to the bottom of cole, and again yoked to a horse, the coles would be dragged quite complete to the stacking and where they would in turn be built into a "gilt" or screws of hay for winter fodder. The gilt was a rectangular stack and so called because it was shaped like the body of a young sow and like the sow or gilt, rounded on the top so that water would run off. Incidentally, this particular type of stack was known on the other side of the Moray Firth as a sow of hay rather than a gilt of hay.

Finally – a short word about life on a croft in bygone days. It was, indeed, a hard life but a full one. The folk were friendly and kindly towards each other. Pastimes were confined to some sort of lighter work of one kind or another. Men mended nets or worked the covers for the creels – we younger ones made our necklaces to sell to the tourists in the summer and meanwhile the women knitted or mended or even made their own clothes. Frankly I would not recommend that the clock should be put back to the times just described, but the passing of one or two aspects of life in those days are to be greatly regretted or even deplored. People were very interdependent in those days, and consequently, thought and regard for your neighbour and relative were of a much higher standard than that practised today. The passing, too, of the community pursuits such as the debating society and the fireside sessions when yarns and stories were swapped galore, is certainly a great miss in rural life – and who knows, when the little "box" has finally had its day, perhaps those who are around for a while in the 21st century, may yet revive some of the more pleasant features of life on the croft in former times.

Ben Green, Roadside, John O'Groats.

A PLANT COT

In January we always made a plant cot for cabbage plants.

The cot was usually eight feet on the square. We selected a dry piece of heathery hill ground at the edge of our arable. We "delled" off the "tirvings" and made them into a fail or divot dyke two feet high. We then dug over the earthy moss and worked this to a fine tilth. The recognised way of sowing was to take mouthfuls of seed and blow it broadcast over the plot. They were covered with a coating of farmyard manure and then we put maybe eight inches of straw on top to keep off the frost. The cot was then covered with wire netting to protect the plants from rabbits and hares.

The straw was removed in March to let the sun in and the cabbage plants were set in the kailyard in early April. We always found that a plant cot in the hill gave better, healthier and hardier plants, than if they were grown on the cultivated ground.

We always kept a few of the best kail stocks and let them go to seed. In October when the seed was ripe, the stock was struck on a canvas sheet and the seed was kept in a jar until January.

We broke out a new cot annually and the following year it grew green the same as the steeth of the lime kiln and this was always increasing the arable land.

David Dunnett, Hillhead, John O'Groats.

HARVEST

(Two Voices)

Oh harvest is a merry time, a cheery time of year;
The birring of the binder makes sweet music in my
ear,
The happy voices echo throughout the golden days;
Oh harvest is a merry month – so everybody says.

Sheives aal weet wi' moarnin' dew,
Sheives 'at so'k ye through an' through
Sheives 'at fill o' thirsels they near cut yer han's in
half,
Trauchled sheives aal heids an' tails,
Lowse sheives fan 'e knotter fails;
Oh Hervast is a merry time if 'at's fit mak's ye
laugh!

Oh harvest is a merry time, a time of pure delight;
The fields of ripened grain go down before the
reaper's might,
And on the golden stubble the sun-drenched
sheaves appear;
Oh harvest is a merry time, a cheery time of year.

Scythan' oot 'e layan' bits, Tidyan' an' tyan' bits,
Tryan' till cut id wan wey far id's flattened by 'e
win',
Stookan' in 'e pooran' rain,
Roon' an' roon' an roon' again;
Oh hervast is a merry time if 'at's fit ye caal fun.

Oh harvest is a merry time, a time of sweet
reward;
The towering loads of grain come in to fill the
waiting yard,
And day by day the fields resound with gaiety and
cheer;
Oh harvest is a merry time, a happy time of year.

Forkan' moarnan', noon, an' nicht,
Beeldan' lods wi' aal yer micht,
Slavan' lek a neeger till get through afore 'e rain,
Racked wi' pain an' weet wi' sweit,
Soartan' screws 'at's lek till heit;
Let ithers hev 'e merry time – A'm no goan' back
again!

Donald Grant, Thurso.

By kind permission of Mrs Mary Grant, "Hillcrest", Caberston Avenue, Walkerburn, Peebles.

Harvest – Duncansby Head in background 1975

Janet and Anne Houston with Ursilla Brown.

CAITHNESS TATTIES

I have no special recipe for cooking potatoes, I merely spend a lot of time steaming them, tasting them and noting down everything to do with their appearance before and after cooking, mostly out of store in February, and not simply out of interest because I make my living as a potato breeder and have done so, in one way or another, for nearly 40 years. I can think of much worse jobs for February days in Caithness and this is what I do.

I tip the samples out of the bags and something about the character of the varieties is revealed by the way they have sprouted, some strongly, some just chitting, the sprouts ranging from clustered to single, from the terminal eye only in some varieties or from several eyes in other varieties. I desprout them, wash them and look at what the powerful

17

people who buy for supermarkets call the skin finish, which should be smooth, clean and bright not scurfy or blemished.

Next I cut the tubers from nose to heel, set one half of each tuber aside and steam the other half. While they are steaming I'll look at the colour of the flesh which can range from white to yellow but is usually an intermediate creamy white or creamy yellow, and can be streaky, marbled or close textured. The cut surfaces of the uncooked tubers may turn brown, a kind of wound reaction, and the degree and distribution of this so-called enzymic browning will be closely related to the amount of after-cooking darkening. By this time the potatoes will be cooked.

I record the colour of the flesh again and whether they have remained glassy or show signs of flaking or sloughing, which is closely related to the dry matter content and will determine whether a variety is likely to be more suitable for boiling or chipping or crisping.

I taste three tubers per sample, which means masticating and spitting out, a messy business, trying to assess flavour. Finally I set the cooked halves aside to cool and record the amount and distribution of darkening the following morning. I can evaluate about two dozen samples a day before I've had enough.

Most of the samples are Caithness grown although I will also have samples of the more advanced selections from England, because cooking quality varies with soil temperature and other factors associated with latitude. Cooking quality is the most difficult character of potatoes to assess because opinions vary and it is difficult to get consistent results. I have learned to trust my first impressions. If I had to think twice about such things as general attractiveness or flavour, I would be lost because there is so little to choose between the merely passable, the good and the very good.

After 40 years, you would think I would know exactly what I am looking for, and I suppose I do, and in that case you might think I must have a favourite variety for table purposes. Actually, I haven't. Above all else I like variety.

Jack Dunnett, Clevnagreen, Freswick.

Footnote:– Dr Dunnett has gained international fame as a potato breeder and in 1989 won first prize at Ingliston with a species named "Nadine".
A.H.

A TATTIE PIT

In days past when crofters did not possess as many outbuildings as they do today, tatties were always stored in a pit. The pit being reasonably close to the house for convenience. In our own case the tattie pit was just outside the garden fence.

The first job in the making of a tattie pit was cutting a supply of heather divads. These divads were cut with a long handled spade which had a semi-circular blade curved slightly upwards in a sort of shallow dish shape.  The spade cut into the heather and a divad approximately 18"-24" long by 12" wide was lifted out. I always thought they looked like a giant slater (wood louse) on its back. Divads from a previous year were reusable or from a number of years before if you were careful with them. Our divads were stored alongside the garden fence during the summer. This had two advantages, one, it gave shelter to part of the garden and two, pieces of peat moss would fall off into the garden and mix with the garden soil.

When the tatties were planted out in the field, Sharps Express were put down in the first few rows, followed by Beauties and then Champions, our main eating tattie. The Sharps being the early tattie were rarely stored in the pit as they were generally lifted after 12 weeks, by the pailful, for use before the main tattie lifting took place. When the Sharps were all lifted, the seed were immediately sorted and boxed. The boxed Sharps were stored in the byre along a couple of rails above the heads of the cows. As the atmosphere in the byre was always warm, the seed were never damaged by frosts.

After the main tattie lifting took place, the Champions were stored at one end of the pit, followed by the Beauties, which were better to eat later. They were all set out in a long triangular shaped pile rather like a Toblerone bar. The new

side view   *end view*

divads were laid heather side inwards, side by side around the bottom. The next layer went on top slightly overlapping the previous row and so on until all the tatties had been covered. This whole process was repeated twice more, with the older divads, until the tatties were completely insulated against the elements. The end product looked something like this:

side view   *end view*

Not only did the layers of divads keep out frost and rain but also sheep looking for a tasty bite. Even if sheep did manage to move a few divads, there were always plenty more underneath to keep them out.

Whenever tatties were required, a pailful would be taken from one end of the pit. It was then over to the water barrel, where the tattie pail would be filled up with water. The tattie chapper (a wooden plunger) was always at hand and this was plunged up and down carefully in the pail of tatties to remove all the excess dirt. The dirty water was then poured off and the tatties were ready to be brought into the house for use. The smallest of tatties were put through the same process before being put in a pan, set on the stove overnight then fed to the hens in the morning.

As the tatties were being used up, the pit became smaller and the divads were set carefully along the fence for the next year's pit.

The horse dung was always used on the tattie ground as it was considered better than the dung from the byre. Unfortunately today, we have no horse dung and burnt oil from a tractor is no use at all!!

Walter Mowat, Balquholly, John O'Groats.

SWEDDIE PIT

Around about the month of May, when the "blackgrun or clean-lan shift" (the turnip field) was being cleared for ploughing, it was necessary to salvage a few turnips for domestic use during the summer months when there was little or no alternative vegetable choice in the Caithness larder of by-gone days.

Accordingly, a few barrow loads of the firmest, unblemished swedes were selected for "pitting". The preferred choice of area was a dry grassy knoll with preferably a good slope to allow rain to drain quickly away. The main requirement was good green, grassy divots which were laid one after another on edge on the ground against the mound of turnips, the builder using one hand and a leg to keep them steady and upright while the free hand endeavoured to place other turnips in such a way as to present convex symmetrical sides. Further courses of divots overlapped the lower ones like slates on a roof and a top coping of divots completed the structure. If the site had a good bed of grass, nothing further was laid between the turnips and the ground, but occasionally rashes or straw might be laid down first.

The most important instruction which was explicitly given to any novice, was that the grassy side of the divot had to go to the inside, otherwise "the sweds wid no keep". This was sound advice, because what actually happened inside the pit was, the nitrogen given off by the green vegetation of the divot grasses, prolonged the "use by date" of the swedes. The chemistry was probably not understood but the result of a good "swed" for the broth" right on into July was what counted.

In recent years, "controlled nitrogen storage" has been used on a vast commercial scale in large insulated buildings to considerably extend the shelf life of apples and other fruit and vegetables. I do not know how the modern method of preservation originated, but the sweddie pits of Caithness just prove once again that "there is nothing new under the sun".

Donald A. Young, Perth (ex-Lybster).

CORN BYKES

These were made in preparation before the threshing mill came, or when the mare was in foal, and room was needed in the barn.

Straw simmons were made (in the barn or even in the kitchen on wet days in winter) by twisting and joining on handfuls of long straightened out straw. They were rolled into balls (about two to three feet diameter) as they made them. (Bere straw was best.)

The size of the byke depended on the amount of grain to be stored. A byke five to six feet in diameter held about 10 quarters, which is 80 bushels. It was built on dry ground by driving in a circle of stabs quite close together to give a large barrel-looking appearance.

Stones were put in the stadle and covered with chaff, sids or straw. Some old bags were spread over this to prevent grain getting mixed with chaff. Straw simmons were very closely woven in and out round the stabs, pressing them down as they worked them up to the top of the wood. The corn was then filled into the byke.

To finish, the corn was piled up in the centre and then very well thatched over (the straw lying up and down to run the water off). This was tightly secured with more simmons and/or old herring net.

The corn is said to have kept better in bykes than in barns.

Magnus Houston, The Mill, John O'Groats.

Corn byke

PEATS AND HEATHER

Tirr Bank – remove top layer of heather roots about one foot deep using garden or lining spade. Cut shiel and tuskar peats and skail (spread out). Set up when firm – shiel in cones, tuskars in herring bones. Cart out to "the hard" when dry and then load up and cart home. Stack was built with

Peat spade

peats sloping out to run off the water.

Boorags or Tirvings were ideal for setting at the back and sides of fire in open hearth. (Heather side towards the fire to give a good smell!)

Dowfer – wet mossy peat used for resting fire.

Peat Neuk – three flagstones set on end with one on top to make a dry cudge for keeping the daily supply of peats. Often set opposite the door. The "bink" where the washing etc. was done was alongside.

Peat meals and also heather was used as insulation or sound proofing in houses. c.1880.

Pot scrubbers – stems of heather whipped closely with string or piece of leather.

Beesom – long heather stems whipped onto a handle.

Lum cleaner – bunches of heather tied at intervals along a rope and pulled up and down the chimney.

Heather simmons – a handful of 10" - 12" lengths of berry heather was twisted and handfuls were joined on by twisting.

"The Strowmas" (Stroma folk) used water from and kept open the Green Bowgie Well when they were working at the peats in the Crogodale Hill. The fresh green patch of grass round the spring can still be seen.

James Bremner, Victoria Villa, Canisbay.

Grandfather Mackay's Saying

Never cut the peats before the 28th May (term-day) because the oil does not rise in the moss before that, and also one might move to a new job after term-day.

Mary Sinclair, Hillside, Gills.

Footnote:– In John O'Groats the "Strowmas" cut their peats above the Breck and also in the Warth Hill. The road up past Jamie Green's, the Breck, was called the Stroma Road.

The peats were carted to the pier, the Crook o' 'e Niss or Stroma Goe at the back of the Niss, by the Groats people and emptied out. They had to be stacked if the weather turned coarse.

The lower end of the family home in the East End was built with stones which were quarried in Stroma. They were brought over as ballast, and could have been given in payment for getting their peats carted.

Sandy Manson, John O'Groats Post Office.

Peat Cutters

Photo, Mrs Bena Rosie, Hillside, John O'Groats.

Back row, left to right:– Alex Dunnet, Eastend; Frank Sutherland, The Shore; Magnus Houston, East End; Ben Laird, Quarryside; Sanny Williamson, West End; Sandy Cormack, Huna.

Front row:– Jim Baikie, Pentland View; Sinclair Rosie, Hillside; Jamie Green, Breck; Jeck Green, Roadside; James Murray, Hotel.

THE PEAT FIRE FLAME

'Twas sittin' by the fireside late
The fire fu' bricht wi' guid black peat'
There lookin' at the am'ers red'
There seemed to form a human head.

There as I gazed it bigger grew,
The eyes were dark an' broad the broo,
The chin wis square determined lek',
The lips they moved as if tae spake.

Tae say the least I wis fu' scared,
For sic a sicht was unprepared,
Ma hair lek bristles stud on end
An' shivers doon ma back did wend.

Ma mooth I opened wide tae roar
A keeked sideways at the door;
But noor a soond escaped ma lips,
An' on the chair were glued ma hips.

Nae mair could a dae but sit quate
An' stare that face richt in the grate;
Till wi' a bang richt at ma back
A turned tae see the dresser shak'.

"Noo what will happin next" a thoucht,
An' scanned ma life for ills I'd rocht;
Some things I'd dun a thoucht wis fun
Took evil shape an' blacks the grun.

A chair cam' clatterin' 'cross the flair
An ethereal form there did sit there;
Then lek the flutterin' o' a bird
A heard a thimblin' quaverin' word.

For me ye needna be sae scared
I've come tae see hoo ye hae fared,
Since a hev left this dismal place
An' entered in the land o' grace.

I've jist come fae the spirit lan'
An livin' there is inco gran';
Where gathered wi' yer lang syne freens
Ye little ken what joy that means.

By this time tae masel' I'd gaithered,
An' says yer nest ye've surely feathered;
If it's sae gran' tae live 'wa there,
For ye were fairly poor when here.

Oh man says he of coorse ye ken
A lived here in a but an' ben'
But hooses canna noo contain
The spirits o' yin great domain.

We flee aboot fae place tae place
Altho' ye canna see wir face;

Aboot puir foulks we often gaither
An' watch their antics on the tether.

Says I, a doot am fair at sea,
A thoucht a' foulks were fairly free;
So gin ye speak aboot a tether
Gae me yer story a' togither.

Oh weel says he, an' then he sighed,
Dae a no' weel mind 'fore a died,
Hoo a hid wi' the rent tae gang
That left me nocht tae stan' ma han'.

Man if ye tak' a cup o' tea,
Far less a dram, he says tae me;
Or gin ye smok' a twarthy fags
Yer taxed until yer claithed in rags.

Puir workin' fouks mak' a' the wealth,
The ither class tak's maist by stealth;
Of coorse o' them wi' see nae muckle,
The "Auld Man" tho' he'll mak' 'em knuckle.

But a' the same it grieves us sair,
That honest workin' foulks nae mair'
That oot o' plenty the'r neglected
That dividends be nae affected.

A focht masel' in the world war
Cam' hame a wreck wi' battle scar;
Then left a wife an' weans doon here
Tae struggle on wi' want tae fear.

That sort o' life it isna fair
Wi' plenty in the world tae share.
That some gang naked, hungry, sick,
An' ithers pompos bloated sleek.

Freen whan fouks leave this mortal sphere
Tae answer for their deeds doon here,
Some tae the questions canna cheep
What has ye done tae feed ma sheep?

The after life it is nae myth
Sae aye speak justice wi' yer pith'
Tae tell fouks aye tae dae the richt,
An' noor let greed their future blicht.

When tae the ballot box they go
Their cross for Socialism show;
They hev the weapon in the'r han'
As powerful's ony in the lan'.

Wi' that table gave a bang,
The chair hi'd sat on rase a' flang;
The fire by this time wis in ase
Whar first a saw ma auld freen's face.

From "The Heather Blooms at John O'Groats" – By John S. Banks, Broo.
By kind permission of Mrs Banks, Knockdry House, Wick.

You cannot set the whole world right
Nor all the people in it;
You cannot do the work of years
In just a single minute.
But keep one little corner straight
By humble patient labour;
And do the work that each hour brings
And help your next door neighbour.
Anon – from Janet Gunn.

The snowdrop tells that winter's here,
The primrose says it's spring.
The gorgeous blooms of warmer days
The summer perfumes bring.
The autumn with it's golden tints
Will beat them all together
With the purple here o'er a' the hills
The bloom upon the heather.
John S. Banks, The Broo.

"EH PEATS"

Eh time hes come tae cut eh peats,
It nearly makes me boke;
If hid wisna for eh wife eh ken,
A widna do a stroke.

A pit eh tusker on ma back,
An set off for eh hill;
And a swear next year I'll pit in oil,
I'm telling 'ee a will.

De'ee realise eh work hid is,
Riving in eh moss;
Till find words till describe hid,
Well, I'm jist at a loss.

First a cut eh divids,
An a throw 'em in eh bank';
If ever 'ee haive done hid,
Ee'l ken hids no an easy prank.

Next a sheel an' clean eh face,
Then I'm ready till begin;
We eh sweat I've lost already,
A must be getting thin.

A clap a spittal in ma han,
An' gie them a good rub;
A say till ma sell I'll cut a chain,
And nip ower till eh pub.

Billy Magee, Lower Gill, Canisbay.

ALLAN'S THRESHING OUTFIT

The Allan Brothers had the first steam engines in Caithness. William the eldest was at Milton, near Wick; Alex was in Mey and Donald at Forse, Latheron; when Alex came to Mey first he worked the meal mill as well as the threshing outfit.

It was always a great time when the mill came to the district. All "hands" in the neighbourhood were recruited as about 20 men were needed for the threshing to proceed smoothly and also of course give time for the local "crack". It was a long day for the millmen as they had to be up before 5 a.m. to get steam on the engine. This was almost impossible when they were supplied with wet foggy peats but not to be outdone, they usually made a raid on the stack and selected nice dry peats for themselves. The steam whistle would blow to summon "hands" about 7 a.m. and down or up the road they would troop with forks at the ready. By the way, John O'Groats "bere" was renowned for being the "choughest in the universe". Awns were so tough the hummlers of the mill used to "jam" and riddles wouldn't work.

As there were no proper roads in the stackyards in olden days the steam engine sometimes needed "paddles" on the iron wheels to tow the mill. The winch on the steam engine was also used when the mill got bogged down. As you can imagine, this left the stackyard completely churned up.

The steam engine had other uses too, apart from working the threshing mill. They used to drag shingle from the shore on a drag line type bucket and tip the shingle into a trailer on the brae head. Boats were often hauled by the steam engine. The winch on the engine was very powerful – in an attempt to refloat the "Linkmoor" at Scarfskerry in the 1930's, the bollards were pulled out of the steamer and the effort had to be abandoned.

In later years tractors took over from the steam, making transport easier and more economical – no more early rising in the morning, getting steam up and devouring a stack of peats. With the shortage of labour, bunchers were fitted to the mill and this made the straw more manageable.

Eventually most farms had their own mill fitted and then finally the advent of the combine put an end to the travelling threshing outfit. The last engine in Caithness was sold in 1951.

Sandy Allan, Mlanje, Heathfield, Thurso.

Footnote:– It was said that at some houses Sanny Allan advised his men to "stick to the loaf when they were told to rax in their hand and fa tae!"

(i.e. Avoid home baking when told to help themselves.)

SCREWS FOR THRESHING

'E steam-mill's in 'e district noo,
We'll get id in 'e morn;
We're needan strae for bedding,
So we'll thresh twa screws o' corn.

We'll thraw 'e necks o' e' twa white hens
They're too owld noo tae lay;
They'll mak a pot o' tasty broth,
For 'e han's on threshing day.

'E beegest poks we've sorted oot,
Weel used an' patched are they;
'E millman's charge is by the seck'
'E beeger' they are 'e less we pay.

Wi' fresh caff in 'e owld bed tick,
Rare comfort we'll hev 'e morn's nicht
We'll loup intae 'e warm box-bed,
An' lie till 'e break o' daylicht.

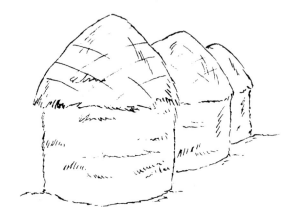

John Geddes, Highlands, Minchinhampton.

Allan's Threshing Outfit at Wester

Photo, Reta Manson, Dwarwick Place, Dunnet.
Sanny Allan on the Clayton and Shuttleworth Steam Engine driving the Robey Threshing Mill (made in Lincoln).

THE CRUISIE LAMP

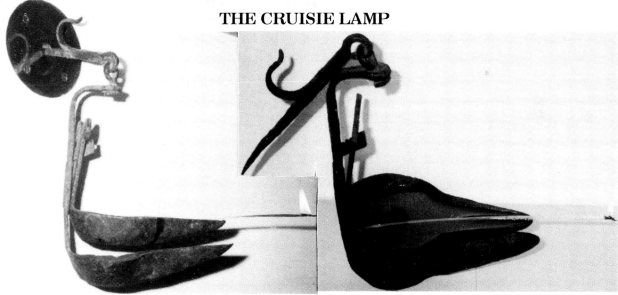

Nurse Cook was very proud of a cruisie lamp her grandfather James Smith made just before he married Janet Campbell in 1853. Paraffin lamps were in use in John O'Groats about 1850 and also tallow candles but it is thought cruisies were still in use because it didn't cost money to burn. It is certain James Smith wasn't making an heirloom although Peter Gordon, Currie, is very proud of having his great grandfather's cruisie.

The spike of the cruisie was stuck into a hole (to fit) in the facing board under the mantlepiece (high in those days) or it could be carried by the hook and hung on a nail.

Silkie (seal) oil, cod and other fish liver oils were used in coastal areas. Hen, goose or animal fats were used in inland areas and had to be heated in the cruisie until liquid. The oil was put in the top goose neb and the under one caught any drips.

Good fat rashes made the wick and were prepared by removing most of the skin by lifting small sections on a pin and stripping it up to the top. A strip of skin must be left on to give back bone to the wick, which was supported by the neb.

There was no need for the cruisie to be lit if the fire was burning brightly.

Barrie Mowat told that c.1910 she remembered the Dunnet sisters carrying a "lowan" (flaming) peat when they were visiting on a dark night. Another peat was trimmed and got ready before they went home.

I am not sure if it is the light or the smell of the peat that draws people, but Charlotte Dunnet's descendants are spread over Canada and the USA (from B.C. to Boston and Edmonton to Key West – the southernmost tip of the USA) and nearly every year some of them come back to find their roots in the East End, Duncansby.

Willie Mowatt says the rashes should be picked when the moon is growing.

Anne Houston, St Magnus.

HISTORICAL NOTES ON THE PARISH OF CANISBAY

These notes deal mainly with the early part of the 20th Century

This is an attempt to describe some of the many changes that have taken place in the Parish of Canisbay during the 20th Century.

Before the decline of the herring fishing in 1914 when war broke out between this country and Germany, many crofters went to Wick for the summer fishing. It started in mid-June and finished by the end of August. Some men had shares in boats, others owned nets. The type of boats were about 40 feet in length and called "Firthies". They had no engines and were propelled by sail. With a good fishing season they did quite well but every year was not alike. The economic situation at the turn of the century was entirely different from what it is today. People had very little money. The housewife went to the shop with a basket of eggs to pay for her groceries. There were no modern conveniences. Many houses were thatched. Though the crofters got security of tenure in the Act of 1885, the Laird still had the power to raise rents which were already high and if anyone couldn't pay promptly they could be evicted.

After much agitation a revised Act was passed in 1911 and the land court was set up. It was 1915 before the first sitting in Canisbay took place. It was held in the Parish Church, and the court could only deal with Holdings under £50 rent. Many applied to get their rents revised, some got their rents reduced by half and anyone in arrears got it cancelled.

The parish is composed mostly of crofts some larger than others and there are also a few farms. There was not much work to be had apart from agriculture. Wages were low, a married man got about £7 half yearly and a house, oatmeal, milk and potatoes. The average for casual workers was 2s 6d for a man for 10 hours per day and 1s 9d for a woman. The price of stock was low. In accordance a stirk would fetch £8 in the early twenties. At that time all farm work was done by horses, with many rearing their own. A common sight on the road was a stallion being led from farm to farm. They were fine big horses and drew a lot of attention. The change from horses to tractors was hastened by the loss of many horses with grass sickness. The exact cause of this fatal illness in horses was never satisfactorily discovered. With the modern machinery of the eighties, one man can work a farm that used to employ three to four men.

The Horse Drawn Hearse

In 1915 the Parish Council purchased a second hand, horse drawn hearse.

It was a rather heavy vehicle but had been well kept and was like new.

Before that time all deceased persons had to be carried shoulder high by those who attended the funeral. The coffin was placed on a bier. The undertaker, generally a local joiner, walked in front and about every 200 yards said "Four men".

That meant that the men carrying the coffin handed over to the four men behind, then stepped aside and fell in at the rear until their turn came round again, which could be several times if the funeral was from a distant part of the Parish.

The average cost of coffins at that time was about £5.

The first driver of the hearse was William Dunnet, East Canisbay who drove for many years. After Mr Dunnet retired, William Cormack, Huna House took over and drove for the rest of the time that the hearse was in use, which was until some time after the 1939-45 war. The charge for the use of the hearse was 15 shillings irrespective of the distance involved.

The hearse was driven at walking pace as the mourners all walked.

After mourners used cars, there were many complaints from drivers who had to drive in low gear, perhaps for miles. The use of the horse drawn hearse was discontinued and motor hearses used.

The hearse shed was located in Canisbay opposite the hall and was demolished in September, 1983, by the Manpower Services.

Shops In The Parish

There were quite a number of shops in the Parish in the early part of the century.

In Mey, David Laing had an extensive business, including an hotel, grocery shop and bakery, as well as selling merchandise of all kinds.

Miss Mackenzie had a small shop in Bunker Road, East Mey.

Alex Begg had a business in Gills, selling groceries, animal feed, etc.; he specialised in rope, many people coming a considerable distance for rope tethers for their animals.

In Upper Warse, there were two shops run by Donald Shearer and Mrs Cormack respectively.

In Canisbay, Alex Taylor had a general merchants business and also had the Post Office; he was also an agent for manure and grass seed.

There were three little shops in Huna owned by Mrs Jessie Dunnet, Mrs Sinclair and Miss Davidson, the latter was a newspaper agent.

At John O'Groats, George Manson had a fairly large shop and also the Post Office. He had many customers including visitors to John O'Groats. Also Williamina Laird had a small shop.

Freswick had three shops run respectively by Mr Gunn, Mrs Bremner and Miss Mowat.

Auckengill had a few shops as well. There are few shops left in the Parish at present.

Joiner shops and blacksmiths played a large part in the Parish, there being three blacksmiths, one each at Mey, Huna and Freswick, also there were numerous joiner's shops.

There must have been a demand for suits and dresses as there were three tailors in Canisbay all working full time. They were W.C. Cuthbertson and Sons, Canisbay, John Sutherland, Huna, and Francis Banks, Kirkstyle. There were also five lady dressmakers, Miss Shearer and Miss Chambers from Mey, Miss Begg and Miss Mowat from John O'Groats and Miss Kennedy from Freswick.

This was the list given in 1928 of people in business:

Banks Donald, sen., boat builder
Banks Donald, jnr., joiner
Begg Alex, grocer, Gills
Begg John, blacksmith, Freswick
Bremner Peter, grocer, Stroma
Bremner Wm., shopkeeper, Freswick
Cormack Jn., grocer, Warse Canisbay
Dundas Matthew, grocer, Stroma
Gunn Peter (Mrs), grocer, Freswick
Houston Magnus, miller, Duncansby
Lees Neil McArthur M.B., Ch.B.Glas., medical officer for Canisbay, Pentland View, Canisbay
Manson Hugh, grocer and Post Office, John O'Groats
Moir Alfd., joiner, West Mey
Mowat Margt. Laird (Miss), shopkeeper, Freswick
Murray Jas., John O'Groats House Hotel, John O'Groats
Nicolson Jas. M., grocer, Auckengill
Rosie Wm., grocer, Newton, John O'Groats
Shearer Donald, grocer, Warse Canisbay
Simpson Hugh, grocer, Stroma
Sutherland Jas., clerk to the Parish Council, inspector of poor for the Parish of Canisbay and registrar of births, deaths and marriages, Canisbay
Sutherland John, blacksmith, Huna
Sutherland John, tailor, Huna
Tait James, joiner, Huna
Taylor Alexander, grocer, Post Office, Canisbay

Canisbay Landholders' Show Committee 1934-1935

Photo, John Dunnet, Seater.

Back row, left to right:– Magnus Houston, The Mill; Donald Dunnet, Quoys; George Innis, Back Road, Gills; Willie Sutherland, Blacksmith; Alex Sinclair, Brabster; George Green, Breck; William Kennedy, Tresdale; James Wm. Shearer, Lower Warse.
Front row:– Jamie Mowat, Burnside Gills; Sandy Bremner, Everly; Alex Kennedy, Tresdale; James Dunnet, Seater; Watt Gunn, Brabster.

The Canisbay Landholders Show

One of the highlights of the year was the "Cattle Show", which was always held in the Tower Park, West Canisbay. It was held in early August and always drew a large crowd of spectators. The exhibits of horses, cattle and sheep were always described by the judges as good quality animals. The show was looked upon as a general holiday. Most crofters and farmers had animals on show. The stock judges were always prominent Caithness farmers. There was a dairy section, and other sections run by the ladies. After the parade of horses and cattle, a variety of sports took place. The show was always visited by Sir Archibald Sinclair MP. In the evening a well attended dance was held.

The show was first held in 1913 and carried on until just before the 1939-45 war. The 1914 show was the day that war was declared.

The Ploughing Association

The annual ploughing match was held in February. It took place in the larger farms like Barrogill Mains, West Canisbay, Tresdale, Warse, Quoys of Canisbay and Quoys of West Mey.

About a dozen ploughs took part. There were two sections, Professionals and Amateurs. The Association Chairman for many years was James Shearer, Upper Warse who used to plough when there was a crofters section and always got the prize for the neatest ends. The secretary was James Dunnett, Seater, himself a good ploughman but his duties prevented him from competing. The judges were former champion ploughmen. The three who generally judged were Messrs. John Leith, Greenland, David Sutherland, Rattar and J.W. Sutherland, Castletown. Apart from ploughing, there were prizes for starts and finishes. Some special prizes were given by different people for oldest and youngest etc.; such prizes were meant for individuals.

The Labour Party

Canisbay was the first place in the North to form a branch of the Labour Party; Alex Matheson, Gills being the forerunner. He had been to Glasgow and met some of the Clydeside members and asked them to come North.

In 1924, James Maxton and Campbell Stephen came to John O'Groats and addressed a well attended meeting which was held in the hall; both were excellent speakers.

A branch was formed that night and John S. Banks of John O'Groats was made chairman, and William Bremner ("Norseman") of Freswick was secretary. A committee was formed and about 40 people became members.

Benefits and Changes

The two great benefits of the century were the Regional Water Scheme and the coming of electricity. We will deal with the water scheme first. It came to the Parish in the early fifties and it was a great relief to many places, for in the summer time water was very scarce; horse and cattle required a lot of drinking water.

Wells and watering stems were an essential part of Parish life. Water had to be carried from the well in pails for domestic use, sometimes a considerable distance, and the stems were for the livestock.

Some of these wells and stems were quite artistically made with local building stone and flagstones. Today they have nearly all disappeared as the houses all have water on tap, with all the modern conveniences, and many of the fields have water troughs fed from the water main.

Electric power came about the same time and opened up a new way of life for the Parish, giving power for lighting and driving machinery and since then, countless electrical gadgets have found their way into the homes; televisions, washing machines, cookers, etc.

Never again will we see a man sitting on a heap of stones, breaking metal for the road. Or men with wheelbarrows carting and spreading the metal on the road, before the horse drawn water cart which sprayed water on the metal. This helped to bind it together, before it was rolled with the steam road roller.

Canisbay Medical Association

The Canisbay Medical Association was formed in the mid 19th century, and as these notes only deal with the 20th century we will have to take it from there. The medical officer for Canisbay in 1906 was Dr Alex MacGregor, generally referred to as Dr Sandy as he was the son of the U.F. Church Minister. He did his rounds on a high bicycle. He was followed by Dr MacDonald who had one of the first motor cycles in Caithness. To get it started he had to push it into gear for a few yards and mount it quickly when it started or he would be left behind.

He was succeeded by Doctors Duffas, Slater, Lees, Junor, Gill, Donaldson, Pyle, Sharp, Walters and Doctors Fraser and Mitchell who are in the practice now.

The Medical Association was worked on the same lines as the Nursing Association. There were two collectors in every district and they formed the committee. They also collected the accounts for medicine for the doctor.

The secretary at the turn of the century was the Canisbay School Headmaster, Andrew Munro. He was followed in office by James Sutherland the council clerk who held the post for many years. The last secretary was James W. Shearer.

When the health service took over in 1948, the association gave them Pentland View which had housed the doctor for a hundred years. Later a new house was built for the doctor in Canisbay and Pentland View was turned into a youth hostel.

The Canisbay doctor also had to attend the people on the Island of Stroma as it was part of the Canisbay Parish. The Department of Health paid a special boating grant for the island.

Canisbay Nursing Association

The Canisbay Nursing Association was formed in the early twenties. In common with other Parishes, a public meeting was held and a committee of management was formed. The secretary appointed was Mrs Laing, Mey.

It was decided to work on a co-operation basis — every person over 21 to pay 4/- per half year. The Parish Council was to pay so much for the people that were entirely in their care.

A few people did not join the association at first as some of the older women thought they could do all the nursing that was required.

The first nurse to be appointed was Jessie Cook. Being a local girl, she understood the people and their ways. Her professional skill and careful handling of a patient was soon appreciated and those who did not at first favour the idea of a nurse, changed their view and joined the association.

The nurse did her

rounds for the first few years on a bicycle. The association then bought her an Austin car which she learned to drive. The car was a great benefit and saved much time. It was better for the sick folk, as the nurse did not go into the houses cold and wet as often was the case.

In 1948 when the welfare state took over, the Nursing Association was disbanded and the Health Board took over. Nurse Cook spent the whole of her working life in the Parish where her services were much appreciated. She retired in 1960 and got a presentation subscribed for by the whole Parish.

She was followed by equally competent ladies. The district nurse has for many years been an integrated part of the health service.

Nurse Cook's Presentation

Photo, courtesy, J. McDonald, Shore Lane, Wick.
Jessie Cook, Mrs Jean Gill and Dr John Gill.

From reminiscences told by the late Dannie Nicolson, Canisbay, to Colin Mackay, Heatherbell Cottages, John O'Groats.

TRANSPORT

The changes in the modes of transport are spectacular, local, national, and international. In my young days passenger traffic was conducted by a covered coach called the "Barrogill", which left Huna in the morning via John O'Groats taking the Warth Hill Road to Wick. The horses were changed about half way at the top of the hill at Auckengill. All male passengers had to vacate their seats on coming to a steep rise on the road, and walk to the top of the brae. This was some improvement on previous procedure. When the coach came to the

base of a brae the horses were halted, and the driver would shout — "First class passengers keep your seats, second class passengers come out and shove."

Before the Warth Hill Road was constructed, the coach plied between Mey and Wick and also carried the mail. Mail was not heavy in those days. Mail for John O'Groats was deposited at Canisbay and taken from there by a postwoman who delivered the same in the district. The mail coach left John

O'Groats, via Huna and Canisbay for Wick in the forenoon, returning by the same route at night. At New Year time when traffic was heavier, I've known the mail to arrive after 11 o'clock at night. The post office was also the local shop, and the recognised rendezvous for the young. When the mail arrived we went into the shop, often sitting on the counter to provide more floor space. The Postmaster spread out the letters on the front counter, and proceeded to read all the names and addresses. When there was a letter for your house you shouted "Here" and it was passed to you. Should you be next to someone there was a letter for, you put your hand over his mouth to prevent him saying "Here" until after the Postmaster had laid it aside. When the person who was muffled got released, and asked for the letter, the postmaster being a fussy person, would give a lecture on the importance of paying attention to him. The coach for mail was of the small waggonette type, pulled by a single horse mostly, although provision could be made for a pair.

A good story is told of Archie who drove the mail coach in my time. The horse, through force of habit, always stopped at the hotel at Keiss. A stranger who was on his way to John O'Groats one night, when the horse stopped, asked Archie, "Is this where you change horses?" Archie replied in his usual genial way, "No, No, No, this is where we change wir breeth!"

At the beginning of the present century the internal combustion engine had made its impact as a means of propulsion. In Wick particularly, the old established "carters" with their horses and long carts, were reluctant to give way to the then modern motor. I can remember when I started haulage in 1920 with a model T Ford ton truck, I had to blow the horn repeatedly to some carters, before they slowly guided their horses to permit me to overtake and pass. This phase soon passed as the motor established its permanency in this field of service. Before my time I have heard my granny tell how she would carry a herring net on her back from John O'Groats to Wick, and twine for another on the homeward journey. I heard of one man from Freswick who carried a boll of meal (10 stone) on his back from Wick to Freswick, 13 miles. He rested once letting the boll of meal down on the parapet of the Bridge of Wester. He was named Bremner, and although not a giant, was an extraordinarily strong man.

The horse and cart was used extensively in my young days. The first time I was in Wick was when I was about four years old and I went in a spring cart with my uncle. When the mare was unharnessed and fed in a stable in a back lane near the Station Hotel, my uncle took me by the hand and we climbed the stone steps at the south end of the hotel, which led to Bridge Street. I gazed, and most likely gaped, in wonderment as we walked along to the other end of the street. My attention was rivetted on a stationer's shop, Arthur Bruce, with a great variety of toys in the window. I have seen many fine emporiums since that day, but the amazement which that shop window created within me has eclipsed all I have subsequently visited. That first journey took three hours, and the mare was a lively lass. Now with the modern motor car I feel I'm wasting time if I take more than 15 to 17 minutes. There were no rolled roads at that time, so there was a difference in speed and comfort compared to some of the billiard table surfaces of today.

The "Barrogill" and the mail coach belonged to a Coaching Company, directed from Wick. The first independent operator was a former coach driver who was on the "Barrogill". He was Alex. Gunn who had a house and stable at the 'Ha, John O'Groats. He operated his coach for some time but was unable to keep horses which had to be replaced repeatedly. Then there was John Horne who was doing some carting; he started a coach and likewise only lasted a short time. After him came David Sutherland, who like John Horne was doing some carting and then branched into coaching. He too gave up and was superseded by an Edinburgh man named Charles Walker. He brought some old cars up here, and this being something of a novelty, succeeded in lasting some time. I remember he had one old car. I think it was a De Dion, and he had a body on it in wagonette design. He thought he could improve on the solid hard rubber tyres. He had iron rings made to fit the rear wheels, holes punched in them similar to that in the shoes for horses, to take cogs for frosty icy roads. He had the wheels shod in Wick with the iron rings, but needless to say, he never got the car up the incline at the old Kirk, Wick. He tried hard, but as the wheels were spinning, all that the car produced was sparks, and plenty of sparks, as the iron rings spun on the hard bluestone road.

The first really beneficial motor transport came when a Caithness company put out a fleet of four twin cylinder, solid tyred, chain driven, Albion vehicles. One of them plied between Thurso and Mey, driven by Daniel Mowatt who later took over the John O'Groats to Wick run and drove buses ever after until he retired. The one between John O'Groats and Wick was driven by William Bremner, who later emigrated to Canada and came over with the Canadian Forces during the First World War. After the war he farmed at Auckengill until he retired. That company had their office and garage in Thurso. They also had buses running west as far as Tongue.

R.S. Waters, a Wick ironmonger and auctioneer, then started a bus business. His first bus was a Halley solid tyred, chain driven vehicle. It was made in Glasgow and was reliable and stood up well to hard work. The body was made in Wick by a coach builder. It had the front seat full width and could comfortably accommodate three passengers and the driver. There were two seats along the sides and a compartment at the rear for carrying the mail bags.

From, "The Heather Blooms at John O'Groats", by John S. Banks, Broo,
by kind permission of Mrs Banks, Knockdry House, Wick.

THE WEATHERGLESS

Some folk think hids oot o'date
Wi' weather forecasts o' wir fate
But half 'e time they've got id wrong
When Michael Fish is no on song

If 'e gae 'e gless a tap
'E needle will move fore and aft
Tellan 'e fae morn till noon
O' 'e weather comman soon

Anither thing 'ats fair misleedan
Is 'e temperature they're givan

They call id celcius noo-a-days
At pits 'e owld fowk in a daze

A wish 'at they wid use hind sicht
An leave id all in Faranheicht
If 'e live in Caithness eel hardly get attention
Forecasters think wur funny fowk and hardly
    worth a mention
But if yer gless is dodgy downt ever be doon cast
Jest turn on yer wireless for 'e Orkney forecast.
Walter S. Rosie, Novelty House, John O'Groats.

LANDMARKS

March Stone Between Mey and Rattar

A Parish is defined as "an ecclesiastical district" and as far as I can find out, no one knows when these boundaries were marked. It is said march stones were used in the days of the Vikings and that they may even date back to Pictish times. The march stones which marked the boundaries between estates often had initials on them.

On the Moss of Mey, near the White Bridge end of it, is a "march stone" which marks the boundary between the Mey and Rattar estates. It has M on the Mey side and R on the Rattar side. It is situated about 40/50 yards in from the road on the south side, and it is made from red sandstone. This is the "march" between the Canisbay and Dunnet Parishes.

Warning Signs at Gills

The Braes o' Gills had warning signs. They were eight to nine feet high and had a triangle on top of them. They were known locally as the "danger poles". There were three of them, one at the west side of the braes, one at the dyke of the Ha, and the other at the east side of the Braes. They provided entertainment for the boys of the place who spent a lot of time climbing them. The poles eventually disappeared after the new road, which bypassed the braes, was opened in 1948.

(The braes were then called Stewart's Brae, Ha Brae, Big Ha Brae and Johnnie's Brae.)

Mile Stones

During the invasion scare early in the 1939/45 war, the mile stones were buried by the road men. Some have been dug up in recent years when road widening schemes have taken place and they can be seen at the top of Harley, at Freswick, Canisbay, near the old church and at East Mey.

Carved M

Colin Mackay, Heatherbell Cottages, John O'Groats.

The March Ditch

The march boundary between John O'Groats and Freswick runs from the red cliffs of Fastgeo, south of the Loch of Lomishion and between the Lint Lochies to the Warth Hill Quarries.

M.H.

JOHN O' GROATS RIFLE CLUB

The Rifle Club

As ah reach for ma glesses an pick up ma pen
Ma thochts wander back tae the year nineteen ten
Ma faither hed telt me fat happened wan day
Fan ae teacher an pals walked ower tae Mey.

Twas ae first day oh January, they'ed six mile tae go
An they wur all SOBER??, ma dad telt me so
They hed risen richt early an wur all feelan fine
An they planned tae reach Mey fore ae clock hed struck nine.

Fae Freesick an Auckengill they all cam at day
There wis also some worthies fae roond Canisbay
So they all cam the gether inside Mey Drill Hall
Fat they planned tae do wis tae benefit all.

They wanted tae start Rifle Shooting ye ken
Sae decided tae start up a club there an then
Wae branches in Freesick an in Auckengill tae
As weel as in Canisbay, Groats an in Mey.

Noo, whit wis ae name oh iss new club tae be
They wanted tae please everybody ye see
They thocht lang aboot it an adjourned for some grub
Twas then it wis called Pentland Rifle Club.

Then Captain Mackenzie, a great leader o' men
They appointed their secretary richt there an then
Hae promised hae'd do ae best at hae could
Tae get ae club on hids feet an go-an richt good.

In those far off days, a hale thousand round
Oh bullets cost them much less than a pound
Today they wid lift up their hans in despair
If they knew at noo hid cost forty pound mair.

So they formed a committee an all cast their votes
And decided tae hev their headquarters in Groats
Fan their plans were all finished they all walked oot
An wae loan oh some rifles held their first NEW YEAR SHOOT.

On at New Year's Day their numbers were few
Boot in no time at all ae list fairly grew
At ae end oh at month coontan both boys an men
Ae membership rose past a hunder an ten.

They later decided it wid be all richt
For them tae go shootan each Setterday nicht
On each ither nicht there wis no much tae do
Cept feedan ae cattle an milkan ae coo.

Then ae club wis enrolled wae the S.M.R.C.
Wha controlled aw ae shootin in a hale countree
Two two rifles hed never been used here before
They were first in ae north tae bring em tae fore.

Noo before iss fowlk spoke aboot sheep an o' coos
Aboot horses an stirkies an peegs an o' soos
An also o' plooan an sowan their oats
Or o' lapsters an partans they catched in their boats.

Boot noo all they spoke o' wis rifles an scores
Every time at they entered in each ithers doors
Their weman could no get a word in at-ta
Ae shooting wis drivan em near up ae wa.

So news o' ae shootin it fairly went roon

An wis no very long gettan ower ae SOON
A treachras bit water an through Lellan's Bore
It got held up at last on ae Stroma men's shore.

Mind ye Stroma men aye were ae first aff their marks
Tae pilot strange men sailing by in their barques
Boot noo they did hear how tae hev some good fun
Wae ae use o' some bullets an a point two two gun.

So they started a branch in ae year nineteen twell
An ae Pentland Club membership greatly did swell
They went at ae shootin wae greatest oh will
Learnan tae shoot wae ae greatest oh skill.

They made Taylor ae C.M. an Moir the R.O.
Robertson an Dundas on committee did go
There were Sinclairs an Wares an Simpsons as well
Smiths, Bremners an Allans, Mansons an Campbell.
Those were ae names oh those brave Stroma men
There were probably mair ah jist dinna ken
They hev long departed ae place o' their birth
Boot memries still linger oot there in ae Firth.

Noo ma uncle Johnny ae shoemakan man
Till keep his sicht clear hed a winderful plan
On Setterday hae did peel ingans galore
Tae wash oot his een as ae teers did doonpour

Ma faither wis one oh those keen shootan men
Hae wis there at the start in ae year nineteen ten
Hae taught me tae shoot an ah thoucht hid wis great
Before hae left ae club hae wis seventy eight.

The years hev rolled by an these men are all gone
Boot ah'm sure they'ed be gled at ae club carries on
An on each New Year's Day everybody goes oot
Tae show aff their skill at ae NEW YEAR'S DAY SHOOT.

Ah first joined ae club in ae year thirty two
An ah thoucht ah wid show them jist whit ah could do
Boot on New Year's Day wae the shootin all past
Ah wis fair disgraced for ah hed cum in last.

Boot the years hev gone by an ah've been up an doon
An ah still go oot shootan though nae mair a loon
An on New Year's Day ah still try my best
Tae get a good score an tae show up the rest.

Ah still sometimes manage tae get near ae top
Boot ah dinna worry if it turns oot a flop
Ah'll still keep on shootan as best as ah can
An let awbody else try tae beat ae old man.

If ye think at ae language ah'm usan is bad
Its a lang time since ah went tae school as a lad
They taught me the English boot hid's no for me
So ah'm usan ae words at cum easy ye see.

If ye dinna ken fat ah'm tryan tae say
Jis write tae St Magnus an ask for Nancy
She's a teacher so she can translate hid for you
Sae ah'll jist pack it in an feenish off noo.

George M. Steven, Seaview, John O'Groats.

John O'Groats School Rifle Club 1912, George T. Mackenzie – Headmaster

Photo, David Dunnet, Hillhead. Names, Donald Mowat, Victoria House, John O'Groats.
Back row, left to right:– Donald Cameron, Lower Stemster; Beilie Bain, Hillside; Hugh Green, Biel; Jeck Green, Roadside; Sinclair Rosie, Hillside; Will Cormack, Huna. Front row:– Walter Steven, Corner House; George Steven, Corner House; Bob Begg, East End; Donald Mowat, Victoria House; Jim Baikie, Pentland View; Ack Dunnet, East End; Magnus Mowat, Linnequoy.

Pentland Rifle Club 1910-1970
Diamond Jubilee January 16, 1970 at John O'Groats House Hotel

(Some founder members and present members of the club.) Photo courtesy, Northern Studios, Bridge Street, Wick.
Standing, left to right:– George Steven, Seaview; James Nicolson, Auckengill; Sandy Matheson, Auckengill; Laurence Brown, North House, Alex Mowat, Roadside; Willie Mowat, Broo. Seated:– Donald Henderson, Skirza; John Mowat, Victoria House; Will Dunnet, St Leonards, Canisbay; James Donn, Warse; John Dunnet, Hilltop, Auckengill; John S. Banks, Broo.

31

A RECITATION BY BILLY STEVEN AT A RIFLE CLUB

Although I'm young, I've joined the club
A shooter for to be
But the rifle's near as big's myself
I'd like you all to see.

At first I couldna hit a thing
The shots they went sky high
The members they all stood well back
When I did have a try.

But on New Year's Day I took the gun
And at the target shot

I did the very best I could
And wondered what I got.

My faither's score at the shortest range
Was forty two you see
So I waited till my score came up
And boys ?? I'd forty three.

Says I, I'll show you how it's done
And I know when I grow up
I'll even beat George Manson then
And win the NEW YEAR CUP.

NB. George Manson won the cup that year.

OWER WEEL OFF

A'm strackid in ma chair 'e nicht, 'mang things 'at
   should content me,
Readan 'e "Groat" wi' 'lectric licht, a TV screen
   fornent me.
A've power till wash an' dry ma cleys an' mak ma
   bite o' meyt,
A'll slyster non mair o' ma days nor cut or skail a
   peyt.
Ma fire, wi barries, never fails just fan 'e switch
   says when,
A'll reet nae mair wi' spownks or spails or tak 'e
   kenlin ben.
A telephone sits on ma bink, ma roddy's black wi'
   tar,
Heyt watter spottan in ma sink an' at ma door a
   car.
They'll pit a hom-help eyne til me fan A go in a
   crile,
A'm pampered lek a VIP tho' pitten til 'e jile.
'E ambulance takes me til Week if A get rayal ill,
An' tho' she never kens A'm seek, 'E Queen'll pay 'e
   bill.
Yit wur ill pleysed, lek awns o' bere wis sticken in
   wur sark,
Wur greetan efter something mair, lek spent lambs
   in a park,
A stirk, 'mang gress 'at's green an' thick, stans
   bellyan an' booran
An' kaiman til get owerr 'e dik' far gosk an trock is
   flooeran.
'E lambs' an' stirkies' troubles smit till tinkler an'
   til toff,
Tho' hid's a thing we'll no admit, lek them wur
   ower weel off.
Contentment is 'e greatest boon 'at man wis ever
   granted,
Bit noo thir's manny a hairy loon 'at disna seem til
   want hid.
Ye'll see a chiel wi' pelly chin, face lek a scooren
   cloot,

He disna ken his luck is in 'cas hid wir nivre oot.
Tho' perfect health hes aye been his, is Jock a
   happy chiel?
Na! Na! He kens'na fat health is 'at niver wis no
   weel.
Twa days o' teethag comes yer way, 'en fan 'e pain's
   departed,
Yer ten times happier a' 'at day than weeks afore
   hid started.
Ye've masked a' day in bowg an' mire, sockid fae
   kep til boot,
'At nicht yer gledder at 'e fire than if ye'd noor been
   oot.
Hid's jist wur thinken 'at's diseysed. A sometimes
   hev 'at notion
'At some o's micht be still illpleysed tho' in 'e lan' o'
   Goshan.
Hid's no 'e pounds 'at's in wur nev 'at maks his gled
   or weary
Nor yit 'e boachies[1] 'at we hev 'at maks wur herts
   feel cheery.
Wur pey's no beeg, bit we can live 'at's no fat maks
   his sore,
Hid's jist 'e fact 'at manny a spiv, 'at's on 'e dole,
   gets more.
We most be workan fan we can, leyve doles til
   sweerer shither,
Saint Paul an' Burns said every man on earth
   should be wur brither.
An' Robbie said til kindly scan 'e faults o' fowk we
   meet,
An' try til help them a' we can, no blacken them wi'
   sheet.
An' niver niver most we grudge success til ither
   men,
Nor yit wur neebour's deeds til judge whither thir
   freend or fren[2].

Willie Alexander, West Canisbay.

[1] Keepsake   [2] Stranger

PENTLAND UNITED – OVER THE YEARS

The first time Pentland United hit the headlines was about 1934 when Canisbay and John O'Groats formed a football club taking up the title. Mey had a team in the rural league in 1930, then about 1936 merged with Pentland United and to the present day play under that banner, adopting the Heart of the Midlothian colours. The team had the unenviable record of never winning a trophy until 1963 when they defeated Keiss at Sir George's Park, Thurso by six goals to two, to win the

Pentland Football Team

Photo, Jimmy Magee, Dervaig, Mey.

Back row, left to right:– Gordon Mackenzie, Dunnet; Mackie Sutherland, Scarfskerry; Bobby Magee, Canisbay; Will Mackenzie, Dunnet; Sandy Mackenzie, Barrock; Willie Mitchell, Glasgow; Bertie Fraser, Canisbay.
Front row:– John Gill, Canisbay; Jimmy Magee, Canisbay; Sandy Swanson, Mey; Tommy Geddes, Mey; Sanders Sinclair, Thurso.

Pentland United F.C. Highland Cup Winners 1987

Photo, Tommy Geddes, Thurso.

Back row, left to right:– Duncan Gray (co-manager), Colin Henderson*, Willie Sinclair*, Clair Robertson*, Angus Mackay, Gerald Davidson, Donald Coghill, Terry Mackay, Jim Farquhar, Dennis Manson (co-manager), Alistair Ham (president). Front row:– Steven Kemp, Alistair Budge, John Sutherland*, James Bruce, John Begg*, Callum Grant*, Ian MacDonald, Donald MacMillan.
Pictured at beginning of Season 1988 with the Highland Cup won in Season 1987. * Those who would have qualified under old rural rules.

Mackay Cup. The team on that momentous occasion was as follows:

John Angus, Barrogill Angus, Jimmy Mathieson, John Leslie Robertson, Gordon Mackenzie, Ackie Banks, Bertie Fraser, John Gill, Tom Anderson, Will McKenzie, John Bain. Reserves: Ian Morris and Billy Sutherland.

All of these players are indigenous except Tom Anderson, an Orcadian who was working at Philips Mains at the time. The rules then were, you either had to be born in the parish or living there for over two weeks, thus excluding holidaymakers.

The captain that night was Jimmy Mathieson from Gills and he joins that long and illustrious list who have had the honour. Amongst these were – starting from 1946 – Bill Magee, Davie Geddes, Donnie Manson, John Les Robertson, John Bain, Bertie Fraser, Jimmy Magee, Sandy Swanson, Gordon Harris, Ian Morris, Duncan Gray, Jimmy Farquhar, Sandy Sinclair (Thurso) Ian McDonald (Thurso), Callum Grant and the present day skipper Jocky Begg. I am sure I missed out some, but they will be included in the next edition of this book!!

Success again eluded them until the Rural League joined the County League in 1975 when, with the aid of coaching and the influx of players from outwith the parish, they went from success to success, winning several trophies including the County League and Highland Cup.

During the first years of the war little football was played in the county. In 1944 and 1945 several games were played between Mey v Groats and Canisbay resulting in a selection which entered the Rural League after its reincarnation in 1946. The team that took the field in Halkirk on that memorable evening was on the following lines.

Tommy Geddes, Davie Geddes, Sandy Allan, Jim Rosie, Ally Sinclair, Jock Geddes, Willie Jack, Ian Allan, Bill Magee, Clare Fraser, Duncan Cameron.

The result that evening was a 2-2 draw.

Taking 1952 as a criterion, Pentland United's record for that year was as follows:

League (1952)

HOME

Pentland United 3	Stirkoke	1
Pentland United 3	Watten	1
Pentland United 2	Bower	4
Pentland United 4	Halkirk	0
Pentland United 1	Castletown	0
Pentland United 6	Keiss	0
Pentland United 0	Staxigoe	5

AWAY

Stirkoke	3	Pentland United 2
Watten	4	Pentland United 2
Bower	0	Pentland United 1
Halkirk	1	Pentland United 4
Castletown	2	Pentland United 0
Keiss	2	Pentland United 2
Staxigoe	3	Pentland United 2

Mackay Cup

Pentland United 0	Halkirk 2
Keiss 1	Halkirk 3

Patterson Cup

Pentland United 2   Watten 5

The line up at that time was roughly as follows:

Tommy Geddes, Davie Geddes, Danny Banks, Donnie Manson, Sandy Allan, George Sinclair, Don Shearer, Bill McIvor, Jock Shearer, Billy Dunnet, Bill Magee.

Other players around that time were Andrew Dundas, Patty Manson, Charlie Manson, Donald Cameron and Sandy Manson. Those results would probably have given us a higher position in the league than we normally occupied.

The Patterson Cup was gifted by a commercial traveller who regularly frequented the John O'Groats Hotel pre-war when the McKenzies were mine hosts.

The Mackay Cup was presented by J. "Abrach" Mackay, the venerable Castletown County Councillor. Later Dr Gill donated the Gill Shield to intensify the great rivalry between Keiss and Pentland. Focus now seems to centre around the more glamorous County Championships and the Highland Cup, both of which have graced the Pentland sideboard lately.

Later on, Walter Long (a Dounreay employee) donated another cup which bears his name.

Though having the largest catchment area – Freswick to the burn of mid sands in Dunnet – parts of that area proved very infertile in football talent. It is difficult to recall a star that emerged in Freswick and in the earlier days only a few emerged from the Dunnet, Brough and Scarfskerry area. Stroma, because of its isolation, only provided one player when a Bill Robertson came over by boat for several games in the 50's. About this time Pentland crossed the Firth to play a friendly in Stroma. The result escapes me but to give it a real bit of island authenticity, the goal posts had been substituted by oars! In the late 40's and 50's Pentland United easily commanded the biggest travelling support with two (Morrison) buses often the order of the day for away games.

Intense rivalry still exists, but it seldom matches the hostility shown in pre-war days, especially at Staxigoe when often the Pentland United visitors had to reverse into the haven of Banks and McRae's bus with their "civvies" over one arm and the free arm shielding against a hail of clods and divots.

Venues like players changed frequently. The Mey pitch was situated in George Laing's park with entry from Cameron back branch road.

This field was also used by the Black Watch and Royal Scots stationed in the Mey plantation and castle during the last war. The goals were constructed of tubular steel poles widely used in the beach defences at Dunnet and Reiss sands. John O'Groats had their pitch on the links along from the hotel. In 1946 the team played in a Tresdale field just behind what was then the doctor's house. In the 50's Pentland moved down the road to a west Canisbay field near the bottom of the Canisbay road where they stayed until the 70's. Since then the venue had gradually "gone west" via the Mey Hotel to its present site in Dunnet where it now enjoys its first dressing rooms.

Some of the venues had their own special peculiarities. Keiss had an enormous crossfall where players with one long leg and one short leg found it very handy; the playing surface however was quite good. Watten at one time had a field criss-crossed with sheep "roadies" (paths) and the standing joke was, it made life easy for the defenders as all they had to do was stand in the roadies as the forwards were bound to come that way! On reflection, Pentland must have been famous for its cow pats causing severe staining to shorts but a great asset to those defenders who favoured the then popular sliding tackle!

Looking back it could be said that the team's lack of success was partly due to its wide catchment area. With the lack of communication and transport, organizing a practice was almost impossible as telephones and cars were a scarce commodity in those days. Teams such as Castletown and Halkirk etc. had their football fields in their respective villages, thus arranging a get-together did not pose such a problem.

Teams, as players, come and go – Bower, Killimster, Wick Scouts, Stirkoke and Staxigoe have departed – hopefully only temporarily. Who would have thought that Staxigoe would ever be defunct, when for decades they always were amongst the top teams in the league.

I will not be tempted along the hazardous road of picking Pentland's greatest players, but I could name some very young players, some as young as 15 years, who were thrown in at the deep end in a game much rougher than that of today's, when tackling from behind and charging the goalkeeper, were the norm.

The oldest player to hold his place consistently was George Sinclair, Gills, who turned out regularly in his 44th year – George by the way is still going strong. The most prolific goalscorer was probably John Gill who on more than one occasion scored double "hat tricks". The name Gill immediately conjures up his even more famous father, Dr J.P.B. Gill who from 1938-1968 was the main driving force behind football in the area.

Comparisons will inevitably be drawn between the present team and the Pentland of yesteryears and I believe that most over-50s would admit that the Manson and Gray coached teams would have proved too hot to handle for most of the teams of the pre 60's era.

In those days some of the Rural League players could play for town teams which at that time was considered a higher grade of football, and I well remember a certain Pentland goalkeeper playing for Pentland United, Thurso Pentland, Thurso Select and Rural League Select all in the space of five nights. Under present rules this can no longer happen, but it certainly cut out the need to train!

No team functions without a committee and over the years Pentland has been lucky in this respect, especially when you have members like Alistair Ham who has served 35 years on the committee, 25 of these as president – well done Alistair, and thanks for your help in the research.

On the lighter side, it would be impossible for six decades of football to pass without its funny side emerging. In an end of season, nothing at stake, league game in Stirkoke, Pentland United could only muster 10 men. One of our travelling support – a strapping youth of 18 who had no interest in football let alone in playing the game – was persuaded to strip and upon entry to the field of play was instructed by the captain to play inside left, to which he replied "where dey ah stan for at?".

In conclusion we wish a now successful Pentland even more success and if this is not to be, there is always one honour that cannot be taken away from them, the honour of playing for the most northerly football team on the mainland of Britain.

Tommy Geddes, 3 Houston Terrace, Thurso.

"EH GEMME"

[This crofter lived in a remote area and these were his first impressions of a football match.]

Ah wid noor hev geed till eh gemme at aa if id wisna far ma sister's loons at wir hame fae Glesgo far thir holidays. They preeged an antled at me till at last ah joust geed far pice sake.

When we got ere thir wis a dreffel oh chiels wi different reeg oots on em, kickan baas in aboot baith goals. Then a chiel fa maist hev been in chairge (ah thought id wis eh Grieve but eh loons telt me id wis a referee), blowed his whistle, then they aa started kickan eh wan ba, an iss seemed till be eh main problem eh whole night – a shortage o' baas.

Eh parkie they played in wis marked oot aboot eh size o' a beeg heidreeg, an when eh ba geed ower iss line a seegnalman wid wave a flaggie an eh whistlie wid blow an they wid throw eh ballie back in till eh heidreeg again. Far masel ah thought a Shire netting fencie wid hev saved a lok a trouble here.

Noo an again a chiel wid get tirled. Wan chiel got a right thresh an' he got up an shook his nev right furnent eh referee an' he wis right mad aboot id. Eh fowk aboot hann wis aa shoutan "fowl" which dumbfounnered me a bittie as ah couldna see a henhoose in sight anywhere. Efter aboot three quarters an oor they stopped an hed a half-youkin an some oh em wis sookan oranges an gushalan in Irn Broo an stuff, but nane o' em wis taken a peece. Efter they feenished they set tae again an eh shither watchan wir gettan excited, shoutan an roaran an some wir usan bad words, an ah wis gled id wis prayer meeting night in Canisbay an eh Minister wisna aboot hann.

Thir wis even mair excitement when a beeg far-splet chiel came rinnan in an kicked 'e ba against eh couples an gluffed 'e goalie, an no twa meenads efter, anither chiel kicked 'e ba right passed him. He made a great gromish at 'e ba tryan till kep her an if id wisna far 'e scroo net id wid hev landed in 'e West Canisbay brether. Thir wis a lok o' right swack loons oot ere an some o' em wid jump an give 'e ba a kinnap wi thir heids – yin couldna be good far yir heid an ah wid hev thought id wid be bad faar making ye beld.

Thir wis twa chiels wi thick ganzies on em (ma nephews caad em goalkeepers) fa wir affel lazy an hardly iver ran aboot – ah doot yin chiels wid hev a job gettan work anywhere. By iss time a lok o' 'e owlder merried men hed joust aboot blown thir pocks an some o' 'e younger chiels wir hirplan an sochan, an ah think they wir aa gled, when 'e referee blowed his whistle far lousing time. Ah wis watchan 'e fowlk lievan eh parkie, an ah kent some o' em hed come fae as far awey as Doungasbay an Lochen, an ah could swire thir wis some fae Week – ah can eisy pick em oot by thir funny twang.

Next day ah wis at 'e scuffler an ye can afford till let yer mind wander a bittie at 'e scuffler, no lek if ye wis working wi 'e neep sower or 'e back deliver – an ah wis thinkan ah fair enjoyed masel yestreen an if id's no fit far 'e hey next Thirsday nicht ah micht go an watch anither game.

Tommy Geddes, 3 Houston Terrace, Thurso.

First Prize at Groat's Gala 1975

Photo, Bet Brown, North House, John O''Groats.

Left to right:– John Mowat, Douglas Leith, Betty Mowat, Anne Mowat, Alex Mowat behind saddle,
(Tommy between the shafts died in his 36th year in 1976).

TINKLERS

Tinklers are a race of people who have practically disappeared from our midst, at least as we knew them. Now they live in council houses, do ordinary jobs, and have generally merged into the community. No longer are they the colourful carefree nomads we knew. I don't know if they have retained their distinctive accents, but in all probability they have lost that link with the past as well.

The tinklers we knew travelled the roads with their packs and rings of tin. Their means of transport was always a spring kert, and on this they loaded their belongings. Sometimes they "sailed" on the kert, but often walked behind; that is, the womenfolk walked! The men sat on the corner of the kert puffing away at a blackened pipe, or chowing a wad of tobacco. They normally had one or maybe two dogs and they trotted behind, tied to the back of the kert by a length of rope. The bairns ran barefoot alongside, without a care in the world, and the pace was always leisurely.

They slept in low brown tents, seemingly very simple affairs made of canvas which they threw over a sort of framework, and there was usually a kind of funnel protruding from the top or side which served as a chimney. They must have been very smoky, but a tinkler's theory was, "Where's there's reek there's heat", and this no doubt applied. They usually pitched their tents on heathland – the Warth Hill and the top of the Hill of Auckengill being popular resting places in our district. I don't know what kind of fireplace they had, but the fuel was always peat – for wasn't their camping site just beside the peat banks, and there were always plenty of clods for the gathering.

The men folk weren't particularly industrious, although they did make and sell tin ware which they carried slung over their shoulders on a wire ring. They made tin pails, skellads, sighers (sieves to those who have never used a sigher), fillers (or funnels), basins and jugs with a varying degree of skill as far as soldering went.

The story is told of the crofter who was working his land with a very nervous horse. A tinkler happened to come along with his ring of tin, and the horsie kept shying as he heard the jingle of the pails etc. Although asked to make less noise and get on his way, the tinkler thought this good sport and kept hitching up his tinware, making it clatter even more loudly, and the poor mannie had more and more difficulty in controlling his terrified horse. At last in desperation he dropped the reins, grabbed a stick and made after the tinkler who ran for his life, but the crofter gave chase and laid about with the stick with such good will, the skellads, pails, basins etc. came adrift, and he never let up until the hapless tinkler was left with only the ring around his neck, and a trail of his battered wares littering the fields! These were the days when retribution was swift, and justice meted out to suit the crime.

All tinklers had the knack of begging worked out to a fine art. They begged automatically. I don't know if they were so very poor; some were possibly better off than we were, but to beg was second nature to them. "Could ye spare a puckle o' tea – or sugar – or meal – or a skin o' pork – or a skint o' milk" and if there was a man selling tin, he would ask for "a chow o' tobacco" or "Hev ye any horse hair aboot yer han?" Tinklers always had space to accommodate any goods they might get; they always came prepared! We never refused to fill their milk pail, and usually they got some oatmeal or a couple of bannags as well – they never left empty-handed, and I am sure we were none the worse of the lavish tinkler blessings showered on our entire household. The bairns who were as adept at begging as their elders, were, as I remember them, mostly bonnie bairns with their rich auburn hair, often curly, suntanned faces and gleaming white teeth.

One day a tinkler lassie about nine or ten called at our school and the teacher brought her into the classroom where we were doing "quick adding" with a circle of figures on the blackboard. This little girl who only attended school in the winter months joined in, and added her way around the figures with a speed and accuracy none of us could match, then went on her way, no doubt well rewarded for her efforts, and held up to us as an example for many months.

Tinkler babies never had a pram, and didn't need one. Arriving in the world with the minimum of fuss and ante- and post-natal care unheard of, they were on their travels almost immediately. Tucked up in a tartan plaid tied firmly around Mum, they were secure and snug in all weathers, and every new baby was assured of a welcome and usually a bundle of baby-clothes when Mum went on her rounds.

The packs they carried were well filled and must have been really heavy. Sheets, towels, underwear, overalls – they had quite a selection, and some favoured a basket which contained reels, elastic, tape, buttons, "lacers", pins and needles. We were always fascinated to see what each pack or basket held, and also by the many rings, mainly silver or maybe tin, each tinkler lady wore.

We were never frightened of our tinkler friends – we had no reason to be. They lived their lives as they knew, went their own way, and hurt no one. They came round year after year. How they survived the winter is their secret but once spring arrived, there they were: Jack the Dowgman, Crooked Mattie, Isaac, Glide Annag, Leizie, Crooked Andy, Beig Jean – and many more whose names I have forgotten.

Once when my Father was setting up peats, a tinkler loon came and asked for some. "If you give me a hand here, you can have as many as you can carry", he was told; and the lad worked with a will and truly earned his pay. This bank was always referred to afterwards as "The Tinkler's Bank"!

But that is all in days gone by. No more do we see their squat brown tents with the blue peat smoke rising to the evening sky against a background of heather, nor do we hear the strains of "Heilan' Laddie" rising and falling in the twilight as a tinkler piper marched up and down outside his tent.

There is little room on our busy roads for a tinkler convoy of "spring kerts", barefoot bairns and mongrel dogs moving carelessly along; and anyway, nowadays they would all have motor transport of some sort.

But whenever I see someone with thick curly auburn hair, laughing eyes and flashing white teeth in a sunburnt face, I travel back in time, and wonder if their name is Macaphee.

Clara Clyne, Strathesk Grove, Penicuik.

A Weel Kent Face

Lizzie MacPhee was born in a cave at Lossiemouth in 1904. She stays in Fearn now and says she misses seeing us and that she never felt better or happier than when she was doing her rounds here.

Lizzie MacPhee

Footnote:– Camp sites were chosen which had shelter, water, fuel and grass for the horsie. They were at the Warth Hill Quarries. The Hill Dam, Duncansby and the Mey and Brabster Quarries.

A.H.

SCHOOLING AND SCHOOLS IN CANISBAY PARISH

In 1696 the Scottish Parliament enacted – again – that a schoolmaster should be appointed in every parish in the land. According to Calder, in the Second Edition of his "History of Caithness", 10 years later, in 1706, Canisbay got a school under this "parochial scheme" as it was called, thus taking pride of place with Wick and Thurso as the first parishes in Caithness to fulfil the legal requirement.

This school was just to the north of the Old Kirk.

It had taken a long, long time and four Acts of Parliament for the vision of John Knox and his fellow reformers – a school in every parish – to be realised in Canisbay. Most of Caithness, and indeed of Scotland, would have to wait a long time yet. Still, prior to this it seems that there had been at least two attempts by the Church to get the heritors (landed proprietors in a parish liable to pay public burdens) to face up to this particular responsibility as these two extracts from the Session Records show:– (i) "May 30, 1653 Hew Groat ordained to write to Thomas Taillour that he come to teach the schoole in Cannasbey according to his engagement wtout longer delay". We cannot tell whether he came or not but again (ii) "October 28, 1660 . . . the minister with them (the elders) yt were present, having consent of the rest, condescended and agreed with Donald Reid Skinner to be schoolmaster at Canisbay, for teaching the young children that suld be sent to him, and for his paines 5 bolls of victuall was promised him in the yier, whilk he thinking too little yet accepted to undertake the charge, and to enter with all convenient diligence provideing the said 5 bolls victuall be duelie payed, and that he may have furniture of peats to supplie his present need." Whether the meal or the peats were lacking we do not know but the 1643 Act under which these attempted arrangements were made proved as ineffective as its predecessors, making necessary in due course the 1696 Act leading in 1706 to permanent schooling in Canisbay.

Then in 1723 The Society for Propagating Christian Knowledge* (usually abbreviated to The SPCK) founded a school in Stroma with a salary of 200 merks, (£10 sterling). It was attended by 50 or 60 pupils and was said to have been one of the most charitable creations of the Society. Shortly afterwards the Society set up another school at Mey. At the publication of The First Statistical Account of Scotland in 1793 these aforementioned were still the only schools in the parish. There had been no change in the legal salaries of the teachers throughout the whole of the 18th century and in 1790 the Parochial School salary was £18 while that of each of the two SPCK Schools was £10.

* **Note** – "The Society for Propagating Christian Knowledge, founded in 1709, was an arm of the established church whose "concern was not about the intellectual and secular interests of the people, but to instruct the children in the principles of Christian – especially of Calvinistic – faith; for

religion formed the main part of the school instruction, the chief object of reading being to know the Bible and the Catechism. . ." – Henry Grey Graham, "The Social Life of Scotland in the Eighteenth Century."

Despite its narrow aims it had a valuable educational effect on the Highlands and indeed on all Scotland.

The people were willing enough to learn and letters written to the lairds show that they were sufficiently well educated to look after their own interests. Also the Reverend John Morison tells us in the Old Statistical Account of 1793 that, "The pronunciation, as well as the language of the peasantry, is better than what prevails among the vulgar (i.e. common people) in the more southern counties. The better sort, and especially the fair sex, speak as well and with as little peculiarity of accent, as their equals in any part of Scotland." We cannot ignore the fact however that, as long as bad roads and distance from school often prevented attendance, the benefits of education had not yet been fully realised. By the end of the first decade of the 19th century the salary for the parochial school had gone up to £30 and the school was attended by 170 scholars.

By the time of the New Statistical Account, the Reverend Peter Jolly tells us that in 1840, in addition to the parochial school and the two SPCK schools, there was one subscription school at Freswick, and two private schools. The exact location of the private schools is not recorded except to place them "in the remote and poorer districts." (However, an estate map dated 1877 shows a school marked where the Skirza Road joins the A9, and another in Slickly.) The parochial school was, of course, still the most important and the teacher's salary, together with what he got as Session Clerk, amounted to £45 per year. The SPCK teacher in Mey got £15 and the Stroma teacher £10 with £4 paid to his wife for teaching sewing and knitting. The subscription school at Freswick which had been founded in 1812, gave a salary of £14 but the teacher got no fees from pupils, as was the case in the former schools, while in the two private schools the teachers "on their own adventure" earned only between £5 and £8 each.

Education about this time, the mid 19th century, was making rapid strides in Canisbay Parish. The Reverend Jolly says, "The branches principally taught in all schools, are, English, reading, writing and arithmetic. All between six and 15 years of age can read, but the females are not commonly taught to write. There are none upwards of 15 years who cannot read, except a few aged individuals. The district most in want of the means of education is the inland part of the parish, where the population is too small to be able to support a teacher, and too remote to benefit by the schools already in existence." Jolly's contribution to the New Statistical Account was followed in three brief years by the Disruption in 1843. The Free (South) Church was founded and with it a Free Church School. Now we have two schools operating in the heart of the parish, the advantage probably lying with the newly constructed school beside the newly constructed church, supported by a large percentage of the parishioners. Possibly in response to this situation, in 1864 the parochial school was transferred to a new building in the centre of the village. This became the responsibility of the Parish School Board in 1872 and remained in use till it was replaced by the present building in 1974.

The passing of the 1872 Education Act, with its tacit recognition that schooling of the people was the responsibility of the state, gave further impetus to educational development in Canisbay parish. The Canisbay Parish School Board was set up with responsibility to provide education of a national standard by certificated teachers in schools built for the purpose. Education now became compulsory for all children between five and 13 years of age. From the implementation of the Act up to almost the middle of the present century, education was provided at seven schools in the parish; at Auckengill, Brabster, Canisbay, Freswick, John O'Groats, Mey and Stroma. All, with the exception of Brabster which had a smaller roll, and for a time (at least until 1923) was run as a "Side School",* were staffed by a Head Teacher who taught the older pupils and an Assistant who took the younger children. This Assistant might be a so-called Pupil Teacher who, as the name implies, was more often than not a school leaver who had shown some academic promise and done well as a pupil and was engaged in effect as an apprentice teacher under instruction from the Head Teacher. As was quite normal with the apprenticeship system a monetary guarantee had often to be given that at least a year's work would be completed by the said Pupil Teacher. After about five years as a Pupil Teacher, young ladies – it seems that young men were seldom if ever considered for this position – could gain entrance to a Teacher Training College and become certificated. Many could not afford to go and remained in post as Uncertificated Teachers.

* **Note** – Side Schools, a feature of this time, were schools with small rolls often in isolated areas run under the supervision of a senior Head Teacher of a larger school in a contiguous district; in Brabster's case, Canisbay. No records relating to Brabster School have been found in Canisbay School Log Books after 5 January, 1923. So it might be reasonable to assume, other evidence lacking, that from then until its closure in 1955 it stood as a school in its own right.

To the above seven schools were transferred all pupils from such as the Free Church and SPCK Schools which hereafter ceased their function. It is worth noting in passing that though a new school was needed at Auckengill, within the Canisbay Parish boundary, because it would serve much of the quoad sacra parish of Keiss its building was undertaken by the Keiss School Board which had assumed responsibility for the Auckengill School after the passing of the 1872 Act. Its first teacher when it opened in 1886 was James Maxton father of the well known socialist MP of the same name. One imagines that his radical sentiments would have been well received in Canisbay parish.

To the schools under the new School Boards were appointed teachers like Maxton holding nationally recognised certificates and paid the going rate for the job. The "going rate", was, as it always had been, a breadline subsistence one – though fortunately few descended to the state of one luckless dominie at the beginning of the century (not in Caithness) who was schoolmaster, precentor, clerk, beadle and gravedigger: all for a total annual income of only £8 sterling.

As we reach the first decade of the 20th century we find that the situation established by the 1872 Act had endured recognisably but one particular change is worthy of remark . . . While the Parochial School Boards were responsible for the affairs of education in the parishes they derived their authority from, and ultimately were answerable to, the Scotch (sic) Education Department. The latter exercised its authority through the Inspectors of Schools. As had been the case since 1862 the amount of annual grant assigned to the Boards related to three components; (A) attendance – 20 pence per pupil with a minimum of 400 attendances; (B) order and discipline – 7.5 pence per pupil if excellent, 5 pence if good; (C) passes in reading, writing and arithmetic – 15 pence per pass. The Inspectors visited the schools annually and tested each pupil. In other words "payment by results"! Clearly the pressure on teachers and consequently on pupils was intense. Lucky were the able pupils, quick on the uptake, for they had a comparatively serene passage. Sadly many others bore mental – and indeed physical – scars, as teachers tried to drive in what the poor youngsters could not take in. Moreover while the duller pupils were overtaxed the quick ones were equally often underestimated and unstretched. Mercifully this disadvantageous system of financing education was abandoned in 1890 but old habits died hard and both James A. Green in his "Groatie Buckies" and John S. Banks in his "The Heather Blooms at John O'Groats" record how, in their school days at the turn of the century, the foregoing circumstances still prevailed. The Head Teacher's word was law and all work had to be done as he said. One lady, sadly no longer with us, used to recall how she got her mother to help her with her homework. Consequently though the answer was right it was not set out as Mr MacKenzie required and she was asked how this came about – who had helped her?

"My mother."

"And who do you think knows better – your mother or I?"

When recounting this story she used to say that, to her eternal regret, with head bowed she answered, "You, Sir".

There is no doubt however that as we move

towards and into the 20th century, greater liberalism extends into education with regard to both administration and the curriculum. Education had been free throughout Caithness for the compulsory age range from 1889 and from 1892 fees were also cancelled for the higher classes. For schools in Canisbay parish there was a down side to this, for along with free higher education we see the beginnings of centralisation which continued in Caithness right through to 1967 and beyond. Down the years Caithness, and not least our parish, had a proud record of educating the "lad o' pairts" (the "lass o' pairts" was not to get the same consideration till some time later) at the local school till he was ready to go to college. Now at a stroke it could be said that rural pupils were disadvantaged and the rural dominie lost a valued stimulus and a source of pride. An appendix to this contribution shows a few examples of work from these bygone days. That done by some older pupils shows considerable maturity to say the least. Parents from the east side of the parish who were ambitious for their children's further education now had to send them to Wick or, at least for a start, to Keiss where since 1899 the upper school had been recognised as a separate secondary department. Similarly parents from the Mey area had to get their academically inclined children to Castletown or Thurso. The journey from John O'Groats to Inverness now takes less time than that to Wick did then. So needless to say not all who showed academic promise were able to avail themselves of this "free" opportunity. It is worth mentioning here, however that the seven parish schools were of equal standing with the exception of the aforementioned side school, Brabster. Despite this equality of status there is no doubt that Canisbay at the centre of the parish had extra kudos. Some parents anxious to do their best, as they saw it, for their bairns would send them to Canisbay. This obviously involved arduous travel so that this option was sometimes taken up when the children were older and better able to stand up to the rigours involved.

For those lacking in means, promising but needy pupils were sometimes the concern of benefactors who had made their way in the world. John Kirk, a provost of Wick, left over £10,000 in trust for educational purposes in the parishes of Wick, Bower and Canisbay. In 1907 John Gunn F.E.I.S. writes of this fund. . . "the proceeds are applied to furnish school bursaries of the value of not less than £5, and not more than £10, and tenable for two years. In addition a sum of £25 is devoted yearly to supplying books and clothing to necessitous children."

He continues that Peter Keith of Canisbay House bequeathed, "£1,000 for the education of youth of the parish of Canisbay which will be managed by the School Board. The sum will be invested, and the interest will be given annually in a bursary or bursaries, as the Board may direct, which will be called the "Keith Bursaries"." In January 1893, the School Board decided to devote the proceeds to paying one bursary, of the annual value of £20, and

tenable for two years to attend a Scotch University or a Normal (i.e. Teacher) Training College; and another of £8 annual value, also tenable for two years, to be spent in attendance at a Secondary School. It is worthy of note that Peter Keith's two sons had both been dux pupils of the Royal High School in Edinburgh, the elder in 1890 and his brother Arthur Berriedale Keith in 1893 of whom it was said, – John O'Groat Journal, July 1893 – that in his 15th year he was the youngest dux the school had produced. No doubt these successes had some influence on the father's decision to give some financial encouragement to other lads o' pairts.

The liberalism I predicted, before being diverted into this glance at the hard facts of educational life is, for all that, discernable. As the scholastic bread and butter ceased to be dependent on the "the three R's", the emphasis on Reading, 'riting and 'rithmetic, though it was never lost sight of, eased slightly and we see expectations from the Inspectorate that, depending on the school's locality, subjects like Cookery and Sewing (for girls of course), Gardening, Navigation – perhaps with some Astronomy – and Woodwork (for boys of course) and Nature Study should receive some attention. You will see from the appendix that even French was attempted in 1903 probably as a gesture of solidarity with the newly signed Entente Cordiale between Britain and France.

Unlike in England where school Boards were replaced by Committees of County and County Borough Councils in 1902, in Scotland it was 1918 before a Bill was passed abolishing the School Boards and replacing them with ad hoc education authorities. Consequently until then, though Government finance for schools no longer depended on pupil passes, the school Log Books report not infrequent threats of refusal of Grants under various Articles relating to such matters as attendance and condition of schools. There is a unique snapshot of the condition of Canisbay's schools contained in a "Report by H.M. Inspector re Schools under Canisbay School Board" in 1905. This report had to be copied into the Log Book of every School in the parish and is of such general interest as to be perhaps worthy of reproduction here.

"Report by H.M. Inspector re Schools under Canisbay School Board" Dated 30th November, 1905

(Taken from Canisbay School Log Book)

The schools in the parish were visited on the 1st November by the Department's Inspector and the Medical Officer of Health for the County of Caithness who will be glad to meet the Board to discuss any of the points raised in this report.

General Condition of the School Buildings and Playground

Regular Inspection of the School buildings by the Managers is strongly recommended and it should be the duty of the Head Teacher to report to the

Board when repairs are necessary, with a view to the schools always having an air of tidiness and order. The rones for example should not have been allowed to remain out of order at Freswick Public School and the girls' playground at John O'Groats Public School should have had fresh gravel put on before the advent of wet weather.

Offices (These were the toilets)

The offices are badly kept at all the schools, they are specially dirty and dilapidated at Mey and Freswick Public Schools and except at Canisbay Public School are of a bad type. There are no urinals. The state of Mey Public School again calls for adverse criticism and unless there is great improvement it will be necessary to deal with the matter under Article 32(b) of the Code. Generally, however more attention should be given to cleanliness. Every part of the floor must be brushed every evening, and both it and the woodwork washed at least eight times a year; the maps and apparatus should be dusted every day, the walls should be brushed down once a week, and washed with distemper once a year. The walls of the offices should be limewashed regularly.

Heating

New grates of a type to be suggested by H.M. Inspector are wanted in both classrooms at Freswick Public School, and the Infant Room at John O'Groats Public School. There should be a thermometer in every classroom.

Lighting

Lighting is satisfactory except in Mey Public School where it is poor in the main room owing to the northern aspect of the windows. It would be much improved, however, if the walls were kept clean and the woodwork painted a light colour. The window sashes are not well fitted in this room.

Ventilation

Ventilation is unsatisfactory at Freswick and Canisbay Public Schools. In the former case, sash ventilation might be tried; and in the latter, properly constructed inlets and outlets should be made in both classrooms as well as in the cloakroom. Some of the books kept in the classroom at Freswick Public School are very musty.

Seats

The seats in the Infant Room at Freswick Public School have no backs; at Canisbay Public School they vary in height from 13 inches to 15 inches and are therefore unsuitable for young children; whilst at the other two schools they should be shifted so that the feet of the pupils may rest on the floor.

Water Supply

A water supply is not introduced at any of the schools. At Canisbay Public School the arrangement whereby water is not obtainable after 10 a.m. is not good; and the pails in which the water is brought to the school are not clean.

Cloakrooms

The porch at Freswick Public School does not give sufficient accommodation for cloaks; it is moreover in disrepair and very dirty.

This report should be copied in the log-book of each of the schools under the Board.

☆★☆★☆★☆

We do not need much imagination to realise that living and growing and working in school was no bed of roses in 1905 but we should not forget that life on the crofts and in the cottar houses was hard too.

From the late Robert E. MacCallum's researches it is clear that one head teacher, the uncompromising George T. MacKenzie of John O'Groats School, strove unremittingly to fulfil the requirements of the Department, both regarding the curriculum and the school itself. From the educational point of view, under his headship the school got consistently good reports, as indeed it continued to do after his time. In trying to ensure that the School Board faced up to its obligations he was perhaps rather less successful, as some of the following extracts from his Log Book entries may indicate: –

9 March 1906

The School supply of coals has run out, and the master is supplying the deficiency from his peat stack till the Board is informed.

Note:– Anent this it is perhaps worth mentioning that it was only in 1894 that the Scotch Education Department issued a circular that pupils need no longer carry a peat to school thus ending a long tradition – a tradition which has it that dodgers who came without their peats were usually kept well away from the fire.

12 March 1906

A severe snowstorm accompanied with frost. Thermometer at 9.30, one hour and a half after fires are supposed to be on, stood at 33 degrees. (i.e. one degree above freezing!)

18 June 1906 – Annual Report – remarks by Department

Immediate attention should be paid to the terms of His Majesty's Inspector's report communicated to the Board on the 30 November last with regard to the offices (toilets). Payment of a grant without deduction under Article 32(b) of the Code has been allowed only after considerable hesitation owing to the Board's delay to remedy the defects mentioned.

22 October 1906

A fisherman's Meeting was held on Saturday night. Visited the school at 10.30 p.m. and found the floor as usual dotted with expectoration. This morning these places were still unwashed and the floor unswept, the school cleaner alleging that she had not been paid for the work done after the previous meeting of the same description. This state of matters is all the worse that the classrooms had been just washed out and were hardly dry.

In accordance with H.M. Inspector's instructions I report this entry to Clerk of School Board.

29 October 1906

Two meetings were held in the school on Saturday evening lasting from 7.30 to 10.30. This morning the school was more than usually filthy, and the headmaster closed the school during the morning sederunt till the school cleaner could wash and brush out. Reported 5/11/06.

2 November 1906 – Excerpt of the Minutes of Canisbay School Board.

There was submitted a letter from Mr MacKenzie dated 22nd October, as to the use of the school Room at John O'Groats for meetings at night. The Clerk was instructed to remind Mr MacKenzie that he should see that the parties getting the use of the school have the School Room properly cleaned out after their meetings.

Note:– In fact this was no part of the Head Teacher's duties.

9 November 1906 – Excerpt of Minutes of Canisbay School Board

The obligation sought to be laid upon the headmaster by the foregoing Excerpt of Minutes would lead to serious complications which must be avoided at all costs, and the obligation is therefore declined.

There the matter seems to have rested!

☆★☆★☆☆

These Inspectors' Reports and Head Teacher's Log-Book entries have taken us into the first years of the 20th century – not within living memory perhaps but certainly into the folk memory of us born in the 1910s, 20s and 30s. From here on many of us can relate, by way of our own recollections or the reminiscences of parents and grandparents, to school life throughout the century which has now almost run its course.

The Classroom Environment

So what was it like to be at school in Canisbay Parish into and through the first half of the 20th century? Basically the school buildings were all very similar dating as they did from the Act of 1872. All, with the exception of Brabster, were two-teacher schools, though, as time went by, rural depopulation affected them up to the war in 1939 and beyond. Till then and through to the end of the war in 1945, children could complete their schooling, up to the school leaving age of 14, at their local district schools.

As mentioned, the buildings with some minor

modifications did duty well into the second half of this century. In Canisbay School for example the main room had been divided by a wood and glass partition into the "big room" and the "peedie room" so that the other lesser room to the north could serve occasional use as a cookery room. It could also serve other purposes – for example, I can well remember being banished there for being disruptive in the "peedie room" while the senior girls were in at their afternoon sewing lesson. There I stayed after all the school had gone home, in mortal terror that I had been forgotten about and would have to stay "locked up" all night. Miss Taylor, later Mrs Docherty, was wise enough to let me "stew" a little and taught me a salutary and unforgotten lesson!

The classrooms of the two teacher school up to these days and beyond were sparsely furnished. The Head Teacher had a desk with drawers and the Assistant had a table, perhaps with one drawer. The pupils sat in double desks of which the seats and the tops hinged up. A neighbour might occupy a desk on his own. If he got up and sat down again without looking he was liable to sit on the floor because you had raised the seat. Great hilarity among the class and stern rebuke from the teacher! These desks had superseded the long forms which in earlier days took perhaps 10 pupils. The main teaching aid was the blackboard and each room had one on its easel which also served as a display stand for maps or any other of the few visual aids available to the school in these days. Then there was a cupboard for books and copy books. This might bear a small plate with the names of the Coats Brothers of whom it might be said that they did as much to encourage book provision in Scotland, though on a smaller scale, as did Carnegie. These along with the teacher's chair, the coal scuttle and the fireguard pretty well completed the inventory.

Mention of the coal scuttle brings up the subject of heating. The "big room" and the "peedie room" each had an ordinary open fire at one end. In the "big room" particularly this was quite inadequate for the Caithness climate. The subject is often mentioned in the log in terms like these:–

20 January, 1922, "On very cold days the main room is so chilly that much of the scholars valuable time is lost in performing exercises to warm themselves" . . . from Canisbay School Log Book.

A glance at old school photos of this era will show that the children are well and warmly turned out, as certainly they needed to be. In the summer however it was quite usual to go to school barefoot. Indeed this was the done thing in Aberdeenshire as well, for Sir Maitland Mackie tells in his book, "A Lucky Chap", how he had boots to wear to school but he left them at the end of the farm road so as not to be different. I well understand that! My mother in a moment of incomprehensible aberration bought me a scarlet – scarlet! – blazer when I was about seven. I wore it once. Life could be very unpleasant if you were "different".

To continue with the theme of physical conditions,

obviously the weather played a critical part in the well-being of the pupils and thus of the schools. When children arrived at school wet after a long walk the teachers did their best for them. Though facilities for drying off were absent they would be allowed to stand by the fire for a time. Outside, the playground was pretty rough and hummocky but that in no way detracted from the bairns' enjoyment in its use – continual references in the Canisbay School Log Book to pot holes in the shingle from the gate to the school door notwithstanding.

The normal school day was from 10.00 a.m. till 4.00 p.m. with a break in the morning, "the Interval", of about 20 minutes and a Lunch Hour between 1.00 p.m. and 2.00 p.m. In the winter months this Lunch Hour was shortened to a half hour and school closed at half past three to allow the long distance travellers to get most of the way home before complete darkness fell. For lunch, those who did not have time to go home, the majority, would have a bottle of milk and a "piece" of flour scone, oat cake or "loaf" with butter and jam, cheese or some other spread. Some went to a nearby house where it would be arranged for a kindly body to provide a cup of cocoa and possibly something to go with it. Money was scarce in those days but it was surprising how many occasionally managed to have a copper to spend in the local shop at "play time".

The Curriculum

We went to school to learn, "The Three R's" basically, but our teachers had sufficient breadth of vision to introduce us to a wide variety of interests. Mind you, the interests you were allowed as a pupil then were distinctly sexist. If you were a girl you did sewing: if you were a boy you did gardening! I do believe still, the boys had the best of it. That apart, our learning days passed serenely enough. Sufficient pressure was applied only to ensure we did our best, and we were given every encouragement to take an interest in books. For many of my generation access to books opened a door to great excitement. Books, being readily available, through the library boxes which came to the school every term, filled a slot later taken up by radio and now by television. Then we had also the less well regarded material like the weekly comics, "The Rover", "The Skipper", "The Adventure", "The Champion", "The Girls' Crystal", "The Beano", "The Dandy", "Tiger Tim" and many more.

Growing up in the late "30s" meant we were living in stimulating times. Unapprehensive of the imminent dangers, we were excited by the threat of war. As I have indicated, our Head Teacher always kept us in the picture, to the extent of taking his radio into the school to let us hear broadcasts on critical situations.

Tools of the Trade

The wireless, of course, was a sophisticated piece of equipment in the 30s. Most of our everyday tools were much more commonplace. Until the late 30s slates and slate pencils were in use in the Junior (Infant) Room. Infinitely durable, they took years of writing and never wore out. The one problem they had was cleaning. The recommended way was to have a cloth (clootie) and some water but more often than not it was done with a spittle and a sleeve – if the teacher's attention was elsewhere.

When we went through to the "Beeg Room" we used jotters or exercise books. These we provided ourselves and they had one serious drawback from the pupils' point of view. The evidence was there in graphite perpetuity of the "slovenly" manner in which your work had been done. "Slovenly" seems to be a word I remember from these days.

Copperplate hand-writing was the acceptable norm then and copperplate writing books were issued every Tuesday and Thursday afternoon for practising correct letter formation. The ink-wells sat in the desks all through the week during which foreign matter by accident or design was accumulated. The results on the copy-books can be guessed. Yet the handwriting produced by the schools, was and is a credit to them.

Discipline

However harmonious the classroom scene was most of the time, discipline had to be kept. The strap was the instrument of discipline, used only as a last resort, after too many warnings had been given and the teacher's patience was exhausted. Different teachers, of course, had different "fuse lengths"! The pupils knew this very well. Some teachers could sear more cuttingly with the tongue than with the belt.

"Laurence Brown, you really are the most unimaginative boy!" I'm sure this was true but why do I remember that comment and not any of the dozens of times I deservedly got the strap?

A group of us boys when we were about the top end of the school actually pinched the strap for a while. The idea was to destroy it but it proved indestructible and really became an embarrassment to us. In addition, Mr McColl made so little fuss about the matter that I think we were sorry for him and slipped it back in its drawer. Nothing more was ever said about it.

Games and Pastimes

Of course when the serious business of feeding the mind and the body was over there was always some time for play, and the pranks and pastimes pursued were many and varied. Usually the boys and girls went their separate ways at this but sometimes they would play together; usually at games like "Hide-and-Seek" or one of the many variants of "Tag". One of these latter, at Canisbay, was "Kaybie". (This is just a phonetic spelling as I have never seen the word written.) Up to 1940, at least, it took bursts of being popular, till it would be displaced by the next craze. Every interval and lunch hour the cry would go up, "Kaybie! Kaybie! 'e loons against 'e lassagies". It was a complex game and the rules are quite beyond my ability to explain here but if there are others out there who remember, "Kaybie, Kaybie, butter and cheese, Come and get me, if you . . . please!", and how it was played it would be worth reviving. It may have been forgotten after 1945 when all the pupils over 12 went to High School. There does not seem to be any reason why it should not again become popular. Oddly I have never heard of it being played anywhere other than at Canisbay. In this it is not like "Knotty" the Caithness version of shinty or hockey played with kail runts or whin branches for sticks and a cork from a herring line, or anything remotely suitable, for a ball. Knotty or notty was popular at the turn of the century and is now happily having a revival; though not in this parish as far as I know.

In genetic terms two other "sports" of "Tag" were "Dowgs an' Rabbads" in Canisbay and "Lee-a-Lawley" in John O'Groats. In both, certain areas of the playground, usually the corners, were safe bases for all those who were "Rabbads" in the former or "Freemen" in the latter. When the "Dowg" barked the "Rabbads" had to run between bases. The "Dowg" armed with a tennis ball or the like tried to hit as many as he could between bases. Each one hit became a "Dowg" and joined the hunt till all "Rabbads" were eliminated and the game started again. "Lee-a-Lawley" was similar but it was played without a ball and therefore probably had an older pedigree. A "King" instead of a "Dowg" shouted, "Cum-a-Lee" to start the game. Those he could "croon" (touch their heads) as they ran between bases became his subjects and joined in the chase till all the Freemen were subjected.

In games like the above, a fair means had to be found to determine who was "It", "Dowg", "King" or whatever, and to this end there were innumerable counting out rhymes which could be the subject of an investigation on their own. The girls, as I remember, were better at these than the boys; as they were at all bouncing ball and skipping games. In this area the boys, like myself, tried to cover up their inadequacy by clowning around. There was a game or rather an activity that allowed the boys to get some of this out of their systems. Called "Chargers", intellectually at least it showed some knowledge of the knights of old. A beeg loon would take a peedy chiel on his back and they would charge and wrestle with another pair until one or other was couped. While there were never any league tables, reputations could be made this way.

Not all free time was spent in the playground. Occasionally there occurred an event beyond the school dyke of such dramatic import that it demanded all our attention. Such an event was the purchase, by Willie Alexander of West Canisbay, of the first tractor in the parish, and a Fordson at that! The rumour had been going around and we had heard all the discussions on the pros and cons of tractors versus horses. This fine morning we could not believe our luck when we saw the tractor ploughing the park behind the "New Hooses" right forenent the school. Nobody thought of going to the lavatory at the interval – it was pell mell over the Manse Road dyke to see this new wonder. We followed the ploughing combination up and down the furrows like maas, sagely shaking our heads and rehearsing the discussions we had heard in adult company; how it would burst the drains; how it would pack the grun'; how the seed would never take, etc., etc., and not caring a button because it was about the most exciting thing we had ever seen, apart that was, from Wildy Allan's steam mill or the road roller. We hardly heard the bell, and few of our "pieces" were eaten that day or the next. But then "the shine went off it" and just as suddenly we found other things to do in the playground.

As far as the boys were concerned, while all of the above exercised us from time to time, and we even played cricket for one glorious summer in 1940, nothing really competed with football as the predominant game. It was played in wet or dry and the tackety boots worn universally then made a fair substitute for football boots. We played it with tennis balls, sponge balls, and six inch air filled balls from "Woolies" which lasted no time; but what we really wanted was a proper football and our resources did not run to that. However we hit on the idea that we should collect around the village for a "School Football". We made out a notebook and called first on Doctor Gill. We knew he was interested in football! He started us off well. Next we called on Mr Cameron, the United Free Continuing Church Minister who then occupied the School House. He also was sympathetic. We should certainly have asked Mr McColl, the Head Master for a donation too but he was beyond our reach after school as he stayed in Mey at that time. This was a pity as it turned out. However by the end of the evening's collection we had made more than six shillings, quite a tidy sum in pre-war terms, and we were very pleased with ourselves. Next day however the balloon went up. News of our entrepreneurial venture reached the school staff. The problem seemed to be that we had collected for a "School Football" without proper authority! The Head Teacher was quite "laid back", (to use a term unknown then) about the matter and obviously didn't really want to know but the Assistant was incensed and insisted that the money should be returned. However we kept our heads down for a while and when things had cooled, took the money to Wick where we bought a football at Arthur Bruce's for six shillings and sixpence. It was not a full size football but it was better than anything we had had before and it lasted us for many a day.

Amenities and Toilets

Although many games were played in the "interval" there is no doubt it was there as a toilet break. Amenities in Canisbay School at this time were basic, as of course they were elsewhere. Until August 1935 when, along with a stove, a sink with running water was installed in the cookery room the only source of water was one cold tap in the porch/cloakroom with a chipped enamel mug to drink from. The coats were hung there on two sturdy coat racks. If they were wet when they arrived they were still wet when they went home. Perhaps they were even wetter, for taps being something of a novelty, we found that great fun could be had holding ones hand under the running tap and squirting water all over the place. Retribution might follow but this game has never died out. However to have one tap with running water in the cloakroom represented paradise when compared to the toilets. The sanitation in these was rudimentary. For the boys, what was called in these days a "zinc pail" did duty as a urinal in the lavatory. Boys will be boys and they were not too fussy about using it – especially if there was a competition going on to see who could pee the highest! Pity the poor cleaner who at that time was a saintly lady called Mrs Nicholson, our next door neighbour, whose kindness to me as a boy I shall never forget.

It is worth remembering that the Inspector's Report in 1905 made no particular criticism of the Canisbay School toilets – indeed they seemed at that time to be the best in the parish. However from then over a period of almost 40 years successive reports by His Majesty's Inspectors continually draw attention to the insanitary condition of the "offices". Yet not till October 1941 did Canisbay School get flush toilets and even then the semi-rotary pump supplying the water was not working properly. There was grumbling about all this of course but as far as I can remember most of us as pupils did not think too much about it. Probably the majority of households in the district or indeed the parish were still without the "luxury" of bathrooms and flush lavatories before the War of 1939/45.

While much of the above detail refers specifically to Canisbay, substitute the names of Auckingill, Brabster, Freswick, John O'Groats, Mey and Stroma and throughout the period, circumstances would have been very similar in all the schools. They all had the same calendar of events and they all had the same obligatory visiting officials though Stroma might be less likely to be taken unawares by these.

The March of Time

Dwindling rolls, unfortunately, saw some of these become single teacher schools – Auckingill in 1921; Freswick in 1943; Stroma in 1944; Mey in 19??. In 1937 John O'Groats too became a one-teacher school, its roll dropping at one stage to only 11 pupils. It made a come-back however and in 1948 its two-teacher status was restored, helped by the transfer of the six pupils from Freswick which was then closed.

From 1933 however, motor bus transport from John O'Groats to Wick meant that pupils east of Gills could travel daily to Wick High School and pursue higher education there if they and their parents were so minded. Such pupils from Mey and

Gills had the advantage of transport to the Higher Grade School at Castletown a couple of years or so earlier. The practical outcome of this was that through the late 30s and into the war years more and more pupils transferred to the High School at the end of Primary Seven and the "Advanced Division" of pupils seeing out their compulsory years of education (up to 14) in the primary schools shrank. Then in 1946 the new Education Act separated Primary and Secondary education at the end of Primary Seven and gave all Canisbay parish children compulsory free access to Secondary Education in Wick – or Thurso, for the Mey pupils. It should perhaps be mentioned that pre 1946 while the Secondary Education was free the bus transport had to be paid for by the pupils. However the Education Committee provided bursaries which neatly covered this cost. From now on, though, free school transport was provided for all children under eight living over two miles from school; and those over eight living over three miles from school. They might still have to travel some distance to catch the transport on its route. At this time, too, school meals were provided for all children who wished to take them. A charge was made for these but this could be waived if family circumstances were financially straitened.

Despite these improvements in school welfare the decline in school rolls has persisted through the years. Writing for the Third Statistical Account of Scotland in 1952, John Mowat gives the following pupil numbers for the parish down the years:– 461 (1834), 454 (1874), 372 (1901), 302 (1914), 135 (1949), and he tells us that of the last 135 the High Schools had 23. These telling figures are reflected in a sad catalogue of School closures. The seven schools built in response to need after the 1872 Act were picked off one by one as their numbers fell below sustainable limits and modern day transport made the parish smaller. In bare statistics the melancholy story looks like this:–

1948	Freswick transferred to John O'Groats	6 pupils
1955	Brabster transferred to Lyth	6 pupils
1957	Stroma transferred to Keiss	2 pupils
1962	Auckengill transferred to Keiss	8 pupils
1969	Mey transferred to Crossroads	20 pupils
1974	John O'Groats transferred to Canisbay	33 pupils

And so after nearly 300 years, the historical clock has gone full circle. Though the souls of the districts may yearn for their lost schools, the Parliamentary Enactment of 1696 has been perversely fulfilled!

There is ae school in the parish!

Laurence Ollason Brown, The North House, John O'Groats.

Primary School Work – Canisbay School 1865

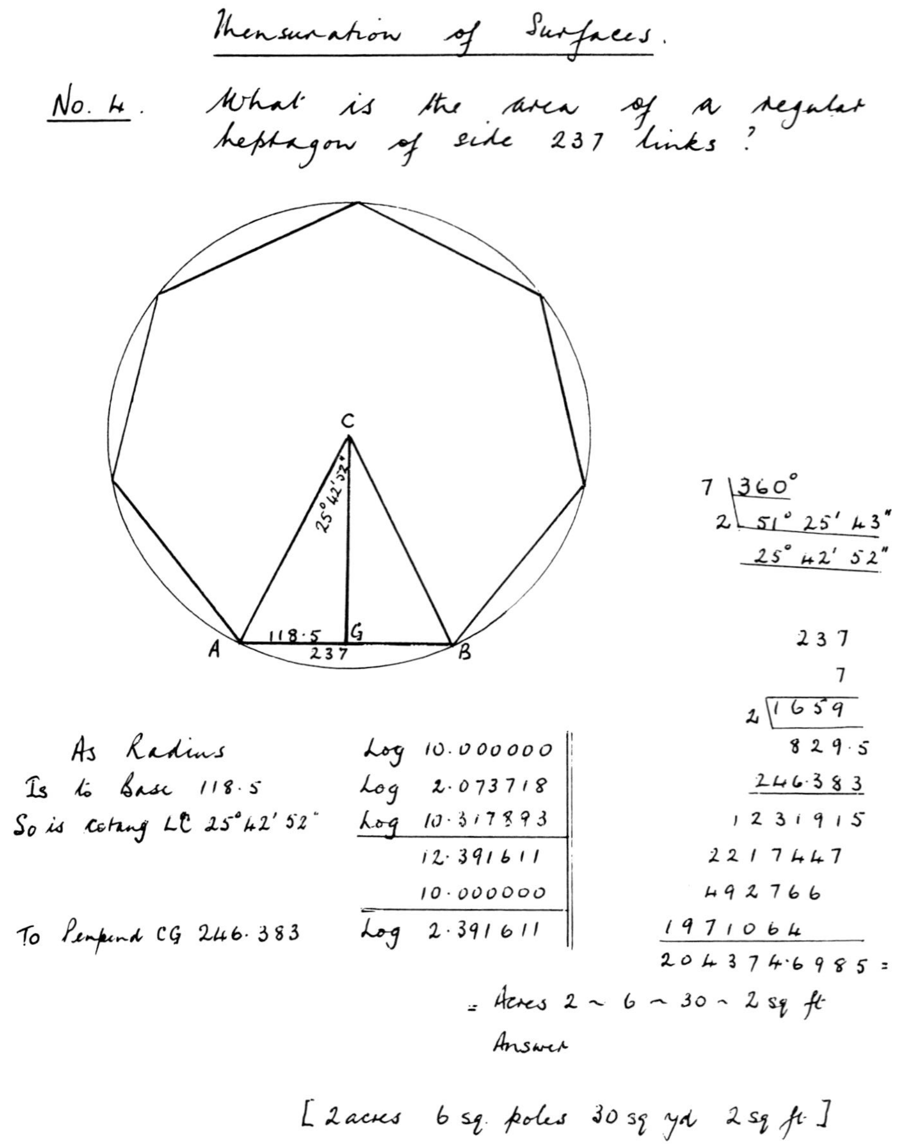

Mensuration of Surfaces.

No. 4. What is the area of a regular heptagon of side 237 links?

No. 1, From the 1st equation $x + y + z = 53$. To find the value
$x + 2y + 3z = 105$ } value of x, y,
$x + 3y + 4z = 134$ } and z.

2d Equation	$x + 2y + 3z = 165$
1st Equation	$x + y + z = 53$
By subtraction	$y + 2z = 52$ (H)
3d Equation	$x + 3y + 4z = 134$
2d Equation	$x + 2y + 3z = 105$
By subtraction	$y + z = 29$ (B)
Equation (H)	$y + 2z = 52$
Equation (B)	$y + z = 29$
By subtraction	$z = 23$

No. 2, $5x + 8y = 124$ } $15x - 10y = 100$ | $10x + 16y = 248$
$3x - 2y = 20$ } $15x + 24y = 372$ | $24x - 16y = No$
          $34y = 272$ | $34x = 408$
          Ans $y = 8$ | $x = 12$ Ans

No. 3, $x - y = 2$ } $5x - 5y = 10$ $5x + 2y = 120$
$5x + 2y = 120$ } $5x + 2y = 120$ $7y = 110$
          $7y = 110$ $y = 15\frac{5}{7}$
          Ans $y = 15\frac{5}{7}$

No. 1, $4x + 3y = 31$ $12x + 9y = 93$
$3x + 2y = 22$ } $12x + 8y = 88$
          $y = 5$ $x = 4$ Ans

$9x + 6y = 66$
$8x + 6y = 62$
$x + 0 = 4$ Ans

As Radius   Log 10.000000
Is to Base 118·5   Log 2.073718
So is Cotang ∠C 25°42'52"   Log 10·317893

                   12.391611
                   10.000000
To Perpend CG 246·383   Log 2.391611

7) 360°
2) 51° 25' 43"
      25° 42' 52"

      237
        7
    2) 1659
        829·5

    246·383
    1231915
    2217447
    492766
    1971064
    2043746985 =

= Acres 2 ~ 6 ~ 30 ~ 2 sq ft
                Answer

[2 acres 6 sq. poles 30 sq yd 2 sq ft.]

A Page from William Houston's Count Book

William Houston's Mensuration Book was too fragile to photocopy so his grand niece Catherine MacLean, Duart, Auckengill transcribed this page.

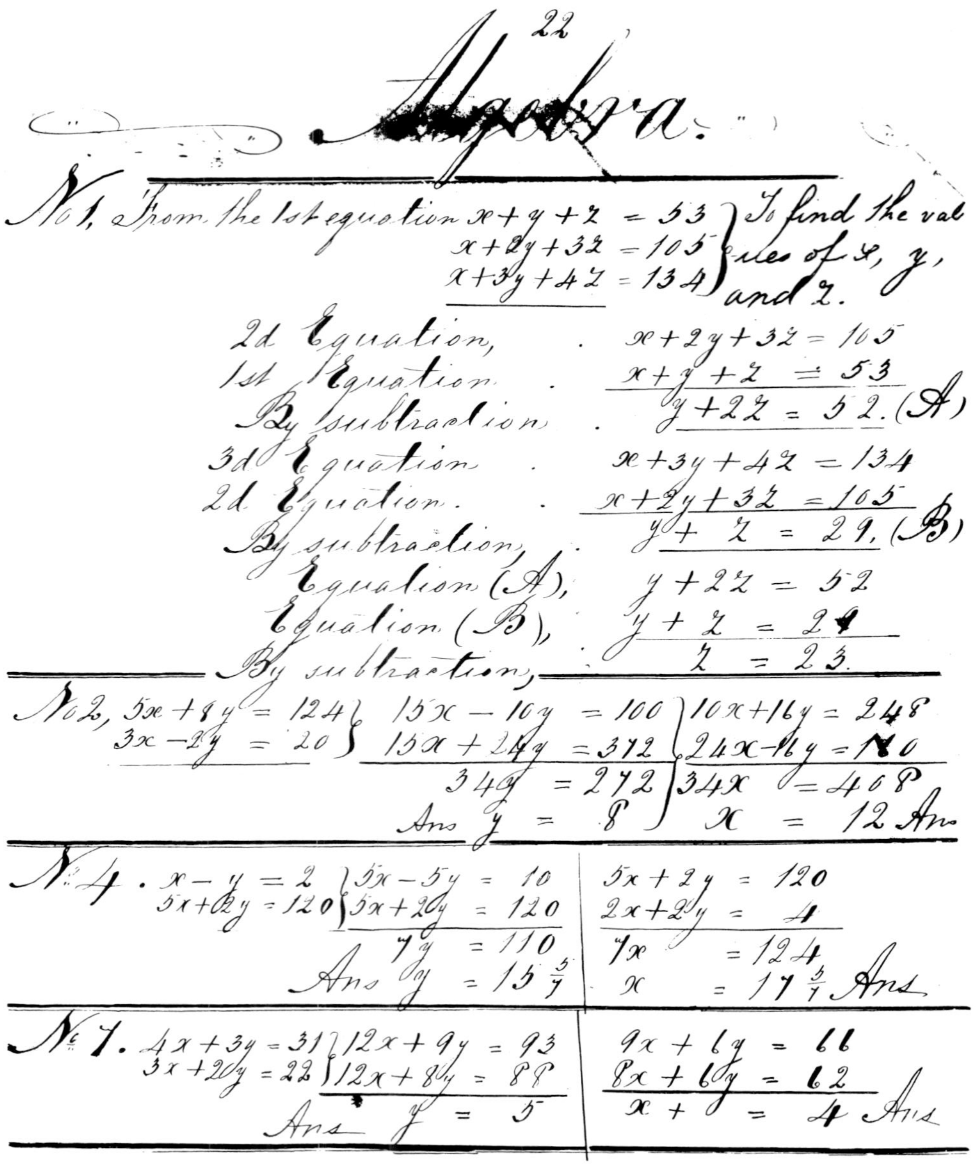

Canisbay School 1874

Inventory

Valuation of Goods on Hand March 31. 1874

Page from David Houston's Book-keeping Jotter.

John O'Groats School 1903

NOV 10 1903

The Weather in Harvest.

The weather this harvest has been very wet, and a good deal of the corn has been destroyed through the wet season. The harvest is the most important part of the year for the farmers. If the weather in harvest was not dry the country people would lose all their year's work. The people must be very active to get their corn and potatoes secured from frost and rain. The farmers had to put in their corn with the moonlight as the weather was so wet. There was much trouble in getting the corn cut this harvest because the land was too wet for the reaping machines to work.

Good — Newcatched!

Magnus Houston's Exercise Book – Teacher Mr Duff.

47

John O'Groats School 1903

Specimen of Dictation Exercise.

Begin the first line about an inch from the margin, writing very open and clear. The Examiner will read out the full stops only, so you must supply the others. Punctuate during second reading, and correct all errors on the final reading.

Specimen of Dictation Exercise.

Begin the first line about an inch from the margin, writing very open and clear. The Examiner will read out the full stops only, so you must supply the others. Punctuate during second reading, and correct all errors on the final reading.

Printing for Map-Drawing.

A B C D E F G H I J K L M

A B C D E F G H I J K L Mᶜ

a b c d e f g h i j k l m n o p q r s t u v w x y z

a b c d e f g h i j k l m—

Some Copybook Writing by Vina and Clara Houston – Teacher Mr Duff.

John O'Groats School 1904

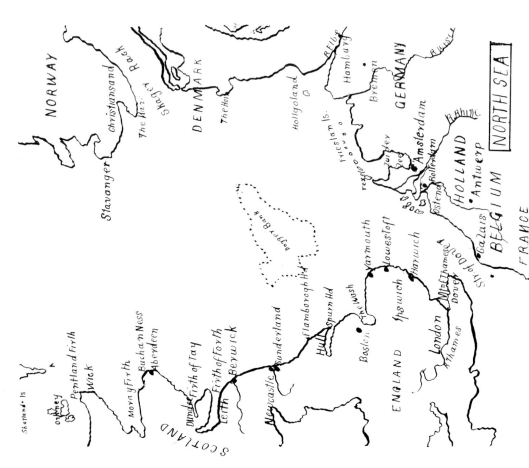

NORTH SEA

Shetland Is
Orkney
Pentland Firth
Wick
Moray Firth
Buchan Ness
Aberdeen
Firth of Tay
Dundee
Firth of Forth
Leith
Berwick
SCOTLAND
Newcastle
Sunderland
Flamborough Hd
Hull
Spurn Hd
The Wash
Boston
ENGLAND
Yarmouth
Lowestoft
Harwich
Ipswich
London
Thames
Dover
Sheerness
Mth of Thames

Dogger Bank

NORWAY
Stavanger
Christiansand
The Naze
Skager Rack
DENMARK
The Horn
Elbe
Hamburg
Helgoland
Friesland Is.
Zuyder Zee
Bremen
GERMANY
Russia
Amsterdam
R. Rhine
Rotterdam
Ostend
HOLLAND
Antwerp
BELGIUM
Calais
FRANCE

W. Good – 4. 11. 04.
4. 7. 04.

Malcolm Houston's Mapping Book.

Canisbay School c.1868
"Counting Out"

Zeentie veentie vantie vaig
Is ell dell dum and daig
Is irky birky stanan rock
Is an dan doosh.
Magnus Houston taught his grandchildren
this rhyme C.1938.

Primary School French
in John O'Groats School 1903

Now we've begun to learn some French
And this is what we say.
For thank you it's merci beaucoup
If you please is s'il vous plait
The child's l'enfant the ma's maman
The girl is la jeune fille
The father's pére the sister seur
The family – la famille
Le chien, the dog, le chat the cat
Le souris is the mouse
Open the door – ouvrez la porte
La Maison – that's the house.
Une tasse de thé is what we say
To have a cup of tea
Bon is good and non is no
And yes is just oui, oui.

William and David (Author of 'E Silkie Man) were the brothers of Magnus Houston (Miller). William who wrote "An Order for Hay", designed and drew out the plans for the new meal mill 1901. He was the son of the above William.

Magnus, Vina, Clara and Malcolm – family of the above Magnus.

John O'Groats School 1886
Teacher Mr Robert Arnott

An order for hay
Mrs Todd x an old widow who lived in a small village near a market town. She was very simple in her manner so the villagers could have cheated her in many ways over and over again. One day when she was standing in her door there past a cart load of hay for market and she cried to the boy who was driving the cart that she wanted some hay.

The boy drove up to her yard and with some difficulty got the horse and cart through the narrow gateway. He then went on the top of the load and with hay fork on hand cried "Now then how much do you want." "Will you give me as much as will make a hens nest for I have been wanting it for a long time Good x

William C. Houston

The Old Mill and Brig at John O'Groats

From a painting by John Nicolson 1888.

It was here that generations of young Houstons played.

Wick High School Pupils 1921

Pupils were all in the same class and came from the north side of Wick.

Photo from Frank Sutherland, Viewfirth, John O'Groats.

Back row, left to right:– David K. Sutherland, Newton, John O'Groats; Barry Mowat, Viewfirth, John O'Groats; Dinie Green, Roadside, John O'Groats; Annie Gunn, West End, John O'Groats; Meggie Alexander, Lyth; Lily Shearer, Upper Warse; George Rosie, Freswick. Front row:– Lily Alice Mowat, Keiss; Magsie Gunn, West End, John O'Groats; Frank Gulloch, Stemster, John O'Groats; Nancy Rollof, Auckengill; Nellie Cuthbertson, Canisbay.

Wick High School

Photo, Nancy Houston, St. Magnus.

The field was there, and there were ponies in it in 1927 when John Ross began at Wick High. He never said if he dreamt of being Rector but he did dream about a lovely black shaltie in the field.

50

WICK HIGH SCHOOL

From 1873 until 1911, Mr William Dick was rector of Pulteneytown Academy until he became rector of Wick High School to which all secondary pupils were transferred in August 1911.

The new High School was completed in time to coincide with the return of pupils to school after the summer holidays and the opening ceremony took place on the 23rd of August, 1911.

The "Groat" gave a very full report of this ceremony and a detailed description of the building itself. The space devoted to the architectural features is or would be unusual today. These features included the Scottish baronial style of architecture, the stepped gables, octagonal towers etc. The freestone facings came from Hopeman in Morayshire – nothing of interest is omitted. The internal features are described in the same minute detailed style, for example the pitch pine blocks of the hall floor which were laid in herring-bone pattern were 12" x 3". The tower rooms on the second floor were intended for classes in meteorology although it seems that future generations were quite unaware of their function in this part of the curriculum.

A feature of the female teachers' room was a gas pendant lit by electric ignition. To light this gas, one had merely to press a button placed at the doorway.

The "Groat" report continues: "The classroom walls and friezes have a decidedly soothing and restful effect" (It seems a pity that this decor was subsequently changed and it would seem highly desirable to revert to it at the earliest opportunity in the interests of a quieter life for all concerned – J.R.).

The desks were placed not less than 12" apart thereby eliminating the danger of spreading contagious diseases from one pupil to another.

The total cost was £10,000 excluding the gymnasium and the manual workshop. As is usual, not everyone was pleased, the suggestion being that something less than the size and grandeur of the new school would have been quite sufficient.

The work of the first session began on the day following the opening ceremony with an attendance of three hundred pupils. The staff consisted of the rector, four principal teachers – English, Mathematics, Classics and Science – and eight assistant teachers.

An entry in the log book for 9th October, refers to the appointment of Miss Elizabeth O. Begg as an assistant teacher. Another teacher with first class certificates from the Edinburgh School of Cookery, Atholl Crescent, was appointed at an annual salary of £60. Miss Begg took up her appointment on 8th November, 1911.

In the following year, 1912, the entry for 25th December reads: "As today is Christmas day the school will continue at work until 2 o'clock pm and will then be dismissed for the day." Two days later the school was closed for the New Year holidays and did not reopen until January 6th.

John Ross, Northfield, Wick.

"Counting Out" Rhymes

Eetil ottel black bottle
Eetil ottel out
Standing on a mantelpiece
Like a shining thrupney piece
Eetil ottel black bottle
Eetil ottel out.

Barbara Steven, Seaview.

Eetil ottel black bottle
Eetil ottel out
If you want a piece and jam
Just walk straight out.

(Stroma Version)
Robbie Dundas, Huna.

This is the man that broke the barn (big toe)
This is the man that stole the corn (first toe)
This is the man that ran awa' (second toe)
This is the man that telt it aa (third toe)
Poor peedie pinkie king o 'em aa
Fell in 'e gutters and paid for it aa.

Alex Dunnet, West End.

Skipping Rhymes

The wind and the wind and the wind, blows high
The rain comes tumbling from the sky.
Jonathan Miller says he'll die
For his lover rolling high.
She is handsome she is pretty
She is the girl of the golden city
She has lovers one, two, three
Pray and tell me who they'll be.
(– A, B, C, D – – when out, that is initial of lover)

Joey Bremner, "St Clair".

Teddy-bear-teddy-bear climb upstairs
Teddy-bear, teddy-bear say your prayers
Teddy-bear, teddy-bear say goodnight
Teddy-bear, teddy-bear that's alright.

Peppery – One, two, three – slow then fast
Nan Fraser, Canisbay.

Cobbler, cobbler mend my shoe
Have it done by half past two
Half past two is far too late
Have it done, by half past eight.

Sina Houston, The Mill.

TABLES

Rule of Thumb

Knuckle	= 1 inch = 3 barleycorns.
Nail	= 2¼ inches (first two joints index finger).
Hand	= 4 inches (when measuring horses).
Hand	= 6 inches (thumb to first or middle finger hand outstretched).
Span	= 9 inches (thumb to pinkie hand outstretched).
Ell } Cubit }	= ½ yard. Tape taken an inch over tip of middle finger and held with thumb. Measure over back of hand to elbow.
Fathom	= 6 feet. Outstretched arms over chest.
Yard	= 3 feet. Chin to outstretched arm.

Linear

12 inches	= 1 foot.
3 feet	= 1 yard = .915 metres.
5½ yards	= 1 rod, pole or perch.
40 poles	= 1 furlong = 220 yards.
7.92 inches	= 1 link.
100 links	= 1 chain = 22 yards.
80 chains	= 1 mile.
10 chains	= 1 furlong.
10 cables	= 1 nautical mile (6080 feet).
8 furlongs	= 1 mile = 1760 yards = 1.61k.

Nautical

6 feet	= 1 fathom.
100 fathoms	= 1 cable.
3 miles	= 1 league.

Area

144 sq. inches	= 1 square foot.
9 sq. feet	= 1 square yard.
30¼ sq. yards	= 1 square pole.
40 sq. poles	= 1 rood.
4 roods	= 1 acre.
16 sq. poles	= 1 square chain.
10 sq. chains	= 1 acre.
840 acres	= 1 square mile.
100 sq. metres	= 1 square decametre.
10,000 sq. metres	= 1 square hectometre = 1 hectare = 2.471 acres.
100 hectares	= 247.1169 acres.

Weight

1 silver 3d piece and old halfpenny	= ¼ ounce.
1 old penny and old halfpenny	= ½ ounce.
3 old pennies	= 1 ounce.

Avoirdupois

16 drams	= 1oz (ounce).
16 ounces	= 1lb (pound).
14 pounds	= 1st. (stone).
2 stones	= 1qr. (quarter).
4 quarters	= 1cwt (hundred weight).
20 hundred weights	= 1 ton.
10 stones	= 1 boll.
16 bolls	= 1 chalder.
1 Firlot	= ¼ boll.

Troy

24 Grains	= 1 pennyweight (dwt).
20 pennyweights	= 1 ounce.

Dry Measure

2 gallons	= 1 peck.
4 pecks	= 1 bushel.
8 bushels	= 1 quarter.
5 quarters	= 1 wey or load.
2 weys	= 1 last.

(1 bushel good quality oats = 42lbs.)

Paper

24 sheets	= 1 quire.
20 quires	= 1 ream.
500 sheets	= 1 ream (printing paper).
2 reams	= 1 bundle.
5 bundles	= 1 bale.

Capacity

1 minim	= 1 drop = 1 grain.
60 minims	= 1 drachm.
8 drachms	= 1 ounce.
20 ounces	= 1 pint.
1 drachm	= 1 teaspoon.
1 mutchkin	= ¾ pint.
1 chopin	= 1½ pints.
2 ounces	= 1 wine glass.
5 ounces	= 1 gill.
4 gills	= 1 pint.
2 pints	= 1 quart.
4 quarts	= 1 gallon.
9 gallons	= 1 firkin.
4 firkins	= 1 barrel.
36 gallons	= 1 barrel.
42 gallons	= 1 tierce.
54 gallons	= 1 hogshead (ale).
63 gallons	= 1 hogshead (wine).
84 gallons	= 1 puncheon.
126 gallons	= 1 pipe or butt.
2 pipes	= 1 tun.
4 baskets	= 1 cran = 1 barrel (750 herrings).

Money

4 farthings	= 1 penny.
3 pennies	= 3d piece.
4d	= 1 Groat.
12d	= 1 shilling 1/-.
2/-	= 1 florin.
2/6	= 1 half crown.
5/-	= 1 crown.
20/-	= 1 pound £.
21/-	= 1 guinea (still used at bull sales).

Decimal Day 15th February, 1971.

½ new penny	= 1.2d.
1 new penny	= 2.4d.
2 new pence	= 4.8d.
5 new pence	= 1/-.

1st August 1969 ½d ceased to be legal tender.

14th October 1969 50p coin to replace 10/- note.

1st January 1970 half crown ceased to be legal tender.

August 1972 circulation of 1d, 3d and 6d ended.

1982 new 20p coin introduced.

21st April 1983 £1 coin introduced.

RECIPES FROM YESTERYEAR

INDEX

Stroma Hard Fish

Gut cod and remove heads. Starting at head end split them down on both sides of the bone as far as the stomach, using a very sharp gully knife. Remove bone and slit down the side of bone to tail. Wash out the blood and the black film using scrubbing brush. Wash fish. Sprinkle the bottom of the barrel or tub with salt. Lay fish skin side down and sprinkle on rough salt. Layer up fish and salt in the barrel. Leave for about three days in salt. Remove and allow to drip through netting spread over a wooden framed rack. Do not leave out in the rain and bring in before the sun goes down and dampness falls.

Hang in kitchen if necessary until the salt dries whitish and they are hard and properly cured. (Do not force the heat.) They can then be kept packed in boxes. They were packed for selling in boll-bags which held a hundredweight dried cod.

To use:– Cut up and soak overnight if wished or bring to boil and boil gently 20 minutes. Drain off water and pour on more boiling water and leave until the tatties are ready. Melt butter in a cup at side of stove and pour over fish when served.

Alex Wares, Seaview, John O'Groats.

Salt Herrings

Have the herrings as fresh as possible (avoid spent ones). Roose in rough salt five to six hours. Pinch below gills and just pull out the long gut. Keep opening small and leave in roe or malt. Place layer of rough salt in half barrel or firkin. Pack herrings in tightly on their backs in wheel shape with heads to outside of barrel. Pack centre of circle, heads to tails. Put a good covering of salt on that layer and then layer up with herrings and salt until the barrel is full. Cover and keep in cold place. Herrings cured in wood are best because, the wood seems to soak up the oil and prevent the "after taste". After some weeks empty "dirty" brine from barrel (bung about half way up side of barrel) and fill up with strong solution of brine.

To cook:– Put into cold water, bring to boil and simmer for about 25 minutes. Pour off water. Fill up with boiling water and simmer for a further five minutes.

Hugh Simpson, Skirza.

To Fry Salt Herrings

Wash herrings, bring to boil and simmer 10-15 minutes. Roll in oatmeal and fry. They taste better than fried fresh herrings.

Charlie Simpson, Dalziel House, Wick.

Brandered Salt Herring (1687 recipe)

Soak salt herrings in cold water four to five hours or overnight preferably. Clean, split and bone. Cover with oatmeal (not oatmeal batter). Lay on brander and toast over an open peat fire. (Any other fish will do.) Try it on a barbecue. Result excellent.

Morris Pottinger, Isauld House, Reay.

Fried Fresh Herrings in Oatmeal

Remove heads, clean and split herrings. Remove back bone by pulling away from tail end. Press herrings into oatmeal. Fry, split side down in a little hot margarine or fat until oatmeal browns slightly. Turn and fry lightly on skin side.

Sina Houston, Mill House, John O'Groats.

Cuddings

Clean, split and steep in salt and water two hours or to taste. The salt enhances the flavour and you cannot beat them boiled or fried.

Charlie Simpson, Dalziel House, Wick

Scraid Sellags

Sellags – very young saithe about five inches long.

Peltags – two year old saithe about seven inches long.

Often large shoals came in at Huna, and at Himral, North End Pier and Harbour in Stroma. Chewed boiled tatties were spat on to the water to attract the fish.

The sellags were scooped up in a sellag poke (strong handle stuck on to a metal ring about four feet across. The ring was covered with about half inch mesh netting.)

Gut fish (heads could be removed or left on). Roo with salt (throw in gowpenful coarse salt and row or turn fish well in it). Tie string around tails and hang up to dry on a nail on gable end of house.

Sellag Poke

Bring inside at first sign of rain. When cured and dry, hang in kitchen until required.

To cook:– Soak in cold water. Boil gently until skins begin to turn back. Eat very hot with plenty tatties and butter.

Robbie Dundas, Stroma View, Huna.

Huna Scraid Sellags

Gut sellags but leave head on. Lace on to fencing wire, through under gills and out at mouth. Hang out to dry until firm and shrivelled. Do not leave out overnight or in rain. Hang up in kitchen until required.

To cook:– Remove heads and soak overnight. Boil 10 minutes.

Walter S. Rosie, Novelty House, John O'Groats.

Sillocks on Brander

Clean fish – keep livers. Place livers in the fish. Roll them in flour. Place on brander and turn to cook.

Mrs C. Robertson, The Cottage, Canisbay.

Chappit Heids

Favourite Stroma Recipe

1 cod head	*1 cod liver
2 middle cuts cod	Pepper and salt

Wash cod head and remove eyes. Wash liver and place in head. Put in a pan of cold water along with the cod. Add salt. Boil gently for 30 minutes.

Remove liver from head. Set aside. Remove the bones and skin from the head and the cod. Flake the fish. Mix fish and liver together. Season to taste. Best with plenty pepper. Heat up if necessary. Serve with boiled potatoes.

* Ling livers considered better than cod.

Elizabeth Bruce, Bellevue, Huna.

Jeannie Simpson's Liver Pies

(Croppan Heads)

Cod or haddock heads (use more haddock heads accordingly)
Cod, haddock or ling livers
Oatmeal – a bit more than you have of livers
1 chopped onion
Seasoning

Wash heads and remove gills and eyes. Mix oatmeal, onions and livers until the mixture will form into a ball. Season it well.

Pack into heads and boil gently in salted water 30 minutes. (Often an extra bit of fish was boiled with the heads.) Serve with mashed potatoes. The bree makes lovely fish stock.

Stroma and Midtown, Freswick.

Some used beremeal because it held together better during cooking.

Boiled Limpids

Wash limpids, put into a pot with cold water and bring nearly to boiling point. They are ready when they are just leaving the shell. It is very important not to let them boil which makes them tough and only suitable for bait.

Mrs C. Robertson, The Cottage, Canisbay.

Boiled Crabs

Crabs are at their best when the corn is ripe. Choose heavy crabs.

Place in cold water for half an hour or so until dead. Wash and place in boiling water. Boil 20-30 minutes depending on size. Drain (claws down). When cold remove claws and edge out the breast. Remove "flaps" and then press the head down into the shell and discard all that comes away with this. Remove gills (deadmen's fingers). Pick out all white and brown meat and use as required.

Ina Manson, Stroma and Newton.

Boiled Lobsters

Cook as for crabs. Allow 20-25 minutes boiling depending on size.

Whelks

Wash well in three clean rinsing waters. Place in salted water and boil 15-20 minutes. Drain and leave until cold. Remove "scale" and eat with a large pin.

George Gunn, The Bungalow, John O'Groats.

Jeannie Leitch's Hare Soup

1 fine brown hare	Onion
Turnip	Potatoes
Carrots	Salt and pepper

Skin hare, cut off head but catch all blood and keep in a separate bowl. Wash hare thoroughly and cut into two or three pieces. Put into large pan, cover with cold water and boil slowly until tender – one and a half to two hours. After an hour or so add chopped and diced turnip, carrots, onion and potatoes (if preferred add mashed potatoes).

When meat is tender remove from heat for a minute – then gradually stir in the blood (stirring all the time so that blood does not curdle). Bring slowly back to boil and serve. Can add thickening if wished (flour and water mixed to a paste).

Brabster.

Stuffed Baked Rabbit

1 whole rabbit (skinned and cleaned)
Oatmeal stuffing
2-3 thin slices home cured ham or bacon rashers
3-4 medium onions

Stuff the rabbit and place in roasting tin with a little water and the whole onions. Sprinkle the rabbit with flour and place the ham over the carcass. Add seasoning. Cover with greaseproof paper. Bake in moderately hot oven until tender (half to one hour). Remove paper and baste well. Thicken gravy with a little blended flour and add one teaspoon gravy salt.

Serve with baked jacket potatoes and mashed neeps.

Mrs Georgie Kennedy, Tresdale, Canisbay.

The Headmaster in John O'Groats c.1900 was Mr Duff whose father was manager of a bacon factory in Aberdeen. Mr Duff passed on his recipe for "the cure" to the locals and they considered it the best in the parish.

Ben Green, Roadside, John O'Groats.

Mrs Alexander's Cured Ham
The best in Canisbay

1 leg pork

Take about 1lb ordinary sugar and the same in bulk of fine salt and one heaped teaspoonful of saltpetre. Mix thoroughly and rub on pork. Repeat after two days and leave two days. Dry with a cloth. Make up a mixture of four pounds rough salt, half pound demerara sugar, one heaped teaspoonful ground cloves, a heaped teaspoonful pepper, mix and rub in. Rub in every second day night and morning for a fortnight, then twice a week for next fortnight. Take out in four weeks time and hang up. Put a small pinch saltpetre on bone.

given by Cathie Mcleod, Lochend.

Laing's Ham Cure

For 30lbs pork:

2¼lbs salt	1½oz salt prunella
1½ gallons water	1oz pepper
¾lb brown sugar	½oz cloves
1½oz saltpetre	

Tried and tested throughout the Parish.

Cured Ham

14lb leg of pork	1lb brown sugar
1lb rough salt	½pt vinegar
2oz saltpetre	

Put meat in large wooden tub and rub all over with saltpetre. Leave until next day. Wipe dry. Mix salt and sugar and rub well over pork. Pour over vinegar and leave two days. Rub pork well each day and turn. Baste when sufficient liquid has formed. Do this for three weeks. Drain and hang in warmish place for a week to drain and dry. (Usually hung near the fire from a large hook in the kitchen ceiling). Cover with tent of brown paper or newspaper and hang just inside the kitchen door or in the passage. Slice and fry.

Jean MacRae, Croftlea, John O'Groats.

Jeannie Leitch's Pork and Kale

Home cured pork (about 2lbs)	Water
Cabbage – home-grown	

Put pork in large pan. Cover with water, and boil for an hour or more. Wash and clean two or more cabbages. Then divide each into four or more sections, cutting out centres. Add this to pan, bring back to boil, and boil for half an hour or less. When ready lift cabbage out of pan, strain and serve with slices of the pork. Delicious!

Brabster.

Lizzie Cook's Salt Pork

Cut pork into suitable pieces. Place pork on wooden table and rub each bit really well with rough salt, especially on skin side.

Pickle:–

¼lb saltpetre	2 handfuls brown sugar
6-8 handfuls rough salt	Large kettle boiling water

Place hot water in pail and stir in sugar, salt petre and salt. Stir until dissolved and keep adding salt until the pickle is strong enough to float an egg. Allow pickle to become cold. Scald a small barrel or round wooden tub and sprinkle the bottom with rough salt. Pack in the pork. Pour pickle over to cover. Place lid on barrel and leave in a cold place. To use, soak overnight and cook whole or sliced.

If the meat begins to rise in the brine, weight down with a boiled wooden board or plate.

Freswick.

Nan Dunnet's Potted Head
"The best ye can taste"

1 pigs head	Salt and pepper
4 trotters	Mustard

Split head, remove eyes and any loose bits of bones. Scrape skin really well and wash head. Rub in plenty of salt and leave to soak in cold water for half an hour. Sear toes with red hot poker until the hooves can be prised off. Place thoroughly washed head, trotters and seasoning in a large pan, cover with cold water and bring to rolling boil. Remove all scum and then simmer three to three and a half hours. Remove all meat and a little fat from the bones and shred. Strain liquor and boil uncovered to reduce it a bit. Add the meat and simmer 15-20 minutes until it is reduced enough to form a jelly. Check seasoning and pot into small bowls.

Seater, Canisbay.

Hannie Green advised to boil an old hen and add the meat to the potted head! (It certainly works well with a frozen fowl.)

Isobel Dunnet, Seater.

Margaret Baikie's Black Puddings

1 quart pig's blood	Salt and pepper
1 quart milk	Ground cloves
1lb fresh suet	Cinnamon
½ loaf bread (2lbs)	Mixed spice
Beremeal	

Cut bread into cubes and place in pan with milk and warm gently (not hot). Pour into large dish containing the blood. Add melted suet, seasoning and beremeal until mixture is a soft paste. Pack loosely into pudding skins. Prick well with darning needle and boil very very gently for three quarters to one hour. Drain and dry as for white puddings.

Tanghead, Scarfskerry.

White Puddings or Mealy Puddings

Wash and clean skins in the ebb or burn. Then steep overnight in mixture of salt and water. Turn outside in and wash in clean water.

Filling:–

| Oatmeal | Chopped onion |
| Finely chopped suet | Salt and pepper to taste |

Tie one end of pudding skin. Flype or have half of the skin turned outside in on itself. Hold skin open and pack in filling using fingers. This way the skin turns up and over the filling as you work. Push down and tie into puddings leaving space for the stuffing to almost double in size. Prick with darning needle, before and during cooking as they swell up and rise in pan.

Boil slowly for three quarters an hour. Drain and hang up in ceiling to dry thoroughly. Store packed in oatmeal in girnal.

Mrs C. Robertson, The Cottage, Canisbay.

Mutton

It was usual for two families to share an animal. One family killed a hogg and then a month or two later the other family killed one and repaid the mutton.

Salt Mutton

The carcass was hung first for two to three days. (The legs were kept whole for "mutton hams" and cured as for pork.)

Cut mutton to suit number in family

| 1½-2lbs coarse salt | 1lb soft brown sugar |
| 1 gallon water | ½oz saltpetre |

Pour boiling water into a small barrel. Add sugar, saltpetre and enough salt to float a potato. Skim and leave until cold. Sprinkle salt in bottom of barrel. Pack in mutton with layer of salt where the pieces touch. Pour pickle over to cover. Store in cold place. Change pickle after three to four weeks.

Lollie Brown, North Dale, Fetlar.

Reested Mutton

Remove mutton from pickle after two weeks and rinse with cold water. Hang outside to drip. Hang up near the fire where there is a steady even heat until cured.

Reested was considered better than salt mutton and it was best dried by a peat fire.

David Nicolson, Cunningsburgh, Shetland.

Reested Mutton Stew

Slice mutton and soak four to five hours. Drain and almost cover with boiling water. Simmer gently one hour. Add sliced onion, carrots and turnips and simmer three quarters an hour.

Lollie Brown, North Dale, Fetlar.

Tattie Soup

Cut the reestit mutton into small pieces and boil up for a few minutes. Pour off the water and add fresh water. Bring to the boil. Add sliced onion and blocks of potato and neep and simmer until tender.

The vegetables soak up the salt and the result is a beautifully flavoured soup.

Georgie Nicolson, Hayfield, Cunningsburgh, Shetland.

Oatmeal and Cabbage Soup

4oz cabbage chopped fine
1 or 2 onions chopped fine
3oz carrots grated
1oz oatmeal
2pts stock or 1pt stock and 1pt water
Oil or butter for lightly frying vegetables.

Fry up vegetables, but do not brown. Stir in oatmeal. Add stock and boil half an hour.

Quick, easy and very, very good.

Laurence Brown, North House, John O'Groats.

Vina MacLean's Oatmeal Stuffing

1 cup oatmeal
2oz margarine or hen fat
1 large onion chopped finely
Salt, pepper and mustard

Warm margarine in pyrex bowl and mix in remainder of ingredients (no water). Use for stuffing a fowl or steam three quarters an hour and serve with mince or stew.

"Duart", Auckengill.

Nurse Cook's Clapshot

Use ⅓ turnips and ⅔ potatoes

Boil sliced turnips in salted water for 15 minutes. Add whole peeled potatoes and cook for 20 minutes until potatoes are tender. Drain, add 1-2ozs butter and mash well. Season and serve very hot. Left over mashed neeps and tatties may be used.

Newton, John O'Groats.

Bashed Neeps

Drain boiled turnips. Add one tablespoon oatmeal and mash well. Stand for five minutes to allow meal to absorb liquid.

Keith Muir, John O'Groats

Beest Cheese

2pts beesty milk (the first milk from a cow newly calved)
½pt fresh milk or water to thin it
1 dessertsp sugar
A little salt

Mix and place in ovenproof dish and cook in cool oven until set. It can be cooked very gently at side of fire until set like crowdie.

Mrs Ada Muir, Parklea, Canisbay.

Annie Houston's Cheese

Mix two gallons of the evening and morning's milk. (i.e. slightly acid and usually skimmed). Set at side of fire until it reaches blood heat. Stir in one teaspoon cheese rennet mixed in quarter cup cold water. Leave until curd is firm enough to cut. (Splits with clean break over finger.) Cut into half inch cubes with gully. Heat very gently taking a full hour for it to become lukewarm. Stir slowly by hand every now and again. Remove from heat and stir for a bit to give a firm springy curd. Allow curd to settle and pour off whey. Stir again and drain curd through rough cheese cloth.

Line scalded cheese mould or hoop with scalded wrung-out cheese cloth. Mix tablespoon salt into curd and fill mould. Fold cloth ends over curd. Place closely fitting "follower" on top with weight on top to press. Turn cheese and keep increasing the pressure and leave under full pressure until the following morning. Ripen cheese on a clean board in an airy place for three to four weeks, turning and rubbing it every day.

(Before cheese presses were fitted with ratchets and thumb screws, the lever method was used. Cheese mould was set on bink or table outside kitchen window. Stout six foot plank set on top with one end tucked under projecting windowsill lintel. Pail of water hung on other end and shore bools set on as required to increase pressure.)

Mill House, John O'Groats.

Maggie Dundas's Crowdie

Skimmed milk which has just turned slightly sour is used. Place in warm place until it reaches blood heat and curd is set. Leave to cool a bit. Stir gently to break up curds and whey. Allow to drain through colander or sieve. Place curd in bowl and mix well with some salt and cream. Shape into flattish balls and serve on small plate or willow pattern saucer.

Stroma and Huna.

Stroma Straw Strainer for Cheese Making

Choose 9-10" long fine straw (Airline or Sanday Oats).

Lay them close and straight to form mat. Thread and sew together at sides and centre using double thread and darning needle. Make second mat to lay at right angles on top of first. Place in cheese hoop and use in place of cheese muslin.

Elma, Matthew and Robbie Dundas remember their mother making this in Stroma.

Curds or Yearned Milk (Junket)

Place warm newly milked milk in small bowls or heat milk until lukewarm. Add a sprig of butterwort to each or stir in a few drops of rennet and leave to set.

Elma Moar, Quoyawa, Huna.

Annie Houston's Butter

Cream was collected for about a week. Stir well after each addition of cream. Ready for churning when it was mildly acidic and had thickened slightly. Start churning slowly and then increase to steady pace (one revolution per minute). When noise changes to a 'plash' (the breaking stage) turn slowly until the butter grains are slightly larger than sago. Drain off butter milk. Add cold water and give a few turns to wash butter. Drain off this milky water. Add salt and water to butter in churn, and give a few turns. Leave 10 minutes or so for butter to firm. Lift on to board and press and beat out moisture using scotch hands. Butter ready to shape when texture is smooth and free from moisture droplets. (Test by cutting with scotch hand.)

Salt Butter

Pack butter into glazed earthenware jar. Cover with thick layer of salt and then parchment paper.

To use:– Cut into small pieces and soak in water. Rework and make up.

Mill House, John O'Groats.

Broon Plate

Place good ladleful of the sowans gruns (the bottom of barrel) in pan. Stir sowans in barrel and add a ladleful to pan. Stir while bringing to the boil. Cook until thick. Dish hot like porridge and serve with milk. It can be served cold.

James Simpson, Stroma.

Brose

Place good handful oatmeal and a little salt in brose bowl. Stir in boiling water from kettle until the mix is fairly soft. Stand for a minute or two and eat with milk.

Mutton, neep or kail bree could be used instead of water.

Ian Angus, Bayview, Freswick.

Burstin

Burstin is bere corn dried in a pot until "roasted" and then hand ground. Makes a rich brown meal which can replace wholemeal.

It was often made at the beginning of the harvest and used for crackins.

Elma Moar, Quoyawa, Huna.

Alex Dunnet's Crackins

| 8oz oatmeal | 1-2 onions chopped |
| 3-4oz dripping | Salt and pepper |

Melt dripping, add onion and brown slowly. Add oatmeal and stir over gentle heat until cooked. Serve with chappit tatties.

West End, John O'Groats.

Thick Milk and Meal

Toast oatmeal or use Burstin.

Place milk which had soured and turned thick, in individual bowls and sprinkle with a little oatmeal just before eating. (It is best to put a little oatmeal on at a time otherwise the meal absorbs the moisture and goes soft.) Try this with yoghurt.

Sinclair Houston, Barga, Thurso.

Clootie Dumpling

Gowpenful flour	Shake ginger
Knob butter	Hint nutmeg
Daudie suet	Dicht spice
Puckle sugar	Clewie treacle
Skintie baking soda	Twrik syrup
Handful currants	Grain salt
Lockie raisins	Twa eggs
Droppie sultanas	Sap milk
Touch cinnamon	Strupag sour milk
Kenning cloves	

Steer till weel elted. Butter centre of lint clootie and shake on layer of flour. Place mixture in centre. Tie allowing space for dumpling to swell. Boil in broth for two hours.

(The flour that seeps through "clootie" makes good livering in broth.)

Nancy Houston, St Magnus, John O'Groats.

The "alfins" could be sliced and eaten cold or fried.

Ben Green, Roadside, John O'Groats.

Bere-bread

6 handfuls (1½lbs) beremeal
Good handful plain flour
Level dessertspoon baking soda
Sour milk or buttermilk to mix

Make up fire so that you will have a hot fire ready to use when the flames go down a bit.

Brandered Bere-bread

Make the mixture stiffish. Take about a quarter and knead out to a bannock about half inch thick. Bake on a fairly hot brander until risen and light brown underneath. Turn and bake on other side until dry in centre.

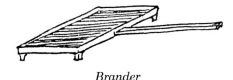

Brander

Bere Bannocks

(Mix makes six bannocks). Make up above mixture, as soft as you can handle. Knead out just over quarter an inch thick. Bake on moderately hot girdle. Heat of girdle can be adjusted by raising or lowering it on the kettle hook. (A few wing feathers tied as a brush was used to dicht the girdle.)

Miss Lizzie Cook, Skirza.

John O'Groats Pudding

Recipe used by Betsy Dunnet when she was housekeeper in the John O'Groats House Hotel 1877-1888. She married Magnus Houston (Miller).

At ebb tide gather sea-moss (carrageen – plenty still growing on "the Maggie Rosie"). Wash well to remove grit and sand. Spread out on a sheet on the bleaching green until bleached and dry (three to four days). Store by tying in clean pillowcase and hanging in dry airy place.

Allow small handful of moss to each pint of milk. Place in pan with a little sugar. Bring to boil and simmer gently until the milk begins to thicken (approx. half an hour). Strain and serve warm or pour into wetted small bowls or cups. Turn out when set and serve with cream.

Variations:– Add very well beaten egg after straining. Boil with a few dried or fresh elder flowers.

Mill House, John O'Groats.

Maudie Ham's Flour Bannocks

1lb plain flour	1 rounded teasp. bicarb of soda
½ level teasp. salt	1 rounded teasp. cream of tartar
½pt buttermilk	

Bannock Turner

Place girdle to heat gently. Mix ingredients to a soft elastic dough with buttermilk. (The softer the dough the lighter the scones.) Divide into four. Knead lightly into a ball and roll out using plenty of flour. Place on fairly hot girdle and pat out the bannock fairly thin. Cook three to four minutes. Turn and cook the other side.

Lochend.

Daisy Houston's Oatbread

1 cup oatmeal	Small knob dripping
Pinch baking soda	Salt

Make well in centre and quickly stir in enough boiling water to make a paste. Knead out very thinly to a circle using oatmeal. Rub well with small handful of oatmeal to whiten. Flip bannock and rub other side. Cut into quarters and shake off loose meal. Cook on moderately hot girdle until crisp and dry on top side. (The corners curl up. The oatcakes are not turned.) Crisp off in cool oven. Make second bannock while first is cooking.

The Ha, John O'Groats.

Brandered Oatbread

Knead out an oatbread mixture almost quarter inch thick. Bake on moderate brander and then crisp off the top side.

Clean dry peats were arranged around the hearth and the oatbread was set up against them to crisp. Flat iron set on end was also used.

Miss Lizzie Cook, Skirza.

Pancakes

2 handfuls flour
½teasp. baking soda
1 teasp cream of tartar
2 teasp. sugar
1 egg
Milk to mix   *Girdle*

Mix to a thick cream consistency. Drop off point of spoon on to fairly hot greased girdle. By the time you get the last on, the first is ready for turning. (For the bairns you should make cats, dogs or rabbits with the scrapings of the bowl.) Use a bit of skin from the cured ham for greasing girdle.

Rena Dunnett, Coach Road, Wick.

(Her mother, the late Mina Manson said "The name was Struma and the Struma wey was the richt wey.")

Sowans

The loveliest drink you can get for quenching a thirst.

2-3 gowpenfuls sids
½-1 gowpenful oatmeal

Place in wooden firkin, buoy or a large earthenware jar. Fill up nearly to the top with cold water. Set in cool place to ferment. Stir every other day. Taste bree after 12 days and then every day until it comes to your taste of sourness. Pour through a sieve and throw away sids. Return sooans to barrel to keep (it won't get any sourer).

To use:– Stir up until milky and drink. Perfect for bad stomachs.

Don Wares, Seater, Canisbay.

Maggie Dundas's Sooan Scones

1 breakfast cup flour
¾ breakfast cup sooans
1 teaspoonful Borwick baking powder
Pinch salt

Mix carefully to a smooth thin batter and mind ye don't droon 'e miller. Bake on a hot greased girdle until brown on both sides.

Stroma and Huna.

Don Wares says "spread with butter and rolled up they're hard to beat". "Spread when hot with syrup and they're magic," insists James Simpson.

Tattie Scones

1 breakfast cup mashed tatties   Pinch salt
1 dessertsp. butter   1 teacup flour
1 level teasp. baking powder

Mix mashed tattie with butter, salt and flour till it holds firmly. Roll thinly and prick with fork. Cook on hot greased girdle until brown on each side.

Elma Moar, Quoyawa, Huna.

Beit Egg – a great tonic

Beat egg with a little sugar in small bowl. Stir in boiling water and drink right away.

Beatrice Brown, Glamis Road, Wick.

Treacle Ale

1lb golden syrup   1oz fresh yeast
8oz black molasses/treacle   ½oz ground ginger
8 pints water   Rind of 1 lemon

Put syrup and treacle in large bowl. Cover with boiling water. Stir until syrup and treacle have melted. Add ginger and thinly peeled lemon rind. When lukewarm add yeast. Cover and keep in warm room for three days. Carefully syphon off liquid into bottles without disturbing sediment. Cork tightly and keep one week before drinking. Cheers!!!

Rosemary Laird, Heatherbell Cottages, John O'Groats.

Toddy

Heat mug by filling with boiling water and pour off. Place one teaspoon sugar in the mug and half fill mug with boiling water. Top up with whisky (at least half gill or to taste). Drink very hot.
"Better canna be".

David Dunnett, Dunroamin, Freswick.

Smiddy Ale

Malt is bere sprouted about two thirds the length of the grain and dried on the kiln and then bruised.

1 stone malt   1 teasp. baking soda
1½lbs sugar   8 gallons of water
3oz yeast, bakers yeast

Have the boiler ready with the eight gallons of water, place the malt in a muslin bag and keep bag slack tied with string, because the malt swells when in the hot water. Place malt and sugar into the boiler to infuse until water comes to the boil, and then boil for one hour. Strain the mixture into the brewing barrel for fermenting and allow to cool to blood heat and add one teaspoonful baking soda. Start the yeast off by mixing it with a little of the cool brew before stirring it into the mixture to ferment. Cover with a clean linen towel or napkin and keep in a warm place in the kitchen. Stir after one day.

When it has stopped fermenting, usually in five to six days, skim the surface. Place one teaspoonful sugar in spotlessly clean screw top beer bottles and syphon in ale, filling to one and a half inches from top. Screw on top tightly and leave to mature two weeks at least. Store in a dark place which is cool, or the bottles could burst.

(Hops are used to make beer bitter and to give flavour. They are not used in ale.)

Wm. S. Mowatt, Smiddy, South Ronaldsay.

PLACE NAMES OF CANISBAY

JOHN MOWAT F.S.A. (Scotland)

John Mowat was a well known authority on northern literature. He gifted his very valuable library of books to Caithness. This, the Mowat Collection, is housed in the Reference Section of Wick Library.

John Mowat was born and brought up at Skirza House, Freswick. He went to Glasgow to work and became director of A.H. Hamilton's Paint Manufacturers.

He was a founder member of the Glasgow Caithness Association and was said to exemplify the county in word and deed. He married Georgina Dunnet from Wick, and we are grateful to his daughters Mrs Margaret Ross and Mrs Jessie McGregor for permission to use their father's articles and for their good wishes for the success of this book.

Photo, Mrs Jessie McGregor.

THE CORNER THAT CRADLED ME

Let me transport you to the brown, heather slopes of the Warth Hill which dominates the fringes of our dark grey coast. Face the south, and on the horizon from Noss Head to the far hills of Reay in the west we have an unmatchable Caithness panorama. Beyond, and mingling into the skyline, are the distant peaks of Sutherland, blue and black. Nearer "the long flat lands of Caithness" are glimmering in our sight. Nearer still and at our feet are the black peat-banks of Canisbay, fringed with a coastline of rocks and bays and sand. We turn "widdershins", but as no fisherman would, and from the sweep of Sinclair Bay to the Men o' Mey there is no bonnier or braver coast. In the dimpled hillsides are the hamlets of as brave a people. Visualise the scene as you have seen it in sunshine and storm, or, as now, in the softer light of a late autumn morning, you catch the peculiar glamour of the rugged moorland. Think of Swinburne's picture of "sky, and shore, and cloud, and waste and sea."

If we have caught the spirit we can pass over the Doug's Nose, so truly named if the north wind blows sharp and snell. In the hollow lies Nybster, the new homestead of some ancient Viking and still the home of one of their race, John Nicolson, artist and antiquarian, whose stately form and strong, rugged face might have stepped out of one of his own old-time pictures. This is the homeland of the "Persians". How and why we know not. Tradition has it that it was the pastime of the boys of Kirkhill to throw down "divads" on the peculiar people from the shores of the Pentland Firth until the parish gave to the Royal Burgh a provost and some bailies. Here we have the breeding place of a vigorous race, the home of the Mowats, the Mansons, the Dunnets, the Bremners, and the Groats. From the cold and sterile land they wrung a scanty livelihood, and from the treacherous sea an uncertain supplement. In the stern fight with nature, men were made. But with the passing of the crofter-fisherman there have been increasing changes and now there are fewer lums that reek on the hillside twixt the heather and the north Sea. But –

"There dwells a wife by the Northern Gate,
And a wealthy wife is she;
She breeds a breed of roving men,
And casts them over the sea".

Back at the grey dawn of Northern history the Norse sea king was playing his part at the making of them.

There are landmarks round which romance and heroism have gathered. Buchollie Castle is one of them. This grim old ruin was for centuries the home of the Caithness Mowats, and perched as it is on a beetling cliff, it is difficult to conceive a less inviting residence. Centuries earlier it was the ideal stronghold of the rover and it was the scene of a siege of great determination and daring resistance which reveals the stuff of which the race was made. Freswick, the Fras-vik of the Sagas, comes early into our homeland story. Here the hardy Norseman made his earliest landings and a sure wintering for his galleys. Master Skeggie lavished hospitality on his rover kinsmen ten centuries ago.

Rounding Duncansby Head we face the swirl of the stormy Pentland as many a stout ship has done since the days of yore – the theme of many a pilot yarn. Gone are the white-winged Atlantic clippers; gone are the barques of the hardy Norsemen; gone are the Arctic whaling fleets. And what have we left? Only a commonplace tramp or trawler. Of all the bold headlines in the Northland County, Duncansby is the grandest of them all. The recently erected lighthouse, standing white on the crown relieves the loneliness but lends to the immensity. The village of Dungal was the home of an early Caithness chief who became a friend of the invading Norsemen by marrying one of their daughters and giving one of his own to be a Viking bride. So his township was a centre centuries before the coming of the famous John O'Groat.

For generations John O'Groats has been the Mecca of the thousands who seek "Scotia's outmost rim." Year by year, increasing numbers of tourists of all nations, of all ranks and all descriptions visit this quiet spot with the house of the beautiful legend.

Close by the whitest of sands, a new house satisfies the needs of the hurrying tourist and the green mound near by holds the secret of the house that John built. The vision of the old peace-lover and his eight-sided house has found so sure a place in our county story that it need not be repeated.

One more glance ere we say farewell to this enchanted ground. Northward and westward stretch the cornfields of Canisbay dipping low to the shores of the Firth. Out in the ceaseless eddying tide sits Stroma, "the island of the stream", an emerald in a sea of turquoise blue. But it may be different when the stormy winds do blow and only a ridge of black looms through the driven spume. North to the far horizon lies the Orkney Isles, holding in their bosom Scapa Flow, that base of adventure and achievement in the days of war.

Nestling by the Pentland shore is the kirkyard which holds the dust of the elect, and the kirk and manse associated with one of Scotland's grandest songs of praise. Let us bare our heads to this corner that cradled you and me –

"And we shall boast the North our natal clime,
The clime whence came our fathers, and forget
At times, perchance, that we were doomed to roam
Through life 'mid scenes more lovely, but less loved."

John Mowat, Skirza.

SOME PLACE NAMES OF CANISBAY

The place-names of Caithness have not yet received the attention they deserve. The Celts and the Norsemen were at the making of them.

The parish Canisbay is the most distinctively Norse in Caithness. In this parish were some of the earliest Viking settlements. As a basis the Ordnance Survey Map has been used, but this has been supplemented from old maps, charters, and local tradition.

The writer is indebted to Mr William Bremner ("Norseman"), Freswick, and to Mr George Green, The Breck, John O'Groats, for helpful descriptions of local place-names.

Some modern and commonplace names have been omitted. In the order of arrangement the coast-line has been roughly followed from the south boundary of the parish at Nybster, working north to Duncansby Head, and west to Mey, giving group headlines to various townships. *[Note – John Mowat's Norse references have been omitted.]*

Canisbay Parish probably took its name from the township of that name on the shore of the Pentland Firth and surrounding the pre-Reformation church. The name is first mentioned in an ecclesiastical document of Bishop Gilbert, about 1222, in which it is spelled "Canenisbi". The following are later forms; Cananesbi, 1223, 1245; Cranesby, 1275; Cananby, 1276; Canyby, 1437; Canesbi, 1445; Cannasby, 1455; and so on until 1620, when Pont's Map gives Conansbay, and thereafter Canesby, Cannisbay, in 1744.

There is some difference of opinion as to the derivation. D.B. Nicolson gives it as meaning King's Town, or Village. Pont's Map of 1620 gives Conansbay, and Dr Joseph Anderson, accepting this spelling, thinks the name is derived from an early Celtic chief, Conan, viz., Conan's by, b'ye bœr, a farm. J.B. Johnston, in Place Names of Scotland, favours "Canon's bi", the clergyman's place. The oldest part of the village lay around the present pre-Reformation Church built on the site of an earlier church dedicated to Saint Drostan.

Nybster and Auckengill District

Nybster. Farm on a rocky place facing the sea.

Aukingill or Auckengill. Hákon's gil.

Rockhill. A croft standing on a rocky rise.

Half-Way-House. Farmhouse originally built as a wayside inn, half-way between Wick and Canisbay now called Summerbank House.

Summerbank or Nybsterhaven. The summer landing place for boats. Old name: "Crookmooth," crooked entrance.

Hell Berry. A flat rock near Summerbank.

Brough Head. So named from the remains of a broch on the headland.

Sgarback. "A high cliff promontory of a curved form bearing the name *Sgarbach*. . . it runs from the edge of a deep ravine on one side to the cliffs on the other."

Milton of Aukingill. Site of old mill.

Ruff o' Aukingill. A small projecting reef of rocks. Also *Ruff* of Freswick, *Lang Ruff*, etc. (an animal's tail applied to a reef).

The Hullion. A sunken rock on the coast at Aukingill.

Point of Sorta. Old name of fisherman's "meeze" for the headland above the *Ruff*, as seen from the north, projecting beyond the nearer land. "Meeze is one of the landmarks by which a fishing-bank is found, or the term for a fishing-bank itself.

Samal's Geo, or Samuel's Geo. Took its name from a man who lived in the vicinity. It had an older name, "Carl Geo".

Dias Geo. On the south side of *Brough Head* with the remains of a cairn.

Tarry-Geo, or Tarriegeo. Seaweed gathers here, seaweed geo.

Dounal, or Doonal. Noisy channel.

Black Score. So named from a black fissure in cliff.

King's Geo or Kingan Geo. Near Buchollie Castle. There is a tradition that King James V landed here on his voyage around Scotland.

The Tippet or Tippad. Near King's Geo. A pyramid-shaped rock.

Castle-Geo. The creek or landing-place below Bucholie Castle.

Buchollie Castle. Commonly called *Buchles' Castle.* Also often printed "Old Freswick Castle". The seat of the Mowat family in Caithness, probably so named from their estate in Aberdeenshire, viz., Balquhollie. It has been identified, by P.A. Munch, as the Lambaborg of Orkneyinga Saga, the strong-hold of Sveinn Asleifarson, the famous viking, who fortified the borg, which was afterwards blockaded by Earl Rognvald. Sveinn made his escape by being let down by a rope into the sea and swimming to the nearest break in the cliffs. Mr A.W. Johnston suggests that the broch at the Ness answers the Saga description of Lambaborg better than Buchollie. Here we have an actual *borg*, with a well-built stone wall at the land end, and the rocks *projecting out seawards*, as described in the Saga, whereas Buchollie is a peninsular rock *lying parallel with the shore*, without any evidence that there had been a borg upon it.

Backless. A croft on a sloping ness or point.

Hill o' Harley. On both sides of the hill-rise the soil is shallow and rocky, (hard slope).

Craw Hillock. Craw, a sheepfold.

Crocans. A piece of marshy grazing moor to the S.W. of Aukengill, locally associated with "crow", rheumatism in cattle.

Tooags. Two round mounds inland between Freswick and Aukingill.

Freswick Township and District

Freswick. The township on Freswick Bay was an early landing place of the Vikings.

Ruff of Freswick. The sloping headland or reef running out to the south of Freswick Bay.

Horse Geo. A green slope down to the beach used for grazings horses.

Selly Geo. Seals' geo.

Lyberry. A rock with a sloping back and a deep water face, used as a common fishing place for lythe or saith.

The Taa. A toe of land, a rock submerged at high water.

Skrithe. A dip in the rock strata on the south side of Freswick Bay. A landslip.

Tang Head. Spit of land running out into the sea.

Cletts. Two rock pillars, nearly as broad at the top as they are at the base.

Rives. Low-lying rocks running out into the sea (reefs).

Sannypeel. A creek with a sandy bottom in which the fishing boats could lie before hauling up, or after launching (peel for pool).

Lodberry. A rock at the entrance to Sannypeel, once used as a pier for the loading of vessels. In former times the grain from the home-farm was shipped from this place (loading rock).

Freswick House. At the mouth of the Burn of Freswick, built by Sir Willliam Sinclair of Freswick 1670. Old local name for the farm is "Burnside", in documents "Burnsyde". Pont's Map 1638, gives "Burnsyde" with Castle.

Burnsyde, Burnside. Barony of Burnsyde and mill, 1549.

St Modden's Chapel. Site of pre-Reformation chapel, around which lingered popish rites. Sir William Sinclair built, on the old site, a modern building with vaults which was never used and has been in decay for over a hundred years.

Braidrigs. Originally the rigs belonging to the tuns and worked on the runrig system. The rigs were held by tenants alternately, none holding two adjoining rigs. According to this plan the tenants had equal shares of good and bad land. The rigs were separated by a ridge of uncultivated land.

The Links. The sand dunes along the shore of Freswick Bay.

The Fitches. Reclaimed mossy ground. Meadow land on the banks of a river.

Shilling Hillock. Near the old mill of Freswick. A shilling-hill, a hill or eminence used for winnowing corn.

Blaeberryquoys. Crofts or farms below the present county road, added to the Mains Farm shortly after 1800.

The Heather. Local name for several crofts, probably having been reclaimed from the hill pasture.

Easter-Wall. An old charter name for a district on the south side of the burn of Freswick, comprising, or adjoining, the district now known as "the Heather".

Tothal Gill. Gill of the infield.

Braid Gill. Broad gill. Gill o'Brabster.

Wolf Gill. Said to be where the last wolf was killed in Caithness.

The Elf Mire. So named as elf-stones (arrow-heads) were supposed to be found there

The Drum. The ridge of the burn of Freswick.

The Fall 'E Drum. The place or a fold for the ingathering of sheep or cattle.

Tofts. Locally called Tafts. A group of houses or home-steads.

The Haas. The haa, i.e. hall, the chief farm in a township in Caithness.

The Slugs. A broad swamp about quarter of a mile long, near the N.W. boundary of Freswick arable land. A miry puddle.

The Priest's Mire. Slightly to the north of the Slugs. Local tradition makes it the place of the murder of a priest in pre-Reformation times.

Wester Quoy. A patch of pasture near the southern base of the Warth Hill.

Hags. A piece of broken moor touching the boundary between the lands of Mey and Freswick. Applied to a ravine or cut-like gap in a hill.

Well o' The Ward. A well in the north-west of Freswick.

The Birlers. An irregular burn, flowing through sloping clay banks, past Wester Quoys.

Gurquoy. Part of a holding.

Everly. *Overley*, over slope.

Outertown. At the outer circle of the township of Freswick.

Mire of Trowskerry. *Ow* in *Trow* pronounced as *ow* in *how*. A mire of hollows and swamps, traditionally associated with trolls or fairies, being in the vicinity of the Warth Hill, the place where the fairies were last seen.

Hill o' Kirshan. The west-ward ridge of hilly moorland between Freswick and the low-lying districts of Canisbay on the north.

Warth, or Wart Hill. The highest eminence in the district. Eastward is the Black Hill, so named from its dark heathery surface. On the top of these ward-hills are usually a heap of stones, the ruins of ancient watch towers or beacons used for signalling purposes. The kindled fires on the wards could be seen from long distances.

Gyres. Gore or strip of out-lying grass in the moorland.

Gyer, or Giar Hill. Westward of the Warth Hill, has patches of green on the slopes.

Loch o' Lomishon. An inland moorland loch. Loch of the ember-goose.

The Shons. A tract of boggy moss.

Shons of Brabster. The pools.

Lint Lochie. A loch so named from the abundance of cotton-grass which whitens the black bog and was at one time gathered and spun. Cotton-grass loch.

Black Lochie. A loch in the black moss.

Dyans. A marshy piece of moorland stretching from the base of the Warth Hill.

Dyssetter. The boggy pasture.

The Brow, the Broo. The rise to the north-west of Freswick township.

The Red Row. A row of four cottar houses, probably so named because of their being built of red sandstone.

Midtown, or Midton. Local pro. "Mittan", middle enclosure.

The Heckler. Originally "The Heckler's Well". A well made in connection with the lint-spinning industry about 1794, and used for bleaching purposes.

Watt's Well. Name of a well.

Quoy Angus. Locally understood to mean the black quoy from its black mossy soil. Also called "The Gutters".

Quoy Dykes. The dykes of the quoys between which was the old cattle or cart track or "caa".

Caa Road, and The Caa. The ancient track passing through the township. There are several *Caas* in other parts of the parish.

Sonsiquoy. The quoy at the end of the sands, or links, of Freswick.

Red Head. Red sandstone cliff on the north-west side of Freswick Bay.

Ferrad. A boggy place, an impassable place.

Feetonsquoy. Wizard's quoy.

Clavey Green. A sloping green break in the cliffs.

Jenny Harrow. Name of a well. Probably a contraction of "Jenny Harrow's Well", from the name of a woman who lived in the neighbourhood.

The Brack. The slope.

Watress. The watery field. (A water course, or a road alongside water.)

Slack o' e' Stack. A hollow between two hillocks, used at sea as a *meeth* or landmark.

The Haven. Old natural landing place now replaced by a pier.

Corff-House. A house or shed for curing salmon and keeping nets.

The Pow. A large pool of water left by the tide between high flood and ebb.

Skirza, Skirza House and Skirza Head. Old forms: *Skirssarie* (valued Rent Roll, 1683); *Scourzie Head*; *Skersarie* (old parochial map); either a shealing or a gravel beach.

Craigwell. An iron-stone spring at Skirza Head. Well of the rock or craig.

The Slate. Flat rock surface under Skirza Head with outlying rock known as "The Stane o' e' Head".

The Selkie Stanes. A common resort of seals.

Lang Ruff. A long projecting submerged rock.

Rushie Geo. Horse geo.

Effie's Geo. Muddy geo.

The Nevs. Rocks north of Effie's Geo, the naves or hub.

Skippie Geo. Ships' geo.

Howburn Head. Half-way between Skirza Head and Duncansbay Head, appears on Thomson's map of Caithness circa 1832, attested by several prominent proprietors and Peter Manson, surveyor. *Howburn Point*, on map attached to Henderson's *Caithness Agriculture*, 1812. Not identified.

Staish Rocks. Placed on Black's map to the south

of the stacks of Duncansby. A stithy, anvil.

Wife Geo. Named from a stack in the centre which resembles a woman.

Fause Geo, or Fast Geo, or Fasgeo. The geo of Fasi.

Crogodale. The winding valley of the Duncansby Burn; name now applied to hill.

The Stacks of Duncansby. Locally designated: Muckle Stack, Peeri Stack and Tom Thoom.

Fishgeil. Sometimes called *Fish Scale*. A large flat reef of rocks partly submerged at high water. There is a channel between the reef and the cliffs large enough for a fishing boat at high water. Fish channel.

The Girns. In this place the cliff slopes gently, and is covered with grass for some distance from the top, in marked contrast with the perpendicular cliffs on either side. It is said to have been a fox lair, when these animals abounded in Caithness.

Partan Girns. A flat shoal jutting out from the beach at The Girns, through which deep channels run, noted for being a good place for fishing lobsters and crabs locally known as *partans*. The shoal probably took its name from the adjoining cliffs, The Girns.

The Stridin Man. A rock near Fasgeo having the appearance of a striding man.

Duncansby and District

Duncansby. The old spelling in local records is "Dungasby", and is so pronounced by the older inhabitants. The farm of Dungall, black foreigner or Dane.

Sannick. A sandy bay, west of Duncansby Head.

Maigie and Cuttiecraig. Fishing rocks near the bay of Sannick. **Maigie** is a kist-shaped shoal with the rocks sloping seaward, submerged at high water. There is deep water between it and the land.

Flutheran. A long sharp-pointed skerry, that is only submerged at high water with spring tides, and surrounded with water at half tide.

Fliss, or Fless. A flat skerry in the bay of Sannick submerged at high water.

Gibscraig. A high stack near Duncansby Head, which from its leaning appearance is likely to topple over. Viewed from the land it appears to be leaning outwards towards the sea, and viewed from the sea it appears to be leaning inwards towards the land. Hence the old local rhyme:–

"If Gibscraig faa's ta 'e lan',
Dungasby 'ill sink for sin.
If Gibscraig faa's till 'e sea,
Dungasbay hid spared will be."

Shinsclave. The valley north of the Head of Crogodale, a grassy slope with perpendicular cliffs on either side, with a footpath winding down to the beach and a small burn running down the slope.

Humlie's Hole. A cave in the face of Duncansby Head, probably caused by the action of the waves wearing away the lower strata of rocks.

Lang Geo o' Slates. A geo at Duncansby Head.

The Knee. A pierced rock at the point of Duncansby Head.

The Bocht, or Bucht. A place where sheep were gathered for shearing. Several boghts at the seaside were used for this purpose, such as this one at Duncansby Head and the Bocht o' Mey. (Scotch, *bught*, sheep-fold).

Quiniclave. The place of an old water mill in a valley, north of Shinsclave, where a footpath also leads down to the beach and a burn falls over the cliff. Quern cliff.

The Beil, or Beild of Duncansby. A hollow where cattle or sheep from the common pasture were collected and *beilded* or folded at night. Most townships had a *beild*. Place for resting and milking.

Faal of the Beil. A fold; at one time a turf-walled enclosure for sheep, but now only a green square patch in the heath.

Baxter Rock. To the south of Duncansby Head. It is a sunken shoal, a ridge or rock still below the surface at low tide. The hidden or blind skerry; is now applied to the rock itself.

Knapster. A stony ridge covered with heather.

Thirl Door. An opening through a small promontory south of Duncansby Head. (A whisk or stick for whipping milk.) It may have been applied to the outer support or pillar of the opening, or to the churning surf washed through the opening.

Geedikettle. A curious wide and deep cauldron-shaped depression on the edge of the cliffs near the stacks of Duncansby.

Kill o' Flux. Right opposite the Big Stack. In this cliff there is a gentle bend projecting towards the Stack, and deep channels run between the cliff and the Stack, in one of which there is room for a small rowing boat.

The Oss. The mouth of a burn.

The Gloop. A cave with an opening to the surface at its inner end.

Lyskerry. A flat sloping rock near the Gloop.

John O'Groat's House. So called after John de Groat of traditional fame. Also the Ferry-house of John O'Groat. Now the popular postal name for the older name of Duncansby.

Pentland Firth. The Sagas give Pettlands-fjoror, Pictland's Firth; 1403.

The Soon. The sound between Stroma and the mainland.

Nis, or Ness of Duncansby. A point or headland.

The Dale. A small inlet sloping in from the Ness or point of Duncansby.

Braid Ebb. A level part of the beach seen at low water east of the Ness.

Blego. A small geo running into a shelly beach. At the outer entrance is a half submerged flat shoal. On one side of the geo are large boulders of blue lava or molten rock.

Ironcraig. Volcanic rocks of ironstone near the Ness.

Robbie's Haven. A landing place for small boats west of the Ness.

The Eastin. The east end.

The Breck. A piece of uncultivated land used as common pasture.

Linniequoy. Level ground covered with heather close beside a burn.

Heppers. A tideway in the Pentland Firth to the east of Stroma. The Hoppers.

The Swell. Probably the Swelkie of Stroma.

Hell Ebb. In Alex. Bryce's Map of 1744, three names appear to the east of Stroma, viz.: The Swilkie, Hell Ebb, and the Boar. Death ebb.

The Bore of Duncansby. A line of breakers which at flood-tide extends from the Ness of Duncansby to the east end of the eddy of Stroma.

Lellan's Bore between Stroma and the Mainland.

Glitteriequoy. A level bit of ground in the centre of the township. Glittering quoy.

Plashmire. A wet marshy place near Stemster.

Burn of Lynegar. A small burn north of the Beil of Duncansby.

Leens and Leen Burn. Pasture land with burn in centre. Leens is the Scotch for low-lying land.

Rutherland. A clearance (of wood or heather).

Swartigill. The black gill.

The Tarnies. Small lochs in marshy moorland.

Lady's Kirk. The remains of an old Roman Catholic chapel, a short distance east of John O'Groats House, dedicated to the Virgin.

Knockin Stane. A rock, east of John O'Groats which at one time had a basin-shaped cavity in which the people used to *hummel* the awns from their bere, or barley. So called from its resemblance to a *knocking stone,* a stone bowl in which corn was knocked with a wooden mall to remove the awns.

Winnin Hill. A place where, in olden times, the corn was winnowed.

Geats Hole. A small geo running into a sandy beach, where refuse was thrown. At the outer entrance are large boulders, and in the centre a circular pool often containing sea-weed. The Knockin Stane forms one side of Geats Hole.

Ferry Haven. Now the pier at John O'Groats, at one time the haven from which the ferry-boat left for Orkney.

The Knickels. Two shoals, one at each side of the entrance to the Ferry Haven. The top of each shoal is round or clew-like in appearance, and both are submerged at half tide. There are deep channels around both the Knickels.

Hammers. The old name was *Haimers.* The name at one period was applied to a jib-shaped piece of ground near the beach, and also to a flat skerry jutting out into the sea. A narrow channel runs through the shoal. The beach is sand, and a small burn at one time flowed through the corner of land which was known as *Haimers* or *Hammers.* It is situated within a hundred yards of Ferry Haven.

Jubigill. *Wester* and *Easter Jubigill,* small ravines east of John O'Groats.

Hang. A small bay. At the base of the surrounding cliffs there is a grass flat called "Ha' Green", about 25 yards wide and four feet above high-water level suitable for a fold. "Ha' Green" takes its name from the adjoining Ha' of Duncansby.

Point o' Hang. A reef of rocks below the mill of John O'Groats.

Fulligeo. Often full of rotten seaweed (foul geo).

Stobie's Hole. A cave near Scarfskerry Point frequented by tinkers.

Seater. In Pont's Map, 1638 *Setre.* A residence, seat, mountain pasture.

Stemster. In 1674, *Stembuster* (Groat charter). A farm-steading near John O'Groats. There is a green mound divided from the steading by a deep gully, through which a burn runs, said to cover the ruins of an ancient keep or stronghold belonging to one of the Earls of Orkney who kept a governor residing there. The places called Stemster in Caithness, occur where there are or were standing stones (farm of the standing stones).

Huna. A crofting township two miles west from John O'Groats, situated at the foot of the Mool Hill. On Huna links are the remains of a Picts' village and several burial cairns. It is supposed to be the burial place of Earl Hlóoer, who, the saga states, was buried at Hofn in Katanes, about 975. The haven of Huna is a sandy beach.

Scarfskerry Point. East of Huna, a common resting place for cormorants.

Mool Hill. Between Huna and John O'Groats. From the east end of the Pentland Firth it looks like an animal's snout.

Tresdale. A low lying stretch of ground which might be termed a valley, strath or dale. Near Tresdale is Trooskerry, traditionally known as a place where the trolls held high revelry.

Stroma

Stroma. Straumey, stream island.

Culliegeo. Knoll geo.

Himral. Lobster channel.

Larquoy. Clay quoy.

Nethertown. Lower. In a charter of 1687 part of it was bounded by the dyke of Tofts on the south, the sea on the east and north, and the burn of Ramigo on the west. Ramigo (pronounced *ramma*), ravens' geo.

Treesgeo. Driftwood geo (trees' geo).

Swelkie. A dangerous tidal whirlpool off the point of Stroma. The myth about the magic quern, *Grotti,* which grinds salt to make the sea salt, is too well known to be repeated here.

Punnie. A house in the rock once used for smuggling, and still intact. A small fold or pound.

The Castle of Mastik or Mestag. A detached stack north west of Mell Head. On the top are the ruins of what is said to have been the residence of a pirate. There was once a draw-bridge between the stack and the adjoining cliff. Probably called "Mey Stack", as it stands across the Firth from Mey or sea-mews' stack.

Mell Head. A round lumpy promontory.

Langaton Point. A long point at the north, nearest the Swelkie. Usually called Langa-tan.

The Gloup. Gloppan, noise.

Barney's geo. The geo of Bjarni.

Duthie Geo. Black geo.

Button Geo. Head of a bay.

Falla Geo. Geo of the fell.

Lamieclett. A long point with a deep geo at one side and the other side sloping down to the sea. Exposed to the continuous beating of the west sea. Klett of Lambi or noisy clett.

Geirieclett. Klett of the gore.

Scar Craggan. Notched crags or it sometimes means a tail in the sea, a concealed rock jutting into the sea.

Geo of Bagwa. A little geo with sloping bank.

Sgeir Gut. Skerry hole.

Mow Skerry. Narrow skerry, or sea-mews' skerry.

Finnies Haven. An old landing-place facing Orkney. Near by are the remains of early settlement and burial place. Finn's haven.

Sgeir Bhan. White skerry.

Hammer. A sharp projecting rock.

Savin Skerries. Seven skerries.

Tarry Berry. A rock covered with sea-weed, with deep waters around, used as a fishing rock.

Clettog. A rock surrounded by the sea at high tide. Small clett.

Geo or Flendie Clett. A landing-place for boats. The stack is of thin slatey formation (a splinter of stone, a flinder).

Geo of Gougan. A long geo with water in it and full of foam in stormy weather. In summer it is a mooring place for boats.

Corbie Tuag. Ravens' mound.

The Kirk of Stara. Cannot now be identified.

Canisbay Township and District

Canisbay. The township on the shore of the Pentland Firth.

Quoys. Quoys of Canisbay. Enclosures or pens.

Niss, or Ness of Quoys. The point opposite the farm of Quoys.

Lyrequoy Well. Below Kirkstyle.

Old Distillery Well. The distillery has long since been out of existence.

Kirkstyle. The farm beside the church.

Kirk of Canisbay. Early site dedicated to St Drostan.

Clay Potts. West of Canisbay, clay soil.

Scaabank. A small sandy channel below Canisbay church. Several large boulders form one side. Often full of sea-weed.

Slaeal, also Slayel. A narrow inlet quite close to Scaabank always covered with green slimy weed.

Haa o' Warse. The ancient hall of the Groats of Warse.

Smiddys or Smyddies. A place-name associated with Warse, in Mey charters, 1574, also part of the Groat lands.

Fowltail or Fooltail. Locally called Fooltel, adjacent to Warse, also Groat lands.

Pyper's croft. Associated with Warse, Smyddies and Foultail, in old charters of the Groats. Location doubtful. There was a family of pipers in a neighbouring croft within the last century, but this name goes back to the 16th century. There was a traditional Pyper's Croft near the Haa of Duncansby.

Brabster, Slickly and Inland District

Brabster. Broad farm.

Brabstermire. Broad-farm mire.

Craighill. A low hill in Brabster district with a craig at one side.

Shons of Brabster. The tarns of Brabster.

Thomson's Field. Between Gills and Brabster.

Stroupster. The big farm.

Fields of Brabster. There were six tenants in 1697 (rental).

Schoolery. The Shealing of Earl Skúli, killed in battle 975.

Slickly. A sinking in the ground, or hill-slope.

Toftranald. Ronald's toft.

Rigifa, Hill of Rigifa. Ridge hill.

Nissetter. Lowest setr.

Philips Mains. Originally *Nissetter*. Renamed after Louisa Philips, wife of the 14th Earl of Caithness.

Grottesoft Moss. If *Grott* is not a personal name, then the moss or moorland of the giant's toft.

Crackersfield. Green fields in the moor between Brabster and Mey, at one time reclaimed into seven crofts, but now back to sheep-grazing.

Holland Mey, or Maik. *Hole o' Mey* (Pont), 1638. Was at one time large commons, but now a farm. "Hollands", once a local name for "commons". The land is raised but not high in the sense of a hill. There is a ruin of an old tower in one field. *Holland* may be high land, which would be applicable to the hill commons.

Gills and Mey

Gills, Gills Bay, Gills Haven, Upper and Lower Gills. A small narrow glen.

Haa o' Gills. The hall or chief house, the residence of the laird.

Soe-Skerry. Sea skerry.

Thomas Peels Rough. Locally called "Tammies Peel". Boat shed of Tom's pool or creek; "rough", may also be applied to a reef or point.

Deubie Gill. *Jubigill*, deep glen.

Sheavie Gills. Unlevel up and down ground. A rough paddock.

Pirly Craig. Crest of the craig.

Kealy Craigs. Keels, applied to mountain range.

Head of Crees. The point at the east side of Scotland's Haven. Holy-rood Head.

Mey. East and West Mey. A field or plain.

Scotland's Haven. On the east side of the haven is the head of Crees, and on the west, St John's Point.

Scoor Berry. Score rock.

Blae Geo. Blue geo.

Fa'en Craig. A geo with overhanging rocks and falling stones.

Bale Geo. Geo of the grassy bank.

Barberry Head. Needle-rock head.

Mallie Geo. Pebble-beach geo.

Blackenberry. A black point of rock with one deep water face.

Rocks o' Girsal. Also called Girsal. A stack or clett. Witch's pillar.

Fas Berry. The rock of Fasi.

Braes o' Gerstal. Grassy braes sloping down to a sandy beach (enclosure for milking cows).

Mealin Tang. An oval-shaped boulder.

Fulligeo. Full of rotten sea-weed.

Liath Skerry. A fishing-place for lythe.

Men o' Mey. A tidal current, or bore, at the west entrance of the Pentland Firth, commonly called "The Men of Mey", or "The Merry Men of Mey".

St John's Point. Named after an old chapel in the neighbourhood dedicated to St John.

Hunspow. Name of a farm. Dog's pool.

Barrogill Castle. Originally called Castle of Mey, or House of Mey. Near by is the site of an ancient burial cairn or barrow. The gill would come down the burnside to Fulligeo, hence there would be the barrow and gill of the borg.

Berriedale Arms Hotel. Opened when the shipment of flagstones was taking place at Philips Harbour.

Philips Harbour. Named after Louisa Philips, wife of James 14th Earl of Caithness. Formerly "Wester Haven".

Wester Haven. The haven of Mey. There is also an Easter Haven.

Trows Geo. Trolls geo.

Tang Head. A spit of land running out into the sea.

Redcastle. A geo with red sandstone cliffs and a block of red sandstone detached from the cliff. There is a tradition that there was a building at the inner end of the geo which collapsed and fell during a night of festivity held inside.

Harrow. Near Barrogill Castle. A heathen place of worship. A hamlet or dwelling.

Scorrie Moss. Bird (Scorrie) moss.

Watty's Craig. Water craig.

Hasty Loup. A detached rock with a space of water between it and the shore. There are several "loups" along the coast (horse leap).

Rotten Geo. Geo of ember geese.

Tree Geo. Driftwood geo.

Geo o' Bedsdale. Geo of the pasturedale (a fold for animals).

How Skerry. A rocky point on the foreshore in a line northwards from an old mound (mound's skerry).

John Mowat, Skirza and Glasgow.

March said to April

I saw three hoggs on yonder hill
And if you'll lend me days three
I'll find a way to gar them dee
The first of them was wind and weet
The next of them was snaw and sleet
The third of them wis sic a freeze
It froze the birds' legs to the trees
But, when the three days were past and gone
The silly poor hoggies came hirplin home.

Ethel Dunnett, Heatherbell Cottages.

A dry "Lent" means a fertile year.

William Dunnet, Quoys.

Rain in May makes the hay.

Sandy Green, Upper Gills.

"The Schochad Storm" – the later it comes the coarser it is.

Lizzie Cook, Skirza.

Clear moon – frost soon.

Johnny Green, Huna.

Evening red and morning grey
Is a sure sign of a better day
Evening grey and morning red
Makes the sailor shake his head

Betty Ham, Hoyview

If Candlemas day be bright and fair
Half the winter's to come and mair
If Candlemas day be wet and foul
Half the winter was past at yule.

Alex Dunnet, West End, John O'Groats.

Mackerel sky, mackerel sky
Never long wet, never long dry.

Muriel Aitken, Organist.

Grass in March – none in May.

Lily Kate Farquhar, Viewfirth.

AUCKENGILL

Auckengill School circa 1900

Photo, Catherine Matheson, Auckengill Post Office.

Teachers – George Stalker and Miss Isabella Begg. Back Row:– Ina Nicolson, Roadside; James Nicolson, Half-way House; George Miller, Old Post Office; Bob Stalker, Schoolhouse; Murdo Mackay, Quarry, Nybster; Wm. John Taylor, Dog's Nose; Lizzie Jane Rosie, Dog's Nose; Georgina Leith, North Keiss; Jean Gunn, Burnside; Edward Rigby, Nybster; Donald Begg, Smiddy, Freswick. Second row from back:– Robert Keith, Mid Auckengill; William Manson, Nybster; Alex Manson, Nybster; Charles Keith, Mid Auckengill; Peter Gunn, Burnside and Canada; Alan Duchart, Roadside; John Banks, Roadside; Dane Charleston, Milton; Alex Campbell, Nybster; Magnus Nicolson, Nybster.

Third row from back:– Marjory Cormack, on holiday; Annie Stalker, School House; Maggie Campbell, Nybster; Mary Rosie, Dog's Nose; Maggie Mackay, Quarry, Nybster; Bill Nicolson, Half-way House; Jean Nicolson, Half-way House; Bessie Nicolson, Half-way House; Ella McGregor, Hillside; Janet Mowat, Rockhill; Kate Nicolson, Roadside; Jessie Leith, North Keiss. Front row:– Robert Mowat, Backless; Peter Miller, North Keiss; Willie Nicolson, Roadside; Mina Begg, Nybster; Maggie Nicolson, Roadside (teacher); Barbara Manson, Nybster; Barbara Rosie, Dog's Nose; Jean Rosie, Dog's Nose; John Cormack, Dog's Nose; Katie Nicolson, Half-way House; Jim Miller, North Keiss; Willie Stalker, School House; David Cormack, Dog's Nose; Tommy Manson, Nybster.

Footnote:– James Maxton was teacher in Auckengill (17.12.1874 – 31.7.1877). He was grandfather of present MP for Bridgeton, Glasgow, John Maxton.

Two men wished one another a Happy New Year over a dram in an Auckengill house. One said he hoped the New Year would not be like the last one for wind, because everytime he had stepped outside, his bonnet blew off his head over the house and invariably landed in a pail of water!

C.M.

Katie Bairdie

Katie Bairdie hed a hen
That wid toddle but and ben
Wisna that a dainty hen?
Dance Katie Bairdie.

Katie Bairdie hed a coo
Black and white aboot the mou'
Wisna that a bonnie coo?
Dance Katie Bairdie

Katie Bairdie hed a cat
Always sittan on the mat
Wisna that a lazy cat?
Dance Katie Bairdie

Katie Bairdie hed a grice
That wid skate upon the ice
Wisna that a cliver grice?
Dance Katie Bairdie.
Malcolm MacLean, Duart, Auckengill

Auckengill School c.1912

Photo, Catherine Matheson, Auckengill Post Office.

Teachers – George Stalker and Miss Lizzie Jane Murray. Back Row, left to right:– James Coghill, Hillside; Charles Begg, Dog's Nose; Katie Nicolson, Schoolhouse; Alex Begg, Milton; Maggie Begg, Smiddy, Freswick; Bob Begg, Nybster; Belle Dunnet, Quoys; Ina Rosie, Dog's Nose; Jackie Cormack, Roadside; Robert Begg, Smiddy, Freswick. Second Row, from back:– George Nicolson, Schoolhouse; Jean Dunnet, Quoys; Nell Simpson, Milton; JohnGeorge Begg, Smiddy, Freswick; John Murray, Dog's Nose; Ella May Coghill, Dog's Nose; Lizzie Cormack, Dog's Nose. Third Row, from back:– David Stalker, School House; George Cormack, Dog's Nose; Maggie Coghill, Hillside; William Simpson, Milton; Maggie Coghill, Dog's Nose; David Simpson, Milton; Peggy Nicolson, Half-way House; Murdo Rosie, Berryhill; Lizzie Coghill, Hillside; John Robertson, Roadside; Mary Service, Quoys. Front Row:– John Service, Quoys; John Rosie, Berryhill; Netta Taylor, Dog's Nose; Lil Wylie, Berryhill; Annie Begg, Dog's Nose; Bella Begg, Dog's Nose; Katie Rosie, Berryhill; Cathie Coghill, Dog's Nose; Mimie Dunnet, Quoys; George Coghill, Hillside; Sinclair Coghill, Hillside.

Auckengill School

Photo, Jessie Sinclair, 9 Main Street, Keiss.

Auckengill School 1923

Photo, Catherine Matheson, Auckengill Post Office.

Back Row:– Teacher, Miss Margaret Nicolson; Jean Steven, Hillside; Johan Dunnet, Quoys; James Cormack, Roadside; William Mackenzie, Mid Auckengill; Markie Levack, Roadside; Betty Steven, Hillside; Tottie Service, Quoys. Middle Row:– Winnie Steven Hillside; Aggie Service, Quoys; Peggy Service, Quoys; Jenny Kennedy, Roadside; Rita Swanson, Rose Cottage; Nellie Begg, Nybster; Nellie Mackenzie, Dog's Nose. Front Row:– Jack Steven, Burnside; Angus Begg, North Keiss; Tom Steven, Burnside; Edward Begg, Nybster; William Mackenzie, Mid Auckengill; James Service, Quoys.

It is of interest to note that three boys in front row – Angus, Tom and Edward – married three sisters from John O'Groats, Lena, Ella and Winnie Steven.

Auckengill School 1931

Photo, Catherine Matheson, Auckengill Post Office.

Back Row:– Robert Bain, Ocean View; John Matheson, Quoys; Jack Sutherland, Summer Bank; George Manson, North Keiss; John Nicolson, The Shop. Middle Row:– William Nicolson, Roadside; Minnie Mackay, Hillside; Minnie Sinclair, Strupster; Isobel Manson, North Keiss; Peggy Mackay, Hillside; Chrissie Bain, Ocean View; Jenny Hendry, Rose Cottage; Jessie Nicolson, The Shop; Catherine Nicolson, The Shop. Front Row:– Margaret Nicolson, Roadside; Jack Clyne, Nybster; Malcolm Steven, Hillside; Sandy Nicolson, Roadside; William Steven (Wing Commander), Hillside; Donald Sinclair; Strupster; William Nicolson Roadside; James Nicolson, Roadside; James Begg, Nybster.

Auckengill School 1936

Photo, Catherine Matheson, Auckengill Post Office.

Back Row:– Teacher – Miss Margaret Nicolson. Donald Sinclair, Strupster; Angus Anderson, Burnside; David Anderson Burnside; Malcolm Steven, Hillside; Robert McGregor, Nybster. Middle Row:– Margaret Nicolson, Roadside; Chrissie Matheson, Hillside; Margaret Sinclair, Strupster; Peggy Keith, Burnside; Ella Steven, Hillside; Ella Begg, Hilltop. Front Row:– Don Robertson, Roadside; Jack Sinclair, Strupster; James Bonnell, Nybster.

Auckengill School 1946

Photo, Catherine Matheson, Auckengill Post Office.

Back Row:– Teacher – Miss Margaret Nicolson. Murdo McLeod, Roadside; John Gunn, Burnside; Helen Burke, Hilltop; Chrissie Oag, North Keiss; Elizabeth Bruce,Greystones; David Cormack, Roadside. Middle Row:– Alistair Cormack, Roadside; Sandy Matheson, Hillside; John Nicolson, Roadside; Alistair McGregor, Nybster; Willie Leitch, Berryhill; Donnie Miller (Taxi's) Burnside. Front Row:– Andrew Manson, Ha; Effie McLeod, Roadside; Margaret Burke, Hilltop; Frances Oag, North Keiss; Margaret Nicolson, The Shop; Barbara Manson, Ha; Helen Gunn, Burnside; Jean McLeod, Roadside; George McLeod, Roadside.

AUCKENGILL

Auckengill Picnic at Sannick 1951

Photo, Catherine Matheson, Auckengill Post Office.

Miss Margaret Nicolson, Teacher; Barbara Manson, Roadside; Winnie Begg, North Keiss. Back Row:– John Gunn, Burnside; Barbara Manson, Ha. Middle Row:– Andrew Manson, Ha; Alexander Bruce, Keiss Garage; Murdo McLeod, Roadside; Elaine Begg, North Keiss; Jean Manson, Ha; Millicent Begg, North Keiss. Front Row:– Minnie Begg, North Keiss; Dolina Bain, North Keiss, Annamay Begg, North Keiss; William Manson, Ha; Allan Gunn, Burnside.

Auckengill School Before It Closed 1962 (Picnic at Lybster)

Photo, Catherine Matheson, Auckengill Post Office.

Back Row:– Yvonne Oag, Roadside; Mrs Margaret Oag, Roadside; Annamay Begg, North Keiss; Louise Matheson, Parkview; Doreen Begg, visiting. Middle Row:– May Manson, Rose Cottage; Jean Cormack, visiting (Keiss). Front Row:– Sandy Budge, Nybster; Margaret Cormack, visiting (Keiss); Edith Nicolson, Roadside; Ronald Oag, Roadside; Marlyn Wisely, Nicolson Cottages; Sheena Wisley, Nicolson Cottages; Margo Matheson, Post Office.

AUCKENGILL

The district known as Auckengill begins north of the lighthouse which is located on the cliff top to the north of the harbour. Long ago when boats were expected, a lantern was placed in the aperture, at the top of the structure. Another light was set in the upstairs end window of the "Halfway House". When the two lights were in line, the boats were on course for the entrance. When the vessel dipped the Halfway House light, it turned to port and the quay head lay ahead.

Further to the north are the "caves" and to the south east of them, in the "ebb" is a "stranger" stone from the Ice Age. A line from this stone to one similar, approximately a half mile inland in a north westerly direction, marks the division between the parishes of Canisbay and Wick.

Beyond the "caves" is "Greenie Geo" and "Winnie Geo" with the headland of Sgarback nearby on which are the remains of a broch. Also near here is the stump of a standing stone and a stone cairn.

Further along is Lang-back, a rocky outcrop, and off shore is the Selkie's Stone, visible at low tide.

The Milton area comes into view a bit further along and in this area there is a wealth of historical ruins. Near to the beach head is a Korff House used for drying fish – to the north east of this one the remains of an ancient mill – further to the north is a barn, with a grain drying kiln on the end. In the same area is an ancient bridge which carried the main road over a stream in days gone by. A stone pillar was built to reinforce the bridge so that it would take the weight of the threshing mill. The steam engine

did not go over the bridge but crossed the burn by a wee track on the upper side and then pulled the mill over the bridge. All of these buildings and the bridge have been repaired recently by some members of the Wick Heritage Society. The name Milton dates pre 1700. During the great days of sail, small boats left the Milton beach with pilots to guide the great sailing ships through the Pentland Firth – to this day one can still see the marks in the soft stone made by the keels during the launching and hauling of the boats.

As one travels further, one sees the "Clett" which in days gone by was a favourite place to fish for "peltags" and "sellags". Numbers of people could be seen fishing in the evenings.

A few hundred yards northwards is the area where the Grimsby trawler Hassett was wrecked on 18/9/1953. Further to the north lies "Samuels Geo", the largest on the Auckengill coast. In days of yore it was a haven for fishing boats. Mooring rings and chains can still be seen on the rocks, as well as stone steps leading down the grassy slope to the beach. After leaving "Samuels Geo", going north, one notices the cliffs are higher with near vertical rock faces and no inlets of any size with the sea washing the cliff face most of the way.

We reach the ruins of Buchollie Castle. This was the seat of the Mowats until 1661 when it was sold to William Sinclair of Rattar. The "Castle Geo" near by terminates the northern end of the Auckengill coast line.

Circular Kiln

Looking down into the kiln showing at the bottom where the fire was stoked and ashes removed. Top left – the door to the kiln was reached by steps inside the barn.

Donnie Robertson, Springwell House, Auckengill

JOHN NICOLSON

John Nicolson was born at Stemster, John O'Groats in 1843. His father and grandfather were both farmers. He attended the old Free Church School in Canisbay and had often been heard to remark, that there he took "pride of place" at the bottom of the class. At an early age, he developed a liking for sculpture and clay-modelling. The clay he procured from the hill at Stemster and his first efforts were at pipe-making. These were smoked by the Canisbay fishermen and crofters and were in great demand.

He came with his family to the "Half-Way House", Nybster, Auckengill in 1858, and after his father's death, continued farming there, until he died in

1934.

In his early years at Nybster, John Nicolson took an active interest in the social and intellectual life of the community. He started a Debating Society which flourished for many years and took a very active part himself in all the debates.

He became keenly interested in the early history of the county and collected many old and valuable documents of great interest. He was particularly interested in the period of the Norse occupation of Caithness and his knowledge of Caithness family history, was probably unrivalled. Many people all over the world approached him, concerning their Caithness ancestry.

He sketched and painted most of the local "worthies", pilots of the Pentland Firth, etc., and many of the public men of Caithness. Some of these sketches and paintings can be seen in the John Nicolson Memorial Exhibition, housed in the old school Auckengill. It was from one of his sketches that the artist sculptured the figure of Calder, the well-known Caithness Historian, which stands on the brae overlooking Wick riverside. Of all his oil-paintings, the best known are the Groat Family and Canisbay School Board – the latter now owned by H.M. Queen Elizabeth, the Queen Mother.

John Nicolson and Family, Half-Way House

Photo, Reta Manson, 22 Dwarwick Place, Dunnet.

Back:– Peggy – Mrs Alex Sutherland, Jessie – Mrs Andrew Bremner, Katie – Mrs William Black; John Nicolson, Andy Bremner, Teenie Nicolson. Seated:– Mrs John Nicolson with Neenie Swanson.

John O'Groats Family

Painting by John Nicolson. Photo, Alistair Sutherland, Summerbank.

Left to right:– Janet Nicolson née Manson (John Nicolson's mother); Jane Nicolson née Mowat (John Nicolson's wife); John Bain, Burnside; Magnus Houston, The Mill, John O'Groats; ? Manson; John Nicolson (the artist); Margaret Nicolson (with boar's head on salver); James McKenzie (grandfather of David John, Keiss); George Manson; Cudler; (in front of J. McKenzie). John Banks (ancestor of Banks, Drapers, High St., Wick); ? Manson.

Although he admired the works of the great masters, his pictures of the sea, fishermen and boats, have qualities all their own.

John Nicolson wrote very little. This was a great pity as he was a born story-teller and his yarns, humorous and otherwise, of old Caithness, were innumerable.

It was when Sir Francis Tress Barry came to Keiss Castle, that he started active antiquarian work. He supervised the excavations of various brochs, a work over which he spent a great deal of time. His observations were minute and accurate and were published by the Antiquarian Society. It was at this time that he obtained his first-hand information about the brochs and their inhabitants. He had a good collection of broch finds which can now be seen in the Memorial Exhibition, Auckengill and also in the National Museum of Antiquities, Edinburgh.

During the salmon fishing season, John collected salmon with a horse and cart from all the small harbours between Mey and Keiss and delivered them to Wick. It was on these journeys that he gleaned all kinds of stories and made observations of possible sites of brochs and cairns. In the surrounding district in which he lived, there are no fewer than 20 brochs and cairns.

For many years, he took a keen interest in education and was chairman of the Keiss School Board. He was a devout churchman and took an active part in the Church of Scotland.

Shortly before he died, the Caithness Research Society had decided to honour him by presenting him with a bust of himself executed by Mr Scott Sutherland (the sculptor of the Commando Memorial at Spean Bridge). Unfortunately, he died before the presentation could be made. This bust can now be seen in the Memorial Museum, Auckengill.

John married Jane Mowat in 1874 and they had 11 of a family, John, Janet, David, William, Christina, Jane, Elizabeth, James, Kate, Margaret, and Ellen.

John Nicolson and his wife are buried in the graveyard at Canisbay Church. Many of his sculptures can be seen there – the most important and notable is the stone he erected to his father and mother, and where he himself is buried. Many knowledgeable people say that this is his finest piece of sculpture.

Alistair Sutherland, Summerbank, Auckengill.

THE OLD PILOTS OF THE PENTLAND FIRTH

Not so very long ago the pilots of the Pentland Firth were indispensable to shipping. Every vessel sailing through the Firth, with its numerous currents and tides and dangerous rocks, had to call upon the services of a pilot to steer them safely on their course. A perfect knowledge of the Firth was necessary as well as of seamanship.

Now all is changed. Towards the end of last century, the coasts and waters were properly surveyed and steam navigation became general. The pilot was no longer required, and now their occupation is gone.

Apart from a chapter in the history of British shipping, the Pentland Firth pilots have left little by way of memorial, with the exception of the two settlements – Pilot Row, near Staxigoe, and Crosskirk, which is about five miles west of Thurso. These were built about 100 years ago and were really the pilots' outposts. The men who lived in Pilot Row came from the north-east parts of the county. The Andersons were from Sannick, Duncansby; the Bruces, Wares, Bains and Rosies from Freswick; and the Mansons from Nybster. The Crosskirk men went from Stroma, and Steven and Smith were common names.

In my early days, the piloting was a regular occupation, and I knew many of the pilots intimately and often heard them relate their experiences. I remember being told by Mrs Donn, Auckengill, who has been deceased many years, that when her father, whose name was Steven, boarded a whaler to take her through the Firth, the captain came along with an axe in his hand and said – "If my ship takes ground your head goes off at the block and lies there!" – pointing to the other side of the ship. Needless to say, Steven was more than usually careful of his charge.

The pilots were, of course, ideal men for the Navy, and during the Napoleonic war the pressgang undertook to gain some of them as recruits. One day James Mackenzie, a Mey man, along with another two, set out for a brig, but on their way they became suspicious of her. An Orkney boat was lying nearby preparing to sail home, and they pulled close around her. When out of view, one of the men hid beneath the sail. The brig proved to be a Government ship, the captain of which hailed them and sternly demanded where the third man was. "Oh" came the ready reply. "He has gone home with his boat to Walls." The ruse was successful and MacKenzie's boat was left untouched as, by law, two men had to be left in a boat.

About 80 years ago, by far the best known among the pilots were Donald Cook, Skirza Head; James Miller, Nybster and Donald Wares, Pilot Row, and their crews were the most prominent men among the pilot boatmen. Other men might know the Pentland Firth as well, but there was a strength of character about these three which placed them far above the ordinary.

At times rivalry among the pilots became very keen. A close race for a ship between a Nybster and a Freswick boat resulted in the former winning with the other coming immediately behind. As the Nybster men were putting their boat snug after making, as they thought, victory secure, the rival pilot jumped into their boat and boarded the ship, and by getting first on deck got the prize. On a later occasion Nybster was avenged. Another close race between the same two boats found them approaching a ship side by side, so close that John Manson, one of the Nybster crew, was able to jerk the sheet from the hands of the man holding it. The delay thus caused to the Freswick boat lost them the ship. Manson, who always went by the nickname of Haman, died not many years ago. I knew him well, and the action referred to was characteristic of the man.

Veterans of Auckengill and Nybster 1900

THE OLD VETERANS OF AUCKENGILL & NYBSTER.

E 4681.

Photo, Peter Miller, Westlands, Freswick.
Back Row, left to right:– John Nicolson (boy), Half-Way House; James Miller, Old Post Office; George Stalker, School House; William Manson, Nybster; William Levack (boy), Roadside; Malcolm Manson, Nybster. Middle Row:– Andrew Dunnet, Berryhill; John Steven, Nybster; Donald Levack, Roadside; George Manson, Nybster; James Begg, Milton; Mr Milliken (with hat), teacher in Keiss. Front Row:– Peter Miller, John Nicolson, Half-Way House; Tam Bain, Red Tams; Charles Dunnet, Dan Rosie's.

It was not always easy for a good pilot to be a good Kirkman. The sight of a ship signalling for a pilot tempted a man, however devout he might be. It is now a good number of years since a Duncansby man was taken to task for going to the ships on a Sunday. On a fine summer Sabbath morning, a ship was seen at the back of the Head with her flag up. John Smith and one of his

boatmen set out for the Ferry Haven. They had difficulty in launching their boat and the man's wife, who was putting her cows to grass, went to their assistance. When the facts became public she and her husband, who were both Kirk members, were hauled before the session at Canisbay and charged with Sabbath-breaking. Their punishment was fixed at perfect church attendance for one year. One Sunday in winter a terrible storm broke out. I have heard my father (who was then in the Ha' of Duncansby) speak of it and of how Mr and Mrs Dunnett went to the church at Canisbay where they formed the entire congregation. That was when services were three and four hours long. They duly fulfilled their obligation. Smith, who was not a member of the Kirk escaped scot-free.

James Miller, Auckengill was a pilot of great skill. After taking a ship through the Firth he saved it from what appeared certain shipwreck. He had taken a ship through and received his fee, but the captain, being in need of men, refused to land him. Miller went into the forecastle. The ship then, in a long tack approached too near Hoy Mouth and when she stayed off it was within a point of the Old Man. On the next tack the tide began to rock the ship on to the Kirk rocks. Preparations were made to abandon her as soon as she struck, when Miller took charge. Taking the wheel, he told the captain to get ready to clew up and get out an anchor. Within a few minutes he had the ship anchored at the Holms in Stromness Harbour. All that in a pitch dark night, with only the lighthouses to steer by. The captain sent him home with an extra fee. Miller was carried away by ships a number of times, and through that he had one time to walk from Limerick to Dublin. So much kindness did he experience at the hands of the poor country folk on the way that he always spoke appreciatively of them and invariably used to say – "I'll never bad use an Irishman's dog."

Though it is more concerned with smuggling than piloting, I will tell of an escapade of four Auckengill pilots which took place in my young days. They had received their fee in kind, and in the form of a supply of duty-free rum, sufficient to fill their water keg. They landed near the Old Castle at Keiss, and two of them set out for a public-house in the village to sell the liquor. They got to the back of the Inn and one, jumping cautiously over the dyke to see if the coast was clear, met the policeman making his last round. "You're late with the girl the nicht," said the constable. "Dae ye never sleep?" was the reply given in a tone loud enough to warn the other pilot, who pushed the keg through a window into the house and left in a hurry. The policeman suspected nothing, but it was several weeks before the crew summoned up courage to reclaim their cask and obtain payment for the rum.

The last of the pilots were Donald Bremner and Simon Bremner, Freswick, and George Manson, Auckengill. In the pockets of his jacket Donald Bremner always carried a Shipwrecked Mariners' Society's medal, a half-crown and a handkerchief. The medal was to enable him to return home if carried away, the half-crown to pay for the boat that would land him and the hankie to "dicht" his nose while he was on the cold quarter-deck. That was his usual equipment. He and three companions from Auckengill were once carried away through a storm striking their ship. On that occasion their boat, which, I may add, was the last of the pilot boats, was lost. Though she was tidily arranged, the ballast heaved, she filled and the tow-line holding her to the ship broke. She was picked up by a Buckie crew and taken back to Auckengill little the worse of the "drooning". Donald Bremner and George Manson died within a short time of each other in the early years of the war.

Before coming to an end, I must mention an incident to show how creditably Auckengill figured in piloting. In 1861, 14 square-rigged ships were wind-bound between Noss Head and Duncansby Head. When they did get through, six of them were piloted by Auckengill men, there being four pilots from the Nybster and two from the Milton boat.

Now the pilots are almost forgotten, and that is a pity, for they were a class of brave and skilful men, accustomed to battle with the storms and dangers of the Firth. Of their brave deeds many a thrilling story could be told.

Notes by John Nicolson, Nybster.

ALONG THE AUCKENGILL / FRESWICK SHORE

The Smuggler's Cave lies southward along the slate from Greeniegeo towards the caves. This is on the north side of the Lighthouse. This cave has a hole of water about five to six feet across and one and a half feet deep with a boulder in the middle lying across its entrance. Once inside you can see the binks or shelves where the Auckengill Worthies set their smuggled tobacco, whisky, rum and other contraband.

A mine was washed into the big cave c.1941, (the one with the pillar in the centre) and was embedded among the boulders. This mine was defused by experts. My father had two mines of the cone type in his shed at the time and I can tell you he was lucky that they were not live when they were washed up. The officer in charge was more than alarmed when he discovered the mines had been dismantled and the bits, any of which could have been live, were set here and there in the shed.

Wildgeo lies about half way between Samuel's Geo and Kingan's Geo, and to get there take the peat road that starts just south of the parking-sign near the top of Betty Begg's Brae. A German destroyer came ashore at the point of Wildgeo in heavy seas when it broke away from the tug towing it south from Scapa after the First World War. This used to be a great place for lobsters which were rusty coloured from hiding in the wreck.

To get to the caves go down the more open geo on the south side and take great care because the path is eaten away at the foot. At stream tide (i.e. when tide is at its lowest) one can get through a hole here into the main geo.

N.B. It is only safe to be through here for half an hour on each side of the tide before it starts to flow.

There are two lots of caves and in the cave on the north side which runs out in a north east direction to the sea, there are stalactites hanging like icicles from the roof and some stalagmites rising from the floor. Further out and jutting out in Wild Geo is Gyants Paw and it was said that Sweyn's treasure was buried at the paw.

Note: It is no longer safe to go out on this paw because where the snib is about three feet wide it is eaten away underneath and there is a drop of about 100 feet to the sea.

The Buchollie Well is in the top half of the grassy slope on the north side of the geo. The sides of the well are rust covered from the iron-ever water filling up and running over. There are quite a few iron-ever wells in the district. When I was young I carried many pails of water (using a hoop) for drinking and cooking.

In the summer I had to fill a tub for the horse, cow and calf from our well. We always liked to have our 'pig' (two gallon clay jar which came in at the shoulders and had a cork stopper) filled with water from the Castlegeo well when we went to the handlines in the "Snowdrop" because it was the best water and kept well. I've never tasted anything finer than a cool drink from the 'pig' on a warm day at sea. When we fished from Auckengill we used to fill our 'pig' using the "stroopie" (piece of rhone pipe) from the well in Torriegeo where the water trickles out of a crack in the rock face. This is just a few steps north of Melvyn's Tower and John Nicolson hollowed a bowl to a depth of one and a half inches in the sandstone below it to collect the water so that one could drink straight from the bowl. It is still there and one can get to this well even at high water if the sea is calm.

A favourite place to fish for sellags, peltags and cuddings was at the south end of the Castle Rock, and it was possible to fish here when it was too rough nearer Auckengill. To get down one must go along past the outhouse buildings and then descend very carefully on to the slate rocks at the south end. The 'Tippet' is a conical shaped rock lying about 15 feet on the sea side of the Castle Rock and I've sailed through this narrow channel in a small boat.

It is possible to clamber down into Kingan's Geo and then with low water one can go through the cave under the Castle Rock which opens out to the sea opposite the Tippet.

It was my father Wm. Nicolson who told me most of this when we lived at Laughton House.

Jimmy Nicolson, Croft House, Auckengill.

AUCKENGILL

Summerbank Oars Men c.1885

Photo, Catherine S. Matheson, Auckengill Post Office,
Will Gunn (junior), Colin Sellars, George Begg, Will Gunn (senior).

Summerbank Boatmen c.1885

Photo, Peter Miller, Westlands, Freswick.
John Nicolson, Half-Way House; Will Gunn (senior), Seaview, Auckengill; George Begg, Roadside; Will Gunn (junior),
Seaview, Auckengill; Colin Sellars, Salmon fisher.

Auckengill Fishing Fleet 1883

Photo, Jessie Sinclair, 9 Main Street, Keiss.

Families and friends on the Braehead. John Nicolson (boy first left); Peter Gunn (extreme left); Will Gunn (front of mast); Alex Campbell (boy seated); John Simpson (with braces), Bill Nicolson (boy); Donald Levack (standing behind Bill); Peter Steven (boy in light cap); John Steven (right of his son Peter); Robert Mowat (seated beside Donald); John Nicolson (seated front). [The pier was built in 1891.]

A Great Catch c.1900

Photo, Reta Manson, 22 Dwarwick Place, Dunnet.

Left to right:– James with his father John Nicolson; unknown; unknown; George Miller (black beard); Thomas Manson, Nybster, with gun; Willie Gunn; unknown; unknown.

Names from Catherine Matheson.

THE LOBSTER FISHER'S DILEMMA

Twas on a sunny April day,
Allan and Peter sailed away,
To look their creels at Stroma Isle,
It would only take a little while.

Off they set in Peter's boat,
No finer yawl was e're afloat,
They set their course for Lang-a-toon,
Before the ebb came roaring doon.

But the tide they hed misjudged a bit,
Because the flood was running yet;
So back they went to Wardie-geo,
For a flask o' tea then back they'd go.

Now Allan he scoffed his tea first,
Because he hed a powerful thirst,
But Peter's bowgie it was sore,
He'd too much beer the nicht before.

His poor gums they were aching too,
Wi yon false choppers in his moo,
So Peter whipped his falsers oot,
And rolled them in an oily cloot.

The warm tea helped soothe Peters bowg,
He licked his lips lek any dowg,
He put his engine into gear,
The slack tide it was very near.

Big lobsters were in Peter's head
As he threw off his crusts of bread,
He saw them floating on the swell,
He saw that oily rag as well.

He turned the boat as fast he could,
But it didna do him any good,
The oily rag was gone from view,
And so were Peter's false teeth too.

Now every day when the weather is fit,
Allan and Peter go back there yet,
And what they are looking for all the while,
Is a lobster with a bright white smile.

Jim Begg, Auckengill.

JAMES SINCLAIR – FOUNDER OF BLENHEIM

James Sinclair born 1817 at Nybster was the fourth son of James Sinclair and Christina Campbell. William was the oldest son and he was a boatbuilder in Pulteneytown about 1845. He later returned to Nybster and had the farm of "Soorooks" (Alan Richard's now).

James Sinclair had a merchant's business in High Street, Wick, before emigrating to New Zealand.

He was married by the Rev. John Mackay, Lybster on the 14th May, 1850 to Christina, daughter of John Sutherland, Merchant of Hillhead, Lybster. Because of ill health, he decided to emigrate to New Zealand and booked passages for himself, wife, son and nurse (afterwards well known as Mrs Charles Brindell).

They sailed from London on the "Agra" in November 1851 and arrived in Wellington on the 3rd March, 1852.

In the following month he moved to Nelson, South Island, where he started business with a stock of

James Sinclair in his 75th year.

Photo, Ethel Jack, Scarfskerry.

goods he had taken out from Manchester.

Hearing good reports of the Wairau Valley he went there in October 1852 and set up business at Beaver. He started an agitation which culminated in the separation of Wairau from Nelson, to create the new Province of Marlborough.

James Sinclair was one of the first members of the Provincial Council and held his seat until 1876. Although repeatedly pressed he declined the office of Superintendent, but his popularity and political influence made him a power to be reckoned with.

With the help of Mr W.H. Eyer and Mr Henry Dobson he succeeded in setting up Blenheim (earlier known as Beaver) as the Provincial capital.

Later James turned his attention to the question of river conservation and matters municipal, including the new layout of the town with Caithness names in honour of his homeland.

Notes by Magnus Houston, The Mill House, John O'Groats

A Sea captain from Auckengill who had sailed round Cape Horn many times on sailing ships used to say when there was a gale blowing "This is nothing – I've seen the wind that strong at the Horn I'd be afraid to open my mouth in case it blew a hole out the top of my head."

C.M.

THE ORIGINAL ST CLARE HALL

The hall was taken over from Orkney in 1920 and had been a canteen and cinema at Lyness during the war. It was brought over by the sailing smack Danish Rose. The sections were put over the side of the boat and then towed ashore like a raft. They were carried up the beach and then taken by horse and cart to the site and erected.

The hall was blown away in a gale and the two men who were inside trying to secure it at the time were very lucky to escape with their lives. It was said that the whole hall rolled a number of times before the floor burst apart and the men were thrown out before the whole thing collapsed.

Some pieces were blown as far as the Milton, and one of Jeckie Nicolson's (the shop) screws was cut in half by one of the ends "flying" into it. The hall was about twelve feet shorter after it was repaired and re-erected.

Jimmy Nicolson, Croft House, Auckengill.

Footnote:– The rafts were towed ashore by the vessel's small boat and the local boat the "Groatie" owned by Bill Nicolson, Summerbank. He named his boat the "Groatie" because this type of boat was very scarce, small and beautiful just like the John O'Groats cowrie shell.

M.S.

THE ST CLARE HALL AUCKENGILL 1923

Photo, Jessie Sinclair, Main Street, Keiss.
Left to Right:– John, Teenie and Jean Nicolson with two friends. Bill Nicolson on bicycle.

The St Clare Hall opened in 1921. The statues of the soldier and sailor were sculpted by John Nicolson as a tribute to those who served in the Great War. The soldier was modelled on Donald Budge, South Keiss and the sailor on William Bremner, Keiss.

Due to the realignment of the A9 the statues had to be moved. A bottle containing interesting artefacts was found in a recess under the statue of the soldier.

The contents, including coins from Germany, Russia, China and the United States, were carefully extracted from the bottle by an expert and then framed. The letter – datemarked Auckengill, 14th July, 1921 – gives a fascinating insight into what concerned people at the time.

"The gate has been erected to commemorate the Great World War of 1914-19 (sic), when the Germans strove with all their might, ruthlessly and inhumanly to lay the whole civilised world under the heel of a despotic and tyrannous militarism," it reads.

Donald Budge

Photo, David Budge, 5 South Street, Keiss.

William Bremner

Photo, Annie Bremner, Cletten, Keiss.

"Trampling underfoot all recognised laws of warfare and the rights of peoples, they waged war on land, sea and in the air, but our Nation's manhood responded gallantly to the calls to arms, and with our Allies and overseas forces, at length turned the tide of war and so thwarted the presumptuous aim of cunning and savage foe.

Stage Curtain

Now "our boys" wear their medals and war decorations in honour of their country while William II, ex Kaiser German Empire, dethroned and disgraced, seeks refuge in Holland, content to wear wooden sabots."

It records that the names of historic battles in which "our heroes engaged" are engraved on the gate.

The contents of the capsule – which also includes fragments of cloth and a snippet from the John O'Groat Journal – will be on display in the museum.

Bill Nicolson painted the St Clare Cockerel on the stage curtain in honour of Admiral Sir John Sinclair who was invited to open the hall in 1921. He was unable to attend on the day and it was Ex-Provost Mackay, Thurso, who did the honours.

Catherine Matheson, Auckengill Post Office.

Footnote:– Sir Walter Scott described this family as "The lordly line of high St Clair" in the Lay of the Last Minstrel.

"AMATEUR RADIO – THE FIRST FIFTY YEARS"

My first encounter with amateur radio began about 50 years ago. I had graduated from the crystal set, to a one valve receiver, mainly for the purpose of listening to trawlers, which abounded on the seas during those days. While tuning around, I came across two people talking, one English, the other with a foreign accent, which turned out to be someone in France. Around the same area, I could hear others in conversation. I could not think what they were – eventually from a radio magazine, I came to the conclusion they were other radio amateurs.

I built various types of receivers throughout the following years, some with up to four valves, also some WW II surplus gear was used. Better aerials were erected, enabling me to listen to radio amateurs world wide. Eventually, I used to keep a log of the calls heard. In the 1950's, I learned morse code, which enabled me to hear stations that used morse, or as it is known "CW". By 1952, I decided to "have a go", at this transmitting! In May I sat the City and Guilds examination for radio amateurs, also a morse code 12wpm morse test in order to get my own personal call-sign. Having passed both exams, I applied to the Post Office in London, and was granted my own personal call-sign – GM3 JDR.

While living in hope of a licence, I had constructed a simple low power morse code transmitter. I may add here, that mains electricity had come to the area about 1952; prior to this, everything was battery operated. One day, the long awaited brown envelope arrived, containing the documentation, "what to do" and "not do, on the air"! – The licence.

I remember my first contact, using my simple transmitter, was with someone in West Germany. Eventually more complex transmitters were built, which enabled me to talk to Australia – China – USSR: In fact, where there are other radio amateurs, I could speak to them; about their weather, what they did etc., using morse or telephony.

Having spoken to King Hussein of Jordon, various Sheiks in the Middle East States, the recent Arctic expeditions, doctors, ships captains, ministers of religion – in amateur radio there are no politics or religions, many famous people like Senator Goldwater, Brian Rix and the late Rajiv Ghandi, to name a few, were licencees.

I still enjoy the hobby, nowadays most transmitters/receivers etc. are bought, though some still make their own equipment.

Donnie Robertson, Springwell House, Auckengill.

The chairman at an Auckengill Christmas Treat had a look behind stage to see if the next turn was ready to carry on the show. He turned around and announced to the audience that the teacher was undressed in the back. In actual fact the truth was that the teacher had not quite got the children dressed ready for the stage. Naturally the audience fairly enjoyed this slip of the tongue.

C.M.

Auckengill Worthies c.1932

Photo, Reta Manson, Dunnet.

Back Row:– Charlie Begg, Charlie Leith, Geordie Begg, Alex Begg; John Simpson. Front Row:– Johnnie Kennedy; John Nicolson; Tom Manson (on holiday); Sandy Steven; Robbie Mowat.

Auckengill Post Office c.1920

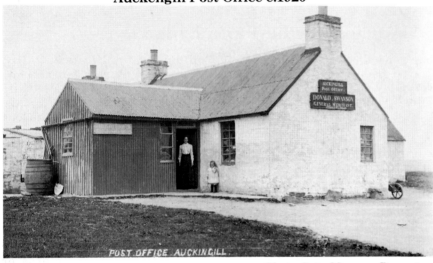

Photo, Reta Manson, Dunnet.
Catherine Swanson with her daughter Neenie. – Note the water barrel.

A CAITHNESS MILLWRIGHT

At Auckengill in the early 1930s, the late John Robertson made three threshing mills for local crofters. They were designed to fit into the small barns which were on the crofts. Wood for the construction was purchased from Wick Sawmill. The drum and certain other items of hardware were purchased from firms in the south, and some of the other iron work was made at the Freswick Smithy. Only one mill remains of the three - it had been located in a derelict barn, with no roof, resulting in most of the woodwork having rotted away. It has been brought back to Auckengill by John Robertson's grandson, who has restored it to the original working condition, in the premises where it was originally constructed.
Donnie Robertson.

An Auckengill man known as Tor went south to work in Edinburgh driving a horse carriage in the city. When he came home on holiday he said that the tatties down there "tasted lek rubber BAWS".

C.M.

Two men wished one another a Happy New Year over a dram in an Auckengill house. One said he hoped the New Year would not be like the last for wind because everytime he had stepped outside his bonnet blew off his head over the house and invariably landed in a pail of water!

C.M.

DUNNET'S COACHES

Charles Dunnet was born in 1855, married Jessie Bain in 1881 and in 1883 commenced the first regular carriage of goods and passengers between Keiss and Wick, although prior to that date he did occasional haulage work for individuals using – 1, Long Cart; 2, Spring Cart; 3, Machine. Among the first passengers carried were pupils from Keiss and the surrounding area attending Wick High School who lodged in Wick and required transport on Monday morning and Friday evening. Transport for Keiss fishermen, to join boats in Wick, had also to be provided on Monday morning returning Saturday evening.

The service was not long in operation when it was found necessary to make two daily trips to Wick using two horses and taking approximately two hours for a single journey. Passenger transport was only part of their business. Fish, crabs, general merchandise, the needs of the crofting and farming community also the fishing and boat-building industry had to be catered for.

The carting of stones for the building of houses etc., and for use as road material, took care of any

Dunnet's Coach on "A9" near the Milton Road, Auckengill

Photo, Jessie Sinclair, Main Street, Keiss.

Gunn Re-union (* brothers and sister).

Back of coach, Left to Right:– Charles Dunnet; William Reid, Boatbuilder, Keiss (Bert's great grandfather); Jessie Ross (married Peter Gunn); Ann Robertson (Mrs Gulloch). Front of coach:– Tom Gunn; Alex Nicolson (went to Canada); Jean Gunn (Mrs Charleson); Nell Gunn (Mrs Lennox); ?; Margaret Budge, Stain, going to visit Harr Begg, Smiddy, Freswick. Front, Left to Right:– Will Gunn (went to America, died in Florida); *Alex Gunn (on holiday from America, died in Chicago); Eliz. Mowat Nicolson (Mrs Alex Gunn, Maggie Nicolson's aunt); *Tom Gunn, Auckengill; Ann Reid, (Mrs Wm. Gunn, daughter of boat-builder); *William Gunn; ?; ?; Gunn from America; Peter Gunn (married Jessie Ross) went to Australia; Will Bremner (Annie and Martha's brother); *Catherine Gunn (Mrs McAngus, Helmsdale).

spare time that the operator might have had.

During the early years of the business, Charles Dunnet continued to follow his herring fishing for short periods, fishing from Wick and as far away as Stornoway. The service continued in his absence by hiring additional horsemen.

Andrew Dunnet, the younger son of the family who was born in 1900, commenced work in the business during the First World War. He used a horse lorry for the carriage of goods while passengers sat on removable seats on the same vehicle. Following his marriage in 1921, he introduced to the business the first motor vehicle, a model T. Ford which could be used as a platform lorry or with a detachable wooden pen known as stocksides for the carriage of livestock to the auction marts and elsewhere. Also a lightweight body with seats and windows could be secured to the platform for the carriage of passengers. A type of roof rack was fitted on the body for the carriage of goods. In the event of the interior being full up passengers raised no objection to travelling on the open roof. It was also not unusual for passengers to find that they were travelling with a calf or young pig or other goods in a sack on the floor.

The earlier vehicles introduced by Andrew Dunnet included:–

SK 738 Model T. Ford. All purpose.
SK 1020 Model T. Ford. All purpose.
SK 1231 4 Cylinder Chevrolette 12 seats. Passengers only.
SK 1623 6 Cylinder Chevrolette 14 Seats. Passengers only.
SK 1905 Thornycroft 20 seats. Passengers only.

Other vehicles included private cars for hire. One of the earliest was an Argyll, purchased in the first instance by John Dunnet, the elder brother of Andrew, who emigrated to California and started a successful Garage and Filling Station in Kenwood. Another private car which caused considerable interest was an Essex, purchased for a nominal sum and removed from the ill-fated American cargo ship Pennsylvania, which went ashore on the Island of Swona in the early 1930's. The vehicles and motor cycles were mainly packed in boxes and being aware of the numbers for a complete set of boxes, ensured a complete vehicle.

Towards the end of the Second World War a new Bedford utility bus joined the fleet SK 2743, followed shortly afterwards by a similar model SK

Andrew Dunnet
Berryhill Auckengill c.1865

Photo, Catherine Matheson, Auckengill Post Office.

2886 and a new Thornycroft Lorry SK 2895.

In 1947 the forerunner of the luxury coaches arrived. A Bedford SK 3033, with the then new Duple body affording the last word in comfort at that time, was the talk of the travelling public in the north. No doubt this vehicle pioneered the way for the present fleet of Bedfords, Fords and Volvos, the latest with toilet and TV which carry the name of Dunnets Motors the length and breadth of the country and the continent, clocking up thousands of miles annually.

Let us remember Charlie Dunnet and the two horses; a brown horse with the unusual name of Forest and the grey mare who started it all by walking twice daily to Wick, six days per week, 52 weeks of the year in all weathers and covering a staggering total of almost 10,000 miles with no Ministry of Transport or EEC rules and regulations, and the tachograph a hundred years away.

Murdo Sinclair, 9 Main Street, Keiss.

Pictured left:– Andrew Dunnet on the steps to the front door of Freswick House. He was ghillie to the Laird of Freswick and one wonders what was in the caisie?

It was Andrew's son Charles who started Dunnet's Coaches in 1883 using a horse and now their sizeable fleet of luxury coaches can be seen throughout the country and the continent.

THE HASSETT

The Hassett, a Grimsby steam trawler outward bound for Iceland, ran aground in heavy seas below Berryhill on the Ruff of Auckengill, 18th September, 1953.

The Wick lifeboat could not close in on the Hassett because of the wild breaking seas. The destroyer HMS Scorpion was also at the scene. Sadly five of the crew were swept overboard before the Wick L.S.A. team got a line aboard and rescued the remaining 15 seamen by breeches buoy.

Everyone who helped at the rescue was presented with a wallet inscribed thus:– "Presented by owners and underwriters of Grimsby Trawler Hassett for services rendered to her crew when wrecked at Auckengill, Caithness."

Barry Almond, the skipper's son was a lad of 16 when the Hassett was wrecked. Last year, he was a crew member on the Solitaire BF.99 a seine-net boat, and when it was berthed at Wick he came out to see us. He said he would never forget the terrifying experience nor would he forget the warmth and kindness of his rescuers.

Donnie Robertson, Springwell House, Auckengill.

BACKLESS

Houses and steading.

Incised stone round window.

Remains of circular kiln upper end of barn.

Winnowing doors in barn.

The 1841 census returns shows that David and Elizabeth Rosey with their family Andrew, Marjory and Murdoch lived in one house and that Malcolm and Elizabeth Dunnet with Andrew, 17 years, and Eliz., seven years, were in the other house. David Rosey is down as farmer and Malcolm Dunnet as cooper. Backless is a bit from Auckengill harbour and it is not sure if Malcolm had a business there or if he worked at the sizeable cooperage at Keiss.

It is certain that Malcolm Dunnet married Elizabeth Davidson on 23rd March, 1822, and that they moved from Backless to the back of Berryhill with their family Charles, Andrew and Betty. Charles married Bella Leith and it was said that when their family Sutherland, Malcolm, Alexander, William, Elizabeth, Jean and Isabella were very young they had to tether them (by the leg!) in case they fell over the cliff. The foundations

Large hallan stone above fireplace with handy cupboard at side. Ship's timber lintel over window. Round stones in gable.

The wall press and groove for "Heilan couples". Note use of round stones.

"Wall units" (there are another three fine ones not shown). The small windows indicate it could have been a milk house or workshop. Latterly used as a hen-house and the hens nested and laid in "units."

of the house can be seen and some of the garden wall right at the edge of the cliff at the top of Charlie's geo.

The Sinclairs were the last family to live at Backless, before the three sons and one daughter Daisy emigrated to America about 1930. Before them it was Robert Mowat and family who moved to "Rockhill".

The buildings are a lasting memorial to the pride, skill and care that went into their construction. One can see the thought that went into the planning of the houses and steading, not only for convenience but also to use selected stones and boat timbers successfully. Large dressed stones are an obvious choice but contrivance to include round stones can also be appreciated. It is hoped that someone can throw more light on the families who built and lived and worked at Backless.

The last house to be built is the one end on to the road and the close-up of the window shows some incised stones which it is thought came from Buchollie. The kiln is unusual in that it is square built on the outside and rounded on the inside. The barn doors were built opposite each other east and west to provide draught for winnowing. The man doing the winnowing stood between the two doors shaking a large type of sieve which was sometimes supported from the couples. The corn fell straight down, the "tails" and strumps of straw were light and blown to the side and the chaff was blown still further over.

There is a drystone dyke running for a considerable distance round the field in front of Backless and stone built dykes are very seldom seen on crofts in the parish. Rhubarb still flourishes in the walled garden.

Margaret Wares, Seaview Hotel. Bena Rosie, Hillside, John O'Groats. Jessie Sinclair, Main St., Keiss.

The mast, sails and oars were pushed in at hole in gable and slipped along above couple baulks. The pigs house would be roofed with local slate (Freswick Mains in background).

Photos, Magnus Houston.

ROBERT MOWAT – BACKLESS

Robert was the son of John Mowat (joiner) married to Barbara Banks, and they appear in the 1841 census as living at Freswick. John and Barbara's family were:–

James – Pilot and father of John Mowat historian.

John – Minister – Studied at Knox college, Toronto and graduated in 1881. He later returned to Freswick and lived at Backless with his brother Robert. He moved to Skirza in 1917 and died in 1920. (Maggie Mowat opened the shop there in 1923).

William – Died in 1866 aged 24.

Catherine – Married William Robertson and lived at Longhope.

Robert – (twin with Catherine) married Margaret Dunnet, Quoys, Canisbay and moved to Backless where they farmed and raised 10 of a family. Seven of the family emigrated and the ones who stayed in this country were proud to tell how well they had all done.

The family of Robert and Margaret Dunnet were:–

Margaret – Spinster who farmed Rockhill after the death of her father in 1940.

John – Went to San Francisco. He was a builder and worked at the re-building of the city after the big earthquake there. He had one son Robert.

Barbara – Married James Kennedy and they emigrated to Alberta.

William – (Bill) married Gertie Inglis and also went to Alberta – no family. (Robin still has the tool-box Bill made when an apprentice joiner.)

Elizabeth – (Lizzie) was cook to a lawyer's family in a large house in Barnton, Edinburgh, where she met and married Alexander Inglis. This was one of the early families to own a car and Alex was chauffeur. Family – Alexander, Robert and Hunter. (Father of Robin Inglis now living at Skirza.)

Janet – Married James Sutherland and went to Berkeley, USA. Family – Elizabeth and Catherine (Kay).

Katherine – Married twice (1) Pope, (2) Elliot, emigrated to British Columbia.

James – Married Alice Provan and was a fruit farmer in California. He learned his trade as a farrier at the Golspie Tech. This is the James Mowat whose displenishing sale notice follows.

George – Married Tibbie Bunting. He was an engineer with Bruce Peebles, (a big heavy engineering firm in Edinburgh and Glasgow) before he emigrated to San Francisco. Family – Irene and Margaret.

Robert David – Tragically fell down the south side of the narrow causeway at Buchollie Castle in 1906, aged 14, whilst collecting gull's eggs and died a few days later. The family left Backless about 1918 and moved to Rockhill, Auckengill.

Gail Inglis, The Shop, Skirza.

Danger! – Keep Away

"Livvieallan"[1] or "Greenteeth" lived at Quarryside, Auckengill and at Himral, Stroma, and were terrifyingly wild.

Robbie Dundas, Stroma View, Huna.

[1] Long ago someone in a towering rage was described as "wild as the very leviathan". Bible Reference – Job. 41. This monster (of the Nile) could have been the crocodile because it has 30 teeth each side of each jaw which lock into each other, and the teeth are seen even when the mouth is closed. This wild crooked wriggling serpent or crocodile = satan.

Betty Begg's Brae

The brae got it's name from Betty Gray who married Alexander Begg and lived in a house on the sea side of the road further up the brae than the "Sodjurs".

Betty Gray's half sister Charlotte Robertson married Andrew Dunnet whose photo is shown on steps of Freswick house.

Alexander Begg was the father of George Begg, miller at Milton and grandfather of Ak who lived at Hilltop.

Catherine Matheson, Auckengill Post Office,

Auction Sale

➤ AUCTION SALE OF ➤

MOTOR CAR,

Fishing Boat, one 7.9-H.P. Engine, Motor Cycle (Beardmore), Blacksmith's and Joiner's Tools, &c.,

AT

ROCKHILL, AUCKENGILL, PARISH OF CANISBAY.

On Saturday, 17th March, 1928

SALE AT ELEVEN O'CLOCK FORENOON PROMPT.

There will be sold by auction at Rockhill, Auckengill, Motor Car, Boat, and Blacksmith's and Joiner's Tools, belonging to **Mr JAMES MOWAT, who is leaving the County.**

Two-Seater Motor Car, in good running order; 2¾-H.P. Motor Cycle (Beardmore) first class condition, complete with Speedometer, Lamps and all Tools; Boat, 13-feet Keel (Decked Yawl), Mast and Sails and fitted for Engine Power, first class condition; Bellows; Boring Machine, 0 to 1½ inches; Steel Vice; Anvil; Turning Lathe; Blow Lamp; 3 Sets Stocks and Dies, 0 to 1¼ inches; Beam and Weights; 2 Benches; Hammers; Spanners; a quantity of Iron and sundry Blacksmith's Tools; also, a number of Joiner's Tools, including--Planes Bead and Feather; Braces; Wood and Steel Drills; Saws; Squares; One complete Set Carving Tools, &c.

Also, AUCTION SALE OF

FARM STOCK, IMPLEMENTS, &c.

AT

MILTON, AUCKENGILL, Parish of Canisbay,

For Mrs B. SIMPSON who is giving up the Croft, viz. :--

1 CROSS RED POLLED COW, 5 years old, time up 14th April.   Box Cart, Plough, Set Harrows, Scuffler, 2 Sets Ambles, and the usual Implements of the Farm.

Some HOUSEHOLD FURNITURE, &c.

Sale at Three o'Clock Afternoon or immediately after Jas. Mowat's Sale.

TERMS—Cash at each Sale.

Motor Conveyance from WICK AUCTION MART at 10 o'clock a.m.

ALEXANDER SINCLAIR, Auctioneer.

Notice of Sale from Sutherland Manson.

Cottages at The Milton, Auckengill, c.1930

Photo, Douglas Cameron.

The main feature is the croft occupied latterly by the household of Alex. Begg. The buildings, now in ruins, include the barn at the extreme right which contains at its landward end, a circular corn-drying kiln. There are two opposing doors, so aligned as to produce a through draught to assist the winnowing process. In recent years the kiln has been restored by the Wick Society.

The dwelling-house and steading are continuous, while the byre in front with conspicuous muck-hole may have been of later constructions. The men appear to be building a hay "scroo" or "gilt" using material from surrounding "coles".

In the foreground, the field slopes down to a burn. The man-made channels on the bank near the steading indicate the site of a mill, possibly of the click mill type with undershot wheel. Its operation gave the name Mill Town to this area, nowadays known as the Milton. The derivation of Auckengill as the "croft by the burn", may have its origin here.

More than a hundred years ago in the corner of the beach below the barn, rested the local boat. On a signal from a sailing vessel requiring a Pentland Firth pilot, it was launched by the crofter-fishermen into the natural haven nearby.

The small thatched cottage with one chimney and a water barrel at the gable end was built for James Begg on his retiral. On the horizon can be seen a small rectangular stone cairn constructed by local antiquarian John Nicolson. To the left of the cairn is the farmhouse and steading built by Charles Dunnet who moved with his wife and family from their former home situated a few yards from precipitous cliffs. After the Dunnet family, the house was occupied by W. Bremner and finally by Dan Rosie and his family.

It is noticeable that crofts had very small fields with no fences. Fishing was necessary to augment meagre agricultural resources.

Lilian Cameron, 125 Rose Street, Dunfermline.

FRESWICK

Freswick School 1920

Photo, Mrs Tommy Munro, Harley.

Back Row, left to right:– William Sinclair, Backless; James Sutherland, Midtown; Ellison Gunn, Road End; David Cook, Skirza Head; Markie Sutherland, Midtown; William Rosie, Harley. Middle Row:– Bena Henderson, Hilltop; Daisy Sinclair, Backless; Nellie Bremner, Heather; Barbara Rosie, Heather; Lily Henderson, Hilltop; Joanna Rosie, Harley; Annabell Donaldson, Midtown; Cathie Rosie, Harley. Front Row:– Donnie Wares, Midtown; Mitchell Bain, Tofts; John Bremner, Midtown; Robbie Kennedy, Pentland House; Robert McKay, Tofts.

Freswick School 1929

Photo, Ian Angus, Midtown.

Back Row:– Willie Munro, Freswick Mains; Robert Dunnet, Skirza; Bobby Sutherland, Freswick Mains; Donald Wares, Midtown; John Bremner, Midtown; William Henderson, Heather. Middle Row:– Jessie Bain, Midtown; Margaret Tait, Midtown; Ella Tait, Midtown; Betty Wares, Midtown; Lily Bremner, Tofts; Minnie Wares, Midtown. Front Row:– Jack Henderson, Heather; Robert Bremner, Midtown; William Bain, Midtown.

Freswick School 1941-42

Photo, Margaret Rosie, Midtown.

Diagram of Heads

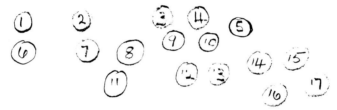

1, Margaret Henderson, Callymuir; 2, Barbara Henderson, Heather; 3, Magnus Henderson, Callymuir; 4, William Cormack, Midtown; 5, Robert Henderson, Heather; 6, Janette Henderson, Skirza; 7, Lena Henderson, Heather; 8, Betty Robertson, Midtown; 9, Laurene Bremner, Tofts; 10, Eileen Henderson, Road End; 11, Gena Henderson, Heather; 12, John Rosie, Heather; 13, Barbara Ganson, Midtown; 14, Margaret Bremner, Midtown; 15, Violet Cormack, Midtown; 16, Nan Bremner, Tofts; 17, Helen Henderson, Callymuir.

Freswick School

Photo, Elizabeth Munro, Harley.

LEST WE FORGET

Freswick Picnic c.1927

Diagram of Heads

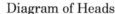

1, Andrew Donaldson, The Row, Freswick; 2, Addie Bremner, Keiss; 3, Katie Bremner (Mrs Mowat), John O'Groats; 4, Ellison Gunn, Road End; 5, Willie MacRae, John O'Groats; 6, Lizzie Cook, Skirza Head; 7, Alex McLeod, Heather; 8, Jeannie Mowatt, The Broo, John O'Groats; 9, Chrissie Mowat, Skirza House (on holiday); 10, ?; 11, Lottie Mowat, Skirza House (on holiday); 12, Lily Bremner (Mrs Kennedy), Tofts; 13, Hamish Sutherland, Midtown; 14, Ada Baikie (Mrs Mowat), Keiss; 15, Margaret Mackay (Mrs Bremner), Midtown; 16, Bella Bremner (Mrs Wares), Freswick; 17, David Dunnet, Mount Pleasant, Freswick; 18 Jack Mowat, Skirza House (on holiday); 19, Nannie Bremner (Mrs Jeffrey), Sonsiquoy; 20, Sandy Bremner, Everly; 21, Maggie Begg, Hilltop; 22, ?; 23, Maggie Coghill (Mrs Munro), Auckengill; 24, Robert Bremner, Midtown; 25, David Wares, Midtown; 26, Robert Dunnet, Skirza; 27, Harry Begg, Hilltop; 28, Lysbeth Laird (Mrs Angus), Skirza; 29, John Calder (Scout), John O'Groats; 30, Elsie Buchanan, Wick, or Bella Cormack (Will Cormack Sodger's wife); 31, John Bremner, Midtown; 32, David Cook, Skirza Head; 33, Lizzie Laird (Mrs Dunnet), Broo; 34, Mrs H. Sutherland, School House, Freswick; 35, ?; 36, George Green, John O'Groats; 37, Nellie Thomson, Wick; 38, John Tait, Midtown; 39, Lizzie Green (Mrs Bremner), Tofts; 40, Bella Mowat (Mrs Bremner), Tofts; 41, David Bremner, Tofts; 42, Mrs Bremner (on holiday from Fife); 43, Donald Bremner, (on holiday from Fife); 44, Robert Sutherland, Freswick Mains; 45, Donald Bremner, Heather; 46, Mimie Green (Mrs Calder), John O'Groats; 47, Donald Bremner, Windygates, Fife; 48, Nellie Henderson (Mrs Tait), Freswick; 49, Maggie Banks (Mrs Sutherland), Freswick Mains; 50, David Sutherland, Freswick Mains; 51, Annabella Donaldson, The Row; 52, Sandy Lyall, Brabster; 53, Alex Munro, Freswick Mains; 54 Bella Kennedy (Mrs Bremner), Tofts; 55, Will Bremner, Tofts House; 56 Willie Gunn, Road End; 57 Jackie Sutherland, Freswick Mains; 58, George Sutherland, Freswick Mains.

Daniel Mowatt took the photograph and the addresses are all Freswick unless otherwise stated. Names from **Mrs Bena Rosie**, Hillside, John O'Groats and **Miss Lizzie Cook**, Skirza.

94

Buchollie Castle

Photo, Magnus Houston.

The remains of courtyard and some outbuildings on the peninsular rock. In front of the Castle the narrow neck of land which had been cut through by a trench seven feet wide and nine feet deep – originally spanned by a draw bridge.

BUCHOLLIE CASTLE – THE SWANSONS AND MOWATS

Photo courtesy of Country Homes and Interiors.

Buchollie as Lambaborg

On a grim and forbidding site on the south side of Freswick Bay, and about five miles south of Duncansby Head at ND382658 are the gaunt ruins of Buchollie Castle, the first of seven medieval castles which dot the next 20 miles or so of the Caithness coastline making it the most castellated stretch of coast in Britain.

It was here, about 1140, that Sweyn (Norse "Svein", a youth) Asleifarson, the Caithness-born scion of a noble Norse family, built his fortress – then known as Lambaborg. He was one of the most colourful, resourceful and daring of the many heroes who flit across the pages of the Norse sagas. On one occasion he was besieged in Lambaborg by Earl Rognvald – the builder of St Magnus Cathedral – whose displeasure he had incurred. When his provisions were almost exhausted he and his companion-in-arms, Margad Grimson, got themselves lowered to the sea from the hundred foot high castle rock by means of a rope and then swam along the shore to safety. Sweyn was a pirate and robber, but these occupations were regarded as honourable in his Viking world and he could claim the genuine friendship of the saintly King David I. During his career he menaced the whole western coast of Scotland, the Isle of Man, and Ireland until finally ambushed and killed while leading a raid on Dublin.

The Swansons

After Sweyn's death a curtain of complete silence falls on Lambaborg. It is not known whether the property was transmitted to his immediate descendants but the evidence would appear to be that it was not. His descendants, the Swansons, multiplied greatly in the north, but never achieved clan status, notwithstanding the fact that in ancient and honourable lineage they equalled many other families who did, and especially their kinsmen, the Gunns, who were descended from Gunn an elder brother of Sweyn. They had no territorial designation, no clan chief, and no coat of arms. The inference is undoubtedly that they never possessed lands, being recognised merely as a sept of the clan Gunn throughout the course of their history.

The Mowats

It was not until the early part of the 14th century that Lambaborg came to life again in history, but then under its new name of Buchollie. We have no definite date as to when the Mowats came to Freswick bringing the name Buchollie with them from their estate of the same name in Aberdeenshire, although we do know that in the reign of King Robert the Bruce, the monarch granted them a charter of the lands of Freswick. However such charters were sometimes merely confirmatory, stamping on possessions the Scottish royal seal of a particular family who might have already inherited them through intermarriage with a Norse family whose previous legal titles were held from the Norwegian crown.

Norman Descent

The Mowat family derive their name from Mont Hault (meaning High Mount) in Normandy, but later Latinized to de Monte Alto. Like many other noble families who followed the Conqueror they settled in England and were given the task of keeping the Welsh marches. Their first castle, built by Robert de Monte Alto was Molde or Moulde from their own surname. The modern town of Mold in Flintshire grew up around the site of this castle. By 1260 their seat was Howarden Castle on the Cheshire side of the border, but in 1329 the first baron of the line died without a male heir and the title became extinct. Branches of the family had spread in England and are now known by the surname of Maude.

Arrival in Scotland

The first of the name to settle in Scotland was another Robert de Monte Alto who was invited to do so by King David I. He was a younger son of one of the barons of Mold, Flintshire. King William the Lion granted Sir William de Monte Alto the lordship of Fern in Angus and his descendants for the next two centuries were prominent landowners and justiciaries in that county, holding many appointments and offices under the crown. Another Sir William de Monte Alto fought with King Robert the Bruce at Bannockburn, was a member of the Scottish Parliament and was one of the signatories of the famous Declaration of Arbroath in 1320. By the 13th century some members of the family were

spelling their surname as de Mohaut, evolving towards the present spelling. After 1410 there is no further mention of the de Monte Altos of Fern, and the representation of the family devolved on the Mowats of Buchollie, Aberdeenshire, who had sprung from the Fern family. This was the branch, who by means unknown, acquired the landed estates of Freswick and Harpsdale in Caithness. They restored and reconstructed the old castle of Lambaborg and changed its name to Buchollie, but the change of name affected the castle only and not the lands which continued to be known as Freswick.

Mowat Branches in Caithness

There were many offshoots of the Mowats of Freswick. One important branch was the Mowats of Brabstermire and Slickly who in turn had a branch in possession of Swinzie (now Lochend). Members of the Mowat family migrated both from Aberdeenshire and Caithness into Orkney and Shetland where several Mowat families appear as landholders; others as merchants and traders. In Shetland the name is often spelt Mouat. The name also appears at an early date in Norway – a son of Andrew Mowat of Hugoland, Shetland, became a distinguished Admiral in the Norwegian Navy with large estates in that country.

In 1661 Magnus Mowat of Buchollie sold the family estates in Caithness and 66 years later the then laird John Mowat disposed of the Aberdeenshire Buchollie Castle, later largely rebuilt by the Duff family, and renamed Hatton.

Landless and Chiefless

The Mowats are unhappily both landless and chiefless. Sir Thomas Innes, Learney, the late Lord Lyon King of Arms has said that "a chiefless clan, like an orphan family is an imperfect group." That the Mowats of Buchollie were Chiefs of their name is signified in their coat of arms with their "supporters" – a distinction only given in Scotland to Chiefs of their name and peers of the realm. The Mowats do not have a clan association – nowadays a first requirement in the tracing of a Chief. That there is someone walking the earth today who unknown to himself and his clansmen is entitled to the "undifference" arms of Buchollie there cannot be the slightest doubt.

The Castle Today

Looking at the castle today it would appear that there is little left of Sweyn's original structure. The earliest Norse strongholds were square box-like buildings three or four storeys in height. With extremely thick walls of about eight feet with the doorway on the first floor level facing the sea. The site is almost an island stuck onto the mainland by a very narrow strip of land cut through at the neck by a dry ditch. The old Norse keeps rose straight up from the far side of the ditch but slightly offset from the line of the drawbridge to allow access past the building to the rear. Today's ruins have an entrance facing where the drawbridge stood and a vaulted passage leads through the keep to the courtyard beyond. It may well be that at Lambaborg extremely thick walls were unnecessary for its defence owing to the natural impregnability of the site, as in a similar position at Castle Gunn in Clyth of about the same date, the walls were only three feet thick. An unusual feature of the ruins is that the ground and second floors were vaulted while the intermediate first floor was of wood. At the second storey level facing the landward side there are the corbelled remains of a projecting turret. The narrow courtyard behind the castle has the remains of out-buildings on either side of it. There are no signs of how the castle was supplied with water. It is clear that the present buildings for the most part date from the Mowat occupation, the main keep being 15th century architecture, closely resembling Girnigoe which is known to date from somewhere between 1475 and 1494.

References

Henderson – Caithness Family History – Douglas.

McGibbon and Ross – The Castellated and Domestic Architecture of Scotland – Douglas, 1889.

Curle – Inventory of Ancient Monuments of Caithness – HMSO, 1911.

St Clair – The St Clairs of the Isles – Brett, 1898.
David B. Miller, Old Stirkoke, Wick.

CANDLEMAS FAIR

"Caanelmas" was held on the outskirts of Freswick alongside the old track from the Orkney ferries. (the hillside overlooking Buchollie Castle and about opposite the now derelict smiddy.)

It was never a cattle market to the same extent as other Caithness Trysts. It was more a mingling of pleasure and business, when the crofters and fishermen did not have too much outside work to do. At the beginning of the 19th century there was a considerable trade between Orkney and Caithness in horses. Several hundred horses were brought across the Firth at the cost of 1/- to 1/6 depending on size. Many would find buyers on the "Caanelmas" to be in readiness for the downlay. They were replaced by young staigs imported from the West Highlands. Candlemas was a festive occasion when ladies wore blue or black hooded cloaks with mutches and bords (ribbons) of spotless white. The males sported the broad Kilmarnock bonnet with distinctive top and checked band.

The fair proper was held on Tuesdays but in its heyday lasted three days and often most of the week. Servants were exempt from ordinary work and there was all the preliminary work of brewing ale and preparing food for man, beast and strangers from a distance. The refreshment booths or tents were the main shelters. The merchandise in the stalls consisted of farm produce, home made linen goods, rugs, plaids, brogues, wooden bickers (brose bowls?) horn spoons, nick-nacks.

The old custom of "handfasting" was said to be observed in a measure on the Candlemas Fair. A young man and girl would meet and pledge their troth to each other for one year by joining hands (get engaged).

Bargaining was a fine art with a sharp wit. After considerable beating up and down of the price, a bargain would be struck and an adjournment would be made to the tent to drink the "feet ales". A bargain was never considered fully ratified until "feet ales" were pledged and drunk in ale or whisky by both seller and buyer. The scaling (ending) of the fair brought the usual spate of sore heads.

Candlemas notes by John Mowat, Skirza and Glasgow.

Candlemas

Canisbay folk reckoned they needed to have half of everything still in reserve at Candlemas – straw, hay, turnips, potatoes, girnal, kailyard, peats, etc.

First comes Candlemas and then the new mune
The first Tuesday efter that is fair Fostern's e'en
That mune out and the next at its height
The first Sunday efter that is Peace Sunday right.

This rhyme must have originated when the Canisbay Kirk was Roman Catholic and has been handed down through the generations.
Magnus Houston, The Mill, John O'Groats.

Candlemas (2nd February)

The day the child Jesus was taken to the temple, candles were lit to remind Christians of the "Light of the World". It was a feast day between Christmas and Easter and at a time when people needed cheering up. Fostern's e'en – I did not find a Saint Foster, so guess it was a day when people were well fostered because all the meat and animal produce had to be used up before the "fast".

Fastern's E'en – Eve of Lent – Shrove Tuesday.

Easter Sunday – Known as Peace Sunday "Peace be with you".
Father Canon MacDonald, Thurso.

FRESWICK CASTLE

Freswick was one of the two estates on the Scottish mainland of the Viking Jarls of Orkney, and as such its owners were closely allied to the Norwegian, Scottish and English Royal Houses and also the ancestors of George Washington. The Jarl's kinsman Sweyn Asleifarson (who lived at Freswick) is recorded as going from Freswick to Aberdeen as the Ambassador of the Norwegian

King to treat with the Scots King at a time when this part of Caithness was part of the Kingdom of Norway.

The tower is 1580. The foundations are Viking and the north wall of the dungeon has exposed stone work of the earlier Viking Hall mentioned in the Orkneyinga Saga circa 1153.

Freswick Castle was rebuilt in the 17th century by the great grandson of the fourth Earl of Caithness. It has two dungeons, one is located below the Laird's drawing room and is reached by a secret trap-door in the floor. The other, a "bottle neck" dungeon is in the ancient bridge. The Sinclair Coat of Arms is carved on a square red stone seen above the entrance to the dungeon.

The drawing room is situated in the old tower c.1580. The red sandstone doorways carry the original mason marks. The great hall on the lower floor with its vaulted ceiling, has a swey above the large open fire in the inglenook. The stone staircase shows skilled mason-work with the "roundels" on the end of each step forming a perfect column rising from the ground to the top floor. A "swastika", the mark of the master-mason is carved on the roundel of the bottom step.

The castle is surrounded on three sides by water and it is only the fine golden sands of Freswick Bay that stand between it and Norway.

Gerald Newell, Freswick Castle.

The Drawing Room

The Laird's Drawing Room

The Circular Stair

Photo, James P. Campbell, Rose Cottage, Halkirk.

The Great Hall

Photos, Gerald Newell.

FRESWICK MAINS OR BURNSIDE

Photo, Peter Miller.

Burnside or Freswick House

Freswick House was built about 1760, lightning hit a chimney in 1768 and damaged a wall from top to bottom, also damaging most of the windows.

The house is not a castle. It does not have the battlements which would entitle it to that distinctive title. It was always known by local residents as "The Burnside".

The last laird died in 1838 and was buried in Bower. His funeral was long remembered because of the large numbers of mourners and retainers who were present. Owing to the lack of roads, the funeral had to cross the moors by "bridle tracks" to Brabster. When the front of the cortege reached Brabster, the last of the mourners were just leaving Freswick House, a distance of about three miles long.

St Moddoan's (or Maddans) Chapel with a burial vault underneath is now roofless.

The fine stone built doocot is in excellent condition. It is bell-shaped with the door and pigeon ports facing south. The roof is off, but you can see the rows and rows of nesting boxes. The boxes start about seven feet above the ground. Pigeons were not kept for their eggs but for the valuable supply of meat they provided all year round. They were so easy to pick up quietly once they had roosted for the night. Two courses of projecting stone encircle the doocot, and the flagstones fit together exactly and jut out to prevent rats climbing up. The birds used these binks or rat-courses when alighting. Inside the cot there was plenty of room in front of the nest-boxes for the doos to perch. The pigeon droppings made excellent fertiliser and were used in the kitchen garden.

There is a good example of a bottle dungeon set into the bridge, and it is considered that examples

Photo James P. Campbell
Steven J. Campbell aged six in the bottle dungeon

Photo, James P. Campbell, Rose Cottage, Halkirk.

The Burnside Bridge showing the Sinclair Arms carved on a block of red sandstone above the window in the bottle dungeon.

kennels (nothing remains now) with all the dogs were a good 80 yards away.

It is said that Donald Wares was the last person to be jailed in the bridge. He had caught a witch taking "freet" and had thrashed her severely. It is thought that the taking of "freet" was still being practised about 1800.

One of the methods of taking "freet" used in Freswick was to trail a simmon tether over the grass where a neighbour had his cow grazing. This was accompanied by some chanting or mutterings and was done very early in the morning when the tether left its trace on the grass heavy and wet with dew. The milk was "creamed off" the cow when she crossed the track of the simmon tether. Donald Wares was not jailed for thrashing the witch but for taking the law into his own hands and not reporting her to the laird and the kirk session.

of this are now rare. The sound of running water and the plop of trout rising in the pool on the lower side of the bridge would add to the torture of prisoners likely fed on salt beef.

Prisoners were lowered down into the dungeon through a trap-door in the bridge and it is not so long ago that the iron bars which covered the window rusted away.

There are no accounts of anyone going mad in it and one can conjecture over possible ways of getting food and water to prisoners. The large

Later the "Burnside" was the farm house of Freswick Mains, and is now a private residence.

Peter K. Miller, Westlands, Freswick.

HARVEST AT BURNSIDE FRESWICK.

Photo, Peter Miller, Westlands.

A fine stackyard overlooking Burnside 1965

On one occasion in harvest time the laird's lady came out with bread, cheese and home brewed ale, to the field where the tenants were busy sheaving. Whilst they were enjoying their lunch the lady amused herself by making some sheaves. Wares who was watching her efforts told her to square up the arse of the sheaf. She replied "Don't use that nasty word, Donald, call it the stubble end of the sheaf".

At nightfall a scrumptious dinner was served to the harvest workers in the large dininghall of the Castle. The lady came down to the basement and summoned all the assembly to follow her up the dark winding and dimly lit staircase to the hall. When near the landing she suddenly remembered that she had not seen Wares among the crowd. Afraid that she had offended him on the field and that he had gone home, she stopped and called out to those following in the stairs. "Anyone seen Donal Wares?" That worthy who was close behind her cried, "Here he is Ma'am just behind your stubble end."

From "Efter Dayset Yarns in Memory of the Poet", by Simon Bremner.

FRESWICK MAINS

Although much of the settlement has been washed away by the sea including the remnants of a boat yard, (which disappeared about 1950). Freswick has no shortage of historic connections with the sea. From the Stone Age up to the last war Freswick Bay was an assembly point for ships. A century or more ago Freswick provided pilots to guide the ships through the Pentland Firth. From an archaeological aspect Freswick is of special interest. There is the Broch and Pictish dwelling at Ness Head, and a 16th century doocot.

The most important of all is the Viking settlement of the 10th and 12th centuries. It would seem that a thousand or more years ago these seafarers from Orkney and beyond, chose to come to Freswick Bay rather than to Gills Bay.

Much of the site has been eroded by the sea, but many very interesting items were found during excavations. These included a special type of pottery, quern stones and a beautiful bronze pin carved to a Norse design. The Norse people, apart from their war-like exploits brought many skills over to Freswick. It is known from the Orkney Sagas that a battle was fought by Erik of Norway on the place where our home is now built.

Another structure of interest is the chapel with fine round windows which was built about 350 years ago on the site of St Modams (10th century?) Roman Catholic Chapel. Old customs die hard and one can sympathise with parishioners for crossing themselves and going on their knees around the ruins, but this was very much frowned on by the ministers and elders of Canisbay Church.

4th March, 1654 – Session book of Cannasbey "Donald Liel to make public confession, for coming out of Stroma on a stormy day, superstitiously to go to Maddan's Chapel in Freswick."

Frank Gulloch, Freswick Mains.

Freswick House

Footnote:- The stone steps in the staircase are of two different kinds – some were quarried from the ebb below the castle and the remainder came from the Brabster Quarry.

Willie Bain, Midtown, Freswick.

Photo, Sina Houston, John O'Groats.
Chapel and Doocot to left of Freswick House.

The anti-invasion concrete blocks from the 1939-45 War.

The round windows in the chapel – sadly the roof is off.

EXCAVATIONS AT FRESWICK LINKS

Archaeological investigation of Freswick Links was undertaken by Dr Colleen Batey and Professor Chris Morris between 1979 and 1982 (whilst both employed at Durham University); work was concentrated on gaining and understanding of the Viking (10th Century AD) and Late Norse (say 11th to 13th Centuries AD) activity at the site. The exciting results will shortly be fully available in print, but here a brief preview is offered!

Excavations at Freswick Links have been undertaken intermittently since the beginning of the century, although only two excavators in the past addressed themselves to the Viking age and later Viking period settlement at the site – A.O. Curle and V.G. Childe. The first recorded excavations (in the 1890s) were at the Iron Age broch on the Links, now surviving only as a stony mound, by Sir Francis Tress Barry of Keiss Castle. He distinguished the broch tower, of the type so familiar to the visitor in Caithness, and also a group of buildings lying outside. Although there were traces of Viking activity on top of the mound, they were not especially noted at the time of excavation. Further work was undertaken by A.J.H. Edwards in 1924 and 1926, when "crude stone structures" or earth houses were examined and found to be dated before the arrival of the Norsemen in Caithness; these may have been associated with the Picts. Several other people have worked less formally at the site, providing material for several museum collections throughout Scotland and beyond!

The Viking Village Curle and Childe Excavations 1937-38

Photo, Margaret, Rosie, Midtown, Freswick.
Left to Right:– Simon Bremner with barrow, William Wares, John Tait, John Henderson, William Cormack.

Curle's Excavations Buildings IV

Peter Miller, Westlands in Viking house.

The work of Curle and Childe at the site indicted the significance of the Vikings there. Even today, there are very few recognised Viking settlements in Caithness – one at Huna and another at Roberts' Haven near John O'Groats and at Freswick – this is a sharp contrast to the picture in Orkney, especially when one remembers that both Caithness and Orkney (as well as Shetland) formed the Norse Earldom lands! The material recovered by both Curle and Childe formed a starting point for the more recent work. Large numbers of artefacts were recovered and many more are in private collections in the county. Through a detailed study of these, it was possible to see that the settlement at Freswick dated to the period of the 11th and 12th Centuries rather than the period of the initial Viking incursions of the 9th Century. So far there is no evidence to support an early Viking presence in Caithness, a handful of fine pagan graves from Reay, Castletown and Westerseat near Wick all date to the 10th Century, and this is the earliest dating we have in the county for the Vikings.

The renewed interest in the site of Freswick, which remained the only excavated Norse site on mainland Scotland until the more recent work at Whithorn in the SW, concentrated on the eroding deposits along the exposed sand cliff edge. Within the eroding half mile stretch were traces of buildings, midden debris and countless animal and fish bones. Through detailed examination of the cliff edge deposits of midden it has been possible to understand more fully about the economy of the site. The most significant element to be recovered is fish bone material, and through sieving large amounts of the middens which were still in position (i.e. in from the cliff edge), several of the very small bones from fish were recovered. These are the ones which are very difficult to recover because they are very fragile and prone to breaking, they survive much better when the soil is sieved in water. The fish represented are primarily cod, ling and saithe, often one metre in length, but sometimes up to two metres. Examination of this material is very slow and requires great patience, it is being undertaken by Andrew (Bone) Jones, of York who finds the results very exciting. . . There is certainly evidence of large scale fishing at the site, conceivably on a commercial scale, but this may be modified by the final study of this material. Even so, it is very important because it has not been identified on this scale at any other site in the North or West of Scotland, despite the examination of large amounts of midden deposits! Preliminary work at Roberts' Haven nearby suggests also the presence of large fish, but much work needs to be done at that site yet (it awaits funding!).

As well as fish bone, there is also evidence of the animals which were kept at the site – cattle, sheep/goat, pig and horse for example. However, the numbers for study are much fewer than with the fish material. Bird bones have been found too, gulls and auks especially, but also some rock dove and goose are present. All the bones are very fragmented, and this may suggest that the midden material itself may have been put onto the fields for manure – this is not unexpected of course.

We also have evidence of cultivation on the site in the form of "plough marks" and there are many remains of burnt seeds, mostly oats and barley. However, a pollen core which was taken by Jacqui Huntly nearby does not show that these were being cultivated at the site. This is a mystery, but may be explained by the bringing in of already threshed grain to the site.

In all this, I have not mentioned the building remains examined. Both Curle and Childe recovered the remains of rectangular dry stone built structures, and in our work, we too recovered incomplete buildings at the cliff edge, the rest having fallen into the sea! However, the most interesting results came from a re-examination of one of the buildings that Curle excavated – and some local people who visited us during the work, may well have seen the building exposed. We concentrated on trying to understand the building sequence, which was complex due to several rebuilds, but also to see if the midden from the building had different things in it than that at the cliff edge (as it now is, several metres of the land having been lost since Viking times). The house middens included several smaller fish, for example, of the more tasty varieties such as haddock!

The complementary work which was undertaken by us in the basements of Freswick House, to the south of Freswick Burn, shows us that the site was rather larger than anticipated. Instead of halting to the north of the burn, the middens and buildings clearly continued to the south. The middens found contained similar items to those further north as well as a large amount of coarse hand-made pottery which is chaff tempered and found everywhere at Freswick, and has entered the literature as "Freswick Ware"; it is not only found in Freswick of course. . .

So several years later, we are still working on this material – it is remarkably rich, and has formed the basis of two Doctoral theses – my own and that of Andrew Jones. The time and patience required to examine all aspects of the material recovered is immense, as all those who work with us already know! However, without the funding of Historic Scotland (Scottish Development Department [Ancient Monuments] as it was known at the time of the excavations) and their belief in the importance of the results, none of this work would have come to fruition. Our debt to them is enormous as it is to the landowner Frank Gulloch, whose patience is also infinite when it comes to archaeology. We have taught several generations of University Archaeology students the methods of archaeological practice on sites in Northern Scotland, and many of those who came to Freswick are now working in units throughout the country. We all have happy memories of Freswick and friends made at that time.

Dr Colleen Batey, Assistant Keeper Archaeology, Kelvingrove Museum, Glasgow.

Grass in March should be eaten in March.
Peter Miller, Westlands.

A time for everything and everything is in time.
Alex' MacGregor, John O'Groats Post Office.

Sae mony mists in March ye see
Sae mony frosts in May will be.
Willie Mowatt, St Margaret's Hope.

If the cock goes crowing to his bed
He'll be sure to rise with a watery head.
Malcolm MacLean, Duart.

A Saturday's storm never saw Monday's morn.
Jim Rosie, Freswick.

A peck of March dust is worth its weight in gold.
David Dunnett, Hillhead.

Gollans – little bits of rainbows
– a sign of deteriorating weather.
Dodie Gunn, John O'Groats.

When the wind is in the east it's neither good for man nor beast.
John Dunnett, Heatherbell Cottages.

Stray Finds From Freswick

These artifacts were found by Simon Bremner and his family. 1938-1950.

Left to Right:–Beautifully made bronze horse-shoe pin. Nail mark decoration on shoe which swivels neatly on pin. Bronze pin showing coiled head. Flat headed pin. Bronze pin with curled head. Bronze pins with thistle heads. Metal tweezers.

Coins found included James VI Twopenny piece 1623 (diameter 17mm).

Left to Right:– Piece of steatite cooking pot. Bone and antler pins and toggle. Two small bone whorls. Two stone whorls used in spinning.Two bone comb pieces. Metal buckles. Three bone chess or game men.

Three headed thistle legend IACOBYS · D · G BRIT – continued on reverse – FRAN & HIB · REX

Actual size.

Obverse

Lion rampant with two dots to show it is two pence.

Legend means James, King of all Britain, France and Ireland.

Actual size

Reverse

Margaret Rosie, Midtown, Freswick.

FLEET – PAYMASTER JOHN BREMNER R.N. 1837-1898

John Bremner was born in Freswick, the son of Alexander Bremner and his wife Catherine Sutherland. He was educated locally and when he was 16 went to London to pass his examinations for the navy. John Bremner was a tall, well built, good looking clever young man, and he was lucky in all things that he tried – so much so that his comrades excluded him from games of chance because he would win all! He was at the taking of Sebastopol (1855) in the Crimean War and was the first person who was landed from the fleet in the deserted town. The "Ganges", a huge vessel of the wooden type was one of his first attachments and he was on the "Centurion", a new and first class battleship with the latest improvements in gunnery, and with a complement of 900 men under his financial care when he died. He was a man of high ability and was noted for his service on land as well as on sea.

Catherine Sutherland, his mother, was the grand-daughter of a proprietor from Ross-shire, who, because he took the side of Bonnie Prince Charlie in 1745, fled to Caithness after Culloden. It was because the Laird of Freswick was sympathetic to the Covenanters that he let some fugitives have a bothy in the area now known as the Heather.

(The 1841 Census shows Catherine's father William Sutherland aged 85 living at the Heather.)

Fleet Paymaster John Bremner claimed to be a close relative of James Bremner, Civil Engineer, and raiser of sunken ships. John Bremner's niece Johan Bremner married Peter Miller and they had a family of three. James the well loved postmaster at Freswick, Alexander was the highly respected Principal of the Baptist College, Glasgow, and Johan who felt the lure of the sea, sailed to the Falklands c.1925 and taught there for many years. Isabella Begg, later Mrs Byron from Hilltop, Auckengill taught along with Johan Miller in Stanley.

Sheena Cook and Vina May Warner's family notes. – From, Pearl Cook, 1 Hood Street, Wick.

Footnote:– John Bremner attended the Free Church School at Canisbay and had as classmates David Matheson, Huna, founder of the Post Office Savings Bank of Canada (cousin of Sir Oliver Mowat) and James Leith Bremner (nephew of the highly esteemed headmaster George Leith) author of "The Pilot of the Pentland Firth".

Notes by John Mowat, Skirza.

'E DIPPING

We only hed a twa three sheep,
Fae fifteen till a score,
Bit fan hid cam' till dipping time,
I'm gled we hed no more.

We hed them herded in a pen,
'E collie keepan watch,
Some o' his helped till dip them,
Ithers were 'ere till catch.

'E day's work started early,
'E box wis set in place,
Wi' dripping boord fixed at 'e end,
Shored up wi' bools in case.

Hid slipped doon at 'e far end,
An' 'e sheep ran helter skelter,
Shaking themselves till everyone,
Was covered wi' dip an' water.

Then back an' fore wi' muckle pails,
'Etween 'e pond an' trough,
We cerried fraucht aye efter fraucht,
Until there wis enough.

'E dip wis broucht in solid chunks,
We cowped them in a cowgie,
Then added water boiling hot –
Watched by 'e collie dowgie.

Fa couldna stand 'e smell o' dip
So stopped weel out o' wey,
He kent we had designs on him,
Till keep his flechs at bay.

'E melted dip wis added tae
'E water in 'e dipper,
Stirred roond an roond till richt well mixed,
'E smell wis strong an' bitter.

We all were dressed in oilskins,
Wi' wellies on wir feet,
Bit fore 'e day wis ended,
We'd all be soakan weet.

Abody took their places,
('E dipper wisna wide)
Ane at each side, two legs apiece,
An' a third chiel held 'e heid.

'E first sheep catched wis lifted in
An' cowpid on her back.
Her heid held up gripped by 'e loogs –
She wis no too fond o' 'at.

They sometimes sprawled roond, a bit,
T'was all of no avail,
Tho' when they splashed we near got drooned,
Faigs dip maks yir een gail.

We turned them back upon their feet,
'An stood them on 'e boord,
Stroking 'e water fae their fleece,
Waste we could no afford.

Then glorious freedom once again,
They shook themselves lek fury,
They didna think much o' their bath,
An' made off in a hurry.

An' so on till they all were dipped,
'E toop wis aye 'e last

We didna try till cowp him,
'Bit all chist held him fast.

An' slushed him ower wi' pails o' dip,
Until his fleece wis drooken,
No keb could stand an earthly chance,
They all fell oot forfochen.

'E dowg by now hid left for hom
He wisna taking chances,
He mint he'd hed a dip efore,
Ye could tell by his backward glances.

The dipper then wis emptied,
An' laid ower on hids side,
'E hol far hid hed stood, filled in,
Wi' fails cut thick an' wide.

Then we set off hom' bedraggled,
Wir han's a yellow broon,
Wir faces kind o' jaundiced,
Drippan fae feet till croon.

Bit gled at 'e chob wis feenished,
An' e sheep mair or less keb free,
A first class bluebottle deterrant,
Bloom dip laced wi' D.D.T.

Far 'e sheep were in beeger numbers,
'E best o' 'e fun wis denied,
They were pushed one by one in a muckle tank,
Till sweem till 'e ither side.

None o' iss pechan' an' heavan',
Wi yowes as heavy as lead,
Ane at each side two legs apiece,
An' a loog grip supporting 'e heid.

Hids all different noo at 'e dipping,
E' hard work is cut mair than half,
For us hid wis manual labour,
Bit we also hed many a laugh.

Lek 'e time when 'e grun wis fair slidy,
Roon 'e dipper lek thick tattie soup,
One chiel took a skite an' overbalanced,
An' landed on top o' 'e toop.

Ye couldna say he wis delighted,
In fact he near snapped aff wir nebs,
Fan we asked if he thocht he wis flechy
Or chist taking precautions 'gainst kebs.

Hid's a while since I helped at a dipping,
But I still mind 'e smell o' e' dip,
An' 'e gallons o' watter I cerried,
Till 'e dipper wis fu' till 'e lip.

An' e' wecht o' 'e yowes fan e' cowped them,
Yir hair soaked wi' Bloom Dip Shampoo,
Yir hans looking lek ye hed boiled them,
An' covered wi' strands o' weet oo.

Nae bathroom wi' modern shower fittings,
Wi water 'erehot fae a tap,
A beeg basin fill wi' 'e kettle,
Helped get rid o' 'e most o' 'e dip.

But when nicht cam' ye needed nae rocking,
Chist wearily climbed into bed,
Fell asleep as yir head touched 'e pillow,
Aye 'e dipping hed turned oot nae bad.

Clara Clyne, Strathesk Grove, Kirkhill, Penicuik.

THE THRESHING

The Hendersons (Sons of Wildie) threshing for Peter Sinclair, Seaview, Keiss, 1973.

Photo, Peter Sinclair, Keiss.

Left to Right:– David Rudhall, forking from screw; James Harrold, South Keiss; Jack Henderson, The Heather; Brian Cormack, the boy in foreground. Fordson Major driving the mill.

Photo, Peter Sinclair, Keiss.

Jack Henderson, feeding the mill; James Harrold, South Keiss; ?; Ronnie Blair, looking round end of mill; Amy Robertson with headsquare; William Henderson, The Heather; Robbie Robertson, Keiss. Massey Ferguson driving the baler. (House on left with lum – Neil and Eleanor Harrold, Butcher, Wick. White House, Bill and Margaret Mackay, Butcher Shop.)

The Freswick Young Men's Mutual Improvement Association existed from 1884-1904

Minute of a meeting in November 1886 was written in verse by John Bremner, The Poet. The clerk then called the members' names.

"And you may think it queer, Sir, but whether it was John or James,
They always answered, "Here Sir",
But absent ones he markéd so,
To keep the thing compactly,
The number then he let us know,
Was twenty one exactly."

Early Education in Caithness – **Bob MacCallum.**
Kind permission of Mrs Ena MacCallum, 13 Stray Court, Prince's Villa, Harrogate.

The Threshing

Photo, Elizabeth Munro, Harley.
Wildie Henderson, The Heather, on his steam engine getting set for the threshing.

SIMON BREMNER AND THE POET

My father, Simon Bremner, wrote his book in 1937 and chose this title for his notes as a tribute of affection and admiration for John Bremner, "The Poet". John was his neighbour and lived at what is now called The Poets Croft in Midtown, Skirza.

I am vexed that I have none of his poems and am always hopeful that some of his rhymes may have survived. He was a very clever man but he had no desire to do other than work his croft which he loved. When he was an old man, Freswick folk wondered why he was working so hard building and repairing a dyke. His reply – "I would lek to leave hid the rod I got hid". He died in 1941 and was in his 80s. The dyke can be seen from the road, still standing well.

Simon Bremner

John Bremner

Margaret Rosie, Midtown, Freswick.

Flying Man of Freswick

Simon Bremner was there in 1918 when the RAF was created by the merger of the Royal Flying Corps and the Royal Naval Air Service. He survived the "War in the Air" where life expectancy for combat airmen was even shorter than the awful trenches which they flew over in their fragile machines.

Courtesy of John O'Groat Journal.

EFTER DAYSET YARNS IN MEMORY OF THE POET

Freswick 1780-1830

In the period that will be mainly treated, from about 1780-1830, the coastal district of Skirza could boast of "40 able bodied fishermen". Its total population must have been close on 200. At the present time (1937) in the same area there are only 20 inhabitants. How did so many people manage to exist in so restricted an area? Money was scarce but then very little of it was required. Ten pence per day was good wages.

The laird of Freswick, who died in 1838, had two handymen employed on his home farm (James Cook and Donald Wares). Some piece of work they did pleased the laird so much that he proposed to raise their wages from 10d to 11d per day. The grieve remonstrated about this. "No, no laird that will never do, why that is more than your best ploughman is getting". The people resorted to many expedients in order to eke out a livelihood. Meal was more plentiful in the inland Caithness district but owing to the high duty salt was nearly unobtainable, so the coastal people evaporated salt water and the salt they obtained was bartered for meal. The rate of exchange was a "straiket pail of salt for a heapit pail of meal".

Fish was plentiful and even after the laird's share had been deducted from a "tide" and every-day needs supplied, there would still be some left to salt away for using in rough stormy weather.

Seabirds, especially guillemots, were caught in large numbers by the simple expedient of dropping a herring net from the top of the cliffs over the entrance to an "oakie cave". A waiting boat made a great noise with oars etc. and the frightened birds flying out from their "binks" were entangled in the net and promptly secured. These, too, were salted for use in winter or stormy weather. Cormorants, before being cooked were buried overnight in the "kailyard". This was said to take the fishy taste away from their flesh.

When a young man got married, if no house or croft was obtainable, he simply built a house on some piece of waste ground that was handy. The houses of that time were very primitive, being narrow, low and with one common doorway for people and animals. A gable built partly of stone and turf separated the cattle from the living room or kitchen. Near the centre of this room a low wall or flagstone set on its edge in the floor served as a "back" to the open fireplace. There were no wooden partitions or inside doors in the houses, instead of these mats or frames of pleated straw, "flets", were used. A common saying "Nae fire nor flet in the hoose" meant a cold, bare, empty house. Wooden beds were not used in Freswick until about 1800. In 1778 the "Six Sisters" of Whitehaven, Capt. Drury, was wrecked at the burnmouth and a greatly prized supply of wood was obtained by the people. There was a south east gale at the time and the ship found herself on a lee shore and was unable to tack seawards so the captain decided to run the ship ashore on the sand in preference to getting smashed on the rocks. In running before the wind and sea the vessel struck an outlying rock and the huge wooden tiller struck the captain and killed him instantly. The rest of the crew were all saved. The rock on which the ship struck was afterwards known as "Drury stane".

After the young man had built his house he then enclosed an acre or so of the scattald around the house with a stone or turf dike. This piece of ground was trenched and grew alternate crops of bere and oats. A corner of this enclosure nearest the house was always kept heavily manured and used for a cabbage garden or kail yard. A heavy crop of cabbage was very essential as potatoes and turnips were not in use and except for some medicinal herbs vegetables were unknown. Cabbage served as a very important item in the menu of the time.

There was at least one public house or inn in every district. There were two in Freswick and the usual price of whisky was 1/- a bottle. Money being scarce the people could not afford even that, so they made a very good brand of whisky for themselves in the bothies that were so snugly hidden in the banks of ravines that cut through the moors. In Freswick the remains of two such bothies can still be seen. The last whisky that is known to have been made in the district was made for a local wedding that took place on the same date as Queen Victoria's wedding. Illicit distilling might have continued to a much later date but for an unfortunate accident.

A raid by the gaugers was expected and two men were told to hide the pot and other smuggling appliances. They did so and immediately afterwards they went to sea in a pilot boat and were drowned. The marks or "meases" (cross bearings) of the place on the moors where the pot was buried were unknown to anyone except the two men. As they ran past their home to join the waiting pilot boat some members of the household shouted "where did you hide the pot?" The reply was "We've a meese on e' Corbie hillock" (a well known landmark). The pilot boat foundered in "Ley lans bore" (the date probably one year before the birth of the late King Edward). In spite of diligent search it was many years afterwards before the pot was accidentally discovered during peat cutting operations. A cow was killed by falling through the roof of one bothy and it was abandoned.

Many raids were made by the authorities before the second bothy was found. It was cutely made in the side of a deep ravine in the burn of Dister. Dister adjoins Hesterval, the modern Heather of Freswick. Hesterval means horse vale or field. Legend says that it was the arena of the stallion fights staged by the Norse inhabitants of the district. An aerial photograph shows an area of about six acres enclosed by a low turf wall. On a calm frosty Sunday morning during the month of November a gauger was sitting on the summit of the Warth Hill examining the moorlands that stretched out all around with the aid of a telescope. One particular spot appeared to attract his attention. In the calm frosty morning atmosphere a thin column or rather pencil of smoke appeared to be rising from the moor a couple of miles away. The officer hurried to the spot guided by the trickle of smoke and discovered the long sought for bothy. Distilling had been carried on during Friday and Saturday nights and apparently the fire had been too carelessly smothered. The plant was removed and the hut destroyed but the smugglers were not discovered.

Another smuggling episode in which the people of Skirza were involved turned out disastrous for all concerned. A few adventurous spirits led by Peedy Will of Pentland Pilot fame bargained with the master of a ship trading with the West Indies to deliver to them on the return trip two large casks of rum. One fine afternoon the ship hove to off the bay and two yawls set out to her for the rum. One of the boats was short of a crew and two men, Rob Mowat and Campbell Wares who were getting a boat ready for the herring fishing were persuaded to accompany them on the promise of a share in the rum. The authorities in Wick got wind of the business and before the yawls got to the creek with their cargo, customs officials were there awaiting them. The yawls then made for Rushy Goe, a large land locked goe at Skirza Head accessible only from the sea. The rum was hid in one of the large caves in the landward end of the goe. Not to be beaten the Customs people summoned a revenue cutter to their aid. The cutter anchored in the bay and sent a boat with an armed crew to secure the rum from the goe. When the boat approached the goe it was met with a fusillade of stones, turf, etc., thrown over the high cliffs by the women of the district. The cutter boat's crew had to retire utterly discomfited. No more attempts were made by the authorities to secure the rum. They contented themselves with getting the names of the shareholders in the venture. The two men who had assisted now backed out of the business as it appeared to be turning out disastrous. The rum casks were taken out of the goe as soon as possible and brought to "Aul Anrus" house in Skirza where the contents were divided among the shareholders. All sorts of receptacles "leems", capable of holding rum were requisitioned and still there was some rum left in the second cask. "Awnrie" (Andrew) who though not a shareholder had been entrusted with the division, now asked some onlookers to have a drink. Mulliken, a noted worthy, was the first to eagerly avail himself of the generous offer. In telling the story afterwards, Awnrie said "Och, och, but Mulliken took a fierce drink." The fireplace was in the middle of the kitchen floor and before long many of the partakers of the free drinks were tumbling in the ashes! The smugglers were summoned to the court at Inverness and had to walk there. They were fined £100.

During the 18th century the ordinary people of Caithness were very illiterate. Nearly all who could read and write fluently were ministers and tutors to the landed families and were importations from the south. These learned men found in north east Caithness, an alien language. Many of the words used by the people were unknown to them. Even many of the vowel sounds had, and still have, no equivalent in English. These words and vowels were derived from the Icelandic or Old Norse – the language of the Norse settlers in Caithness. When the men of letters had to write a place-name, word or surname they did not take the local pronunciation of the word into account but just wrote down what they thought the word should be in English. (The local pronunciation of a word generally provided a sure clue as to its origin and meaning. That pronunciation had been handed down from generation to generation.)

Thus the surnames Magnuson (pronounced Mawnson, the "g" having a "w" or "y" sound) became Manson. Ole and Jok, became Auld and Jack. Place names suffered the same. A glaring example of this mutilation is Hestervall. Only a few years ago a learned gentleman looking for the derivation of this name said it meant "east valley". In reality the name is pure Norse and is the plural form of horse field or horses' vale.

Many and varied expedients were used to earn a few shillings. A common device was selling limpets to the line fishermen of Wick. An old woman now long deceased used to relate that her mother told her that one fine morning in October when the daylight came in she counted 18 young women taking limpets in the "ebb" at Fastgoe. They had to walk about a mile across the moor to reach the Goe and then descend over 200 feet to the beach by a steep winding narrow path. After filling their "caisies" with limpets these young women or girls, aged from 16 to 20, set off to Wick, with their burden of limpets. Each girl carried as many limpets as would bait one sma' line. The price was 1/-. After disposing of them they had to walk home again. It was a recognised custom that they always stopped and had a glass of ale at the "Plover Inn", Reiss.

These caisies, straw plaited receptacles designed for carrying on the back, served a lot of purposes. Wheel barrows and carts were not used and the place of these in the crofters' daily work was taken by the caisie. The straw of which the caisie was made was carefully selected and termed "nocks of gloy".[1] Different caisies were used for various purposes. A somewhat larger and more open one was used for carrying peats, fish and farmyard manure. Closer pleated or woven caisies were used for holding grain.

Every year it was the duty of the tenants to manure a large field belonging to the laird's home farm with seaweed. The seaweed had to be carried in caisies from Freswick Sand.

As there were no rotation grasses, cattle roamed about anywhere after the harvest had been secured. They sought the shelter of their respective byres at nightfall.

A deep wide trench extended along the length of the byre and all the dung mixed with ashes from the kitchen was thrown into this pit. When spring came the contents of the pit were carried to the land for manure. Two caisies were used for this

[1] Gloy – cleaned straw used for making caises (straw baskets). It was tied into small sheaves called Nocks of Gloy.

purpose. When the wife was carrying a full one to the land, her husband would be filling the other in readiness for her return. A cured sealskin was secured over the neck, shoulder and back of the woman carrying the caisie full of manure.

The laird's handymen, James Cook and Donald Wares were two well known worthies. Their natures were entirely different. Cook was diligent and willing to please. while Wares did not care a hang for anyone. In describing them to a friend the laird said. If I was to tell them that I was thinking of shifting Freswick Castle to another site, Cook would reply, "Well laird it might not be easy but we could have a shot at it." Wares would answer "Just listen tae the aul feel deevil noo." (Just hear what the old foolish devil proposes to do now.).

The removal of tenants was very common. If anyone incurred the displeasure of laird or tacksman, he would be promptly removed from his home to some outlying part of the estate. Or it might be that he and his family got removed altogether from the district. These forced removals gave the families of Anderson, Bruce and Wares to the Staxigoe and Broadhaven area.

The first Anderson to settle in Skirza was Murdo Anderson from Foula. How or why he left Foula is not recorded. Most probably he got "blown awa" during a fishing trip and got picked up by a ship and landed at Freswick. His son William Anderson, met the tacksman one day while crossing Freswick sands. In the course of a heated argument about some trivial matter, the tacksman in order to emphasise his part of the argument, prodded William in the stomach with a cane that he was carrying. William's hasty temper rose and looking round he found and grabbed a hefty "swart" (a large stout tangle) that was lying handy on the sand. With well directed whacks from this formidable weapon, Will belaboured the fleeing and thoroughly frightened tacksman right across the sand. Will got his removal notice next day and left soon afterwards with his family for the Broadhaven district.

The harvest that year (1800) was late and disastrous. A gale of wind and snow at Christmas blew the unsecured stooks to the beach. The new tenant of Anderson's croft sent word to Anderson at Broadhaven asking for instructions as to what was to be done. Anderson replied "Try and save the minister's share and let the rest be going." This new tenant (Auld Awnru) did not enjoy possession very long either. A party of herd boys discovered a seal on the beach of Fastgoe on a Sunday. What was to be done with so valuable a prize? To kill the beast on Sunday was out of the question, because in doing so, all the powers of the kirk session would fall with no uncertain hand on them, Aul Awnru's oldest son "Peedy Will" of Pentland pilot fame was the ring leader of the herds and under his direction the problem was solved by building a wall or pen around the seal, out of which he could not escape. The herds came back on Monday and killed the seal. The tacksman got notice of the business and

Aul Awnru was summoned to his presence. Aul Awnru's argument, that the laird's share of seals only applied to seals that had been captured in the "seal coves" of the estate title deeds, was sound, but the tacksman would not listen to it. "You may just as well say that the kelp on the shore does not belong to me." So Aul Awnru got flit to a small inhospitable place in Mybster. He was too good a tenant to be in disgrace for long and in a year or so he got back to Skirza on condition that he would allow his second son, Donald, to be his heir to the croft. Peedy Will married Maggie Cruickshanks and had a public house in Canisbay for a number of years. The place is now known as "Maggie's Corner" and is at the T Junction of the moor road from Everly, down to Canisbay. (Aul Awnru lived at Sunnybraes, Skirza).

The prefix "apel", "peedy", "beeg", muckle", "aul" or young did not necessarily mean diminutive, very large, or very old or very young. Peedy Will was so called to distinguish him from his older cousin of the same name Beeg Willie. Aul Awnru was likewise called to distinguish him from his nephew Young Awnru.

The houses in different parts of a township were generally grouped together so as to form a little hamlet. Their arable land radiated outwards in narrow strips from this common centre. During the long winter evenings the women spun balls of thread from wool hemp and flax. The wool and flax balls were taken to the local weaver and made into blankets, "scourers" and linen sheets and larms. The hemp was spun into fishing lines and cordage and twine for herring net meshing. While the women were thus occupied the men were engaged in net meshing and caisie making.

A general practice was for the occupants of a couple or more houses to take their work with them to another house and while carrying on their tasks, songs, recitations and old stories and traditions enlivened their labours. The light was supplied by the large open peat fires and cruisie lamps (one or two) which burned fish or seal oil with a rush wick. For special nights selected peat "clods" were set aside. These burned and gave a brilliant light. As there were no windows in the walls of the houses, it was lighter inside the dwellings at night time than during the day. Two small openings in the thatch at the wall tops on each side served as windows. The leeside opening was kept open and the weather or windward closed up with a bundle of straw.

The first windows in the walls of a house were regarded as great novelties and the mistress of a house with these windows used to brag about them to her acquaintances. "They gave her such fine light for piping her boards" (ironing the ribbons of her head dress).

Young men who had been at the previous summers whale fishing would be telling their adventures with ships and whales among the ice of the "straits". Others again might have returned from service with the Hudson Bay Company in the north west.

John Henderson, brother of Donald Henderson, Skirza died in that company's service. David Kennedy of Freswick was one of the smartest of the Caithness whale fishers. The whaling ships carried large crews and had a large spread of canvas.

In favourable winds stun sails were set and it sometimes happened that in running out the stun sail boom (a long light spar extension to a cross-yard) the halyards were overlooked. In an English whaler hailing from Hull, Kennedy was the only man aboard who would reeve the halyards of the stun sail boom once that boom had been run out in position. The difficulty of the job may be guessed from the fact that the yards had footropes for steadying the sailors when aloft, but on the long slender stun sail booms there were none. Kennedy, through the ship being caught and crushed in the ice, had to spend a winter in the Davis Straits.

An American sailing ship, the Lincoln, was wrecked under the cliffs at Skirza head. A fishing boat's mast was taken from the haven and run out over the cliffs with tackle through the pulley in the end of the mast and the entire crew were hauled to safety. They grumbled at being wrecked in such (to them) an outlandish place. Kennedy, who had been assisting in the rescue work, said to them, you have nothing to grumble about, you are in a civilised land. Here am I that was wrecked on the shores of Davis Straits and had to live nine months with the "yaki yaws" (the whalers' term for the Esquimaux). The "Lincoln" was from America with logs and became a total wreck. She was a "copper fastened" ship. The copper bolts were of no value to the people of the district, but iron was eagerly picked up. They always had to bring their own iron to the smith.

Many and varied were the tales that enlived the informal "after day set" gatherings. Witches, fairies, ghosts "foregawns" and warnings were believed in and were as real to the people of that period as the cinema and wireless are to the present generation.

Fairies played an important part in the lives of people and on certain occasions were unusually active. In general, the little people were harmless and ready to do a good turn to those who reverenced them but they could be malevolent to anyone who slighted or mocked at them.

Scotty the tacksman was inordinately fond of sea or hand line fishing. For this purpose he kept a yawl near the burnmouth and when he wished to go fishing he would hurry to the cobbler's shop and shout inside. "Come on boys we'll go fishing." He was always sure of getting a crew. The same reliable man was always the skipper of the boat and he used to have heated arguments with Scotty regarding the unsuitability of the tide for proceeding to sea. Scotty finished the argument by saying, "You speak about your "nor burlts" and "sou burlts" but we will go fishing when it is a good day and never heed your tides." This did not please the skipper and crew and it was decided to teach Scotty a lesson. One fine day at the height of the stream tides they proceeded to sea with Scotty. They paid no attention to tides but went where he desired. The result was that Scotty lost his line and they were in grave danger of being carried through the Pentland Firth. When at last they reached the burnmouth, Scotty stepped out of the boat, turned and said, "Men after this we will go a fishing when you think it is suitable and at no other time." For some reason or other Scotty gave his skipper's croft to another member of his crew, and one day shortly afterwards as they were proceeding to sea as usual, he said to the skipper "go aft and shot the rudder." The man replied "No Mr S. you get him to shot the rudder to whom you gave my croft." This man was told to do so but getting the rudder on a large yawl in a tide way was no easy matter and required a lot of practice. The newcomer fumbled the job and was in danger of losing the rudder. Scotty told him to leave off and asked him how many cabbage plants he had planted in the skipper's former kailyard. (Planting the cabbage was preparatory to taking possession of the croft.) He replied that he had set 850 plants. "Well," said Scotty, "I will pay you for them and you stay in your own croft," and to his former skipper, "go and shot the rudder and stay in your croft." This was now promptly done.

After the death of his parents, George Bremner better known as "Clubby", an only son, left the district and started business in Wick. His first venture was a charge house or public house. It became very popular with the natives of Canisbay and Clubby found himself in hot water with the authorities for sheltering or hiding wild-doers from "doon e 'country". On one "Hill market" day some of Clubby's cronies from Skirza were outnumbered and got the worst of a row that took place. Asking Clubby's advice, he told them to go to Corners shop and buy sooples[1] as he had just got a large supply in. This was done and returning to the market field thus armed, they soon settled old scores with all and sundry.

Wick's only policeman raided Clubby's establishment in a vain search of the miscreants who were said to be hiding there. Clubby used very offensive language to the guardian of the law and asked what right he had to interfere with "lads o ma ain toon". The "lads" had to leave Clubby's drink shop in such a hurry that they had no time to pay for drinks consumed. One of the young men, probably the leader, was John Mowat, and his father went to Wick and called on Clubby the next day. He told him that he was to pay for the drink that had been consumed and unpaid for and how much was it. Clubby scratched his head and then called on his wife "Bawbie, go ben and see how much they left i' the cowg[2]."

Disposing of his public house, Clubby next started a general store on the site near the present shop occupied by Alexander Reid, Flesher.

He walked twice yearly to Edinburgh ordering

supplies. His provisions for the long journey consisted of a bag of oatmeal. Any handy spring or burn supplied the water necessary for moistening the meal to make it more palatable.

The merchants in Edinburgh with whom Clubby plied his orders belonged to his native district. On one occasion this merchant and some friends treated Clubby, on one of his visits, to a high class dinner in an eating house. Looking at the spread of good things Clubby remarked "A michty difference this, Mr Miller, from the bere bread and brochan o' e' Mittans o' Freswick.

With this half yearly supply of goods he took passage North in a trading smack. He could neither read nor write and his system of book keeping must have been unique.

Clubby's grave in Canisbay churchyard in the Bremner's "ground" is marked by a large flagstone with the letters G.B. rudely formed and deeply incised.

Clubby had two sisters. One was married to Robertson. From this family are descended the Robertsons of Freswick, Keiss and Wick.

¹ A stout stick about four feet long made from wood which did not split easily and was the part of the flail which beats the grain.

² Keg or small barrel.

A Herd Laddie Story

Alexander Manson was the eldest of the family. He lived with his parents in a little cluster of houses or hamlet called Tafts. The houses, six in number, were on the edge of the moor called the "park o' Tafts". Their arable ground stretched fanwise in long narrow strips south east towards Freswick bay. His father died when the eldest boy was ten years old. The neighbours were very kind and helped the widow and family to carry on with the croft. In order to help to pay the rent the laird took the boy into his employment as a herd. The laird's cattle were sent out to the moors in summer and the "dey" and her milk maids instead of going to a shelter in the hills took possession of Manson's house where butter and cheesemaking was carried on all through summer and early autumn and the widow and children had to remove to the barn.

After the cows were milked about eight or nine o'clock in the evening, it was the herd laddie's job to drive them away out to the distant pastures in the valleys of the burns and ravines, and to stay with them all night and bring them "in aboot" in the morning for early milking. Just fancy a laddie ten years old staying out with the cattle on the hill all night. His mother always made him take two dogs or rather the dog and bitch (Bob and Fan) along with him. When he said he only wanted one with him, she insisted saying "Watch Fan, she will give you warning and Bob will protect you."

The cattle would roam about and eat at first, but before darkness came on they would wander to some familiar "beiling place" and lie down until the morning. The herd ladie would select a comfortable sheltered, dry place and go to sleep with his dogs for company and warmth. The cattle were up and feeding or making for fresh pastures at the first streaks of daylight. In midsummer it was barely dark at all. Where the cattle went the herd had to go too and lead them homewards for the early milking. There were generally a number of "herd hooses" scattered over the two or three miles of pasture. These were rough roofed shelters in the sheltered banks or brae of a ravine and were used by the herds, when the cattle were in their vicinity for the shelter from rain or cold, and for cooking

purposes. Manson would get a bottle of milk, a bere bannock and a "bulk" (lump) of cheese from the "dey" when going on his nightly watch. One night the cattle selected a "beiling" place far up the "battens" of Stroupster. They were astir early and they followed down "the Toethal" a tributary of the main stream, eating the short, sweet, dew-covered grass.

The sleepy herd boy watched them from his comfortable shelter of a large clump of rushes and heather. When about half way down to the main stream, to the herd's surprise, the cattle showed signs of uneasiness and suddenly left the course of the burn and cut across a "flow", (pronounced like "plough") where they would reach the main burn about half a mile further inland. The herd, now thoroughly awake, rose and stretched himself, lifted the coat he had been lying upon, and followed down stream. He was anxious to know what had disturbed the cattle and also he had night lines for trout set in the broad "pow" or pool at the junction of the burn and its tributary. As he neared the place where the cattle had changed their direction, the two dogs began to show signs of uneasiness. At a sharp bend in the burn Bob whimpered and cowered at his feet. Suddenly as Fan went round the bend she halted and showed every sign of terror. She snarled and her hair stood on end. The herd jumped the narrow stream and made to pass Fan in order to see the cause of her terror. Without warning she half turned and attacked her master. As she sprang at his throat, the other dog, who, in spite of his terror, had been watching her closely, rushed forward and throttled her. Dazed and in consternation the herd ran back round the bend and called to Bob. Reluctantly the dog released his hold of the other dog and ran to his master. Fan sprang to her feet and giving vent to a pitful howl she dashed away up the burn and soon disappeared. In his hurried glance round the bend the herd had seen nothing to account for the terror of the dogs. He then remembered his mother's warning "Don't try to pass Fan if she gives you warning." He now changed his direction and crossed the moor in the track of the cattle. Bob appeared to be pleased at this move for he danced and capered in front of his master. They reached the cattle grazing quietly in the valley of the main stream and following it downwards he lifted his lines and secured a half dozen of fine plump speckled trout. Making for the nearest herd hoose he quickly cleaned them and had a couple roasting on the hot stones round the fire which he had started. The delicious trout proved a welcome addition to the herd laddies's dry bere bannock, 'e wir "kitchy" tae his piece. Trout used to be plentiful in the burn and its numerous tributary streams. The fill of the washing tub of fine trout was said to have been taken by a dragnet out of one long narrow pool. This pool was known afterwards as "Curley's pow", so named after the owner of the dragnet. Manson took the cattle home for the early six o'clock milking and reported to his mother what had happened. She said they would never see Fan again and this surmise proved correct.

After the morning milking was over, Manson's younger sister, Ester, eight years of age took over and attended the cattle all day. Her brother would have a few hours sleep and then do some necessary work on the croft and be ready again at nightfall to take charge of the animals.

The herd's father, James Manson belonged to Mey. His father Alexander Manson was a noted Pentland Firth ferryman. His services were in much request by south country horse dealers to ferry animals from Orkney to the mainland.

The Pentland Pilots

Skirza appears to have been the home of the earliest recorded pilots of the dangerous northern waters and channels. Finlay Mowat was the name of the first pilot, according to tradition and history. He went on board a ship as pilot for her to Orkney and she turned out to be a pirate vessel and was captured and Finlay had a narrow escape in being tried for being a pirate. A flat gravestone in Canisbay Churchyard (the inscription of which is now probably illegible) recorded the names, among others, of Simon Bremner, aged 17, drowned Candlemas Day 1812; Donald Bremner, aged 68, his father, drowned Candlemas Day 1816; Andrew Bremner, son of Donald, drowned Candlemas Day 183? and William Bremner drowned Candlemas Day 1816.

These men were all noted Pentland Firth pilots. Donald Bremner's father was William Bremner and his mother Jinny (Jessie) Laird, whose father was Finlay Laird. This Donald Bremner commemorated on the stone was the next recorded pilot after Finlay Mowat and his maternal grandfather Finlay Laird was probably a nephew of Mowat. Bremner possessed a yawl of his own and hired four men, three of them his half-brothers, to man it. Their pay was a shilling each for every ship that they piloted through the Firth. Thus if the fee was £1 Donald pocketed 16/- and the crew got 4/-, but most probably the fee would be 10/- – 4/- for the crew and 6/- for the pilot. after a time Donald's half brothers struck for different conditions. A conference was held and it was decided to have two pilot boats, the one boat to be in the charge of Donald with his youngest brother William as second pilot. The other boat was skippered by Donald's other half-brother Andrew Bremner (Aul Awnrie) and his brother Alexander as second. Each boat was six oared and the remainder of the crews were selected men from the other Skirza families of Bain and Henderson. The new plan worked well, ships being plentiful but competition from neighbouring creeks such as Auckengill, Staxigoe and Broadhaven becoming more pronounced, it became necessary for the Skirza pilots to obtain larger boats and meet the ships farther at sea – well out in the Moray Firth. The season did not start until about the middle of March. Before that date it was dangerous to go piloting as there was a "Bran" in the sea. The pilots first trip during the season was called "Branning". The meaning and derivation of these terms are now lost.

The original main creek or haven was at or near the north end of Freswick sands. Tradition says that it was the scene of a boating disaster on a Candlemas Day in which a large number of men lost their lives and also that the majority of these drowned were Bremners. The haven was afterwards deserted in favour of the creek at Skirza. The tragedy probably happened about 1700, as in 1654 there were many families of the name in Freswick but in 1735 there appears to be only one.

On a fine afternoon in early spring Candlemas Day 1812, Donald Bremner, along with his sons and three nephews, all youths in their teens, went handline fishing just outside the bay. As the tide was getting done, a whaling ship stood in towards the land in order to shun the first rush of the south going flood tide. As the ship approached the bay, Donald and his crew of youngsters pulled to her. The ship backed her mainyard and when the boat drew alongside, the master recognised Donald as an old chum whom he had not seen for some years and invited him on board, and in his cabin treated him hospitably. In the meantime another yawl put off from Skirza with a number of young men anxious to get berths for the whale fishing on board the ship. They tied their boat astern of the other one. the ship was in charge of a pilot from Staxigoe named Wildridge, whatever was his reason he gave the necessary order and "filled on" the vessel. The two boats were soon in difficulties and the first boat either broke or was cast off with the result the both collided and were upset. The ship was immediately hove to and a boat lowered to pick up the men struggling to keep afloat. The accident was seen from the shore and a boat was manned and was also quickly on the scene. Donald's son managed to get on the keel of one of the boats and drifted north on the tide.

As he was fairly safe the men in the water were first picked up. This done, one of the boats set off to get the young man off the keel of the capsized craft. By this time it had drifted into the tide rip of Skirza Head and he was flung off the keel and disappeared. Three men in all were drowned, Simon Bremner, James Matheson and John Mowat. Mowat had his young son a boy eight years old along with him and he was heard to exclaim "I'll lose my bairn through your capers this day." The boy was saved and he lost his life.

On board the ship as one of the regular crew was a man from Stroma named Sinclair, nicknamed "Cairnie". At the time of the accident he was busy aloft. In his hurry to share in the rescue work, it was said that he slid down a back stay to the deck and flung a coil of rope to the men in the water. This done he helped to get the boat launched. When he hauled in the rope he found that the eight year old boy had got entangled in the coils and was thus saved. The pilot was blamed for the mishap. It was said that he was jealous of Donald being so long with the captain and was afraid that he might be put ashore and Donald taken on as pilot and that he got way on the ship to hurry the departure of the boats. More probably, he being in charge, got afraid for the safety of the vessel as she would be drifting towards Skirza Head with the strong north going tide. The bodies of the drowned men were recovered some days later in the bay of Sannick, Duncansby.

At the time of the accident a man and his wife were busy "geeding" their land about a quarter of a mile from the shore. He was filling the caisies in the byre with the hard packed winter dung and she was carrying it to the bere land. Each time as she returned she told her husband about the position of the ship and boats. "There appears to be some commotion on the ship," she told him, "and I sees some things floating in the water away from her." He took a burden of the manure on his back and went to the land to see for himself. As he was long in returning the wife went to see what detained him. He was running for the haven. At a glance his practical eye had taken in the details of the accident and he was in time to join the yawl and take part in the rescue work.

"Aul Awnrie" was an ideal pilot and skipper. He was a clever seaman, bold and daring and resourceful, but cautious when there was need to be otherwise. If his knowledge and experience told him that he was right, then it was no use for his crew to say otherwise or try to alter him. Donald, though older, and a clever brave seaman, was more reckless and impetuous.

As one of the pilot boats was getting worn out, a new one was ordered from the carpenters at Stromness and on Candlemas Day 1816 a boat left Skirza to go to Stromness to take delivery of the new boat. Stromness was reached without incident and the boat paid for, launched and got ready for crossing the firth.

In Stromness at the time were a number of whale fishers belong to Caithness who had been unable to get berths on ships for the season. The pilots agreed to take them across to Caithness in the new boat which was to be skippered by Donald. Andrew in charge of the older boat, tried to hurry their departure, saying that there would be little enough flood tide to take them to the Southard. At last getting exasperated at the delay in getting the bags and sea chests of the rejected whalers on board, Andrew, with his brother Alex and Bain and Henderson for a crew, left Stromness in the old boat. With his usual skill and knowledge Andrew took full advantage of what little flood tide was still left and in due course reached Skirza. The new boat leaving a little later, got caught in the strong west going current and was swiftly carried towards Stroma and the dreaded Swelkie. They still might have got clear but at a critical moment, an oar broke and threw the rowers in confusion. As the boat was being drawn into the Swelkie, watchers on Stroma saw one of the whalers rise and lift a chest and hurl it into the whirlpool. It was believed that something bulky thrown into the whirlpool would choke it and render it harmless. A few seconds later the boat disappeared in a boiling tide race. The names of the men who were drowned with Donald and his youngest half brother William are not now known, but it is believed that they belonged to the Mey district. The name of one was either Harrow or else belonged to the district of Harrow.

After this disaster the pilots had perforce to carry on with the old boat until another new boat was built. Some time afterwards, Andrew had to pilot a ship to Stromness and while there he found that the new boat was ready. He decided to take her across the Flow to South Ronaldsay and at the ferry station there he might be able to pick up some passengers who would help him to take the boat across to the mainland. When near Burwick (the ferry station) Andrew found that he had good suitable tide and a fair wind and in order to save time he carried on alone across the Firth. It was said that he used his big sea coat spread on an oar for a sail. At any rate he reached Skirza alone with the new boat. John Bain familiarly known as "Aul Jock" took Donald's place as skipper of the second pilot boat. In seamanship and a thorough knowledge of the Pentland Firth, he was no doubt "Aul Awnrie's" equal. He was more outspoken and not so reticent as Andrew. His temper was more hurried and in spite of his sound knowledge and judgement, he would give in to the advice of his crew. This trait, on two occasions, very nearly proved disastrous. The pilot boat was lying at the Pentland Skerries waiting for the ebb tide to slacken before venturing to attempt the crossing to the mainland. After some time of this forced inaction and waiting, some of the crew began to murmur and say that surely the tide was well run now and that it was time to be going. "Aul Jock" apparently lost his patience with them, for he gave orders to get under way, at the same time saying they would find out that the tide was still too strong. Before they were half way across, Bain's views were justified, they were being carried rapidly by the strong ebb tide towards the Firth. "There is only one thing we can do," said Bain "keep her ramping full and try to catch Stroma." Would they reach the island or be drawn into the dreaded Swelkie? The watchers on Stroma viewed the terrific race with misgivings. The yawl was carrying full sail and pulling three weather oars with Bain grim and resolute at the helm.

Some of the watchers turned their backs not wishing to view the impending disaster. The race was won with not many yards to spare. Bain ran the yawl high and dry on the smooth sloping rocks and tore the bilge off the boat in doing so.

At certain times of the tide there is a very rough tempestuous strip of sea to the southward of the Pentland Skerries. It is comparatively narrow in some parts only about 100 yards wide but it extends from near the Skerries to three or four miles to the south. This long narrow tide race is formed by the south setting flood tide of Brough sound going with the main flood streams of the Firth which first sets east-south-east and then later south-east. It has been stated before, that keen rivalry existed between the pilots of the various creeks and many a hotly contested "strive" or race took place between the rival pilot boats. In these contests the boat from Nybster had a certain advantage as the North setting tide ran for about nine hours out of the eleven and the Skirza boat had about three miles of that tide before they were on equal terms with the other boat. One morning a ship was sighted standing towards the land well to the "Nor'ard" (north). The boat from Skirza under Bain and a boat from Nybster were soon away on that ten mile race. With sails and oars the two boats converged on the ship, the Nybster boat being well to the southward. With her main yard backed, the ship lay waiting the pilot boat but she was well on the outside or seaward side of the wild tide strip of Broch sound. As the Skirza boat drew near to the tempestuous roost, sail masts were lowered and the crew tried to row the boat through the heaving broken seas. They soon found this was impossible and all oars were taken in, with exception of two which tried to keep the boat's head to the wind. Two men kept baling until the boat "bore" out of the broken water. They still managed to reach the ship before the rival boat which had crossed the roost farther south where it had spread and merged with the main flood stream.

On another occasion the pilot boat skippered by "Auld Awnrie" had a somewhat similar experience. A ship was waiting on the east of the tide rip which was a mass of heaving breaking billows. An Auckengill boat was approaching the ship from the southward and the Skirza boat was much nearer the ship from which she was separated by that wild stretch of broken water, What was to be done, were they to give in and return? Andrew ordered the sail and mast to be lowered and then told the crew to row along the side of the roost. "We should find a "lithe" (a break or joint, in this instance a break in continuity) in it somewhere where we get across." His keen experienced eyes soon detected such a comparatively smooth place and without hesitation he steered for it and the boat got across with little trouble and reached the waiting ship long before the rival boat got near.

When ships requiring pilots were plentiful, it was customary to put a member of the pilot boat's crew in each ship until perhaps there would only be two men left in the boat. If the weather was fine these two would get another ship and go "through" with her with the boat in tow. When they got west to about Holborn Head, they cast off and set about collecting the rest of the crew from other vessels.

It was not always suitable for the boat to go through with the ship and in that case the pilot had to be put ashore with the ship's boat or by some fishing yawl that they might meet. The pilot then had to walk back to his home.

It was said that Andrew set up a record by walking twice from Thurso to Skirza in 24 hours. It appears that he went through with a ship in the early morning and after leaving her at Thurso and walking back to Skirza, he immediately joined the pilot boat which was just setting out to another vessel. He went with this ship and after a quick run through the Firth, was landed at Scrabster and immediately set out for Skirza, all within 24 hours.

On one occasion Andrew was put ashore by the ship's boat near Lower Dounreay. As the tide was out and the boat grounded before getting alongside the reef, Andrew took off his shoes and stockings and waded ashore. He sat down on the rock and put on his footgear again while the boat was returning to the ship. Scrambling over the reef he made for the brae. To his dismay he found that the ridge he was on was separated from the land by a narrow deep channel with fairly steep perpendicular sides. He had been put ashore on a long island reef. He waved and called to the boat but the sailors thought that he was waving them goodbye and carried on to the ship.

On that lonely part of the coast there was no house in sight, no one near who could help him in his dilemma. As the tide was starting to come in the channel would soon get wider, so removing his shoes and stockings once more and tying them round his neck Andrew jumped as far as he could. After a struggle he managed to get hold of tangles and seaweed on the opposite side and working along the face of the reef he at last found some footholds where he managed to haul himself out of the water and so to safety. After a short rest, wringing the salt water out of his clothes, he set off on his long walk home.

Andrew died, leaving a family of four sons and one daughter. At the present time his descendants are to be found in every quarter of the earth.

A Skirza fisherman who died a few years ago remarked to his son-in-law, I was at the sea as a boy with "Aul Awnrie". I was at the sea with his son your grandfather. I was at the sea with your father and yourself and now I have been afloat with your sons – five generations of the same family.

In walking from Thurso to Freswick, the pilots cut inland at the Links of Dunnet and went by Inkstack, Brabster and Scoolary. Between Scoolary and Brabster they reached the head waters of the Freswick burn and they followed its course to their home district.

A noted member of the pilot boats crew in Young Awnrie's time was "Strowma Geordie". His mother a Gills woman, was married to John Bremner in Stroma. She died while her son George was very young and her people in the Ha of Gills took the child and fostered him. He married and settled down in Skirza, his wife was Isabella Bain. They were a pious, God-fearing couple and their only son was a regular harum-scarum rascal. He was the youthful leader in all kinds of pranks and mischief. Joining the navy he went to the east and it was said that at the seige and capture of Peking "Strowma's Jock" as he was locally known, was the first of the attacking party over the walls of the city. It was reported that Jock had been captured by Arab slave dealers whilst he was on patrol duty on the African-Arabian coast. This was told to his father and he was informed that the slaves and prisoners were shackled together two and two in the chain gang. The father remarked "Lord hae mercy on e' puir deevil 'ats chained tae oor Jock" –

a reference to Jock's restless nature. Petty Officer Bremner succumbed to fever in the Red Sea.

Willam Bruce, who kept a public house at the haven of Skirza was also one of the early pilots. Business prevented him from going with the pilot boat on one occasion and his son Robert eagerly seized the opportunity and went in his place. The pilot boat had a successful trip and returned to the haven after putting four of its crew on different ships. As the wind was light and the tide not suitable, the ships tacked to and fro near Freswick Bay.

William Bruce met the boat on its return. He enquired of the returned crew "Who did they put on that ship and the next one?" He was told and then asked "And who did you put on that big ship that is not standing to the land?" "Robbie," he was told. "Whatna Robbie?" he queried. "Your son Robbie" was the answer.

The old man was dumfounded. "What does he ken about the Firth" he grumbled, "ye were daft tae pit him on a big ship." "Haud yer tongue, Willie" replied one of the crew, "there was no-one born a pilot, we a' hid tae learn." "That may be" said Willie, "bit a' that Robbie kens aboot the Firth is that he was ance at Malcolm Rosies's shop in Duncansby for snuff!" After the Bruce family left Skirza and settled in Staxigoe, Robert Bruce became a noted Pentland Firth pilot.

Raiders

From very early times the people of the coastal districts were the victims of many raids by rovers from the sea. It was even put forward by some authorities that the immensely strong fortresses (brochs) of the north were the strongholds of pirate leaders who settled there and harassed the inhabitants. No tale or tradition exists or has come down to us from these early periods.

The next raiders were the Northmen from Norway and Denmark. After repeated raids continuing over many centuries many of the raiders settled on the best land in the north. some legends and tales of these times still exist.

It appears that the Pictish inhabitants had established a beacon station on the Warth Hill. A smoke signal by day and a blaze of fire at night warned the inhabitants of the approach of sea raiders. Cattle would then be driven to secret folds or pens. One very large pen can still be seen, very artfully hidden in the side of a deep ravine, about a mile inland from Freswick sand. The beacon on the hill had frustrated many a carefully planned raid

before the Norse got a footing in Caithness. They determined on revenge and under cover of fog or haze a large galley lay off the land until nightfall and during the night – a fine evening in October – she was beached on the sand at Freswick with the flowing tide. A well chosen armed party silently made their way inland to the hill. Crossing a moor they came across a stray ox which was promptly killed and its reeking hide cut into strips and taken along with them. Reaching the base of the hill the party separated and converged on the summit from different directions.

The sentry was passing near the beacon pile and the remainder of the guard were lying round the watch fire in the shelter of a large boulder (the fairies kist). They were taken completely by surprise and slain. Then in a spirit of bravado the signal pile was lit and the bodies of the guards thrown in the flames. Another version tells that the seven captives were bound with the strips of reeking hide and thrown alive on the burning pile!

From Efter Dayset Yarns in Memory of the Poet by Simon Bremner, Midtown, Freswick.

Candlemas Day is now always the 2nd February.
It used to be about the 3rd-5th February.
Old Candlemas Day is the 13th February.
(Old New Year's Day is the 12th January.)

On Candlemas Day
If the sun shines before noon
Winter isn't half done.

At five o'clock on Candlemas Day
You can see a white horse a mile away.

Margaret Rosie, Freswick.

FRESWICK WRECKS

The "Gerona" ashore at Skirza 1892

Photo, Courtesy of Wick Society.

The "Gerona" ran head on to the "Shoal of the Slate". It was said that the crew and passengers were brought off by a breeches buoy made out of a cran basket.

It was also said that Donald Henderson's father got £100 for allowing the main hawser to be put round his house (house used as anchor) so that the ship could be winched off. The house had been newly slated and renovated, so Donald must have had some anxious moments! The house stood the test and is still standing firm, now occupied by John Hall.

S.S. "Willesden" stranded at Freswick 1911

Photo, Margaret Rosie, Midtown, Freswick.

The "Willesden" went ashore in fog on Skirza Head and was refloated later.

The "Alibi" wrecked at Freswick 1877. The "iron wood" (does not float) timbers from this boat were used for strainer posts all over Freswick and many can still be seen standing fast. There is one at the roadside where the track goes down to the shore near the chapel.

Sometimes when there has been a movement of sand after a storm, some ribs of the "Alibi" can be seen towards the southside of the bay.

The "Kentucky" went ashore on the "Shoal of the Slate" Skirza Head in thick fog. She was towed off when the weather settled.

The "Kentucky" at Wick 1921

Photo, Margaret Rosie, Midtown, Freswick.

FRESWICK FISHERMEN AT SKIRZA HOUSE C.1885

Photo, Lizzie Cook, Skirza Head.

Standing, Left to Right:– Mrs Colin Sellars with child, ? , William Gunn, James Begg, Peter Miller, John Nicolson, George Begg, William Gunn (junior), Colin Sellars, William Wares. Seated:– Salmon Fisher, Salmon Fisher, John Bremner, Pat Manson.

Traditional salmon cobles had three sets of rowlocks – so in this well preserved photograph of so many handsome stalwart salmon fishermen, one can assume they constituted two six-men crews with two young "prents" (handy for filling needles with twine and maybe actually mending an occasional "half-leg" at sea!?)

In the background, there is a traditional salmon-net dock where nets were hoisted up on pulleys in order to dry, or be mended, or cleaned of various types of seaweed or clay. .

In the middle of the group, one can discern Peter Miller and William Gunn holding up a quite heavy handbarrow. . . .(so both are excused for not smiling. .!?)

To the left of the photograph – Robbie Mackay? and William Gunn are tying corks on the top rope of a new "leader".,

Mrs Sellars is helping with that task, by creating a slight but necessary tension on the rope, Pat Manson appears to be splicing the rope.

The horse and cart will have been loaded (in those days with heavy cotton twine) – for the new "leader" – then several fathoms at a time coiled onto the hand-barrow and "fed" to the other crew members to have the bottom rope stitched on – also the top rope which has to be "corked". (No-one had a more patient or peaceable horse than John Nicolson).

Description from George Crowden, Cedar End, Castletown.

What tales these men could have told of piloting great ships through the Pentland Firth and the halcyon days of the herring fishing.

This Freswick pilot was taking a large "four master" through. A clootie dumpling boiled in a bit of canvas was handed down to the men in the pilot boat. They said the skin was a little "tough".

J.D.

Freswick Fishermen c.1885

Photo, Reta Manson, 20 Dwarwick Place, Dunnet.

Back Row:– John Nicolson, Half-way House; George Begg, Roadside Auckengill; William Gunn (junior) Seaview, Auckengill. Middle Row:– Salmon Fisher (reading paper); Pat Manson, Freswick; Peter Miller, Freswick Post Office; James Begg, Milton Auckengill; Colin Sellars; Salmon fisher. Seated:– William Wares, Skirza; John Bremner, Tofts; William Gunn (senior), Seaview, Auckengill; ? ; Mrs Colin Sellars with child. – Names from Catherine Matheson.

Cavelling Fish at Freswick c.1900

The largest cod were set out first, then the next biggest and so on until they were divided as evenly as possible. Then there were were different ways of cavelling. Each man took a stone or bit of wood or something and they were given to someone who did not know who owned the items and he set one on each pile of fish.

The "Someone" was not a crew member.

When Checking The Gless

A quick rise after low,
Foretells a strong blow.
  Bill Sinclair (Pattie's Bill), Huna and the Cairn.

If the grass grows in January it grows the worse for it all the year.
  Lizzie Cook, Skirza.

Goats' beards and mares tails,
Make tall ships carry small sails (gales).
  Elma Moar, Huna.

Photo, Margaret Rosie, Midtown.

Left to right:– John Bremner, Tofts; Robert Mackay, Tofts; Unknown; James Mowat, Skirza House.

VESSELS GROUNDED OR LOST IN VICINITY OF FRESWICK

1778	Six Sisters	A wooden brig of Whitehaven ashore below Freswick Castle; crew saved but captain lost. Total wreck.
1877	Alibi	A wooden brig, south side of Freswick Bay; total wreck. (*Brig of Peterhead. 4/4/1877. Sold for £76 to A. Reid, Keiss.*)
1887	Henri Aiden	Norwegian brig, at Skirza Head; total wreck.
1892	Gerona	S.S. 4000 tons of Dundee. Some cargo dumped and refloated after about a week.
7/1897	Ohio	S.S. Near Berryhill Auckengill; some cargo dumped and refloated after some days.
1898	?	A German N. Lloyd S.S. Near Fastgeo; refloated five hours later. (*Norddeutscher Lloyd.*)
1898	Cremona	A Norwegian S.S. Struck Long Ruff Skirza Head. Took local pilot aboard and later beached near Dunbeath.
1899	Skidby	S.S. 3500 tons of West Hartlepool. Near Freswick Pier; warped off next high water.
1905	Harriet	S.S. Ashore Slate Skirza Head. About 1000 tons; Dumped lot of cargo – (pig iron) and refloated following day.
1906	King Harald	S.T. GY.479. Near Freswick Pier; refloated in eight hours.
5/1907	Strath Clyde	S.T. A.336. East of pier; refloated after seven days.
7/1907	Loch Stennis	S.T. A.632. Near pier; warped off after six hours.
1908	Briton	S.T. A.101. East of pier; refloated after 20 hours. (*21/7/1915. Sunk when minesweeping off Harwich.*)
1908	Chiangkiang	S.T. A.798. East of pier; refloated following day. (*12/4/1917. Sunk by U-boat 30 miles NE of Buchan Ness.*)
3/1910	Mormond	S.T. of Fraserburgh; north of Fastgeo. Total wreck, crew saved. (*A.293. Bought by Andrew Walker, Aberdeen in 1909 from Fraserburgh Steam Trawling Co.*)
6/1911	Willesden	S.S. of London, 7000 tons, below Freswick Castle; discharged bunker coal and towed off after eight days.
1912	Fraser	S.T. H.951 Red Head; towed off three days later. (*17/6/1917. Sunk by mine off Boulogne.*)
1912	Velox	Coaster of Wick. South side Freswick Bay; refloated next day.
1915	Hamlet	Minesweeper. West of pier; towed off next day by Naval tug.
2/1920	Kentucky	S.S. of Copenhagen, 4000 tons; Skirza Head, salved 9/3/20.
6/1923	City of Florence	S.S. of Ellerman line, ashore at Fastgoe at low water; refloated six hours later.
5/1925	Salacon	S.T. GY.55. Slate Skirza Head; warped off six hours later. (*7/9/1940. Sunk by mine off Spurm Pt.*)
1926	Senator Heidman	S.S. In distress off Skirza Head; drifting in and north. Picked up by S.T. Firsby of Granton and towed south.
7/1928	Neptune	Belgian trawler; struck south side Freswick Bay in dense fog. Floated off drifting north and sinking; crew to boat and landed Warse. Vessel sank in middle of Freswick Bay.
5/1930	Marconi	S.T. H.488. Summerbank; refloated after seven hours. (*20/9/1941. Lost by collision off Harwich.*)
8/1930	Dunleith	Coaster of Beaumaris. North of Buchollie Castle; lost quantity of empty barrels; refloated after 12 hours.
5/1931	Robert Gibson	S.T. SN.30. Back of Freswick Pier; refloated in seven hours.
6/1933	Malacolite	S.T. GY.162. Slate Skirza Head; refloated in seven hours.
6/1933	Ormonde	S.T. GY.157. Slate Skirza Head; refloated in seven and a half hours. (*16/1/1941. Sunk by air attack off east coast of Scotland.*)
6/1937	Bayflower	S.T. H.487. North of Buchollie; refloated after 10 hours. (*Sold Grimsby 1939. Renamed "Saon" minesweeping. Broken up 1958.*)
9/1939	Navarre	S.T. At Skirza Head. Crew taken off. Became total wreck.
1953	Hassett	S.T. GY.489 at Berryhill Auckengill.
1959	Stellatus	South of Buchollie Castle; aground for several months then broke up and sank.

The Malacolite (6/1933) and Ormonde (6/1933) entries are bracketed together as "Same Day".

(S.S. – Steamship; S.T. – Steam Trawler; A– Aberdeen; GY – Grimsby; H – Hull; SN – North Shields)

From a list drawn up by James Miller, Freswick Post Office.

Additional information in brackets from Sutherland Manson.

INTRODUCTION TO YARNS OF PENTLAND FIRTH

David Grant, A.C.P., F.E.I.S., was author of the "Yarns" of the Pentland Firth.

Mr Grant came north to Caithness in 1857, and was parochial schoolmaster at Canisbay until 1861. He quickly caught the spirit of the north and delighted in the folk-tales which were then current round the Pentland Shores. He was not long enough in Caithness to master the northern doric. Hence the "Yarns" are written in English. His son Mr Henry Keith Grant, writes:– "Such Merits as his English verse possesses I attribute to his residence in Caithness. The grandeur of the ocean, and the cheerful courage with which the fishermen and pilots plied their callings filled him with admiration."

True, there are oft the whistling winds and the clamorous bursting surges; the terrors of the "dreaded Pentland's rough and rapid flow," with all its eddies and currents, and "the bold and beetling crags where whitening breakers roar." But there are also, in summer and autumn days, the glory of sunrise and sunset – vast pageants of colour and splendour – and all the glories of "the sea that bares her bosom to the moon." With all this the pilots of long ago were familiar. If they did not always appreciate its aesthetic and poetic glamour, they imbibed its spirit to the full, and became living embodiments of the Scandinavian sentiment that still clings around the Islands and the northern Caithness coast. They had much lore and many tales of derring-do which strongly appealed to Mr Grant's poetic temperament. In putting them into pleasing lines, rich with melody, he did a fine service to our far northern coast. Several of his pieces have the true tang of the sea. Hardy and daring men were the pilots in the 19th century days of sail. Ever on the outlook for ships, they lost no time in putting to sea when a vessel hove up on the horizon, and there was frequently keen rivalry between the boats as to which would "get" her. When competition was very keen, as many as four or six boats engaged in a vigorous race after one "prize", and whether in wind or calm the little craft

were handled with consummate skill. The pilot's fee usually varied in accordance with the generosity of the shipmaster, and was occasionally supplemented by a supply of tobacco or liquor – luxuries eagerly coveted by the venture-some pilots. This led to a considerable trade in smuggling; and thrilling exploits are still recounted on the Pentland shores of pilots landing contraband goods under the very noses of the Officers of Excise. A larger fee was expected for the piloting of a three-masted ship or barque than for an ordinary brig, schooner, or sloop.

Mr John Mowat, F.S.A., Glasgow (son of Mr James Mowat, one of the pilots) informs me that there were men with the knowledge of pilots in nearly all the fishing communities east and west of the Pentland Firth entrances. But there were strategic points on the coast line. These were at Freswick, Auckengill, and as far south as Staxigoe to the east, and at Brims and Sandside in the west, with a colony of Stroma pilots in the centre, to pilot east or west as the tide or occasion required.

The pilots had no characteristic uniform, but in seamanlike appearance they were of a very definite type. In the course of their occupation they were not infrequently "carried away" on the ship they were piloting. This was usually due to storms coming on and the vessels being blown out into the Atlantic without getting in touch with a west-coast landing-place. These men were known afterwards by the names of the ports to which they had been taken – "Savannah", "Jamaica", "Quebec", or as the case happened to be. The story of a Freswick pilot being carried away is excellently told in W. Leith Bremner's narrative poem, "The Pilot of the Pentland Firth." Pilot Mowat was one of those who had the experience of being carried across the Atlantic. He was taken to Quebec in his slippers in 1870. Much more could be written concerning both the pilots and their times. The foregoing, may suffice to give the reader some impression of Caithness seafaring life at a period that now seems remote.

R.J.G. Millar, John O'Groat Journal Office, Wick, July 1931.

Note:– Donald Cook **(Uncle Dan)** was the son of Wm. Cook and his wife Margaret Bain. Donald was born in 1786 and married Margaret Manson in 1814. His brother James born 1789 was the great grandfather of Willie, Bella, Annie, David and Lizzie Cook. Donald Cook's daughter Barbara (b.1821) had the croft after her father. Babbie's croft lies between Lizzie Cook's and Donald Henderson's but is a bit further out on Skirza Head. Bella's grandson George Simpson has the croft now.

John Dunnett, Heatherbell Cottages.

Left to right: James Cook, grandson of James b.1789; John Miller, Salmon Fisher, Halcro, Bower and Donald Robertson, Midtown, Skirza.

Carrying a net on a hand-barrow from Skirza Salmon House

Photo, Christine Simpson, Midtown, Freswick.

121

UNCLE DAN, THE PENTLAND FIRTH PILOT

EXPLANATORY NOTE:– Except about an hour during "slack water", or turn of the tide, the current of the Pentland Firth averages nine or ten knots an hour, and cannot be stemmed by a mere sailing vessel. The pilots, by taking advantage of the numerous eddies, know how to hold their own; but few entire strangers attempt the passage of the Firth without the assistance of a pilot; and before education introduced a better morality, many a shipmaster was mulcted in double fees, as in the manner set forth by our pilot in his yarn.

My Uncle Dan was a moral man,
And seldom drank or swore;
My Uncle Dan was an honest man
While he kept his foot on shore.
But, strange to tell of my Uncle Dan,
Whenever he touched the brine,
His notions always got confused
On the laws of yours and mine.

On shore, dishonest shrank abashed
At the sound of my Uncle's name,
For ne'er was he known to lift a plack
To which another had claim;
But once upon board, such odds and ends
As landsmen could scarce conceive
Would find their way to my Uncle's pouch,
And never ask owner's leave.

The skippers who sailed the northern seas
Knew Uncle's faults to a man;
But they also knew that their ships were safe
In the hands of my Uncle Dan;
For Britain never produced his match
At steering a vessel to berth,
And none in Caithness better knew how
To pilot the Pentland Firth.

Bay and creek, and skerry and ness,
And eddies great and small;
Ebb and flood, and reef and roust,
My Uncle knew them all.
The shores and the seas from east to west
He knew for a hundred miles,
And the wells and flows, and sounds and hopes,
To the farthest Orkney Isles.

Or east, or west, or north, or south,
Wherever the wind might veer,
Blow high or low, run ebb or flow,
My Uncle knew whither to steer
But to my tale, 'twas an autumn morn,
If I do aright remember,
Exactly fifty years ago,
Come the first of next November.

A smartish breeze was ruffling the ebb,
An hour and a quarter run,
When over the eastern waters rose
The sober November sun;
And, rounding Noss head, a gallant barque
Attracted my Uncle's eye;
For he knew she signalled a pilot out
By the red flag half-mast high.

"Get ready, my boys," cried Uncle Dan,
To myself and cousins three –
To "Rob o' the Rock" and "Tom o' the Hole",
And "Peerie Will", and me.
"There's a pilot required for yonder barque"
(And he chuckled and rubbed his hands);
"A stranger here, I know by his gear,
And the awkward way that he stands."

"Get out in haste, and pilot him west,
For the highest fee that you can;
But leave a shot in the locker, my boys,
'T will be needed for Uncle Dan.
Run him up the way of the Men of Mey,
And tell him to stand to sea,
And then make off for fear of squalls";
And my Uncle redoubled his glee.

We launched our boat, the Mary Jane,
And dashed across the tide,
Till we reached the barque, made fast a rope,
And climbed the stranger's side;
We found the barque of Jonathan's build,
And her master a swaggering blade,
"Guessed" he hadn't seen a "clearance" like ours
Since he entered the timber trade.

He reckoned our "squires" didn't thank their sires,
Nor much approve of the "spec' "
That cleared their "lots" of their timber plots,
And squirted the juice on the deck.
He screwed us down, and lower down,
Begrudging our meanest fee;
But I got charge of the Yankee barque,
And west away stood we.

We rounded the rocks of Duncan's Bay,
And skirted the "Western Bore",
Standing now upon Stroma Isle,
And now upon Canisbay shore;
Tacking here with the breeze abreast,
And there with the breeze abaft,
From eddy to ebb, with little away,
But a wondrous show of craft.

And we left him west of the Men of Mey'
But little the Yankee "guessed"
That the wind and tide would soon unite
With a force he could never resist,
He fought them long, but in spite of his teeth,
He lost upon every tack,
For the westerly wind and the eastering flood
Were carrying him swiftly back.

And down he went upon Swona Isle,
Where he narrowly 'scaped a wreck,
Down till he easted Skirza Head
And my Uncle stood upon deck
Nor failed my Uncle to find a berth,
Where the barque at anchor could ride,
Until he could pilot her west the Sound
With the flow of the westering tide.

He sorely blamed the "lubberly swab"
Who'd played the pilot before,
And cleverly pocketed odds and ends
From out of the yankee's store.

FRESWICK

But Jonathan's "eye-teeth had been cut,"
For a Yankee 'cute was he;
And he fathomed our plans and Uncle Dan's
'Ere he entered the open sea.

And, asking my Uncle down below,
He plied him so hard with grog
That the old man's tongue outran his wits,
And his brains were lost in fog.
He drank and drank, till at last he sank
With a heavy gurgling snore,
And lay completely spirit-logged
On Jonathan's cabin floor.

He lay – he knew not how long he lay –
Entranced in his drunken sleep;
Nor if't was the tide or the Yankee's barque
That carried him out to the deep.
But, lo! when he opened his drowsy eyes,
A 'wildered man was he,
To find himself in his little boat
Far out in the open sea.

Outstretched in a punt of nine feet keel,
Unmeet for the slightest gale;
With naught to shield his shivering frame
Save a shred of tattered sail;
Without his pickings, without his fee,
With never a pipe to smoke,
With a racking head and a parching throat,
My Uncle Dan awoke.

He started up and gazed around
With a wild, bewildered stare;
The barque was gone, and he was alone,
With the ocean everywhere.
He looked to the east – the cloudless sky
Gave hopes of a tranquil night;
He looked to the west, the setting sun
Went down in a blaze of light.

He looked to the north, he looked to the south,
But as far as the eye could sweep,
Around and around the only bound
Was the meeting of sky and deep;
With never a boat, with never a ship
With never a floating thing,
Save only he and his tiny punt
In the midst of the mighty ring.

He had battled the Bores of Duncan's Bay,
He had tossed in the Men of Mey,
He had weathered the wrath of wind and wave,
Till his hair was scanty and grey.
The raging winds and the roaring floods,
He had battled them like a man,
For there wasn't a braver stept in shoes
Than my brave old Uncle Dan.

But now, though he sat on a smiling sea,
On an evening calm and mild,
His head dropped over his helpless breast,
And he wept like a sucking child;
For how could he pass the dreary night
Afar on the open sea,
In the sprites of the deep, the ghosts of the drowned,
In the Finmen's company?

He wasn't without his trust in Heaven –
Your seaman is seldom so –
Though he oft forgets the Power that saves
When the storm hath ceased to blow;
Though he bid religion pass today,
And call again tomorrow;
Though he's oft a thoughtless, dissolute dog,
He's seldom an Atheist thorough.

Your blinded advocate of chance,
Whom the churchmen cannot reform
Who laughs at faith, and sneers at hope –
Put him out to sea in a storm.
Put him far at sea in an open boat,
And alone like my Uncle Dan,
And I'll lay you my yawl to a schooner's punt
You would find him an altered man.

My Uncle thought on his friends at home,
The wife he might ne'er see more,
And wrung his hands, and wept and prayed,
As he never had prayed on shore.
'T were long to tell how he lay becalmed
On the broad Atlantic's breast,
Or number the risks of his tiny bark
When a breeze sprang up in the west.

'T were sad to hear of his raging thirst,
With nothing to quench its fire,
Or the hunger that gnawed his vitals up
With the fangs of fierce desire.
Enough to say that a second day
And a third dread night had run,
Ere a coaster picked my Uncle up
At the rising of the sun.

Nor ever again was my Uncle Dan
The pilot he'd wont to be;
He would never climb to a stranger's deck,
Nor hear of a double fee.
He pulled an oar with a feebler stroke,
And steered with unsteady hand;
He was ever the last to put to sea,
And the first to spring to land.

He never went west of the Men of Mey,
Nor into the open seas,
But he shivered and shook in a nervous fit,
Like a sail in a ruffling breeze.
Some twenty years have passed away
Since my Uncle stowed the oar,
And hoisted sail, to stand, as we trust,
For a fairer, happier shore.

And this was the last advice he gave
To myself and my cousins three –
To "Rob o' the Rock" and "Tom o' the Hole",
And "Peerie Will" and me:
"Let Conscience stand at the wheel", he said,
"And Honesty heave the log;
Keep a sharp look-out on a Yankee ship,
And be sparing of Jonathan's grog;
Beware of the wicked one whose nets
Are spread for the soul of man,
And whenever you think of a double fee,
Remember your Uncle Dan."

From Yarns of the Pentland Firth by David Grant.

123

THE MOWAT COLLECTION

Skirza House c.1910

*Photo, Joan Slater, 31 Rodger Drive, Rutherglen, Glasgow.
Mrs John Mowat (Georgina Dunnet) with mother-in-law Mrs James Mowat
(Margaret Reid) and her son James and daughters Peggy and Jessie.*

Salmon House and Beach at Freswick where "The Wanderer" lay

*Photo, Joan Slater, 31 Rodger Drive, Rutherglen, Glasgow.
John and Georgina's Family on holiday. Left to right:- Peggy, Lottie, Jessie and
George (twins), James, [John and Chrys also twins would be too young to be on
the shore].*

"The Wanderer" c.1925

*Photo, Joan Slater, 31 Rodger Drive, Rutherglen, Glasgow.
Pilot James Mowat, Skirza House in his boat mending lobster creels.*

"The Peggy" 1937

*Photo, Joan Slater, 31 Rodger Drive, Rutherglen, Glasgow.
The boat was named after John Mowat's daughter. Scott was an excellent and
very special dog. John Mowat with his sister Maggie, daughter Peggy and
grand-daughter Joan.*

The Mowat Collection

Four Generations 1934

Photo, Joan Slater, 31 Rodger Drive, Rutherglen, Glasgow.

John Mowat with Pilot James his father, Peggy his daughter and Joan his grand-daughter.

SOME OLD CANISBAY CUSTOMS AND SUPERSTITIONS

"Old Customs! Oh I love the sound!
However simple, they be;
What'er with time hath sanction found,
Is welcome and is dear to me."

There were various wells said to possess the curative virtue, to which people afflicted with particular ailments resorted at certain times and seasons. The "Wall o' e' Warth Hill" was one of these. Here the seekers after health went in search of their quest " 'tween sin and day". Perhaps associated with this superstition is the old custom of "creaming the well". To be the first at the well on New Year's morning was to get the "cream" of the well, which meant beauty and happiness to the fair one who secured it. A wisp of straw was left in the well to indicate to the next comer that the well had already been "creamed". It was usual for a lad and a lass to go together as soon as possible after the stroke of 12. The custom has long been obsolete, but even in the memory of the writer the

wisp of straw was placed in the well as a practical joke on an early rising maiden to show that someone had been before her.

The custom of "castin the heart" was a superstitious ceremony which lingered long. It was considered necessary as a cure for all who suffered from the result of a fright or from a lingering sickness. The heart was supposed to be out of place or spirited away by an evil Jinnee. The services of one skilled in the casting of the heart was often in request, and every district had its representative. The performance, with slight variations, was carried out as follows. Over the head of the patient was held a common sieve and under it a wooden "bicker" containing newly drawn spring water. Molten lead was then poured through the eye of a scissors, which passed through the sieve into the water and separated into small pieces. These were carefully examined to find one of the shape of a heart. If not successful the process had to be repeated on alternate days. At the end of each performance the patient had to take a drink of the water and also wash face and hands with it. When the leaden shape of the heart was secured it was sewn into the clothing of the sufferer, or hung around the neck until recovery was complete, and as a proof against future trouble. To be effectual both the patient and the performer had to be fasting when the ceremony was carried out.[1]

Under the date of 18th February, 1724, there is the following reference to a case of supposed ability to cure by sorcery. "The minister reports that he is credibly informed that Margaret Bain, spouse to James Donaldson, in Nybster, professes to cure diseases, and has lately practised her skill in this parish particularly on David Bremner and Euphans Doull, his wife, in Freswick, and on a child of William Cormack's in Auckengill and others; that she practices her art in different methods, and by different ceremonies, upon different diseases. One of her cures particularly, is this. She takes a stockine (stocking), a horn spoon and an unscoured woollen thread: she lays the stockine on a stool and some of the yarn upon it, and sets the patient thereon: then takes the rest of the thread and wraps it about several parts of the patient's body, particularly the arms, breast, and head, then ties the end of the thread to the kettlecrook with her own hand, and crosses the fire three or four times, going against the sun – all the time muttering some unintelligible words, shaking and pulling all the joints in such a way as if the devil were in her. Then she raises the patient from off the stool, and if the spoon, which was on the outside of the stockine, be within the stockine, and the thread which was with it be wrapt about it, she reckons her cure performed."[2]

Animals were subject to three particular forms of disease, "forespoken", "elfshot", or "ta'en by the fairies", and were treated accordingly. The cure for "forespoken", or affected by the evil eye, was a drink of water off silver or out of a vessel in which silver had been placed. A mixture of oatmeal and salt, called the "lib-for-spoken", was then poured down the throat of the animal. Previously some skilly person had stirred the mixture with a steel needle and muttered over it some incantation. The secret of this remedy was said to have passed away with James Cook, Freswick, a century ago. The salt and oatmeal preparation was only effectual when applied by one having skill in such matters. "Lib-for-spoken" was used in several ways as a proof against the power of the evil eye. It was sprinkled on boats setting out for the fishing, and fishermen were said to secure a portion, which was put in the "forestep" beneath the foot of the fore mast. Oatmeal and salt were also used for "saining" ie., to secure a blessing. An old woman in Duncansby, named Kirsty Loutit, used it in this way. A neighbour had come to give her a "yokin's" ploughing. Before he was allowed to start, the horses and plough had to be blessed and sprinkled with the oatmeal and salt which she carried in her apron, because she said the folk will be "aystin" me.[3] While doing so she muttered this incantation:

"Preserve man and beast;
Stryth,[4] pleoch and gear, go on."

The symptons of "elfshot" were a languid appearance, hard breathing, and disinclination to take food. The skilly man professed to find holes in the underskin, which they sought for very diligently. The supposed marks were rubbed with "forls" or "elf stones", or "soap stones". Two tablespoonfuls of salt were dissolved in water, and a little poured in the ears and down the throat of the animal. A silver piece had to be put in the water when the salt was dissolving. A much more elaborate performance had to be resorted to in dealing with "murrain" or "heasty", as it was called in Caithness in olden times. When the disease was discovered the charm doctors were immediately called to superintend the raising of the "need fire", the relic of an old Druidical custom. On an island with running water on either side was erected a circular booth of stone and turf, over which was set a "heilan" couple of birch wood. An upright pole was fixed from the crown of the couple and inserted in an oblong socket in the ground. Between the upright pole and the couple leg was fixed a horizontal beam, the pointed ends of which fitted into sockets. On the centre of this beam, which was called the auger, was fixed four short arms or levers. When all was completed, men were called who had already divested themselves of most of their clothing and everything containing metal. Two by two they turned the auger, while others drove wedges on the offside of the upright pole to press it harder on the lever. By constant pressure and friction the end of the auger would take fire, and from this the "need fire" was immediately kindled. All the fires in the infected farm were quenched with water and rekindled from the "need fire". The smoke of the new fire blown on the cattle was supposed to arrest the plague. To prevent the spreading of "blackquarter", a disease prevalent among young cattle, the infected beast was taken to a house, which no cattle were ever after to enter, and there the heart was taken out and fixed to the byre. While there the other cattle were free from the risk of the disease spreading.

In the Sibbald MS. Collection in the Advocates' Library, Edinburgh, there is a curious letter from Mr Mathew Macaile, apothecary, dated 5th March, 1683, which has the following reference to "Heasty, a disease incident to the cattle in Caithness": "The Beasts in Caithness are often troubled with a disease which the people call Heastie, because it putteth them in a rage, and killeth them suddenly."

The "taking of freet" was practised by the necromancer with more or less sincerity even within the past hundred years. The method generally adopted in Caithness to charm away the produce of a neighbour's dairy was the trailing of a hair tether or simmon over their grazing pasture between sun and day, when the dew lay wet and heavy. When the cow crossed the track of the hair tether she became yeil or her milk yielded no butter. This state of matters is described by Burns.

"Thence country wives wi toil an pain,
May plunge and plunge the kirn in vain,
For Oh! the yellow treasure's taen
    By witchin skill.
An dawtit twall pint Hawkies gain
    As yeil's a bill."

The story is told of a good man getting up one morning to find a notorious person parading his pasture. He set off in pursuit, and succeeded in capturing the hair rope, which he took home with him and threw behind a "meal-girnal". The first time the goodwife went to churn she was amazed at the unusual quantity of butter produced. As there was no other explanation the horse-hair rope behind the girnal was associated with the matter. It was brought out, and when cut there flowed from it a copious supply of rich cream. But the cutting broke the spell, as future churning brought no superabundance. The same process has been associated with a heather simmon.

Many peculiar practices, now long obsolete, were associated with particular days. Eel (Yule) and Ne'er's day were the beginning of festivities which continued more or less until Candlemas. On New Year's day young and old turned out to the ancient game of "Knotty". First footing on New Year's day lingered longer than most old customs. But in bygone times the "first foot" formed quite an important part in the destinies of the northerner. In going on a journey or to a new job, or even setting out on the ordinary calling, some were careful to note the first living creature they met, and by it judged their success.

Fosterne'en was celebrated by a dish of Scotch brose for dinner. The brose was served in one large wooden bicker, and the whole company sat round with spoons and partook. On "Peace" Sunday everyone had eggs for breakfast, and those who had no poultry begged their "peace eggs" from the neighbours.

The "cutting-aff-piece" is still kept up in the harvest home ball, but it is shorn of the glamour of the principal reaper throwing all the shearing hooks over his head to see how many would stick in the ground, and how many of the reapers would live to shear another year. Nor do the shearers now sleep with the last hand of corn they cut below their pillows to dream of future husbands. The old customs associated with births, deaths and marriages were many. Before deaths there were always those who had "foregangs" or saw "lichts" or had "dreams". The hearing of the "death watch" or the ticking of the "Jacky Mill" was a sure sign of a death in the family. The "lyke" or "lye-a-wake", with all its forms of feasting, so much out of keeping with the solemnity of the occasion, is now of the dim and superstitious past, but the remnant of it, in whisky and bread and cheese at funerals, became a deeply engrained use and wont in the habits of later generations. The old wedding ceremony was the period for feasting and display, and few were daring enough to break a custom, which very gradually took on milder forms. It was a period of feasting which lasted for more than a week, and sometimes the couple were run into expense which took them the greater part of their married life to clear off. To begin with, there was the "cantrag" or contract night, then the house-to-house visitation by the bride and bridegroom giving "the bids". The ceremony proper began with the "feet-washing" night, which preceded the wedding day, and the feasting continued next day and night without much interruption. It was resumed on the evening of the third day, when all the invited guests gathered together to a "house warming" for the newly married couple, which was often held in an ale-house, and which was perhaps with some measure of truth called the "filling-foo" night.

These are but lights and shadows of a dim past, perhaps more of shadows than lights, because the shadows left the deeper impress, and the perspective may be somewhat blurred by the process of time, but we will not think less kindly of the people who held to them with some sincerity.

[1] Calder's Sketches from John O'Groats, P.226.

[2] Canisbay Kirk Session Records.

[3] Caithness phrase, meaning: they would wish to take away her luck. It also occurs in the Caithness saying: 'em at aysts 'e silk goon will get the sleeve o't.

[4] Work-animals.

"The bids" = *invitations*

Notes by John Mowat, Skirza and Glasgow.

THE SEVEN STONES AT RUSHIE GEO, SKIRZA HEAD

Long, long ago there was always a threat of raids or invasion so people were usually on the alert. This story was handed down by my father from his grandfather and I'm not sure how long before that.

An old woman living in a house beside the Broch near the "Hole of the Head" saw men climbing up the rock at Effie's Goe. She thought they were raiders, but instead of running for her life decided to tackle them. She took off her good knitted wool stocking and put a fair sized stone in the toe. She clobbered them with this as they put their heads over the brae.

Photo, James Rosie, Midtown, Freswick.
The Cairn can just be seen on the left

They had no chance to explain that their ship had gone on the rocks. A young lad was the last, and he assured her he just wanted to get back home to his folk in Aberdeen. She spared his life and was very good to him and so too were the Freswick folk. They gave the unfortunate sailors decent burials on the little promontary at the head of Rushie Goe and placed large stones to mark each grave. The stones are there to this day.

The young lad hoped that the seas would turn up the captain's iron box which had gold galore! A pilot got him aboard a ship that was bound for Aberdeen and there is no need to tell of his mother's joy.

Freswick with its grand sweep of bay, sandy beaches and green fertile land has always been attractive. The links is the site of, possibly, the biggest Viking settlement in Caithness. Then as now Freswick was aye being taken over!

Lizzie Cook, Skirza Head.

Footnote:– We checked and saw the seven boulders which varied in size but were roughly rectangular. There is moss and lichen growing over them and the grass is well up the sides, but they are all there, some of them just about six feet from the edge of the cliff.

James Rosie, Midtown, and John Hall, Skirza.

———

James T. Calder wrote "The Graves of the Mariners on Skirza Head" in "Sketches from John O'Groats in Prose and Verse" published 1842. It would seem from it that the ship was wrecked c.1742.

Ethel Dunnett, Heatherbell Cottages, John O'Groats.

SKIRZA TO THE BIEL

Hole of the Head

The House at Wife Geo showing coastguard shelter.

Take the Skirza road to the last T-junction and to the right in front of you is Effie's Geo. Rushie Geo lies to the south of it and Skirza Head itself is to the south of that.

The rough stones which mark the sailor's graves are set at the head of Rushie Geo. On the headland between Rushie and Effie's Geo stands a Broch known locally as the "Mound". There is a well at the entrance to the "Mound". Dr Curle carried out excavations here in 1937-38 but now the site is very overgrown.

It cannot be over emphasised that **very great care** must be taken when looking around here.

About 20-25 yards from the "Cairn" (built with stones from the Broch) is the "Hole of the Head" which must go down a depth of about 120 feet to the sea where there are three entrances to the "Hole".

It is an awesome and very dangerous hole and there is nothing to indicate its position until you are on it, and then you realise why so much care must be taken when approaching it. As far as I know it has never been fenced off but it is hoped this will be done soon.

Long ago a man with a one horse plough used to cultivate the ground around the "Hole" on that wee headland, and I never heard of anyone falling down the "Hole".

Effie's Goe is accessible with care, and near its mouth, one small entrance to the "Hole of the Head" can be seen at low water. It is supposed that McAlpine's purse containing a fortune is still at the bottom of the goe!

Next, it's north round the Bocht to the Long Goe, and it is said that from there a cave runs right into the Warth Hill!! The slate quarry is just on the north side of the Long Geo bordering the Skirza quarry. Billy Sinclair has the quarry now, and it is hard to believe that the beautiful, cassied

Skirza Quarry December 1991

bottom is natural. It's a good 50 yards square, level, and nature's work can be clearly seen.

The clay holes are lying just to the west of the quarry. Before the days of cement and during the last war when it was unobtainable or too expensive, clay was dug and carted for building houses and steadings.

Raised grassy topped hillocks can be seen all over the Freswick hill and it was there that birds of prey were trapped. The mounds were built up about two feet high with divots and had a long stab or post driven into them. A round gin trap was secured to the top of the post.

Hawks, falcons and eagles hover when searching for prey and a handy post where they can perch, rest and view for movement on the ground attracts them. It was the game keepers job to preserve the grouse, pheasant and other moor birds and he must have walked miles checking these traps. The fresh bright green grassy topped mounds still show up well against the heather.

At one time it was planned to take the main road to John O'Groats round from Skirza to Duncansby. Last century the road was started and it was made standard width with ditches at each side. (Cost however eventually dictated that the shorter route over the Warth Hill was taken.) Keep going northwards over the end of Skippie Geo and you are on this road. George Angus continued on with this road for carting his peats and in places had to dig down three-four feet to make a good rock bottom road.

The "Railway" begins after the peat road and is the track over the mires to Wife Geo. It is a good description because it looks like an overgrown railway line. In the summer David Matheson who lived at Skirza (the Cook's house) grazed his sheep on tethers at Wife Geo. The distance was nothing, but in fog or in the darkening there was considerable risk. It was David who set 20-25 marker stones along a track on firm ground, and bridged the mire ditches. He called his road the

"Railway" and it takes you past the house at Wife Geo right to Gibson's House at Fastgoe.

There was a good quarry at Salt Skerry, lying half way between Skirza quarry and Wife Geo and it still can be seen from the "Railway". A lot of stones from this quarry were built into the Freswick pier because of their heavy solid quality. Fishermen from Groats and Freswick came with horses and carts to get stones from the Salt Skerry quarry for ballast in their creels. The heavy blue stones did not shatter, were easy to split by chisel and they lifted cleanly off the bed. They were ideal for weighting down creels because they sat flat and steady. It was thought that lobsters and crabs might shy clear if there was movement from a rocking or light stone.

Robbie Mackay, Tofts, a coastguard during the Second World War, built this wall close to the fireplace to make a shelter just big enough for sitting in. The good workmanship shows he enjoyed building it.

He carried a bag with peats over on his back to make a fire, when he started his watch and he would have needed it all in such an exposed place. It is understood that Wife Geo was "Half-way House" and that the Freswick and Groats coastguards met up there.

There is a track from Wife Geo that will take you right round to Duncansby Head and another, if you look carefully will take you to the Biel.

In 1956 it seemed no trouble at all to tow a binder from Skirza over to the Biel. It was not shaken separate, nor did it need any welding by Billy – it just never worked better!

About 1890 there were four families living at the Biel – Bremners, Greens, Cooks and Rosies.

Now there is just Billy and Betty Bremner, and as yet no new settlers, but with a tarred road from Groats to the front door one never can tell!

John Dunnett, Heatherbell Cottage, John O'Groats.

JOHN GIBSON, FASTGOE

John Gibson was connected with an abortive distillery venture near Kirkstyle Canisbay. After it failed, Gibson built a house in a sheltered nook at the top of the steep slope going down to the beach at Fast Goe. A wilder more lonely spot would be hard to find. It is situated between the township of John O'Groats and Freswick. The want of a road round this part of the coast is badly missed. Visitors who have been guided to Fastgoe Head are all loud in their praises of the cliff scenery and magnificent view. They all agree that it is the finest in the north. The scenery is fine in Summer. Magnificent cliffs and goes cutting far inland, with the Stacks of Duncansby, Duncansby Head and the Pentland Skerries and Orkney in the distance make a view long to be remembered. In winter with an easterly gale and spray and spindrift being flung over the 200ft cliffs life must have been very

uncomfortable.

Gibson was a good scholar and possessed a library of his own. He assisted Calder with his history of Caithness, indeed much of the credit for this publication is due to Gibson. He was quite fearless but very unassuming. During a great easterly gale in the winter of 1870 a Norwegian brig was running blindly under bare poles for the Pentland Firth. Once in the Firth she would be in smooth water. But fate decided otherwise and the brig missed the firth and safety by half a mile. She went ashore near the Stacks of Duncansby and was smashed to fragments and all the crew drowned.

In the afternoon following the sea tragedy, Gibson from the top of the cliffs, saw some bodies of the drowned crew floating in the surf in the "Houp of Fastgoe". From an intimate knowledge of the set of the tides he calculated that some of them at least would be cast ashore about midnight on or near the beach of Fastgoe. It is risky reaching that beach in daytime when there is a heavy sea running, as one has to descend the goe and traverse under the 250 foot perpendicular cliffs with always the danger of an exceptionally heavy wave washing right up to the face of the cliff. To get round is only possible when the tide is full out as at high water to half tide the bottom of the cliff is awash and swept by heavy seas.

At midnight, after the tide receded, Gibson lit his lantern and with his staff in his hand, went down the goe in that pitch darkness and howling gale and essayed that perilous journey round to the beach. He found four bodies and part of another and carried them on his back to the foot of the cliffs where the sea could not reach them. How he managed to do so can only be guessed as the "ebb" which he had to traverse is a mass of huge boulders lying tilted at all angles. In the morning willing helpers took the bodies up the cliff to Gibson's barn. There they were reverently wrapped in sheets supplied by Gibson's wife and later buried in Canisbay churchyard. A niggardly Parochial Board would not even recompense Mrs Gibson for her sheets.

Gibson on being asked if he was not afraid or nervous during his self imposed task, replied, "What, afraid of a dead man! No I might well be afraid of a living man, but of a dead man never."

From – Efter Dayset Yarns in Memory of The Poet by Simon Bremner, Midtown, Freswick.

'E PUFFIN

When ye walk along 'e cliff tops
Ye'll find birds o' every kind,
Oakies, terns an' cormorants,
An' kittywakes ye'll find.

Gulls o' different breed an' size –
We call them all a "maw"
But 'e Puffin is 'e odd man out
He's different fae them a'.

He toddles lek a penguin'
He's a muckle-coloured beak.
He's naething lek a scorry,
Mair a parrad wi' webbed feet.

They say 'e Devil oot o' spite
Made mock o' God's creation,
An' added bits an' pieces
'At were oot o' a' proportion.

'At's how 'e donkey's loogs are long,
His cry mair lek a wheeze,
But 'e Puffin surely landed
Wi' 'e Devil's masterpiece.

His neb is maist byornar,
Hid's yellow, blue an' red,
Shaped lek a triangle
An' half as beeg's his head.

Wi' his colourful extremities
Ye'd expect a brilliant sight –
But his stocky little body
Is chist plain black an' white.

He disna use a nerrow bink
High on a sheer cliff face
Till make a nest lek ither birds
Fa clamour for a space.

He goes ashore an' deegs a hole
Til make himself a nest
Any soft-lek soil will do –
But a rabbad burrow's best.

His neb is chist 'e very dab
For shovelling oot 'e earth.
He makes a really thorough job
An' dells for all he's worth.

Then lines hid weel wi' bits o' gress
An' feathers soft an' warm.

The eggs pure white wi' pale brown spots
Are snug an' free fae harm.

If an unwary han' should reach
Intil 'e nest so stealthy,
'E neb goes into action
Wi' a drive 'at's maist unhealthy!

Ye'll take yer leave immediately
Ye widna want til linger;
At best ye'd get a nasty nip
Or mebby lose a finger.

So Puffin eggs are quite secure;
Their nests are weel protected.
Nae egg on earth is worth 'e risk
If that beak gets connected!

But if ye're walkan ower 'e dunes
Ye could get a fearful gluff
If ye heard sounds beneath yer feet
Far 'e bent is thick an' rough.

Ye think o' ghosts an' pirates
'At fairly maks ye shiver,
But hids chist a pair of Puffins
Sittan' bletheran til each ither.

They're no beeg but they're hardy
An' can fly far oot til sea
Skimman smoothly ower 'e waves
An' fishan for their tea.

'E fish chist dinna stand a chance
Against a force so great
'At can swim beneath 'e water
An' nab them while ye wait.

An' when 'e winter storms blow hard
Wi' sleat an' drivan' rain,
Ye'll find them far away from lan'
But flyan' hom again.

We watch them wi' affection
In groups upon 'e rocks
Wi' their red an' blue an' yellow beaks
An' their scarlet-coloured socks.

When we walk along 'e cliff tops
They're 'e birds we look for most.
Long may they make their burrowed nests
Around our northern coast.

Clara Clyne, Strathesk Grove, Kirkhill, Penicuik.

THE FORT DYKE

This dyke runs east to west where the side road "forks" to Clevnagreen and Sonsiquoy. James Matheson (married to Jean Davidson), Carrier carted for the shops and district using a longcart. The Mathesons had the Bayview croft. Jess Matheson was very good with horses, and got the credit for gathering the stones off the land over the years and building this fine boundary dyke between them and Clevnagree. It is seven to eight chain long and must be a full six feet wide and six feet high.

There is a similar but smaller dyke running along the foot of Willie Bain's land. (In Aberdeenshire these dykes were known as consumption dykes because they consumed the stones.)

Ian Angus, Bayview, Freswick.

FRESWICK LINEN INDUSTRY C.1800

Murdoch Campbell or his wife Catherine is said to have taught locals to spin linen. An abstract from his spinning book shows he was distributing lint to 80-90 women spinners in the district. He then collected the finished yarn and sent it for weaving to a cousin. Linen Draper, Abbeyhill, Edinburgh. [There was a movement at this time to develop the linen industry in Northern Counties.]

The balls of flax were also taken to the local weaver to be made up. [In 1970 Nurse Cook had "The Clootie" – a small tablecloth which had been woven from flax grown locally. It was very special and she had childhood memories of it being used when they had visitors from the "sooth".]

Women also spun hemp which the men made into ropes and nets. Wool was also spun and knitted. They took hanks of wool to the local wool weaver who made it up into tweed or blankets for them.

Local names too, show there was a good going linen industry. The Lint Lochies are to the east of the road over the Warth Hill. The Heckler's Well is a strong spring in the Mittan (near the schoolhouse). Hempriggs, the Dyer's Well and Boiler's Burn are also in Freswick.

The 1841 census records show that George Shearer, Freswick was a linen and woollen hand loom-weaver and that Alex Bremner and Wm. Bruce sen., Skirza were farmers and spinning dealers. (No others mentioned in this parish.)

The flax was carefully pulled by hand and tied into small sheaves. After the seeds had been removed by coarse combing (some were kept for seed and the remainder made into linseed oil and used for waterproofing) the sheaves were soaked to rot the fleshy parts of the stems and free the flax fibres. The stems were beaten or passed between rollers to crush and break the woody parts and scutched to remove the straw from the linen. The flax bundles were then combed or heckled to separate and straighten the fibres and remove the tow. The long fibres were wet-spun to make fine linen and the short ones or "tow' were dry spun into coarse yarn.

Miss Jessie B. Coghill, Keiss says there used to be a lint mill beside the burn in Lyth. The remains of the lade can still easily be seen, and the actual mill itself is 400 yards or two park lengths north of the school. It is thought to have been driven on the click-mill principle. The mill itself formed the lower part of the miller's house. On more than one occasion sheaves of flax were found during peat-cutting in the Quores Hill. Alex Annal tells there were lint mills in South Ronaldsay but as far as is known there is no local tradition of a lint or flax mill along the Freswick Burn. Gibbags of heckled flax would have been distributed to the spinners thus obviating the need for a mill. The flax grown locally would likely have been scutched and heckled by hand.

Murdoch Campbell's shop was at the house on the Groats side of Priory Antiques, situated on the dry ground at Tofts. The bridgeless tracks from the Orkney ferries of Duncansby, Huna and Scarfskerry converged there before the track went through the wet marshy ground and over the ford on the Freswick Burn.

Murdoch Campbell died July 1806 and is described as "Merchant in Freswick" on his tombstone (a table stone lying just to the south of the porch window in Canisbay Church).

The inventory of the shop, shed some light on the way things were at the time. The articles valued at current prices of the period consisted of drapery, hosiery, ironmongery, earthenware, drugs and an assortment of fishing materials. The absence of groceries would indicate that the housewife, with milk and meal of her own required little else!

Prints varied from 2/- to 3/- a yard, check 1/6 per yard. Mankey 1/- per yard. Linen 3/- per yard. Red flannel 3/- per yard. Red plaids 15/- each. Coarse napkins 3/- each. Considerable stock of thread and buttons showing all garments were home made.

Earthenware and household articles included: – White plates 2d each. Blue edged ashets 6d each. White bowls 3d each. Egg cups 1d each. Cups and flatts 1d each. Bread baskets 1/- each (common table article). Metal pots 3/- each. Pewter plates 3/- each. Pewter teaspoons $1\frac{1}{2}$d each. Wool cards and weaving reeds both 3/6 each. Spectacles 3d each and cases for same 1d. Pen cases 1d. Ink holders 1d. Bibles 2/6 each and even gold edged note paper!

Black sugar (liquorice), ginger, pepper, tobacco, and snuff all priced at 3/- per lb. Included in the assortment is salts, essence of shina, flower of brimstone, molasses, indigo, logwood, British oil, madder and copperas. The quantity of the above indicates a considerable trade in home dyeing. The old "lit-pot" and navy blue scourin petticoats were then the fashion. Candlewick in quantity suggest homemade tallow candles.

Coffin handles, coffin tacks, double and single nails, screwnails, shoemakers knives, awls and files, hand lines, fish hooks, hemp and tarry ropes – even mousetraps added to the collection. His ledger accounts showed his customers included all ranks of society:– The Right Hon. the Countess of Caithness; Captain Campbell, Barrogill Castle; Captain Sutherland, Brabster; Lieut. Magnus Hogston; John Mowat, ferryman, Huna; James Dunnet, post, Duncansby; James Manson, heckler, Lyth. Several from Castletown, Thurso and Burray. The majority were accounts from the parish and the predominating names:– Laird, Mowat, Dunnet, Manson, Bain, Bremner, Kennedy and Groat.

Murdoch Campbell's grandchilden included:–

James Sinclair, Nybster who sailed to New Zealand on the Agra in 1851 and was the founder of Blenheim.

Peggy Sinclair who married (2.12.1833) Donald Mowatt, The Broo, John O'Groats.

Betsy Sinclair (Howdie) who married (28.5.1846) Magnus Houston, Miller, John O'Groats.

William Sinclair who married (15.1.1836) Ann Mackay. He was a boatbuilder in Wick and at Newton, John O'Groats before taking the farm "Soorocks" Auckengill (Alan Richard's now).

Gibbag = roll of flax for hand-spinning. "As white as a gibbag" describes head of a grey haired person.

Sources:– Notes on a Freswick Shop by John Mowat, Skirza and Glasgow. Information from Daniel Mowatt and from family records.

Anne Houston, "St Magnus", John O'Groats.

Footnote:– Sandy Bremner, Everly had a small cloth or tray cloth which was hand-woven from lint grown and spun in Freswick.

C.C

Freswick Mill
(Sea-side of Bridge)

Photo, Elizabeth Munro, Harley

James Miller
On Back-delivery

Photo, Elizabeth Munro, Harley.

Freswick Post Office 1936

James Miller

Photo, Peter Miller, Westlands.
With Elizabeth and Peter Miller

Near Maggie Mowat's Shop

SMUGGLER'S HIDE

Concealed, with great ingenuity, on the north facing wall of an outbuilding at a croft in Tofts Freswick, is a small secret cavity. Being placed in close proximity to the chimney it would be the ideal place for storing smuggled tobacco ensuring it would be kept dry and hidden from the prying eyes of the exciseman. To the casual passer-by the small stone opening would be very difficult to detect from the many other carefully dressed Caithness red-stones. The size of the cavity measuring approximately 10" x 7" x 12" suggests it was only used for the storing of tobacco and not spirits.

Laurene Miller, Westlands, Freswick.

'E WARTH HILL

'Ere are many names in Caithness 'at are worth a
word or two
Bit iss ane in particular is weel worth quite a few.
Hids mebby no a mountain bit famous chist 'e
same,
Ye pass hid goan till John O'Groats 'e Warth Hill is
'e name.

Ye dinna need yer climban gear till get ye till 'e top
An' 'eres plenty bools for sittan on if ye should
want til stop,
Bit fan at last ye reach 'e Cairn ye dinna hev a care
Ye stan' an' gie yer loungs a fill o' good clean Warth
Hill Air.

An' gaze oot ower 'e glorious view 'at stretches
miles and miles,
'Ere's Morvens lyan till 'e sooth an' north 'e Orkney
Isles,
'E crofts spread oot lek patchwork twilt, 'e peat
smoke curlin' high,
'E Red Rod twisting roond aboot an' an antran car
goan by.

'Ere's Stroma chist a loup away – a place o'
memories dear,
'E Pentland Firth wi' a hids moods, 'e Skerries lyan
near,
'E Hill o' Kirshan till 'e west and Brabster farther
ower,
'E Noss Head Licht and Freswick Bay 'e Castle an'
'e pier.

An' John O'Groats hoose by 'e shore, a spot o' world
wide fame,
It doesna matter far ye go abody kens 'at name.
There's Huna an' 'eres Mansie's Mill, his meal wis
aye 'e best,
Along the road the Auld Kirk stands, that's far wir
fore fowks rest.

There's a tracey o' peat banks wi' their tuskers
spread oot flat,
Or rued in hillags dryan off their clods an inky
black.
There are lochies glimmering in 'e sun far hill ma's
make their nest,
An' purple heather long an' thick far hairy brottags
rest.

Ye'd maybe see a dragonfly wi' irridescent wing
An' note the muiran's harsh "Go Back!" An' hear
the lairag sing.
The whirr an' flap o' schochad wings as they come
swoopan low
An' lang nebbed fawps give plaintive cries as on
their way they go.

'E cairn hidsel' is worth a look although noo gettan
worn,
'E sculptured letters showan signs o' passan years
an' storms.
Most o' the stones are scattered roond and covered
wi' the heather
Bit it used to stand oot bravely defying wind and
weather.
Till his hid wis a magic place an' lyan in wir bed,
We'd picture fairies dwellan there – 'ats fat 'e ould
fowk said.

In fact on summer mornings 'e sun high in 'e sky
Ye'll see them dancing on 'e skyline – if ye hev a
seean eye.

On Jubilee and later on on Coronation Day,
We built a muckle bonfire 'ere wi' grand firework
display,
'E lowes were seen for miles aroond, a truly
splendid sight,
An' stars an' rockets did their best till beat the
Northern Lights.

Fan wartime wis upon us 'e army climbed 'e hill,
An' armed wi' picks an' shovels they laboured wi' a
will,
They dug an' tunneled underneath their eye upon
the coast,
I wonder how the Fairies liked their Warth Hill
look out post.

An' Tinklers passing on their way here made a
camping spot.
Ye'd see their low grey tents spread oot wi' wisps o'
blue peat smoke.
One winter day a tinkler bairn made her
appearance here,
An' we christened her there an' then "Warth Hill"
an' the name stuck year by year.

Ye'll hardly see a Tinkler noo, they all hev settled
doon,
An' pit away their ring o' tin for gran' jobs in 'e
toon.
A council hoose now taks 'e place o' canvas for their
home.
Aye changes are a way o' life, bit 'e Warth Hill
stays 'e same.

So if ye're feelan jaded an' ye're tired o' city sounds
An' ye're lookan for a corner far peace and quate
abounds,
A mossy carpet neath yir feet an' air that tastes lek
wine,
Far 'e sun dips doon beyond 'e hills in a glory that's
divine.

Chist come ye hom til Caithness an' ye'll soon be
fine an' fit,
Pit a bannag in yer pockad an' yir strong shoes on
yir feet,
Tak 'e roadie through 'e heather an' keep walkan
on,
Until ye reach 'e cairn far fairies dance.
On top o' 'e Warth Hill.

(Muiran or muirhen = red grouse)
Clara Clyne, Strathesk Grove, Penicuik.

Footnote:– I would like to record the part played
in the building of bonfires on the top of the Warth
Hill by the late John Nicolson. He built the cairn
celebrating the 1897 Jubilee, with a sculptured
stone in the same. He added sculptured stones on
subsequent coronations, except the last one, when
both he and the cairn were no more. The cairn was
levelled during the second World War, machine
gun nests taking its place.
**From the Heather Blooms at John O'Groats
by John S. Banks.**

THE WARTH HILL

The modest height of the Warth Hill belies the panoramic view from the summit. On a clear day, to the south, the distinctive profiles of Scaraben, Maiden Pap and Morven can be readily identified. The western boundary of the county falls just short of the twin peaks of the Griams and runs northwards to meet the ocean just beyond Sandside Head. In the distance beyond the Griams lies Ben Klibreck, with Ben Loyal and Ben Hope further to the north. These Sutherland peaks are more than 70 miles from the Warth Hill.

The seaward horizon stretching from Dunnet Head on the north coast to Noss Head near Wick is broken by the Orkney Islands, with the bulk of Hoy sheltering the lower lands of Walls and South Ronaldsay from the Atlantic waves. In the Pentland Firth the smaller islands, of Swona and the Pentland Skerries together with the Caithness island of Stroma, channel the flow of water into very strong tide-rips which are quite obvious from the hilltop.

The placename Warth is probably derived from the Old Norse "vartha" meaning "to watch". Warth is therefore cognate with the many Ward hills on the Orkney Islands. Indeed this system of inter-visible "Watch" hills continued along the north coast of Scotland where there are a number of Bens and Cnocs called Freiceadain which in Gaelic also means "to watch or guard".

A second meaning of "vartha" is "a cairn", so it is not surprising to find a large bronze-age cairn on the top of the Warth Hill. In 1910 the cairn was described as about 57 feet in diameter with a kerb of large stones measuring two feet to four feet in length and one foot to one foot six inches high running along the south edge. About six feet in from this kerb were a number of large stones set point upwards. When excavated in 1870 a rough stone cist was found 17 feet in from the south side. It was aligned east/west and measured three feet six inches long, two feet four inches wide and one foot nine inches deep. Inside were the remains of a skeleton.

Six feet from the east end of this cist was a well-like hole about 20 inches square with dry-built sides. It went down to natural soil level but contained only black ashes.

Many years before a second cist had been exposed, three feet from the south west corner of the first one. It measured four feet six inches in length, two feet three inches in width, and one foot eight inches in depth. It also contained a skeleton. Unfortunately few traces of these features have survived to the present day.

A grassy mound 120 yards south of the excavated cairn may be the less disturbed remains of a smaller cairn.

In fact traces of human activity are scattered over the hillside, ranging in date from the cairns which are approximately 3500 years old to a number of foxholes dug during the Second World War by the army on a training exercise.

Some 20 yards west of the large cairn is the stump of a standing stone surrounded by a circular "path" two feet wide and 17 feet in diameter. No obvious use or date can be suggested for this enigmatic structure.

When the climate deteriorated towards the end of the Bronze Age, peat gradually spread up the hillside. The quarry on the lower slope provides a ready made section revealing the depth of peat, and the underlying band of grey clay on top of a very thin iron pan. This iron has leached from the base rock which is noticeably paler towards the interface.

George Watson, 14 St. Andrew's Drive, Thurso.

FRESWICK ESTATE PAPERS

The hundreds of papers kept by SINCLAIR OF FRESWICK were deposited in the Scottish Record Office in Edinburgh. The catalogue of nearly 170 pages has the reference GC (Gifts and Deposits) 136. Some examples are:

701	1813 June 28	Copy of minute of Commissioners for Highland roads and bridges concerning the road from Wick to Huna.
253	1817 July 7	Decreet of division of the island of Stroma between Sinclair of Mey and Sinclair of Freswick.
1298	1816 February 26	Circular to the proprietors and farmers in Caithness from Sir John Sinclair promoting a new system for the cultivation of flax.
932	1829 February 29!	Advertisement for estimates for building a bridge over the burn of Freswick with specifications and sketches.
740	1830 January 4	Advertisement for contractors to build bridges on road from Keiss to Huna.
941	1831 January 14	Letter to Wm. Sinclair of Freswick from tenants in Freswick expressing their concern at receiving a summons of removing, after they had started to build houses on the new lots at Skirza and Skirzahead
957	1835 April 14	Account due by William Sinclair of Freswick to John Stephen and Fraser McBeath in Wick for building an inn at Nybster
987	1846 November 2	Petition to William Sinclair of Freswick on behalf of tenants of Nybster and Auckengill for a harbour at Somerbank to enable them to prosecute the herring fishing.
994	1847 April to July 2	Letter engaging George Mowat to superintend the work of clearing out Summerfield (or Nybster) Harbour.

Douglas Cameron, 125 Rose Street, Dunfermline.

JOHN O'GROATS

John O'Groats School (Peedie Room) c.1898

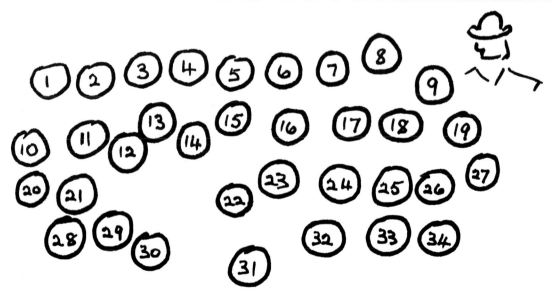

Photo, Magnus Houston, The Mill House, John O'Groats.

Teacher Mr Alexander Duff. Pupil teacher Miss Lizzie Begg. Back Row, Left to Right:– 1, Lizzie Ann Steven, Snowflake; 2, Vina Houston, Mill House; 3, Vinie Mowat, Viewfirth; 4, Clara Houston, Mill House; 5, ? ; 6, Jimmy Sutherland, Newton; 7, Willie Sutherland, Newton; 8, John S. Banks, Broo; 9, Peter Duff ; 10, Alex Bain, The Ha; 11, Donald Smith, Breck; 12 Lizzie Begg, Biel Road; 13, Jimmy Dunnett, East End, 14, Mrs Duff (Annie MacKenzie, John O'Groats Hotel); 15, John Bain, The Ha; 16, Magnus Houston, Mill House; 17, Hugh Manson, Post Office; 18, Robert Begg, Beil Road; 19, Malcolm Houston, Mill House; 20, ? ; 21, Annie Gunn, Midtown; 22, Ella Duff, School House; 23, Jessie Bella Laird, Quarryside; 24, Jessie Maggie Laird, East End; 25, Maggie Mowatt, Broo; 26, Jemima Horne, Lower Stemster; 27, Sinkie Steven, Snowflake; 28, James Banks, Broo; 29, John Matheson, East End; 30, Willie McKay, 31, William Manson, Post Office; 32, Vinie Sutherland, Newton; 33, Lizzie Green, Breck; 34, William Mowatt, The Broo.

John O'Groats School 1922/23 (The Woodwork Class)

Standing Left to Right:– Jimmy Dunnett, Hillhead; George Steven, Rose Cottage; Alex Mowat, Roadside; George Green, Beil; Mr Arthur Brown, Teacher; William Mowat, Linnequoy; David Gunn, West End. Seated on Lower Left:– Richard MacKenzie, East End; Sinclair Dunnett, Westend.

John O'Groats School 1924

Photos from Laurence Brown, North House, John O'Groats.

Teacher:– Arthur Brown. Back Row:– Willie Mowatt, Broo; Nellie Bartlett, East End; Jean Gulloch, Newton; Emma Gillanders, Hotel Croft; Agnes Wood, Lighthouse; Cathie Smith, Breck; William Gulloch, Newton; Sinclair Bremner, Nessdale; Sinclair Dunnett, West End; Betty Laird Midtown; Ella Steven, Seaview; Margaret Gillanders, Hotel Croft; Lildy Gunn, West End; Arthur Rosie, Burnside. Third Row:– Barrie Cormack, Huna; Tina Steven, The Ha; Chrissie Dunnett, Hillhead; Donnie Laird, Midtown; Richard MacKenzie, East End; Lily Gillanders, Hotel Croft; Lizzie Bonnell, Lower Stemster; Alex Mowat, Roadside; Alex Bremner, Nessdale; Sinclair Williamson, Broo; Davie Steven, Rose Cottage; Lizzie Cormack, Huna; Lizzie Dunnet, West End; Edith MacDonald, Stemster.

Second Row:– Mary Steven, Fernhill; Alice Wood, Lighthouse; Lottie Dunnett, Hillhead; Beatrice Brown, Schoolhouse; Jessie Gunn, West End; Lena Steven, Seaview; Cathie Bonnell, Lower Stemster; Clara Cormack, Huna; Vinie Cormack, Huna; Margaret Steven, Fernhill; Mary Banks, Broo; Annie Green, Roadside; Winnie Steven, Seaview; Cathy Gunn, West End. Front Row:– Doddie Gunn, West End; Alex Gunn, West End; Willie Rosie, Burnside; James Mowatt, Broo; Alex Bonnell, Lower Stemster; Jackie Steven, The Ha; Sandy Green, Biel; Davie Banks, Broo; James Steven, The Ha; George Steven, Seaview.

John O'Groats School 1931

Photo, Mrs A.B. Henderson, 24 Robertson Square, Wick.

Teachers:–Mr Alex B. Henderson, Keiss; Miss Lily Alice Mowat, Pie Shop, Keiss. Back Row:– Sandy Dunnet, West End; David Dunnett, Hillhead; Danny Gulloch, Newton; Johnnie Laird, Midtown; Willie Mowatt, Broo; George Steven, Seaview; John MacDonald, Lighthouse; Will Rosie, Burnside; Ben Green, Roadside. Second Back Row:– Ethel Reid, Lighthouse; Betty Gulloch, Stemster; Bella Green, Biel; Mabel Cormack, Huna; Lottie Dunnett, Hillhead; Mary Steven, Fernhill; Annie Green, Roadside; Joey Dunnet, West End; Chrissie Green, Roadside.

Third Row:– Margaret Laird, Midtown; Barbara Sutherland, Last House; Ivy Rosie, Burnside; Nan Dunnet, West End; Millie Steven, Seaview; Cathie Gunn, West End; Joey Green Roadside; Beth Shearer, Quarryside; Minnie Gunn, West End; Mary Manson, Post Office; Chrissie MacLean, Lighthouse. Front Row:– George MacDonald, Lighthouse; John Sinclair, Pentland View; John Mowatt, Broo; Magsie Houston, The Ha; Willie Laird, Midtown; George Manson, Post Office; Ally Sinclair, Pentland View; Sandy Manson, Post Office; Willie Gulloch, Stemster; Jim Gulloch, Newton; Jim Rosie, Burnside.   – **Names, David Dunnet, Hillhead, John O'Groats.**

John O'Groats School

Photo, Laurence Brown.

JOHN O'GROATS

John O'Groats School 1938-39

Photo, Elsie Cowe, The Ha, John O'Groats.

Back Row, Left to Right:– Jim Rosie, Burnside; Frank Sutherland, Last House; Magnus Houston, The Ha; James Shearer, Quarryside. Third Row:– George Green, Breck; Bessie Manson, Post Office; Sheila Dundas, Fernhill; Isobel Manson, Post Office; Nana Sinclair, Pentland View; Ella Laird, Midtown; Ismay Firth, Lighthouse; Elsie Houston, The Ha; Sandy Cormack, Huna. Second Row:– Marie Sinclair, Pentland View; Tina Green, Breck; Clara Firth, Lighthouse; Betty Green, Biel; Greta Smith, Lighthouse; Flora Green, Biel; Ethel Laird, East End. Front Row:– Jim Bremner, Biel; Clarence Sinclair, Pentland View; Kenneth Dundas, Fernhill; Norman Smith, Lighthouse; Billy Bremner, Biel; John Green, Breck.

PLAYTIME IN THE BOYS' PLAYGROUND AT JOHN O'GROATS PUBLIC SCHOOL

A Game Called Dumps

George Green, now of Halkirk, and I were talking the other day about a game we used to play at school. It was an all boy's game. In fact it was played against the wall that divided the boy's playground from that of the girls but that was the only connection the game had with the girls. In those far back days every boy wore a "bonnad" which was sometimes a gey tattered headgear but it was always worn out of doors and this particular game depended entirely on it. It was played mostly in the mornings before the bell rang but sometimes it was the main boys' game in the "little playtime". Somebody would shout: "Come on and hev Dumps"! At that call sign all the boys would pull off their "bonnads" and run to lay them at the foot of the wallie between the playgrounds. They were laid out very carefully just as a bird would make a nest – rounded and smoothed just as a bird would do. They had to be laid fairly close till each ither but not too close so that everybody would instantly recognise his own bonnad. Once that had been done the boys would stand on the imaginary line

within reasonable throwing distance. There was always a hand ball about and somebody would be chosen to start the game and throw the first ball. He would stand on the imaginary line and slowly and carefully take aim at whatever bonnad he chose. Then he flung the ball. If he failed to put the ball into any bonnad that was a point against him and he had to have another go. Now what happened if he managed to "bed the ball"? The owner of the bonnad "bedded" ran forward, grabbed the ball while all the other players ran like mad for the opposite wallie – that is the dyke beside the Breck road. The chap with the ball flung it into the running mob. If he hit someone that boy became the next thrower and the one who managed to hit the running target scored a point. But if he failed to score he lost a point and had to start from scratch again. The points scored led to many arguments and I never fully understood how it worked. Nor did anybody else I believe. Nor did I ever find out why the game was called "Dumps" – probably because all the bonnads were dumped on the ground.

Sandy Green, Roadside, Gills.

139

LEST WE FORGET

John O'Groats School 1955-56

Photo, Margaret Steven, Oldhall, Watten.

Teachers:– Ben Green, Beth Shearer (Mrs A. Banks). Back Row:– Carol Dunnett, The Breck; Pearl Tait, Freswick; Donald MacPhee, Freswick; Donald Bremner, Everly; Bill Mowat, Roadside; Grant Bremner, Everly; Ian Steven, Caberfeidh; Hamish Steven, Caberfeidh; George Green, Freswick; Moira Dunnett, The Breck; Elizabeth Sutherland, Freswick. Middle Row:– Billy Dunnett, Heatherbell Cottages; John Banks, Broo; Sandra Kennedy, Freswick; Elna Rosie, Hillside; Catherine Harper, Lighthouse; Lesley Harper, Lighthouse; Minnie Banks, Broo; Ina Dunnet, West End; Alistair Mowat, Roadside; George Florence, Seaview. Front Row:– John Mowat, Roadside; Babs Mowat, Nessdale; Elizabeth Bremner, Tofts; Maureen Banks, Broo; Jennifer Steven, Fernhill; Elizabeth Green, Freswick; Christine Green, Freswick; Ian Randall, The Ha.

OH TO SEE ONCE AGAIN

There's a dear, old homely countryside
On Caithness northern shore
It's John O'Groats, famed far and wide
Where I'd live for everymore:
To see the stacks of Duncansby
Like sentinels in the sea
And the bonnie shining pearly sands
Where I ever long to be.

The Pentland's many fickle moods
Aye vivid in my dreams
In storm, the "Bores" in fury break
Their white crests hissing gleam:
But, on a calm and summer night
Lap softly o'er the sand
I still can hear their lullaby
Though far on foreign strand.

To see a view as bonnie as
The distant Orkney Isles
With Stroma in the foreground
You would travel many miles:

Although that well loved countryside
Is now far far away
It's ever in my foremost thoughts
My thoughts are there today.

Come quickly here, the transport,
And take me once more there
To that dear old-world corner
With its bracing northern air
Though I've roamed the whole world over
There's nought like it to me
Oh, John O'Groats! that well-loved spot
Washed by the Pentland's Sea.

I will ever sing thy praises
Will pay homage to thy charms
And ne'er forget the happy days
I've spent within your arms
I live in hope to come again
And should that be my lot
To once more grasp your welcome hand
O well-loved cradling spot.

From "Gleanings" by John Ross, Albyn, Gills.

Footnote:– The above poem was originally by Bill Mowat, John O'Groats and then was altered slightly, and lengthened for him, by his grand-father John Ross.

John O'Groats School 1974

(Just before the school closed for good)

Photo, Bet Brown, North House, John O'Groats.

Teachers:– Mrs Winnie Graham, Mrs Bet Brown. Back Row:– Gordon Mackay, Heatherbell Cottages; Hugh Manson, Post Office; Peter Harrold, Freswick; Isobel Angus, Bayview, Freswick; Mrs W. Graham, Schoolhouse; Lorna Manson, Post Office; Sandra MacKenzie, Sunray; Ursilla Brown, North House; Isobel Mary Leitch, Rowena; Margaret Gulloch, Freswick; Alan Cormack, Midtown; Andrew Cowe, The Ha; Kevin Green, Heatherbell Cottages; James Davidson, Elmes; Kevin MacGregor, Newton; Mrs B. Brown, North House; James Rosie, Freswick; Neil Morris, Lighthouse; Stefan Rochan, Seaview Hotel; Brian Cormack, Midtown; William Davidson, Elmes.

Front Row:– Karen MacGregor, Newton; Angela Cormack, Midtown; Yvonne Cormack, Midtown; Janice Rosie, Freswick; Wendy Cormack, Huna; Irene MacGregor, Newton; Mary Ritchie, Huna Post Office; Liz Sinclair, Ha Cottage; Jennifer Cormack, Midtown; Laura Steven, St Rowan; Janet Houston, Mill House; Susan Manson, Post Office; Pauline Wares, Tofts, Freswick; Eleanor Ritchie, Huna Post Office; Clair Davidson Elmes; George Simpson, Freswick; Calum MacLean, Freswick; Eric Green, Heatherbell Cottages; William MacLean, Freswick; Don Mowat, Victoria House.
(Absent:– John and Shona Turnbull, Lighthouse.)

Counting Out

Eerie oarie ower the dam
Fill oor pocks and let us gang
White fish, black troot
Eerie Oarie you are oot.

Katie Bremner and schoolmates recited this rhyme in the Groats School c.1920.

Pupils held their clenched fists in front of them for this one

One a tattie, two a tattie, three a tattie, four
Five a tattie, six a tattie, seven a tattie more.
(Pupils out on "fours" and "more")
Alex Dunnet, West End.

Bouncing Ball Rhyme

One, two, three, a-leerie
Four, five, six, a -leerie
Seven, eight, nine a-leerie
Ten-a-leerie – postman.

Janet Gunn, Mey

Skipping Rhyme

I am a Girl Guide dressed in blue
These are the actions I can do
Stand at ease, bend your knees,
Salute to the King, bow to the Queen
Turn your back on the sailor boys,
1-2-3-a peppery.

Nancy Mackenzie, Heatherbell Cottages.

TOURISM

Tourism is today one of the bedrocks of the economy of North-East Caithness.

Yet it has the right to be considered alongside fishing, agriculture and craft-type manufacturing as one of the truly traditional industries of the area.

Mankind has, of course, made journeys since the very dawn of his time on Earth, but in the context of the North of Scotland, recreational travel – as opposed to trips involving trade, settlement movement and military campaigns – can properly be dated back to around the middle of the 18th century.

These early travellers to the Far North undertook what would be described as "expeditions" today – the first road linking Caithness to the rest of the Highlands was not built until 1803.

Many of the early travellers kept diaries, often for publication, and by the 1760s there were clearly enough of them for at least one local family to have realised that there was an economic value in "groatie buckies" at John O'Groats. Bishop Forbes in 1761 writes that he and his party had unsuccessfully searched for our prized cowries on the beach, but as he was leaving on horseback he was approached by a young lad who gave him a few. He records the boy's surprise on being handed a sixpence – probably worth at least £10.00 in today's money. The boy's mother and an older brother, who probably lived in the settlement at "Henderson's Brae", (a couple of hundred yards inland from the site of Jan de Groot's House) then came on the scene with a stockingful – and the woman had a measuring "cog" for 2,000 shells, for which she charged one shilling. The making of groatie buckie strings – necklaces made from the shells – has a local history going back at least a century earlier and, incidentally, is the oldest known craft in Scotland, dating back to Mesolithic times, with the "original" pierced 6,000-year-old-shells from an archaeological dig on Oronsay Island, in the Inner Hebrides, being on display at Edinburgh's Queen Street and Glasgow's Hunterian museums.

When Sir Walter Scott looked towards John O'Groats from the deck of a lighthouse tender in 1818 doing a tour of Orkney and Shetland, he recorded a large building as being prominent there. He was, of course referring to the Girnals, now the building operated by the John O'Groats Knitwear Company, but then considerably higher when it had its role as storage depot for loads of bere and oats collected in lieu of rent by the local estate, and held there before being transported by small boats to Staxigoe, from where it was exported to Scandinavia. That the Groats family existed there can be no doubt, nor that they held the ferry concession (a Crown privilege) for c.300 years. The romantic story of the "eight-sided house" was first recorded by Rev Dr John Morrison of Canisbay c.1790, and he claimed his sources went back to the mid-17th century – and one of our most famous ministers would not be fibbing, would he?

Scotland's national bard, Robert Burns, talked about from "Johnny Groats House to Maiden Kirk" (Kirkmaiden in Galloway) as being from one end of Scotland to the other, and the desire to visit Lands End and John O'Groats as representing the extremities of the United Kingdom, certainly dates back to the mid 19th century.

Elihu Buritt, an American, became the first man to walk the route in 1865, and within 20 years "End to End" cycling records were being recognised, with the first motor car arriving at John O'Groats in 1896.

But far more important was the arrival of the railway in Wick in 1873. It is really from that date that we can date modern tourism, although it was confined to "the gentry" – a term which undoubtedly included the "nouveaux-riches" of Victorian times.

From day one, the Highland Railway relied substantially on tourism – and like lines in other parts of the country, actively promoted recreational travel – and as shooting lodges, grouse-moors and deer-forests spread throughout the Highlands, the railway made an excursion to John O'Groats possible. It was to cater for precisely this trade that the John O'Groats Hotel was built in 1875, and its popularity got an immediate boost from a visit in 1876 from no less than Queen Victoria's oldest son, the Prince of Wales (later King Edward VII). And he was on hand to officially open the "Royal" Bridge at the Mill, which carried the first-ever road into John O'Groats, a public-sector necessity if the new hotel was to prosper. (Today the bridge retains the same design, but was doubled in width in 1939 as part of the A836 reconstruction under the Crofters' Counties scheme.) The route to the "End of the Road" was of course via the Hilly Kirsan, Maggies Corner, Canisbay and Huna, whose inn was also rebuilt at the same time. It had been the earlier road terminus, and the place where the earlier travellers stayed. The "Red Road" over the Warth Hill, with its deep peat-bogs, had to wait another 20 years, before it was built.

The tradition of young boys selling postcards and groatie buckies to tourists was well established long before the end of the century, and it was in 1902 that the "Old Grocer", George Manson, changed the name of the Post Office and postal district from Duncansby to John O'Groats – a move of considerable positive significance for the area. It was he, too, who introduced the first "imported" souvenirs – made at the Goss family's china pottery in Staffordshire. The number of motorists visiting rose steadily up to 1914, but these were hand-built vehicles outside the pockets of working-class people, and indeed in that age when servants were cheap, were often chauffeur-driven. Mass tourism – if that is the right word – got underway in the inter-war era. Assembly-line cars such as

Morrises, Fords and Austins, while still outside the price-range of most locals, were being bought by skilled tradesmen, although motor-cycle combinations were a commoner mode of transport for tourists from the mill-towns. Bus operators Smiths[1] of Wigan, started the first "charabanc" tours (as coach trips were then known) in the early 1920s, taking Lancashire mill workers to the Far North – and they were quickly followed by Autey's of Bury taking their "Wakes-Week" trippers North, while Alexander's of Falkirk, Lawson's of Kilsyth and Edinburgh's SMT were all taking "Fair" holidaymakers from Central Scotland to John O'Groats by the 1930s. Cycling holidays were immensely popular during the years of the depression, and a group of unemployed Manchester lads made three trips North in one single year.

The local reaction was the opening of the tea-rooms by Mrs Camilla Steven (at the Seaview Hotel site) and Banks and MacRae's business selling knitwear etc., while "Sanny" Williamson sold tourists his "curios and antiques" at his camping site at Roadside. Then, too, the groatie-buckie sellers were active in their greatest numbers, the best of them mirroring fashion trends by making necklaces using small china and "bugle" beads in many colours interspersed in patterns between the shells.

It was at this time, too, the John O'Groats House Hotel was significantly extended – although the architectural standard using non-traditional materials may have left something to be desired – and it was graded as Three-Star by both the AA and the RAC, with the Royal Scottish AC also giving it plaudits and for six years using it as the UK start-off point for the Monte Carlo Rally, an event which oozed class, brought January business (a large team of journalists covered the event) and unbuyable publicity to the area.

In the post war era, tourism continued to increase. Two coach companies – Glenton of London and Southdown of Brighton – started bringing overseas visitors in numbers. These were mainly from the "White Commonwealth" and the United States. Coaches bringing tourists from Europe, made their appearance in the late 1950s – while rear-engined Renault cars, often with the Paris 75 number-plates and later the ubiquitous VW Beetles, started arriving at John O'Groats as the German economy started its booming period.

The main local response was the opening of a number of "Souvenir shops" – the Last House (as a business) and the "First and Last" (in its original form) date from this time, but at least four others are no longer in business. Coronation Year in 1953 brought a special boom – groatie beaded strings in red, white and blue were made by the hundreds (and probably low thousands) by the groatie buckie sellers that year and sold at three and six per necklace.

The 50s – before the era of Mediterranean holidays in the sun – also saw a significant increase in accommodation locally with the building of the Seaview Hotel and the expansion of the Caber Feidh guest house in what was once known as Rose Cottage.

By the end of 1960s even young locals were flying to "Costa" holidays, and the competition for the traditional working-class trade from the North of England and Central Scotland was becoming fierce. The biggest investment in the 1970s in John O'Groats was by the public sector, with the building of the harbour and a subsequent deepening scheme being most significant and enabling the traditional Jan de Groot route to Orkney from the old Ferry Haven to re-open. This was a factor in saving the tourist trade from serious decline – coupled with the vast increase in Europeans visiting the North and added to Brits who were now having second or third holidays each year, which meant a significant increase in the length of the season.

By the 1980s it was apparent that the retail sector, which had moved up-market, and had replaced imported goods with UK products (and often those made in the Highlands under the stimulus of the Highlands Development Board) was employing several hundred people elsewhere in the country, and a policy of trying to substitute some of those goods by those manufactured on the spot was instituted under the Highland Regional Council's Local Plan Consultations, which drew virtually everyone in the local tourist trade to a meeting in Canisbay Hall, where a framework for developing John O'Groats was agreed.

This resulted in the Highland Development Board and the Regional Council investing around £1 million in workshop units, which are already proving their worth by providing year-round employment. The policy agreed involved essentially attracting more visitors to John O'Groats and keeping them there longer – and official figures on length of stay (for non-ferry visitors) clearly show that much has been achieved.

John O'Groats is fortunate in having a substantial number of natural assets. These include a superb landscape of the Orkney Islands on the Northern horizon; the only Shell Beach on the Eastern side of the UK, which has the country's greatest number of separate shell species; the international-standard cliff, geo, sea-stack and cave scenery at Duncansby Head which houses the finest accessible sea-bird colony on the UK mainland, as well as the fine curving beach at Sannick. It has also some fine man-made attractions – the only square-towered lighthouse in Scotland and the unique Meal Mill coupled with the oldest military bridge in the Highlands.

---

[1] Their direct descendant company Smith's, Shearing's Happiways, still sell John O'Groats tours – the firm is now part of the giant Rank Organisation.

Bill Mowat, Roadside, John O'Groats.

THE HUNA INN AND JOHN O'GROATS HOUSE HOTEL IN THE 19TH CENTURY

Both the Huna Inn and John O'Groats House Hotel played a significant part in the life of the local community in the 19th century. Some evidence of this is still there, to be found today, in the pages of a substantial brown leather bound volume filled with entries in faded ink which served as the hotel register in Huna[1] from 1840 until 1876. It was also used from 1876 until 1880 in the John O'Groats Hotel, and this would have been along with the very fine leather bound visitors book presented by the proprietrix Mrs Thomson Sinclair of Freswick when the new hotel was opened by H.R.H. Albert Edward, Prince of Wales.

The faded entries tell us the names of the guests, sometimes their status, the purpose of their visit and their nationality. There are entries for visitors from America, Italy, Japan, China, Belgium, France, Switzerland, Ireland, India, Argentina, Germany, Norway, Holland, Persia and New Zealand. There are also descriptions of various functions held at the hotels and attended by the local community.

From the 1871 census returns we know that Huna Inn had four rooms with windows, which gives some indication of the accommodation in the inn at that time.

Many of the entries refer to the excellent fare provided by Mrs Manson who was responsible for the hotel until 1867 and by Mr and Mrs Mackenzie who leased it, with the farm, until they moved to the John O'Groats House Hotel in 1876.

There are longer entries which are of great historical interest in themselves.

We learn, for example, from this entry written in copperplate and dated March, 1856, of the extended role fulfilled by the Minister in the local community. It also provides us with a glimpse of contemporary sporting activity.

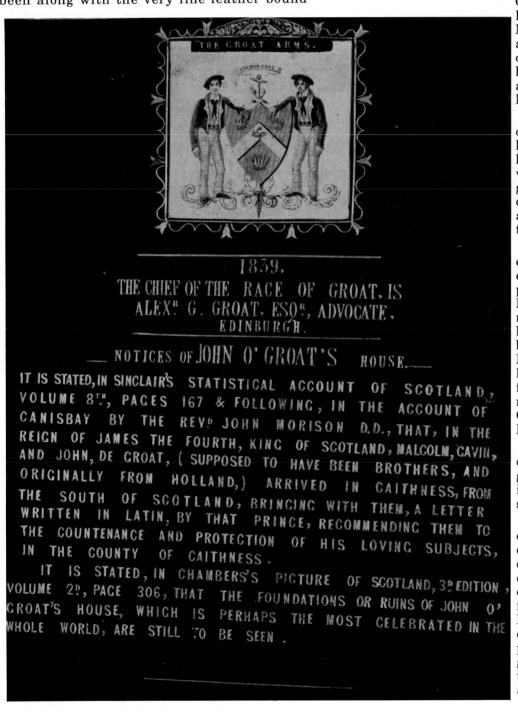

Front Page of Huna Inn Album

John O'Groats Dispensary

"The far flung John O'Groats House has been long styled the Lands End; the Parish of Canisbay on which it is situated being the most northerly Parish in Scotland. Being equi-distant from the Burgh of Wick and the Town of Thurso to the extent of 17 miles. It may easily be supposed that a good many years ago the poor but honest and industrious population of the district suffered many hardships and privations which their more favoured neighbours knew little about. No doubt they then had the parochial minister and schoolmaster among them but with these exceptions and the kind and benevolent Laird of Brabster they had no-one living amongst them to whom they could look for advice and assistance. With regard to the minister, from the time of the incumbency of the reverend John Morison D.D. who was an excellent classical scholar, an eloquent and accomplished preacher and clearly beloved by the whole of the parishioners down to the present time, this parish has been highly favoured so far as regards their spiritual preachers but for many years these gentlemen had not only to administer to them in spiritual things but also to their bodily ailments. It will be born in mind that there were no regular roads for communication with the towns in those days but tracks through a wild and barren moor; and there being no medical officer nearer than Wick or Thurso, before their assistance could be brought to bear upon any sufferer in this distant locality often, and to the regret of sorrowing relatives, they came too late. The parson, therefore, in the first place was invariably consulted for all manner of diseases and adminstered such simple restoratives as he thought necessary.

Thus matters continued until between 20 or 30 years ago when Dr Sinclair[2] came to practice in Wick, and the state of the roads and communication with this long neglected Parish forced itself upon the notice not only of the Proprietors of Land therein, but of others also interested in the improvement of the soil and the welfare of the inhabitants. It fell to the lot of Dr Sinclair to be very generally called to prescribe for the inhabitants of this district, and ultimately a mutual attachment sprang up between them. He saw that from their remoteness from either of the towns, their quiet and unobtrusive habits as well as their honesty of disposition and general good character, that they had before then suffered much and were sadly neglected, while they saw in him a young man, easy of access, kind and warmhearted, ever ready and willing to sympathize with them in their troubles and at all times most anxious to strain every nerve to alleviate their sufferings. In the course of time this bond of union between them was destined to be more closely connected and it was agreed that Dr Sinclair should devote one day of the week to administer to their wants and necessities, and by the kindness and courtesy of the Reverend Alexander Whyte, present incumbent of the Parish and of his predecessors in office a room was set aside at the manse for the purpose of affording accommodation for the doctor and such of his patients as could visit him there. Those not being able to do so he visited at their places of abode.

We live in a time when the schoolmaster is abroad (ie. the importance of education is becoming widely recognised) and thanks to the indefatigable exertions of Mr Calder the worthy parochial teacher of the district, traces of its being so are now to be found in all parts of the parish. The inhabitants, thankful and grateful as they are and will continue to be to the ministers of the Parish for the handsome manner in which they gratuitously gave up one of the rooms in the manse for their benefit – sometime ago resolved to erect a dispensary for their own accommodations and having applied to the late Right Honorable Alexander Earl of Caithness and his amiable and talented son Lord Berriedale, they at once in the most handsome manner not only gave a convenient and well adapted site but handsomely subscribed to the fund for its erection. The dispensary was accordingly built and finished and Monday, the third day of March, 1856, was fixed for opening it up to the public.

It was opened in a solemn and appropriate manner and a number of Dr Sinclair's friends were present on the occasion from many parts of the county. After the doctor had attended to the wants and wishes of his patients, the day was spent in a very happy manner, some of the party betaking themselves to the gathering of John O'Groats buckies; others to view and admire the grandeur of the cliffs of Duncansbay with its magnificent stacks while others enjoyed themselves with the sports of the field – coursing – when the greyhounds in a very short space of time ran down fine hares.

The parties afterwards assembled in the larger room of the dispensary and partook of an excellent dinner with the etceteras which had been brought from Wick and Thurso for the purpose. The party then joined in dancing and spent a most happy evening which was interspersed with vocal as well as instrumental music and at an early time separated with united wishes that all should soon meet again."

☆★☆★☆★☆

Many of the contributions in the album are written in verse. It opens with the following verses signed "Naval Surgery Service, 19th October, 1840."

Good reader beware! 'ere you take pen in hand
To add to this volume's mixed store;
That your offering be sense or at once take your
    stand
With the fools who have written before.
One thing is made clear in this album's quaint
    page
(And the fact I've no doubt you'll admit)
Tho' the journey to Huna may benefit age
The air is most fatal to wit.

There are innumerable odes to John O'Groats in the album which seems to have provided an inexhaustable source of inspiration. There are a striking number of entries in the album which refer to shipwrecks in the treacherous waters of the Pentland Firth, entries by government wreck officials as well as records written by survivors.

DAVID GRANT'S HANDWRITING

First page of a 20 page entry of ballads, all written in the same hand.

These Huna Inn Album Poems by David Grant were later included in "Yarns of the Pentland Firth" published by Peter Reid, John O'Groat Journal Office, 1933.

The Dominie's Yarn, or A Harbour of Refuge at Wick

This moving appeal with a political ring is dated, 11th August, 1858.

Those who have seen the Bay of Wick in a gale from the German Ocean can alone realise the dangers to which the fisherman who trawls from that port is exposed in the prosecution of his perilous calling. I have had frequent opportunities of observing to what fury the waters of the bay are lashed and with what force the billows are hurled against the Caithness shores from Noss Head to the End during such storms. In particular, I was at Wick during the gales of September 1857. I stood at the height of Pulteneytown when the lifeboat put out to the assistance of the Dutch galleon. I saw the boat dancing over the surging waters, light as a seabird, till she had shot ahead of the galleon and turned to run alongside, and received the ropes from the men on the bows of the belabouring craft. I shut my eyes for a moment when that wild cry burst from the shore and that wave greater, swifter and more sharply crested than all the others came careering on, broke upon the galleon and submerged the lifeboat and its gallant crew. When I looked again, what a change. The dripping mariners clung to their plunging vessel. The lifeboat crew were helpless, the boat torn from their grasp floating beyond their reach. Two of the brave fellows themselves struggled with the waves beneath which one of them was doomed to sink. The boat drifted in at the mercy of the surge against which she would sometimes stand up and do battle like a desperate living thing. That sight has often recurred to me with terrible vividness. Often since that night have I thought of our unsheltered coast and of how small a portion of our nation's 60 odd millions of national revenue would suffice to give us a harbour of refuge. Often have I looked to the more favoured south with its broad rivers and deep ravines bridged over, it's great valleys filled up, its mountains cut through or bored under, its very cities and towns riddled beneath with the iron routes of commerce and thought how comparatively easy it would be to enclose the Bay of Wick so as to make it a complete shelter for the Northern fisheries and trade.

An Appeal for the Northern Fishermen

Were I a man of consequence
In a place of high command
I would cry unto our gracious Queen
That rules our native land.

I would reason with the minister
That guides the helm of state
And wrestle with the parliament
When it sits in grave debate.

I would tell of thrice 500 boats
On a tempest-ridden sea
With never a creek on all the coast
Where a dozen dare to flee.

A coast from which the mountain waves
Are hurled in sheets of foam
Where the fishers find the fiercest surge
On the threshold of his home.

I would point to mothers, husbandless,
And children sparely fed
To hoary age and helpless youth
Sustained on parish bread.

To those whose brave supporters 'scaped
In distant ocean's roar
And perished at the feet of friends
Along the Caithness shores.

I would say to those in places of power
By whom the laws are made
To free the fishers from needless risk
When out on their perilous trade.

To free his wife from anxious nights
And her morning of painful doubt
And the nervous fears that chill her blood
When the winds are loud without.

What matter to her that Britain boasts
The mastery of the waves
When the Northern fishermen year by year
Are swept to watery graves.

When oft as the thundering surge is heard
And the angry tempests rise
They find themselves and their helpless boats
At the mercy of seas and skies.

What matter to her that our navy rides
Unmatched by a foreign foe
When she and hers must shiver in dread
As oft as the breezes blow.

When danger looms on their weather bow
And certain death on the lee
When all save the westerly breezes sweep
The face of the German sea.

We spend our gold and poured our blood
For the unbelieving Turk
Can nought be done for brothers at home
Have we nought for Christian work?

We armed our fleet to scour the seas
And battle for negro rights
Is there none to look to the Northern shores
And plead for defence for the whites.

It is not squadrons of armed ships
Maintained at a vast expense
It's only a wall against the waves
We ask for the fisher's defence.

A haven to which he can run in a gale
Is all the protection we seek
A fourth of a million of paltry pounds
To spend on the Bay of Wick.

David Grant, Canisbay, 1858.

Many of the entries record the disappointment of visitors at the absence of any sign of an original John O'Groat's House.

James Heyworth, August 1848

"I came here expecting to see the last remains of John O'Groat's House, perhaps half a wall but time has not permitted it to be so for naught now remains but a mound of soil".

Entry dated 1854. . . Visited John O'Groat's House this morning saw nothing remaining of the house nor any mark whereby a visitor might find out the place where it once stood.

16th September 1859

"The fog remains, the man is gone
His building has not left one stone
Or vestige on the barren shore
In vain the mystery we explore
'Tis but a name and nothing more."

September 1875

O backwards backwards may we again wander
To this noble Northern land
May we feel the breezes blowing
Fresh along the mountain side
May we see the purple heather
Let us hear the thundering tide
Be it hoarse as Corryvreckan
Spouting when the storm is high
Oh! Let us see dear John O'Groats
Once again before we die.

25th November, 1871 Warrington

Copy of a letter from John Taylor junior written after a journey from Lands End, John O'Groats, to Lands End in Cornwall.

Dear Mr and Mrs Mackenzie, According to promise I write these few lines to you to inform you that we reached Lands End in Cornwall last Saturday evening, November 18th. Since we left your house on Monday, September 18th to the time we reached Lands End we were never in any kind of conveyance and never crossed a single ferry. The total distance we walked is 1360 miles and it took nine weeks to walk it. Please make a memorandum of this near our entry in your album. . . With kind regards. . . believe me to be yours very truly.

1881 Marked Peoria. U.S.A. Sinclair John O'Groats House

What's in a name? Tis everything
To this small mound of earth
Leading the feet of men to tread
The sands of Pentland Firth.

Only a name! and legend quaint
Of a father who could ill
Abide the quarrels of his sons
And so to keep them still

He built a house with eight fair fronts
Where, when their meals were spread
Each of the eight proud sons might feel
That he sat at the head.

A peaceful man was John O'Groat
Me thinks it was his wife
That left the temper to the sons
And John was tired of strife.

He little thought his house of peace
Would give him world-wide fame
And that the shells upon the shore
Should bear his humble name

Some say they are the tears he shed
When all was broil and strife
Now they are pure and pearly gems
Fit emblems of John's life.

What though the traveller find no house?
He is considered lucky
If, after searching well the sands
He finds a "Groatie Buckie".

24th February, 1876

Doctor Alec Mitchell was presented with a handsome dogcart and harness in recognition of his valuable services as doctor of the parish; present the undersigned representing the numerous subscribers towards the testimonial, Captain Keith occupied the chair.

Peter Keith, Barrogill Castle; Reverend James MacPherson, Minister of the Parish; David Meiklejohn, Secretary of the manse; John Mann, schoolmaster, John O'Groats; George Reid, Farmer, Brabster; David Patterson, Farmer, East Mey; James Robertson, Duncansby; Hugh Mackenzie, Huna Inn; Thomas Robertson, Duncansbay; William Leith, Canisbay; Andrew Simpson, Mey; Molvendy, Montevideo, guest of Dr Mitchell.

JOHN O'GROATS HOUSE HOTEL

February, 1876

A new John O'Groats House was nearing completion as various entries in the Huna Inn Album record.

5th April, 1876

"Hotel about to be opened. The visiting party unanimously decided that the smoke room was without doubt the best room in the hotel, a circumstance which they considered very unfair to the ladies and decidedly selfish on the parts of those lords of creation who designed the establishment. They have much pleasure in recommending the Inn kept by Mr and Mrs

Mackenzie for any parties visiting John O'Groats."

22nd April, 1876

"Hope that the hotel may act as the nucleus of what may ultimately be a favourite resort of those seeking something new in the form of a watering place and summer residence."

A prophetic statement as we know that the Duc de Guise took over the hotel for his family and staff for an extended period one summer (four to six weeks). Legend in the Mackenzie family has it that "the antics of the foreigners were viewed with great curiosity by the locals. . ."

H.R.H. ALBERT EDWARD, PRINCE OF WALES FORMALLY OPENED THE JOHN O'GROATS HOUSE HOTEL 6th OCTOBER, 1876

Marie Caithness 1876

14th Earl's Coat of Arms

This photo is from a large framed photo of a painting by V. Lawlor with the 14th Earl's coat of arms underneath.

John O'Groats Hotel 1888
(before the porch was added)

Left to right: Betsy Dunnet (house keeper, later Mrs Magnus Houston), Robertina, Annie and Mrs Mackenzie, James Ross (coachman, butler, etc., from 'Sunray' or Bartletts) Joanna Mackenzie. Hugh Mackenzie at the Horse's Head.

gentlemen for the 20-year-old "Old Pulteney".

The Hotel, leased from William Sinclair Thompson Sinclair, Laird of Freswick, soon established an international reputation for itself under the management of Hugh and Elizabeth Mackenzie. He a master carpenter and farmer, originally from Tongue and she from Castletown. Married in Edinburgh, they were to establish a reputation for the hotel which is referred to in the following terms in newspaper clippings.

May 1890; Mr and Mrs Mackenzie's names have become household words in the country and the fame of John O'Groats House has spread from San Francisco to Japan ". . . an old fashioned house at the shore where great comfort, great convenience and a good deal of ready assistance were always to be had by those who frequented the house either on business or pleasure."

An undated clipping records the visit of Andrew Carnegie and party to the hotel (which they reached by horse from Thurso): "They all sat down to a capital luncheon prepared in Mrs Mackenzie's best style. The salmon was excellent, the roast mutton (from sheep reared on the farm) was so good that they all took a second helping. The fowls of course were tender and tasty and other accompaniments in the form of puddings and salads left nothing to be desired."

Another clipping, undated and published in connection with the publicity for the Thurso–Gills Bay railway extension refers to the hotel in the following terms: "John O'Groats . . . an especially excellent and commodious hotel, the landlady of which is said to be one of the most interesting personages in the county and the best informed on local traditions and history."

The hotel had a well stocked wine cellar and Mrs Mackenzie supervised all the cooking (done on peat burning ranges) and the daughters worked alongside the maids in this family business.

We know that Princess Alexandra, Earl and Countess of Caithness, Duke and Duchess of Sutherland, Lady Fanny, Lord Berriedale, Duke of Pomar, Rev. J. MacPherson and Rev. R. MacGregor were present. The album tells that the entertainment was provided by Forest Knowles and that his concert company sang a medley of national songs specially arranged for the occasion. The octagonal table was polished to perfection and our family treasure, the fine china teaset used by the Princess and ladies, but it is not sure which crystal glasses were used by the Prince and

The Mackenzie Family, Tain.

Elizabeth and Hugh Mackenzie and Family 1897

Left to right: Annie (Mrs Alex' Duff), Robertina (Mrs Alex' Cormack, Wick), Albert Edward John Hugh (b.20.1.1877) married Isabella Davidson and Joanna (Mrs James Ross).

Edward Mackenzie on the pony's back with brother William at its head. Note the fine dressed red sandstone from Gulloch's Quarry at the Warth Hill. (Mr William Munro, Thurso had the contract for building the hotel.)

[1] John O'Groat Journal, 18th October, 1839 – Establishment of daily mail gig, Wick to Huna.

Notice to Travellers
Public Conveyance from Wick to John O'Groats House

A mail diligence carrying three passengers, starts from Leith's Caledonian Hotel, Wick every day at 6.00 p.m. for Huna and leaves Huna every day betwixt 12 noon and 2.00 p.m. A mail boat from Orkney crosses everyday, weather permitting. Passengers and parcels (at moderate fares) booked at Leith's Hotel and Post Office Huna.

[2] This was Eric Sutherland Sinclair – See "Times Gone By" Vol 1. page 14, 26th December, 1927.

Prince of Wales visit to Wick, John O'Groats and Barrogill

Detailed account in John O'Groat Journal, 12th October, 1876.

". . . the royal train of five carriages swept onwards at the rate of eight miles per hour . . . At Keiss the fresh horses are straining upon the start and yeho they are off again. Hugh Falconer had the honour of driving the royal carriage from Keiss to John O'Groats. . . . At Nybster, John Nicolson had the jaw bones of a whale formed in an arch over the road with a freestone lion and flower vase at each base. Flags flying at every house (route was through Freswick, over Hill of Kirsan, down through Canisbay, past Quoys to Huna and John O'Groats) . . . carpeting of John O'Groats shells and buckies spread on the road and new bridge at Duncansby Mill . . . tasteful, elaborate, effective decorations at John O'Groats House Hotel – masts, oars, flag staffs, wreathed with greenery and flying flags, bunting, banners. . . . four to five hundred of a welcome party . . . refreshments all round at expense of Wm. Sinclair Thomson Sinclair. . . . A bit of an accident happened at the starting from the Inn, which to many was a lucky and welcome stoppage. The horses in the Prince's carriage stood back and shyed when near the floral arch. Immediately two or three brawny fellows rushed down from the slopes on each side of the avenue where the crowds were collected, and seizing the carriage by the wheels, very soon landed the whole hypothec on the other side, amid enthusiastic cheering and waving of hats and handkerchiefs.

The Prince seemed to enjoy the thing immensely. He smiled, took off his bonnet, thanked the people, and being right again, they sped away, waving a graceful and pleasant adieu to the honest men and bonnie lassies of John O'Groats. . . . Barrogill Castle . . . Royal Standard hoisted . . . A guard of honour of the Mey Artillery Volunteers under command of Captain Keith and Lieut. Mitchell at the front of the castle. Royal salute given, the band played the National Anthem. . . . Welcome to Barrogill . . . guests . . . luncheon . . . Prince and Princess planted two trees in front of castle . . . Royal Party left at 4.30 amid the cheers of spectators . . ."

Courtesy of John O'Groat Journal.

Footnote: The Lord Lyon King of Arms, Sir Malcolm Innes of Edingight, KVCO (grandson of the 18th Earl of Caithness) made a search in the Public Register of All Arms and Bearings in Scotland (founded 1672) and found no person of the surname Groat had recorded Armorial Bearings therein and found no reference to this name in earlier Armorials.

A.H.

Footnote: My grandfather Donald Mowatt and my granny Margaret Smith married, 3rd March, 1880. Theirs was the first wedding in the John O'Groats Hotel. Prior to this it was usual for couples to have the marriage and reception in the bride's home.

Jane Mowatt, The Broo, John O'Groats.

John O'Groats Hotel c.1895

Photo, John Muir, Silverknowes Brae, Edinburgh.

Left of Photo: The Store (later the mill stable). The Old Mill (later the threshing mill). The Ha Barn (site of present mill). Nurse Cook's Cottage and steading. Large well built peat stack belongs to the Last House.

RAINY RATTLESTANES – THE STORY OF JOHN O'GROATS

In the bonny North of Scotland in the days of long ago.
Beside the mirky Pentland Firth where stormy waters flow
There lived a man who ferried folk to Orkney in his boat
And now he's known to all the world, by the name of John de Groat.

   Rainy, rainy rattlestanes, dinna rain on me,
   Rain on John O'Groats house, far across the sea.

Now Johnny was a Dutchman, and a young and roving lad
He came and asked King James the fourth if he could buy some land
"I want to run a ferry boat from Caithness to Orkney,
And if you'll let me have the land I'll start it right away."

King James the fourth consented, and so Johnny sailed away,
Up the coast of Scotland round the head at Duncansby
He settled there beside the sea, and far as I can tell
A flagpole stands upon the spot where Johnnie chose to dwell.

Across the stormy Pentland Firth he ran his ferry boat
In summer and in winter time he kept his ship afloat,

He prospered very quickly and his wife had seven sons
Who later ran the ferry that old Johnnie had begun.
At the yearly celebrations of the landing in Caithness
The seven sons all quarrelled as to which of them was best
So John de Groat commanded them "Go off back home again
And when you come back next year, it'll all be settled then."
So Johnnie went and built a house, with eight sides round about
And on each side there was a door, each son went in and out
Inside there was a table which also had eight sides
And that is how old John O'Groats is known the world wide.

Bill Steven, 7 Athol Drive, Giffnock, Glasgow.

P.S. From Elsie

In the bonnie North of Scotland there is still a ferry boat
On the Pentland Venture you may go across from John O'Groats
It's run by Ian Thomas and a crew that's hard to beat
So John de Groat's old ferry boat is now brought up to date.

John O'Groats c.1900

Photo, courtesy of Wick Society.
Hugh MacKenzie, Hotel-keeper, welcomes Hubert Egerton, motoring pioneer, on a converted bicycle driven by a petrol engine. Left to Right:– John Green, Biel (grandfather of Johnnie, Havengore); Frank Sutherland, Last House; John Steven, shoemaker, Rose Cottage; Hugh and Willie Manson, Post Office, William Steven, Seaview.

Wheelbarrow Versus Motor Car c.1900

Photo, courtesy of Wick Society.
Sanny Mowat in the barrow (great grandfather of Bill and Walter). Hubert Egerton in a Werner of the type before 1901.

Richard MacKenzie at the Helm of the "Amy" c.1948

Photo, David Sinclair, 9 Maurice Place, Edinburgh.

The dining room was added c.1932. Mr Murray had a small lounge added 1928. Donald M. MacKenzie put the big lounge on in 1939. The new bedrooms and bar were added to south side of hotel 1938/39.

The Silvery Sands c.1925

Photo, Sutherland Manson, Bower Court, Thurso.

Shows pier built 1897 or 98 by congested District Board Act.

John O'Groats House Hotel *Early Photo of Hotel c.1877*

Photo, Don Wares, Seater

Card sent to Mr John Robertson, Salmon Fisher, Achastle, Lybster, 1904.
Message – How are ye John? You may expect a call Wednesday if its a fine day — wife and other arrangements permitting.
Maggie R.

Mail Bus at Hotel c.1879

Photo, Hamish Donn, Lower Warse.

JOHN O'GROATS HOUSE HOTEL

John O'Groats Hotel c.1925

Corridor leading to bedrooms. Door on right opens into drawing room.

Drawing Room (upstairs – room in tower.)

Smoking Room (downstairs – room in tower)

Pictures from Hannie Green's collection.

A lot of people have visited John O'Groats House Hotel. Since it was built in 1875, people from all over the world from the man-in-the-street to the rich and famous, have made the long journey to one of the world's best known hotels. Fortunately their visits here did not all go unrecorded. At the hotel to this day, are kept the Visitor's Books which record who came here and when, dating back to 1876, the year the hotel opened for business.

The more modest of the well-known personalities of the day simply signed their names, enjoyed their stay and left. Those of a more flamboyant persuasion who never could abide anonymity, ensured that their passing through this hotel was recorded for posterity with not only a signature but with poems, drawings and a full account of what they saw and did whilst here.

The books have, in the past, also been used as a political springboard. On 17th September, 1910 the principal suffragette, Emily Pankhurst, travelled from London and left her "calling card" in the book of that time in the form of a poem to further her worthy cause. It reads:–

*A young man from far
John O'Groats
Wore a top hat and 17
coats.
And explained he had
sworn
That such clothes should
be worn
Till the day when all
women have VOTES!!!*

Truly a great find amongst the thousands of signatures contained in 24 books.

The original books are large, expensively bound in tooled brown leather decorated with gold lettering and trim. In later years some were bound in suede and leather. However the increase in the cost of such luxurious binding in later years reduced the size and quality of the books to little more than exercise books – indeed some probably were.

One of the most famous and regal personages to grace the hotel and sign his name in the book, in 1876, was his Royal Highness the Prince of Wales, later to become King Edward VII. It was he who opened the hotel and during his stay he also planted two trees in front of the Castle of Mey and opened the new road bridge which replaced the ford at Houston's Mill to the west of the hotel on what is now the A836. Regrettably, vandalism, or probably souvenir hunters existed then as now, and the page in the register containing his signature was removed.

In the main, the books contain page after page of unrecognisable names. Some were never even guests. The Scottish licensing laws prior to the 1960's made bars close on a Sunday and to get an alcoholic drink on the Sabbath one had to be declared a "Bona Fide Traveller". This meant that one had to have travelled over 10 miles to qualify for this status and thus be allowed to order a drink in a hotel. This curious anachronism gave rise in the books to page after page of guests with very local surnames!

Whilst poring over these lists, occasionally a name jumps out of the pages.

"28th September 1905 – Andrew Carnegie – Skibo Castle" – together with "Louise and Margaret Carnegie."

The great man himself, whose magnificent castle on the north shore of Dornoch Firth so recently passed into the hands of a former owner of John O'Groats House Hotel, the renowned world-class yachtsman and entrepreneur, Peter de Savary.

A hotel overlooking such a volatile stretch of water such as the Pentland Firth, becomes, occasionally, involved in the business of the seamen who pass by. Some less than fortunate individuals did not pass by, but became victims, or survivors of the shipwrecks which lie in their hundreds at the bottom of the Pentland Firth. The 12 knot ebb and flow of the tides here, combined with the most ferocious of storms, have led to the death of many a good or unwary sailor. One such captain, Hans A. Nielson of the Norwegian barque "Branda of Christiana" was stranded on Dunnet beach, 12 miles west of John O'Groats, on 31st March 1878. The fate of the barque from Mandal in southern Norway is not recorded as the entry is brief but all hands were saved and the Lord was praised – in Norwegian – in the books of the John O'Groats House Hotel.

A jump forward in time of 15 years and this entry appears:

"From a Ships Reck crew – which was rescued by the Huna Lifeboat – having three hours in the rigging and then four hours in the lifeboat – being received by the manager of the John O'Groats House Hotel and made comfortable. With many thanks by all the crew."

The crew signed their names after this entry together with their station aboard the vessel. A cross reference puts this crew as being possibly from the Grimsby trawler "Sylanion" and the entry says she was later refloated by a salvage vessel. The captain's name does not appear among the signatures.

In the early days of the hotel it was visited by many a noble family and the road to the hotel would have been lined with expensive Rolls Royces and Bentleys. A wooden house, known as the bungalow, was built to accommodate the guests' servants and chauffeurs and the hotel boasted it's own generator to supply electrical power. The black shed that used to house this generator still stands but now serves as a store room.

The Earl of Caithness's signature appears in the book as a result of his yacht, "Francesca", being moored nearby. Throughout the books are sprinkled the signatures of Lords, Ladies, Knights and noblemen from Britain and abroad together with their families and friends.

The two world wars coloured the book with the ranked names of servicemen from all three British services and others from Commonwealth countries when they were based nearby. During the 1939-45 conflict, the three airfields of Wick, Skitten and Castletown must have given a lot of custom to the hotel as would the enormous naval presence in Orkney's Scapa Flow – a scant 10 miles across the water.

One mysterious serviceman's entry was made by a Lieutenant Johnston, Royal Navy, who gave his address in the book as "H.M.S. Ark Royal – Sunk!". The date of this entry is in 1940, yet the aircraft carrier Ark Royal was not torpedoed and sunk until 13th November, 1941. Research reveals that, as Ark Royal was such a prestigious target, the Germans claimed, through "Lord Haw-Haw" on radio broadcasts, to have sunk the carrier many times. Thus the entry in the 1940 book was a light-hearted reference to this propaganda. In point of fact, one particular German pilot returned to his squadron claiming to have definitely sunk Ark Royal with his bombs. He became a national hero overnight and this happy state of affairs lasted until it was revealed that he had subsequently been invited to dine aboard Ark Royal by the ship's officers some weeks later!

As progress through the books is made to the present day, the entries become less and less eloquent. Degenerating into a strictly functional role of recording name, address, nationality and car registration number. This is a sad decline and, regretfully, an indication of how modern technological entertainment seems to have robbed us of the need and ability to record and discuss the experiences in our lives, such as a holiday at John O'Groats.

If we took the trouble to write in books, such as these, our thoughts and feelings, then they would remain a poignant record for ever.

Brian L. Johnstone,
Manager, John O'Groats House Hotel.

First Charabanc at John O'Groats Hotel c.1920

Photo, Ivy Sinclair, late of Ormlie Hall, Thurso.
In front, Jack, Jim and Ada Laird with Ivy Sinclair (Grandchildren of Mrs Calder who had the hotel)

THE GOLF COURSE

George T. MacKenzie (Teacher in John O'Groats) was instrumental in preparing the nine-hole John O'Groats Golf Course. He is also credited with "resuscitating" the golf club according to the minutes. The course was opened in September, 1902 by Master Mervyn Sinclair, son of the Freswick laird, Captain Sinclair. 50 golfers from around the county gathered for the opening of the course which stretched for 2815 yards, almost from the door of the hotel along the links and the course was rated as a par 40.

Bailie Rae of Wick referred to the hotel visitors book when he told that a party of experienced golfers from London, Edinburgh and Glasgow had been the first to introduce the game of golf to the shores of the Pentland Firth in 1887. "These gentlemen gave their united testimony to the superiority of the course at John O'Groats to those of St Andrews and Musselburgh."

Courtesy, John O'Groat Journal Files.

Overheard – At John O'Groats pier during the Glasgow Fair, as an elderly visitor stared out to sea. Summoning his consort from the treasures of Walter's Stall, he pointed excitedly at a white buoy floating in the wave-chop some 30-yards out. "Aw c'mere hen. C'mere and see iss. Erra berr ower err – erra polar berr!"

Keith Muir, Newton, John O'Groats.

LEISURE HOURS OF BYGONE DAYS

I do not intend to start to portray what people did for leisure or pleasure at the turn of the century and onto the outbreak of the First World War, but there was one pursuit that I have been asked to mention and that is the famous "Riddlag". I have mentioned previously how the big herring fishing boats were hauled onto the beach every Autumn, by Allan's steam engine. As space was at a premium, these big herring boats were berthed on the beach at the harbour, as close to one another as possible. The distance between them would be a matter of a few feet but room enough for the young folk to fix up swings between the boats. Ropes were attached from the gunnels of the boats at midships, and as these boats stood a good many feet from the

ground, then the swings were quite lengthy and therefore swinging was long and strong and not for the faint-hearted. This was a great source of entertainment and socialising for the teenagers, and not only was the "Riddlag" patronised in the evening twilight but on into the night when moonlight was available.

The "Riddlag" became the accepted meeting place for the youth of the district and many a romance began as the result of sessions on the "Riddlag". Accidents, too, mostly of a minor nature occurred at the "Riddlag", but I must assure you that the "Riddlag" was held in high esteem and much spoken of by generations of our forefathers and foremothers, at and after the turn of the century.

Ben Green, Roadside, John O'Groats.

Overheard – David Gunn, a John O'Groats fisherman, was accosted on the pier by a tourist, who pointed to Stroma and asked "Is that Skye over there?" "Naw," replied David, pointing upwards, "That's it up there!"

A tourist, watching the Pentalina ferry from Orkney arriving at John O'Groats pier, turned to David Gunn and asked him if the St Ola would be able to come in to John O'Groats. "Oh yes certainly," replied David. "Mind, she'd never go out

again, but she'd come in no bother at all!"

Keith Muir, Newton, John O'Groats.

Petty Officer David Gunn R.N.R., H.M.S. "Prince Leopold" awarded D.S.M. with oak leaf bar in November, 1944, for gallantry, skill, determination and undaunted devotion to duty during the landing of Allied forces on the coast of Normandy. He was coxwain of a landing craft.

From Caithness and the War, by N. M. Glass.

Groatie Sellers

Groatie Chains

Photo, Joey Bremner, St Clair, John O'Groats.
Back Row:– David Steven, Caberfeidh; Alex Bremner, Nessdale; James
Mowatt, Broo; Malcolm Green, Roadside; Donald Laird, Midtown. Front
Row:– Alex Gunn, West End; George Gunn, West End; Willie Mowatt, Broo.

Photo, George Steven, Seaview,
John O'Groats.

"FAN I WIS CHIST A LOON"

Hed disna seem at long ago, fan ah wis chist a
loon,
Fan lof wis fower pence hae'penny, an' a shirt wis
half-a-croon
We gethered Groaties – in a cham char, aal along 'e
shore
An' wi' a darner in a cork 'e holies we wid bore.

Wi' bonny beidies an' some threid, 'e necklaces we
strang
Single eens, an' double eens, an' some wi' pendants
hang
There wis no televeeshan then till glower at half 'e
nicht,
'Ee chest pumped up 'e tilley lamp till gie ye plenty
licht.

'Ee keept them in a boxie efter Players or Gold
Flake,
An' thocht aboot 'e money at yer Groatie strings
wid make
Fan 'ee selt them till 'e tourists 'at came by
charabang
For fan we were chist boyags 'e tourist trade began.

Weel, 'e summer finally came' roond, yer boxie in
yer han',
'Ee took off on yer owld bike, fan 'ee saw 'e
charabang.
'E ither loons were 'ere as weel, so ye'd till be gey
bowld
An' confront 'e tourist wifies, till get yer stringies
sowld.

They didna understand weer townge, ciz they were
fae 'e sooth,
An' we aye thocht they spoke wi' marbles in their
mooth!

Boot we saide we made them aal wursels, an' let
them take their pick,
Two shillings for a double, an' a single, one an' six.

'E time 'ee always selt 'e most, wis' 'e fine an' sunny
days,
Fan 'e tourists viewed 'e islands, an stravaiged
eboot 'e braes.
Boot 'at wis aye 'e days at hid wis fit for colan' hey-
Or thinan' neeps, or kertan' peits – for at 'ee got no
pay.

Or yer faither wid be flightan' fan 'ee took off doon
'e rod,
For a charabang wis coman', an 'ee howped till
make a bob.
Boot he'd want 'ee till doze 'e lambs 'at day, as sure
as fate –
'Ee'd do hid aal fan 'ee came hom', boot och, he
widna wait.

Weel as ah say iss wis 'e start o' aal 'e tourist trade.
Boot we saw' 'e writing on' e wa' fan a new law wis
made.
Without a hacker's licence hid wis made very plain
That boyags sellan' Groatie strings we'd never see
again.

So – we coled 'e hey, an' thinned 'e neeps, an' dozed
'e lambs as weel,
Kerted 'e peits, an' beilt 'e stack, an' geid back till
'e school.
Boot ah'll aye mind 'e Groatie strings, fan ah wis
chist a loon,
Fan lof wis fower pence hae'penny, an' a shirt wis
half a croon.

Elsie Cowe, The Ha, John O'Groats.

The Proposed Harbour at John O'Groats

JOHN O'GROAT'S HOUSE.

SWAIN'S "NATURE".

THE

Proposed Harbour

AT

JOHN O'GROAT'S.

T HE population of the Parish of Canisbay, within the districts of Duncansbay and John O'Groat's, are almost entirely composed of crofters and fishermen. Unable, as many of them are, to subsist on the products of their land, they are largely dependent for support on the harvest of the sea.

The fishing grounds in the vicinity are excellent, and the fish are unequalled for superiority of quality by those caught anywhere along the coast of Great Britain. The only hindrance to the extension of the trade of the district and to the development of its fishing industry is the want of harbour facilities. Some years ago, with the

help of the late proprietor—Mr Thomson-Sinclair—and their own labour, the inhabitants erected a small landing pier. This pier proved a great convenience in calm weather, but it is totally inadequate for the requirements and the aspirations of the community.

Some time ago a Committee was formed with a view of promoting a scheme of Harbour extension. Plans prepared by Mr J. J. Cronin, C.E., Wick, were submitted to the County Council of Caithness, and were approved of by them. They have also received the sanction and approval of the Board of Trade. The proposed Works are estimated to cost £650. To meet this expense a grant of £450 has been obtained under the Highlands and Islands Act, and contributions amounting to £100 have been subscribed for locally and in the county. There is still a balance wanted of £100. This sum must be got before the grant will be available or the undertaking can be gone on with.

In these circumstances, the Committee are reluctantly compelled to appeal for help to natives outside the county, and also to the generosity of friends at a distance.

We may add that the Pier when completed will not only be an acquisition to the people of this locality, but will be a benefit to the people of Stroma, and, it is hoped, will prove a refuge to passing craft in stormy weather.

The proposed Pier will be within a stone's throw of the site where John O'Groat erected his historic house. It is probable that the "goe" which will form part of the basin of the harbour was used by him when he launched his boat out into the deep.

Any contribution which you may be good enough to send will be thankfully received and duly acknowledged by,

HUGH MACKENZIE, C.C.,
Chairman of Committee,
JOHN O'GROAT'S ;

or,

A. DUFF,
Secretary of Committee,
SCHOOL HOUSE, JOHN O'GROAT'S.

THE PIER JOHN O'GROATS

The "Rosebud" (WK 446) c.1950

JOHN O'GROATS JETTY

Copyright : J. Adams

Photo, Emma Sinclair, 3 Cluny Gardens, Edinburgh.

The "Rosebud" was built in Flotta in 1906. She was bought from a Keiss man in 1912 by Sanny Mowat (great grandfather of Bill and Walter) and is still going strong.

The "Garrivale" in the Firth. Herring Nets on Pier c.1930.

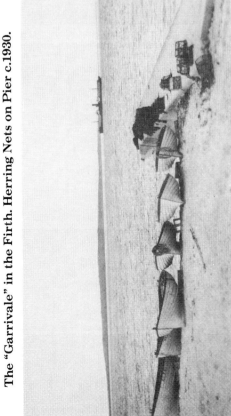

Photo, Alice Steven, Corner House, John O'Groats.

Sinclair Steven was well acquaint with the captain of this tramp steamer and he stopped every time he passed for Sinclair to give him lobsters, crabs or even cuddings. The "Garrivale" was intended for the Suez Canal and was built with the decks narrower than the main hull to cut down on canal dues.
Dodie Gunn, the Bungalow, John O'Groats.

The "Pentalina" Arriving At The Pier On A Fine Summer Evening 1974

Photos, Magnus Houston, Mill House.

The "Pentalina" an ex air-sea rescue craft ran as a ferry between John O'Groats and Orkney in '72, '73, '74. She was skippered and owned by Captain Bill Banks, St Margaret's Hope. Alfie Tait on the bow. Alex Mowat on pontoon. The pontoon was constructed from the jib of a crane and attached to a large tank which rose and fell with the tide.

159

Prize Catches at Groats
"Trink" to East of Present Harbour c.1880

Photo, Moira Bremner, Victoria Villa, Canisbay.
Left to Right:– Sinclair Dunnet, Grandfather of Alex Dunnet, West End. Donald Mowat – Grandfather of Donald Mowat, Victoria House. John Laird – Brother-in-law of Camel Laird, Last House. All viewing a bull seal.

'E Day's Catch c.1880

Photo, Billy Steven, "St Rowans", John O'Groats.
Left to Right:– Unknown; James Laird; Willie and Frank Sutherland, Last House, viewing handline caught cod from the "Soon". The cobbled section jetty would have been the first man-made landing area at John O'Groats and no doubt was used when crofters carried the grain down on their backs from the "store" for shipment.

John O'Groats C.1880

Photo, Sandy Manson, John O'Groats Post Office.

There are five ferthies berthed. The "Britannia" – Jeck Houston, East End. "The Isabella" Greens, Roadside and Biel.
"The Isabella Elizabeth" – James Laird, Quarry Side and Tommy Dunnet, Auckengill. Note, too, that the beach and
seaweed is almost up to the Last House. It was said that once the house was surrounded by water at a very high tide.
The ground has been built up over the years. An upturned salmon coble can also be seen.

SALMON FISHING AT JOHN O'GROATS

The Salmon followed the line of the coast and there was quite an industry at Harrow, Gills and Freswick which all had salmon bothies.

Salmon fishing was also carried on from John O'Groats. Iron rings fastened securely to a rock, show where they used to anchor the nets. It is worth looking for these rusting rings at Hang, and then just east of the Last House, about the Crook of the Niss, the Back of the Niss, and at the Rock because the rings are likely still there. It's some time since I walked along "the Coastline from the Burnmouth to the Niss" but I certainly saw them in these places. If I remember rightly, the salmon nets used to be kept upstairs at the east end of "The Store". There were other nets, oars and masts also stored there.

As far as I know, the ice-house at John O'Groats was used by salmon fishers first and in later years by the hotel. Ice was collected off the mill dam and carted there.

Alexander S. Manson, John O'Groats Post Office.

OVERHEARD – Robbie Cowe was smoking his pipe on the braehead at John O'Groats, watching Jimmy Simpson loading his large Hereford bull into the "Boy James" to take him in to Stroma. The bull was in a cattle crush, dangling in mid-air, hanging from the old crane at the end of the West pier, when a tourist coach disgorged a chuckle of old wifies from Yorkshire about him. "Eeh ba goom," squawked one such, "What are they doin to that poor cow?" Robbie, ever ready with the bon mot, replied "I think if you look closely madam, you'll see that poor cow is a bull. And can't you tell from the smile on his face, he's going on his holidays to the island." "Ooh, whatever is he to be doing going over there?" asked another blue-rinse, "Weel, I reckon pretty much the same as you do on your holidays!" was Robbie's reply.

Keith Muir, Newton, John O'Groats

In September, 1980, **Keith Muir** became the first person to swim across the inner sound of the Pentland Firth. Guided across the tides by Jimmy Simpson, the Laird of Stroma, Keith left Stroma just west of the beacon, and arrived in John O'Groats harbour just 65 minutes later. The event was sponsored to raise funds for the hospital appeal.

A.H.

John O'Groats Harbour 1990

Photo, Brian Johnstone, Manager, John O'Groats House Hotel.
The harbour reels under the onslaught of the worst gale in living memory in September 1990 when four boats were lost here and 22 sunk in harbours between here and Thurso.

John O'Groats From The Air In 1991

Photo, Brian Johnstone, Manager, John O'Groats House Hotel.
The harbour, hotel, shops and crafts units lie at the end of the A9 to the left.

John O'Groats From The Air c.1930

Photo, Sinclair Houston, Barga, Thurso.
A bit of the "Ha Green" can be seen below the brae at the top left of this photo.

The pier – the top end was built on pillars and paid for by the Lighthouse Co., and the pier was sloped, to ease the rolling up of barrels of oil and stores. Boats were hauled up and berthed at each side of the pier.

The Lighthouse Store – white building in foreground. The building to the north of the lighthouse store was a corrugated iron garage which Mr Murray had built when he was in the hotel. This would be about the time that cars were becoming popular with the hotel guests. The store is clearly seen and the Hotel croft to the west.

The sailhouse can be seen and the green infront of the hotel which was used for the spreading of nets.
Alexander S. Manson, John O'Groats Post Office.

HOME

There's a corner in the Northland,
In old Caithness that I love,
And it's bordered by the moor and by the sea,
I know it's wild and windswept,
With no sheltering hills around,
But there's not a place on earth so dear to me.

Oh I love the stormy Pentland,
With its mighty whirling tides,
And I love the white shell beach and rocky shore,
I love the purple heather,
The peat banks and the bogs,
Round the windswept Caithness home that I adore.

Have you walked along the coastline
From the Ness to Skirza Head?
Have you seen the mighty cliffs and geos galore?
Have you seen the stacks of Duncansby
Stand boldly in the sea?
Like sentries keeping watch upon our shore.

Oh I love the mighty towering cliffs.
Where seabirds make their home.

On the binks and in the crevices they boast.
I love the thundering winding geos,
Where seal and otter roam,
Round that wild and rugged rockbound Caithness
    coast.

Have you wandered on the sandy beach
From the Burnmouth to the Niss?
Have you stood where John O'Groats House used
    to stand?
Have you seen the panorama of the Orkneys and
    the Firth
With Stroma and the Skerries near at hand?

Oh I love my northern birthplace,
By the stormy Pentland Firth,
And although out in the world I have to roam,
My heart is aye is Caithness,
With the people that I love,
In the corner that to me is always home.
    Hugh Manson, The Grocer, John O'Groats.
(He wrote this when in Medicine Hat or Winnipeg c.1912)

Spritsail Rigged Stroma Yole

Lugsail Rigged Stroma Yole

Pencil drawings by Derry Ross, White Broo, Canisbay.

Spritsail and Lugsale Yoles

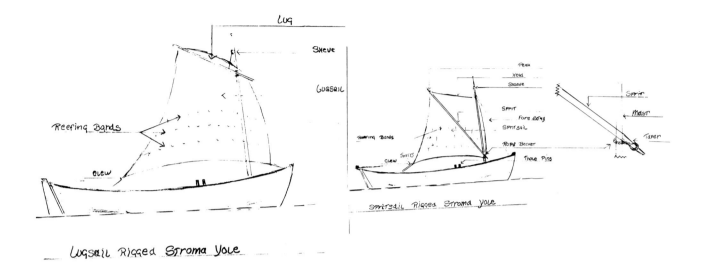

Lugsail Rigged Stroma Yole

DAYS OF SAIL

The Stroma and Orkney yawls used a similar rig for sailing and there were two distinct types of sails used on the yawls. Firstly, and the more popular type, was the sproot sail, almost always used on the smaller yawls. This was a quadrilateral of canvas edged with rope, and was stretched to catch the breeze by a long rounded stick or sproot. Regular handlers of the yawls seemed to prefer this rig, as it appeared to be more responsive to the helm – and remembering that sailing on this coast often involved tides and ever-changing winds then hence the reason for the sproot.

To illustrate my point I should tell of old Sandy Mowat our neighbour at Roadside who entered his boat for a regatta in Reiss Bay. His own sproot sails being a little the worse for wear, were exchanged for the day with sails from Green-the-Breck's boat which had recently been built by John Banks, the carpenter at the Back Road. Old Sandy set off with two crewmen for Reiss Bay and returned with the trophy. His success was largely put down to the sproot sails, for the majority of the competing yawls used the lug sail, which I'll come to shortly. Sandy, when coming up to the marker, was able to get his crewmen to slip the sproot from the sail with the end falling into the water rounding the buoy on a tanner (sixpence) and then heading along the next leg in great style with the sproots on the fore and main sails being hastily replaced.

The sproot stretched from a rope becket near the foot of the mast to the high corner of the quadrilateral as shown in Derry's illustration.

The other type of sail, usually used on the larger yawls, was the lug sail. This sail had a wooden boom along the top and was hauled up for spreading on a block and tackle along the mast. It should be noted that when turning, this sail had to be lowered to the deck which was a longer process than that with the sproot. Hence the reason for the quick turn by the sproot idea.

The boat belonging to Sandy Gunn called the "Hope" sported a lug sail which was rather novel compared to the sproot or sprite sails used at John O'Groats. This boat, later bought by Willie Mowatt of Old Schoolhouse, St Margaret's Hope, remains in the man's possession.

Ben Green, Roadside, John O'Groats.

The "Hope" on a day trip from South Ronaldsay

Photo, William S. Mowatt.
Left to right: Steven Manson, John Rosie, James Omand, George Rosie, Brian Thompson, Mrs Anne Omand, Mrs Betty Rosie, John Brown. William S. Mowatt at the helm.

165

**Camel Laird née Shearer on her
100th birthday 1924**

*Photo, Barbara Steven, Seaview, John O'Groats.
One of the first sewing machines in
John O'Groats.*

All pleased! c.1927

*Photo, Barbara Steven, Seaview, John
O'Groats.*
Teenie Sutherland, née Laird; Barbara Steven,
née Sutherland; Lizzie Sutherland, née Mowat.

A BUT-AN-BEN – THE LAST HOUSE

When recently carrying out renovations to the "Last House", John O'Groats, a lot of history was uncovered as regards the building itself, and some artifacts. The inside of the house was completely stripped, all ceilings, partitions, plaster, wood floors, etc., were removed. It soon became obvious that the east-end of the building had been the original but-an-ben, and that the other part had been added at a later date. The dividing wall between the two parts is two and a half feet thick (as are the outside walls). This shows that the dividing wall would have been the outside west gable. It is known that the new part was added shortly after Willie and Campbell Laird (Camel) came to the but-an-ben in 1845. The exact age of the but-an-ben is not known but could be pre-1700.

When the walls were completely stripped down to the stone, it was discovered that hardwood logs, part of ship ribs, had been used along with the stone in the building of the old part, as much as 30 per cent in the north wall (still in perfect condition). After removing some stone, a bink or binkie was found. It was a recess set into the wall four feet by two feet, about three feet from ground level. It would have been used for the storage of fresh water, milk, etc. Being in the north wall it would be the coolest part of the house. In the east gable the hole for the open fire was found; the iron ring for holding the top of the swey was still there, but the aise hole was filled up with cement. There is evidence where the old couple-legs were stuck into the wall now filled up with stone. When the wood floors were removed, the original Caithness flagstones were found to be in good order.

A very interesting artifact was found under the floor; it was a quern, a meal grinding stone in good condition. In the loft space above the ceiling, a portrait of the late Rev Roderick MacGregor was found in good condition. He was the first Free Church minister in Canisbay (1845-1890) and was Camel Laird's minister.

In 1913 the thatching was removed, and replaced with Caithness slates, which are still in first class condition today. Thatching was a skilled operation. Purlings (strips of wood) were fixed between the couples, spaced close enough to hold the divots in place. Sarking was not normally used, as it is with slates. The divots were cut in the hill with a flachter spade, with the heather retained on one side. The divots were placed on the roof in rows with an overlap. After the roof was completely covered with divots, winlins of straw were put on top, and held in place with simmons. The simmons were made of heather or straw, twisted together to make a rope. Before the simmons were put on, a row of benleens (long flat stones) were placed along the bottom edge of the roof, which the simmons were tied to. With the high Caithness winds, more fixing was necessary than in some other parts of Scotland.

With the new souvenir shop built at the back, the old house has been turned into a museum.

Except for the pointing, the walls have been left bare. The original open fire with a swey and a Victorian fireplace can be seen. The Caithness flagstone floor is in use, and the "binkie" is there. The windows, doors and the porch have been replaced, but all in the old style. The first porch was built about 1929, and became well known for its lovely display of pot plants.

A good crop of tatties at the Last House c.1880

Photo, Robert Cowe, The Ha, John O'Groats.

There are picture displays, depicting life on Stroma, "Shipwrecks of the Pentland Firth", John O'Groats of yesteryears, old farming methods, and Caithness harbours of the old days.

On the wall is a "Family Tree" of the "Last House" residents, going back to Willie Laird's mother Christian Groat, born 1797, whose father John Groat had "The Ha", and was a descendant of John de Groat. There is also a "Pen picture" of each resident who lived in the Last House since 1845. Camel Laird's telegram which she received from King George V in 1924 when she was 100 years old, and the telescope which her husband Willie Laird got from a shipping company for helping to save the lives of the crew of a ship which ran aground below the Ha braes can be seen. There is a photo of the first wireless set brought to John O'Groats by Willie Sutherland about 1922. He and his mother are also in the picture.

An interesting occurrence of the early wireless days can still be remembered by the Sutherland family. The family would be sitting round the wireless on a winter evening, when suddenly the sound would stop. Once more the young boys of the district had removed the aerial wire which came through the back window, and without the outside aerial the set was useless. This was a ploy that kept the young boys in entertainment during winter evenings.

There is a collection of artifacts depicting the way of life over the last 150 years. Most of the local people made a living from crofting and fishing and the tools, utensils, kitchen ware, etc, used can be seen.

Camel Laird in front of Boathouse c.1900

Photo, George Steven, Seaview, John O'Groats.

The Boat House

The upturned boat was in place at the "Last House" from about 1885 until 1960.

At the end of its fishing career, the boat, "The Britannia", was bought from Jeck Houston, Eastend, for £2. Camel Laird and her son-in-law Francis Sutherland had it erected upside down, on a two foot high stone foundation. It was turned into a very useful wash house, store, hen house, pig house, and toilet.

The hotel washing was carried out in this wash house for many years by the women of the family. Camel, her daughter Teenie, and later Teenie's daughter-in-law Lizzie (my mother).

The reason that it survived so long, was that it received a coat of tar yearly by my grandfather (Francis) and later by my father Frank, until the Second World War.

Frank Sutherland, Viewfirth, John O'Groats.

John O'Groats Guides and Brownies c.1946

Photo, Elsie Cowe, Ha, John O'Groats.

Left to Right:– Mrs Daisy Houston, Mr Donald M. MacKenzie, Miss Janet Leitch. Back:– Julia Laird, Jessie Dunnet, Nina Green. Front:– Minnie Banks, Shirley Green, Elna Rosie, Ruby Kennedy, Elizabeth Banks, Sandra Kennedy, Kathleen Kennedy. Alex Dunnet, West End and Spark in charge of transport.

The John O'Groats Girl-Guides Song

John O'Groats in Caithness
A long way away,
That's where we come from
There's where we stay
Very near the midnight sun
Just by the sea,
I would like you all to come
To John O'Groats with me.

A long beach of shell sand
Shines clear and white.
A heather hill behind us
Orkney just in sight.
Stroma in the tide way
The Skerries far a-lee.
I would like you all to come
To John O'Groats with me.

Mrs Daisy Miller,
Teacher, John O'Groats' School.

"Have A Go" in John O'Groats Public Hall 1948
(Wilfred Pickles Radio Programme)

Photo, John Adams.

Back Row:– Pearson Brothers; ? ; John Thompson, Lighthouse; Alistair MacKenzie, John O'Groats Hotel. Front Row:– Barnie (with the money); James Cormack, (Cuba); Magnus Houston, Mill House; ? ; Kitty Sutherland, Haster; Mabel Pickles; Jean Gill (wife of Dr Gill); Wilfred Pickles; Nurse Cook, Newton; Violet Carson (Ena Sharples) at piano.

Nurse Cook got over fifty proposals of marriage after the broadcast!

Chorus:– Come on Joe – Come on and have a go,
Its easy and it costs you nought to make yourself some dough.
So come along and join us, don't be shy and don't be slow.
Have a go Joe – Have a go.

John O'Groats Dramatic Club 1955

En route to Inverness to the Scottish Finals after winning the Caithness Cup

Photo, Courtesy of J. McDonald, 8 Shore Lane, Wick.

Left to Right:– Ella Laird, Willie Laird, Beth Shearer, Ben Green, Jim Shearer, Magnus Houston, Anne MacKenzie, Malcolm Green, Angie Banks and Jamsie Mowat (Keiss) in the bus.

THE OPEN AIR

What a tremendous change today on a Sunday afternoon at John O'Groats shore. In 1947 John Creelman and I used to go along the brae-head and call out texts to family groups on the shore. We had no musical instrument with which to regale the folks. John Creelman was the singer, and he was more strong than sweet! It lapsed for a short time when John died suddenly at Fassberry but was revived when Sandy Cormack, Slickly, and his family got a car and they as a family were there. They had music and singers and he himself was a gifted preacher. Some of the local Christians were there also and, without the aid of loudspeakers, the singing could be heard on a quiet day at Huna and the Eastend, John O'Groats.

In the days when cars were not so plentiful, three buses ran to John O'Groats from Thurso and three from Wick. When cars became common the buses discontinued their service, but the people still came. There have been some lovely Sundays when the thoroughfare has been quite congested, but the car park has relieved that. Nowadays there is usually quite a number in the ring, and with the loudspeakers (supplied by the Wick contingent, of which the Calders are the main supporting group) the group singing, duets, solos, testimonies are heard and appreciated by many people. Some visitors, not knowing the set up, have offered different sums of money to help in the work, and seem very surprised when their offer is refused. Throughout the years there have been some preachers whose names have created quite an interest and over the years the Hotel has changed hands a few times, but so far no owners have objected to the Open Air being held on their ground, for which the Open Air are grateful.

Alexander S. MacGregor, Post Office, John O'Groats.

D'YE KEN JOHNNY HOWKSTAN?

Two young men, brothers, whose surname was Horne, joined the Hudson Bay Co., and in due course proceeded to the "Nor West". Being diligent and hard working they prospered and in a few years they amassed a considerable sum of money.

Business reasons took them to Quebec and they thought it would be a good idea to try and get a letter and money sent home to their aged parents in Skirza. They went to one of the numerous wharfs where sailing ships were loading and discharging cargoes. At this particular wharf two ships were berthed. One of the vessels had just arrived from England. The other vessel was loaded up and getting ready to sail for home.

The two captains were old cronies and were walking to and fro on the wharf and as the brothers approached, were laughing at a joke that one of them was telling.

The brothers made known their errand and the captain of the homeward bound ship readily agreed to take the letter and money and do all in his power to get the same delivered. He invited them on board his ship and in the captain's cabin the brothers were hospitably entertained. "Now", said the captain, "I must tell you what we were laughing at when you first accosted us. As you come from the North of Scotland do you by any chance know Johnny Howkstan?" "Man Alive!", replied one of the brothers, "I was serving with him before I came out here, and a better master I could not wish for." The captain then told them the joke.

It appeared that on his homeward voyages when approaching the western end of the Pentland Firth, he always took a pilot from Crosskirk aboard. In the vicinity of Duncansby Head, the pilot would be transferred to a waiting yawl and landed at Huna. In the late spring when his seasonal occupation was finished, Johnny with his yawl and a crew of two hefty lads in their late teens, used to meet the homeward bound ships, and, for a small sum, take their pilots ashore. It was in that way that our captain became first acquainted with Johnny.

When the pilot was getting ready to leave the ship and board the waiting yawl, the captain gave orders that a good measure of rum should be handed down to Johnny and also one for each of the two young men who formed his crew. To the captain's amazement, Johnny first drank his own share of rum and then drank up the other two. The captain went to the ship's rail and upbraided Johnny and asked him what he meant by drinking up his crew's share of rum. "It's like this captain", explained the unabashed Johnny, "I widna lek it tae be said that I was the means of learning thae young lads to be drunkards, so just to put temptation out of their way I drank their share masel."

The captain asked the brothers if Johnny could be trusted to deliver the money and letter. "Trusted", replied one of the Hornes, "If Johnny promises to do a thing only death will stop him from carrying it out."

The money and letters were handed over to the obliging captain, and when the ship reached the eastern end of the Pentland Firth, sure enough Johnny and his yawl were there as usual. The captain handed the letter and money to Johnny and made him promise to deliver the same to the aged parents in Freswick. He also gave Johnny two bottles of rum, one for himself and the other for the aged Hornes.

As soon as the yawl reached the land, Johnny, without going home, set off across the moors to Freswick. In his own words, "Nae gress grew 'neath ma feet until I put the letter and money in the hands of the delighted and thankful old couple." Johnny never even took the cork out of his own bottle until his mission was accomplished.

Efter Dayset Yarns in Memory of **"The Poet", Simon Bremner, Midtown, Freswick.**

THE JOHN O'GROATS KNITWEAR BUILDING

(The Store House is marked on the 1817 map of Duncansby)

It is understood that the Laird of Freswick had this built as a store in the days that crofters paid their rent in grain. The bere or oats would then have been shipped to Staxigoe or Thurso for sale or export.

The bere or oats used to be carried on horseback and this was a very slow process as the horses could only carry two caisies with half a boll in each. It would have been a step forward when the grain was sent by boat. Alex Gibson, minister of Canisbay, wrote in June 1837 that all Freswick's boats both in Stroma and elsewhere were carrying victuals to Staxigoe to a ship he loads there, and that there wasn't a boat to be got on this coast for any consideration. (Ref. "The Mey Letters" edited by John E. Donaldson.)

It must have saved a great deal of organisation and inconvenience to have the grain stored near a pier so that it was ready for shipment when the sea was calm and the weather dry.

After the tenants stopped paying their rent "in kind" the store was taken over by the hotel and guests were able to stable their horses in part of it.

A stone stairway at the west-end of the store led up to a large loft which often had nets and oars etc., stowed at the east-end of it. My father and mother told me about many of the grand dances that were held in the loft in their young days. This was long before there was a hall in John O'Groats or Canisbay. They collected money and bought a melodian (boxie), and Daniel Mowatt and James Rosie, Burnside, often played for the dances.

As a young child I can remember clearly the old store, steading and small house which is now the John O'Groats Knitwear. From our front windows we looked on to the old buildings; this would be about 1930.

The store was at the east-end of the complex and was much the largest building. The house at the west-end ran north and south with the door on the east side and the byre and stable in between it and the store. It belonged to the hotel (Mr Donald MacKenzie). The byre housed the three cows which supplied milk for the hotel.

Mrs Ina Gillanders lived in the house with her daughters and looked after the cows. She did the milking, fed them, and in fact did everything for them, including carrying the milk to the hotel. Her brother-in-law, Mr George Green, cultivated the hotel ground and supplied all the feeding for the animals; this was done later by his sons.

She was a very busy woman, but always had time for the young people and always had a smile on her face. She had an open door for young folks, and I have happy memories of visiting Ina when very young. I can remember, one Hogmanay, her walking into our house with a jug of milk in one hand and her arm in a sling. When asked what was wrong with her arm, she replied, "Oh I just fell and broke my arm" (she was a hardy lady).

About 1934-35 the store was turned into the hotel garage. The loft was removed, a new roof put on, and two large sliding doors erected, one in the north side and one in the east gable. I can clearly remember the excitement each January when the garage would be full of cars preparing for the Monte Carlo Rally. Before the Second World War, many cars going on that Rally left from John O'Groats.

During the war, very little use was made of the garage, except for the storage of two old cars (Rolls) belonging to Mey Castle. The young boys spent many hours trying to start the old cars and success was achieved with one of them. I'm not saying how they (or should I say we) got into the garage.

In 1973 the garage became a pottery, which kept going until 1979. The Knitwear Company then turned the whole complex into what it is today.

Frank Sutherland, Viewfirth.

Hotel, Crofthouse, Store and Lighthouse Store c.1930

Photo, Walter Mowat, Balquholly, John O'Groats.

The Fidelity – 1st Motor Boat in John O'Groats, 1913

Photo, Frank Sutherland, Viewfirth, John O'Groats.
Left to Right:– Sinclair Steven, Johnnie Laird, Willie Mowat. Standing:–
Ben Laird.

JOHN O'GROATS

The snow white sands o' John O'Groats
Reminds me of the ways
We lads and lassies wandered by
In far off Caithness days.

We searched for groaties – wee bit shells
That lurked in shallow pools
We climbed o'er rocks – wild jagged geos
And fell o'er slippery bools.

Oh lovely land of rugged rocks
Of sunsets' scarlet glow
Of bonnie boaties on the tides
That back and forward flow.

Your silvery sand lies secretly
Your seabirds swirl and soar
O'er braes and bent and rabbit runs
On bonnie Northern shore.

Chorus:
Oh John O'Groats, Oh John O'Groats
Your fame is now world wide
The native lads and lassies all
May sing your name with pride.
Mrs Daisy Miller,
Head Teacher in John O'Groats.

THE WAY THINGS WERE

Photo, George Steven, Seaview.
William Steven with Beauty and Nance drawing the binder c.1930.

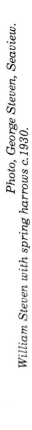

Photo, George Steven, Seaview.
William Steven with spring harrows c.1930.

Photo, David Dunnett, Hillhead.
Washday at Hillhead c.1938.
Note the stones set to shelter the fire under the three legged pot. Jeannie Dunnett wringing clothes and her daughter Chrissie tramping clothes.

Photo, David Dunnett, Hillhead.
David Dunnett at Daisy's head with David and Tibbie Dunnett in cart c.1928

In The Tatties – May 1928

General Election approaching – 28th May polling day. Setting tatties in the field where the foundations of Walter Mowat's latest venture is situated.

Left to Right:– Fanny (brown face) and Nellie, Fanny's daughter – a splendid pair. Aunt Ina – Mrs Gillanders then living in the cottage. Sir Archibald Sinclair MP calling to talk to my father who was prominent in the local Liberal Party at that time. Mimie – before she went to train as a nurse in Glasgow. George Green, my father, about to close the tatties – horses and plough ready. Malcolm – then 13 years-old. Yours truly – with the battered pail, then seven years-old. In the background, the chauffeur driven Rolls Royce – the stamp of the aristocracy at that time.

Ben Green, Roadside, John O'Groats.

PREPARATIONS FOR A WEDDING IN DUNCANSBY

During the early part of last century, a wedding was to be held in Duncansby. As there had been a poor crop of bere, ale was in short supply, and so a boat was dispatched to Orkney, where evidently liquor was more plentiful.

A number of men gathered at Sannick haven for the boat's return. Unfortunately just as they were nearly ashore, the boat capsized.

The story goes that everyone was so busy rescuing the ale, that some time elapsed before a crew member was discovered missing. Eventually he was found partially covered with seaweed, but alive, although cold and unconscious.

They carried him to the nearest house, where he was put to bed between two young women, which was the usual treatment for someone in his condition in those days.

Later, when a concerned relative called to ask if he would live, the owner of the house, who was "a bit of a character", replied, "Aye, he'll live, I only wish I was in his place."

Ethel Dunnett, Heatherbell Cottages, John O'Groats.

OLD MARKET AT LYSKERRY

Jamie Green, The Breck, and later my neighbour in Rowena, told me that his granny (Elizabeth Banks, born 1850, who married John Steven, Snowflake) remembered seeing the Orkney cattle coming ashore with simmons tied round their horns.

The Orkney men sailed straight across from Burwick to Sannick, thus missing the Boars and giving them a good passage. (This is the course the Pentland Venture usually takes.)

The boats would have come close in, and then the cattle would be put over the side with their simmon halters. They were caught and held or tied in the Orkney Pen.

The pen was on the lighthouse side of the Sannick burnmouth. It had a stone built dyke round it, and was on the flat strip of land above the Lyskerry rocks and below the brae.

The stone dyke remained long after the cattle sales stopped, but then when the houses were built the stones just disappeared!

I remember as a boy walking along the shore with my father and having this pointed out to me.

Alexander S. Manson, John O'Groats Post Office.

The Shamrock at Robbie's Haven c.1936

Cutty Craigs and Sandsberry,
Flotherum and the Fliss,
Sanniehol and Backlass
Lie a' beyond the Niss.
(A favourite of Sinclair's.)
Joey Bremner, "St Clair",
John O'Groats.

Bairns and lambs are most likely to arrive
When it's flood tides (if everything is
alright)

Three brothers, David Dunnett in
boat, Alex beside the boat and Isaac
looking on.

David Dunnett, Hillhead,
John O'Groats.

FISH FARMS AND FINDS:

A preview of Archaeological discoveries at
Robert's Haven, Duncansby Head Common Grazings

Today the shallow bay of Robert's Haven at the Ness of Duncansby, is the quiet abode of sheep, sea birds, seals and occasional human visitors. Approximately three-quarters of a millennium ago it was a very different place. Archaeological remains have begun to reveal that this site may have been part of an important estate with a bustling fishing station in late Norse times.

In archaeological terms it is both disastrous and advantageous that coastal erosion has cut deeply into the sand banks of Robert's Haven. The action of the sea, undoubtedly hastened by extensive sand quarrying in the 1940's and 1950's, has revealed midden layers and associated walls which had previously been covered by thick deposits of windblown sand. This erosion severed the site, but also led directly to its discovery by Dr Colleen Batey, now of the Kelvingrove Museum, Glasgow, during an archaeological survey of the Caithness coastline in the early 1980's.

Dr Batey's discovery has raised several interesting questions. First, in the most pragmatic terms, it remains to determine more precisely when the site was occupied. The deposits at Robert's Haven are very rich in finds, primarily fish-bones (mainly from whitefish such as cod, saithe and ling), shells and sherds of dung or chaff-tempered pottery. These discoveries alone cannot pin-point the site in time. However the geographical location of Robert's Haven, the thick fish middens and the pottery all have close parallels at the excavated Norse site of Freswick. A Viking style bone pin (now in the John Nicolson Museum) has also been recovered by Mr Murdo Sinclair of Keiss from the vicinity of a stone foundation about 150 metres inland. It would seem that Robert's Haven and its surrounds were occupied within the period of Norse influence in Caithness – sometime between the 10th and 14th centuries. The fish middens were probably deposited towards the end of this time-span, but a more precise date requires radiocarbon analyses and the study of time-specific artifacts.

The subtleties of dates aside, it is particularly interesting that two broadly contemporary sites in the Parish of Canisbay, Robert's Haven and Freswick, reveal extensive middens dominated by whitefish bones. Similar middens have also been discovered at Norse sites in Orkney, such as Quoygrew at the Biggings Farm, Westray. Could these middens all represent the waste from an export fishery? This idea is consistent with historical evidence for a stockfish trade of enormous importance in medieval Norway, the parentland of the Norse Earldoms in Scotland. As early as the 11th century, for example, dried whitefish were exported from the Lofoten islands in Northern Norway. Stockfish was shipped, via Bergen, to England and the continent where it served purposes as diverse as Lenten fare and military rations. If an export exchange in whitefish occurred in Norse Caithness, this pattern contrasts with the early modern period when herring and salmon formed the keel of the county's fisheries.

Alternatively, the possibility can't be dismissed that the Robert's Haven middens were simply a domestic rubbish pile. In later centuries, the 1700s for example, cod fishing in Caithness was a relatively small-scale activity which crofters used to supplement their subsistence needs.

To decide between these options requires a close examination of what rubbish was left in the middens at Robert's Haven. Are the fish bones the waste one would expect from stockfish production?

In historical descriptions of dried fish preparation, some bones were cut out while others were left in place to give the finished product more rigidity. Does the midden contain only a narrow range of finds which could be associated with fishing and fishers such as fish bones, shellfish for bait, boat rivets, hooks and line weights? Conversely, does it include a wide variety of domestic rubbish such as cereal grain and chaff, mammal bone, personal ornaments and spindle whorls. By studying the bones, seeds and artifacts from Robert's Haven we could come closer to an understanding of Duncansby's past fishers and farmers.

With the kind consent of the Duncansby Head Common Grazings shareholders an archaeological sampling project at Robert's Haven is currently trying to do just this. It aims to recover as much information as possible from the site before it is completely swept into the sea. The project has just begun (1992). Detailed laboratory analyses of the recovered materials will go on for some time. Nevertheless it is possible to outline a few tentative discoveries.

First, the bone in the Robert's Haven midden is almost all from fish, primarily cod. If it was a general household midden, domestic animals must seldom have been eaten (unless their bones were discarded elsewhere). Second, the deposits are large, approximately 25 metres of exposed midden, over a metre and a half deep in many places. Third, the layers are relatively undisturbed. Bones from the same fish are frequently discovered together in their correct places. The fragile rays of single fish fins and patches of fish scales have even been discovered in clusters. This suggests that the midden accumulated very rapidly, before dogs or other scavengers could avail themselves of the tasty morsels.

It is premature to interpret these findings. We must await laboratory analyses of the finds and the results of radiocarbon dating. Assuming for the moment, however, that Robert's Haven dates to the period of Norse influence in Caithness, the archaeological remains can be illuminated with some scepticism from *Orkneyinga Saga: the history of the Earls of Orkney*. This saga, which is thought to have been written by an Icelander around A.D. 1200, frequently refers to Caithness and specifically to Duncansby.

Sagas are a dangerous source of "history" to be used cautiously by archaeologists. At the best they are mixes of historical narrative, political propaganda, literary convention and literary invention. Nevertheless, the stories in *Orkneyinga Saga* may include grains of useful information. For example, the saga associates Duncansby with the Earls of Orkney and their representatives. Its writer obviously considered Duncansby a farm of some considerable importance. The first relevant passage refers to the 11th century. At this time Earl Thorfinn stayed at Duncansby with five longships. He was waiting for his adversary, King Karl of the Scots, whom Thorfinn later defeated in a sea-battle at Deerness in Orkney. Several subsequent passages refer to Duncansby as the farm of Olaf Hrolfsson who was described as the Earl of Orkney's representative in Caithness. In the 12th century he was responsible for raising levies in Caithness for Earl Paul. Olaf was eventually burned in his house by a rival band who then looted the farm – another testimony to Duncansby's assumed prosperity.

Beyond the potential historical legitimacy of the *History of the Earls of Orkney, Orkneyinga Saga* provides an entertaining picture of how a nearly contemporary Icelander chose to portray life in 12th century Caithness. No stories are so telling in this regard as those surrounding the infamous character Svein Asleifarson. Svein was the son of Olaf Hrolfsson and Asleif, a woman praised for her intelligence and character. The tales of his piratical Viking exploits are too numerous to recount, but several relate directly to Duncansby. A particularly informative episode transpired on Svein's return from a successful piratical excursion in the Hebrides. The raiders sheltered at Duncansby (which now belonged to Svein) to divide their acquisitions. There were five captains on the expedition, but Svein, surrounded by his local followers, chose to claim all their shares as his own. His explanation for this arbitrary decision, that the voyage had been his idea, was not particularly popular. Nevertheless, the other captains were not in a position to demand immediate retribution.

This episode might have ended thus had it not been for the depredations of another saga character, Margad Grimsson. Svein had left Margad in charge of his stewardship of Caithness during his expedition to the Hebrides. The brutality with which he executed this office angered several influential chieftains. They complained bitterly to Rognvald, then Earl of Orkney (incidental he had become sole earl of Orkney through the work of Svein!) who decided that Svein had finally gone too far. Rognvald, accompanied by a collection of Svein's enemies, arrived in Duncansby only to discover that the estate's master had fled to his castle, Lambaborg. Margad, Svein and their followers stocked Lambaborg with supplies looted from the Earl's local farms in preparation for the siege which inevitably followed.

The location of Lambaborg has been variously identified as Buchollie Castle, Ness Broch and Freswick House (all near Freswick). This debate is a little immaterial, however, given the possibility that *Orkneyinga Saga* is not what we currently think of as history. The important light shed by this story need not be lost in the shadow of speculation regarding Svein's castle. The saga shows us a society in which Earls and their chieftains held sway over large estates which must have been capable of supplying them with surplus resources. It was a society in which central authority was limited, where Norse warlords continued to wield considerable power within their spheres of influence.

To return for a moment to the excavations at Robert's Haven. Did the fish whose bones were discarded there fill the stomachs of farmers whose agricultural goods had been taken as dues (or by more direct expropriation)? Alternatively, was a trade in stockfish a source of wealth for insatiable figures such as Svein Asleifarson? Were the middens now exposed by the sea rubbish from a surplus producing fishing station? These are questions the *Orkneyinga Saga* allows us to ask, and which continuing studies should allow us to answer.

It is perhaps unfair to end this short note while Svein and Margad lay trapped in Lambaborg. As the Saga story goes, they both escaped by being lowered into the sea from the precipice on which Lambaborg stood. They swam to safety, and were eventually welcomed at the Scottish Court of King David Malcolmson. Before long, however the incorrigible Svein was reconciled with Earl Rognvald and returned to the Earldom.

Acknowledgements

Many people have made the archaeological investigation of Robert's Haven a successful and exciting research project. Thanks are more than deserved by the shareholders in the Duncansby Head Common Grazings. Without their generosity and interest the project could not have occurred.

My archaeological assistants, Ms Heather Henderson, Mr Robert James, Ms Sarah King, Mr Sinclair Manson and Mr George Watson, were the most competent, accommodating and inspiring crew a project leader could wish to work with. Last I must thank Dr Colleen Batey and Professor Christopher Morris who have provided immeasurable assistance with the Robert's Haven project. As a Nova Scotian, the early history of Scotland has always fascinated me. I sincerely appreciate the welcome I received in Caithness.

James H. Barrett, B.A., M.A. Department of Archaeology, University of Glasgow, or 468 Beaver Bank Road, Halifax County, Nova Scotia.

Extract from Census 1841

"Comprising so much of the parish of Canisbay as lies between Huna Inn and Canisbay Distillery, both inclusive, comprehending Huna, Seater, Quoys, Tresdal, East Canisbay and Kirkstyle (12 pages).

Remarks:– There is a small increase in the district since 1801. One family consisting of three males and four females emigrated from this district to Pictou, Nova Scotia, on the 5th June, being the only persons emigrated from this parish to the Colonies or Foreign Countries during the past six months."

L. Davidson, Permission of the Controller H.M.S.O.

Did James have his roots in Canisbay?

FIRST BOARDING HOUSE JOHN O'GROATS *(VIEWFIRTH)*

The late Mrs Barbara Mowat along with her daughters Kate and Vina, started the first tourist accommodation in the area, about the middle 20s. Mr Sinclair, supervisor at the building of the Duncansby Head Lighthouse, lodged there from 1921-24. About 1930, they became a "Cycling Touring Club of Great Britain" registered station. Along with two bedrooms in the house, they had a new wood bungalow with two bedrooms, which gave them four bedrooms for let.

Although about 50 per cent of their visitors were cyclists, motor and pedal, they had many who came by car and a few by bus. They even converted part of the barn in summer as a garage with a sliding door in the gable (two cars).

By the mid 30s they were getting the same people back year after year. One of the best known, was an Admiral Lane, who came with his wife for many years. Many families kept in touch by letter with Kate and Vina long after they retired. They kept a few lodgers during the war, most of whom worked at the sand plant. By the end of the war, they were not so fit, so retired in 1948.

The bungalow was sold to Mr George Manson, Canisbay (Charlie's father) and became the Canisbay Post Office for a number of years.

Frank Sutherland, Viewfirth, John O'Groats.

Photo, Billy Steven, St Rowan, John O'Groats.
Mowat sisters, Vina, Jessie and a shy little Mary.

"THE BENACHIE"

The "Benachie", The "Benachie"
You know the name as well as me
A seine net boat from the town MacDuff
Ran aground and gave her crew a gluff

On the Ness of John O'Groats
This place has claimed a good few boats
Her mast it lay right on the brae
We all thought she was there to stay.

The men from Groats and Canisbay
Came swarming there that very day
What they took I cannot tell
But all they left was just the shell.

There she lay all forlorn
They even pinched her very horn
Wishing they were Samson's men
To carry her bodily off with them.

Three men from Wick saved her soul
But in their pockets left a hole
They bought her for a hundred fivers
Their occupation deep sea divers.

They made a road right up the brae
But didn't do it in a day
Days it took was three or four
They think their task is now half o'er.

Now for Wick they must advance
To get her there they take a chance
Trailer they have made by hand
And think the job they've done is grand.

Lorries to tow they must seek
The outlook seems very bleak

Cormack's transport do their deed
For money is the thing they need.

Saturday morning about 11 o'clock
Off they head for dry dock
Two lorries in front they have the knack
And one behind to hold her back.

A police escort they did ask
For getting to Wick was a terrible task
Their journey's o'er they took great care
And if in Wick visit her there.

Anne Ross, Haven Fiord, Gills.

The "Benachie" November 1971

Photo, Colin Mackay, Heatherbell Cottages.

SATISFIED EXCISEMEN!

There was said to be a few good working "stills" in Duncansby in the early 1800's, and my great grandparents claimed to make very good whisky. George Houston and Barbara Houston were married in 1827 and lived at Nessdale. George a crofter fisherman also did some tailoring and got a mention in Calder's History of Caithness. He killed an eagle which attacked him on the top of the Muckle Stack by stabbing it with his tailor's shears. He was also a very well known fiddler who taught a good number of the local lads to play the fiddle. Barbara was a clever, capable, well educated and very religious woman. She prided herself in being able to quote passages of the scriptures and told about the fine sermons preached by Peter Jolly and Finlay Cook. It is handed down that her husband drove her in the spring cart to Dunnet to the sacraments which lasted from Thursday to Tuesday. It is worth noting that in 1843 Peter Jolly, (who transferred to Dunnet in 1845) one of the most loved of Canisbay ministers remained with the established Church and that Finlay Cook in Reay, one of the most eminent ministers in the north elected to join the Free Church.

Long ago distilling for family use was not considered a crime but more a case of necessity.

Babbie was distilling one day when someone shouted "There's the excisemen!" She lifted the end of the featherbed and put the "still" in under it at the back of the box bed and then shook down the feathers a bit and covered it all over. She was in the box bed with the patchwork quilt pulled up and nursing the baby before the excisemen got through the door. She asked them what they thought of her new born bairn?? – the bairn (my granny Isabella Houston) was a month old so this must have been the end of October, 1836 and would have been the first of the new season's malt. Meanwhile Betsy (later Mrs Gordon Dower) a very talkative child was given boiled egg to prevent her giving the show away when the exciseman was asking questions. Betsy loved boiled egg and each time she opened her mouth to speak was fed another spoonful. The others in the family had to do without their egg that day but the excisemen went in peace.

On another occasion Barbara was at the mending, with a foot on the cradle rocking the baby when visitors came to the door and were asked in by Betsy. (It could have been John Houston, b.1834, who lived at the top of the East End and had the "Britannia" who was in the cradle or perhaps James b.1832.) Barbara spotted the man had two thumbs and realised this was none other than Wm. Hare who had turned Queen's evidence and escaped punishment when his partner Burke was convicted of suffocating or strangling their victims and selling the bodies for dissection. Burke was hanged in Edinburgh in 1829. Hare took over Mid's

Croft above Willie Mowatt's, The Broo. He cut peats – the like of which no one had ever seen in Duncansby! (Irish style it turned out to be.) He had a wife and five bairns with him and they left as suddenly as they came.

Mrs Isabella Houston Coghill, South Cannigall, St Ola, Orkney (formerly Sonsiquoy, Freswick).

THE JOHN O'GROATS COASTGUARD RESCUE COMPANY

The Queen Mother with the John O'Groat Coastguards in the Castle of Mey when she presented these founder members with long-service medals in 1981.

Photo, Kevin Green.

Back Row: Allie Sinclair, Johnny Green, Robbie Cowe, P. Prosser (Inspector), George Manson, Bill Bremner, Cdr. Michael Woollcombe, John Mowat, Willie Laird.

Middle Row: Sandy Dunnet, Will Rosie, Norman MacInnes (Station Officer), John Sinclair.

Front row: George Steven and Clarence Sinclair.

The John O'Groats Coastguard Rescue Company was formed in 1960 soon after the loss with all hands of the Aberdeen trawler "George Robb" at Queenie Cliff, near the Stacks of Duncansby. David Gunn was the auxilliary in charge and I was his first mate.

The company met regulary for rescue exercises with special emphasis being placed on cliff-top work. The team rescued cows, sheep and dogs trapped on ledges down the face of high cliffs and it should not be forgotten that these were very frightened and unpredictable animals. I took over from David, and George Manson took over the watch keeping section.

The John O'Groat team were very proud to win the first annual competition for the David Gunn memorial trophy which was gifted in his memory by his wife. The contest took the form of a sea and cliff-top rescue drill at the Gills Bay cliffs.

We were proud too and very thankful when we rescued the crew of the Banff registered seine-netter "Benachie" which ran aground at the point of the Ness on 24th November, 1971. George

Manson was the officer on watch. It was 4.00 a.m. and black dark when we mustered the company. We got a line aboard the vessel which was rocking badly in a heavy swell and brought the four men off by breeches buoy in less than half an hour. Skipper Watt said "she keeled over so far to port, that water was coming over the rail and was so deep that it was over the tops of our boots. We were ready to abandon ship when she rose again and overturned the life-raft we were trying to right." William Watt and his son Colin, along with Robert Hepburn and John Robertson all from Macduff were glad to see our car lights and hear a Lossie voice on the loud hailer.

I retired in 1987 and the company is now in the capable hands of John Mowat with William Mackenzie the first assistant.

One could think that with all the modern high tech equipment ship wrecks would be a thing of the past but we have not quite reached that moment in time because it was just last year (February 1993) the "Bettina Danica" ran aground on the Clett, Stroma.

Robert G. Cowe, The Ha, John O'Groats.

"THE SKIRZA"

James Cook, Skirza Head let George Manson and myself have the boat for £2. We took her on my father's lorry to the garage at the Old Post Office where we put a new "skin" on the "Skirza" and did extensive repairs. We fitted in an old car engine (two cylinder Brit) which we got from our Uncle Willie in Wick. The propellor shaft came out of an old model T. Ford and the propellor we got from Malcolm Green. We decided to have the "trials" on the Mill Dam at the Biel and since John Rosie, Hillside, my grandfather, knew the Dam he took the helm! This was his first time in a motor boat so he set his matches in the rim of his cap (to keep them dry) and then put the cap on back to front in case the wind blew it off. There was fair good speed in the "Skirza" and it was lucky there were no rocks in the Hill Dam because we went aground once or twice. It was a great occasion, and my grandfather spoke about it for many a day and praised the advantages of modern inventions – no oars to pull or sails to set.

George Manson, myself and Johnnie Green set off to catch cod and we were told a good place to start was "off the Stroma Road". It was the first time any of us had been out ourselves to the handlines and we knew very little about the tide. We hadn't got properly started when the tide took us round the back of the beacon and we had a sore struggle

Willie Laird (sitting), friend, Allie Sinclair, Andrew Sinclair at the helm, 1948.

to make it back to the pier at Stroma. Johnnie was dispatched to the Co-op shop for lemonade and pies because by that time we were starving. Some Stroma boys told us when to leave and the course to take for John O'Groats. Jim Smith and Jessie had started the handlines and were getting fish but we decided we had better head for home. Cathie and Joey were working in the John O'Groats Hotel at this time and many was the fine cruise we had in the "Skirza" after that.

Allie Sinclair, Swona View, John O'Groats.

DUNCANSBY HEAD LIGHTHOUSE

One of the most eventful periods in the history of the John O'Groats district was the building of the lighthouse at Duncansby Head. There already had been a fog signal at the head and this had been necessary for the passing ships during the 1914-18 war, but a government decision after the war to go ahead with a lighthouse as well, caused a tremendous stir, not only in the immediate vicinity, but throughout the parish and as far as Wick.

After extensive surveying, mapping out roads, etc. work on the construction commenced in May 1921. The main contractor was an Edinburgh firm called Finlayson, and as much hauling of stones, sand, cement and so on was required, there was a need for horses and carts, for as yet the motor truck had not come to the

Photo, Nell Sinclair, Robertson Creascent, Keiss.
The windmill used for pumping water to Duncansby Head.

fore. Most of the skilled labour were Edinburgh employees of the firm, and they found lodgings in the croft houses in the vicinity of the job. Many friendships were made between the Edinburgh employees and the local people and this remained for many years after the lighthouse beamed out over the land and sea. Most of the labourers were

recruited locally, not entirely from John O'Groats, but from all along the north coast to Dunnet and down the east coast to Keiss and beyond.

As the herring fishing at this time had gone into serious decline many who had plied the fishing came to work at the "head", to use the expression

The Lighthouse Tower, Duncansby Head

Photo, Laurence Brown, North House, John O'Groats.

A broch was knocked down and removed from the site before the tower of the lighthouse was started. Francis MacGregor built the white block corners and base of the tower. Mr Sinclair, Inspector of Works, is in the front of the photo. Second on left – John Bremner, Nessdale. Mr Scott is top right.

Katie Mowat, Nessdale, John O'Groats.

At the Building of Duncansby Head Lighthouse

Photo, Ian Angus, Midtown Freswick.

Back Row, left to right:– Bill Gunn, West End; James Rosie, Burnside; James Green, Breck; ? ; D.B. Gunn, Wick Clerk of Works. Middle Row:– Donald Sinclair (The Inspector's son); ?; John Green, Biel; Johnnie Dunnet, West End; Wildie Cormack, Huna; ? ; ? ; Mr Sinclair, The Inspector of Works; Mr Meiklejohn, Wick; Mr Scott, The Foreman; Donald Muir, c/o Victoria House; ?; Sandy Williamson, Broo. Front Row:– George Dunnet, West End; Peter Gunn, Midtown; ? ; Wildie (Mack) MacKenzie; Alex Ross?, Gills; Frank Begg, Biel (brother of Matron Begg); Willie Steven, Seaview.

of the time, to make a living. I'm not certain, but I believe a labourer's rate at the time was about a shilling an hour. I do know that at the outset the pay for a horse and cart plus driver was £1 per day. And so in the early 20s John O'Groats and district enjoyed a welcome boom which lasted for the best part of three years, and at the end of it many found it difficult to scrape a living, and thereafter followed a period when many young men and women were forced to find work elsewhere – it was a period of emigration. In fact, the exodus continued throughout the later 20s and well into the 30s, as can easily be demonstrated by the steady decline in the school roll. The decline continued until World War II came along, and the demand for food brought the Government subsidies to the crofts and halted the drift to the cities and abroad – many had of course to go and serve in the forces. What has happened since is another story and must wait for the time being.

To go back to the lighthouse briefly, I should say that the stones used for the dwelling houses at the lighthouse came from the same quarry as did the Queen Mother's renovation at the Castle of Mey.

The first principal lighthouse keeper at Duncansby Head was Mr Cromarty, a native of South Ronaldsay, Orkney. His wife hailed from Watten, Caithness and they had one daughter called Chrissie who trained as a teacher, became Mrs Murray, and is still fit and well, residing in retirement in Argyle Square, Wick. She and I started school together at John O'Groats in 1926, when Mr Arthur Brown was the headteacher – Miss Robertson from Keiss was the infant teacher – and I am pleased to tell you that Chrissie Cromarty and I remain firm friends until this day.

Ben Green, Roadside, John O'Groats.

Duncansby Head Lighthouse

DUNCANSBAY HEAD LIGHTHOUSE JOHN O'GROATS

Photo, Walter Mowat, Balquholly, John O'Groats.

Light Established:	1924
Engineer:	David A. Stevenson
Position:	Latitude 58° 38.6' N – Longitude 03° 01.4' W
Character:	Flashing white every 12 seconds
Elevation:	67 metres
Candlepower:	596,000
Nominal Range:	24 nautical miles
Structure:	White tower 11 metres high.

—ooOoo—

There are 31 steps to the top of the tower. The tidal streams flowing through the Pentland Firth earned it the title of the hell's mouth in the days of sail, and it is still a place where unwary ships can become the plaything of the sea. As the waters of the wide Atlantic flow into the North Sea and ebb in the opposite direction, they set in motion a welter of eddies, races and overfalls, and in the neighbourhood of the Pentland Skerries they run at a speed of 10 knots. So dramatic are the effects that each of these tide races has been given a name – the Swilkie, the Bore of Huna, the Wells of Tuftalie, the Duncansby Bore, and the Merry Men of Mey.

181

In 1914 during the First World War, a temporary fog signal was provided at Duncansby Head close to John O'Groats to be replaced by a permanent lighthouse after the war.

The traditional round tower has been abandoned (curved walls require interior fittings made to match) even the concrete lantern tower is square.

During the Second World War, and on the eve of the invasion of Norway, Duncansby Head Lighthouse was machine-gunned by a German bomber, but fortunately no-one was injured and no damage was caused.

In 1968, a high power racon (radar beacon) was installed. It has now been replaced by a low-power self operating type, which can be particularly useful as a warning where the coastline is not conspicious on a radar display.

With thanks to Mr Perkins – Admin Officer.
John Muir, 17 Silverknowes Brae, Edinburgh.

Stacks of Duncansby

Rocks that rise in giddy grandeur
Cliffs where dwells the eagle grey,
Chasms, caves where wild waves thunder,
Form the charms of Duncansby.
Anon – From Huna Inn Visitor's Book.

THE CHARMS OF DUNCANSBY

Pearly sands along the beaches,
Stretch from Hang to Sannick Bay,
Like a myriad sparkling jewels
Laved and washed twice every day.

Out at sea the Bores are tumbling,
Getting ready for the fray,
As the flood-tide gains momentum
They are quickly brought to bay.

White-tipped billows spitting fury,
Break in clouds of foam and spray,
Shutting off the inner passage
As a wall each stormy day.

Woe betide the luckless mariner
Forced to cross that angry ford,
Should this ship emerge sea-worthy
Neptune then has been aboard.

From Sannick cliffs rise sharply upwards
Undulating geos and caves
Screaming seabirds in their thousands
Vie with music of the waves.

The Knee and Gibbs Craig, noble pillars!
The latter leaning out to sea.,
Guarding 'gainst what might befall
Foretold in ancient prophecy.

But the grandest sight by far,
Three hundred feet above the sea,
In scenic grandeur unsurpassed
The stately stacks of Duncansby.

Nature's architect was matchless
In the dim and distant past
When he framed these glorious statues
Out of all the holocaust.

Weathered by the stormy Pentland,
Lashed by billows flecked with foam.
Standing there serene, unruffled,
With a charm that's all their own.

What a sight on first beholding,
At once they cast a spell o'er me
And many others likewise minded
Who are blest with eyes to see.

Oft have I stood in silent rapture,
On the rocky ramparts there,
Drinking draughts of deepest pleasure
From that view beyond compare.

Enshrined in every exiles bosom,
In far distant foreign lands
Pulling ever at the heart strings,
The cliffs, the geos, the pearly sands.

These are some of nature's pictures
To be seen from day to day
Praise and thanks are due the artist
For the "Charms of Duncansby".
From "Gleanings" by John Ross "Albyn", Gills.

Footnote:– "Gleanings" – a book John Ross wrote for Alex Mowat, his son-in-law in 1957.

TRAGEDY AT JOHN O'GROATS

We regret to report that a boat containing three young men, Pentland Firth pilots from Duncansby, was capsized at sea on Wednesday 25.3.1868.

The men, respectively named George Houston (26), David Manson (24), and John Dunnet (20), all unmarried, went to sea in the fore noon with the intention of prosecuting the line fishing and also piloting some vessels through the Pentland Firth, which were in the offing.

The day turned rough and the wind rose to almost gale force, and when last seen by some Stroma people, the boat[1] was a considerable distance east and south from Duncansby Head.

A French fishing vessel, bound for Iceland, went to the rescue, but as she did not communicate with the shore, it is feared that the three men perished before aid could be given.

The three were industrious and highly deserving young men.

Courtesy, John O'Groat Journal.

[1] See page 240, column 2 – top line..

THE DUNCANSBY BOAT

It was the year of sixty eight,
March the twenty fifth day
The wind blew strong from the south, south-east
And raised a raging sea.

Far to the east a Frenchman seen
Coming quickly sailing in
For Newfoundland Bank he steered his course
Though tossed by sea and wind.

A pilot boat was quickly launched
And manned by three o' a crew
To try the boat their intention was
Because that she was new.

One of the mothers of that daring crew
Said it was far too wild a sea
But the answer that he gave to her
"If we canna fight we'll flee."

Away they went so boldly
No danger did they dread
Until they came to a well known place
The flood of the Red Head.

'Twas there they met with the wildest part
It was too late to turn
There they met with a raging sea
The boat, she foundered, she never returned.

Some Stroma people saw them last
When they went o'er the head
But they were never seen again
For they are numbered wi' the dead.

(Some verses missing – last verse ends)

Many's the loss has Duncansby got
For her wild and troubled sea.

Words – Ethel Dunnett, Heatherbell Cottages.
Tune – Nancy Farquhar, Hillside House, Huna.
Music – Jennifer Ferguson, Virum, Newton Hill, Wick.

DUNCANSBY SEA-SONG

This is one of the last rhymed sagas or sea-songs from the parish and many thanks are due to John Laird, East End who often repeated and thus preserved the story of the Duncansby Boat and to Angus MacLeod who liked singing it to his family.

The sea-songs usually extolled the exploits, dangers and tragedies of the sea and seamen. Long ago they were sung or recited at "efter daysets" so that the young could learn and the old remember and that the people and events would not be forgotten.

Ethel told me she thought it was when they started having concerts in the school c.1890 that these sad songs were stopped. It was entirely different hearing these sagas sung round a peat fire when there was time to think and ponder, from hearing them in a crowded hall in an atmosphere of entertainment.

The death certificates are dated 25th March, 1868 and the familes were next-door neighbours in the East End.

George Houston – Son of George Houston and Barbara Houston.

David Manson – Son of Alex Manson and Jane Dunnet.

John Dunnet – Son of Malcolm Dunnet and Catherine Houston.

Charles Ferguson's great-great-grandmother Helen Dunnet, married to William Dunnet, was the aunt of John Dunnet and of David Manson and lived on the next croft to George Houston. John Dunnet was our granny's brother.

Anne Houston, St Magnus, John O'Groats.

THE MILLERS OF WIFE GOE

My mother was one of a family of nine who were all brought up on a small croft on the cliff top at Wife Goe, midway between Skirza Head and the Stacks.

At that time there was also a croft at Fassgoe, half a mile further north, where John Gibson and his wife lived. John Gibson was very musical and my mother told that he would come over in the long dark winter evenings and entertain them all with his Jew's harp – an occasion very much looked forward to.

On the 25th November 1891 my Granny Isabella (Sutherland) Miller was killed when she fell over the cliff. The staig was loose (tether not staked down) and it was thought that "skwacking" seagulls could have risen when she went to flit the young horse and that he had shied and knocked her over the edge.

The following year the family moved to a croft at the West End, John O'Groats. (They had intended to flit on the 6th November, 1892 but it was postponed because that day the "Gerona" was to be refloated.)

This croft had belonged to James Sutherland who went to "Cairns of Heatherow", Bower and then to "Gillfield", Wick. This was a big undertaking for a crofter fishermen.

Donald Mowat, Victoria House, John O'Groats.

Victoria House c.1895

Photo, John Muir, Edinburgh.
Mrs John Mowat (Katie Sutherland) seated – Great-grandmother of John Mowat. Mrs Jock Mowat (Maggie Miller) with child in arms. David Muir and his wife Mary Mowat (sister of Jock) and their family on holiday from Leith.

This was one of the first houses in Groats to have a slate roof. Photos were printed from "Magic Lantern" glass plates, which we think were taken by James Mowat before he went to New Zealand. James was the brother of Mary Mowat, my granny and he left the "glass-plates" in Leith with her.
Moira Bremner, Victoria Villa, Canisbay.

THEY CAME FROM WIFE GOE

Photo, Moira Bremner, Victoria Villa, Canisbay.
Mrs Isabella Miller seated with two of her daughters, Isabella seated and Christina standing.

William Miller who took the croft at Wife Goe, after a Mowat family left, was the son of Donald and Christian Bain.

William Miller married Isabella Sutherland daughter of Alexander Sutherland (Hedger) and Isabella Manson. They brought up a family of nine on this small isolated croft, with nothing between them and Norway, as my granny used to say.

Now a word about the family:–

1. Donald was engaged to Jessie Dunnet (sister of the coxwain) but he died a young man in 1899. Jessie later married Sutherland, "Gillfield".

2. Isabella married John Dunnet, coxwain and they brought up James, William, Bella, Malcolm, Donald, Maggie and George at Huna (Adam Flockhart's now) moving to Seater after George was born. There was some panic at Huna once when Maggie (aged two-three) was lost for hours before she was found in at Wattie Ross's back – both sound asleep! He was an old man then and often had a lie down in the afternoon. Sandy Sinclair, Stroma, moved to "Rosie's" or "Adam Flockhart's" after the Dunnets moved to Seater. Once when my grandfather was anxious to get the lifeboat launched, he took two sons with him and it was not until my granny got down to the pier that she realised what he'd done. She said this was not to happen again or she could be left like Widow Douglas from Clyth. (A reference to Clyth boat lost c.1880.)

LOCKIE BROTHERS TRAILING TRAIN LOAD OF CATTLE TO RAILROAD
DAVE   JAMES BILL   JOHN DAN   GEORGE

*1940, the six Lockie brothers near Yellowtone River (**HX** was their livestock brand).*

3. Christina (Teenie) married James Lockie whose ancestors came up as shepherds from the borders and the same Lockies as Peter and Bill who went to New Zealand.

Christina and James Lockie took their courage in both hands and emigrated to Montana, and the family here felt so sorry for them having to leave behind all that they held most dear.

They got land – staked their claim – built a log cabin and that was them started. Their nearest neighbours were many miles away, so they had to be self sufficient and masters of all trades. Once when her husband had gashed himself very badly, Teenie stitched up the wound with a darning needle after using whisky as an antiseptic, and it's likely that Jamie got a drop of that too.

They had six sons, and before long their ranch "Sheffield" measured 60 x 40 miles. Wheat was the main crop in Montana and here at Seater our folk were proud to show the photos they sent home of their horse drawn binders and trailers of corn. For many years they raised 2500 horses annually and sold them to the American Government.

When they wrote that they had 1500 steer that was just the stirks!

4. Williamina (Wildy) married Andrew Mowat, Linnequoy, and their family was Magnus, Ida, Jean and William. Ida lives with her nephew Andrew in the Black Isle.

5. Margaret married John Mowat, Victoria House and had three of a family Donald, Bella and Betty.

6. George married Isobel Dunnet and they had three of a family, William, Jenny and Isobel. They stayed on in the family croft at the West End until they moved to Calder Mains. At the May term 1914, George along with James Dunnet, Seater and William Kennedy, Freswick received tenancies of holdings on Calder Mains, Halkirk, which was broken up by the Department of Agriculture. James Mowat, Stroma, followed a few years after that. (George Miller was in the RNVR and was called up to the Royal Navy in August 1914.)

Taking on and stocking a holding was no small consideration for crofters even in that day. George Miller and his wife retired to Lyth and later moved to the Dog's Nose. They are buried in the family grave in Canisbay. Their son's name also appears on the tombstone. Sergt. William Miller fell South Italy 18.1.1944 aged 32 years.

7. Jessie married James Rosie and they stayed at Burnside, John O'Groats where Arthur, Will, Ivy and Jim were brought up.

8. Lizzie was engaged to Jimmy Laird who was drowned in February 1908 when his yawl the "Kruger" was run down by the Aberdeen trawler "Ben Eden" north-east of Duncansby Head where they were fishing cod. Gilbert Laird (Garibaldi) his father and William Laird his cousin were lost in the same tragedy.

Lizzie later married Bill Livie and they settled in Montana – the letters home said they were no distance from Teenie – just 150 miles or so and they visited each other often!

Lizzie's daughter Jimmy was a great favourite at Seater.

9. William married Lena Olive and they had two of a family William and Elizabeth. He was in banking in Toronto, had a good head for business and did very well there.

The descendants of the family from Wife Goe are now scattered over the world, and those of us in the parish are pleased and proud when they come "home" to find their roots and relations.

John Dunnet, Seater, Canisbay.

THE "ROCKET LEE" ON LOCH OF LOMASHION

Photo, Lizzie Cook, Skirza.
Left to Right:– Donald Bremner, Biel; David Cook, Skirza and
Jim Bremner, Biel.

We bought the "Rocket Lee", a 12 foot creel boat from Scarfskerry about 1946.

We had the boat at the "Rock" which is no distance from the Biel and kept it there summer and winter hauled up on the beach.

A piece of rock fell through the skin and after patching it temporarily we sailed it to Freswick to repair it. After repairing the boat we took it by tractor to the calm waters of the Loch of Lomashion to try it out and make sure it was sea worthy.

The loch was about six feet deep in the middle.

Jimmy Bremner, Victoria Villa, Canisbay.

JOHN O'GROATS

Would you like to come to the far North of Scotland
To view the lovely islands and the boats
To meet the kindly folk and get a welcome
And see the far-famed land of John O'Groats?

We could take you to that rocky northern headland
With its lighthouse flashing warnings out to sea
You could view the lovely sunsets over Stroma
With the Skerries standing out upon your lee.

You could wander round the "goes" and watch the
sea birds
We could show you all the rugged cliffs and stacks

You could ramble o'er the blossom-laden moorlands
With gentle breezes blowing on your backs.

You could walk along the lovely pearly beaches
And gather "Groatie Buckies" in the sand
Then you'd watch the rolling waves and foaming
breakers.
And ships upon their way to distant lands.

If you ever want to leave the busy city,
Or, when you tire of "sowing your wild oats"
Then find a home and settle down for ever.
In our dear northern land of John O'Groats.

Janet Gunn, Emohruo, Mey.

CHILDHOOD MEMORIES AT THE BRECK SEVENTY YEARS AGO

Johnnie was not quite seven when the First World War started. I was not quite three. My earliest memory of it was when our other brother Jamie went off to join the navy in 1915, or was it in 1916, and seeing my mother kiss him goodbye. Kissing among the grown-ups of our family was not common so that is probably why I remember it. Johnnie and I did our little bit for the war effort by not taking sugar in our tea. When we were both having tea we abstained but when one was absent for any reason the other took sugar as usual. Of a normal child's toys there was none, as Germany had been the great provider prior to the war. We invented our own with sea shells. Our interests of course were largely bound up with the animals on the croft – horse, cow, sheep, pig and the family sheep dog. We had a separate kind of shell representing each – big and small "buckies" we called them. At one stage we collected loads of the

biggest kind for my father to build into a "lime kiln" as he called it. The big heap of buckies had peats piled around them and the outside had a strong padding of "divots". Air holes allowed the whole to be set alight and after days of burning, the centre was left as pure white lime which he used for his building projects as cement would be used today.

Imitating what the grown-ups did was of course standard. It was still the days of "cupple" drains in the land, when suitable small stone slabs were laid roof like in straight deep channels and then covered by smaller stones to hold them in place. The water needing to be drained away would find its way into the "cuppled" channel and then wind its way into a ditch or burn that had a natural flow. We were close to the hill where an old peat bank, long since abandoned, gave us the right medium to practise what father was doing in larger fields.

The Duncansby burn ran through our croft from the hill dam where the water gathered, to the mill dam where the water was available when the miller needed its power to drive the great mill wheel. Shutting and opening the hill dam was a family task. A tartan shawl hung from an upstairs window at the Mill House was the signal to let water down and the increased flow to the miller brought joy and interest to us boys. There were trout and eels for our sport and paddling in summer was the elixir of delight.

Mr Brown our headmaster taught us clay modelling on our slates and afterwards we were sent to wash them in the burn. Inevitably this became a wild melee and the slates sometimes suffered cracks and breakages. Then there was a price to pay.

Vaguely, I suppose I worried a bit about the war. Jamie had been torpedoed once and was twice in the water. I understood we would all be killed if Germany won the war but I lost no sleep over it. I remember we got a half holiday on the day the war ended. That was better than being killed.

George Green, Gerston, Halkirk.

Major Green is far too modest to tell about his part in the Second World War. The following paragraph is from his brother's book. – A.H.

George Green M.A. Edin. M.B.E.

"He joined Officer Corps University of Edinburgh and T.A. before War. Called up 1940 5th Seaforths. Served in the 5th Battalion North Africa and rose to rank of Major. Awarded Military Cross. Served in Normandy. After the war, returned to teaching as Headmaster, Crossroads. Served in T.A. long after the war. 1984 Vice Lieutenant, County of Caithness."

From "Groatie Buckies" by James A. Green, Rowena, John O'Groats.

DUNCANSBY DUCK

When I was a young chiel in John O'Groats, we had a neighbour called George Bartlett who was, as they say, 'deaf as a post'.

George was reputed to have lost his hearing in the trenches of World War I. He was awarded the Military Medal for carrying back to the British lines a wounded Caithness man – one of the Clynes of Noss. When any local enquired of George as to how he acquired the Military Medal he always laconically replied "shotin scorries".

In the summer of 1945, my father and my uncle Mac were at the 'lapsters' or lobster fishing around the Stacks. The pickings were poor that summer – there were no lobsters about.

My brother John and I were both home from school for the summer holidays. My uncle Mac had been out fishing cuddings for bait one evening and a Caithness man on holiday from London (he was a butcher by trade) had come out for the fishing trip. He lamented on the scarcity of food in the wartime metropolis and proffered the opinion that the numerous scarfs or cormorants around the cliffs could be sold to the hungry hordes in the capital if suitably disguised as palatable fare.

Now, nobody in Duncansby could ever remember the Groaters being so hungry that they took to eating scarfs. The opinion of the Stromas was sought and the verdict of that "sheither" was that you had to bury the bird in peat meals for three weeks and that even then you had to use all your culinary ingenuity to disguise the taste.

There was no sign of the lapsters "coming on" as they say. One fine day, my brother and I borrowed my father's single barrel shotgun – Mauser – (an ancient weapon of doubtful provenance). A box (25) of 12 bore cartridges was purchased.

Raking the flocks of scarfs sitting around the Head could hardly be defined as sport. There were however, some exciting moments when scrambling over the wet slimy rocks trying to retrieve the carcasses.

Seventy-five birds for 25 cartridges – that was not a bad return for openers. We loaded them on the train at Wick for Smithfield Market. A week later a postal order arrived for 15 pounds. Four shillings for a scarf! It was unbelievable. The creels were abandoned and for the next two weeks, the cliffs resounded to the clamour of two shotguns firing right and left as the boat edged its way into geos, round the Muckle Stack, Skirza Head and as far west as Dunnet Head.

Scarfs fell from the cliffs in dozens, often accompanied by chunks of rock dislodged by the reverberation. The weather was perfect and the sea as calm as one could expect around these shores.

On the best day we bagged 240 scarfs. The news spread and competitors arrived on the scene. Young lads were shooting the birds from the beaches and sending them by post to London. The GPO complained of the stench.

However, the scarfs had developed a keen sense of survival. After three weeks, they literally took flight and deserted the Duncansby cliffs for safer havens. The great hunt was over. They came back after a few years but, by then, the Sassenachs had lost their appetite for Duncansby duck.

I wonder what they tasted like???

George J. Green, Riyadh, Saudi Arabia.

Footnote:– George Bartlett and Lieut. Daniel Miller Clyne were in the 5th Seaforth Highlanders. George received the Military Medal for going out under enemy fire and carrying Daniel Clyne back to the British lines. Sadly Daniel was killed on the 23rd July, 1918 aged 22 and was buried in Rheims.

Helen McGregor (grand-daughter of George Bartlett), 4 Balimore Place, Thurso.

SINGLE-HANDED TO THE AMERICAS 1985

The Zuleika (Lion class designed by Arthur Robb 35ft L.O.A. 24ft L.W.L.)

Route Map

Patrick Green sold his shareholding in a small engineering consultancy to rebuild Zuleika and make this voyage. After his return to Cornwall he spent 18 months as chief instructor of a sailing school based on the Solent, prior to taking up his current appointment as a lecturer in electronics at Saltash College, Cornwall.

After a year of work in which Patrick Green had virtually taken his boat to pieces and rebuilt her, he still wasn't ready to sail, but he went anyway. The last his family were to see of him for eight months was the diminishing gleam of his sails as the yacht Zuleika slipped into the blackness of the night at Polruan on the River Fowey in Cornwall.

A few moments earlier, his wife Rosemary had reminded him he hadn't made a will, so he signed one in the car park of the pub where he had said his goodbyes to his family and friends.

He didn't really know why he was going; he had only a rough plan of where he was going. Ten thousand sea miles later he knew of course where he'd been; and a greater understanding of why he done it.

Patrick Green was then 40 years old, a Scotsman from Caithness who's Celtic sense of duty gave him pause for thought about leaving his wife and three sons (one not yet a teenager) ashore while he

explored the oceans and himself. But his stronger sense of duty to himself had burned brightly enough for everyone waving him away to wish him well. Patrick's sense of duty was inherited from his father; had his father been on the quayside in Polruan, and not at home in Caithness, he would perhaps have suggested that Patrick's duty to his family should over-ride his duty to himself.

It is at times like these that Celtic folk turn to poetry; Rosemary, an honorary Celt because she was married to a Scot and lives in Cornwall, had written "I hope that your journey brings you the sense of achievement and fulfilment that you are looking for. . . and that you return at peace with yourself." A cousin, a nun, had written the complete wish: "That you will find all that you are seeking and know all that you find." Patrick Green is not a religious man, but he does and did believe in the fates, a formless ruling force, but a force which nevertheless may be bent and applied to advantage with planning and methodical preparation. Patrick was a methodical romantic, whose favourite phrase is Inshallah. . . (God willing).

At seven o'clock on the dark Tuesday evening of 15th October, 1985, Patrick sailed the 35-foot sloop Zuleika away from Polruan and headed south. He had three friends to keep him company, Leonard, a toy lion mascot, Martha, the Aries self-steering gear, and Tony, his electronic satellite navigation aid. Two hours later he had sailed less than six miles.

Twenty four hours later, he declared himself well satisfied with a run of 120 miles, a daily run that would seem inadequate months later when Zuleika flew with the trade winds under spinnaker notching up 170-plus day after day – reckless maybe, but exhilarating to the boundary of belief for a sailor single-handed; just him and his boat using the wind with perhaps no other human within a thousand miles. But by then Patrick would have crossed the equator twice and the Atlantic once; now he had still to clear the busy shipping lanes approaching the Bay of Biscay.

Sailing single-handed requires two disciplines above all others, sleep and food. Patrick was no cook, so the joy of making his first successful omelette deserved a photograph. A few days later, eight days from Polruan, he made porridge rather less successfully. He told his diary "It definitely smelt funny; like old socks; like me after eight days at sea. As I couldn't throw myself overboard, the porridge went instead." Zuleika had two taps in the galley, freshwater and saltwater, drawn from the ocean (good for cleaning and dishwashing, saving valuable fresh water supplies). He'd mistakenly drawn salt water to make the porridge. "The salt water smelt OK, but combined with the basis of all Scotland. . . the porridge was definitely off. I was reduced to Alpen."

Two days later with 1000 miles between him and Polruan, Patrick picked up a radio beacon from Porto Santo, a giant mountain top which rises thousands of feet from the floor of the Atlantic Ocean, just 20 miles from his first destination of Funchal, the bustling and beautiful capital of Madeira, even taller; so tall it has three separate climatic zones from shore to mountain top. When he saw Porto Santo he told his diary "This island looks fantastic; those mountains must be magnificent walking. " He dropped the anchor and pumped the bilges dry. Zuleika was a wooden boat, and like all wooden boats, she leaked a little. That day it took just 24 strokes of the hand-pump. There would be days when it took more than 500; it is perhaps as well that Patrick couldn't foresee the future. Three days later, and after walking Porto Santo, Zuleika sailed into Funchal.

It was Madeira that changed the style and reasoning behind Patrick's voyage; all his planning, and reading of similar voyages, had undervalued the impact of friendships formed within the close community of long-distance sailing – a community that immediately accepts new members, simply because they have sailed into the harbour. Patrick Green had expected to learn something of himself by sailing the oceans; he undoubtedly did; but he learnt much more because of the people he met when he stopped sailing. It isn't easy to sail away from new found friends simply because a preconceived timetable dictated departure. So Madeira taught him to tarry, and the nature of his voyage changed. Other stops at the Canary Islands and the Cape Verde Islands meant more friends, more tarrying. He even flew to England for a week from the Canaries to collect spares and to see the family. It meant when he headed west across the Atlantic, that he would have to shorten his intended route of a figure-of-eight triple crossing of the ocean, first to Brazil, then South Africa, and back up to America. Patrick Green is a single-handed sailor, but not a solitary man, and if a man's friends are the better for having met him, he too must be the better for having met them.

In spite of that he tells his diary that he never felt lonely at sea; on the contrary at the end of a long sea passage, often of weeks alone "I feel I don't want to make any landfall; I am fully occupied and interested in the challenge of my world, and yes – I don't have to think of where I am and what to do about it."

On 3rd January, 1986, Zuleika headed west from the Cape Verde Islands towards Brazil; not the shortest distance across the Atlantic – it involved crossing the equator. He had been at sea, away from home, over Christmas, and he was already looking forward to next Christmas, "I am sure my relationship with Rums and the boys will be different after this trip; next Christmas will be the best ever."

Three days later the motion of the boat, the rolling, the constant movement and noise coupled with snatched sleep, and the self-discipline of studying navigation text books, caused Patrick to write in his diary of his doubts. "In the end it's not the sailing that gets to you, it's the headaches, and particularly the leaks (Zuleika was leaking badly). It's worth writing these feelings down as I know, that once anchored, there's such a pleasant sense of achievement, you tend to dismiss all that is behind and forget the not so good bits."

A small yacht in a vast ocean is a very small place. Single-handed sailors know there is no second chance. . . Martha was steering the boat; if Patrick fell overboard, she would continue sailing towards Brazil, leaving her human crew to certain death in her wake. Patrick used a harness to anchor himself to Zuleika only in bad weather; the day before his 41st birthday he had found a number of flying fish dead on deck "I cast them back into the deep, as I have no stomach to eat them and deeply regret my intrusion into their world which brought them death. It made me think of the chances of them landing on my deck in the whole of the ocean and comparing it with the probability of my hitting a whale or a large ship. I do think of it but I can't let it dominate, or I couldn't operate. Like falling overboard, it's thoughts of the boys that provides the discipline."

As Zuleika moved south west, approaching the equator, it was HOT. "The heat gets to me and I seem to drink pints. Today I've probably drunk six pints. The heat is also a major reason why I'm so tired."

The following day Patrick sailed Zuleika to within

150 yards of one of the loneliest and most dangerous places on earth, the Rocks of St Peter and St Paul, a thousand miles from Brazil. The twin rocks, which barely break the ocean swell, rise like dragons teeth from the floor of the Atlantic five miles below. Finding them without hitting them is as fine a test of ocean navigation as there is. Although Patrick carried Tony, his satellite nagivation system, it was a back-up; useless if Zuleika's batteries should fail. His primary navigation aid was his sextant, and he saw St Peter and St Paul through the optical eyepiece as he was taking a sight. "This has to be one of the milestones of my life. For some silly reason, I've always wanted to go there. . . I should say come here!" One day later Zuleika crossed the equator; Patrick took "a wee dram" and splashed a few drops over the side to share it with Neptune, one of the fates, Inshallah.

During this part of the voyage, Patrick was doing a lot of reading, staying under shade trying to keep cool. "I have just finished reading "A Key to the Stars", received by me as a class prize for Primary Seven, Crossroads School, 1955/56. It's taken me 30 years and a few thousand miles to read it, but what's the distance to Brazil compared with the distant galaxies and the 880,000 years it takes for light to reach us from Andromeda."

More too about Patrick's childhood when he had been awoken that morning by a dream so vivid it made him cry. . . a dream of an old man unknown to him, a dream with an immensely sad ending, of people who have contributed, but are then lost.

"I do have a very strong impression of my childhood and the community of the north, of Caithness; a way, I believe, of longing for the predictable, protected society of a child, and a consciousness of simplicity of lifestyle. Perhaps it's the gap in distance and time between me and it. Perhaps I fear its passing, its people, its old folks I grew up with, and yet I have seen some of them die without this feeling. Perhaps I am lucky that I still have that, a place I know, people, houses, seashore, climate." Patrick swears he is not into philosophy, but single-handed sailing does change people.

In the meantime, Patrick was driving Zuleika hard to windward, racing, as he says, to the next phone box to call home. It was the determination to drive hard and keep sailing which made Zuleika leak, the timbers of the hull being pulled apart by the pressure of the wind in the sails. "Have just pumped the bilge, water over the floor of the cabin. I know I haven't pumped for three days but this is ridiculous; 525 pumps on the main bilge pump. Hot work." That is a Scottish understatement, it would be hot work in the Arctic, let alone a few miles south of the equator.

Patrick anchored Zuleika at Itaparica, opposite Salvador in Brazil on 26th January, 1986, one week after making his first Brazilian landfall. He stayed for seven weeks, mostly trying to trace letters from home with the help of yet more sailing friends, Argentinians who could speak Portuguese. It was also in Brazil that Patrick declined the offer of female crew, the first of three offers he was to be made before reaching America.

The oceans are sailed by a gypsy-mix of peoples from across the world, all of them united by one common denominator; the sea. Later Patrick was to write, having been called on his short-range radio by a passing ship, and holding a long conversation: "Strange how everywhere today, people don't trust people, yet amongst seamen (not that I would say I am of their ranks) there is an instant bond. Even professional seamen to yachtsmen." That call came from a professional seaman, who, when he enquired of Patrick how many people were aboard and was told "Just me", there was a long pause before the man replied: "Jeeesus Christ".

Within such a bunch of yachting vagabonds as are ocean sailors, relationships blossom, sometimes wither, and offers of partnership from women, often suntanned beauties, are not as rare as they may be ashore. Patrick's polite rejection of three proffered partnerships made him a rare vagabond indeed.

Zuleika headed north from Brazil, towards the Caribbean island of Martinique, on 6th March, 1986, on the longest single passage of his eight months at sea, almost 3000 miles. It meant crossing the equator again, and it almost killed him; it reinforced his faith in Inshallah.

On 13th March, one week into the voyage, damage to the sails left Patrick with no alternative "There is nothing for it but to go up the mast." A yacht remains stable on a rolling ocean because it is moving, and heeling one way or another because of the pressure of the wind in the sails. Take away that stabilising pressure and the yacht becomes a cork, bobbing and pitching at will. . . bad enough for those on deck. For the ONLY person on board to climb a mast of such a lurching vessel is supremely dangerous. Patrick had to do it twice, the second time because he made a careless mistake the first time.

"I cannot describe my ascent. I tried watching the waves to forecast when the mast would whip; I tried jamming my feet and toes between the sail and the mast; I tried to cling to the mast with my thighs; I tried to brace myself between the mast, sail and rigging. In the end I didn't have to think of methods; I clung desperately anyway possible. The bosun's chair (a canvas seat hoisted up the mast by the block and tackle) was so tight into my crutch that my testicles are pushed forward in a lump. If I crash them into the mast, pass out and lose my grip, I've had it." He did reach the damaged sail halyard, replace it with another rope, and get down. But he had led the replacement the wrong way round the rigging. . . he had to go up a second time. It can be compared with trying to climb a giant's fishing rod while the giant is casting for trout over Niagara Falls. "I had screamed at the powers on the horizon "Haven't I done enough?" The horror of having to go up a second time had been too serious to scream at my own stupidity." He did climb again, and he came down safely. He wore his safety harness for days afterwards, conscious that he was too tired and too bruised to avoid falling overboard.

With repaired rigging, Zuleika was sailing days later like a racehorse. "Bows crashing into each wave, sending jets of spray aside and behind as she raced through the night. To me this is one of the best bits of sailing, flying to windward in the dark, flying spray showing white in the moonlight. Then you feel you walk the edge, set up the trick and gamble your judgement; but you know the margins are narrow."

Three days later "I have a Scotch at my feet, celebrating over 300 miles in two days." It got better, as good as it can get in a 35-foot boat. . . an average of 170 miles a day for seven days in succession. But in spite of such exhilaration, Patrick was questioning his motives "Gather your determination and what's left of your strengths and capacity, for without that there is no survival in this emptiness. Like all romantics you sail in the hope of a new horizon, although you know inside it isn't there."

Zuleika dropped anchor in Fort de France, the capital of the French island of Martinique, at dawn on 29th March, 22 days after sailing from Brazil, and leaving a wake of 2799 miles. Again Patrick

was delayed by new friends, the first of whom, a French couple, helped him complete the four hour search for a working phone to call home to Polruan.

Three weeks later, after days of swimming, picnics, folk singing, not a few rum punch parties, and a coat of varnish for Zuleika, Patrick sailed north towards Antigua. On board was his brother-in-law Nigel who'd flown from England for a West Indian cruise. Problems with an electrical back-up self-steering system delayed him in Antigua, he headed north on the penultimate leg of his 10,000 mile voyage to America on 29th May single-handed again. And questioning his motives.

"A few days on land and the sea exerts all its pull and appeal. Why do I relate so much to the sea. My journeys have not as such brought awareness, perhaps more a realisation of where I am and that life still has potential. The sunset tonight, as always, was sad; an end of today, and for some inevitably, no tomorrow."

Zuleika made harbour in St George's, Bermuda, on 6th June, and six days later set sail for Newport, Rhode Island, sailing into the Gulf Stream and flat calm. "I floated with the onion peelings alongside and had my end of the southern latitudes sunbathe. Have felt only so-so, may have been sea-sickness but I suspect it's more to do with my attempts at diet. Empty stomachs and the sea just don't go well together."

Pat and family aboard Zuleika

Left to Right:– Stuart, James, Rosemary (Rummy), Pat and Mark.

On 18th June, 1986, Zuleika cleared customs at Boston, USA. Patrick Green's family flew out to join him for a holiday, and he decided to sell the boat. The last entry in his diary of 10,000 miles is a list of the requirements for his next boat. It ends: "Having established my pen to paper, I leave it for now."

Patrick and his family live at 19 Glenwood Road, Mannamead, Plymouth. He has bought another boat. Pat is the son of George H. Green and his wife Isobel Myron.

This article was written after conversations with Patrick who allowed me to read his personal log of the voyage.

Tim Hurst, Central Television.

One ship sails east and one sails west
While the self same breezes blow
It's the set of the sails and not the gales
That send them where they go.

When the wind backs and the weatherglass falls
Be on your guard 'gainst rain and squalls

Wind before rain let your canvas (sails) remain
– fine sailing weather
Rain before win' get your canvas in
– storms ahead

When the wind backs against the sun
For the nearest port you'd better run.
William Ham, Hoy View.

THE FIRST THRESHING OUTFIT OF ALLAN BROTHERS C.1905
Fowler Engine – Robey Mill

Photo, Jean MacRae, Croftlea, John O'Groats.

Sanny Allan at the wheel of "Maggie". Left to Right:– Geordie Miller, Meg Williamson, Sanny Ross, Jock Green, Sanny Williamson, Danny Mowatt, Mike Gulloch, Davie Banks, Bill Mowat, Eric Ross, Isy Smith, Robbie Dunnet, Bill Gunn (child), Jockal Williamson, Sandy Gunn forking, Davie Ross on the mill. The threshing was taking place on the site of Croftlea.

A THRESHING ON THE CROFT

Allan's Steam Mill pulled in at the croft belonging to John Williamson – Jockal Williamson in the picture. He was well known as a pessimist, and consequently when one was pessimistic in our house you were referred to as a "Jockal".

Geordie Miller resided where the late Bessie Dunnet lived and the house is about to be occupied by a young couple, I am pleased to say. Don Mowat and his Orkney bride are shortly to take up residence. Geordie Miller left John O'Groats and settled in Lyth, returning to the Dog's Nose, Auckengill to retire.

Meg Williamson also known as Maggie – daughter of Jockal and sister of Sanny Williamson was a great character and eventually left John O'Groats to reside and work in Wick.

Sanny Ross, Upper Gills – I don't quite understand why he should be there, unless he was doing a job for someone who would normally be giving a hand at the mill and just came along to help. He was a mason by trade.

John Green, my uncle, would be doing his duty as a neighbour.

Sanny Williamson is clearly on his own territory. He is Jockal's son. Sanny, like sister Meg was quite a character and would very much be the

supervisor on such an occasion.

Danny Mowatt, from the "Broo", resided where Willie and Jean Mowatt now stay. He was the father of Daniel the bus driver, and was married to Meggie Smith. Notorious for his moaning about his rheumatism, the weather or whatever. Oft repeated saying of his "I would be alright if it wisna for my fillad."

Mike Gulloch known as Mikie – bachelor, brother of the well-known character Jim who lived in a one chimneyed house beside the Queen Mother's Quarry. House now demolished. Mikie lived at Plashmire, a small croft south west of where Alex and Peggy Dunnet dwell – the croft is now incorporated in Davie Bank's holding.

Davie Banks married to Katie Smith – sister of Meggie (already mentioned) – father of the late John S. Banks. Lived at Windy Ha' the house now owned by Mrs Ella Banks. Was a roadman whose beat was the "Red Road" stretching from Freswick over the Warth Hill through John O'Groats and into Huna.

Bill Mowat – our much appreciated neighbour and friend of the family – was a stalwart of the herring fishing – and in his fishing career lived on 14 different herring boats, mostly owned by Wick skippers. Walter Mowat, grandson, now occupies the croft.

Eric Ross – also known as Sanny – farmer at Stemster, bachelor, eventually gave up the farm but built the house where Marge and Andrew Sinclair later lived known as Little Stemster. He also kept 25-30 acres of the land of Stemster a holding now belonging to John Mowat, Victoria House. The lady who kept house for Eric was Katie Swanson from Shore Street in Thurso. Came to work at Stemster when 14-years old and stayed at Stemster and Little Stemster all her days. She is the only person I have come across locally who could neither read nor write. Eric by the way was an amateur vet.

Bill Gunn born 1903 died of an undiagnosed disease in 1933. Drove John S. Bank's lorry for a good number of years – was the oldest son in the Gunn family.

Sandy Gunn crofted where Maggie Gunn now dwells. He was also an ardent herring fisher and was popular with the younger generation because of his canny approach. A very hard worker.

Davie Ross – I do not know but I assume he was Sanny Allan's assistant as normally two men travelled with the mill. He came from Keiss.

Isy Smith, sister of Katie, who was married to Davy Banks (roadman) and also sister of Meggie Smith married to Dannie Mowat, ran the croft which Davie Banks now occupies. She was a good and kindly soul and well known for her generosity. Her brother Joe Smith, of one hand fame, lived there and without Isy's help would have found it difficult to work the croft. Eventually, another sister retired from house-keeping in London and lived out her days with Isy.

Ben Green, Roadside, John O'Groats.

"Jockal" or John Williamson was a well known worthy. In early manhood he was press ganged into the navy, and was on one of the old sailing Men of War. Many a hair raising tale he told concerning this period of his life. He then went whaling in Arctic waters, and he'd tell of experiences he had in the whale boat, after the harpoon had made a successful throw. They had many long and dangerous fights with the whale, as they were hauled along at the whale's will, until the final kill. John with the slow spoken comical phrases usually prefaced his yarns, "My dear man," and loved telling of the bargains he made while a cattle dealer in Orkney.

From the Heather Blooms at John O'Groats by John S. Banks, The Broo.

The Caff Seck

The Threshing was always done on a fine dry day and the caff seck was filled when the first of the corn was threshed in September. The chaff in the seck after a year's wear would have flattened and shrunk down a lot.

The caff seck was emptied and the black and white ticking was well shaken out and then filled with lovely sweet smelling, round springy fresh, new chaff. It was filled to give a mattress of about 18 inches deep.

Robbie Dundas, Swona View, Huna.

THE WEDDING

My sister Lottie was married to Donald Shearer on the 2nd of December, 1921. I was 10 years old at the time and my brother Johnnie was just about 14 and ready to leave school. He is dead now and so is Donald Shearer. Lottie is still hale and hearty nearing 90 years of age. I am 10 years younger so my memory is probably a little better but, apart from Lottie herself, there is no-one else I can consult.

It was the first wedding in our family of seven and I was the youngest so, to me, it was a great occasion. It was what one might call a house wedding. My parents might have held it in the John O'Groats hotel but it had been booked for the wedding of Matty Innes and Geordie Sinclair on that same night. Both Donald's family and ours were very populous so going farther afield would have been difficult in view of expense and transport. As far as I can remember, cooking and baking went on for days. Neighbours were involved and there was much borrowing of cutlery and crockery as the wedding meal was to be held in the new Comrades' Hall where its successor still stands today. I have no idea of numbers but the whole business of getting enough tables and seats must have been quite a headache.

The great day arrived at last. The actual marriage ceremony was held in the best room of the house and people packed in or clustered around the door as best they could. The local children regarded the wedding as a kind of school picnic. Many of them, invited or uninvited, crowded in with the guests, but cakes and apples were distributed to these young visitors later.

Altogether it might be called a packed house and there was little room even for the bride and groom to stand together. In a neighbouring house and a previous wedding, the bride had fainted with the press and heat but nothing of that sort occurred in our case. The minister was Mr Forbes who was not only a popular minister but also did much unpaid doctoring as well. He had considerable experience in that line and had no doubt studied medicine at one time.

However there were no need for such ministrations and, after all the customary greetings, kissings, etc. the wedding guests formed up to march down the Breck Road to the hall. A piper led the way. He was Dunnet to name. Donald and he had each worked a pair of horses on Warse farm after the war. Much was the noise and confusion. My interest was divided between the piper and my brother Jamie making preparations to fire a volley or two of 12 bore from our old Mauser shotgun. This he did but there was so much noise that nobody except myself seemed to notice. When I grew older I jaloused that such must have been an ancient custom to scare away evil spirits. I know nothing of other spirits but brother Jamie and his pal, Ben Laird, had bought a small cask of beer which was duly ladled out and some was still left next morning. Big Jeck from the Roadside was passing with one or more carts from work on the Lighthouse Road. He told me much later that he had been invited in for a mug from the cask. I think he said the horse and cart made their own way home!

But I am going on too fast. Remember I was only 10 and Johnnie, though older, was only a boy at school. Both of us were left to our own devices. As you can imagine, these devices were mostly concerned with emptying odd plates of cakes, buns and puddings. Probably we were tired as well but my last memories of the wedding were both of us being violently sick thanks to the unusual abundance of unaccustomed fare.

The dance, of course, followed the meal after the dinner things were cleared away. There was no band. Bill Nicolson from Auckengill played the fiddle with an occasional volunteer to give him a break. The relief would mostly be a boxie but the mouth organ was not unknown. Bill was paid five shillings for his night's work but nobody knew how he managed for transport. I don't know how that wonderful night ended as I wasn't there at the end. Somebody must have decided that I had had enough.

George H. Green, originally John O'Groats, Later Bilbster, Crossroads and Gerston, Halkirk.

EARLY BUS SERVICE, JOHN O'GROATS TO WICK

Archie MacLeod, a Castletown man, ran the coach service between John O'Groats and Wick, for many years but just before the First World War, a man called Charlie Walker appeared in John O'Groats with a motor driven bus (he had come from Edinburgh) and commenced the first bus service on the route. The new quicker service soon saw the coach off the road, but Charlie was short of back up, and before long found it necessary to sell out to R.S. Waters who also had the hardware business in Bridge Street, Wick. It is at this junction that "Daniel" Mowatt comes into the picture – as a young fellow he had spent a lot of his time with Charlie Walker, and his bus, and was naturally curious about the working or the mechanics of the engine. As you can imagine the bus of that period, and especially the engine, was constantly needing attention and repairs, so here was Daniel's chance to get to know a bit about it. And so when Charlie sold out to R.S. Waters, Daniel was the natural choice to drive the mail bus between John O'Groats and Wick.

Buses in those days were not only used for the carriage of passengers. As well as the mail, lots of goods such as feeding stuff, even calfs and piglets were often transported in the buses. Daniel also ran the dried fish from Stroma via the Fish Shed at Huna to Wick. He would make a special trip back to Wick in the evening after delivering the mail, with the fish, and I believe the following morning passengers were faced with the wonderful aroma of salted fish. (Just as well we weren't in the EEC in those days.)

R.S. Waters bus enterprise paid off in the early days and a second bus was put on the road. This one was driven by Willie Macrae who was first married to Cathie Banks and later to Jean Gunn. The two buses were garaged in a wooden shed, the site of which is now George Gunn's bungalow. It was on the same spot as Charlie Walker first had his enterprise – in fact it was the south east corner of the croft at Roadside and in return for the rent of the sublet, my father received the princely sum of 10/- per annum.

R.S. Waters' twin bus service did not last long – traffic had decreased with the failure of the fishing and the start of the long depression, and it was at this point that John S. Banks and Willie Macrae started their own bus service. Daniel, however, carried on driving the mails for many years after.

I am now writing about the early 30s when Banks and Macrae went on the route. Their first bus was a Chevrolet chassis with a body built by J.S. Banks and my brother George who was a joiner, having served his apprenticeship with James Tait at Huna. The construction took place in John S. Banks' garage at the Broo where the Novelty House is now sited. The bus turned out to be very satisfactory and ran the route for a good many years. John S. Banks had previously started a haulage business in the area and his lorry was driven by Bill Gunn, the oldest brother in the Gunn family at West End.

Somewhat later, Sandy Sinclair went into the haulage business, and his business, though somewhat changed in character, still exists in the name of A. and W. Sinclair, Pentland View.

Ben Green, Roadside, John O'Groats.

St Thomas grey, St Thomas grey
The longest night and the shortest day
St Thomas Day 21st December

Johnnie Moar, Huna.

February fills the dykes. March mucks them out.
(Heavy snow in February is followed by heavy rain.)
Barbara Steven, Seaview.

AS HID WIZ

Building the peats out on the shell wings 1937

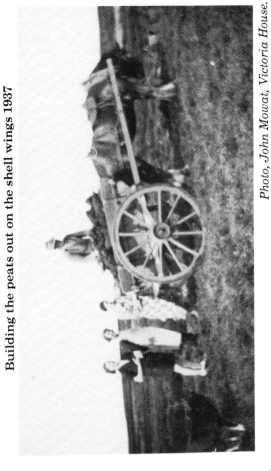

*Photo, John Mowat, Victoria House.
Second left, Bessie Dunnet with Annie and Donald Mowat. Topsy a peaceable mare and Nell the dog.*

Peat cutting at Warth Hill 1976

*Photo, Nancy Houston, St Magnus, John O'Groats.
Johnnie Banks cutting the bottom peat. Magnus Houston and James Dunnet scaling, Janet watching.*

Half yoking in the Ha stackyard 1947

*Photo, Elsie Cowe, The Ha.
Lil wearing sun bonnet. Sandy and Peggy Dunnet, Laurence Brown, John Dunnet, West End.*

Davie Banks carting his granny's peats c.1940

*Photo, Nell Sinclair, Robertson Crescent, Keiss.
Jock in the shafts. "The rubber wheels from an old Essex car – not off the Pennsylvania".*

A GOOD 'GROATS CROFT

There was this Groats crofter and he used to tell that one particular year he had such a crop of oats, that in fact when he leant the sheaves against the telegraph poles the heads were touching the wires! The tatties were that big they would not go in at the barn door and the neeps were so enormous he couldn't get them through the cutter. His carrots beat all, for the only way he could lift them was pulling them by the shaws over his shoulder, like pulling a backie!

I'm thinking this is a yarn – Ed.

Pen drawing – Gordon Inglis, South Road, Wick.

HIDS ALL CHANGED

Charabanc (tourist bus) at John O'Groats, Post Office

Photo, Sandy Manson.
George Manson, my grandfather, built the store on the left with its old English style roof, which was flat on the top to give more room. Notice too, the crane which was a hand powered winch type, used for lifting bags of flour, sugar and feeding stuff into the store.

Cure for toothache?

Fill yer mooth wi' water
Add cod-liver oil
Haud ye heid beside the fire
Till it begins to boil;
(No guarantee given.)
Sandy Manson,
John O'Groat Post Office.

John O'Groats Post Office c.1950

Photo, Barbara Banks, Braeburn, Broo.

Song of Happiness

Sing a song of happiness
Dispel all thoughts of care
Help make the world a pleasant
   place,
Frown now if you dare!
Thrust aside all signs of gloom
Meet troubles with a smile.
Shed happiness on all around,
You'll find it worth your while.
Forget to grieve and worry,
Sing a happy song;
A happy thought, a kindly deed
Helps the world along.
Anon – from, Janet Gunn,
"Emohruo", Mey.

POST OFFICE, JOHN O'GROATS   *Copyright—J. Adams*

John O'Groats Tea Rooms c.1925

Photo, George Steven, Seaview.
This was the first coach party to come for tea with Sandy Fetchie the driver who brought many more tourists here over the years.

MIND ON

Land yachting 1932

Photo, George Steven, Seaview.
Left to Right:– Sandy Manson, George Manson,
George Steven, (jib sail on frame of motor bike).

Operation Snowdrop 1955

Photo, George Manson, East End.
Royal Navy helicopter. George and Sandy Manson collecting the
mails. (Seaview House in background).

The Mail Bus in a "Cutting" February 1955

Photo, Sheila Wares, Seater.
Conductress Sheila Manson in bus. Driver Willie Mowatt
took the photo.

Tea Rooms 1955

Photo, Sheila Wares, Seater.
William Florence on a mountain of snow.

Butlin's Walk 1959

Photo, George Steven, Seaview.

The "Victory" leaving Groats c.1951

Photo, Magnus Houston.
Willie Bremner, Glencairn at the helm. The "Britannia"
or "Hope II" anchored in the isles.

SEEDTIME AND HARVEST

A Standing Crop of Ripe Corn

Jim Rosie on International binder and Magnus Houston on MF35 Tractor.

Starting a Screw at the Mill Brig

Jim Rosie forking, David Dunnett making the stadle and Janet learning to skip!

Preparing to Sow

David Dunnett, Hillhead, ready with sowing sheet.

Stooks

A good crop of oats at Danny Gullochs.

SEATER TO SANNICK

I would like to take you a walk along the shore from Seater to Sannick Bay. It was difficult to know where to start or finish but who better to accompany me on the first lap than my good friend John Dunnet, Seater. John has few equals in his knowledge of Huna, its customs and traditions. His family have resided there for many generations taking their living from the land and from the sea. We set out on a lovely May afternoon and first of all John says, "I'll show you the grave of the Englishman." We went across his land and then through Quoys to the shore. Just above the high water mark there is a head-stone two and a half feet wide, eight inches thick and standing two feet high. It is a rough stone but we could decipher no inscription. There is a smaller stone at the sailor's feet, and, as was the custom, he faced the rising sun. It is believed the body came ashore from the wreck of an English ship and was buried here by Huna fishermen. Whether by accident or intent the grave lies exactly in a direct line between the Kirk of Stroma and the Old Kirk manse in Canisbay.

We continued along the shore towards Huna. In January 1993, there was an exceptionally high tide accompanied by record low pressure in the Atlantic and the ensuing storm caused a great deal of erosion along the coast. John pointed out that fences which had been seven or eight yards back from the beach were now right at the high-water mark. Running out from the boundary between John's land and Quoys is a large spit of shingle known as the "Point of the Spur". Rounding the Spur we came to the Haven of Seater. Before the lifeboat slip was built, the Huna and Seater fishermen all kept their boats here at the mouth of the burn. It is a wide pebble beach of maybe 100 yards with protective reefs running out to each side. John remarked that David Gunn, John O'Groats, a noted fisherman, ardently believed that the Haven of Seater, excavated into the land was the best and safest place for a harbour on our coast. There were 20 or so big "silkies' lying sunning themselves on the East rocks when we walked past. We climbed up on the brae and crossed the Seater burn to see the boats' oasts or noosts. There are at least four oasts excavated into the brae – 20 feet long by 10 feet wide. They were shaped to match the underside of the boats which were hauled up into the oasts in rough weather and for protection from winter storms. There is also a flat area which has been excavated maybe for curing fish or perhaps kelp.

We then proceeded on top of the brae and 40 yards west of the smiddy house there is a raised mound with flag stones set in an irregular pattern. Whether it had Christian or Pagan significance, John was not sure, but we both agreed it is far too elaborate for a sheep shelter. We came back onto the beach below the houses and walked on to the slip. The lifeboat station was established at Huna in 1877 and standing at the shed looking down the rails was, for us, a poignant reminder of the brave men who manned the open boat with only oars, sails and their knowledge of the Firth to guide and assist them. We both marvelled at the construction of the slip (1890) – massive stones some eight feet by five and 16 inches thick, hammer dressed and fitting exactly. It has been battered by, and weathered all the storms in the Pentland Firth for over a century, and is a credit to the man who designed it and the men who built it. Mr William Bremner, Freswick (Norseman's father) a stone mason at the building of the railway viaduct over the River Spey was foreman at the slip. When I was a boy "**the**" place to go for sellags[1] was to the Huna slip and the main method of catching them was with the "sellag pock'. It consisted of a round iron ring four and a half feet diameter, covered slackly with a knitted net, the mesh being slightly smaller than for herring and weighed down at the centre with a small lead sinker. It was suspended with four ropes from a wooden pole held by the fisherman. The second half of September and October with an evening flood-tide was "**the**" time for fishing. Limpet bait was leeped in a bucket, that is covered with boiling water before removing them from the shell. The man working the pock would lower it in the water, chew the bait and spit it over the ring. Limpet bait was considered to be the best for "bringing in" the sellags, so that was used first and then boiled potatoes were spat over the pock. The sellags swarmed after the bait – the pock was raised quickly and on a good night two or three pints in bulk would be secured with every lift. The experts with the pock in those days were Will Cormack, William Rosie the post and Daniel Mowatt. We used to hurry home with the fish, clean them, roll them in flour and fry them. The excitement of going to Huna, the crack there, and the anticipation of the feast always engendered an enormous appetite and I still consider there is no dish quite like a plate of fried sellags straight from the sea. John told me, that in his father's time, a long net would be laid at low-water and as the tide flowed in, it would be dragged ashore by two or three men at each side and often pailfuls of sellags would be landed with every haul. The sea and sea shore was a great provider of food. My mother was born and raised in Upper Gills and her granny, born in 1830, stayed with them. She would often tell the bairns to be careful and thrifty and would say "I remember the days of the famine", and when she spoke of that time my mother said her voice changed completely and she pronounced it as "the faymin". This was when the potato crop failed in Caithness, as it did in Ireland and caused the historic famine in 1844 and 1845. Many people from Bower and inland areas came down the Brabster road to Gills and Huna to get fish and gather limpets and whelks etc. It is said that in Caithness, after the potato was established, there was never an extreme shortage of food because a small area could produce a large quantity of the best of nourishment, also the old crop lasted until the new crop was ready. This led to maybe overdependence on the potato, with disastrous consequences in years of crop failure, due to blight.

Huna was at the very heart of a very busy community occupying a key position in the Parish and was the focal point for all the Stroma traffic. There was an inn at Huna long before the John O'Groats Hotel was built and it was formerly the landing place for passengers and mails from Orkney.

But to continue with our walk – just to the East of the lifeboat shed there is a concrete area which was the floor of the fish shed, built 1926 by a firm Davidson from Glasgow, for buying, selecting and sending south, line-caught fish from local and Stroma boats. John's uncle George was the man in charge and great is his regret that the "books" belonging to the firm have been lost for they would have provided a great record of the fish landed in times past. The shed was erected by Alfred Moir, formerly of Stroma but at that time working from Mey. It was an accepted fact that Stroma salt-fish was the very best that could be got.

Staying above the brae, a hundred yards further on, is a small mound known as the "Rickan Hillag". When a boat was wanted over from Stroma, people went to Willie Sutherland the blacksmith for a small winlin of straw and it was burnt here, in full view of the island as a signal. From here, almost to the Huna Hotel, there was extensive removal of shell-sand for agricultural purposes in the 1940's. This part of Huna was the site of an historic and very important Norse settlement. Dr Colleen Batey, Kelvingrove Museum, has written that Huna is the only site of a Norse boat burial to be even suggested for mainland Scotland.

Past Huna Hotel just below the brae is a big flagstone well. The Huna district in a dry summer was often very scarce of fresh water, and I can well remember Will Cormack coming everyday to the mill wade with his cattle. The regional water scheme in 1953 was indeed a blessing for such places. The shore is rough here and strewn with big boulders. John says that at low water with spring tides, lobsters would be stranded in pools and easily caught from the land in the days when lobsters were plentiful.

Now we come to the Peat Goes. Before 1945, Stroma was owned by two proprietors – the North End by the Freswick Estate and the remainder by the Mey Estate. As there was no peat moss left on the island, the Stroma people cut their peats on the mainland. The Goes are long trinks with flat rocks on each side which allowed the boats to come well inshore. A stack of peats entails of a lot of hard work for anybody, but for the Stroma folk it was doubly so, as you can well imagine. Quite a few of the North End men cut their peats in John O'Groats at Crogodale and the peat road going past the Breck is still known as the Stroma road. I have heard my grandfather saying that with a wet Spring, which made a late "down-lay" of the crops, the crofter-fishermen from Stroma, desperate to get their land work completed and their boats ready for the Wick herring fishing on the 3rd of June, would already be cutting peats in the Groats' hill when the sun was rising out of the sea, and that in the middle of May it would be 4.00 a.m. My grandfather had a tremendous respect for the Stroma men both on the sea and on the land. John and I then walked along the beach until we came to Scarfskerry Point, so named many centuries ago, likely because the scarfs stand out on the skerry rock shaking their wings dry, as they still do today. We then realised that time had caught up with us, so we climbed up on the brae and walked across the lands towards the smiddy. On the way John said that at the turn of the century, from the Mool Hill to Kirkstyle there were 10 crofts, all with Dunnets, and most of these families were not closely related.

Just to refresh my memory I went back to Scarfskerry Point a few days later. I remember Daniel Mowatt, the Broo, saying he had seen as many as five men working sellag pocks from the two deep goes that run into the beach here, and that before the lifeboat slip was built, this was the premier spot for fishing sellags on our shore. Just to the east, in the face of the cliff are three caves known locally as the Stobie Holes. In 1934 a man by the name of Jamie Street lived here – the last cave dweller in the Parish. He had been in the Royal Signals in the first war and for some reason "took to the road". Ben Green told me the local folk were very kind to this man and he in return taught the boys morse and signalling. Good battery torches were coming into fashion then and "morseing" to Stroma, Orkney and ships in the Pentland Firth became, among the youth, a very popular hobby.

Walking along from the caves, we come into the sweep of Foligoe or the Whale's Goe – a wide beach of rough shingle. Coming up from the shore to the top of the cliffs is a man-made waar road used by horse and carts. Just looking at it, one can realise the enormous amount of time, effort and hard work which must have gone into its construction. Seaweed or waar as it is always called here, has since time immemorial played a very important part in manuring crops and improving arable land. In the First Statistical Account of Scotland, published in 1793, Dr Morison wrote "The shores of the Parish are exceeding valuable yielding about a hundred tons of kelp in a favourable season which is near as much as is made in all the rest of Caithness – 20 tons of wet seaweed yielding one ton of kelp."

Going on towards the back of the North House, the shore is rocky with big loose stones. Sinclair Rosie, Hillside told me the best stone land-rollers commonly known as "tirlags" were taken from here and in fact, he said one still lies in the ebb almost completed. Stone rollers which were quarried would often "board" or split and it is easy to understand that if stones from the shore would crack, the "tirlags" would have been broken long ago. Just below the North House one can see where a big lintel or roller has been split off from the rock-face by drilling holes six inches apart. Millstones have also been quarried here, for close by on a big flat rock the stone has been dressed away to leave a full-sized millstone – four and a half feet in diameter and 10 inches thick, almost ready to be burst off the bed. The work must have been carried out by my own forebears although I never heard it mentioned and I can only guess why it was abandoned.

From the brae-edge here a waar road leads down to the burn-mouth. My father used to say that an enormous quantity of seaweed came into the burn-mouth in spring with easterly winds. The men from the Broo and Midtown came on to shore with their carts at the hotel for a short cut, and went through the Hang-gate and then carted half loads from the beach up the Waar road to the top of the brae. The burn-mouth at that time was all shell-sand with the result, that not only was sea-weed being applied but also lime which was most beneficial to the peaty soil. I remember Jeannie Dunnett from the East End saying that after the advent of steam fishing trawlers in the 1890's there never again came such large quantities of waar onshore. (The trawls broke up the growing seaweed before it had matured.) At the same time the trawlers were blamed for a lot of things, including the decline in herring and cod fishing.

On 23rd February, 1941, Elsie Cowe's brother Magnus, aged 16, found what turned out to be a mine on the shore here. He carried it up to the waar road and went home and told his father. They both went back – the mine exploded killing Magnus instantly; her father Malcolm died later that same evening in hospital. This tragic event and sad day is often remembered and spoken about in our district.

Close beside the brae, just west of the burn, clear evidence can still easily be seen of William Sinclair's boat building stance. He had learnt his trade in Wick and he built big herring "Ferthie' boats here. Hamish Donn says the last herring boat to be built at the burn-mouth was the "Britannia" which belonged to John Houston, East End. She was a very successful boat and eventually ended her days as a shed at the Last House. In September 1857, William Sinclair's son David, aged ten, was taking a stirk out to the grass, he had tied the tether round his waist – the animal bolted – the boy was dragged off his feet and killed. After this tragedy, the Sinclair family felt they could no longer stay in Newton and took on the farm in Auckengill where Alan Richard now resides. William Sinclair's brother James emigrated to New Zealand as a young man and founded the town of Blenheim in 1876.

There were several very skilled boat-builders in the Parish during the latter half of the 19th century and none more so than John Banks, the Back Road, Newton. He had served his time with Banks at Harrow, and it was said he had a good eye for a boat. John S. Banks says in his book, page 57, "Highlanders from the North coast of Sutherland did like a John Bank's boat." Cathy Manson, East End, told me her grandfather had a boat built here in 1890. The crew walked most of the way from Skerray, Sutherland and sailed the boat home. My information from Ben Green is that Banks built Sinclair Steven's boat the "Ivy" and Green the Breck's boat among many others. Banks's son William founded Banks the Drapers in High Street, Wick.

But to get back to the burn mouth – Donald Mowat, Victoria House, told me he came down to the mill with his father during the great snow storm of January 1918, and they walked across the gill which was level from side to side. The snow came from the south east and he said a lot of sheep on Duncansby Head drove before the storm and were drowned at Sannick. When the snow eventually melted, Kennedy's and Beel Cook's boat was found to have been flattened by the weight. All that now remains of the burn mouth haven is the concrete plinth which secured the hauling winch.

Coming up on the east side is another waar road, and recent coast erosion has exposed its very careful strong construction – starting off with huge stones cassied side by side. Walking round the point we come to the Hang-gate and then the Snib. Lying on the beach are two millstones – part of an Orkney schooner's cargo wrecked here. This part of the shore above the high-water mark is known as the Ha Green. It used to be extensive but with the removal of the shell-sand for agricultural purposes during the 1939/45 War and consequent and subsequent coastal erosion, very little of the Green now remains. It is a lovely walk on a sandy beach from there to the John O'Groats Hotel.

Duncansby Mains or the Ha was made a farm in the early 1800's and extended from the Mill to the Stacks of Duncansby incorporating the hotel ground, fields above the burn, Duncansby Head Grazing and everything on the north of the dry-stone dyke, which runs from the camping site to the lighthouse road. In 1901 the proprietor, Admiral Sinclair, agreed to reduce drastically the size of the farm, and let the ground so released to the surrounding crofting tenants, as enlargements to their holdings. Many crofters in the East and the West End took advantage of this offer. Duncansby Head Grazings was shared among 28 crofters – in fact all who expressed an interest. The original souming was: a horse and two sheep; or six sheep per share. I have heard the older generation recalling it was a great sight to see sometimes over 20 horses and several foals, all galloping over the grazings. With reseeding, ditching, draining and liming, the share has been increased to 12 sheep and their followers. The Duncansby Head Grazings has proved a great boon to all concerned and its success is due entirely to the good co-operation between the shareholders.

In 1901 the tenant of the Ha was Edward Mackenzie, who also ran the John O'Groats Hotel. They then moved to Hilton, just south of Tain, Ross-shire, where the family farm to this day. Edward missed John O'Groats very much and used to return every August to the lamb sales and stay in the hotel.

Now on to Billy Steven's camping site. I am quite

sure this ground has never been cultivated since it became part of the Ha early last century. The grass is always kept short with the result you can see an excellent example here of ridge and furrow cultivation, a method used to dry the soil before underground drainage was practised. The ridges are six yards apart and run with the natural gradient. There is also a very good example of ridge and furrow cultivation covering a large area at the Head of Mey. From the camping site there is a good sandy foot-path leading on to the shore at Willie Laird's burn and here, half-way between the high and low watermark, is the Knocking Stone. On top of this big rock there is a natural basin-shaped hollow resembling a knocking stone, in which bere was knocked with a wooden mall to remove the awns. Now whether this rock, because of its location, was used as such is difficult to imagine but at the same time, just to the east is the Winnin Hill, where in olden times the grain was winnowed.

Moving on we come to the sites of the two Pre-Reformation Catholic Chapels, St Mary's and Ladykirk. Very little evidence of them remains today, only some loose building stones lying on the shore above the high water mark and a few built in a dyke there. In 1969 several hundred coins, dated 1600–1700, were found here. Whether the coins had been hidden for safe keeping in time of conflict or placed in the walls for whatever reason, I suppose will never be known. Dr Raymond Lamb, County Archaeologist, Orkney said in a recent article "that medieval churches were never built to stand isolated in the country-side, but erected near to the most important settlements in the district." This area was certainly of great significance in those times and much evidence still remains of the inhabitants presence, in form of the fish middens and Norse buildings. Good stone walls were exposed here several years ago when the grazers were digging foundations for new dipping fanks.

Next we now come to the concrete sea wall built in 1980. The work was done under a community aid project and the local men employed were William Rosie, William Laird, John William Laird and Clarence Sinclair. Of all the improvements done on the common grazings, this surely gives the most benefit. Previously winter storms continually broke down the fences on the beach allowing the sheep to stray. David Dunnett, Hillhead told me that when the "Thyra" struck head-on at Queenie Cliff in 1914 part of her cargo was big pitch-pine logs. A large quantity was salvaged by the shareholders and rafted round Duncansby Head to the Niss. Sanny Allan, Millman, Mey came over with his steam-engine and saw, and cut up the wood into fencing posts. The fencing around the cliffs was erected by two brothers Cormack, who later on had a holding on Lochend, Barrock. (Prior to this there was a fail dyke².) They were most excellent fencers and although much has been renewed recently, a good portion of the original fence remains. Galvanised strainers and stays were used and were fixed in round holes drilled into large boulders. A mixture of molten lead mixed with sulphur and known as "Devil's Blood" was poured around the strainers and they are as firm today as they were when erected.

We now cross the Muckle ditch and on to the fine sandy beach known as the Crook of the Niss and at the east side of this bay lies Robbie's Haven. It has been of great importance over the centuries and especially during the 19th Century when the sailing ships going west took a local pilot aboard off Duncansby Head. Piloting was a very precarious occupation with the first man reaching the ship getting the fee. The Duncansby pilots – a very special breed – came mostly from the East End, launching their boats from Robbie's Haven where now only the roofless ruins of their "sail hoose" remains. What tales those stones could tell of the piloting of large sailing ships through the Firth particularly the great emigrant ships from northern Europe and Eastern Britain, outward bound for the Americas with hundreds of passengers cramming the rails for one long last look back.

Some of the East End crofts were small and it is said a good percentage of their winter living came from the cod-line and the kailyard. From Robbie's Haven to the point of the Niss, the beach is rough and covered with stones. It has been the graveyard of many a good ship even in recent times. Just east of the Niss lie the Iron Craigs. This must be one of the most accessible, and best examples of volcanic rock in the North. It is fascinating to see how the molten mass has solidified trapping stones of every description.

From the Niss to the Snib of Sannick is really a lovely walk – a wide beach made up of millions and millions of shells of every shape, colour and size. Our part of Scotland is much affected by the Gulf Stream and these shells are carried through the Firth by the warm waters of the North Atlantic drift and deposited south of the Skerries in an area known as the "Sanny Riddles". Easterly storms throw them up on the beach here. Near the Snib of Sannick the ridges of rock come in almost to the brae and the biggest trink is known as the Stroma Haven – another goe used for transporting peats to the island.

Round the Snib we come to the beautiful bay of Sannick, a long stretch of fine clean white sand. On 12th April, 1650 the Marquis of Montrose landed here from Orkney with 1,500 fighting men in support of the King. He marched to Thurso, cut overland to Dunbeath and was defeated at the battle of Carbisdale on 27th April. Montrose fled to Ardveck Castle but was betrayed by the Laird of Assynt and hung at the Mercat Cross in Edinburgh on 21st May, 1650. John Buchan says in his book "Montrose" that "Tears ran down the hangman's face as he pushed him off the scaffold and a great sob broke from the crowd - - - they had cause to sob for that day was done to death such a man as this country has not seen again."

Well, I am at the end of my walk now and looking east I wonder if that mound 100 yards along on the far side of the burn is a horned cairn?

Archaeologists say the shape is right, the site is right and hopefully time will tell that they are right.

Looking west I can see 40 houses on Stroma silhouetted against the evening sky. The setting sun shining on the Firth puts things into perspective for me – the same yesterday, today and for ever.

[1] Young coalfish.

[2] Turf.

Magnus Houston, The Mill House, John O'Groats.

THE MEAL MILL
The John O'Groats Mill 1903

My grandfather born in 1856 wrote a short history of the family on the first page of a mill ledger and from this I quote.

"The Houston family acquired the John O'Groats Mill in 1750. William Houston one of three brothers was born on a croft at the burnmouth named Swartigill. Previous to this date the mill was worked by John Sutherland bachelor, miller and pilot who was also engaged in trading to Orkney. He carried the mails as well as passengers, cattle, horses and other freight from the ferry haven.

On his last and final trip back he had on board beside the crew three young horses – about half-way across the Pentland Firth being a stormy day in November and probably overloaded with the horses the boat in a sudden squall capsized. All were drowned except for a young horse which swam towards Duncansby and landed at the Niss.

The above Wm. Houston then succeeded John Sutherland in the Mill."

But there certainly has been a mill at or near the present site since long before 1750. Recently through erosion by the burn in spate, a well-built stone wall has been exposed just south of the road-bridge and running at 45 degrees to the main stream. Archaeologists from Glasgow University believe this could be the foundations of a Norse water mill built maybe a thousand years ago.

The concept of milling has never changed and goes back to the very mists of time. It is mentioned in Genesis 18 verse six that Abraham told Sarah his wife "to make ready quickly three measures of fine meal."

Originally the work was all done by hand with quern stones and the principle is still the same today. The lower or bed-stone is fixed and the upper or runner-stone is spun around on top. The dried grain is fed through the "eye" in the centre and as the stone is rotated the grain is ground into meal. The bed-stone is always flat and the runner is slightly concave or, as we say in Caithness, "has a dish in it." Working the quern by hand was very hard work and there is a saying if something is difficult to do, "it is as stiff as the handle of the quern."

The first mechanical mills came to Northern Britain with the Norsemen and were known as "click mills".

There is a good working example in Dounby, Orkney, and several others in Shetland. Such mills were usually set on a lade drawn off a burn so the water supply could be better controlled. The wheel sits horizontally in the side of the lade and is driven round as the water runs past.

A wooden shaft fixed into this wheel comes up through the bed-stone and by means of a counter sunk iron cross-bar the top-stone is spun around. This was certainly a big improvement on the quern. Recently a click mill stone was uncovered beside the old brig. This was a most important special find for us and George Campbell, Dunnet made a simple protective bed for it beside the present mill.

With the click mill the grain was all dried in straw-kilns on the crofts. I have never seen a straw kiln working but on one occasion when I was in Swona, James and Arthur Rosie showed me several examples which they referred to as the "Dutchmen". James explained that this type of kiln made a first class job of drying any kind of grain. The kiln bearers, or simmers, were made of wood and no iron was used in the structure. On Swona the kilns are round shaped like the doo-cot at Freswick Castle, and stand separate from the rest of the steadings.

In the click mill era the dried corn was brought to the mill in kaisies and emptied into the hopper for shelling. Next the hulled grain was carried to the shelling hill where it was winnowed. The sieves for winnowing were circular, covered with sheepskin and stretched over a wooden frame. I have been told a great deal of skill and practice was required to manipulate the sieve to stream the grain in the wind. The shellings (kernels) were then taken back to the mill for grinding. However the great advance in milling came with the advent of the perpendicular or vertical waterwheel and of this type, by far the most efficient is the overshot where the water goes over the top of the

wheel, the weight of water multiplied by the radius giving the horse-power. Before this kind of wheel can function, there has to be at that point a drop of at least the diameter of the wheel plus two feet to allow the water to get away. At our mill we are particularly fortunate in this respect. The meal mills at Watten and Thurso, where this drop could not be achieved because of the lie of the land, were driven by a vertical breast wheel where the water struck at the middle turning the wheel back the opposite way. Consequently much more water was required to generate the same power. For milling, the supply of water is of the most utmost imporatance and my grandfather used to say "a person who would waste water would waste anything."

There is a very interesting map of the "Lands of Duncansby" drawn up in 1817 when the Lairds of Mey and Freswick did a deal. The mill and Newton (the new town of Duncansby) was given to the Freswick Estate and in exchange Mey Estate received Stemster and Lower Stemster. The Stemster burn was also diverted at this time to give more water for the mill. This exchange took place to allow a site for a new mill and mill dam on the Freswick Estate. This mill was erected in 1818 and John Nicolson, Nybster, in consultation with my grandfather, made a painting of the setting as it would have looked at that time. Sandy Manson at the John O'Groat Post Office has the original but unfortunately it has proved difficult to reproduce. Alice Calder has very kindly made this line drawing of the painting. This mill was built close beside the Cromwell bridge with the breast wheel on the east gable and the kiln at the other end. There was only one pair of millstones used for both shelling and grinding.

Sketch of the 1818 Mill from John Nicolson's Painting

Drawing by Alice Calder, Katrins, Sibmister, Castletown.

Circa 1840 iron foundries were established in Wick and Thurso. The Industrial and Agricultural Revolutions were in full swing and new milling techniques were being developed. Consequently a new mill was erected in 1845 by my great-grandfather with two pairs of millstones, one for shelling and one for grinding. Other improvements such as sack-tackle, sifters, elevator belts, separators and fans were also incorporated. In 1888 the same John Nicolson, a contemporary and great friend of my grandfather's, came down to Swartigill and painted the scene as it was then, see page 49.

The middle building with a good smoke coming from the kiln and showing clearly the overshot wheel was the mill built 1845. My great-grandfather made a big wooden gear wheel for this mill and I am very glad it still survives.

The building in the foreground was the threshing mill and barn for the Ha built also c.1845. The two buildings were strategically positioned to take advantage of the one water supply. The bridge in the foreground was built by Cromwells' soldiers in 1651.

After the Marquis of Montrose was defeated at Carbisdale in 1650, Cromwell was afraid this part of the country could again be invaded from Orkney. A garrison was sent North, the horses were stabled in the Old Kirk of Canisbay and the soldiers billeted in the houses of the tenantry. (Recorded in Church Session Records.) During the winter months a great amount of water comes down the Duncansby burn, and so that the troops could be moved quickly in an emergency, the soldiers built a bridge over the burn here. It is reputed to be the oldest military bridge in the Highlands. Although not of unique design, I think it is worth mentioning the stones in the arch are almost all undressed and start an angle of 65 degrees to the horizontal. The bridge built over 340 years ago has been visited by architects and enthusiasts from all over Britain who marvel at its construction and condition. The main road bridge was built in 1875 and opened by Edward The Prince of Wales, before this the wheeled traffic crossed by a ford just south of this bridge.

My grandfather was the sixth son in a family of nine and during the late 1890's, he decided that if he was to stay on in John O'Groats he would have to get a bigger and better mill in order to make a reasonable living. In the summer of 1900 his nephew Billy Houston, an engineer in Glasgow, came north, they both went round all the mills in Caithness and took what they hoped were the best ideas from each. That year a new four horse threshing mill was installed in the steading at the Ha and their threshing mill and barn (in the foreground of the painting) was not required. Plans were drawn up for a new mill incorporating this building and in 1901 the present mill went up.

At this point I would like to give credit to the contractors concerned.

The new mill was built by George Sinclair, East Mey – a legend in his lifetime.

George Sinclair was born at Howe, Lyth in 1843 and as a young man in his teens worked as a carter at the Wick herring fishing which at that time was at its very zenith. In the winter months he was employed building dry-stone dykes in the Mey area and after a very few years he became mason for the Mey Estate, moving to a house at Rigifa. Great progress and improvements were taking place in agriculture then and George took on the contract to erect dry-stone dykes around every field on Barrogill Mains. The stones were quarried on the shore below the castle and these dykes stand today for everyone to see, as straight and as beautiful as the day they were built. He also constructed the dykes on West Canisbay and Phillips Mains.

George Sinclair and his wife Eliz Thomson had a family of 12 sons and one daughter and he would jokingly remark that they had 12 sons and each one had a sister.

His business soon expanded and he began taking on work over a wide area giving much employment and training many local men as masons. In Canisbay Parish his houses included those of G. Manson, grocer, John O'Groats; J. Sutherland, Newton; J. Dunnet, Seater; Alex Begg, Gills; also the East and West Lodges in Mey. He built the Gerston Distillery, major extensions to the Miller Academy and British Linen Bank, also the Lodge and entrance to Thurso Castle.

In the latter half of the 19th century, several large sporting estates were created in Caithness and Sutherland. The most elaborate shooting lodges were the fashion and George Sinclair, in partnership with several of his sons, took on contracts for extensive alterations and improvements to the lodges at Strathmore, Dalnawillan and the Gluth, where even tennis courts were created and Lochdhu Lodge was built from the very foundations. We only have to look at a map of Caithness to understand the enormous scale of George Sinclair's achievements – truly a legend in his lifetime.

The joiner work on the mill was undertaken by John Manson from Thurso. He had emigrated to South Africa as a young man and returned to start up a joinery business in Rose Street. His foreman at the mill was James Sutherland, Freswick from a family of joiners over many generations. James Sutherland and his wife both died early in life leaving two sons Hamish, seven and Marcus, five, who were brought up by their grandparents at Midtown Skirza.

John Bruce, Wick Foundry had the contract for supplying the machinery and fittings. The Bruce family originally came from Kirk and after serving his time as a moulder in Wick then gaining experience in Glasgow, John Bruce started up in a new foundry in Grant Street, later moving to an extensive site at East Banks which included the present Newton Avenue. The machinery was fitted and installed by Donald Miller and Sons, Millwrights, Wick.

The beremeal stones are granite from Kirtomy near Bettyhill, the bedstone being originally from a mill in the Corsback Gill which is across from the Crossroads School. The oatmeal stones were specially made up and known as Derby Peaks. The shelling stones are red-sandstone and were quarried at Dunnet Head.

My father had the greatest admiration for all the tradesmen involved but he especially admired the moulders and millwrights. Casting was a most skilled, exact and even at times dangerous trade. It must be borne in mind that the foundry had first to make new patterns in wood of the gearing etc required, also allowing for expansion and contraction. The complexity of the castings, the ingenuity and the amounts of measurement involved, deserves the greatest praise and admiration. The millwrights were really exceptional men. They had to understand milling, speed, timing and the relationship between them. Their work has stood the greatest test of all, the test of time. One can only wonder what these men could have achieved with power tools and modern machinery. Credit must also be given to Wm. C. Houston who designed and encouraged my

Preparing the beremeal stones

Photo, Rogni Brown, Swartigill.

grandfather to go ahead with the project.

I am in the mill most days in the winter months and it is only now I am realising and recognising the extraordinary amount of dedication, thought and expertise that went into its planning. The simplicity and effectiveness of the machinery never fail to amaze me.

Magnus Houston, The Mill House, John O'Groats.

NEWTON

In a modern day world of rush and hurry, it is good sometimes to sit down and reminisce on years gone by when time did not mean so much; when the days seemed to be longer and the years took longer to pass. In such a frame of mind, I will endeavour as far as my memory serves me, to describe what life was like, what took place in this insignificant part of John O'Groats – but still a place that is dear to one who spent his carefree childhood days and part of his adult life, enjoying the bracing air of the Pentland Firth.

Newton had this unique advantage in the late 19th century and the early part of this century to be served with all the trades necessary for our needs in life.

To begin with, in the house known as The North House, now owned by Mr Laurence Brown, situated at the bottom of the Newton Road, we had the tailor, Mr David Kennedy, who would have one or two apprentices working with him. His wife had a grocer shop to supply all the necessary needs for food and household goods.

The next house, known as Seaside House, was the home of the Sutherland family. William Sutherland was a shoemaker. William and his son James, sometimes assisted by a part-time journey

– man and two apprentices, catered for all classes of footwear – from ladies and gents dress shoes and boots, the strong "tackety" boots for out-door workers, to the sea boots, knee length and full hip length for fishermen all made from leather. It was quite a busy place, where people would often gather and enjoy a good "crack" while waiting to have their footwear repaired.

Sunbeam Cottage, next door now owned by Mr Frank McGregor, was built by Mr James Sutherland round about 1903 when he got married. In the war years, and certainly after the first war, the shoemaker business declined and ultimately closed. Mr Sutherland then became Poor Inspector and Clerk to the District Council, and because of this had to move to a house in Canisbay next door to the old United Free Church. He later returned to Sunbeam Cottage round about 1930, carrying on as Clerk to the District Council until his death in 1936. During Mr Sutherland's stay in Canisbay, he let the house to Mr Wm. Rosie, (father of Mr Walter Rosie who has the novelty and souvenir shop at the Broo, John O'Groats). Mr Rosie and his wife started up a grocer's shop. He also had a horse drawn delivery van, and with his faithful white steed, "Flossy", he brought provisions to many on the west side of the parish who lived some distance from the shop.

In the croft house, later owned by Mr A. McGregor, we had the local joiner Mr Robbie Smith. He was a real character who could see the funny side of every situation, and nothing delighted him more than to get a rise or joke on his neighbours. Here again was a good thriving business with two journeymen and very often two or three apprentices employed to supply all the facilities needed on the farm, in the house, and also catering for all funeral services.

Moving up the Stemster road to the first house, now "Horseman's Cottage", we come to where Mr John Banks stayed. He carried on a good boat building and blacksmiths business, employing a journeyman and two apprentices. We also have the well known landmark in John O'Groats, the meal mill, owned by Mr Magnus Houston, who ground and supplied oatmeal and beremeal for the crofting area round about. An interesting exercise concerning the preparation of the grain for grinding is perhaps little known by this modern generation. In the early part of the century the threshing was all done by the "flail" or small hand driven barn mill, but if I could be personal for a moment, at our croft at Lower Stemster we put in a horse driven barn mill made by a firm called McKidd, Thurso. This mill cost £30 if my memory serves me right – a lot of money in those days. The mill was fitted with a wooden shaft on opposite sides of a spur wheel, to which two horses were attached, although one horse could quite easily drive the mill. It was a sickening job for the horse as he trudged round and round the circular course for one or sometimes two hours at a time. When properly trained they would go themselves with the man tending the straw end of the mill keeping a watchful eye at the back door. With a loud shout of "Whoa" from inside, the horse would gradually ease off, being careful not to stop too suddenly or the shaft would hit him in the heels. The grain and the chaff all fell underneath the mill which then had to be separated or winnowed. This process was completed by using a sieve made with a bamboo cane formed in an oval shape and then covered with a piece of dried sheep or cow hide. The back and front barn doors were purposely built in two halves and directly opposite one another. On a suitable windy day the bottom halves of the back and front doors were removed, thus causing a controlled channel of wind. With the help of the sieve as a utensil for lifting and gently shaking the chaffy mixture in the path of this wind, the grain was successfully separated. It was then put through a hand riddle to extract any empty husks that may have escaped the wind. It was now ready for sending to the meal mill to be dried and ground into meal. This process was later made easier with the purchase of a hand driven fanners.

The threshing of the oats and bere was also catered for by Messrs Allan of Mey with their portable steam driven threshing mill, which visited the district at least twice in the season. It was a big event in the district when all the neighbours, showing the true community spirit, gathered together to help each other. With a blast from the steam whistle, signifying they were ready to start, willing helpers soon responded. The peat stack was raided for the best of the peats as fuel for the engine, and the ladies of the house provided refreshments for the workers. Many a good "crack" was told on such occasions and no doubt some "tall tales" thrown in to brighten the conversation.

My lasting childhood memories of those days were watching with fascination the big drive wheel and the slick, sweet movements of the pistons, with the hum of the mill and its intricate working parts a great attraction for the young minds. While working in the district Mr Allan and his mate slept at night in a corrugated iron clad van, which they towed behind the mill. It had a small stove for heating and two bunk beds. A very amusing incident happened one night which is worth recalling. Some of the youths coming home late at night decided to play a prank on the sleeping occupants of the van. They noticed the van was parked on a slight incline on the road. The temptation was too great for the boys, so with all shoulders to the wheel they started the van moving down hill. It was gathering momentum in spite of only having iron wheels, when Old Sandy Allan awoke. He tried to open the door but found the boys had securely tied them. Realising his predicament and the danger of the fire in the stove being overturned by the vibrations of the runaway van he shouted to his mate who was still fast asleep: "For goodness sake rise oot o' there or ye'll be cremated." Fortunately the wheels stuck in a rut further down the road, thus saving them from further danger. Being a man that enjoyed a good joke himself he took it all in good fun, but made sure after that the van wheels were well dug in at night.

One last resident of Newton who cannot be forgotten was the local nurse, Miss Jessie Cook, who served the parish of Canisbay for many years from the early 30s until she retired in 1959. In the course of her faithful service she had sometimes to brave the stormy boat journey to Stroma, and during a severe snowstorm in 1955 she even was transported by helicopter to Slickly to attend the birth of a child (David Manson).

This trip down memory lane has stirred up many treasured memories of yester years, of days when neighbours and friends had time to chat to one another over the garden wall or at the end of the field. Many a happy evening was enjoyed as neighbours would spend an "after dayset" visiting one another, discussing the topics of the day, mingled with happy banter, with a little gossip to add spice to the conversation.

With all the gadgets and machinery in this modern age, we should have more time, but we seem to be caught up in the ever increasing pace of life.

Should we not stop and think of the peace and job satisfaction our forefathers enjoyed, which we in our hurry seem to be missing?

Dannie Gulloch, 6 Thorsdale View, Thurso.

John Smith and his wife Katie Dunnet, Newton

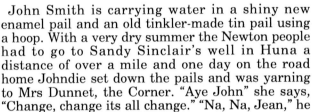

Photos, Margaret Lee Smith.

John Smith is carrying water in a shiny new enamel pail and an old tinkler-made tin pail using a hoop. With a very dry summer the Newton people had to go to Sandy Sinclair's well in Huna a distance of over a mile and one day on the road home Johndie set down the pails and was yarning to Mrs Dunnet, the Corner. "Aye John" she says, "Change, change its all change." "Na, Na, Jean," he says, "there's nae difference on the Mool Hill since the first time I saw it." Katie Smith with spinning wheel outside the house – now Frankie MacGregor's steading behind the new house occupied by Kevin MacGregor (Margaret Lee's mother was a niece of Katie Smith, Jock O' the Burn and Willie Post).

A DEAL AT THE MARYMAS

John Smith, crofter, Newton needed a horse for carting his peats and the harvest, so he went off to the Dunnet Marymas (about 19th August) 1930 and bought one. When he got him home he found the horse wouldn't "back", he didn't lie down and was afraid of traffic.

John went specially into Thurso to see Keith Murray, a noted lawyer and asked what redress he would have on the seller. The counsel given – "My best advice to you Mr Smith is to go to the next market and sell the horse the same way as you bought him!"

Oft related by John Smith.

MEMORIES OF GROWING UP IN JOHN O'GROATS

My father was John Dunnett, my mother Ina Mowat and I was born on 15th April, 1912 and was the oldest. Elizabeth, Isobel, Joey and Alex made up the family.

I started school at age five and my teacher was Miss Nicolson from Auckengill; then after she left it was Miss Robertson from Keiss. Miss Clyne, who married Malcolm Houston, came next and my last teacher was Arthur Brown. I left school when I was 14.

In spring, David Steven and I used to cut peats for some of the people around John O'Groats and for the hotel. When the peats were ready for taking home, Sandy Green and I used to cart them down to the hotel with the horse and cart from the Warth Hill. I always liked the sea and especially going to the cuddings with my dad and uncle Bill Mowat,

and it was usually after supper time that we went. We often went hunting for rabbits in the dark with a pit lamp.

In the winter, I went to work at the meal mill as loft boy. I was promoted to kiln-man in my second year and enjoyed working for Magnus Houston. He was courting Annie Ham in these days and she later became his wife.

In 1930, when I left John O'Groats for Canada, they were all thinning neeps at the Ha – not my favourite job!

I sailed from Glasgow on 5th June and took seven days to cross the Atlantic. I landed at Quebec and took the train from there to Montreal, from Montreal to Winnipeg and from there to Prince Rupert. I had to stay there two days before I got a boat up the coast to Shagway and then got the narrow gauge train to Whitehorse. I got the river steam-boat from Whitehorse to Mayo and arrived there on the 25th June. I then went by car to Wernech Mining Camp where I was united with my uncle, Sinclair Dunnett.

I worked nine months underground in the mine before I got the job of working the mine hoist.

I got married to Mickey in 1937 – ours was the first double wedding in Mayo and we went to Dawson City for our honeymoon. Mickey spent the winter in Mayo and it was there that our daughter Peggy was born in 1940.

In the spring of 1942 I went to work for a gold mining company.

The US Army moved into Whitehorse in 1942 to build the Alaska Highway and I went to work for them as power-plant operator and continued with them for four years. The Canadian Army took over the maintenance of the Highway and I worked with them for 22 years.

I retired when I reached 60, and now am enjoying every minute of my retirement, especially visiting the old home and meeting the family, childhood friends and neighbours.

Sinclair Dunnett, 2330 Auto Road Street, Salmon Arm, British Columbia.

PRAYER MEETING PLACE AT LOWER STEMSTER, JOHN O'GROATS

Round about 1865 there was a strong religious revival movement in the Parish. Sandy Horne was a very religious man who faithfully stuck to his principles. He was a baptist and so strong were his beliefs that he set about building a church. It was carefully and very skilfully built, but then the Laird got wind of his plans and stopped the delivery of slates.

Anyway the building was completed, using shipwood for couples, etc., and the roof was thatched. All was ready and the prayer meetings were held there on Sunday nights. William Dunnet (Ze-beelzie) who lived opposite the Stemster road end, had a strong and true singing voice so he was precentor. Sandy Horne himself had a very fine voice and Lizzie Houston also helped with the singing. The ministers or travelling preachers stayed with the Hornes and the beautiful building work can be seen to this day at Lower Stemster. (William Dunnet was the great-grandfather of the Johnnie Cormack and the Frankie MacGregor generation of Cormacks.)

ANON.

STEMSTER

Our folk came to Stemster in 1903 and we succeeded the Ross family. The Rosses had many talents. Tammy and Jimmy Ross were stone masons and built many of the houses in this area. Sanny (also known as Eric) was a first class 'bone-setter' and was known as the local vet. My grandfather took his dog which had a badly broken hind leg to him to get it set. Sandy was in his 80s then and using white of egg, two small pieces of

leather and a bandage, he worked and manipulated until he was satisfied. He then poured olive oil over the bandage and said to take the bandage off after a week and the dog will do the rest herself. It was a perfect mend and afterwards one couldn't tell which leg had been broken. Sailor Ross was George and Willie was the farmer. My uncle William Gulloch told me that when he was a boy (c.1905) on his way to school that he remembered seeing old Willie Ross aged 90 ploughing with his pair of stots on Little Stemster. Uncle Willie impressed this on me as a child.

John Nicolson's family had Stemster before the Rosses and three days after my grandfather took over the farm, John Nicolson came and asked if he could get the John O'Groat lintel stone and this he got readily. Nothing remains of the house but the lintel stone was recovered from the low field on Stemster not far from the burn. John Nicolson took the stone to Auckengill where he cleaned and renovated it and that is where this photo was taken. It is believed that John de Groat's good lady was a Mowat as is shown by the M. on the stone.

William J. Gulloch, Stemster.

A Stone From Stemster

Mr Nicolson beside the lintel of John O'Groats House. Within the rectangle is John O'Groat's initials, and on the right those of his brother Hugh.

Photo, Jessie Sinclair, Main Street, Keiss.

HUNA

A RETROSPECT

The white sands on the beach lay shining,
A boat-slip jutted out to sea,
Oft have I waded, played and guddled,
With other boys, all full of glee.

Time has changed that spot for ever,
It looks so strange to see it now,
No boaties there that gave such pleasure
To us who watched the boaties row.

These were the happy days of youth,
When time nor worries had no part,
Waiting to see the boats coming in,
Without a care in each young heart.

Our hardy fathers manned the boats,
Their living wrestled from the sea,
Quite contented with their calling,
Precarious though the case might be.

Where is the sand along the beach,
That stretched from slipway past the Ness?
In its place are boulders rough,
Compared with then, oh what a mess!

Commandeered by man-made laws
And carted thither far and wide,
As substitute for lime and used
On land all round the countryside.

The houses still look much the same,
Though silence reigns instead of joys,
When every house was full of folks,
Strong men and women, girls and boys.

How many now would answer, "present",
Of that young care-free gallant band,
Who fished for sellags, peltags, cuddies
And raced and played upon the sand.

A few might do so, very few,
If given me to call the role.
Scattered afar, some here, some there
But Oh! so many; paid the toll.

Where is that spot I here bewail,
It is the spot that cradled me,
"Huna" – that little Caithness place,
Where sounds the everlasting sea.

From Gleanings by John Ross, "Albyn", Gills.

Rose Cottage

There were four similar pavilion gabled houses, thought to be estate built when Seater and Huna was "squared" in the latter half of the 19th century. These houses and several more were built with two gable windows, one of which was often filled with two flagstones, which were sometimes painted to resemble ordinary windows.

Photo, Kathleen Ross, Upper Warse.
John Ross with his parents and family at the door of Rose Cottage, Croft Road.

Footnote:– "When I remember Huna (1900) there were eight boats there and two at the Haven of Seater, twenty able bodied men, six or seven familes of the name Dunnet, eleven Mrs Dunnets there at one time before I came to Gills, now one solitary rep. John Dunnet (Burn) unmarried. The younger ones went to the herring fishing in summer, the older to lobster and cod fishing."

John Ross, "Albyn".

Croft Road, Huna

In 1878 my great-granny widow Margaret Dunnet paid Magnus Banks, Mey £7-10/- in total, for all the wood and joiner work on her new house and steading, now occupied by the Flockhart family. This receipt and the photo of Burn's Cottage p.234 would indicate the new plan of Huna took effect at this time.

John Dunnet, Seater.

SMIDDY ALBUM C.1900

Within this book your eyes may trace
The well known smile on friendship's face
There may your wandering eyes behold
The friends of youth, the loved of old
And as you gaze with tearful eye
Sweet memories of the years gone by
Will come again with magic power
To charm the evening's pensive hour.

Some in this book have passed the bore
From whence no traveller will return
Some through the world, yet do roam
As pilgrims from their native home
Are here by nature's power enshrined
As loved memorials to the mind
Till all shall reach that happy shore
Where friends and kindred part no more.

From flyleaf of Album, Helen Sinclair, Keiss.

THE SMIDDY

Huna Smiddy 1898

Photo, Helen Sinclair, Keiss.

All smiddies were blackened inside by the smoke from the forge, as were the windows but nevertheless were a favourite meeting place for the men of the district where all sorts of topics were discussed. It was here also that the local athletes "trained", under the watchful and selective eye of the smith, for the events in the various cattle shows and galas held annually throughout the county.

The blacksmith was a man of substance and standing in all rural communities, mainly I suppose, because he had dealings with everyone and, along with the miller, was the industrial backbone of any farming area.

Smiddies were usually single storey buildings with a very large door in the middle of the long front wall, flanked on either side by a narrow window or two depending on the length of the building. Under one window, a stone or cast iron horse trough was usually provided, another had a long bench, sometimes made of stone, for the comfort of customers and cronies. Beside the door would be a mounting step or two. These were about three feet high, made of stone and rounded on the top, and were used mostly by the bareback riders of the farm horses brought for shoeing. Tethering posts or rings were also close to the door.

Inside the smiddy, under the windows, would be long wooden benches festooned with tools, hammers of all sizes and shapes from "toffee hammers" to full blown 14lb sledges, tongs, snips, pliers, "nippers" and all manner of cold chisels, punches and wrenches. There would also be

several vices, a guillotine, a hand operated pillar drill or two and a press.

Opposite the door would be the forge, a mighty roaring monstrosity, which frightened the living daylights out of all children when they first saw it but nevertheless fascinated them too with its white hot centre and fierce hot breath. On this wall too, would be the bellows for providing air to the forge. Originally these were very large, fixed versions of the household bellows and were pumped by hand usually with a rope attached to the free leg but as time went on and if a burn was near, water power could be used.

The centre of the floor was taken up by the anvil. Above it, hung on the rafters, was the horseshoe blanks, half completed shoes of all the commonest sizes used in the district. These were fabricated during slack spells, as were the nails for holding the shoes in place. At each end of the smiddy would be racks of different metals, in sheet and strip form. In later days there would also be an oxyacetylene welding set.

In the days before safety clothing as such, the smith wore a thick shirt, sleeves rolled up well above the elbow, heavy worsted trousers usually held up by braces, and a heavy leather belt and a divided apron of leather or "moleskin". Hot metal can cause very nasty burns so the heat of this clothing was tholed in the interest of safety. He also wore heavy leather boots.

The smith's main job was shoeing the many horses used by the farms around the district. This could

Willie Sutherland at the Anvil

Photo, Helen Sinclair, Keiss.

be an easy or difficult task depending on the temperament of the animal. Shoeing was nearly always done outside the big door, horses are not too happy close to fire. The smith would first select four shoe blanks of roughly the right size, pick up one of the horse's hooves and try a shoe against it. This would be done for all four hooves in turn and the shoes would be set in order round the forge heart to heat gradually, curved side closest to the fire. Meanwhile the smith would remove one worn shoe by nipping off the bent ends of any nails protruding through the front of the hoof and using a claw hammer and pincers pull out all the nails holding the shoe.

Once the first shoe was removed it was offered up to the replacement to give an idea of the adjustments to be made. The new shoe was now heated to red heat by the smith's helper while the smith trimmed the horse's hoof using a knife and rasp. This was done to obtain firm material to hold the new shoe. Next the shoe would be formed on the anvil to approximately the same shape as the old one and a hole punched in the middle of the shoe at the front. The punch was left in to act as a handle for the hot shoe. Again the shoe was tried for size against the hoof, any final adjustments made and it was now ready to have the nail holes punched into it. After reheating, this would be done then the shoe would be heated again and set

briefly against the horse's hoof to burn the shoe shape into it and possibly to harden the hoof. The shoe was then cooled in water and nailed on to the horse's hoof. All four feet were done the same way.

To shoe a horse it was necessary to bring the horse's leg up to a comfortable working height and still have control over the animal's movements. This was done by bringing the horse's lower leg up through the smith's legs from behind and gripping the animal's leg between the knees, hence the divided apron. In this position the smith was very vulnerable to a painful bite so the horse was usually given hay or a nosebag with corn during the shoeing.

The blacksmith also made parts for the farm machinery, such as it was, and when the first cars appeared he was usually called upon to make spare parts or to repair the frequent breakages. Quite a few blacksmiths became the first garage mechanics of the 20th century.

David Bruce, Bellevue, Huna.

Footnote:– David Bruce now lives in Huna but he was born and brought up in Wick. David was persuaded to write the next article because the folk here depended so much on "Bruce the Foundry".

THE FOUNDRY IN EAST BANKS, WICK

In Wick there used to be a Foundry where nearly all the local cast iron work was done. They produced most of the railings round the "Big Houses" and Town Council property, as well as street drains, manhole covers, lamp posts and rain water pipes used on houses throughout the town. It was started up about the beginning of the 20th Century by John Bruce, an engineer to trade, who went to South Africa for work and learned iron moulding there. The development of the Wick Harbour was taking place about the time the foundry started, so naturally a lot of the cast iron work was provided by the Wick Foundry. Pauls can still be seen at the harbour with John Bruce and Son, Wick cast into the top.

Work in a foundry today is hard graft, but before the 1939-45 war it was back breaking. There was no such thing as casting benches, all work was done on the floor.

In the foundry at Wick the floor was made up of black used casting sand to a depth of at least a foot, with hard packed paths around the edge of the building. The furnace was situated on one short wall, the other had a door leading to the workshop and office. On one long wall was a hand operated derrick crane, known as the "cran" which swivelled in such a way that it covered the area from the furnace to almost two thirds of the way to the office/workshop partition wall. The opposite long wall had a big sliding door. This wall also held the windows. In the roof were several skylights to allow work to be done away from the windows.

Scattered around the foundry building itself were several outbuildings used to store such things as steel casting boxes, new casting sand, casting box clips and sprue collars. There was also a shed where "Heela", an old soldier, or sailor lived. I never did know his proper name or how he came to live there but he was treated with great tolerance by all the foundry workers.

The actual making of moulds went on every day except Sunday of course and the actual casting took place fortnightly or monthly as space and contracts (jobs they were called in those days) required.

To make a mould the first thing required was a pattern. This could be a wooden full sized model of the required article and in the case of "jobs" nearly always was. The pattern could also be the broken pieces of some gear, wheel pulley, engine block cover or any other piece of machinery. It didn't matter which type of pattern was used the process was always the same. A casting box of a size and depth suitable to take the pattern was fetched from the box shed and split into its two parts. Both halves would be set on the floor, beside each other and one half would be levelled using a spirit level so that there was a slight run in one direction. This was the bottom half. It would be partly filled with used casting sand from the floor around the box and lightly firmed. Into this would be put enough new casting sand (which was yellow in colour) to

completely surround the bottom half of the pattern leaving a depth of about an inch under the lowest part of where the pattern would sit. Next, the pattern was set in place and if a broken piece of machinery was the pattern some delicate jigsaw puzzle work could be called for.

The top half would then be placed on the bottom, clips wedged over the handles on the sides and ends of the boxes so that they could not move. More new sand was shovelled in to cover the pattern to an inch or two over its highest part. The box would then be filled to the top with sand from the floor.

To make sure that the sand was tight around the pattern several different types of rammers and tamps were used to press the sand firmly down. Each time the sand level dropped below the top of the box more sand would be added until no more could be forced down into the box, then the casting box and pattern would be turned over either manually (if small) or by crane and the same ramming process repeated.

Once it was rammed hard the clips would be removed and a wire passed between the two box halves to cut the sand so that the halves could be separated to remove the pattern. When the boxes were parted, some trimming had to be done around the pattern to flatten the sand not cut by the wire before the pattern was removed. Next the pattern was lifted delicately out using a slight shaking motion to clear the sand.

Channels had then to be cut to allow the molten iron to flow and throats had to be fashioned into the top box sand for pouring the iron in and allowing the expanding air to escape. When all this had been done both halves of the moulds were covered in liquid black lead and polished until they shone. The boxes were then put together again, clipped and wedged as before and placed ready for casting. Having been levelled again as before.

Casting was usually done when the floor of the foundry was covered with boxes. Depending on the amount of work. This varied from fortnightly to monthly. Casting was always done using extra "hands" because iron hardens very quickly. These "hands" mostly came from other engineering trades though not always. I don't know the exact details of how they were recruited nor do I know of the agreements reached with their employers (if the "hands" were in work) but they always seemed to be available.

The furnace would have been charged with a mixture of pig iron ("peegs") and scrap gathered from all over the county. On the day of casting, or possibly the night before, the furnace fire would be lit and the heat gradually brought up to temperature so as not to crack the firebrick in the furnace as all its sides were open to the elements. Once the furnace reached the temperature at which the iron started to melt, a close watch would be kept to see if more iron was needed for the casting in hand and to see when the iron was ready, time taken to reach this point varied with ambient temperature, wind direction and quality of coke and only experience told when the iron was ready.

When it was decided that the iron was at the right temperature the furnace was tapped by driving a long steel rod into the sand plugged hole in the furnace outlet and allowing a small quantity of iron to run out into a few rough slot moulds fashioned in the floor sand. If these looked right the first ladle would be filled. Unless all the moulds were big ones this would be a two man ladle used for casting outside the crane range. The molten metal, which glowed white in the gloom, was poured into the casting boxes, through the iron collars, until the iron flowed up through the vent hole. This had to be done quickly as the iron soon started to solidify on top. One of the biggest dangers in casting was pouring too soon or too quickly and allowing the hot metal to land on the cold casting box or collar because the white hot iron flew around like water from a lawn sprinkler, and it stuck to clothing or flesh with equal ease, causing very nasty burns. Hence most men wore corduroy or "moleskin" trousers, heavy jackets with a rag around the neck and a cap or hat. I assume gloves were also worn but I can't remember.

Casting was hot, exhausting work and lots of water or "fizzy" Bremner's lemonade was drunk. (Wick was dry or no doubt pale ale would have been the preferred thirst quencher.) When the day was done the moulds were left to cool overnight.

The following day or the next Monday if casting was done on a Saturday, as quite a few were if I remember rightly, the first boxes were opened and the sand removed from the cast. This was examined for flaws and if passed, the apprentice or most junior member had the job of knocking off the casting sprue and any nibs produced at the box junction. He then had to file down these areas to correspond to the surrounding metal. No easy task as cast iron is very hard and angle grinders were a thing of the distant future.

Once it had cooled down sufficiently the furnace had to be cleaned out and the fire bricks checked for cracks. First the slag had to be broken from the furnace door and as much as possible removed before the manhole was opened and someone had to go in to remove the rest. This someone also examined and repaired the firebricks. A most unpleasant job.

Quite a lot of the material cast had to be coated in tar to protect it from rust so a tar boiler was on the go for several days after casting. The cycle then started all over again.

There were a couple of very small electric furnaces where brass and aluminium casting was undertaken occasionally and I remember a model of a Spitfire cast in aluminium being made. This must have been in 1940, after my father had gone to war with the Territorials and before my "uncle" Jock (actually my father's cousin) was directed to war work in a foundry in Aberdeen.

As a matter of interest, using the same entrance yard in East Banks was a millwright (Miller's), a smiddy (MacDonald's) and the foundry. All of whom operated to each other's mutual benefit.

David Bruce, Bellevue, Huna.

POST OFFICES IN CANISBAY PARISH

There is no record of the date on which the first post office was opened in Caithness, but it is generally accepted that by 1715 offices existed at Dunbeath, Thurso and Wick and between 1755 and 1775 at Achinarras.

The Rev. John Morrison, D.D., when writing about the parish of Canisbay in 1790 for Sir John Sinclair's "Statistical Account of Scotland", gives the population of the parish as 1950, being an increase from the 1481 souls recorded by Dr Webster in 1755. At the time the report was written the public roads in the parish were those leading from Huna to Wick and from Huna to Thurso. Huna was a place of some significance as it was from there that the ferry crossed to Burwick on South Ronaldsay once a week with the mails.

At a meeting of the Freeholders of the County of Caithness chaired by the Rt. Honorable the Earl of Caithness in Wick on 30th September, 1802 resolutions were made concerning "the delays in the conveyance of the Mails to and from the County of Caithness". The third resolution was "That it would be a great conveniency to the Counties of Orkney and Caithness to have a Post Office establishment at Huna, and a weekly Runner from Huna to Thurso. . ." The petition was accepted and the opening of a post office at Huna authorised. The date of opening is not known, but certainly by 1803 it was in existence and was the first post office to be opened in the parish and the fifth office to be opened in the county. The office was closed in 1867 to re-open on 3rd May, 1880 and finally close on 31st August, 1979.

Mey followed in 1826 and still operates from a small wooden hut.

Canisbay came next opening on 28th May, 1867 and is still open, followed by Freswick on 6th June, 1882, closed in recent years. Some 10 years later Auckengill opened on 18th January, 1892 and is still open.

The most recent office to open was Duncansby which opened on 27th June, 1892, but changed its name to John O'Groats on 1st September, 1909. Probably this post office is the most well known outside of the parish and county because of the cachets applied, since at least 1904, to holidaymaker's postcards. These cachets have been triangular, circular, oval and even octagonal in shape, the latter shape fitting in very nicely with the legend of John O'Groats and his eight sided house.

Although not on the mainland, Stroma is very

Postmarks

much a part of Canisbay and during the years the post office was open it probably played a most important part in the life of the community. Although opened on 26th May, 1879 it was 1890 before the island had a postmark of its own. The office closed on 23rd November, 1958 around the time the last of the islanders left for the mainland. Philatelically, Stroma is still to the fore as from time to time local labels have appeared which can be cancelled with a postmark-like rubber stamp showing the name of the island and the date.

Ian Aitchison, 20 Gorse Way, Fresh Field, Formby, Liverpool.

HUNA HOUSE

Huna House c.1880.

Photo, Jimmy Gunn, Emohruo, Mey.

Huna House was extensively modernised and enlarged in 1879. There were seven bedrooms upstairs, and one toilet which was supplied from a "well" in the roof. Bedroom No.1 was to the east, and bedroom No.2, above the front door was the room James Hughes had before he fell to his death down the stairs and after that, it was supposed to be haunted by his ghost. Bedroom No.5 looked out on the Mermaid Rock – a huge rock where sometimes a mermaid can be seen combing her hair. Five of the bedrooms had fireplaces – iron grates with fancy tiles down each side and now, more than a hundred years later these grates are much sought after.

The staircase was very wide with fine carved banisters rising to a large impressive landing with two big pillars supporting the roof, and it was well lit by big double windows. The ceilings were all corniced and in the dining room and sitting room they were very elaborate. Both were big rooms at the front and there was a beautiful, large, creamy white, marble fireplace in the sitting room which was the one nearest the garden.

Most of the rooms had "bell pulls" beside the fireplace which showed up on a big board in the front hallway. Downstairs the floors were all of flagstones with the exception of the sitting room which had a wooden floor. There were two small bedrooms downstairs – one below the stair and one off the "peedie kitchen" which it is thought was also a bedroom in the early days.

The big kitchen which looked out over the sea to Stroma was heated by a large range with an oven at one side of the fire and a boiler at the other. Originally there was probably a scullery or pantry but this division was taken down and it was incorporated in the big kitchen.

We think it was William Simpson from Stroma and his wife Barbara Allan who had the front porch built. They were the couple who built the Huna Mission Hall. Sandy went down to keep Jamie Simpson company after his uncle and aunt died and did not think much of sleeping in such a big house. The wind whistled and the windows rattled and in their imagination they were sure that the ghost was on the move! Sandy's granny [1] took Jamie up to Roadside, now "Norwin", and he stayed with them until he married. Later on when Neil Douglas and his wife Milla Cormack lived in Huna House, Sandy slept in No.3. In those days when the weather was too rough for the boat to get back to Stroma, folk used to stay overnight.

One particular night, Sandy was wakened by a scraping noise on the walls, the door creaked and he could hear shuffling steps. He was in a cold sweat and thought "this is the ghost this time" because the footsteps came nearer the bed and then something was touching the bed. Sandy lay rigid until a voice spoke and this was an old man, Donald Banks, the Bard of Stroma, who had lost his way coming back from the toilet! There was no electric light in these days and the only lamp Milla had left was small, and not much better than a candle. My husband got nearly as big a fright when he came back with the lamp, and saw the old man with his white hair standing on end and in his long johns and nightshirt.

He aye wondered if he was looking for a woman!

Margaret Cormack, Kirkstyle.

[1] Sandy's grandmother Annie Cormack née Dunnet was aye in demand to play the "boxie" when dances were held in the barn of Huna Inn. Jess – a sister of Johan Calder was a lovely singer and entertained the company when there was a pause from dancing.

A PENTLAND FIRTH VISITORS' BOOK

Inns have a fascination. Who will you meet there? – the roystering blades of Dumas – Mr Pickwick and his friends – Bailie Nicol Jarvie with his red-hot poker? They all have been in their time at a good inn fire. And with the wind rising to a gale, and the white fangs of the Men O'Mey, that whirlpool of the Pentland Firth, livid against the sky, you couldn't wish for better than the old inn of Huna. Down by the sea's edge, in the parish of Canisbay by the shores of the Pentland Firth. You could see it far off, from the high moorland road, a light like a will o' the wisp, then a sudden flash at a turning, and at the end – bright lamps, peat smoke, doors flung open wide. Or, it might be from the mast of a tossing schooner, with the Firth racing nine knots, you watched with envious eyes the ferry from Stroma make for the warmth of the old inn. Landsman or seaman, everybody knew Huna. . . But the tide turned. Tarred roads sweep you past to other hostelries today. And the trawlers in the teeth of any gale, run down the Firth. Huna Inn is high and dry. Its doors are closed. And its visitors' book, in well worn calf, is all that remains to tell what the inn was.

Early Entries

It gives a livelier picture than you might think. The opening now. The Earl of Caithness came to that, on a December day in '79, from Barrogill Castle, five miles off, his heir, young Lord Berriedale, with him. And the visitors' book, too, all new and shining, "Presented by Lord Berriedale on his attaining his majority and on the opening of the new Huna Inn" – and then, with the confidence of one-and-twenty, "to remain in the Inn".

Pilots, as you might expect, were Huna's first guests – Andrew Mowat and Daniel Henderson, and most famous of all Pentland Firth pilots, Jock O' the Burn. But the hands that steered so straight by Dunnet Head and Cantick Head, running you, in any weather, clear of the Boars or the Men O'Mey, found the visitors' book a problem. Half an hour was it, or more, for Jock O' the Burn's signature? And Huna, at the sea edge, knew danger. "A collecting box for the Lifeboat Institution." By 6th January – poverty or no – it held 2s 7d. Pilots came from every quarter. The barque "Caesarea", Sunderland to Bergen drops hers here; but so does the "Moby Dick", Sunderland to Singapore. What took a ship to Singapore through the Pentland Firth, and why did she carry a pilot so far? With the spring come the visitors – from Sydney, Australia – a bicycle touring club from Eastbourne – from Canterbury and Berwick-on-Tweed – all men; for these were the awful '80's, with the women "in their proper places", still staying at home.

The Sheriff's Officer

The men, though – unlike the blankness that confronts you in the modern hotel-list – tell you what they do: coachman, driver, architect – ah! a sheriff's officer. Now what brought him to Huna? Smuggling? With the rocks and geos down Duncansby way just made for it, what do you expect? And then – in high June – a wedding! "This merry company assembled here on occasion of George Bain's marriage. He was married on the above date at 6 o'clock p.m. by Rev. J. MacPherson." That is all. No mention of the bride! – John Knox's Scotland, you grimly reflect, where you might be anonymous at your own wedding! There were funeral parties too – black clothes and tall hats in Huna parlour gathering over the glasses after the bitter tramp to the burial. Family parties, too, in July from the Glasgow Fair, and in the wake of the swarming children, as usual, mother. "Mrs G. R. and four children;" "Mrs Swanson and 12 of her grandchildren." Where, you may well ask, was grandpa?

They are cheerful enough though, some of them with a piper; and sandwiched amidst this hilarious crowd, in the neatest of scholary writing, is "James MacKenzie, student Cambridge." Huna delectable and unusual, with its tarry, salty smell, its tonic air that whipped your blood and brought you waves and waves of dreamless sleep, and an appetite – well! – Huna with its queer, nice people, and its ships so close under your window you could hear the sailors talk – Huna was the place every time for a Cambridge undergraduate in the Long Vacation! So must have thought J. A. Robinson, of Christ's, and J. R. N. MacPhail (Later Sheriff MacPhail, K.C.), who followed hard after, in

From a' the Airts

By 1881 the Inn had got a good start. Visitors from Yokohama, from "London, England", and "New York, America"; an English rector. On October 21 cyclists who claim unexpectedly enough the record for slowness. "Bad roads with rain and mud from Bromley to Blair Athol, snowed up (in October) for two days at Dalwhinnie, tremendous easterly gale all the way ahead to Huna." Yet they liked it, "Not a single mishap during our journey of 726 miles." Next year it is Chicago, Manchester, Ireland, Jerusalem, and Kansas, with a Colonel from Shropshire cutting into that jolly medley like the breath of the east wind, though maybe he thawed, with J. Sinclair, Wick, fixing up at his elbow the barometer with its homely rhyme.

> Wind North to East with falling glass
> Don't go to sea – go see your lass.
> From South to West, tho' glass be low
> It oft means rain, and not a blow.

If they talked of the weather – who knows – even England's Colonel might prove a "mixer" on that.

The Toll of the Firth

Sometimes there were wrecks. '83 was a bad year for these – the barque "Margaret Gunn"; SS "Gladiolus" in February; "Prince Victor" from Newport, Mon., in March; with Lloyd's man down from London in the April after. And a Swedish brig another year; a Greenock smack; a Grimsby trawler; on and on. Strange fish came with them, many a time, to Huna – a baby once, on a wild November night at 2 a.m. from a wreck off Stroma; and again, hey presto! a Major-General, complete with "Capt. P. Warner, Mr Rider Haggard, and two valets". Three Customs officers on the heels of that little party! No – you never knew who was on Huna's doorstep, with the Pentland Firth raging.

The moorland road brought odd folk too: Salgano, the African lion-tamer, with a team from Bostock's menagerie; Ira D. Sankey, singing hymns; the pipeband of the 1st Sutherland Highlanders – pipe-major, pipers, drummers, and all (hark to them over the Mey moor!). A honeymoon couple in '86 "on a bicycle built for two"; four old Caithness schoolmates, one home from Hong Kong, the second from Manitoba, the third from Monte Video and the fourth – from Dunnet! An artist from Looe, Cornwall, sketching Huna delightfully in pen-and-ink for the visitors' book; a leisurely coaching tour up from Wales, 1175 miles of it, from July to September. Lord Harris and a sporting party staying for six weeks; the Crofters' Commission in 1890; telegraph linesmen laying the first wires in '93; and who do you think but the Lord Mayor of London one fine August day (did he, by any chance bring his coach?). Someone whose last visit to Huna has been with Thomas Carlyle in 1860, Thomas "in Highland cloak and wideawake revolving many things", Mr D. Lloyd-George; and last of all, on a shooting visit in '97, H.R.H. the Duc de Chartres and the Marquis de Bréteuil. Huna ended with a grand slam!

Parting Shots

Did they all like it? Well – No. "Huna dismal, bleak and barren – Huna windy, Huna rainy – Tides that pass it every day – Mariners they curse and damn it". The gentleman who wrote that (signing initials only) probably did not. Nor yet the shivering penman, under the huge umbrella "trying to find the scenery". But one who described himself, "prentice-dyer at Stockton-on-Tees" found it, in '95 "the most magnificent place in the British Isles", though a visitor from Thornaby-on-Tees, meaning well, no doubt, has it – "A perfect holiday. . . Now for England, home and beauty!"

You may like to leave it with the epitaph of the Cambridge undergraduate.

> N'er in desert land I saw
> Such an hostlery before.
> Charms of which I cannot tell
> Filled me in thy blest Hotel.
>
> Charms that charm not all in vain,
> Charms that cry "Return Again",
> Charms like these I bear away
> On this memorable day.

For that was what the pilots thought, and the shipwrecked folks, gentle and simple, and the merry-makers of long years past, who knew their way by land or water, to the welcome of Huna Inn.

Christina Keith,
Courtesy of the Scotsman Newspaper.

A TALE OF THE VISITORS' BOOK FROM HUNA HOTEL

"I wonder if you know what happened to the Visitors' Book from Huna Hotel?"

My father's brother and sister were Hetty and Alistair Munro and some of their collection of Caithness books came to me recently. I searched through these books and found, to my delight, not one but TWO visitors' books from the hotel, and sat down to read them.

All of life is here, weddings, funerals, organisations having a day out, people stranded by bad weather, crews from shipwrecks, visitors from all over the world and, to my surprise, regular visits from Cycling Clubs from as far as Kent, and even Novia Scotia!

My mother's great grandfather Wm. Simpson, Brough, was the Captain of a sailing ship called "The Flower of Olrig" which carried Caithness flag stones from Castlehill Harbour, so I settled down to see what I could find out about ships.

The first ship to be mentioned is the Steam Ship "Blytheville" which passed through the Firth bound east in September 1880. Some of the first

A page from Huna Visitors' Book

1905
Sept. 3rd

Allan McMillan Sherry Lodge Stromness
Mrs McMillan
H. Hunter, General Floor-sweeper and Rogue
of any description you like, Stromness
George Simpson Stroma Policeman
John Robertson Hall! Stroma.

All waiting for a chance
to get across.

Oh how I would like to be there

STROMA

"wants a i bar"

On the rocks.
(The other two are in the *…*)

Later on, our three friends from the rocks
joined us and oh what a jolly
time we have had, drinking scotch
& best bass etc. Rain is pouring
cats & dogs but on the whole we have
lively times etc & vice versa.

visitors to Huna Hotel in December 1879, were ship's pilots, David Henderson and Andrew Mowat, whose job it would be to guide ships through the treacherous waters of the Pentland Firth. Another pilot visited in July 1882. Peter Soutar, Winchester Terrace, Sunderland, landed from the barque "Moley Don", 1100 tons, going from Sunderland to Singapore. My son, Ragnar, is an engineer on super tankers and the ships he sails to Singapore in, are some 300,000 tons! Peter Soutar visited again two years later, landing from the barque "General Picton".

The waters of the Pentland Firth were always held in great respect. A Lifeboat Collection box was in place in the hotel and when it was opened by D. Meiklejohn, Hon. Secretary, in January 1880, it was found to contain 2/7d.

Bad weather can occur at any time of the year, and in August the following year James and Alexander Coghill penned their thoughts.

"To Stroma in the Pentland Firth
We did intend to go
But from it we prevented were
Because the wind did blow."

Ever mindful of the weather James Sinclair, watchmaker, Wick, fixed up a barometer at the Lifeboat Shed for the use of fishermen and seamen, and left this advice:

"Wind north to east with falling glass
Don't go to sea, go see your lass.
From south to west though glass be low
It oft means rain, and not a blow."

The first wreck mentioned in January 1883 is the boat "Margaret Gunn", WK304 (?). George Doull and Don Waters from Wick survived to visit the Inn. The following year in July the "Edwin and Lizzie" was wrecked on Stroma. The crew came from North and South Shields, with one member from Rotterdam. The next wreck on Stroma found Mrs Johnston and her baby stranded at Huna. Whatever next? In July 1888, among those shipwrecked from "SS Copeland" bound from Iceland were a Major General and H. Rider Haggard. These were closely followed by Customs Officers and a Lloyds Agent. The next year in November, fourteen crewmen from "SS Minna", wrecked at Ness of Quoys, stayed at the hotel. Proving that sea-going is an international pursuit, when the crew of "SS Corinthia" were stranded on Stroma, nine nationalities were represented.

Sea-going does not always involve ships. Missionary canoeist John Ross Brown, Greenock, travelled 2500 miles in his canoe "Mull of Kintyre". His secret of success was "Go when the sea is calm"!

My own memory of Huna is being taken to a Sale of Work on Stroma when I was about ten years old. It was a large family outing and I can remember crossing to the island in a boat very full of people and the water seemed to be lapping over the sides. My own children have all had the opportunity to visit the island as part of their school outdoor activities week and thoroughly enjoyed the experience.

These two visitors' books have given me a lot of pleasure and I shall treasure them always and make sure my family and future generations treasure them also.

Fiona M. Celli, 63 Farr, Bettyhill.

THE CALL OF THE SEA

When James Dunnet the Coxswain's eldest son, set off to get a pair of boots half-soled on the morning of 7th August, 1910 it was the start of a well remembered story, almost a legend. He had walked as far as Gills when the maroon went up to summon the crew of the Huna lifeboat. James, who was a regular member of the crew missed the launch. His younger brother William, my father who had been working in the Huna smithy, and who was not a regular crewman, took his place. The lifeboat went to the assistance of the S. S. "Indian" which had been holed and was slowly sinking. They escorted her into Sinclair Bay, where she was beached and eventually salvaged. Salvage money was paid out and divided between the lifeboat crew, £80 per man. Since William would not have been earning more than 10 shillings per week as a young blacksmith at that time, that was three to four years wages rolled into one lump sum for him. He went down to Clydeside, where he served his time as a marine engineer, and sailed through both world wars, latterly as Chief Engineer with the Ellerman Line, on ships such as the "City of Oxford" and the City of Lancaster".

He had to abandon ship twice, when the "Mardinian" and the "Fabian" were sunk. On the first occasion, early in the Second World War, before the convoy system was fully operational, a U-boat surfaced after torpedoing the "Mardinian" and far from ordering survivors to be machine gunned, the captain saw to it that the ship's lifeboats were adequately provisioned with food and water, and gave them a course for Africa. They were picked up after six days' sailing. William's experience of the Huna lifeboat and other small boats in the Pentland Firth ensured that he knew how to rig a sail. Nobody else in the boat had been under sail before.

Jamie who took over the family farm at Seater in due time, used to say he never grudged the salvage money because it gave Willie his start in life; and my father always had good reason to count himself lucky to have been in a position to answer that Call of the Sea on a foggy morning in 1910.

Jack Dunnett, Clevnagreen, Skirza, Freswick.

The "Indian" aground on Reiss beach with the Huna lifeboat (arrowed) in attendance

Photo, Alistair Ham, Harrow.

The "Indian" struck just off Gibb's Craig at Duncansby Head in thick fog. She was a Leyland Line Steamer with a cargo of rock salt – presumably potassium salt (potash) for use as agricultural fertiliser rather than table salt. Before escorting the "Indian", John Dunnet, Coxswain, put two lifeboat men aboard her, one of whom was Sandy Sinclair, Huna formerly Stroma, which greatly helped to support the salvage claim at a later date.

It was a great night in Coxswain's kitchen when the crew sat round the big table and Keith Murray, who acted on behalf of the lifeboat crew, gave each man a fiver in his hand, with the remainder put on deposit with the British Linen Bank, Thurso.

John Dunnet, Seater.

WHAT'S IN A NAME?

The editor noticed that I had referred to my cousin as Dunnet and signed myself Dunnett and asked why. Strictly speaking I should be Dunnet but the change was made before I was born and so I am stuck with it, and so are my children and my son's children.

A glance through the Highlands Phone Book is enough to show that variable spelling of a surname can be expected whenever some change is possible without altering or much altering the sound, e.g. Brown, Browne, Fraser, Frazer, Stephen, Stephens, Steven, Stevens, McEwan, MacEwan, McEwen, MacEwen, etc. It merely tells us that people like to be different and it would be such a dull world if they did not.

Place names change, too, in the course of time and may lose their original meaning, perhaps because a mapmaker did not understand the local dialect or felt he could improve upon it. In our local history class at Freswick last year we looked at map names and asked the locals how they pronounced them; and also discussed what other names for places and rocks were missing and in danger of dying out.

According to the map there is a rock jutting out to the south of Freswick Bay called Longberry, which is meaningless until you know that the local name is Lyeberry and that "lye" and "berry" are both from old Norse words meaning "pollack" and "rock". So we can deduce that this was known to be a good place to fish for lyes or lythe anything up to a thousand years ago, when the first Vikings landed.

There is also a cluster of ruined cottages to the south of Freswick Bay, called Backless, not the only Backless in Caithness, and surely a meaningless name. Think, however, of backlying ground as ground that lies away from the sun, and remember that leys are meadows, and you arrive at back (lying) leys and the origin of the name becomes obvious – it certainly fits Backless at Freswick.

Finally, greatly daring and just to show how easily it can be done, let me suggest the origin of Dunnet as a name. The local pronounciation is Din'ad, a short step from Din Head or Dun Head, a very suitable name for a brown haired group of people in a predominantly fair haired society. Quite a suitable name, too, for an imposing headland covered with an expanse of brown heather.

Jack Dunnett, Clevnagreen, Skirza.

ACROSS THE WATER

Peter Annal

In 1880 it was decreed that the area of sea called the Pentland Firth, would be recognised by a line from Duncansby Head to Pentland Skerries, then to Old Head, following the South Ronaldsay coastline in a northerly direction to Herston Head and west to Switha; then on south to Cantick Head and follow the south Walls coastline to Torness. From there south to Dunnet Head and easterly along the Caithness shore, finishing at Duncansby Head.

My grandfather Peter Annal was the last man in South Ronaldsay who had been "a hand" on the yawl which crossed the Firth with the mails and passengers from Burwick to Huna. He was born in 1830 at Steen in the south parish, and the sea and the Firth were his life.

When a young man Peter Annal was the youngest hand on the "Royal Mail" – a six oared sail boat that plied between Burwick and Huna every day until 1858 when a steam boat started to give a daily service between Stromness and Scrabster.

The "Royal Mail" was one of the yawls used on the Firth run. My grandfather was also "a hand" on a much larger boat carrying two sails and a jib.

In the two years prior to 1858 there was seldom 48 hours between the crossings. He earned sixpence a day as "a hand" on the mail boat and a shilling if he helped carry half the mails the nine miles from Burwick to Watersund.

My grandfather told me how his mother went to the field and cut a sheaf of oats, took it home and thrashed off the grain on the bilgit stone in the barn. The bilgit stone was a 15"-12" long shaped stone built in the barn wall about three feet above the floor level and protruding six inches out from the wall. She then carried the grain into her kitchen, dried the grain over the peat fire in a frying pan, then ground the grain into oatmeal with a quern, making porridge and oat bannocks. Her oldest son John was 12 years old and when he could not get off in the boat to catch fish, he used the small fish hooks attached to a 60 fathom line with bait on the hooks to catch scarfs at the cliffs. He sometimes would get several home with him. Now, the scarf is not a very tasty bird, not considered fit for human consumption, but hunger was everywhere and a method of making scarf meat edible evolved. A tub was filled with soft clay and the scarf was buried in the clay for more than a week. By that time, the clay acting as a poultice, had sucked out a lot of the oil and impurities and feathers, so I have been told, that after cooking, the meat tasted delicious.

My grandfather was a wonderful man and quite a character! He enjoyed smoking "Black Twist" and liked a dram. He died in 1924 aged 93 and still had a head of towsy curly hair. Here the folk are always looking towards Scotland and his favourite seat was at the table near the window, looking towards John O'Groats. He could tell you exactly how the tide was flowing any hour or day of the week, when to leave for Groats and which course to take. It took me many years to acquire this knowledge, often from trial and error. It would be impossible to convey or learn this type of knowledge from a book. In those days, vessels had no engines, and any mistake in calculation of the tide in the Pentland Firth would mean being swept six miles east to the Skerries or west to Cape Wrath.

Another outstanding thing was a little saying he often repeated when soup was served. It would be "that soup was nearly as good as Betty Manson's"

The "Royal Mail" prior to 1858

Landing at Hoxa from S.S. St. Ola in Androo's Boat

Photo, Alex T. Annal, Myers, South Ronaldsay.

Andrew Lennie in felt hat at the helm, Robert Deerness standing up. – This photo was taken when the yawl lay at the How of Hoxa and used to go out the half mile to meet the "St Ola" before the pier was built at the Hope in 1906. It was said that like others of their day, Andrew and Robert were never willing to say no to a shilling!

or it would be "Betty Manson made better soup than that" – but he never ever did say that his daughter's soup was better than Betty Manson's.

We know that Betty Manson lived at Huna and that the Orkney men got shelter and warmth in her house when the "Royal Mail" could not return until the next day. However, Betty Manson was a generous kindly soul, who always had a large pot of hot soup on the fire when she saw the boat coming and it must have been a godsend to the boatmen, often cold, wet and hungry on arrival.

One thing grandad never told us, was Betty young and beautiful or, was she old and kindly? Was there a budding romance between grandad and Betty that failed when the "Royal Mail" ceased to cross after 1958???

(In Jan de Groot's time one of his sons lived in a house he built near Burwick. He called the house Holland.)

**Alex T. Annal, Myers,
South Ronaldsay.**

THE "CAIRNGLEN"

The S.S. "Cairnglen", built in 1926 and 5019 tons gross, was homeward bound from Halifax, Nova Scotia to the Tyne with a general cargo when she went ashore at Huna. Part of her cargo was transferred to Scrabster by coasting steamers. The ship was refloated at high water with the help of Stroma boatmen while tugs from Hull and a salvage vessel stood by.

Tugs piloted by Stroma men towed the vessel to Longhope for repairs, and it was discovered she had engine damage. The tug "Seaman" (shown at her bow in the photo) towed the "Cairnglen" to the Tyne.

John Dunnet, Seater.

The "Cairnglen" aground off Huna Pier, 23rd March, 1934. The number of people in their best clothes, shows this was taken on a Sunday, when they were walking home from the church.

Footnote:– 1930 – Lifeboat Institution are going to give up Huna Pier. 16th March, 1930 – Council takes over Huna Pier. 9th May, 1931 – Cost of pier estimated to be £720, repairs to defects £120.
John O'Groat Journals.

THE WRECK OF THE "THOMAS DRYDEN" IN THE PENTLAND FIRTH

As I stood upon the sandy beach
One morn near Pentland Ferry,
I saw a beautiful brigantine,
And all her crew seem'd merry.

Then the sea began to swell,
And seem'd like mountains high,
And the sailors on board that brigantine
To God for help did loudly cry.

Their cargo consisted of window glass,
Also coal and linseed-oil,
Which helped to calm the raging sea
That loud and angry did boil.

Then she began to duck in the trough of the sea,
Which was fearful to behold;
And her crossyards dipped in the big billows
As from side to side she rolled.

She was tossed about on the merciless sea,
And received some terrible shocks,
Until at last she ran against
A jagged reef of rocks.

And when the crew did get ashore,
They were shaking with cold and fright,
And they went away to Huna Inn,
And got lodgings for the night!
William McGonagall, Dundee.

Footnote:– The **"Thomas Dryden"** on passage from South Shields to Dublin was totally wrecked at Huna on the 21st March, 1843.
John Dunnet, 52 Staffa Street, Gourock.

HUNA INN

The John O'Groat Journal (20th June, 1867) records – "Huna Inn and Farm have been let to Mr Hugh MacKenzie, late of Reiss. We hope that this celebrated place of resort for tourists coming to John O'Groats will keep up, with its new tenant, the good name it got with Mrs Manson."

Ann Davidson, born in Thurso and married to James Manson, Quoys, must have been a capable businesswoman. The census returns show she was innkeeper in 1841, postmistress and innkeeper in 1851 with her brother-in-law farming the 34 acres. In 1861 she was still in charge of the post office and inn and had also taken over the farm when her brother-in-law retired. She employed one man and two boys. Her son-in-law John Wares was farm manager and her daughter Elizabeth was assistant postmistress. Ann retired in 1867, John Wares set up as a coach proprietor and Elizabeth as a dressmaker.

Elizabeth Manson married John Wares on 15th April, 1859 – one year after the mail service between Huna and Burwick ceased and would have been the "Betty" Peter Annal spoke of so fondly.

Betty's sister Henrietta married John Sutherland who was a shoemaker in 1861, parochial teacher by 1863 and was head teacher when the new school in

Canisbay opened in 1864. Sinclair Davidson, ship agent, was the brother of Ann Davidson and his daughter Henny Davidson had a grocer's shop at Huna.

Sinclair Davidson who married John Dunnet and had the grocer's shop at Burns' Cottage was a sister of Henny Davidson.

The "Groat" records that the new inn at John O'Groats was leased by the owner to Mr MacKenzie of the Huna Inn, 25th February, 1876.

John Calder, son of James Calder, Shipmaster from the parish of Dunnet took over the Huna Inn in 1876. John was the coxswain of the first lifeboat at Huna. Mrs Calder took over the John O'Groats Hotel when Hugh MacKenzie left and her son John kept on the Huna Inn. The late William Bremner of Stroma stated, "Captain Tom Calder from Dunnet was in charge of the "Liverpool" for a number of years and his sister-in-law, when proprietor of John O'Groats Hotel had a picture of this large sailing ship on a wall in the hotel.

Sources:– Census Returns, Canisbay Parish Register of Deaths.
Anne Houston, St Magnus, John O'Groats.

THE "SKIP" CALDERS

The brothers John, Sinclair and Thomas Calder were born in the parish of Dunnet and the old home was "Skips" at the shore, Rattar. I don't know why Captain John Calder (b.1847) gave up the sea but he moved to the Inn at Huna and became coxswain of the lifeboat there.

Captain Tom (b.1852) attended Edward Paterson's navigation classes and was 36 when he took command of the "Liverpool" – the largest sailing ship afloat under the Red Ensign. This four masted, full rigged iron built giant jute clipper for

the Calcutta trade was launched on 7th December, 1888 by Russell and Co., Greenock for the Leyland Co. She was 3500 tons, 333 feet long with a beam of 48 feet, a depth of 26 feet and could stow 26,000 bales of jute – deadweight c.6000 tons. This great ship only carried 34 of a crew and it seems incredible that so few hands could work all the ropes and the vast area of canvas.

The family story tells that there was a fair bit of a fuss and very serious arguments before Tom was persuaded to become master of the split new

"Liverpool". It was not the thought of commanding this huge sailing ship which made him hesitate, but the very considerable worry that his crew might become soft!! The ship had hollow steel masts, which allowed the men to climb aloft via the internal ladders thus getting some protection. It was quite a tight squeeze climbing up inside masts and there were small doors to allow the sailors out on to the yard arms – a sheltered life??

Tom took the "Liverpool" round Cape Horn on her maiden voyage to Melbourne which took 88 days. On her second trip he had to proceed to Norway for an outward cargo to Melbourne and the ship's log details that they brought home: 5045 bales of wool, 29,353 bags of wheat, 3112 bags of flour, leather, tallow, horns and bark.

Sinclair (b.1848), my grandfather, sailed as ships carpenter and sailing master[1] with Tom on the "Liverpool" and told many stirring yarns of these far off days of sail, about rounding the Horn, crossing the line, trade winds, storms, hurricanes and above all else the power of the "Liverpool". (Likely the reason my father stowed away on the schooner "Volant" at Castlehill when he was 12!) Speed had become very important and there was much competition and rivalry in the clipper races.,

The design of wooden frigates and galleons made them buoyant, they sat on top of the waves and as a rule were not driven hard because of the risk of bursting timbers. The long, heavily loaded iron sailing ships sat low in the water and when running hard under a large spread of canvas[2] their main decks would be awash as they ploughed on. Grandfather told that Tom had the reputation of being a hard driver and that he didn't spare the ship, the crew or himself and was noted for fast passages.

The "Liverpool"

Photo, courtesy "Sea Breezes", Cotton Exchange Buildings, Liverpool.

[1] The sailing master was responsible for all aspects of the sails and rigging – setting, trimming and maintenance.

2 "The Liverpool" carried approximately 40,000 square feet of canvas and 20 miles of rope. (This did not include the chains.)
Clair Calder, Ben Nevis, Scarfskerry.

Landing Sheep at Huna c.1900

The shipping of sheep or stirks was always a big day which had to be well planned because so many people were involved. Note one sheep is being held as a decoy, and at that time all the sheep on the island would have been kept on tethers. Note too that the boats do not have engines.
J.D.

Photo, John Dunnet, Seater.

Huna Slip c.1958

Peter Sinclair laden with boxes and a mat under his arm. Jamie Cormack follows with a bed spring and pictures under the other arm. It was Nicky Simpson in a "Tanghead" lorry that took Kate Smith's flitting (with very heavy kists!) to Macarthur Street, Wick.

Photo, Helen Sinclair, Keiss.

HUNA

The old saying goes "After a strong blow from north to south the first tide is the fairest."

It is sure that many a boat would have come with that tide to Huna which was such an important and busy place in days gone by. In the 1940's the islanders hired Sandy Sinclair's lorry on Monday mornings to catch the 6 o'clock train from Wick with their lobsters for the Billingsgate market. They would have had a full load in these days and the Stroma folk would have to be up before the crack of dawn to get their kists of lobsters to Huna in time. During the summer months there was always the threat of the dreaded blue paper saying that some or all of the lobsters had been condemned or were dead on arrival.

The Cormacks, Huna, did a lot of good turns for the Stroma folk and always seemed to be on hand and ready to help. Jamie would give us a run in the car to Groats, Thurso or wherever, and would wait patiently until we were ready to come back. Margaret and Will always had a bed anytime we were storm stuck and couldn't have been kinder.

Willie Sutherland (blacksmith) was a very good friend to the Stroma folk and was always ready to help in any way he could. Often islanders came with items they required urgently and Willie would set aside what he was doing and start immediately on the repairs. Often there would be a lot of boats tied up at the slip at the same time when the men were over to collect provisions and all kinds of goods for Stroma. The Smiddy was a real haven – warm, busy and lightsome, where we got up to date with, and gave opinions on the latest local events and we also listened to our elders yarning about happenings of long ago.

The lifeboat shed was used for storing parcels and all kinds of sundry goods for the island and then after the doors got broken, Willie kept all this for us in what used to be his barn. I never remember him being short of lubricating oil which was so essential and he always had a plentiful supply of fuel for our petrol paraffin engines. The mix was one gallon petrol to 10 gallons paraffin which was not a lot of petrol but we had to go to Groats Hotel for that. Donald MacKenzie and his son Alistair were also very kind to the Stroma men and had obtained special permission from the chief of police to open the bar to islanders, because we worked with the tide. We knew "time" was up when Donald drew his watch out of his pocket and took a long look at it!

The Groaters were loath to accept that we should have this special dispensation and often the merits and demerits of jaykit pookits and jaykad pookads or rabbads and rabbits got a going over!

They say one gets like the folk they live with, but we islanders are proud we come from Struma.

Peter Sinclair, Main Street, Keiss.

Footnote:- Peter William Sinclair's yole the "Kelvin Star" is one of the finest examples of its kind to be seen. Peter Matheson, Heritage Boatbuilding Centre, Scarfskerry has skilfully rebuilt an exact replica of this boat for George Watt, Keith. It is good to know the traditional model will be preserved for posterity.

C.C.

THE "DILIGENT"

The records in the Customs and Excise Office, Wick show: 9th July, 1912. Diligent. Reg. No. WK.382 owner Mr Peter Sinclair (Patty) – licensed for lines and creels.

Teenie Robertson, The Cottage, Canisbay remembers watching her grandpa George Simpson building this boat and also Patty arriving with the "pig" of whisky under his oxter for the formalities of the launching at the North End. She cost £18-12/- to build.

Patty was a very capable seaman, often sailing in weather when most would have stayed at home, and he was recognised for driving the boat, the crew and himself hard. The doctor never hesitated to go with old Patty if he was called to Stroma on a wild night in an emergency, but had been known to postpone the return trip until there was less white water. One must bear in mind that the design of the "Diligent" was ahead of her times and that the 12 + 1 strokes instead of the usual 12 gave her a big head and a hefty draught. She had a succession of different owners.

July 1938 saw Patty's son (Patty's Bill) in charge and in May 1939 she was with the Millers of Keiss and renamed "Lupin". September 1947 she had her old name back but had moved to pastures new with Walter and Angus Manson in Mey. However Stroma bonds are strong and David Crowe and Donald Wares had taken over the "Diligent" by November 1949. She was moored at Thurso Harbour and by all accounts was pushed beyond her limits but proved herself steady and reliable. At this time she also doubled as the rescue boat for the Pentland Yacht Club.

Malcolm Simpson, grandson of the builder of the "Diligent" is recorded as joining her in June 1956. In July 1973 she was back along the coast to Huna and in home waters with Davie Wares. She transferred to Wick in 1980 and was there until Sandy Gunn brought her back to Groats in 1984 and then the register was closed.

Patty's Bill's Peter rescued his grandpa's boat, but the long years and stormy seas had taken their toll and although very tired and sad she still held many fond memories and boasted of hair-raising occurrences in days gone by. She rallied after a few twilight years spent in Peter's barn where he started the restoration work. My brother Ronnie and myself then took on the task of rebuilding the "Diligent" but the credit for the "thick-end" of the work must go to Peter Matheson, Boatbuilder, Scarfskerry who completed the restoration in 1990. The work which took more than a year was the culmination of a family enterprise to return the boat to her original condition. Henry Sinclair, whose brother Patty was the first skipper of the "Diligent", was our great grandfather. Our father Ronald passed on his love of the sea and boats to us and he would have been so proud that it was the sailing skills and disciplines that he taught us that made possible the completion of this bit of family history and sailing the "Diligent" again.

Brian Sinclair, 14 Atton Road, Mansewood, Glasgow.

Brian and son Bruce sailing the "Diligent".

ODE TILL 'E SELLAG

A hardy life he hes till thole
When on his own or in a shoal
Watchin for 'e flies an hooks
Fae Groats till Gills in bays and nooks
'E reason is he's good for bait
Weel known for a partan's fate
In price he's no at far behind
'E cod or haddie an their kind

Cudding, saithe, or coley, call him fat 'e may
Alang wi' chips and gerdin peas, hid's 'e denner o' 'e day
Even as a starter, he is 'e best by far
Better an 'e lapster or even caviar
So if yer feelan hungry don't eat at forran trock
Off 'e go till Huna wi yer Sellag Pock.

Walter S. Rosie, Novelty House, John O'Groats

WILLIAM COOK'S RNLI CERTIFICATE OF SERVICE

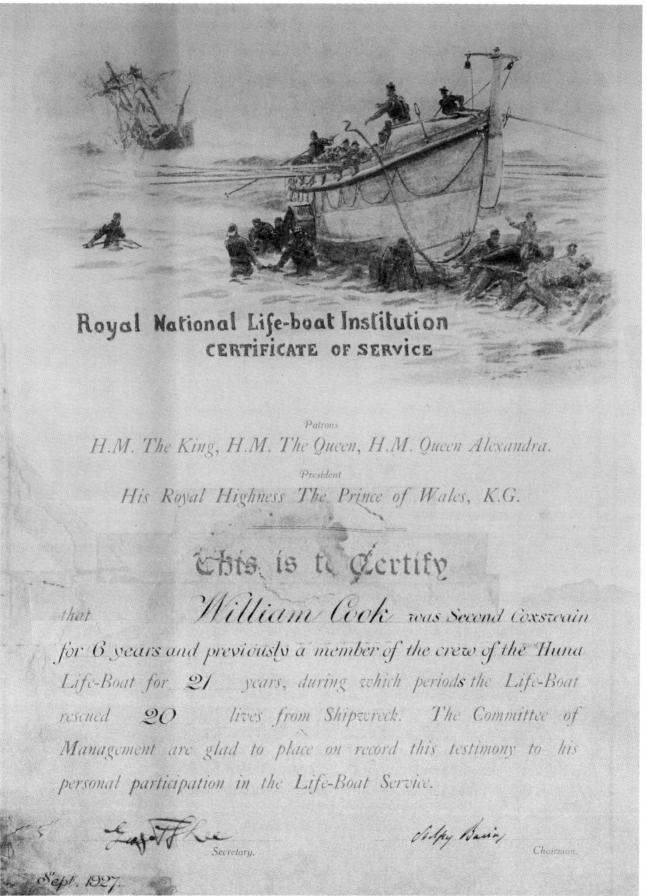

Royal National Life-boat Institution
CERTIFICATE OF SERVICE

Patrons

H.M. The King, H.M. The Queen, H.M. Queen Alexandra.

President

His Royal Highness The Prince of Wales, K.G.

This is to Certify

that *William Cook* was Second Coxswain

for 6 years and previously a member of the crew of the Huna

Life-Boat for 21 years, during which periods the Life-Boat

rescued 20 lives from Shipwreck. The Committee of

Management are glad to place on record this testimony to his

personal participation in the Life-Boat Service.

Secretary.

Chairman.

Sept. 1927.

Peter Gordon, 105 Lanark Road, West Currie, Midlothian.

ROYAL NATIONAL LIFEBOAT INSTITUTION

OFFICERS AND OFFICIALS OF

Huna Lifeboat
1877 — 1930

Coxwains

John Calder	June	1877	– October	1898
John Dunnet	December	1898	– December	1915
Alexander Sinclair	December	1915	– December	1926
William Mowat	January	1927	– March	1930

Second Coxwains

John Dunnet	June	1877	– December	1898
William Kennedy	January	1899	–	1921
William Cook		1921	–	1927
Donald Laird		1928	–	1930

Honorary Secretaries

David Meiklejohn	1877	–	1880
David Dunnet	1880	–	1884
Dr David Lechmere Anderson	1884	–	1885
Dr W.J.H Sinclair	1888	–	1892
John Sutherland (Jnr)	1892	–	1922
William Kennedy	1922	–	1930

This page is intended as a tribute to generations of men from the Pentland Firth area who by their devotion to duty, often at great personal danger and discomfort on lifeboats and fishing vessels gave help to seafarers in distress.

HUNA LIFEBOAT 1877-1930

The Royal National Lifeboat Institution was founded on 4th March, 1824 by Sir William Hillary. His main aim was to organise a national lifeboat service which would provide a means of rescue around the coast of Britain. This ideal took many years to implement fully and even today its requirements are under constant review. During the latter half of the 19th century the Pentland Firth, which lies between the extreme north of Scotland and the Orkney Islands, was one of the main trade routes between Europe and the Americas. The speed of the tides and the sudden changes in the weather conditions caused the loss of many fine vessels together with their experienced masters and crews. Because of the large numbers of shipwrecks in the area the RNLI established lifeboat stations at Scrabster in 1860 and at Longhope in 1874. These, together with that at Wick operated by the Pulteneytown Harbour Trust and funded by the British Fishery Society in 1848, provided the rescue services available. In spite of the distances involved and the fact that these were sailing/rowing lifeboats many fine rescues were carried out. In order to improve the facilities at the eastern end of the Pentland Firth, the RNLI decided in 1877 to place a lifeboat at Huna. The locals agreed to contribute towards the estimated cost of £1100 for the lifeboat and boathouse and to support maintenance of the station.

On the 6th December, 1877 a large number of the inhabitants of Canisbay assembled at Huna to witness the ceremony for the new lifeboat. After the Rev. MacGregor had offered a prayer for the success of the boat it was handed over by the RNLI to the chairman of the Huna Branch, Peter Keith Esq. The lifeboat was named W.M.C. by Mrs MacGregor and then launched and demonstrated its capabilities before enthusiastic spectators. The lifeboat was gifted anonymously to the RNLI by grateful parents in memory of a child whose life was preserved on 6th August, 1873. At their request it was named "W.M.C." It was a standard 34 feet long and eight feet three inch broad, 10 oared self-righting built by Woolfe at a cost of

Huna Lifeboat c.1900

Photo, John Dunnet, Seater.

John Dunnet "Burns" (Bowman); John Dunnet "Moolhill"; John Dunnet "Tailor"; Willie Sutherland, Smiddy; Donald Gulloch, Newton; Jamie Dunnet, Seater (wearing cap); William Dunnet "Mason"; Sinclair MacLeod, Hillside; Wattie Ross, Rose Cottage; William Dunnet "Post" (at tip of sail); Matthew Dunnet, Corner House; John Sutherland, Smiddy; Davie Kennedy, Seater later Tresdale; William Dunnet "Hike"; William Kennedy, 2nd Coxswain; John Dunnet, Coxswain.

£363. The first boathouse was built by J. Charleson for £252, but its site is uncertain.

On the morning of 10th January, 1893 the fishing fleet had set out from Wick for the winter fishing off Noss Head – the weather being pleasant and the water smooth. The fishing vessel "Margaret Gunn" WK 304 skipper John MacLean and a crew of six, had set four nets and was working with lines off Freswick when a violent southerly gale placed the vessel in danger. With great difficulty the nets were recovered, the sails were reefed in and efforts were made to get under the shelter of the land. After a short distance, the mast broke and together with the sail, was swept overboard. It was however, made fast by ropes to the stern. The fishing boat WK 1107 skippered by John Robertson went to their aid, but was unable to make fast the ropes which were thrown, and the disabled boat was swept past Duncansby Head and into the Firth at the mercy of the wind and waves. The danger was considerably increased by the mast in the water bumping against the stern and several leaks occurred. In spite of many difficulties and constant bailing, Gills' Bay was reached about 7 p.m. Two anchors were cast overboard, but the "Margaret Gunn" started dragging towards the shore. In answer to the distress flares, Huna lifeboat was quicky manned and launched. By

skilful handling, the lifeboat under coxswain John Calder, went alongside and rescued the crew of seven landing them at Huna. Shortly afterwards the "Margaret Gunn" was driven ashore and smashed to pieces on the rocks.

At 8.30 a.m. on the 8th August, 1888 the 362 ton Norwegian barque "Minerva" of Langesund (Captain Gundersen) went ashore on the Pentland Skerries. She had left Garston Dock, Liverpool just over a week before with a cargo of salt for Viburg in Finland. All had gone well until Dunnet Head was reached, but there steering way was lost due to the direction of the wind, and the vessel was swept by the tide through the Firth and on to the skerries. When the "Minerva" struck, Huna lifeboat was launched and together with several Stroma boats was quickly on the scene. By that time, however, the damaged leaking vessel had been dislodged from the rocks by the waves and tide, sinking in a short time on the south side of the main island. The crew of nine were able to launch the ship's boat and with the assistance of the lighthouse keepers, land on the rocks. Huna lifeboat, under her coxswains Messrs Calder and Dunnet, recovered the crew with their immediate belongings from the Skerries and landed them on the mainland.

In November 1889 the "W.M.C." was replaced by

Crew of Huna Lifeboat c.1898

Photo, John Dunnet, Seater.

Back Row:– Davie Kennedy, Seater later Tresdale; James Dunnet, Corner House, Huna; Donald Gulloch, Newton; Coxswain John Dunnet, Seater; William Kennedy, Seater later Tresdale; Jockey Dunnet, "Burns"; Matt Dunnet, Corner House, Huna. Front Row:– Jamie Dunnet, Seater; Sinclair MacLeod, Huna; Willie Dunnet, "Post", Mrs Alick MacGregor (wife of doctor); William Dunnet "Mason", Huna; William Dunnet "Hike", East Canisbay.

the "Caroline and Thomas". The new lifeboat was self-righting, 37 feet long, eight feet broad, 12 oared and cost £495. She was bought with a legacy from Mr T. Hackwood of Sydenham. Under certain conditions of weather and especially at low tide, difficulty in launching the lifeboat was experienced. This had to be done through a narrow gap eight yards wide which had to be constantly cleared of large loose boulders. In 1890 the present boathouse was built for £988. The slipway 343 feet long was constructed by Sinclair and Banks for £724. Special rollers were later added at a cost of £100. A winch was also placed on a concrete base in a field at the rear of the boathouse. There were two methods used when recovering the lifeboat. At high tide and in calm conditions it was simply floated on the trolley and pulled up the slipway by winch. The other method was to draw the lifeboat up the beach on the east side of the boathouse, turn it through 180 degrees and enter it through the inland doors for placement on the trolley. The floor of the boathouse had been constructed on two levels in order to make that operation easier.

At 4 p.m. on the 31st October, 1898, the four masted steamer "Manchester City", while on her maiden voyage from Middlesbrough to Manchester to load for America, broke her rudder quandrant two miles off Dunnet Head and began drifting in the strong westerly gale. Two anchors were let down and these held for a time. In answer to her distress signals, lifeboats from Thurso, Longhope and Huna were alerted and together with the "St Ola" and a Grimsby trawler, made for the scene. After launching difficulties because of low tide, Huna lifeboat soon made up under a press of sail. By that time the flowing tide was causing problems and the anchors were slipped allowing the "Manchester City" and her escorts to drive to eastwards. Second coxswain Bill Mowat of the Longhope lifeboat was placed on board the disabled vessel as pilot and although the steering was out of order she was kept off the rocks by using ahead/astern on the engines until past Duncansby Head. The three lifeboats all gave considerable assistance in spite of the mountainous seas in the Pentland Firth and on the way towards Wick Bay. Because of difficulties near Noss Head, Ackergill lifeboat together with the steam tug "Tyne" (Captain David Simpson) went to their assistance. While anchoring at the mouth of Wick Bay awaiting arrival of powerful tugs, the "Manchester City" ranged ahead and two men on the tug, Don Sweeney and Peter Simpson were injured. During the night the "Manchester City" drove out to sea while a jury rudder was fitted. With the Aberdeen steam liner "Loch Lomond" in attendance a course was set for the Cromarty Firth. Two days later, while under light anchors in the Cromarty Roads a sudden gale from the south west drove her ashore on the Nigg sands. She was later refloated undamaged by two tugs and towed south for repairs to her steering gear. The "Manchester City" (Captain Forrest) was 461 feet long, beam 52 feet and dead weight 8600 tons. She had triple expansion engines of 4000 I.H.P. made by Sir Christopher Furness and Co. of Middlesbrough and had a speed of 15 knots.

On the 1st May, 1900 the Swedish barque "Hans" of Landscrona, 1200 tons, with a cargo of rosin worth £4000, lost her rudder, wheel and sails in a strong north westerly gale near Dunnet Head. Lifeboats from Thurso (Coxs. Brims) and Longhope (Coxs. John Swanson) pursued her as she was driven eastwards through the Firth. Huna lifeboat was taken from its shed but was damaged in the launching and had to be recalled. Ackergill was made ready but was not launched. When clear of Duncansby Head, the 12 members of the crew of the "Hans" were taken aboard the steam liner "Celtic" after abandoning ship. Two days later Wick lifeboat was launched when the abandoned "Hans" was driven ashore at Broadhaven. Its cargo was recovered but the vessel became a total loss.

In thick fog on the 21st June, 1900, the Kirkcaldy fishing lugger "Magdalene Hughes" went ashore on the Little Skerry. Two of the crew swam ashore and the remainder (five) were taken off together with nets and belongings by the Huna lifeboat under coxswain John Dunnet. The seven members of her crew were later landed at Stromness probably by the steam liner "Lilian Maud" of Peterhead.

On 6th October, 1900 the fishing steamer "Champion" of Grimsby ran ashore on the Little Skerry and stuck fast. Although Huna lifeboat was quickly on the scene, the crew were rescued by Stroma fishermen just as she arrived. Shortly afterwards nine salvage men set up base in a 12 foot square hut on the Skerry as they attempted to refloat the "Champion". On the 11th November in answer to distress signals from the salvage men, Huna lifeboat set out to the rescue. Because the weather was unsettled and the sea rough, she was unable to land and had to return to station. Next day Wick lifeboat was towed to the area by the steamer "Salisbury", which was helping with the salvage operations, and rescued five men. The other five decided to remain on the island until the weather improved.

In September, 1901 the "Caroline and Thomas" was replaced by the "Ida". She was self-righting, 37 feet long, nine feet three inches broad, 10 oared and cost £903. She was provided by legacy of Miss Ida B. Summons of Hove.

About 3 a.m. on the 29th November, 1902 the steam trawler "Silanion" No.1179 of Grimsby ran ashore east of the John O'Groats Hotel. There was a strong south easterly gale, the night was intensely dark and a heavy land surf was running. When the distress signals were seen from the shore, the lifeboat under coxswain J. Dunnet was hurriedly manned, launched and proceeded towards the stranded vessel. In the meantime the crew of the trawler had launched their own boat, but this was swept away in the heavy seas. Captain Smith, who had been staying at John O'Groats made his way over the rocks and shouted to the shipwrecked crew to wait for the lifeboat. By means of a lantern he was able to guide her to the scene as by then the "Silanion's" lights had failed. With great skill and determination, the lifeboat was taken against the lee quarter and the crew of 10 hauled aboard. Because of the heavy seas running, the lifeboat had to wait for daylight before attempting to land at Huna. Even then it was not possible and she proceeded with the rescued crew to the harbour at Mey. The "Silanion" belonged to the Standard Steam Fishing Co., of Grimsby and was commanded by William Wright. She had been fishing near the Faroe Islands and was on her way home with a catch worth £400. The vessel was two years old and cost £6000.

Early on 8th April, 1902, during hazy weather the Glasgow trawler "Ardgowan" GW4 ran on the rocks about half a mile from John O'Groats. After being fast for three hours, the crew were able to refloat her on the rising tide. Before the vessel could get under way, however, a rapid current caught her and she was swept on to the Ness of Duncansby in a dangerous position. Meantime the Huna lifeboat was alerted and quickly launched. The crew of nine and the captain's son were transferred to the lifeboat and landed at Huna. The "Ardgowan" was later refloated and taken to Wick for repairs.

On the 25th May, 1910 while the fishing vessel "Strathyre" of Findochty (BF 493 and skipper Alexander Campbell) was proceeding through the Pentland Firth on passage from Stornoway to Stronsay, the wind fell away and she was swept by the strong tide on to the Skerries. Shortly afterwards she broke up and sank leaving the crew clinging to a rough raft of spars and buoys floundering in the water. At considerable danger to himself, James MacHardy, one of the assistant lighthouse keepers, swam out and made a line fast to the raft which was then drawn ashore by the other lighthouse keepers. Huna lifeboat had been alerted when the incident occurred but they were safe by the time she arrived. The crew were recovered from the Skerries by the lifeboat and taken to Huna. The "Stratheyre" was valued at £440 and the gear £350 – all was lost.

On the 6th October, 1910 while passing through the Pentland Firth in dense fog, the four masted steamer "Indian" of Liverpool under the command of Captain Bruce bound from Nordenham via the Tyne to Pensacola, Florida, with a load of salt went ashore on the east side of Duncansby Head. Such was the force of the current that the vessel heeled over to a dangerous angle, and the captain fearing that the vessel would flounder, ordered the lifeboats to be launched. This was a procedure fraught with danger and no sooner had the boats touched the water than they capsized and one of the crew engaged in the launching fell overboard and was drowned. Considering that the tide ran at 12 knots it was surprising that the consequences were not more serious. The position where the "Indian" struck was the Rispie – the Keiss vessel "F. T. Barry" had been lost there some time previously. The distress signals were quickly answered by the "Princess Olga" and "Princess Royal" of Liverpool closely followed by Huna lifeboat under coxswain John Dunnet. The vessel

was badly holed in the forward compartments but the watertight bulkheads held and there was little water aft. The crew was preparing to abandon ship with their personal effects when she refloated on the rising tide. The "Indian" proceeded south under her own steam escorted by Huna lifeboat and when in danger of sinking was beached in Sinclair Bay. Huna lifeboat remained in attendance from Saturday afternoon until Tuesday. The "Indian" was owned by the Frederick Leyland Co. Ltd., of Liverpool and was built in Belfast in 1900. She was 482 feet long tonnage 5990 and had a draught when loaded of 29 feet. Her crew of 52 were German and British with a Shetland captain. She was refloated on 17th August after repairs had been made to the bow and went to Newcastle under her own power with salvage tugs "Ranger" and "Linnet" in attendance.

The Huna lifeboat was recorded as having been launched on service 29 times and saved 27 lives between 1877 and 1930. It was then withdrawn and the station closed. By that time the lifeboat stations at Thurso, Longhope and Wick had been provided with motor powered vessels and the Committee of the RNLI felt that there was adequate cover in the Pentland Firth and area.

It is worth noting that during the time of the Huna lifeboat 145 vessels were in difficulties in the Pentland Firth and a large number of these were wrecked. Many others were refloated and crews rescued by the action of local fishermen who in terrible conditions and in dangerous situations gave help on at least 43 occasions.

On two occasions Stroma fishermen were awarded the RNLI parchment for outstanding rescues.

In 1908 the "Royal Oak", a Stroma fishing boat, was swamped in heavy seas near Muckle Skerry. The crew of five kept themselves afloat by clinging to wreckage from the boat until rescued by the heroic efforts and seamanship of another Stroma boat the "Undaunted". They were landed on Muckle Skerry, provided with hot food and dry clothes and taken back to Stroma by the "Undaunted".

In 1912 the "Dubbelmann", a trawler from Ymuiden, ran ashore on the Lother Rock off Brough Ness, South Ronaldsay and was wrecked. Stroma fishermen rescued the crew under very difficult conditions.

This article is intended as a tribute to generations of men from the Pentland Firth area who by their devotion to duty, often at great personal danger and discomfort on lifeboats and in fishing vessels, gave help to seafarers in distress.

Andy Anderson, "Shiloh", Janetstown, Wick.

New moon with old moon in her arms –
sign of storm

Robbie Dundas, Huna.

"BURNS" COTTAGE HUNA C.1880

The home of John Dunnet (A'al Seaman) and his wife Isabella Kennedy.

This is the old cottage at the mouth of the Huna burn from which that Dunnet family took its name. It is thought that it was when Huna was "squared up" that the family built the house now known as Havengore and moved there. The head of Mey is seen on the right and Quoys on left of photograph.

The notice says Mrs Dunnet, Grocer. She was Sinclair Davidson, widow of John Dunnet, who was drowned in 1874 at Huna when the boat was lost. [The men and women on the shore could only watch as the boat was swamped in a terrible sea. The crew all perished with the exception of Tailor John who managed to cling to an oar and was rescued. It was thought that the loss of this boat was one of the main reasons for having the lifeboat sited at Huna.] Mrs Sinclair Dunnet in doorway. Jockie Dunnet (her son) later Roadside, Huna. Kate (her daughter) who married Johndie Smith, Huna. "A'al Seaman" John Dunnet who died 1888 aged 91.

It was A'al Seaman who helped her set up shop and to bring up her family which also included Belle m. M. Elliot – County Durham. Jean m. Alex Banks – Edinburgh – Nova Scotia. David m. Margt. Begg – Flour Miller, Glasgow. William m. Jessie Kennedy – Postman, Canisbay.

Clara Cormack, "Broadcroft", Woodlands Avenue, Kirkcudbright.

DAVID DUNNET "BURNS"

David Nicolson grew up at Seater and it was to David Dunnet "Burns" that he sent the following poems. They were childhood chums and had spent many happy evenings at Huna walking along the shore. David was the son of John Dunnet and Sinclair Davidson.

Lines suggested on parting with a Juvenile Friend – D. Dunnet

Dear youthful friend, we now must part,
I leave behind the false and true;
The pangs shoot through my inmost heart,
When driven from a friend like you.

Although it is Fates stern decree,
Unto this slender hope I cling;
To meet beyond the deep, blue sea,
The thought, it soothes the parting sting.

Yes, Hope, the substitute of joy,
Bids me restrain the melting tear;
Nor time nor distance can destroy
The band which binds two friends sincere.

One glance behind, brings fresh to mind,
The happy hours together spent;
The jocular tale unconfined
Around our circle gaily went.

Or if instruction was the theme,
To elevate our mental powers
Thou did'st impart a bright'ning gleam,
I'll cherish to my latest hours.

Perchance we wandered by the dell,
On Nature's work to learn and muse;
Enraptured, I could ever dwell
With thee, amid the landscape views.

The past leaves pleasant prints behind,
More dark the future does appear,
Where will I seek? Who can I find
So noble, faithful, and sincere?

We yet shall meet, I'll yet enjoy
The smile of thy congenial face,
And friendship pure without allow,
Which death alone, can e'er erase.
David Nicholson.

Letter to Catherine Matheson, Auckengill Post Office from Dannie Nicolson

Canisbay.
11.8.1986

Dear Cathie,

Just a note to thank you for the copy of the verses composed by David Nicolson. They are good, much better than I expected. His education must have been good for that time, hence the wide choice of words. A critic might say that they were too sentimental but leaving home meant a great deal to him.

His mother was a realist and when any of her family emigrated she said they must push on! She was a good mother but showed no emotion and no tears when they left. Six of her family crossed the Atlantic and two went to New Zealand. A sailing ship must have picked David up, and likely some others as well. An agent used to arrange for emigrants to gather at certain places to be picked up. It was a common practice during the Clearances. We will never know the facts, as all the people concerned are no longer with us.

David Nicolson was my uncle David's eldest son. Uncle David and Uncle Bill went to Canada about (1886) and settled in Ontario. They went by passenger ship. They both married but David and his wife both died young. Bill got a farm by time, and his grandson is still there. Bill's granddaughter Jane Nicolson was over about three years ago. She called and we had a long conversation.

Trust you are all well.

Sincerely

Dannie

The Emigrant's Farewell

The ship has lies ready in the bay
To bear me o'er the wester main
The sun declines with waning ray
Behind the purple, heath-clad plain.

One lingering look is cast behind,
On those I leave upon the shore;
Ties now more strongly seem to bind,
Than they had ever done before.

Reluctantly I bid adieu
To scenes o'er which I fondly dwell;
My native land, friends dear and true –
To all – a fervent, fond farewell.

The muffled murmur of the sea
Blends with the sighing on the deck,
As tearful eyes, do gaze on thee –
Scotia! now a fading speck.

The breeze strikes on the snow-white sails
Our ship glides swiftly o'er the sea
Like music on the evening gales
Floats one sweet sound, remember me.

I never, never shall forget
Thee, nor my seat of early joy;
Until my star of life is set,
'Twill be as when I was a boy.

Though roaming o'er a sun-scorched plain,
Or straying by an ice-bound shore;
Or tossed upon the surging main,
I'll think of where I've been before.

And thee – dear one will always hold
A seat forever in my mind,
My thoughts of thee will ne'er grow cold;
Though thou art left far, far behind.

David Nicholson.

The Entrance to Huna Pier

Long ago they used to put a light in the end window of Havengore to guide the boats into the channel. This was especially necessary if the doctor was needed in Stroma or in any emergency.

Meeze on the Lan?

Get Smiddy on Havengore and then sail along until the window showed clear on the west side of Smiddy. Turn east until that same window showed clear on east side of Smiddy. Wheel round, and that takes boat in safely round the Outskerry Rock and in the channel to the pier.

James Simpson, Burnside, Gills.

Huna Pier – Safe Channel from the East

Sail along until you have coxswains chimneys on Geordie Manson's garage, then follow the above instructions. This keeps you clear of seaweed which does not grow on sand.

R.D.

Meeze for Cape Wrath

A jet pilot said radar is no use when they are on low flying exercises, so they must take a meeze on the land. For Cape Wrath they line up Duncansby Head Lighthouse on the Canisbay Kirk. This takes them over Stroma View and out through Gothiegill and over Cape Wrath.

Robbie Dundas.

The English Men

Two distinct rock ledges at the west side of Huna burnmouth seen at ebb tide. When these rocks could be seen in clear view from our house we knew that our boat would be lying high and dry at Huna slip.

Robbie Dundas, Stroma View.

Companion Ferrymen

Venerable and characteristic representatives of the Pentland Firth pilots and fishermen c.1885.

John Dunnet o' the Burn

Murdo Sutherland

Photos from 'E Silkie Man by David Houston.

John Dunnet always regretted Johnston the photographer took him in his working clothes. Murdo knew he would be next so he got changed into his Sunday best. Their large hand tinted portraits hung for many years in the Huna Inn.

A NAUTICAL MISCELLANY

Generally speaking the northern coastline of Canisbay Parish does not feature towering cliffs or natural inlets (geos) which could be confidently rated as geologically formed harbours, but flat rocks and comparatively level beaches possessed certain advantages appreciated by the seafaring fraternity of a bygone age who launched and hauled their boats long before piers or indeed enclosed havens of refuge had become a reality. In some localities boulders would have to be removed to make a safe seaward track but there was no lack of brawny men, then, to do that job satisfactorily. No doubt they looked enviously towards Huna and John O'Groats where sand stretched much more extensively along the shore, even 60 years ago, since when it began an irreversible decline right up to the present day. Lack of direct exposure to the full effect and fetch of waves hurled shorewards by westerly or easterly gales and being sheltered from northerly blasts by the Orkney Islands, has perhaps resulted in this north facing coast suffering a lesser degree of erosion and serration by the remorseless ocean even though the land is at a much lower height above sea level than neighbouring approaches to Dunnet and Duncansby headlands. Gills, Huna and John O'Groats have always been focal points for fishermen in the past because they did possibly, afford reasonable, though far from perfect facilities which were improved later on by piers giving some slight protection from the elements while provision of hand operated winches was a further step in a labour saving direction.

In 1897 it was proposed to make a harbour at Gills which would cost £1000, a large sum at that time, and this would include an anticipated local contribution of £200, but in 1902 construction had still not commenced while the cost had risen to £1250. There were 15 boats fishing from Gills at that period, when the local Member of Parliament, (it must have been near election time), again advocated the need for a harbour. Local people put their case very forcibly and some exaggeration in their claims may be forgiven considering the

237

fishermens' unenviable situation. They stated that during bad weather the greatest part of the Stroma traffic is carried on there, in preference to Huna and John O'Groats, which are in such conditions, unapproachable. Furthermore in their opinion it was the best harbour of refuge between Scrabster and Ackergill while the bay itself sometimes gave shelter to 50-60 fishing vessels, yet despite all that was said, the pier at Gills did not take shape until 1904 and was to be 150 yards long with a breadth of from 10-12 feet. Two years later a proposed pier for the Bocht was mooted also, and the lowest tender from a Donald Sinclair was accepted, a third of the expense for same being met by the County Council. In 1906 there were two big herring boats (ferthies) registered under Gills and Mey viz. "Maggie" WK 111 owned by J. Ross and 53 feet in length while another "Maggie" WK 523 was 45 feet long and owned by A. Swanson. There were still two boats of that size in 1910 with different names "Maggie and Annie" WK 111 owned by J. Ross and three others, and "Magnet" WK 172 owners W. Ham and W. McLeod. No doubt the First World War put an end to their herring fishing operations. In 1936 only two small boats were registered at Gills and they were the "Marjory" WK 604 belonging to Robert Banks and the "Maggie" WK 606 owned by James Shearer. There was a bigger fleet of small fishing craft at Mey.

"Clyne"	WK 169	Wm. Banks and Wm. Dunnet
"Dosilee"	WK 476	Donald Banks
"Liberty"	WK 516	Thomas Dunnet
"Blossom"	WK 519	John Miller
"Lottie"	WK 458	George Sutherland
"Lively"	WK 716	William Manson
"Cathie"	WK 737	Magnus Baikie

Huna really came into prominence when the new rowing and sailing lifeboat "W.M.C.", gifted by a Manchester lady, was stationed there in 1877 after a boathouse and slipway had been constructed to RNLI specifications. Harbour facilities at John O'Groats[1] had been improved also since local boatman James Geddes, touting for Orkney bound passengers and cargo in 1836, stated that there was an excellent coach road from Wick to the water's edge at the point of embarkation for those wishing to cross the Firth. His charges were moderate, he stressed.

Stroma's nearest point of contact with the mainland was Huna though on occasion with an excessive easterly sea running, a landing, by the mailboat especially, was made at Gills. The name Huna according to Horne is derived from the Old Norse Hoefn meaning a haven and this seems a reasonable deduction. In 1902 John Nicolson of Auckengill accidentally discovered and unearthed a male skeleton along with some unidentifiable animal bones close to the shore near the Drill Hall at Huna Inn. Hlodver, a Norse Earl of Orkney, is said to have been buried at Huna or Hofu as it was then called, but no convincing evidence of that interment has ever come to light.

When Stroma was in its heyday, without a single vacant house on the island, Huna must have indeed been a hive of activity with the constant comings and goings of a vibrant community. Such was still the case even after the lifeboat had been removed, when in 1930 the lifeboat shed, as it was called, along with the adjoining slipway had been handed over to the County Council. My youthful memories of Huna are very vivid varying from extreme delight when going home for school holidays to utmost depths of despair when two or three of us young lads abandoned to our fate on foreign soil sat on empty oil drums, not even having the courage to look round as the last link with our island home sped out past the Out Skerry with an ever increasing bow wave while we waited mournfully for the bus which would carry us irrevocably to Wick High School where with trembling hand we proffered our notes of regret from parents, explaining our unavoidably late arrival. Gruffly dismissing us to our respective classes, where, on opening the door we felt the focussed gaze of all eyes, the Rector I think was sympathetic though possibly unable to visualise our early morning bleary eyed morning start, followed by a rough crossing of the Sound with wind against tide and then an "all shook up" lengthy bus run to the Burgh. Those recollections remind me of my first such voyage into the unknown as it were, when on Huna slip I turned to gaze wistfully at a now far distant convoy at which a Stroma fisherman of mature years earnestly advised me to "stick in at yir books an' forget aal aboot ships!" On reflection, maybe a satisfactory compromise was reached!

In those days Huna "Smiddy" was in full swing serving Stroma and much of the surrounding parish as well. You could hear the metallic clink, clink of hammer on iron, on a quiet day before the boat had reached the slip while the broad blackened chimney issued intermittent puffs like smoke signals. Willie Sutherland, the blacksmith, and his father before him always had great rapport with Stroma folk. They understood the "islanders" way of life so nobody at any time was turned away, no task undertaken caused inconvenience whether it was making a set of horse shoes, a plough "sock" needing sharpening or some piece of metal work urgently required for boat maintenance. Time and tide wait for no man and with that in mind the fishermen got priority and a supply of fuel for boats' engines was always supplied on demand. Many a stranded islander appreciated a "windlin" of straw from Willie in order to make a smoke signal on the sand. When a boat was seen leaving the haven the marooned person dowsed a makeshift bonfire with relief, a primitive means of communication which rarely failed to attract attention. The door of the Smiddy was always open sending out a blast of hot air while in the eerie interior light, wreathed by smoke and steam, the blacksmith, wearing his leather apron, forced the bellows lever up and down making the dull red glow of the furnace burst into new life. Armed with a pair of long tongs he removed a red bar of iron from the fire and laying it on the anvil immediately

Father and son John and Willie Sutherland

Photo, Helen Sinclair, Keiss.

fashioned the shape of a horseshoe, while showers of sparks rebounded off his apron to die on the flagstone floor. The old man now retired, sat on a nearby wooden stool, turning slowly in one hand a long handled maul, unable now to wield the hammer yet content to feel the well worn haft like the trusty handclasp of an old friend, as he watched his son plunge the completed shoe into the water tub beside the anvil, where steam erupted with a sharp hissing sound. A name was then chalked upon the finished article and if not collected at the time it was placed at one side of the main entrance along with sundry other items and parcels destined for the isle across the water while other agricultural objects for mainland clients were hung on wall pegs to await collection.

The approach channel to Huna slip was fairly straightforward, though when the tide was low a bowman gave the necessary hand signals to guide the helmsman. A rock known as the Out Skerry when covered could be identified by its iron rod marker and was never a hazard though in bad weather it could sharpen a wave crest to sudden breaking point. There were times during adverse conditions when boats could only lie bow on to the slip and hurried transactions on shore were kept to an absolute minimum so that a return passage could be made before tidal variations took effect. A fisherman whose boat takes the bottom unexpectedly on a falling tide wears a doleful expression akin to that of the ardent motorist who gazes in disbelief at the squashed appearance of an unforeseen flat tyre. At Huna, especially during spring tides, two men were usually detailed to stay by the boat, moving her continuously seaward. Even so it was sometimes necessary to incline a craft until she was listed over on her bilge and could then with boathooks be pushed nearer the slip or to seaward as required. Those were the days when thigh booted fishermen were forced to slide and slither over stones green with treacherous seaweed while their lady passengers shrieked with affected terror or maybe delight as they lurched from side to side arms clasped grimly round male necks to the point of suffocation. As with all small harbours of that era, little in the way of improvement was carried out and Huna was no exception where men shortened their lifespan carrying heavy loads on their backs up and down a slipway where a small winch and trolley running on the rails would have proved a labour saving innovation. Years were to pass before a slight and not very effective extension was added to the end of the existing facility, supposed to enable boats to be reached more easily and still stay afloat. When cattle were taken across from the island in the "big boat", a name which took preference over the "Bee", she was beached on the sand and listed so that animals could step out of her quite easily. The beach had altered by 1949 causing William Bremner to complain bitterly to the Council that the cattle boat had been damaged to such an extent by stones on the beach that it would take £100 to make effective repairs.

There was a man named Sinclair Davidson who acted as Lloyds Agent at Huna in 1866 and his reports of passing vessels in the Caithness Courier make extremely interesting reading. The full rigged sailing vessels "Laurel" and "Canada West" also barques "Alexander Hall", "St Lawrence" and "Harmonia" passed through the Firth in April of that year. The "Hindustan" from Aberdeen. "Cavalier" and "Cornelia" were all full rigged ships bound for Quebec with a fresh east-north-east breeze, he said, while the barque "Loyalist" of Leith was bound for the same port. No doubt these ships would be on the then lucrative trade of coal out and timber home. However the barque "Annie Laurie" and full rigger "Hyena" were bearing up to go north about Orkney. Reports after this unfortunately ceased except for a mention that the "Pride of Canada" with Captain Lyall in command passed through bound from Leith to Calcutta. But this was 8th September, 1871, and Sinclair Davidson had died at Huna two years previously. A house with its gable facing the sea lay vacant for many years and had at one time been tenanted by a lady known locally as "Henny" Davidson, so I was told, who when the Customs and Excise officials planned a visit, pulled down a blind to warn her Stroma friends but whether or not she was related to the Lloyds Agent I cannot confirm.

Shipwreck in those bygone days was an accepted occupational hazard when the only aids to navigation comprised a magnetic compass, soundings obtained by hand leadlines, ship's speed given by the log and the visual observations of a lookout man stationed so as to have as clear a field of vision ahead as possible, but often tragically his warning shout of "Breakers Ahead" came too late for successful avoiding action to be taken. There were many unknown factors affecting ship position fixing at that time. Knowledge of compass errors and their causes left much to be desired, while it was not always appreciated that the rotating log does not record the effect of tide on a vessel's progress and it was not easy to find the depth with accuracy, in fact it would be difficult to get the lead to even reach the sea bed owing to the velocity of the tidal stream. Approaching such dangerous waters, having had bad visibility for days, meant that no definite "fix" could be worked out from sun or stars making the final run through the Firth a hazardous operation, indeed, rendered even more difficult in days of sail should wind decrease to light variable airs. Initially low-powered engine driven vessels could not compete against the full force of vicious tides. Many a ship owed her survival to the local pilot on board yet the voyages of numerous vessels ended abruptly on the sharp fangs of submerged rocky reefs. In days when people had very little in the way of worldly goods the cargo of a wreck was an unforeseen bonus and who can blame them for robbing the sea of some of its prey. Loss of life at sea was as great a tragedy then as it is today and the loss of a Duncansby

boat[2] in April 1868 must have caused deep sorrow when George Houston 25, David Manson 26, and John Dunnet 21 failed to return. They put to sea intending to fish or pilot ships and were last seen from Stroma to be east and south of Duncansby Head. A French fishing vessel on her way to Iceland must have had reason to make a search but did not communicate with the land so presumably her efforts were in vain. In December of that year the skipper of an English smack reported that he had identified the missing boat in Norway where she had been bought in undamaged condition by a Norwegian who was using her for pleasure. If application was made for same by her original owners it was surmised they would get the full value of their craft but this would be small consolation for those bereaved.

In February, 1870, as was quite common on these coasts, wreckage came ashore at Duncansby from an unknown vessel; then a fortnight later four bodies found in Fasgeo were taken to the house of John Gibson, thereafter to be interred in Canisbay churchyard.

There must have been great excitement on 12th August, 1872 when the "William Mitchell" went ashore in the Crook of Ness near Duncansby Head. She was a wooden vessel originally full rigged and had been built in 1856 by J. Johnson and Sons, Stirling, for the Ben Line of Leith. They named her after the founder of the Alloa Coal Co. and her figurehead was a replica of this individual who, with an associate, shared and financed business ventures with the ship's owners, enabling Alloa coal to be carried outwards from Leith and timber homewards from Canada. The "William Mitchell" was 668 tons register, 161 feet in length, 28 feet in breadth and had a depth of 18 feet. Her crew comprised 10 men and a boy and she was well found, having self reefing gear for single topsails while a longboat, pinnace and gig were carried. In April, 1872 she had been sold to J. Rankin and Co., Sunderland, reduced to barque rig and put under the command of Captain Dacres who was also part owner. Bound from Three Rivers, Canada to Hartlepool laden with timber she had no local pilot on board when she went ashore during calm weather with dense fog. Subsequently Hugh Green fisherman and pilot took charge but there was no hope of her refloating as she lay across a reef midships, had 13 feet of water in the holds and eventually her back broke between the fore and main masts. Fortunately ship and cargo were fully insured which must have been a relief to her owners.

A hundred men were engaged in discharging her cargo under the superintendence of Lloyd's Agent Mr Spence, and at first it was optimistically thought that three days would complete discharge, but by 24th September, though 15,000 deals of pitch pine had been salvaged, there were still 2000 on board. However ultimately all the cargo was landed on shore and reshipped while the wrecked vessel was broken up and her gear sold on the shore at Duncansby during October 1872. I was informed on good authority that the beams now supporting the roof of the Old Mill Theatre in Thurso came originally from the "William Mitchell".

A few weeks before the above event the French barque "Espérance" had stranded only a quarter of a mile away, but her gear, sails and casks of oil had been put up for sale at Huna.

During December 1876 another barque the "Eos" of Norway had been driven so far inshore that her crew jumped on to rocks and were thereafter hospitably entertained in John O'Groats Hotel while shortly before in mid September a large ship, the "Rescue" of 1200 tons had run aground on the Ness of Duncansby in hazy weather. Her crew were saved and she was laden with Quebec timber for Hartlepool which consisted of oak, elm and pine logs 40-60 feet long and 20-26 inches in diameter. There were various other vessels which came to grief in this area including the Glasgow steamer "Ardmore" on her way from the Baltic to the west coast of Scotland in August 1899 with a cargo of pitprops, when she struck bottom at the Ness of Duncansby. Despite a fierce gale raging at the time, her crew slid down ropes from her bowsprit to safety. This would indicate she was also fitted with sails. At the ensuing Board of Trade Enquiry local fishermen pilots said if they had been in charge they could not have done more than her captain who had taken a proper course to pass through the Inner Sound.

It was remarked by the court that he should not have kept quite so close to land, however findings concluded that the vessel became unmanageable owing to unexpected tidal influence. There was a narrow escape in June 1907 for a John O'Groats crew when their boat, in which they were fishing in Sannick Bay, was struck and damaged by the Aberdeen trawler "North Coast". At a subsequent trial the trawler was found to be at fault by swinging to port after she rounded Duncansby Head. But in February, 1907 there was a much more serious incident in which a John O'Groats boat, fishing near the Pentland Skerries with other local and Stroma boats was run down by the Aberdeen trawler "Ben Aden" and Gilbert Laird sen., his son William, Gilbert Laird jun. and his son William and John Ross were tragically lost. Later in court the helmsman declared the sun was in his eyes and in avoiding one boat he had hit the other. He received two months in prison for not making a rescue attempt while the skipper who was below at the time was given a verdict of not guilty.

Three years later, in August 1910 to be exact, a large four masted steamer belonging to the then well known Leyland Line of Liverpool went ashore at Duncansby Head in dense fog. The "Indian" built at Belfast in 1900 was 482 feet in length and had sailed from Bremerhaven for Pensacola USA with a cargo of kainite (magnesium and potassium sulphate used as fertiliser) but en route she called at Newcastle for coal bunkers. Shortly after leaving that port, two German stowaways were discovered, resulting in the vessel altering course

for Wick Bay, where the two men were taken ashore in the pilot boat to be repatriated. Arguably there were some folk of the opinion that if she had not made this detour the vessel would have sailed through the Firth without mishap. At first when the "Indian" struck, force of tide listed her over to such an extent that her rail was in the water and the captain, who as it happened was a Shetlander, thinking with good reason his ship might capsize, ordered two empty lifeboats to be launched but they were overturned by the tide and carried away, one being picked up by a Stroma boat, the other by a trawler. Distress signals had by this time brought Huna lifeboat and two steamers belonging to Messrs Langlands Co. The latter attempted a tow but the hawsers parted. When the tide turned the "Indian" floated clear, though down by the head, and proceeded to Sinclair's Bay escorted by the lifeboat, under her own steam. She was beached there until temporary repairs could be executed and then left for the Tyne accompanied by two tugs. The report of an enquiry held in September stated that the Huna Lifeboat Coxswain John Dunnet and John Sutherland a member of his crew, agreed with the ship's master that the tide could run at 10-12 knots and furthermore two steamers were driven ashore that same year close to where the "Indian" had stranded. The captain said he had altered course to starboard to avoid another vessel in the fog but the Court cautioned him with a warning to allow a greater margin of safety in the future. Apart from this episode the "Indian" was a very fortunate ship when torpedoes fired during two separate attacks missed their target in the First World War yet strange as it may seem her final voyage was in 1923 to a German ship breaker's yard.

A bank of fog which came on suddenly caused the Norwegian steamer "Ausgarius" to run ashore on the Ness of Duncansby in December 1910. She was bound for Oslo with a cargo of coal loaded in Glasgow. The wreck was ultimately bought by local fishermen. During the next three years there were various strandings of fishing vessels and even if they managed to keep well clear of land they had to contend with weather hazards. In January 1913 the Cullen steam drifter "Racer" on her way to Buckie from the west coast fishing reported having encountered a heavy sea off Duncansby Head which carried away everything on deck, started the hatches and planking, and her skipper said that had the bulwarks not burst she would have sunk. Presumably this damage was providential in quickly clearing her decks of water.

Several tugs including the Danish "Viking" one of the best equipped in the world at that time, tried in vain to refloat the America-bound Norwegian steamer "Thyra" from the rocks near the Stacks of Duncansby where she had gone ashore in June 1914 but by November of that year the remorseless waves of a south east gale completely wrecked the vessel. Much of her cargo was salvaged by the Liverpool Salvage Co., and taken to Wick but large quantities of jute and linen remained on board. The "Stroma", another Norwegian ship, chose a better locality when she ran aground near John O'Groats Hotel in October 1919. Her captain is alleged to have said he thought Pentland Skerries light was that of Duncansby Head. However despite a north east gale which did not help matters she was fortunate in being refloated though part of her cargo of fish oil from Iceland to Grangemouth had to be jettisoned. If the sands were polluted there would not be many tourists around at that time of the year anyway.

The local community again suffered a sad loss during May 1932 when Sinclair Steven, 68 and his son John, 25, went to the "creels" and their boat was swamped off Duncansby Head. It is interesting to note that a warning light shone forth from Duncansby Head in 1914 but in 1921 a new lighthouse was being proposed which ultimately flashed seawards from 1924 onwards. In February 1916 the Admiralty had erected a fog signal here, no doubt considering the safety of numerous naval vessels in the area, but in January 1920 they had dismantled this aid to mariners.

There were also contradictory statements from the Department of Agriculture who in 1934 stated that they could not give a grant for the proposed extension and improvement of John O'Groats pier, yet in the summer of 1935 they decided to offer £900, which with the Lighthouse Board's offer of £40, would assist in attaining the total estimated cost of £1200.

In 1906 there were only two large herring boats (ferthies) registered here viz. "Isabella" WK 468 owned by G. Green and 52 feet in length, also the "Isabella Elizabeth" WK 391 of 48 feet and they were still there in 1910 but I have seen an old photo showing at least five boats of this size hauled up between the hotel and the last house. In 1936 such craft were but a memory and only small open boats were based there as indicated.

"Ivy"	WK 98	Alex Gunn
"Rosebud"	WK 446	Wm Mowat
"Hope"	WK 529	Alex Gunn
"Lily"	WK 559	Ben Laird
"Sal"	WK 595	Alex Houston
"Alert"	WK 229	Alex Mowat
"Mizpah"	WK 512	Donald Mowat
"Dolphin"	WK 548	William Steven
"Shamrock"	WK 590	Alex Dunnet
"Flower"	WK 598	Donald Laird

There seems to be no record of "ferthies" being hauled up at Huna during the herring boom while in 1936 only the small boat "Dewdrop" WK 455 was registered and she was owned by Stroma man William Simpson who with his wife Barbara tenanted the former Huna Inn latterly known as Huna House.

At the end of March 1936 on a night of dense fog the Finnish vessel "Osterhav" ran ashore two miles South of Duncansby Head lighthouse. Radio had come into its own by this time and Wick Wireless Station received her distress transmissions. Consequently Wick lifeboat escorted the refloated vessel to Sinclair's Bay, where after discharging her paper pulp cargo and making temporary repairs she proceeded to the Cromarty Firth. According to a report in the local press at the time there were four female crew members on board, one of whom Mrs Syjostrum a stewardess, was said to have been shipwrecked no fewer than six times.

During the last war, maritime news was of course subject to the censor and it was only after hostilities had ceased that many facts became available, but most local folk will remember or have heard about the large ex-Canadian salvage tug "Salvage King" built in 1925, which had been brought over to this country from Vancouver. She ended her days one dark night in September 1940 on the Ness of Duncansby where despite efforts by another naval tug, the "Buccaneer" to free her from the rocks all was in vain and she was broken up for scrap, which after being transported to Wick was then conveyed south by rail. The "Buccaneer" lasted until 1946 when during target practice she was sunk by a shell.

A year later in the same month a smaller tug the "St Olaves" built for the Royal Navy in 1919 and requisitioned for the Navy again in 1939 went aground in the same locality as the "Salvage King". The former was towing the water boat "Golden Crown" south from Scapa Flow so both vessels were stranded. Four men reached the shore on a life raft while at great risk to herself, Wick lifeboat rescued the remainder. Possibly the worst disaster in recent memory was the total loss on 7th December, 1959, of the Aberdeen trawler "George Robb", which during a veritable hurricane from the south east, foundered at the Stacks of Duncansby. None of her crew of 12 survived. Sadly a member of Wick Life Saving Brigade died helping to save others on this night of storm and tragedy. Subsequently John O'Groats formed their own Life Saving team which is now always ready for any eventuality.

Certain prominent headlands proved to be literally graveyards for shipping, yet vessels sometimes came to grief off the beaten track as it were, when no doubt vagaries of tide set low powered ships dangerously close to land. In November 1866 the steamer "Battalion" of Leith with a cargo of wheat from Danzig to Dublin stranded on the Ness of Huna but some cargo was jettisoned and she proceeded on her voyage. The following month the brigantine "Scotia" of Inverness, on passage from Liverpool to Arbroath with salt, ran into bad weather off Cape Wrath and survived until she reached Gills Bay where she was wrecked, fortunately without loss of life. The year after her demise there was yet another strong petition put forward by a local seafarer Captain Begg of the schooner "Admiral Napier", for a beacon to be erected on St John's Point, and though this matter came up for discussion at various times nothing came of the deliberations.

On a dark drizzly night in March 1874 the French fishing lugger "Victor et Lois" from Dunkirk towards Iceland went ashore on Quoys Ness. Her crew of 16 and a boy were taken to Huna Inn. Amongst various items in the ship's stores were brandy, gin, rum, etc., so said the local press these liquors were too freely indulged in by the inhabitants which seems to have been the case because six persons were apprehended the following month on charges of theft from the vessel. At about the same time a similar lugger from Dunkirk, the "Notre Dame" stranded half a mile east of Huna but there was no chance of frivolity as she was refloated to arrive in Wick in a damaged condition.

During August 1899 the owners of the Aberdeen steamer "Harlaw" would not be happy, when informed that on a trial cruise after an overhaul, their ship had gone ashore near Huna. It was dense fog, though, and being refloated she was towed to Scrabster for repairs. A couple of years later in June, two Huna fishermen would not be overjoyed either when proceeding to the lobster fishing, for their boat struck the submerged wreck of a steamer at Ness of Quoys which stove in her planking and the water was coming in so rapidly it was up to their waists by the time another boat, alerted by a shore observer, had come to their rescue.

At the beginning of this century a regular visitor to Phillip's Harbour, Mey was the sailing vessel "Lark" which appeared to make consecutive voyages with lime or coal from the Tyne, Sunderland or Shields. Though blown ashore on more than one occasion her stout timbers ensured she lived to sail again.

Ness of Quoys has no doubt in the past been the last resting place of many a fine vessel but the wreck most associated with that locality is surely the stranding of the "Malin Head" on October 1910. She had been built in 1892 for G. Heyn and Sons of Belfast, displaying the white shield with superimposed red hand of Ulster on an otherwise black funnel. Many of this company's fleet passed through the Firth before, between and after the wars until their Baltic trade ceased. The "Malin Head" was bound from Middlesbrough to Belfast with 2500 tons of pig iron on board. There was a strong south east wind causing a fairly heavy sea in the Inner Sound with flood tide. The skipper of a Grimsby trawler coming up astern said that the tide suddenly caught the cargo vessel's starboard bow and before anything could be done she had run aground. The trawler passed a hawser to the stricken ship but it parted after several fruitless attempts at refloating had been made. Then the salvage tug "Ranger" of the Liverpool Salvage association arrived and actually refloated the "Malin Head" but she was making water badly and had to be beached in Gills Bay. Unfortunately during this operation two men from the "Ranger" were seriously injured when a tow rope broke.

The "Malin Head" was refloated in Gills Bay a month later but grounded yet again, then owing to deteriorating weather the salvage vessel was forced to take shelter in Longhope while the "Malin Head" became a total wreck. The "Julius Rutgers", a German vessel laden with oil, grounded near Huna in 1923 as did the Banff drifter "Viola" but both refloated without damage. Next year Huna lifeboat stood by the I.N.S. drifter "Braehead" during a snowstorm until the latter freed herself. The crew of the Grimsby trawler "Akranes" were rescued in July 1931 when their vessel on her way home ran on to the rocks at Longeo, Mey. A ship of 1929 vintage, she was refloated, requisitioned at the outbreak of war and served as a mine sweeper until she was unfortunately bombed by the enemy and sunk in Bridlington Bay in 1941. There was a change of scenery for Huna folk when the large steamer "Cairnglen" went ashore not very far from the seaward end of Huna slipway on March 1934. This vessel owned by Cairns Noble and Co., Newcastle, built in 1926 was homeward bound with general cargo from St Johns, Canada for Leith and Newcastle. A quantity of her discharged cargo was taken to Scrabster by the coasters "Kinnaird Head" of Leith and the "Yewforest" of Glasgow. Three Hull tugs and the salvage vessel "Bullger" of Leith stood by and the "Cairnglen" was eventually refloated, then towed to Longhope for repairs which allowed her to complete her voyage.

During the last war, despite blacked out lighthouses, it was fortunate that the majority of shipping managed to avoid confrontation with this part of the coast. In January 1940 a Naval trawler struck the bottom at Huna but refloated later, while in August 1944 the "Crundick" one of the many fishing smacks from Faroe bringing us fish during those dark days, grounded off Huna but was released by the rising tide to continue her passage to Aberdeen.

Peace had returned by October 1952 when the Hull trawler "St Ronan" bound for Greenland went on a reef at St John's Point. Fortunately a Stroma boat in the vicinity brought the crew ashore except for her skipper and radio operator who were landed next day by Thurso lifeboat. The tugs "Enforcer" and "Salveda" along with the frigate "Widemouth Bay" stood by while the "Whirlpool", a drifter belonging to Metal Industries Ltd., took empty herring barrels from Scrabster to be placed in the vessel's fish hold by which means it was hoped to refloat the trawler but all efforts were in vain because she slid off the reef to become a total loss.

As navigational aids were fitted to the majority of vessels of any size so technical performance was also improved and probably of greater significance the information was more correctly interpreted. Shipwrecks consequently decreased greatly but on September 1953 the Aberdeen trawler "Coastal Emperor" stranded a short distance north west of Huna slip in clear weather with a calm sea and after a few hours of rising tide she came clear without mishap. The rugged coastline southward from Duncansby Head to the Rough of Auckengill has also had its quota of shipwrecks, a resultant, no doubt of vessels in bad visibility being affected by tides and compass error to such an extent that by the time eastern approaches to the Firth had been reached there was quite a large discrepancy between estimated and actual positions.

There were local tragedies, too, for in February

1871, Rev McPherson of Canisbay Church received £2 from the Earl of Caithness while Rev MacGregor of the Free Church there accepted 12/6 from Dr Kennedy for the widows and children of Matthew Matheson and William Geddes, Freswick, fishermen who had lost their lives at sea a few weeks previously. Some time before, in 1865 the schooner "Adelaide" of Thurso had come to grief in Freswick Bay. Her crew were saved but her cargo of Sunderland coal went to the bottom. During the first week in April 1877 the Peterhead barque "Alibi" grounded in the bay in dense fog and although a tug came from Wick, she remained hard and fast, becoming a total wreck which was sold the next month. It is interesting to note that in the 1868 list of Peterhead whalers a vessel of this name is mentioned. Was it the same ship?

Plans were being prepared for the construction of a pier at Freswick in 1894 and work must have gone ahead because in October 1897 the contractors had not been paid as the stones forming the jetty had not been hammer dressed. Even as late as 1898, the chief engineer Mr Brennan then in charge, was still not satisfied with the work executed while his foreman had interfered too much so that his workers from Stornoway had difficulty getting lodgings in the neighbourhood while local employees were far from happy with their remuneration of £1-3/4 to be divided between 12 men. However the pier seems to have been completed by 1899 at an estimated cost of £845.

Freswick, famous for its fishermen pilots paid tribute to the last of that race of men when in 1936 James Mowat aged 96 died. His long seafaring life included an experience as pilot of a sailing vessel which ran into a storm off Cape Wrath and they were carried across the Atlantic, finally making a landfall at Quebec. Ship and crew had been given up for lost but the pilot returned in another sailing ship to the great joy and relief of his relatives and neighbours. The fleet of small boats at Freswick had by 1936 dwindled to five. "Vigilant" WK 158 owned by James Mowat, "W.E. Gladstone" WK 163 George Groat, "Robert the Bruce" WK 221 William Mowat, "Veda" WK 478 Andrew Bain, "Milton" WK 747 Geo. Rosie.

Skirza Head proved to be a dangerous obstacle for vessels making for the Firth as those on the "Gerona" discovered when that steamer ran aground there in 1892 bound for Canada. She was refloated but had to be beached on the sand until further repairs were made before being towed south to her home port of Dundee via the Cromarty Firth.

The summer of 1905 saw another steamer the "Harriet" make contact with the headland on her way from Middlesbrough to Belfast with 400 tons of pig iron and railway fittings, during a spell of dense fog.

The discharge of 50 tons of cargo was enough to refloat the vessel which, on reaching Wick Bay, was considered seaworthy. Two years later the Aberdeen trawler, "Star of Hope", again with

visibility down to nil, mistook Freswick Bay for the entrance to the Firth and this caused her to take the bottom between Skirza Head and the pier but she got clear, made her way to Wick, then finally reached her home port for repairs. A week before the incident another trawler from Aberdeen, the "Strathclyde" had gone ashore in the Bay but was able to heave herself off into deep water using kedge anchors laid out by the "Clan Grant" a fishing vessel from the same port.

There were more strandings at Freswick when both ships were fortunate in being refloated, the London steamer "Willesden" in 1911 and the "Kentucky" in 1920. The latter, a Danish ship of the well known Forenede Line, Copenhagen easily identified pre-war by the broad red funnel band and name in large letters on the broadside, led a charmed life as she went aground again in 1924 on Quoys Ness and survived. This was the same year that the passenger-cargo liner "City of Florence" struck rocks at Skirza Head and refloated on the rising tide. In poor visibility the statutory reduction of speed often proved beneficial when closing the land.

It was March 1928 when the Belgian trawler "Neptune", on passage from Ostende to Icelandic fishing grounds, stranded in Freswick during thick weather. Her engines were put full astern which took her clear but leaking so badly that she rapidly sank while her skipper and crew of 14 augmented by an agricultural student on holiday, hurriedly took to their lifeboat. One wonders what the latter thought of his pleasure trip when they finally reached Wick by the overland route after their small boat had drifted round Duncansby Head to finally make land in Gills Bay. In 1932 the Grimsby trawler "Ormond" managed to refloat after going ashore in the Bay only to be victim of an air attack off the east coast of Scotland in 1941 when mine sweeping.

The Hull trawler "Bayflower" was only four years old when in 1937 she went ashore on the south side of the Bay at Ness Head. She survived and was sold to Grimsby in 1939.

The cargo vessel "Clan Mackinlay" was on a coastal voyage from Glasgow to London when she was bombed and sunk off Freswick with considerable loss of life. Subsequently, much wreckage came ashore including bales of rubber which, after winter storms, still occasionally surface after 50 years of immersion.

South from Freswick Bay, high cliffs are a feature of the coast to where a reef, the Rough of Auckengill extends seawards marked by tide rips and ready to trap the unwary voyager. It was on the south side of this navigational hazard that the steamship "Ohio" grounded and damaged herself severely in May 1897. She had been built in Sunderland in 1888 and was schooner rigged to complement her engines during the first few years of her life. Owned by Neptune Steam Navigation Co., Sunderland, she left Rotterdam with general cargo for Baltimore and had called at Sunderland to obtain bunker coal. The "Ohio" was eventually refloated and beached stern first on Reiss sands from whence assisted by three tugs she arrived at Aberdeen for extensive repairs. Court proceedings resulted in a finding which stated that when soundings of 19 fathoms were obtained, course should have been altered away from the land despite her speed being dead slow. Next year the "Ohio" was sold, renamed "Atbara" and was lost on Haisboro sands in 1907 laden with coal for Pyraeus from the Tyne. In practically the same place in September, 1953 the Grimsby trawler "Hasset" was wrecked outward bound for the fishing grounds and though 15 crewmen were saved, five lost their lives.

The ruins of Buchollie Castle lie approximately halfway between Freswick Bay and the Rough of Auckengill. A mile or so south of this locality the Swedish vessel "Stellatus" was waiting in March 1959 for the main stream of flood tide to ease in the Firth. The weather was hazy and she was set shorewards by the tide, going ashore in a vulnerable position, laden with a cargo of paper pulp. Captain and crew finally left their stricken vessel, subsequently a south east gale sprang up turning a well found vessel into a total wreck.

Many will remember the loss of the West German trawler "Hessen" in June 1987 which having struck rocks near Stroma beacon, drifted east round Duncansby Head and sank, fortunately without loss of life, a short distance to seaward of where the "Stellatus" came to an untimely end.

Early on a February morning in 1993 in good weather conditions, not far from where the "Hessen" was holed, the Danish vessel "Bettina Danica" grounded on the north side of Mell Head at Stroma's south west corner. Only three years old and most recent addition to her company's fleet, she was on passage in ballast from Ireland to Norway. Despite efforts of tugs the relatively small ship remains a rusting bulk, battered and bruised by every winter storm, a constant reminder of unfortunate consequences arising from human error. Fortunately there was no loss of life and pollution negligible. The "Bettina Danica" became another victim of a merciless adversary.

The annual proliferation of shipwrecks often attended by horrendous loss of life has in the present age ended and thankfully so, yet there is no guarantee that despite all the modern scientific knowledge to hand, personal error could not cause a catastrophe in these waters which, considering the size of present day ocean-going vessels, would vastly eclipse any previous incident which has occurred to date.

With gratitude for help given by Thurso Library staff during research of old "Caithness Courier" files.

Sutherland Manson, 6 Bower Court, Thurso.

[1] Could this be Huna?? See advert page 150.

[2] See page 182 and 183.

The "Bettina Danica" stranded on the Clett at Mell Head. Her hatches made a first class bridge over the geo. William Simpson said it was easy to cross on a narrow plank when there was a ship ashore and the adrenaline was flowing!

*Photos, Sina Houston,
Mill House.*

STROMA

Stroma School 1952

Photo, Elizabeth S.Bruce, Bellevue, Huna.

Back Row:– Katie Ord, The Lighthouse; Elizabeth Robertson, Clettack; Isobel Dunnett, Lochside; John Sinclair, Seaview; Malcolm Simpson, The Loch; Andrew Manson, East Side; John Dunnett, Lochside. Middle Row:– Isobel Simpson, The Loch; John Manson, East Side; Ruth Ord, The Lighthouse. Front Row:– Stewart Sinclair, Seaview; David Dunnett, Lochside; Irene Simpson, The Loch; George McCaughey, East Side.

The Stroma School and Charlie Simpson

Stroma School is situated about the middle of the island between Nethertown in the north and Evertown in the south. There were two classrooms "the small end" for the younger pupils and "the big end" for the older ones. Originally it was a two teacher school but like most schools of their era, the teachers were assisted by a pupil teacher. As the roll dropped it became a one teacher school.

Beside the school was a building known as the "Cookery" where in the past, girls were taught cooking and the boys woodwork. In later years this building was used for holding dances. The school was also used to hold meetings, whist drives and concerts. Both the school and the "Cookery" were used for night classes. The women did classes in cooking and sewing while the men did woodwork and navigation.

Elizabeth S. Bruce, Bellevue, Huna.

Anvil clouds – Sign of rain.
                    Elma Moar, Huna.

Soot falling down chimney – Rain soon.
          Rena Dunnett, Wick.

*Red sky at night is the shepherd's delight
Red sky in the morning is the sailor's warning.*
                    Don Wares, Seater.

246

THE CHURCH AND MANSE

Photo, Margaret Green, 'Havengore', Huna.

"Church and manse in Stroma built and opened free of debt in 1887." (Brief note from session records but it tells a lot.)

The two communion cups and plates were presented in 1887 by John Henderson, W.S. Thurso. The silver plate was presented by Alice Youngson in memory of her parents (Alex Youngson – Minister 1900-1909). They are in safe keeping along with the Canisbay Communion Silver.

The collection plate has the inscription "For Stroma Kirk erected 1878" on the rim and on the underside "Cast from George II, III and IV copper. G.S.H. 1928". This plate is used every Sunday in Canisbay for the offering.

H.S.

The Communion Table was bought from McEwen, Cabinet Makers, Wick and was made by apprentice John Simpson, youngest son of Malcolm Simpson, sen., The Loch. The table now stands in the vestibule of Canisbay Church.

E.B.

. . . A Stroma Minister's Prayer. "Oh Lord, if it be thy will to send us a wreck, send us a good one."

C.C.

Stroma Wedding Invitations – Marriage to take place on a certain date **or** the first fine day after that.

Guests at Stroma Wedding.

My mother said it was great fun being a guest because a boat all decorated with flags and bunting came specially over to Huna to pick up the guests. Their partner for the night met them at the pier carrying a rolled umbrella over his arm!

Moira Bremner, Victoria Villa, Canisbay.

Painting of Netherton Haven by John Nicolson 1898

Photo from Betty MacLeod, Dwarwick Place, Dunnet.

247

James Simpson junior and senior at Tanghead with Stroma and the "Merry Men of Mey" in the background.

Photo courtesy of J. McDonald, Photographer, Shore Lane, Wick.

RETURN OF THE NATIVE

It was revealed on the 13th December, 1960, that the island of Stroma had been bought by James Simpson, who lived at Lòwland Cottage, Scarfskerry. He was born and bred on Stroma but now farmed on the mainland with his father.

Stroma had been bought by a Yorkshire business man, Mr Hoyland, in 1946 for £4000 and had often been in the news since. When the island went up for sale many prospective buyers from this country and abroad showed an interest, but Mr Simpson's offer was accepted and so once again a Scot became Laird of Stroma.

The Island of Stroma TV Quiz Prize

The above story appeared in the Aberdeen Press and Journal in August, 1958. Although millions of people had never heard of this little isle in the Pentland Firth, it suddenly hit the world's headlines and featured on the BBC television programme "Tonight". The reason was because it had been offered as a prize in an American TV quiz programme. The offer aroused international interest but it was reported that life for the island's 16 inhabitants (which included five living at the Lighthouse) went on serenely. They were too busy earning their livelihood to be distracted by outside events. Of course this idea did not come to anything and in 1960 the island was bought by James Simpson.

Malcolm Simpson, 95 Willowbank, Wick.

WILLIAM'S QUEER CATCH

You've heard of the famous Stroma Isle
Where lobsters have a bright white smile
But now there's something more exclusive
A lobster which is more elusive.

This new discovery I have heard
Was made by William, son of the Laird
'Twas sitting in the end of his creel
And had a funny, softish feel.

It didna even move or flap
When William took it from its trap
And when he set it on the deck
It wouldn'a move a single step.

It lay there just like it was dead
And William sat and shook his head
This fish was really quite fantastic
The ruddy thing was made of plastic.

The like he'd never seen before
How did it reach the Stroma shore
It must have floated with the tide
With "Hong Kong Made" stamped on its side.

He thought of his poor aching jaws
Trying to chew those plastic claws
It looked so real, already boiled
So William just sat back and smiled.

This brand new lobster which was found
Must be the only one around
Though William hopes at a later date
That he will find its plastic mate.

Jim Begg, Auckengill.

248

THE "SQUARE" OR STROMA MAINS

John B. Simpson originally from Stroma, moved from Backless to Larkway c.1904. His eldest brother Hugh was keen to get him back home so that they could go to the fishing together and seeing John was married with a young family, Hugh made over the place to him.

Hugh was the grandfather of Willie Simpson in Switzerland. James, another brother, was a baker in Wick before moving to Glasgow and then Johannesburg. One of his granddaughters, who was head matron in a big hospital in Johannesburg with 24 matrons under her control, brought back a beautiful bible which had been presented by the Baptist Church in Wick to her grandfather.

John B. Simpson's son, James M. Simpson [1], my father, moved to Stroma Mains after his grandfather James Mowat, aged about 80, fell off a cart when the horse scared and died shortly afterwards.

This was sure to be the same Mowats as John Mowat who was miller in Stroma in 1841. The mill was situated down near the shore at the North End and there are a still a couple of small mill-stones lying there and another is set up as a picnic table at the manse.

It was originally planned to have a new meal mill at the Mains and the overshot wheel enclosed in the "lean to" was driven by water from Edward's Loch. However the plan was changed and this became the threshing mill. The barn would hold one screw of corn and still left room to hold the straw from a screw threshed. There was also a stone-built mill course, and if there was a shortage of water the mill was driven by horses. The water wheel must have taken many a hundred thousand turns because the teeth on the wheel are worn thin. The barn windows did not have glass and were just slits on the outside which widened out in a V-shape to the inside, perhaps used for ventilation. The slit nearest the horse course was the "whoa hole" where they shouted out to the horses to stop.

In the second photograph the stone stair leading up to the granary can be clearly seen. This was very handy for the kiln where metal beams still remain. The beautiful stone-built arches to the neep and cart sheds are a credit to

The barn and mill course.

Kiln to left of arches.

Ventilation Slit

those masons of long ago. Besides the byres and stables there was also a smiddy. This workshop was between the main stable and the bull's byre and the heavy wooden base for the anvil is still there.

These were the days when fishermen and crofters liked to give some fish, eggs, milk, butter or whatever they had to certain people in the area to avoid bad luck.

The "Dreadnought" was built as a cattle boat for James Mowat, Stroma Mains, or as it was locally known, "The Square".

[1] James M. Simpson was decorated by the King of Belgium in 1916 when he was awarded the military medal for bravery in the field.

Charles Simpson, Dalziel House, Wick.

THE "MIZPAH" ON DAY OUTING WITH VISITORS C.1895

The John O'Groats boat "Mizpah" is shown being held off Stroma pier by means of a 'bottag' (boat hook) held by Sinclair Mowat, nephew of the owner, Jock Mowat who is at the helm. The head rope is still made fast to the quay. Perhaps Jock Mowat chooses to ignore the camera because he feels uncomfortable pretending to steer a moored boat with sails furled but more likely, as it is high water and not long before or after spring tides by the marks on the beach, he is no doubt wishing the palaver would end soon so that they can get across the Sound before the ebb tide gains strength.

It seems a warm day with the ladies in summer attire and a 'cole' of hay between the road and the top of the brae. The sun is high in the sky throwing shadows directly beneath beached boats. In the Haven, wind is a light southerly but possibly more south easterly in the Sound, while the sea is calm as a mill pond. It would appear to be Sunday with all boats except one hauled up. The great beam of Stroma boats is very noticeable, of course it will be almost another 20 years before the engines are installed. W. Robertson's shop is visible at the top right hand corner of the picture. The passengers look happy and relaxed, confident they are in capable hands. The boat's rowlocks are in place all ready for oars which will turn her head to sea and with all sails set it should be a pleasant trip in idyllic conditions.

John Muir, Edinburgh.

("Mizpah" = May the Lord watch between thee and me while we are apart.)

I.S.

STROMA ISLE FOR ME

There's an island in the Firth,
It's the land that gave me birth,
Surrounded by such treacherous sea,
Stroma Isle for me.

Chorus:-

Not so long ago,
Small boats crossing to and fro
The Pentland Firth is ill to know,
Stroma Isle for me.

As we stood on Huna Pier,
Stroma men in fishing gear,
T'was the life we lo'ed so dear,
Stroma Isle for me.

While the lighthouse sheds its light
Keeping watch throughout the night,
Guide me safely home to thee,
Stroma Isle for me.

Charles Simpson, Dalziel House, Wick.

EARLY MEMORIES OF STROMA

Born nine years before the start of the First World War, I entered a world vastly different from that of today. I was born at The Loch in the North End of Stroma. I had four brothers George, Pat, Malkie and John and one sister, Mary. We lived in a three roomed house built almost at the top of the beach along with my parents, grandparents, an aunt and a cousin.

A new two storey house was started before the war. My grandfather built the house up to the chimney heads and then, when he died of flu in 1919, my father and three brothers George, Pat and Malkie finished the house.

The stones for the house were quarried at Langaton (near the Lighthouse) and in the ebb below Finnies Haven (a short distance from the house). The slates for the roof came from quarries at the shore on the East Side down below Larkway.

When we finally moved into the new house in 1923, I was the first to sleep there along with two cousins home on holiday from Edinburgh – Ciss and Ina Robertson. The new house had three rooms upstairs and three downstairs with a porch at the back. After the cramped conditions of the old house, the new one seemed large indeed. In the years following the war, the family split up, each going their own way. George and Pat went to the herring fishing but eventually George went to America and Pat went to Glasgow, joining the

The "Loch" nearing completion

Peter Simpson (sitting on scaffold). From Left:- Simpson Crowe, Mrs Crowe, Bill Crowe, Teenie Simpson, George Simpson, Malcolm Simpson, Mrs Simpson. Sitting:- Donald Crowe, Alex Crowe, John Simpson, Peter Crowe. Rover – The Dog.

Glasgow City Police Force. Mary went into service ending up in Moffat in Dumfriesshire. John served his time as a cabinet maker with McEwens in Wick and then moved to London. Only Malkie and I stayed on in Stroma; Malkie to go to the fishing with our father and to work the croft, while I helped in the house and worked on the croft.

My father, Malcolm Simpson (known as Ould Macum), went to the herring fishing in the boat "City of Rome" with a mainly Stroma crew. The exceptions were a man Robb from Hoy and James Donn from Canisbay, who later became postman for that area. The boat fished from Wick but was laid up in Holm in Orkney for the winter months.

It was while my father was involved in the herring fishing that he met my mother. She was a herring packer and belonged to South Ronaldsay in Orkney. Her name was Mary Isabella Brown.

After the herring fishing collapsed, he went to the creels and cod fishing with neighbours John Allan and Simpson Crowe in John Allan's sailing boat, the "Camel". Of course he also worked the croft but had no real interest in it, the sea being his whole life. With John Allan and Simpson Crowe he fished for lobsters at the Pentland Skerries staying there for the week, living in the wheelhouse of a wrecked trawler (the "Champion"). This wheelhouse was situated on the Little Skerry. John Allan then got a bigger boat, the "Alpha", which was later converted to motor. The "Alpha", is now in John O'Groats owned by Mr Jimmy Sinclair, Maritina.

Later still my father bought the "Evelyn" from the South End. This boat was built in Stroma by Donald Banks, who had just built a cattle boat for the North End called the "Dreadnought". He built the "Evelyn" next using wood left over from the cattle boat to complete part of the boat. (The "Evelyn" is still in the Simpson family, having been passed down from generation to generation. My brother Pat handed it on to his nephew Malcolm Simpson who has her berthed at Scrabster.)

The "Evelyn" at Huna.

Malcolm Simpson, Malcolm Simpson Sen., Donald Smith, James Allan.

Most of the cod caught was salted and dried and then sold to shops in Wick or taken over to Kirkwall by boat. It was also sold to the "floating shops" when they visited the island.

My father stopped fishing for lobsters when in his early 70s but his last trip to the Pentland Skerries was when he was 80.

My grandfather, George Simpson, was a boatbuilder. He served his time in the North End with Donald Smith who had served his time in Orkney. My grandfather set up his own business and later had Donald Banks, a boatbuilder in the South End, working with him. The boat shed was at the back of the house right at the top of the beach. This was convenient, as the completed boats were launched on to the beach. The boat shed was a busy place, boats being built for the west coast as well as Stroma. If a boat was required in a hurry,

my grandfather would get up at two o'clock in the morning to get it completed on time.

As a child I spent many hours playing in the shed, being very fond of Donald Banks who allowed me to do what I wanted. I spent more time at his side of the boat than my grandfather's.

The boat shed was finally swept away by heavy sea on 25th January, 1937. It was not uncommon for the sea to come up round the old house but on this occasion it was much more serious. We heard the first rumblings of the sea coming up and my father and Malkie went out to see what was going on. The sea was coming round the old house and Malkie caught hold of the stable door. (The old house was now the steading.) My father ventured further out and I can still see him running towards the garden with the sea at his back. He managed to get into the garden and the sea swept him to the front flagstone dyke where he managed to get a grip on a flagstone. He would certainly have been swept away if he had not been able to hold on to the flagstone. Earlier my sister-in-law and myself had helped to haul a boat which was sitting beside the boat shed to a "safer" place beside the garden wall. The sea lifted the boat and swept it up the field a distance of approximately 50 yards.

As a child I had plenty companions to play with. As well as my brothers and sister, I had the Allans on one side, Willie, Stewart, Ida, Barbara and Annie and the Crowes on the other side, John, Bill, Davie, Simpson, Peter, Donald and Alex.

The beach was our play area and many happy hours were spent paddling, making sandcastles and collecting shells and whelks. We also used to catch sticklebacks using nets. Donald Banks, the boatbuilder, used to make nets for me. There was always someone getting knocked into the water, arriving home dripping wet to get a row from our respective mothers. We often used to get rows for bashing our boots against the rocks but little heed was paid to that. Playing in the field was frowned upon, as it was considered we were tramping down the grass required for the animals. We were expected to behave ourselves on Sunday, going to Sunday School when the church came out at one o'clock. My favourite pastime on a Sunday afternoon was collecting groatie buckies on the beach.

When I started school there were approximately 90 pupils attending school. The infant teacher was Betsy Smith, a native of Stroma. My next teacher was Mr James Taylor who was very well liked by all the pupils. When the First World War started he went into the army and we had a Mr MacBeath in his place. It was a happy day when Mr Taylor returned to the school at the end of the war. Betsy Smith became ill and was replaced by Minnie Bain, Myreland, Lyth who later married James Taylor. She taught the girls cooking and sewing. I left school at 14; in fact I was 14 the day before the school opened again. I remember Mr Taylor jokingly saying he didn't think he could let me leave but I was leaving whatever anyone said.

When war came in 1914 George and Pat went off

to serve in the Navy. Warships became a common sight using the area between Dunnet Head and Hoy to practise manoeuvres and gunnery. I remember all the panes on the lighthouse being blacked out except one which shone towards Duncansby Head for the benefit of the convoys. When war ended we were very pleased to see George and Pat come home safely.

Life was very hard in those days with none of the modern equipment we now have in the home. Washing was a major task. First you had to carry water from the well, get it boiled and then start the washing. No washing machines then, just a washboard to scrub the clothes and a scrubbing brush for the dungarees. The clothes were heavier then, most of it having been knitted during the winter months and so took longer to dry. Sheets, pillowcases, tablecloths and towels were bleached on the grass, being left for a couple of days and turned over to whiten.

Meals were simpler then but we had more people to cook for. We had the normal diet of that time, soup, beef perhaps once a week, mutton occasionally and fresh pork when "the pig was killed". The leg was made into ham and the rest salted for future use. We always made white puddings and black puddings. Of course there was always plenty fish and we had dried cod and salt herrings for winter use. We grew vegetables in the garden, carrots, onions and cabbage and had potatoes and turnips in the field.

There were four shops on the island and we went to all of them at some time. Shops opened at nine o'clock in the morning and closed when the last customer left at night, which could, on occasions, be bedtime. You always met someone at the shop and news was exchanged. Shopping could take a long time depending on how many people were around.

I also worked on the croft. We had approximately five acres at home and approximately ten acres at the "school" park which had been part of Stroma Mains at one time. This park was about a mile from the house and it meant walking there a few times in the day. We grew corn, potatoes and turnips and grazed the cows, sheep and horses there. The cows and horses were walked home each evening. I liked the horses best of all and was never frightened of them. Our horse was Prince and we worked with Crowe's next door using their horse Dandy. Later we got another horse, Jock, and Crowe's also got another horse. This made life easier, having two horses each.

Crofting was not easy in those days but friendship was very important on the island and anyone who needed help would always get it from their neighbours.

As well as the shops on the island there were the "floating shops". They were sailing smacks that came over from Orkney during the summer months. They started coming about 1910 and continued until a few years after the war. They came week about, the "Star of Hope" coming to the North End and the "Endeavour" to the South End.

There was always an air of excitement watching for the boats to appear. They had their own small boats and came into the harbour to pick up the waiting customers and take them out to the floating shop. There were groceries, feeding stuffs and drapery available. The women sold eggs to the shop which helped to pay for their groceries, and the men sold their dried cod.

The floating shop at Stroma, March 1924.

Shipwrecks were a common occurrence in those days. When a ship went ashore everything was dropped and off the men went, regardless of the weather conditions, leaving the women to worry until their men returned safely. The Stroma Pirates were well known but the Stroma fishermen saved many lives too, with little thought given to their own safety. My father and his crew received a vellum from the RNLI for saving the crew of the "Marz", a trawler which went ashore at Langaton in the North End.

This is the citation my father and his crew received for the rescue of the crew of the "Gertrud" which went ashore in fog at Langaton in 1934.

H.M. Coastguard, Wick, Caithness.

30th August, 1934.

Mr Malcolm Simpson, Senr, Stroma.

Dear Sir,

I have been directed to convey to you and those who assisted you in the motor boat "Evelyn", the thanks and great appreciation of the Board of Trade for your valuable services, rendered to the crew of the Finnish S.S. "Gertrud", on the occasion of that vessel stranding on Langaton Rock, Stroma, on 1st June, 1934.

On this occasion you, assisted by Messrs Malcolm Simpson Junr., James L. Allan, Donald Smith and Jas. Moodie, took off the crew of 22 and landed them safely under very difficult conditions of weather and tide.

Yours Truly

J. G. Buchanan, Inspector, H.M. Coastguard, North Scotland Division.

[Malcolm Simpson, 95 Willowbank, Wick, has the original citation.]

The "Gertrud" ashore at Langaton

Mrs C. Robertson, (second left) with "Gertrud" survivors

Third left, Cook – fourth left, Stewardess.

My father's boat, the "Evelyn", had set off for the creels towing a skiff, the "Mary", belonging to Andy Simpson, which was used for going in close to the rocks to set creels. When they got to the "Gertrud", they found there were three women aboard, which was quite common in those days on the foreign ships. Malkie got the women and some of the crew aboard the "Mary" and set off rowing for the Goe in the North End. I saw him coming round the tails at the lighthouse and knew there was something wrong. As the "Gertrud" ebbed, more of the crew climbed ashore on to the rocks and the rest were taken to the Goe. My mother and I were kept busy preparing food for the crew. Later in the day they were taken over to Huna to start the long journey home. The women regarded the "Gertrud" as their home and were very upset when she broke up and sank.

During the summer months there was always the excitement of relatives and friends coming back to Stroma for their holidays. A lot of preparations went on getting everything tidied up, beds ready and extra baking and cooking done. Once my sister married and had her family, Johnny, Malcolm, May and George, she always brought them back to Stroma for the entire school holidays. I looked forward to seeing them each year and always went to Wick to meet them and then saw them off in Wick at the end of their holiday. My nephews and niece were always happy to arrive in Stroma but it was a different story when the time came for them to leave. My mother accompanied them on one occasion but on arriving at Huna, Johnny sat down on a fish box, crying and saying he wanted to go back to Auntie Teenie and the red cow. When I grew up there was the occasional trip to Wick to visit relatives and do shopping.

During the winter months there were always whist drives, concerts, dances and box socials. A box social was a dance at which tea was served at the beginning. The unmarried women had to make up boxes of baking for two, cover them with fancy paper and then tie them up with ribbon. The boxes were auctioned, the idea being that the men bought the boxes not knowing who owned them, but the owner of the box was his partner for the night. This was the theory but it did not always work out in practice. A lot of underhand work went on sometimes, men trying to find out which box belonged to a certain woman, but if this was suspected, then someone else would make up a box to look exactly the same, and so things did not always turn out as planned!

There was also night school to attend and I did sewing with Lizzie Manson, a native of Stroma, who later became Mrs Donald Dundas of Warse in Canisbay.

There was always more time to visit people during the long winter nights when stories of times past would be told and retold. And so life continued until the start of the Second World War when things changed for Stroma. A lot of people had to go away during the war and when war ended they found work in the south and made their homes there.

The Stroma people are widely scattered now but the bond which held us together on the island still exists and we like to meet whenever possible and keep up-to-date with all the news of the various families. The Stroma "grapevine" is still very active.

Christina Robertson, The Cottage, Canisbay.

Stroma Record? Four calves in a year? Malcolm Simpson's cross-bred cow had twin calves at end of March 1937 and twins again at beginning of March 1938.

A.H.

When the moon is on her back
Mend yer sheen (shoes) and strap yer thatch

When round the moon there is a broch
The weather will be cold and rough.
(halo round moon = rain)

Alex Wares.

The "Ella" 1947

The "Willowbank"

The yawls were dressed overall for the wedding of Amy Sinclair and Robbie Robertson.

The "Hinemoa" with her flags flying

Baiting a creel

Cathie and Jimmy Simpson, Edderton, all set for Stroma honeymoon.

Hugh Simpson, Burmah.

Turning hay

Hay "Gilt" at the "Cairn"

Amy, Peter and Margaret Sinclair turning hay at the "Cairn".

Bill Sinclair, Donald Crowe, Margaret, Peter and Amy. Robbie Robertson on Beda.

Photos, Margaret Green, Havengore, Huna.

Loading and unloading at Huna 1935

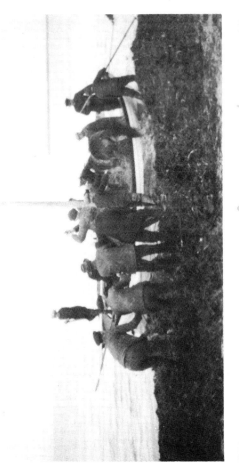

Photos, Helen Sinclair, 17 High Street, Keiss.

SHIPPING HORSES AND CATTLE TO STROMA

Transporting cattle and horses to and from Stroma was a difficult and often dangerous job. On the South Side of the island, the boat which was used was called the Cattleboat but her real name was the "Bee". She had been especially strongly built for the purpose by the Banks family, Harrow, and was jointly owned by several families. The fee for taking an animal across was one shilling a beast and this money was collected by David Sinclair, Redgoe and used for painting and maintaining the boat.

A few years ago, the "Bee" was completely refurbished by the late John William Laird, East End, John O'Groats and is now used as a lobster boat by his brother-in-law John Dunnett.

When a horse was to be taken over to Stroma from Huna, it was a special occasion and it was normal for up to 12 able-bodied men to be involved. First heather divots (similar to ones used on potato pits) were cut at the West Side, and although there was no peat on Stroma there was plenty of heather then. These were taken across along with straw, this was called "booglin". There was no engine in the "Bee" and she was towed by one of the motor boats.

Once at Huna, the boat was turned side on to the shore and a rope was fixed to the top of the mast. The boat was pulled over with this rope by maybe five men until the gunnel was nearly touching the water. The booglin was then spread over the skin of the boat, both to protect it and to give the horse a firmer and surer footing. Many horses which came in to Stroma had never even seen the sea, never mind been in a boat. Between the loading and unloading from a lorry, people the horse was not accustomed to, and with all the other commotion, the animal was usually in a very nervous and excited state.

Now to pacify the horse, the Stroma men used a special ploy. Half an hour before loading they would take the bridle from the horse and tie two or three wisps of black twist tobacco around the bit. When the bridle was put back on, the horse naturally chewed the bit and the strong tobacco juices acted like a sedative. It likely made the horse feel really sick, but it did make the animal much easier to handle.

When safely loaded, the boat was righted by letting go the rope to the mast, and the cattle boat, with maybe six men aboard, was towed back over. To land the horse, once there, it was the same procedure pulling the boat over by the mast etc. It was always much easier to get the horse out of the boat than to get it in.

Every year about the end of May, a bull was hired from the Department of Agriculture in Inverness. Shipping a bull could also be a dangerous business as they are often very temperamental and one year the bull broke loose and jumped over the side of the boat and was drowned.

Another year when they were taking in the Dept. bull, it became very "raised" during the crossing, but luckily they got landed safely. They wondered and worried a bit about how they would manage shipping him back in October! The tobacco treatment was decided on, and so two ounces of black twist tobacco was boiled in some water for two hours. The bull was drenched with a bottle of the liquid and that did the trick!

The Stroma cattle were usually sold fat, or as forward stores rising two years old, and it was normal to ship four cattle beasts at a time to Huna in the "Bee".

Hugh Simpson, Midtown, Freswick.

STROMA

I'm thinking tonight of that beautiful Isle,
My birthplace, my homeland, my dear native soil,
Wherever I wander, no place e'er can wile
My love for my beautiful Stroma.

Oh sad was the day that compelled me to part
From scenes of my childhood so dear to my heart
Now in memory so often the tears quickly start
When I think of my homeland, my Stroma.

Oh, to hear once again the wild sea birds cry
And the lark singing sweetly in yonder blue sky

The scent of the wild flowers, and heather forbye
Fills my heart with sweet memories of Stroma.

The years have rolled by, and tho' distance divide
You're set like a jewel in Pentland's wild tide,
My love, and my memory, will ever abide
Always true to the island of Stroma.

Are you from the isle where I wish I could be?
The gem of the Pentland surrounded by sea,
Let me clasp your hand, if you're from that land,
Our beautiful island of Stroma.

William J. Sinclair, Westside, Stroma.

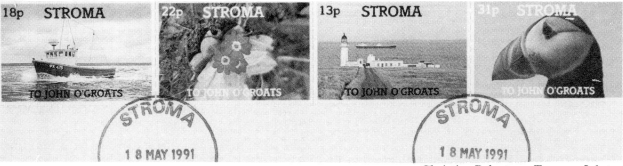

Christine Robertson, Torvean, Inkstack.

THE HISTORY OF THE ISLANDS IN THE PENTLAND FIRTH BY A RESIDENT OF STROMA ISLAND

Donald Banks

Donald Banks, the Bard of Stroma, was born 1870 and wrote this history when he was 78 years old. He was born in the North End of the island quite near to the lighthouse. He left school when he was 14 and his first job was to help with the peat cutting at John O'Groats.

Stroma

Tis a wee wee spot the place of my birth
Quite near John O'Groats, in the Pentland Firth,
Though storms and tempests around us do boil
On mainland their faces with sarcastic smile
Yet surely it never will be spurned by me
For I love Stroma Island surrounded by sea.

I've crept in its coves, its caves and its voes,
I've walked round its peaks its gullys and geos
I've scanned the tides ripple o'er reefs as it glides
And studied the movements of ebb and flood tide
And now there's nothing that can come to me
For I was born in this island surrounded by sea.

I ken that mannie 'ats haudin' a ploo
And that wifie herdin' her coo
And that lassie nursing that babe
And that auld grey mannie takin bait in the ebb
I ken a' the lochies they sail in and a'
And a' the ditches wherein ye micht fa'.

I ken a' the boaties that lie side the quay
For a' things in Stroma are weel kent by me
In winter when storms do rage and do howl
And great sheets of foam rïse from the Punch Bowl
Rise, put on the fire, make a good cup of tea
For this island is controlled by the wind and the sea.

Donald Banks, Bard of Stroma.

Press Gang

One fine summer morning a vessel came along, which turned out to be the brig or cutter to press 18-year-olds and upwards for the Navy, to engage in the famous battle of Trafalgar. The people of the island knew this ship was employed for the purpose. They ran for their boat. Seven men got six oars launched and made off. The brig nearing with an air of wind and the other boat keeping close to the rocks.

The navy then opened fire with their muskets and blew the blades off their oars. The boatmen knew they were done, but to their alarm one of the crew got nerve shock and began all sorts of mutterings and foolishness. The cutter launched their boat and took them to the ship and examined each man. The first two, my grandfather George Banks aged 18 and a man Allan [1] about the same age, were taken. The rest were not the kind of men they wanted and they let them pass. The shocked man got worse – he went to the capstan handlebars and exclaimed "oh this is lek the handles of my grandfather's "plough"." One of the chiefs gave him a halfcrown. He gave a sweep of his right arm and says "hid a grand skeating stane" and threw it in the sea.

The captain said: "I am keeping the two. I'll pay you to supply your boat with oars and tow your boat ashore with the launch. Keep an eye on that fool because he may do damage to himself or some other body." Then the launch went back to the cutter and off she went.

There was no news of the two taken, but afterwards it was known they had been placed in Collinwood's frigates. They were not on the same ship but saw each other at times. Allan never saw his chum after the battle and wondered if he had been killed or had deserted.

The battle came on and the ships were lined out for the fray according to orders. The enemy were getting ready and so too was Nelson, of great fame, with Hardy second in command.

[1] Top-Master William Allan, Stroma, served with Nelson and was at Trafalgar. *From the Veteran's Roll of Honour, compiled by John Horne and placed in the Veteran's Memorial Tower at the North Head, Wick.*

The Battle of Trafalgar 1820

Out came the fleet with Collinwood in charge of the frigates. When the rivals came in sight of each other, it was the time to judge which tack would be the best for the whole fleet to get a broadside charge on the enemy. Collinwood's choice was to beat to windward as far as he was sure he could have the chance to run down on the enemy and cut them off. The old "Victory" never could beat to windward as proved by practice, but if she had to run she could sail with studding sails.

At the next crossing the frigates were well to windward. The order was spread to the whole fleet to look out for the enemy to change from beating to running.

Old saying – When the enemy seeks to run, then yours the victory's won.

Collinwood ran down to close quarters with the enemy – actually so close that musket fire had effect. Just a few volleys were fired before my grandfather was shot through the right arm by an enemy sniper. Grandfather was in the "lookout" or crows nest and had to be lowered down the rigging and was treated. The ship's surgeon amputated his arm between the elbow and shoulder. He was sent home as he could not defend himself.

Nelson put the glass to his blind eye until he got another three volleys on the enemy. Nelson fell mortally wounded and did not survive the hour of victory which was sounded all over the world. Allan survived the fight and after working a "time limit" came home in good health. He met his chum and heard what happened to him. He met up with "the fool" too, who, a week after the press gang raid, was back in his normal mind and everyone believed a very clever trick had been played. We are of Norse descent, therefore the poem.

The Norseman's home in days gone by was on the
    rolling seas,
And there his forebears' did defy the foes of
    Normandy.
Then let us all with heart and hand give honour to
    the brave,
The noble hardy Northern men who rule the
    stormy wave.
The spirit of our fathers do start in every wave,
The ocean was their field of fame. The ocean was
    their grave.
Where Drake and mighty Nelson fell our manly
    hearts shall glow,
Do they sweep through the deep where the stormy
    tempests blow?

Piloting a Sailing Ship

There were four special pilot crews that paid great attention to that vocation, so much so that a continual striving against one another was common. Off in the morning – west for Strathy Point, lie in wait till sailing craft would appear, sometimes pulling six oars. The jute ships were the main catch. Competition became so keen, a "South" boat put a black ball in her bows, the "North" a blue diamond. The captains knew their boats and if it was not the boat he wanted, he would haul away till the other one would come up. No steamers then – anything from a ketch to a four masted full rigger. Barques were the most common.

My father and crew ran a bad storm from north east towing with the Barque "Nina" of Dundee. Smith the pilot sang out "Cut the tow rope and let go and I'll go on to Dundee." Reason:– the squall struck the ship and he could not stow the canvas to halt the ship's speed. The Stroma crew learned a lesson on this matter.

A mainland crew got a big ship off Duncansby Head. They put their man aboard. There was plenty of wind already for the small boat to tow and captain or pilot did not warn the crew to cut the rope. It was a case of immediate swamping of the boat and being towed under and the man aboard seeing his mates drown.

The captain with forethought ought to have hoisted the boat clear of the water. Then he could have turned the ship's bow to the wind and backed his main yards to lay the ship idle until they got the canvas stowed.

The barque continued on her passage. My father being second in command took the helm. The crew left the foremast sails unfurled but brailed up the sail on the mast except about five yards for the purpose of steering, the wind being dead fair (a partial temporary furling). The boat had a fearful run – two men bailing with a pail each – other two taking turns – my father standing at the helm – not a word spoken until they got in over the north tide. Men running to the shore meeting them. Old William Laird the only one who cheered him "Well done Geordie – stick till her, she's wonderful." That was Mr Laird, joiner and builder's father. (Mr Laird of "Catford" a member of the London Caithness has a family there or thereabout yet.)

So the old "Onward" survived and saved her crew perhaps about 60 years ago. She is in fair going order having been repaired and going to the lobster fishing from John O'Groats. The Greens bought her from me about 12 years ago with a good Kelvin engine running well and kept in good order with no complaints.

A Huna boat was lost being embayed and could not clear the land about 700 yards from their landing place. Sutherland saved his life on an oar. Three Dunnets lost their lives. Old Wattie Smith on his way home from Dundee heard about the loss of life in the small boat. "That is my good partner, his son and my son. What a tragedy." When he came off the train at Wick he got the full details of what happened. During his time on the ship his mind was far from being at ease – hence the hoisting of the boat was the main thing that had to be done.

I myself was at one big sailing ship the "Crompton" of Liverpool about which this act or poem was brought about.

I was about 16-years-old then. Old Wattie, my father and I. The boat was afloat and we had nothing to do but loose her moorings, so off we set. My father had been up and had had a look about one o'clock. A fine calm morning – sea as smooth as a loch. The ship was driving back with the first of the ebb tide. She was a four masted barque – fore and aft rig on the fourth mast. A flag was at the fore top. A great chance for a good pilot fee.

We made sure to round the North Tails in case a south boat was in the know. She had 40 of a crew, skipper and wife. We had to see if it was an Englishman. He had the ladder down ready for the pilot to come aboard – which he did.

The captain is to give you money to land at Mey for papers and fresh mutton. It is handier for you to go now as it is the shorter distance. You will have plenty of time to meet the ship west of Dunnet Head.

We met the ship west of Dunnet Head – light wind from south west in this case the boat towing alongside. I was steering – keeping the boat clear of the ships side. My father was having a sleep as he was up early and saw and turned out Smith. She just went right through with nothing to report. Not like me acting as a pilot with the wind east-south-east which is dead ahead, take as many tacks as she could do it in. It has been done by a competent man. The Pentland Firth is sometimes easy and sometimes not. In this case plenty wind to make the stay (change from one tack to another) a little like the check board (draught board) to know what she will fetch and get around (to know the position she will reach and still have enough room to clear the land and come round on a different tack.)

Order "Hard to lee". Swing the main braces with a shanty or sea-song in the doing it. That is an explanation of a sailor's life at sea.

Piloting of a Big Sailing Ship

Speaking and poetry mixed – you understand pilot is talking to the captain.

So well I mind in my younger days when I was just a boy,
A little bit walk, and I fixed my gaze from Dunnet Head to Hoy.
I scanned the waters for white specks coming in from over the sea,
For those were the days of big ships from Calcutta to Dundee.
Oh for a sky of azure blue, and masts, three royals in height,
A sparkling sea of lovely hue, white canvas shimmering bright,
With glass at your eye, if this you could spy, passing through the Pentland Firth.
As the ship draws near, your vision clear – A pleasing sight of worth,
But alas these beauties of silver and grey are not seen in the present day.
Act – "Are you wakin John".

☆★☆★☆

A ship like this – I won't make a bargain for a pilot fee if he won't agree to hoist the boat and crew. We will get two slings under the boat and I'll tell him my crew will take the tail of the brace every time. (Brace – tackle on each end of the yard used to swing it to required angle.) The ship goes round. The tide is all that is driving her west. She is not sailing much, big masts and heavy canvas do not help with calm weather. We will not be long now until we catch her up. She is on the right tack to go in Dunnet Bay. We will see what he says about it. There is going to be wind and that is what I want. When the boat is up on her side I wish her to sail but these three royals have to be stowed and I'll try her if she is trimmed to stay well. (I'll try to see if her depth in the water by bow or stern is such that she would quickly come round on another tack if and when necessary.)

There is sure to be wind before we get back to Dunnet Head. I am not wanting her to be too soon. I'll make sure there is young flood on the Head or else she'll catch the ebb and drive west. I'll wear her out and run back rather than that. (Coming on the other tack by bringing the wind round the stern from one side to the other instead of coming head to wind.)

Maybe if I watch today I might make a second run and that with a wind dead ahead. I'll let him see it can be done but not with any loitering. Surely we will not have too much wind for getting home. That would be another problem to solve.

We might have to go into Freswick. (Thinking of getting off the ship once safely through the Firth. He hopes the weather will be favourable, or otherwise he is considering making a detour into Freswick Bay.) It is our hope that it may keep moderate, as our small boat is not fit for much.

Now you can brail up your sails and put everything in trim, put on two oars and pull round her quarter and see what she is like – that is the side I want the boat hoisted. They will see the boat on her side when we pass Stroma. I hope the "Crompton of Liverpool" – an Englishman – will lie to till I get up (remain stationary until his small boat reaches her).

Good morning, Captain. Good morning, Pilot. You have not been sleeping this morning. Very calm – we were well down in the Firth and look now – she is as far back as ever. What a game – nothing could be done – could not steer without wind. I am glad you have come as I have not been through here and what if I had to anchor a ship like this? Come away to the cabin until I see your terms of pilotage. My terms are this. I am not as much worried about calm as too much wind. A small boat like this will not tow. The first in my agreement is that the boat be hoisted up and the crew come aboard. Then if the wind increases stow the three royals. The pilot fee will be £5 and whisky, tobacco, beef and biscuits. My crew are starving of hunger being so early off in the morning. The first time the bell rings I expect you to have something for them. We can lower it down to them as long as it is like this. We will not hoist the boat until we wear around and get the yards braced for the other tack. We can hoist the boat and stow the royals when we come along the shores west of Dunnet Head. It will take time till the ebb eases off and we find the effects of young flood which is our tide to go through with. I myself am more annoyed about too much wind from this airt than too little. There have been accidents in towing with too much sail and it is dangerous to risk anything. We understand each other. Now that I have had my say he will take heart and maybe all things will come out well.

The ebb should be easing in an hour and a half – she has been driving a fair length of time. We will try her in an hour to wear – there is a slight air more now – not as much as she would stay yet. (Not enough wind to give the vessel enough speed to come head on to the wind and fall off on the other tack. There was always a fear in enclosed waters that a vessel would miss stays, ie., come up in the wind and failing to come round got the wind on the wrong side of the sails which made the ship drive astern and frequently go ashore. In very strong winds this could also demast a vessel as the masts were stayed mainly against a wind coming from any direction but dead ahead.)

The captain of a big ship does not like to be near the land with calms and shifting winds with a strong current of tide. That is all to skill and management without which anybody could get out of position, especially with the tide driving into the land.

Steersman try her round to wear and we'll get the sails braced for standing north. We will hoist the boat off Dwarwick Head, then stow the royals, brace the yards now to suit the airt of wind. There the bells are ringing and we are to have something to eat. Put some down to the men in the boat and a bottle of whisky but the crew are to get grog when the boat is hoisted and the royals stowed. We are a bit from Dwarwick Head yet and the tide has not eased much. There and the wind is beginning to fill the sails. You are better to stow first and boat last. Then before you get too much to do, turn up on the quarter deck for your grog which will be given to each and then scatter out till you get your orders. That is the life.

We have to round the west head of Dunnet before we haul to the wind. I expect to have flood tide to hold her to windward when we come to the east side of Dunnet Head – then we will know what to do.

Steersman is she gripping on the wheel? – (Is she sailing as close to the wind direction as possible?) That is what I want her to do, not to run off the helm. That is the thing for being good in the stays. With tide we never wish the ship to be sailed too close to the wind. Now tighten your braces (haul on the tackle to adjust the yards and sails to the wind direction) and your sheets for close sailing. We are to have a fair day yet, and the tide is good. I intend standing down the Firth a bit as I am to use the forbidden tack. A very dangerous course to steer with any other airt of wind and as if calm she would drive straight in for the high rocks of Stroma. Now we have it and the wind too – she is moving now. "Ready – bout ship– hard to lee." "Swing the myen bryce." She'll not fetch high enough, but we'll stand her cross for Brough.

Lomand by chance we got a good pilot fee man. With the tide below her keel, the wind she sure will feel in a ship like this it's fine to be a seaman.

We have got the grip of the tide for the inner sound drawing us well to windward and next tack we will fetch Stroma easy (we will be able to reach Stroma without changing tack). With this wind we can run off as far as we want. Ready – about ship . . . hard to lee . . . "Swing the myen bryce" (swing the main brace). We are doing well. There is a bad reef inside this which is submerged just now. Rounding this we will haul close to the wind so as to fetch high on this tack (to reach a point well off land on this tack) for the Pentland Skerries but we

will round her soon again. "Look there are the wives on the brae." They'll be singing low:

It's braw to sit and see the ships coming in
It's fine to sit and see the ships coming in
Wi the wee boatie up on the big ship's side
As she sweeps away on the glancing tide.

"Ready about ship . . . hard to lee . . . swing the myen bryce"
It's a long way to Tipperary.

When the sails began to flop
She came round just like a top
We know that with me she does agree man
So it's all at ease, the very way to please
On a ship like this it's fine to be a seaman.

Get my fee ready with my beef, biscuits, grog and tobacco. I am to go off the flood out off the Stacks of Duncansby. When we go around you can give orders not to pull the main brace. Let her lie idle till the boat is launched. Then we will go down to our own craft. We will take anything that is of weight for ballast. We will not let go until our masts are set and everything is in place for going home. Then we will bid you goodbye, good luck and a speedy passage.

The Process of Taking Coals

On the mainland, the public, every time a ship goes ashore, make a hue and cry. Strouma is in for a good time, but if they had to follow the Strouma's coat-tails they would know something else!

They would find officials of authority are soon on the spot to order and direct what can be done. It is only after vessels are given up by salvage tugs that they use their scummers. Some things cannot be taken off the bottom with net bags as coals are taken. They use their own devices, such as nippers or pincers on a long boom and there is nothing of importance to pay for a diver. The elements of a big storm help immensely. They will actually use a long water light for to show them copper or brass with a glass pane affixed. A long boom with a notched gripper – when you pull on the gripper rope it closes in on a pipe. This is only used when needed and certainly not to be taken from them.

Now I must go on to taking all that can be with coal cargoes to lighten the ship so as she might come off. The first order is off hatches and clear the beams, discharge as long as water keeps away from the furnace. The windlass is used steadily.

The steamer's own gear – a sluice, a broad flat with sides maybe 20 inches, slung up for the purpose, with enough incline to run empty. In some cases the outpourings are raised like a pyramid above water. In this way the cargo is good as there are lumps so if the steamer comes off she leaves behind her mark, and some benefit is to be got, but a light ship with bunker coal (engine fuel) is so fine as to run down to the furnace and if put in the water is never seen. In most cases a light ship (not loaded) will come off if there is no part of a rock up through the bottom. If a coal-laden ship is condemned, the only way is to make a bargain with the customs. They will have to pay the tallyman as to the tonnage each boat will carry.

The customs are also there to look after stores etc. – tobacco and spirits a speciality. When the water comes up to the engines, the ship's crew leave the vessel. The Stroma crew having to pay the price put on, start off at once to fill their coal bags and work away like demons while the weather will allow. This is the cleanest and best part, as with a storm or rather after, the land surf would beat and wet the whole cargo. They would just have to wait for a better chance at her.

When the water is above the cargo we have a boom, say 20 feet long, attached to it a three quarter of an inch rod of iron thinned with a cutting face and holed so that net loops can be made for a bag to hold in the coals. Perhaps the first bout (row) is made of wire loops whipped with spun yarn. Then begin on one loop with strong almost trawl net twine let out quickly so as to get breadth at the bottom and continue letting out till the net in size is about 30 inches circular at that. Take none in till about five rows (three separate lengths of strong rope) from the top which has to be about the same in height when hoisting with a three branch strong rope bearing the weight of fully half a hundred-weight of coals letting the water drip out if successful. This would be fairly heavy work with a tripping line using oilskin sleeves – a trudgery business to do but Stroma men take spells o'd. There are generally five men to the cargo boat (small boat carrying coal) meaning five fires to be provided with fuel. So by carrying wet coals they are never dry. The coals are emptied out in a quarry or elsewhere but that job is gone for ever.

We have good lights and good houses and no unseaworthy vessels to be thrown away.

First thing every morning have a look at the timbers in the bottom of the small boat to make sure small lumps of coal did not block the pump or we would have half a cargo of water and lose our weight of coals. (Presumably much water came off the wet sea coal which had to be pumped out regularly so that the extra weight of water meant less coal could be carried. Between each rib (timber) and a boat's planking there should be small holes which allow water to run through towards the pump. Usually thick tar blocked them in any case.)

Everything has to be watched with care. Sometimes we would leave with half a cargo owing to the tide being against us getting to our landing place, and carry it up and land it on a place we could take it again. Back to the steamer and take the full cargo with us this time and take the first landed stuff with flood tide working the whole time at the shore as we could not get to the steamer. Hard work is never easy but we would have warm feet in a bad winter.

There was no play then, everybody working for themselves and everybody has his share when he finished. No idlers when there was work to do for themselves and it was then they could work with a

will, but to work for a master they might be poor labourers!

Dangers to be Shun

East of the lighthouse not far from the land, there is a wild spot not passable in winter or even in summer with a spring tide as the land surf will break to the land from the Swelkie. The cause – stream tides coming from shallow water to a deep cavity – no one knows how deep.

They have special marks on the land and make sure they do not let the boats drift too far north. They must haul in their lines and shift away from the abyss or they will lose every line on the face of rock rising from the depth. This is the worst spot about the island.

The next rock is called Scartan which is outside the burial ground. There is always an eruption, perhaps too much for a small boat, so all fishermen must avoid this place.

The turnover from sail to motor has made matters better and they can shun all these wild spots, and steam up against the tide close inshore. The fishermen have it easy as there is no pulling or setting of sails but far less fish are being caught because they are not there to catch. The seine net is doing what was never done before. They are sweeping the sea, destroying the spawn and taking ashore less than they ruin. They certainly spoil herring as well as white fish.

Salvaging a Boiler and Engines

The wreck which lay longest on the Skerries was the Grimsby trawler "Champion" which lay on the Little Skerry and was burned down and scrapped. I worked here for seven weeks cutting part deck and side to let the engine and boilers out. We had a log and plank passage laid for 60 yards. The logs on the lower side, and the planks of wood to cross and level up the taper of the sloping slate rocks. The parts of the engine first and old fishing boat with broken barrels for dunnage put aboard by cobbles as we could not risk the "Glad Tidings" except on anchor. She was light and was a good asset for the purpose. Then back with the logs for the boiler to be parbuccled along the slate.

There were six of us and we managed famously. We could not have done without a man holding a tail rope to take the strain in case the boiler took a run! One turn had to be made to make a right angled change and this was my job. I just took a look at how the coopers changed the course of their barrels. The boiler had to run from the top of the slate to the edge of the water, so I had to raise high the side to make the turn. Remove the log at the lower side bevelling the edge next to the sea. This made a good fall and more rise at the end to climb. What a grand turn the boiler made – a real beauty when let loose it ran down and got a afloat. Councillor James Mowat, Canisbay on the top and me at his side to help in making her fast for the towing. Ronalson the boss was there and Captain Taylor of the "Tyne" tug. The main thing to see was that this tow rope was clear of being entangled with rocks or boulders, as the coopers will have to run over the wire and give the all clear. One of the cobbles took us off the boiler as we were sitting on the corner like two scarfs on a lump of rock. We were landed and stayed on the Skerry and had to haul the boat. Two went to Wick with the tug and a breeze came on and the wonder was they did not lose the boiler after all our success.

> **Footnote:–** The Skerries lighthouse with its two towers marks the eastern entrance to the Firth, so aptly called Hell's Mouth by the master mariners in the days of sail. It was built in 1794 and after almost 200 years, automation took over and on 22nd March, 1994, it became a remote controlled station.

Saithe Fishing

Just one summer in a lifetime was this fishing known. It was about the year 1886 that there was a good herring fishing with a lot of mackerel and herring in the Inner Sound. The solan geese began to dive and the saithe took to the surface. Shoals of them in spots began to lash the water and they were as thick as podleys (cuddings).

The Stroma boats were quickly on the scene and with sail set, just ran up and down near the play. About 20 fathoms of common handline was used with lead, sprool and a well sized big hook with red cotton or flannel for the fly. I was not strong enough to haul quickly and sometimes I would get a second fish only about 10 fathoms from the boat. (I was gey tired and wished for a breeze to stop the fishing!)

There was no time to bleed the fish but we bled what we could on the passage home by cutting the gills. The boat was well set in the water before we headed home, where they were thrown out. Then home for a nap and back to finish the bleeding.

Sometimes when the weather was fair, we would get washed and dressed and go into Orkney, otherwise we ran the sea.

Rock Fishing

There was good grey cudding fishing on the east side of the island and this was best from half flood to high water. Two floods of the month of May with smooth weather before the podleys set into the rocks. It helps when the wind is blowing into the land and you will see them playing outside for some time before they attempt to come in. There are always plenty when they do come in and I always could kill more than I could carry. They are very good scaled and roasted and freshly hauled, they are always at their best.

Sometimes you may get a lythe but those who throw the line are the masters of this fish. The

motor boats towing three lines pick them up easily. Occasionally you may get a red coddie or a plucker but seldom the golden carp. It is the older men living near the shore who prosecute this kind of fishing. It is a grand sport using fly or ripper but I prefer the limpet myself. (Lythe = Pollack. Plucker = Bullhead. Podley = Cudding.)

Cod Fishing

The Stroma men who were home during the 1914-1918 war got great hauls of cod. Some days they got a ton as they ran the seas. Once, I and the crew had 21 hundred-weights. We took three trips to Thurso with them and sold them to Allan and Sons who had a curing station there.

Lobster Fishing

This fishing is considered by some to be an easy way of making a living and yet not many can take their living out of it.

Special attention must be taken of the marks on the land which give the position of the trinks. It is best to set the creel on a level bottom in a place where the fish can see the bait. After hauling the creel don't shoot it on exactly the same spot, but if you have been successful, place it very near because your first creel would not have been far from a track. They like a sandy bottom and darkness.

My father used to work the rings with wide net bag with three branches of rope with float to keep the bait clear.

They worked with smooth weather, making no noise with the oars. The buoy rope must be plumb. Pull with a sudden jerk and haul as fast as possible. The jerk knocks the lobster to the bottom of the bag and then you must be quick because he is a very smart swimmer after the tail.

Making Whisky

A few details as handed down from olden times.

The people of the island actually poverished the heather moss to get the wherewithal to raise fires for the kilns.

The Customs from Wick came out and measured the long byres. They found one where the inside wall was 14 feet less than the outside measurement. They bent down and followed the attraction of the smell which led them to an underground passage. To their great satisfaction, they found the kegs after whisky, which had been sold to Orkney the week before. They took the kegs away with them as proof of an illicit still, and progress had made a start to do away with it.

The next time, the two gaugers came with guns and went straight to the Punch Bowl to have a look at a cave there. The Gloup, as we call it, is about 60 yards each way and about a hundred deep carrying its full width to the bottom.

At a house nearby, a woman had summed up the situation while she was doing the washing. Now in her words.

"Look here Jimmick – rin up to the Gloup and see if the twa men wi' guns are hauf across mang yon big boulders. Ye'll see them a'right, but lookan up they'll no see ye. I'll be watchin, so wave your cap and we'll be up to gie them a shooer of stanes. Rin doon 'e burn till 'e cavey at the ooter end o' the Ramie o' Kam, and dinna come hame until they be across the Soond."

We went up with five lapfuls of small stanes and threw them down to reach just where they were. Two shots were fired but they did not touch us.

We were back home and I was at my washing before they came back. The tide and time was given for them to cross the "Soond" and we escaped any awkward questions. I guess they would have had to haul in their guns and legs too below the big boulders at the bottom of the Punch Bowl.

They came back with a third man with them. This time it seemed the copper pot was reported on and taken away. —— No More Whisky!

David Banks – Pilot

[The following article appeared in the "100 years ago" section of the Groat of 2nd November, 1991. David was the brother of Donald Banks, the Bard.

"The Stroma Pilot, Mr David Banks, made it safely back home after a harrowing adventure aboard a Norwegian ship. Mr Banks, boarded the schooner "Cupido", of Drammen, in the Pentland Firth, with the intention of piloting her to Stornoway. The "Cupido" was bound for the Isle of Man with flooring boards but was hit by a hurricane 10 miles west of Cape Wrath. The hurricane carried away the top gallant mast, all the deck cargo, the bulwarks and a boat. A couple of days later the vessel tried to make for Shetland but a gale overtook her and carried away the topsails. She finally succeeded in making Westmannhaven in the Faroe Islands. Mr Banks travelled about 35 miles over hill land to Thorshavn where he joined the mail steamer "Laura". On his arrival at Granton, he managed to get a train to Wick under the charge of the Shipwrecked Mariner's Society."
Courtesy of the John O'Groat Journal.]

Donald Banks wrote "An Episode" about this in his History of Stroma. The"Cupido" had been flagging for a pilot, and they wanted a man who would crew with them to Stornoway and then drop him off after he had piloted them through the Firth on their return passage. Donald wrote, they mourned their brother for over a month and then the joy of his safe return. The "Cupido" was repaired and made seaworthy in Thorshavn, and some time later when the "Cupido" was in Wick, David met the captain and was taken down to the cabin where he was treated royally.

Stroma

Swarthy black faced rocks and a piece of grey earth,
That's what makes an island in the Pentland Firth,
The tide runs past and the seas run high,
And every vessel passing do sail close by.
Here we live and here we toil in Stroma little isle,
In the good old days when the people were frisky,
They always had malt and made plenty good whisky.
In hiding with others the whisky they stole,
And hid it again in the Punch Bowl hole,
When sampling the brew they danced in great style,
In Stroma little isle with its mystic smile.
In winter in Stroma there's not much to do,
The gruns far ower weet for haudin' ai ploo,
We thresh wir corn and kert in wir neeps,
Then oot frae the midden we put wur dung heaps.
The loons rin at night aboot to see sichties,
Wi' a sort o' torches and bublack lichties,
They have nothing else their time to pass in,
Stroma little isle with its mystic smile.
In summer the boats are all down and west,
Of course it is cod that is their quest.
But fish being scarce after a whole day's toil,
They just came home and gave the wife the smile,
In Stroma little isle with its mystic smile.
In harvest we are not awfully forlorn,
Some or others here have good fields of corn,
Wi' good Swedish neeps and plenty of tatties,
There's something oot ower to feed wir young gauties,
Wi' rheumatics, the auld folk are just in a cryle,
In Stroma little isle with its mystic smile.

(Bublack lichties – flashing lights usually from torches; Gauties – pigs).
From, History of the Islands in the Pentland Firth. By Donald Banks, Bard of Stroma.

Footnote:– Donald Banks like many other islanders was very interested in his house and they were all keen to get their homes fitted out well and made attractive. Donald had a large collection of glass floats set on a shelf round the ceiling. He had them painted in different colours and decorated with designs of spots and stars etc. Donald gave me his preventive cure against baldness which also promoted the growth of hair. Rub paraffin on the head every night, and he demonstrated it worked for him, taking off his cap and showing how much his grand head of hair had grown.
James McCaughey.

There were lots of stories about Stroma pirates, but not one was ever caught.
Malcolm Simpson, Wick.

CAPTAIN DUNDAS

Alex Dundas

You won't recall Sannag Das, a laddie running barefoot over the rocks and tussocks of Stroma Island in the early years of this century. But some of you may remember Captain Dundas, standing on the bridge of the "St Ninian" – the pride of the North of Scotland Shipping Company's fleet – as he conned her safely between northern harbours, in all weathers and at all seasons, during the 1950's and '60s.

Alex was born in Stroma in 1894, the second son of Matthew Dundas, a well known pilot of the Pentland Firth, and Lizzie More of Sarclet. As with so many of the sons of crofter-fishermen in the north, he was expected to start earning a living early, and so at the age of 13, he was engaged as cook/coiler on a "ferthie" sailing with Sinclair and Andrew Manson and Andrew Wyllie.

No doubt it was there that he learned the art of cooking such esoteric dishes as "crappit heid" and "fish-liver balls", as well as acquiring a basic knowledge of the ways of ships at sea. At the same time, he suffered dreadfully from sea-sickness and that might have been the end of his career but for an unusual spell of fine weather at a time critical for him. And so he persevered, proved an apt learner, left the fishing and sailed in the coastal trade in sailing smacks and steamers. He joined the R.N.R. shortly after the outbreak of the 1914-1918 war serving in charge of trawlers engaged in mine-sweeping in the Cromarty Firth and on the west coast. After the Armistice he volunteered for mine clearance in the English Channel and was with the Dover Patrol.

Returning to civilian life and the coastal trade, and with little book-learning but great determination, he worked his way through courses at the Nautical Colleges in Leith and Glasgow, and gained his Mate's and then his Master's Certificates. With the small wages then prevailing, and no Government grants, one wonders what hardships of preliminary saving went into financing these six month breaks, and enabled him to become, at 26, one of the youngest Master Mariners of his day.

Only after qualifying in this way and establishing himself with the North of Scotland Shipping Company, did he turn to serious courting, with snatched visits to the Shearer household at Lower Warse by sailing skiff from Stroma to Gills while his ship was in one or other of the local ports. These visits did indeed provoke a reprimand on the occasion when he missed ship at Scrabster and had to rejoin apologetically at Wick. Did his motor-cycle break down?

And so he won the hand of Georgina (Ida) and made a home for his growing family in Leith, to suit sailing schedules for the SS "St Rognvald", "St Magnus" and "St Fergus".

The 1939-1945 war found him back in Caithness, in command, variously, of the "St Ninian", the "Tjaldur", and the "Morialta", all ships commandeered for the daily run from Scrabster to Scapa, Lyness or Stromness, ferrying servicemen and materials to and from the islands, contending with the vagaries of weather and the threat of enemy attack, but with a protective escort vessel standing by "in case of emergencies". It was for unfailing attention to duty under these difficult circumstances that he was awarded the M.B.E. on 12th June, 1941.

His post war duties took him back to Leith and culminated, in his being appointed Commodore of the Company and being given command of their splendid new ship, the M.V. "St Ninian", the first of their modern vessels. He served in her until his retirement in 1958, and it was then that he was able to realise his long-held dream – to spend a good part of each year "up north",

The "St Ninian" 1950

and to have his own small boat with its fishing lines and lobster creels by the shores of the Pentland Firth.

And there he lies even today, at rest in Canisbay kirkyard, within a stone's throw – albeit a long one – of his native waters. He lived by his belief in the merits of hard work and education, of devotion to family and loyalty to Country and Company, and by a strong Christian faith. Such were the characteristics of a man made in Stroma.

Elizabeth Sutherland, 88 Colliesdene Avenue, Edinburgh.
George Dundas, 'Pentland', 1 Grants Crescent, Maryburgh.

STILL SIGHTS TO TAKE YOUR BREATH AWAY
[Written for Elizabeth Sutherland née Dundas]

Dear Exile – On a moonlit night, on the Warth Hill road, I still want to hold my breath, lest the mere sound violates the soul-enriching silence and vast acres of dark, sombre, moorland – beauty, all around me.

On a brilliant sunny day, I still gasp when the Pentland Firth comes into view, with the distant grandeur and mystery of Hoy, the nostalgic Stroma, now uninhabited, uncultivated – so no longer a lively patchwork of green, black, gold and purple.

Nowadays, there is no patient gathering of weather-beaten weather-eyed, thigh-booted, nautical maestros, beside the old smiddy, near Huna pier – or any sight of their gleaming purposeful yawls crossing the Firth. Their challenges and playgrounds – the "Men O'Mey" and the "Boars' O' Duncansby" are always flaunting themselves as if awaiting their return.

Remember, before you went to India, you took a long last look at the Pentland Firth and remarked, with hidden emotion, "I'll miss the white horses. . ."

Well, when first I moved a mere 11 miles to Castletown, I too missed the daily, visual luxury of the Firth, but have grown to like Dunnet Bay (dull cul-de-sac by comparison!).

The quite majestic Point of Duff and stately Dwarwick House, and the homely, nestling village of Dunnet are undoubtedly a triple mixture of quiet picturesqueness.

Do you remember Gills? The two braes with the bridges over the burns? The primroses in the spring?

I have never been down there since it has been transformed into a roll-on ferry terminal for Orkney-bound tourists.

When I loved and knew it, there were three "osts" in the brae for boats (11 feet keel, seven feet beam), a narrow pier, a sail-house and a rusting winch – all seemingly adequate enough facilities for the hardy and sober crofter-cum-fisherman.

They would catch cod off the west end of Stroma to salt down for winter to augment a good healthy basic diet (mind soaking the dried cod overnight, in order to soften it, and extract most of the salt, simmering it gently and – m'm – serving it with mashed tatties and thick, white sauce?).

Such an independent, disciplined, rugged lifestyle has gone, I fear, for ever, and with it so much that was good, wholesome and pure – and character building.

Yours affectionately,

Patricia X.

(Patricia Crowden, Main Street, Castletown.)

STROMA ENGINEERING LTD.

A number of houses throughout the country have been named "Stroma" by people who have connections with the island. However, few people will know of a small family firm in Birmingham called Stroma Engineering Ltd.

Sybil Smith was born in Newton Cottage in the North End of the island. She spent her childhood in Stroma and then when she was 15, moved to London where four members of her family already lived, brothers Donnie and Nicol, and sisters Mary and Kit. She also had an uncle and aunt, Walter and Nellie Simpson, whose home was a base for everyone from the north and who were very kind to her.

Sybil worked in London but was eventually bombed out during the war and decided to return to Stroma. This was easier said than done as she discovered she needed a passport to return to the island, because of its proximity to Scapa Flow. It took six weeks for the passport to come through and during this time she had to stay in Galashiels in the Borders. By the time she received her passport, she had decided that rather than go home to Stroma she would stay with another brother, Willie, who was unmarried, and was a lighthouse keeper on Scalpay, an island on the west coast of Scotland.

Sybil lived there for one year but found she was unable to cope with the loneliness and the fact that the local people all spoke Gaelic. She volunteered for "the war effort", the production of war material in factories, and found herself in a training centre in Glasgow. After some time, six girls including Sybil were picked to go to a factory in Birmingham. This was the nearest she could get to London. When they arrived at the factory they found they were the first girls to work there and so everyone made a great fuss of them. Sybil was allocated to the tool room where she met her future husband, Vic Hale. They married in 1945 and have lived in Sutton Coldfield ever since, where they brought up their family.

About 1977 Vic and their eldest son, Stuart, set up a company in Birmingham doing precision engineering. Stuart named the company Stroma Engineering, a name his mother is very proud of. Their daughter Sue became secretary and five years later they were joined by their other son, Graham. And so the name of Stroma lives on in Birmingham, in what was once the very busy industrial belt of England.

Elizabeth Bruce, Bellevue, Huna

WIND POWER

Accumulators, "wet batteries", we called them were necessary for wireless performance. We had two, complete with metal frames fitted with carrying handles. Each consisted of a toughened glass container in which the plates were immersed in a solution of diluted sulphuric acid. A bakelite top was fitted with two threaded studs to hold negative and positive terminals. There was a horizontal embossed line on the side showing prescribed acid level and a pointer activated by acid density. Degree of charge was indicated on a scale which read, full, half full, empty.

George Manson stands at the south gable end of Stroma schoolhouse beside his newly constructed windmill, pleased with the result of meticulous planning and manual labour – no power tools then!

The final coat of paint has just been applied by George and son. Minutes later, a neighbour, accumulator in hand, expressed his approval and suggested a naming ceremony as at the launch of a new boat.

Celluloid containers having a coloured ball in liquid suspension were also being introduced 60 years ago.

While one of our accumulators was in use, its discharged partner was carried to the Stroma Haven sail shed. The "post boat" took it to Huna next morning where by bus, the "flat" battery was transported to a Wick garage for re-charging. On one occasion the battery arrived back having been charged at too high a rate. The build up of gas had cracked the top bakelite plate.

A windmill was constructed for the sake of convenience and to obviate such unfortunate incidents.

The boarded part of the framework could be removed. There was also a small inspection window in the after section. Bolted to a triangular oak boss were the arms on which wooden "sails" were fixed in such a manner that, during very strong winds, one or two blades could be reversed to reduce rotational speed. The method of construction was such that a capsizing momentum was rendered negligible and never occurred.

At the front were two home made wooden wheels, which, when the back legs were lifted, allowed the machine to be easily turned to face the wind or brought round in order to change over batteries. The main shaft was set in ball races eliminating vibration. This shaft carried a round hardwood block and a metal grooved pulley. The latter was connected by belt to a 12 volt car dynamo while round the former hung a rope, a loop of which is visible below the housing in the photo. This rope, meant to act as a brake when pulled downward, was only effective in a light breeze. Frequently friction caused the wood to smoke but the blades kept on turning.

Interior installation was simple. A small switchboard contained a volt meter, ammeter, two main switches and a pot lid cut-out, which opened when the wind fell off, thereby breaking the circuit and preventing discharge of accumulators through the dynamo.

Six accumulators could be charged simultaneously.

The green painted windmill with white sails turning, proved to be a picturesque yet efficient solution to a problem.

Sutherland Manson, 6 Bower Court, Thurso.

MODEL YACHT SAILING

Sailing yachts became a very popular pastime in the years between the First and Second World Wars. All the boats were built in Stroma with the womenfolk sewing the sails. Both lochs used for sailing were in the North End of the island. At first the sailing took place on Edward's Loch but latterly it was on Loch Lomond which was a man-made loch. The sailing took place during the winter months and because of the number of yachts competing, took all day with competitors and spectators alike coming home as darkness fell. In later years, some of the islanders competed annually at Sarclet Loch, south of Wick. On one occasion, Malcolm Simpson (jnr), The Loch, North End took the County Cup home to Stroma.

Elizabeth S. Bruce, Bellevue, Huna.

Malcolm Simpson Sen., sailing his yacht on Loch Lomond. He gave the fine Wedgwood china teaset he won on a different occasion to his grandson and namesake.

Malcolm Simpson's grandson, sailing the "Paragon" on Sarclet Loch. He took first place in 1970 with this boat he built himself.

THE HAVEN, STROMA

Tied up at the quay:
1, The "Victory" – Post Boat – Sandy and George Robertson, Skipper Willie Bremner.
2, "Cormorant" – George B. Simpson.
3, "Dreadnought" – James M. Simpson.
4, "Diligent" – Bill Sinclair.

If you save the heid, you'll glen (gather) hair.

A clattering cairt gangs lang to the hill.

They can carry a tale who can't carry a burden.

Mary Sinclair.

Photo, George Dundas, Maryburgh.

THE "FRUITFUL" AT BROUGH 1911

This photograph was taken just after the "Fruitful" had completed her maiden voyage.

Bill Ryrie on pier. Jimmy Wallace in boat, with Jim Sinclair behind him. (Note ballast on pier).

George Simpson, Stroma built the "Fruitful" in 1911 for Mrs Annie Ryrie in Brough who hoped this boat would perhaps keep her sons at home, because the sea and sailing was in their blood.

The Ryries sold the boat to Donald Smith from Stroma who fitted in a Ricardo engine and put a lot of work on her. He took the boat with him when he moved to Wick. The boat was moored in (at) the river and he fished from Scalesburn.

Jim Crowden had the boat next and then it was bought by Don Wares. Sadly she was lost in the storm at Huna, 19th September, 1990.

James McCaughey, Boat Builder, Wick reckons it would now cost about £6000 to build the "Fruitful".

Photo, Don Wares, Seater.

Recieved from Mrs Ryrie Brough
The Sum of Seventeen Pounds ten Shilling
being the price of a new Thirteen feet keel boat
Sails and material as agreed between her
and George Simpson boat builder Stroma

		£. S. D
First Installment paid		2 — u — u
Second Do	Do	6 — u — u
Third Do	Do	9 — 10 — u
Due amount Paid		£ 17 — 10 — u

Geo_ _mpson

From Jimmy Ryrie, 35 Ashbridge Road, Allesley Park, Coventry.

THE STROMA YOLE

About 300 years ago, two young men, one a Horne and one a Duncan, started boatbuilding in Burwick. A son of the Duncan family (relative of the famous Admiral Duncan buried in Elgin) developed a design that proved its worth in these waters and he became an exceptionally good builder of boats.

It was about 1845 that two well-handed young men, one a Banks and one a Smith, came across from Stroma to learn boatbuilding with Mr Duncan who had a workshop at a house called "The Mey" in Burwick.

The boats they built were of a size ranging one ton but under 20 feet of keel, up to six tons under 30 feet, average width 10 feet. The broad beam gave stability. The stem was curved to allow the boat to be run up easily on the sand, so that passengers could get ashore dry shod. The "rise" or gradient in the bottom (usually called the floor) was a rise of one inch for each foot of width amidship measuring from the centre towards the bilge. After they learned their trade, these two men returned to Stroma and built many boats for Stroma and for sale elsewhere.

Alex T. Annal, Myres, South Ronaldsay.

Footnote:– The boatbuilders in Stroma added their own skills to the original Orkney yole design and in their estimation reckoned they were better boats. The old Stroma men could always tell the difference between the two yoles.

James McCaughey.

Yole (jo:l): s., small, undecked sailing boat; gen. wide and shallow in build. The type is now practically obsolete. It was rigged with two masts – each of which had a fore-and-aft-sail; in addition, it had a jib. [Gen.] This is a form which shows the No. vowel *o* of *jolle*, a small boat, rather than the *aw* of Eng. *yawl*.

From, Orkney Norm, OUP 1929, by H. Marwick.

With thanks to Robert Leslie, Chief Librarian of Scotland's oldest Public Library. Founded as the Bibliotheck of Kirkwall, 1683.

COAL BOAT AT THE HAVEN

This photo shows the coal ship alongside the Haven pier at the South End of Stroma. The ship's derrick has been hauled over by the guy man sitting atop the parapet while another person standing on the pile of coal is removing side links on the bucket so that it may be tipped. There are two weighing machines with scoops attached. In the centre of the picture an islander is shovelling coal into the scoop on the right where George Manson in the white boiler suit, with another person, is holding a sack open to receive the correct amount when registered by the machine. It would appear that discharging has just commenced as there are no filled sacks to be seen, only a few fresh tarred creels on the quay and not a horse and cart in sight. One elderly man seated in the foreground is having a puff of his pipe while awaiting his turn. A shower has left some water on the quay which will no doubt keep down the dust and a man standing near the vessel is still wearing his oilskin. The building in the immediate background is the Simpsons' shed while above it stands the sail shed, then on the skyline is the Robertsons' shop. Three boats, out of commission, are berthed across the road to the right of the shop and beside them lies an overturned steel lifeboat which came from the American steamer "Grayson", wrecked on the west side of the island in 1920.

Two halves of boats converted for storage purposes are placed on the harbour side of the road and to the left of the shop.

Sutherland Manson.

Footnote:– The numbers are still on the beams in the sail shed where each boat owner kept his oars, sails, etc.

Photo, Magnus Houston, Mill House.

H.S.

THE "UNDAUNTED"

The "Undaunted" was built by George Simpson, The Loch, in 1906 for Donald Simpson, West End. She was the first sailing boat built in Stroma with a side deck and was used for all the rough crossings because she had this additional strength.

Donald Simpson, my grandfather, along with his sons William, John, George and Jim were awarded the Royal National Lifeboat Institution Parchment in 1908 for saving the crew of the "Royal Oak" under very difficult conditions.

There were spots near the Skerries which were specially good places for catching cod. Disaster struck in August, 1908 when the "Royal Oak" was at the handlines, more to the north side of the Skerries, and the "Undaunted" was on the west side with both boats fishing well. The "Royal Oak" had an exceptionally large catch and with the weight of the fish making her low in the water, she was swamped in a heavy swell. The crew of the "Undaunted" saw the boat go down so they adjusted sails as quickly as they could and went back. My grandfather said it was terrible with the five men; James and John Robertson, Donald Robertson, David Sinclair and Donald Wares gasping and thrashing in the water and grabbing whatever they could, and in these days few if any of the islanders could swim. The first they did was to get them all one way or another, clinging to the boat and after that it was some job to get them into the boat because they were all big heavily built men and with their heavy wet clothes and seaboots they were just about beat. Grandfather said they were in a fairly smooth trough or hollow between long big rollers and he believed that it was the oil from the fish that calmed the waves and made the rescue possible. They were all utterly exhausted by the time they got landed on the Skerries. The lighthouse keepers were more than kind for they calmed, dried, revived them and kitted them out with dry clothes before they set sail for the haven.

Sybil McCaughey, 24 Louisburgh Street, Wick.

David Manson and Donald Simpson

Photo, Malcolm Simpson, 95 Willowbank, Wick.

Donald Simpson, skipper of the "Undaunted" in front of his house, with Di Robertson's in the background. Old herring net laid over sproots (sprits) set across oars resting on herring barrels make this temporary rack with cod drying on it David and Donald are the grand-parents of Sybil McCaughey and Rena Dunnett.

J.S.

THE "UNDAUNTED" SAILS AGAIN

The "Undaunted" was always in the Simpson family and I was delighted when in 1965, Davie Simpson let me buy my great-grandfather's boat. She was one of the last boats lying neglected at the haven and no one thought I would be able to make anything of her because she had been out of the water for 25 years and was in a sad state. Davie got her ready for the water and patched on canvas because she was so gizzened.

Don Wares volunteered to tow us over, my father came with me in the "Undaunted" so that we could steer and bail. Don got well started towing us, and we were bailing steadily when he realised he had left the dog in Stroma, so he cast us loose and went back for her. There we were near the middle of the Firth, up to the knees in water and bailing for all we were able and no sign of the "Fruitful". Don got "Queenie" no bother at all but when he was turning in the quay the tiller hit the steps and knocked the fastening off the rudder which took him some time to sort. We were drifting towards the "Men O'Mey", bailing hard, drooked with sweat, still no sign of the "Fruitful" and getting a wee bit worried. The top stroke was off the boat and there was not much free-board with her being so full of water and also the boat was loose and flexible, wobbling like a jelly with each wave that hit her. We were drifting in the Firth for about an hour and ended up near the beacon before Don caught us. We eventually got safely landed and hauled up at Huna and were thankful that part was over. The next stage was easy. John Nicolson's lorry was a low loader, adapted for caravans and it was no trouble for him to winch the boat aboard and take her to Wick. It was great to have the "Undaunted" in the back garden at 22 Nicolson Street where I spent many hours working on her over the next two years.

I rebuilt the boat exactly as she was and then fitted in a Brit petrol paraffin engine. She still has half her original timber and, typical of the Stroma yole, is good to handle in any seas. David Simpson was proud to come with us for the trial run and he passed his good old "Undaunted" as **perfect**!

James McCaughey, Boat Builder, Pulteney.

THE "DUBBELMAN"

S.T. "Dubbelman" a Dutch steam trawler belonging to Ymuiden, a fishing port near Amsterdam, ran aground in dense fog on the Lother Rock with the last of the flood tide at 11 p.m. on the 8th May, 1912. John and James Allan, Malcolm Simpson, Simpson Crowe and Donald Wares had just come home from the cod fishing from the westward when they saw the rockets go up, so they turned the "Alpha" and set off immediately. Thomas Budge of Brough, South Ronaldsay in his motor dinghy was there before them and strongly advised the Stroma boatmen against going in to the trawler because the tide was going over the rock and it would be extremely dangerous. They ignored his advice, went in and and under such very hazardous conditions, rescued the crew and landed them at Burwick. The crew were taken to St Margaret's Hope where they were accommodated and got food and warm clothes.

Naturally there was always keen rivalry between Orkney and Stroma boatmen, especially when there was a wreck. William Allan of Burwick was most ill-pleased with the Stroma men for encroaching on Orkney territory.

Two days after the "Dubbelman" was stranded, she was pulled off by a destroyer but sank immediately and they just managed to get the crew off in the nick of time. When the destroyer was hauling off the trawler, the rudder gear of the "Alpha" got damaged. The Stroma crew stayed over until my grandfather Donald Mowatt, The Smithy, got the damaged ironwork and rudder repaired. John Allan stayed with William Allan, Burwick, James Allan and Malcolm Simpson stayed with Malcolm's brother-in-law John Brown, Upper Flaws. Simpson Crowe and Donald Wares stayed with Thomas Budge. Thomas Budge was the boatman for the Pentland Skerries and brought over the supplies for the lighthouse. He also farmed "Brough".

The crew of the "Alpha" was awarded a RNLI parchment for life saving on the 11th July 1912.

The "Alpha" was built in 1903 by George Simpson and with mast sails and oars cost £23. She was fitted with a Kelvin engine in July 1913. John R. Sinclair bought the "Alpha" from Hamish Duncan and she is now at Maritima, John O'Groats.

William S. Mowatt, The Smithy,
South Ronaldsay.

Royal National Lifeboat Institution Citation

At a meeting of the Committee of Management of the Royal National Lifeboat Institution for the Preservation of Life from Shipwreck held at their offices, London on the 11th day of July, 1912, the following Minute was ordered to be recorded on the Books of the Society. That the best thanks of the Royal National Lifeboat Institution to be presented to **Mr John Allan** in recognition of his courageous conduct in putting off in a boat with four other men, at great personal risk, saving the crew of 13 hands of the Trawler "Dubbelman" of Ymuiden, which was wrecked at South Ronaldsay, Orkney Islands, on 8th May, 1912.

Waldegrave	George T. Shee
Chairman	Secretary

The original citation is held by John Allan's grand-daughter, **Jessie Smith, 3 John Street, Wick.**

A Stroma Wren Miss Jessie L. Smith (WRNS), was promoted to Petty Officer. It was 18 months since she had first volunteered, and after six months service she was made a Leading Wren. Miss Smith, who was enjoying a short spell at home on leave, was serving at a Western base. Meanwhile, Matthew Dundas, Robert Robertson, David Simpson, William Smith, Donald Smith, Herbert McBeath and Audrey Simpson WRNS, were also on leave in Stroma.

Courtesy of John O'Groat Journal, 24.4.1942.

Kissing is out of fashion
When the whin is out of bloom.
        Robbie Dundas, Stroma View.

The west wind is a gentleman and goes to bed
(wind will fall at night).
        Willie Mowatt, South Ronaldsay.

Stroma Lighthouse

Photo, Laurence Brown, John O'Groats.

Foghorn under construction

Helicopter landing

"Pole Star" at The Goe

Land sea at The Goe.

Photos, Malcolm Simpson, Wick.

273

THE LIGHTHOUSE

Lighthouse Stair

Photo, Billy Magee, Lower Gills.
Stroma Light made automatic 20.2.96

Stroma Lighthouse is built at the North End of the island overlooking the notorious whirlpool called the Swilkie.

It was decided to build a lighthouse on Stroma in 1894. (Lit 15.10.96.) The lighthouse was manned by three lightkeepers who lived in houses built for them at the lighthouse. The families became part of the island community, mixing socially and having their children educated at the island school.

This was the situation for many years but as time passed, the island community dwindled and in 1961 the Lighthouse commissioners decided that Stroma should become a "rock" station. This meant that the families would have to live on the mainland and are now accommodated in houses in Thurso. A helipad was built near the lighthouse and when the men are due for relief they are flown off the island by helicopter, and replaced by another lightkeeper. In the past, all supplies to the lighthouse were brought by one of the lighthouse ships and transferred from the ship by a small boat to the harbour at the North End – The Goe. This was also the case when a lightkeeper was shifted to another lighthouse. All his furniture, personal goods etc., had to be moved by the lighthouse ship. This is no longer the case of course and most of the supplies to the lighthouse are flown from one of the lighthouse ships, both of which have a helicopter on board, to the island. The ability to use a helicopter has changed the handling of supplies dramatically. It is quite interesting to watch the helicopter flying backwards and forwards from the lighthouse ships to the island with oil drums and other supplies slung beneath it.

Elizabeth S. Bruce, Bellevue, Huna.

STROMA BEACON

The Beacon

Photo, Magnus Houston

An area of shallow water off the south west extremity of Stroma Island extends seaward, formed by weed covered rocky outcrops, partly visible during ebb tide but completely concealed at high water. We can speculate that long ago, a headland may have jutted out into the sea until its softer layers became eroded by the ceaseless pounding of the waves, eventually forming a stack or clett which in turn was gradually demolished, the debris being dispersed by relentless tides. Now only the Skerry remains, a name, given to the locality though in later times "The Beacon" was used in a more comprehensive sense. However certain folk were said to live at " 'e back o' 'e Skerry" and "they wur at 'e creels at 'e back o' e' Skerry" was a familiar phrase in the vocabulary of the island's fishing fraternity.

The main stream of flood tide rushes round and over the dangerous hidden reef and even with ebbing water, the portion of rock revealed for a short period does little to minimise the perils of a close encounter. Local seafarers and others well versed in the hazards of the Inner Sound, shape a safe avoiding course but for the unwary or those for whom familiarity has bred contempt, swift progress can come to an abrupt halt with dire consequences.

The Inner Sound, that part of the Pentland Firth between Stroma and Caithness, has always been regarded as a subsidiary channel by shipowners, the recognised navigational route being the Outer

Sound from Stroma to Orkney even more so as vessels increased in size and draught. In pre-war years, the bulk of traffic through the Inner Sound consisted of fishing vessels and coasters while the occasional large ship using this route was generally under the command of a Captain possessing local knowledge. Radar nowadays reduces but does not entirely obviate risk of stranding yet long before its advent, a navigational aid in the form of a beacon had been constructed and remains a fitting tribute to those engaged in its erection. This is how it all began.

11th July, 1853. From Lloyds the following communication was submitted to the Northern Lighthouse Board and remitted to their engineer.

Sir, I am instructed on the part of the Committee for managing the affairs of Lloyds to submit to you the acompanying extract of a letter received from Mr James Bremner the Agent for this establishment at Canisbay, and to request that you will lay the same before the Commissioners of Northern Lighthouses for their consideration.'

The extract of this letter was as follows:

Skerry of Stroma, Pentland Firth

7th July, 1853.

'On board the Steamer Vessel "Stettin" of Konigsberg.

Stranded.

'The above vessel struck on the Skerry of Stroma, I have examined the master's Chart carefully and find that the ledges are not laid down in it, and during the past 40 years I have known more than 50 sail of vessels damaged and discharged.

There should be a Beacon erected on this dangerous reef, I have often spoken of it.

(Signed) James Bremner.

On 5th October, 1853, the Secretary of State indicated to the Lighthouse Board that a reply had been made regarding the request from Lloyds for the placing of a Beacon on Stroma Skerry. This letter to Lloyds stated that the Lighthouse Commissioners, on their annual voyage of inspection, had inspected the locality which had been long under their consideration to be marked by a Beacon and which had not yet been undertaken because of other pressing demands. However they had now ordered a survey and estimate to be prepared and were hopeful of including it in their work to be undertaken in 1854.

A report by D. and T. Stevenson, "Engineers to the Board" was submitted on 10th October, 1855, also six tenders, the lowest of which was regarded as being "greatly undercalculated regarding the weight of metal in the castings and it was agreed the work could not be done at the amount of this offer." The next lowest estimate of £406.11.0 from Mr Meiklejohn of Westfield Iron Works, Dalkeith found favour and was accepted mainly "because he has experience and ample accommodation and appliances for enabling him to execute the work

satisfactorily" although he had not previously worked for the Board.

Work commenced and a report from Messrs Stevenson (Engineers to the Board) dated 10th January, 1857, indicated that there were difficulties to be overcome but fortunately fears that the Beacon would come to an untimely end because of heavy seas or flotsam (a very real threat in those far off days) have not been realised.

Let the engineers tell their own story.

"The Beacon of Stroma has been in progress during the whole of the available working season, but such is the difficulty of the situation, occasioned by the low level of the rock, the rapid tideway in which it lies, and the heavy seas to which it is exposed that the workmen were seldom enabled to remain more than two hours at one tide upon the rock. An accident occurred which somewhat retarded the work, the large landing boat used for taking the castings to the rock had to be abandoned at anchor near the rock during a gale on the 15th September.

The men reached the Island of Stroma with great difficulty, but the large boat with some heavy castings on board went down during the night and was totally lost. The castings were however subsequently recovered. The most difficult part of the work may now be regarded as finished, the foundation having been prepared and the whole of the soleplate having been laid. It only now remains to put up the pillars of the Beacon which under favourable circumstances may be accomplished in about a month. From the experience gained at this rock it is obvious that the Beacon will be exposed to no ordinary amount of sea but so long as it is not struck by any floating body we confidently expect from the manner in which the whole fabric is secured that it will be able to resist the many heavy seas which it will have to encounter."

On 18th November, 1887 the Secretary included in his Report to the Board the terse statement that "The Beacon on Stroma Skerries, Pentland Firth has been completed."

Another summing up report from Messrs Stevenson.

"Stroma Beacon was successfully completed during the course of the past season. Exposed to a heavy sea in a rapid tideway, this work cannot fail to be severely tried and so long as it is not struck by floating wreck we have every confidence in its stability, but from the rapid tideway which acts across the rock on which it is erected it is peculiarly exposed to the assault of floating bodies which may be drifted through the Pentland Firth. The total cost of Stroma Beacon is £1191.13.10 being £193.13.10 above our estimate."

To those familiar with the construction of the Beacon it remains a matter of conjecture whether the cross bars incorporated in the central pillar were fitted to afford footholds for those positioning the castings which weighed 35 cwts. apiece or were they intended to assist shipwrecked mariners to reach the safety of the upper cage? Perhaps they were planned to provide access should a light be added at a future date?

Prior to the erection of a warning Beacon, no doubt many vessels grounded on the Skerry but these are difficult to define, as wreck reports did not then state specific localities around Stroma's coast. However whether or not it was a case of "cutting corners" in good visibility or not being able to see ahead in dense fog, these vessels made contact with the reef.

The "Golden Eagle", a brigantine with a cargo of wood from Riga for Belfast during a south east gale, became a total loss when she broke her back on the Skerry in November 1859. In 1896 the steamship "Spero" laden with coal was fortunate in being refloated. Three years later, the schooner "Andrew Longmore" of Banff with a cargo of salt for her home port, was swept off the rocks by the tide, then capsized and went out through the Sound bottom up, a derelict.

In 1902 the Grimsby trawler "Silanion" went ashore at John O'Groats and was refloated but her change of name to "St Bernard" did not alter her fortune because she went ashore yet again, this time in 1906 at the Beacon but survived to sail another day.

The Icelandic trawler "Hilmar" grounded one morning in 1936 but only for an hour or two before high water. Two years later the Aberdeen trawler "Cadella" came to grips with the reef but escaped unscathed and continued her voyage to northern fishing grounds. It was 1945 when an air sea rescue launch beached herself beside the Beacon and was refloated with local assistance then towed to Wick.

The fate of the German trawler "Hessen" in 1987 is a recent memory when she came in contact with the Skerry damaging herself to such an extent that after refloating, she eventually sank a few miles south of Duncansby Head.

I wish to acknowledge and offer thanks for the information kindly given by the Northern Lighthouse Board.
Sutherland Manson, 6 Bower Court, Thurso.

Footnote:– Sinclair Davison aged 48 was Lloyds Ship Agent in Huna in 1851 and was still agent in 1861 and the census returns do not mention another ship agent in the parish, so it is likely that the James Bremner on board the stranded "Stettin" was the Keiss Civil Engineer – James Bremner the Wreck Raiser. He would have been constantly writing to Lloyds with ideas for the salving of stranded ships, wrecks and cargoes and being such an influential engineer of proven ability, Lloyds were acting on his advice four days after the letter was written on Stroma. One can but wonder if the David and Thomas Stevenson, Engineers to the Lighthouse Board, who on the 7th September, 1853, signed the plan for the Stroma Beacon were related to Robert Louis Stevenson, whose father Thomas started work on the ill-fated breakwater in Wick Bay on 1st October, 1863?

A.H.

PENTLAND FIRTH MEMORIES

A PRE-1914-18 TRAWLER.

We might consider, looking back on the amount of traffic passing through the Firth 60 years ago, that ships were more numerous then, more individualistic and certainly much smaller than their gigantic counterparts of today, when one vessel can easily carry more than 10 times the tonnage, which put a predecessor of similar type "down to her marks". Speed has also increased as a result of more powerful engines and nowadays the traditional profile of a cargo vessel has changed radically owing to the use of containers and increase in bulk cargoes rendering derricks almost obsolete. Formerly larger vessels preferred to navigate between Stroma and Orkney while the Inner Sound was used mainly by coasters and fishing vessels. No doubt a shipowner would not be too amused if his ship's log book indicated that one of his captains had chosen the more dangerous channel in such treacherous waters as far as the insurance company was concerned. Of course those were days before many of our modern navigational aids had been invented so anxiety was understandable.

A constant stream of trawlers in pre-war days hurried to and fro as they headed home for the market or steamed northwards to lucrative fishing grounds. On a calm summer evening a pall of smoke left by outward bound vessels would linger to form a long dark cloud extending from Duncansby Head to the Skerries. Fishing vessels came mainly from Humber ports their number augmented by ships from Aberdeen and also the European harbours of Cuxhaven, Geestemunde, Ostend, Fécamp and Boulogne to name but a few. Such density of traffic is not difficult to comprehend considering that in 1936 close on 500 trawlers were registered at Grimsby, 300 at Hull

and Aberdeen respectively while near enough a hundred hailed from Leith, Granton and North Shields. Some craft were of pre-1914-1918 vintage, easily recognised by their bridge abaft the funnel. A few of these veterans were still around for a considerable time after the last war. In former days it was not unusual to see 30 or 40 low powered coal burning fishers hastening into Reiss Bay at the onset of a north westerly gale while a few might opt for sheltered anchorage in Freswick Bay. Others of a more restless nature, would dodge along the coast, a mile or two offshore. Some with lights doused might even try a quick "drag" within the limits in the hope of defraying running expenses.

Stroma, for the ship spotter, will always be the perfect vantage point, a pastime to which I became addicted at a very early age. Throughout the years, telescope and I remain inseparable. The time came when I was adjudged old enough to be entrusted with our telescope which rested in the workshed below vessels' names inscribed on the wooden side planking and still decipherable. My first success in this sphere remains a very vivid memory. It concerns a small Tyneside trader which came in from the east, her black funnel decorated with a peculiar white painted symbol causing the owning company to be known as the "Tombstone Line". The letters of her name were read with accuracy "Alacrity" but my pronounciation of same caused hilarity in the house when I ran in shouting "'E "Alice Ritty" is passan close in". Then recollection of the homeward bound S.S. "Heronspool" brings another youthful episode to mind. Her bosun at the time was David Simpson from Stroma. Dunnet Head was well astern when her captain called him up to take the wheel saying "Right, you know these

ANOTHER TIMBER C'RCO

S.S. "DROTTNINEHOLM"

waters, take her through" which he proceeded to do, rounding the beacon without a qualm to head safely eastward through the Sound. Naturally, it was agreed that being so close to home they should give a few blasts on the whistle to alert Mrs Simpson. I was at the shop when Matthew Dundas with a twinkle in his eye, which I was too young to notice, said "go an' tell Davy's wife he's blowan Kate, Kate on the whistle," so I took off across the fields as fast as a six-year-old boy's legs can carry him. She looked bemused for a moment, then asking who had sent me, dawning realisation lit up her features and she gave me "sweeties" as a reward. I trotted triumphantly homeward having to my mind performed an important task to everyone's satisfaction.

Trade seemed quite brisk in the early 1930's though there was a worldwide shipping slump with many vessels laid up. Ships came through the Firth as usual, often listing severely since their deck cargoes of timber had become sodden from spray on one side as they crossed the North Sea. There were few sailing vessels passing and those that did were equipped with a small auxiliary engine. Familiar visitors were the three masted schooners "Asta" and "Sif" from Denmark and we frequently saw a similar type of craft, the Swedish "Isolda" whose owner/captain had his wife and children on board for she was their floating home.

On one occasion prior to hostilities, we had the pleasure of viewing two three-masted barques under full sail coming round the "tails" (Swelkie point) on the flood tide. They were the "Gorch Folk" and "Albert Leo Sclageter", new built training ships for Hitler's naval men, the latter being named after a Nazi terrorist (martyr). As part of war reparations, the former vessel is now the Russian tall ship "Tovarisch" while the latter after being taken over by America, was sold to Brazil but in 1972 became the Portuguese "Sagres II".

Certain passenger liners only appeared during the summer months while others were on a regular run. The Liverpool liners "Vandyck" and "Voltaire" on different occasions went east between the Pentland Skerries and South Ronaldsay en route to the Norwegian fjords. The "Gripsholm", "Kungsholm" and "Drottningholm" of Swedish America line were stately liners resplendent in their white hulls set off by yellow funnels with blue roundels and crowns superimposed, graceful by day, a blaze of light at night – veritable floating hotels. Even more modern and luxurious were the "Pilsudski" and "Batory" built in Italy in 1936 for the Gdynia America Line. Unfortunately, the former taken over as a troopship on our account, was sunk by the enemy in 1940 but the "Batory" known as the "singing ship" from the happy atmosphere on board, resumed her normal run after the war ended but during strained relations with Russia she was no longer welcome in New York and had to be rerouted to India. When she became infiltrated by K.G.B. agents, the term "Happy" was no longer applicable, even her captain found his authority being undermined to such a degree that finally, during refit on the Tyne, he put a few necessities in a briefcase, slipped ashore unseen and caught the London express but being wary of interception at a main line station, he disembarked at surburban Hitchin thus outwitting his pursuers and obtaining political asylum in this country before eventually emigrating to the United States.

The majority of ships coming through the Firth during this period were from Europe and

Scandinavia many owned by the Danish Forenede Line which, having their names painted on each side, were a boon to the spotter when visibility was poor. It is common practice today to use the ship's side as a kind of advertising medium for the owners or trading consortium. Pre-war this was unusual except for an American Company formed by two Irishmen who had made good. Their vessels had Moore and McCormack painted amidships and were usually of 1914-18 vintage called "Hog Islanders" after their birthplace. They were easily identified by an apparently drooping bow and stern which made them appear to bore into the sea as they came round the "tails" (Swelkie Point) on their way to Gothenburg. Other vessels on this run of similar type belonged to the United States Shipping Board. The "City of Flint" was such a ship passing Stroma on 5th February, 1939, hitting the headlines several months later when she sparked off a diplomatic incident. Her intention had been to cross the North Sea and then, taking advantage of the territorial waters of as yet neutral Norway, reach Germany in safety with her cargo, but unfortunately the Germans violated neutral waters, arrested the "City of Flint" and took her to Murmansk as at that time Russia was their ally. When it was discovered a grave blunder had been made, the ship was immediately released but the German Consul in Bergen, who should have known better, was hurriedly recalled and replaced.

It was always an interesting sight to see a salvaged battleship of the scuttled fleet being towed south with tugs in attendance, like seagulls with a dead whale. Then one day in 1934 a vessel which came rolling and tumbling along on the flood tide caused much speculation and discussion, being almost circular in shape with paddles. However it ultimately transpired that this was the "Queen Margaret" on her maiden voyage from Dumbarton bound for Queensferry on the Firth of Forth where she and her sisters plied until construction of the road bridge rendered them obsolete.

Trawlers traversed both channels which comprise the Pentland Firth vis. Outer and Inner Sounds. We saw them all, named after football teams, Lords, Ladies, Lochs, Capes, Saints, etc. Steam drifters with an increasing number of motor boats headed west through the Sound at the beginning of the west coast herring fishing, a procession lasting for days with the main stream going through the Inner Sound. When there was a similar fishing at Wick, a number of drifters would round Duncansby Head in the afternoon on their way to the Hoy grounds via the Firth; English boats easily recognisable by the forward raked mizzen mast and a long slender mast at the wheelhouse as radio had been installed on some vessels.

In 1939 the dark clouds of war were looming ever closer on the horizon and the crew of the small homeward bound German steamer "Henry Lutjens" must have been glad to leave the Firth astern on 28th August of that year. The mighty, yet ill fated, H.M.S. "Hood" appeared in our waters on the last day of August while H.M.S. "Renown" passed our shores the day previous.

The inevitable happened and by the end of September all our modern trawlers had been recalled for conversion to minesweepers and escorts. Neutral vessels hastily painted their national flag and country's name along each side. Soon they began to be stopped and searched west of Stroma. If suspected of carrying contraband, they were taken into Orkney for more extensive examination. Many vessels, in the early stages of hostilities, considered it safer to come north about rather than sail through the English Channel.

There was an initial delay in the formation of convoys but once greater safety in numbers had been proved yet again in this new war, the volume of shipping in our waters increased. Around the Scapa Flow area there was always much activity where sleek grey destroyers merged with their surroundings and escorted battleships with aircraft carriers sailed past Cantick Head on secret missions the details of which would only be revealed long after the armistice had been signed.

The "St Ola", depending on the tide, frequently came close round Swelkie Point on her daily run between Orkney and Scrabster. Extra transport was provided for service personnel by the "St Ninian", "Morialta" and "Tjaldur". Many a person then in uniform, remembers to this day, horrendous crossings either going on or coming off leave in one of those vessels before stablisers became a fact of maritime life. The "St Ninian" ended her days in 1948 at a breaker's yard in Rosyth while the "Morialta", originally built for Australia, capsized and sank in heavy weather on a voyage from Vietnam to Singapore in 1973.

The "Tjaldur" had been on the Faroes to Denmark mail run but on occupation of the latter, she was managed by the North of Scotland, Orkney and Shetland Shipping Co., and after the war was returned to the Faroe Islands where in dense fog, she unfortunately struck rocks off Mjoanes and sank in 1946 when on passage from Thorshavn to Klaksvig.

A large fleet of Faroese fishing vessels went through the Firth during the war with fish to Aberdeen, and it is perhaps a not too well known fact that 125 of their seamen made the supreme sacrifice during these operations. The majority of the Faroese fishing fleet at that time were ex-Grimsby and Brixham smacks, relying mainly on sail but having a very low powered auxiliary engine fitted for emergencies. When the war ended, traffic through the Firth slowly began to return to a semblance of normality, but the number of fishing vessels, or indeed shipping in general, has never attained its pre-war proportions.

The Pentland Firth has witnessed many changes since the days of sail and the need for local pilots, to the mammoth power driven monsters which now forge through our waters, but hazards remain for the unwary, perhaps more so, considering the huge draft and restricted mobility of the modern ocean going leviathans.

Sutherland Manson, Bower Court, Thurso.

THE GLOUP

In Stroma the Gloup is known as the Devil's Punchbowl. A fairly narrow tunnel leads into the area shown in the photograph from the west side. Although the tunnel into the Gloup is narrow, it is possible to take a small boat in at flood tide.

Many years ago the Stroma people made whisky down at the bottom of the Gloup in a cave in the right hand corner. When it is flood tide the cave is cut off which meant it was only accessible at ebb tide. This made it an ideal place to hide a still. Apparently the whisky was considered to be of good quality.

If it was necessary to go down during the night to tend to the still, they took a lantern and climbed down the side of the Gloup, not an easy climb even in daylight. I believe my great-grandmother, Christina Simpson, used to do this when a young woman.

There was always the fear of Customs Officers visiting the island to check on the illicit whisky making and if it became known that a visit was likely, the islanders set off for Orkney and sold the whisky there.

Elizabeth Bruce, Bellevue, Huna.

The Primula Scotica which grows so well in Stroma.

THE KENNEDY MAUSOLEUM

The Kennedy Mausoleum and Church Yard c.1970

Scartan Point where the notorious Well of Scartan can be seen when the ebb tide is running.

In 1659 John Kennedy of Kermuck is said to have fled to Stroma having killed a man Forbes in Foveran, Aberdeenshire. It was also said that John was the grandson of Lady Buchollie and that likely the Mowats helped him find this secure retreat. His house was down near the north pier and the ruined walls of his herb garden can still be seen.

It was Bishop Forbes who in 1762 wrote "This island is famous for having dead bodies of men, women and children, above ground, entire and to be seen for 70 or 80 years free of all corruption, without embalming or any art whatsoever, but owing, it is thought, to the plenty of nitre that is there." The bodies became very brown with time

The pigeon loft c.1970

and it was said that Dr John Kennedy's body was entire in 1750. The roof was off the dovecot before 1762. John Kennedy was reputed to be a doctor of herbs and there were certainly a lot of herbs growing in Stroma and handed down herb-cures were still being used effectively when I was a lad. For example:– drink the bree from boiled tormentil roots for diarrhoea; chew heather roots for heartburn; take nettle soup for rheumatism.

In the long ago when a sailor died in distant seas, the body was hung up in the rigging and by the time they got the remains home they were pickled by the salt spray and sun. I aye wondered if the Kennedy bodies had been given a similar treatment?

The walls of the mausoleum must be two and a half feet thick and the vault rises from a six inch ledge two feet from the floor. The building is some 22 feet high, with doorway and corner stones of dressed red sandstones, which it is said were brought over from Orkney. John Kennedy's initials are carved in relief on the door lintel and 1677 is on the date stone on the south west corner.

The floor of the pigeon loft is about the level of the projecting "course" of flagstones which prevented rats getting up to the nest boxes. (Incidentally there were no rats on Stroma!) There are about 600 large nesting boxes, some still in use last spring, by a merlin hawk, black guillemots (tysties), as well as pigeons.

It's about 20 years since the photos were taken, and the doorway, Elsie Cowe and Nancy Houston are weathering well!

James Simpson, Stroma.

The Laird's Wife at the North End Pier 1902

It was a special day in Stroma when they had a visit from the Laird's Lady and it was reported she was the first member of the Freswick family to visit their tenants on the island for a hundred years. James Simpson, with his boat the "Julia" (named after Admiral Sinclair's wife), ferried her to Stroma where she took a trick with the islanders and a good day was had by all. The foundation stone of this pier was laid in 1900. The "Marinetta" WK 896 is hauled at the East Landing.

James Simpson, Stroma.

Left to Right:– Rev. Alex Youngson; Mrs Alexander Sinclair of Freswick; James Simpson, Skipper (Grandfather of James Simpson, Edderton); Mr MacKay, Factor.

281

THE LAIRD OF STROMA EN ROUTE FOR THE ROBBER'S CASTLE 1980

Wm. MacKenzie and Dennis Farquhar on the stack.
Photo, Robbie Cowe, The Ha, John O'Groats.

At the south west corner of the island is a stack with Castle Nestag or the Robber's Castle on top. It was quite a thrill for me to set foot in the Robber's Castle under the expert team-manship of the Pentland Coastguard crew and I did not feel too apprehensive swinging across in a breeches-buoy.

Robert Cowe, Rogni Brown, Malcolm Calder, Dennis Farquhar, Douglas Hay, Wm. MacKenzie, Jack Morrice, John Mowat, Wm. Rosie and Jimmy Sinclair were the men who took part in this exercise under the command of Robert Cowe. The list of names was put in a bottle and I placed it under a wee cairn of stones there on Castle Nestag or the Robber's Castle as we aye called it.

James Simpson, Stroma.

Right: **James Simpson with his daughter Christine.**

Donald Sinclair's (15) the nearest house was her Granny Chrissie's home. Next is Charlotte Moodey's (16) and John Jolly Sinclairs (17).

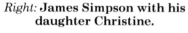

Photos, Alistair Sutherland, Summerbank.

Stroma Toast

Here's to them who wish us well
And for the rest - - - - ye ken yersel!

SWONA

Swona is the nearest Orkney island but is <u>NOT</u> in the Parish of Canisbay. The Rosies came to John O'Groats frequently and always referred to it as Scotland. This expression "over to Scotland" has been handed down through generations of Orcadians from the days when Orkney and Shetland belonged to Norway. James Rosie, a good man with a camera sent these photos on calendars to the Mill House.

James Rosie sails the "Falcon" 1962

The "Falcon" at Longhope 1962

"Falcon" and "Hood" in the Haven 1961

James and Arthur in the "Hood" passing the Clett, Swona 1961

GLIMPSES OF SWONA (SWEYN'S ISLE)

Swona has been inhabited for at least 5000 years and must have been a place of some importance as it is frequently mentioned in the sagas. Halcros (norn spelling hako-kru or hak-kru) inhabited Swona from about 1550 to 1850 when Magnus Halcro came across to South Ronaldshay. Sir John George Halcrow (the last of Magnus's descendants) died in 1992 at St Margaret's Hope. He was entitled to call himself "Sir" because King Robert the Bruce conferred a knighthood on Sir Hugh Halcro after the battle of Bannockburn (1314).

John Rosie born, c.1809, was the first of the Rosie dynasty and his mother Betty was a sister of Magnus Halcrow. John Rosie absconded with the Stroma schoolmaster's daughter Margaret Sinclair (daughter of Margaret Jack) and brought her back to Swona and married her. James Rosie their youngest son married Jean Sinclair of Dean in Graemsay.

Ivor's Biggin's – later Rose Cottage

David's Yole c.1945

Their son James married Isabella Norquoy and were the parents of Edith, Eva, James, Arthur and Violet. That's four generations of Rosies and 180 years of island life. I married Eva Rosie and now our sons Cyril and Martin own the island.

The Swona men built all their own boats up to 30 feet in length. James Rosie, Sen., built at least 23 boats. The "Hood" was approximately 26 feet on deck. The "Falcon", 17 feet, was built for lobster fishing, but specially rigged for sailing in regattas.

It was James Rosie and Jean Sinclair who built the Rosie's home. It was 15 feet wide by 40 feet long and they carried all the stones from the beach on their backs in caisies (handmade straw baskets).

Although in 1774, according to George Low, there were nine families resident on Swona, the time came when the Rosie family were the only inhabitants remaining and this photo of their dwelling house features a building which would not look amiss anywhere on the Scottish mainland, in fact its neat appearance and well tended garden might well evoke the envy of many living in a much less harsh climatic setting. The cottage was lengthened and heightened in 1900, the couples being made from 7" x 4" deck timbers off the "Croma". There was excellent flag and slate on Swona which was used on all the houses.

This is James Rosie wearing his characteristic soft brimmed hat with the wide silk band. He takes his ease on the engine casing, while a young lad "holds on" with the oars allowing Arthur to place recently caught lobsters into a floating "kist". A kist with coamings would prevent lobsters slipping away as could happen with an ordinary kist full of lobsters and low in the water (coamings = raised part round a boat hatch). A small dinghy such as this, demonstrates the Rosies' aptitude for boat construction. Stability of the craft is obviously unaffected by a hefty man leaning over one side. There are two spare oars and a boat hook in addition to the small engine but if necessary three oars on each side could be used. This particular type of boat would be most efficient for lobster fishing in rock strewn restricted areas round the island where size and manoeuvrability counted most.

The Dipping c.1895

On the left wearing oilskins and a "cheese cutter" James Rosie senior, with grand-daughter, Edith. Sabiston brothers wearing braces and James Rosie junior on right. Four men took a leg each of a sheep and lowered it into the purpose made wooden box which was three quarters full of dip and then held it to drip on draining board. The sheep were only kept on tethers during the lambing time and the rest of the year they grazed outside the dykes and could also get down on the shore for seaweed. There was a stone dyke at the Tarfend which shut off about 12 acres and another which ran across from the Haven and closed off about 10 acres at the North End.

James Norquay (grand uncle of Edith Rosie) lived all his life at Upthraw, Swona. His brother John was a lifeboat rescue man on Lake Superior for many years. David Gunn (son of Jessie Robertson) was an agent for "Highland Park" Whisky and left Swona when he was 26. He became a million dollar farmer and had a 40,000 acre ranch on the Argentine Pampas. He died in 1928.

The women as well as the men had to be masters of all trades, and with no shop on the island they learned to improvise. Edith's granny was an expert with the soldering iron and made jugs and pails as well as soldering holes in milk dishes, pans and kettles. She devised this feeder when they didn't have a lamb's teat or even an old teapot. A piece of cloth was tied round the end of the "stroop" and the lamb sucked the cloth and got the milk no bother.

Pet lambs were kept on the tether to prevent them following people into the house.

Edith Rosie feeding appreciative pet lamb.

Geordie Allan's boat at Haven before 1906

Left to right:– George Allan with sons David and Tom, James Norquay.

The surplus stones and shingle from the Hope Pier were used in the building of this pier 1906. George Allan, wearing an oilskin sou'wester smoking a clay pipe with only half a shank and getting his nose burnt.

The Haven with Barth Head, Sound Ronaldsay, in background 1960

"Hood" anchored at breakwater. Alex Annal on the "Cecelia". John Taylor on pier. (Cradle has been washed up.)

Sale of Wreck from "Croma" 1899

The "Croma" was a British steamer of 3187 tons built at Wallsend on the Tyne in 1883. She was formerly a passenger boat and then used as a tramp steamer. She was on passage from Dundee to New York with general cargo when she went ashore on Swona during dense fog on 13th August, 1899. She smashed on to the South Clett – an 18 foot pinnacle of rock and demolished it. Captain Claxton and the crew were all saved.

The Swona men salvaged the cargo and this along with a lot of fittings and furniture was set out on the grass. The sale was extensively advertised, and boats came from all round with the North Isles steamer bring a crowd from Scapa. It was a big sale – bales and bales of jute and canvas, and thousands and thousands and thousands of jars of Keiller's Marmalade. The marmalade was in one pound white 'lame' jars with "James Keiller and Sons Dundee Marmalade – Grand medal of merit Vienna 1873 – Only prize medal for marmalade London 1861" stamped in black on the jars. It was said that nearly 5000 cases of marmalade were auctioned.

Orkney, Stroma and 'Groats boats there with the North Isles Steamer lying off.

The Allans

George Allan's brother William went to Detroit. He owned 22 grain carrying schooners on Lake Superior and employed many South Isles men to sail the vessels during the summer. This went on until 1906 and each year the men came home to Orkney for the winter months. George's sons Tom and William went to Manitoulin Island in Lake Huron where they had a good general merchant's business. The Allans were descendants of Allan Stewart, a fugitive from Culloden who changed his name to Stewart Allan when he took refuge on Swona.

Schooling

In 1704 Margaret Hartice was the teacher and down through the ages the islanders got a good education. The school was a well slated house with three rooms and last time I looked the desks, chairs and some books in the schoolroom were sitting just as they had been left. James told me that during his school years a visiting teacher came each year during the summer holidays to teach them for six weeks and their parents had to do the rest. It was in 1915 that a schools' inspector was so impressed with James Rosie that he wanted his father to send James to University and keep Arthur at home to build boats and fish lobsters. The answer was "only clever people can survive in Swona" and how right was he.

James Rosie, senior on "back delivery" c.1945

Arthur Rosie ploughing with oxen c.1945

James Rosie on Back Delivery c.1945

James Rosie, senior, is seen cutting a field of bere with his Bisset reaper or "back delivery" as it was more usually called.

This ox must have been as strong as any Clydesdale because we would have expected to see two horses pulling the reaper. Oxen were slower than horses but were preferred in Swona because they were less temperamental, easier to train and could be sold for beef when they had a younger animal ready to take over. Note the home made canvas collar filled with straw, and chains passing through the back band to a shortened version of wooden pole held up by a "grubber" wheel. The revolving arms or "flies" were motivated by a chain and toothed wheel system and directed the corn into the blade known as the "knife" which moved laterally through iron "fingers" set about three inches apart. This scissors type movement was imparted to the "knife" by means of a crank, operated in its turn by a small rotating wheel. The broad "fly" furthest left in the picture ejected the corn in appropriately sized bundles behind the machine and those had then to be bound by hand, which task is being carried out by Arthur Rosie on the other side of the field. Almost hidden by the animal is an immaculately built hay "gilt", while a short distance to the left is a directional windmill which operated the threshing mill. The Sabistons lived at Norhead, the white two storey house on the right of Rose Cottage.

We may assume, from shadows cast, that there is a weak "back end" form of sunshine filtering through the cloud.

Mr Rosie, no doubt well aware of the photographer, has a look of contentment on his weatherbeaten face, a natural pose vouched for, I am sure, by all who remember this greatly talented yet modest man.

Arthur Rosie Ploughing with Oxen c.1945

Arthur is ploughing with two oxen on a dry spring day with a cold north east wind and accompanying overcast sky. Hoy shows up faintly in the background and there is a slight motion in the sea around the shore.

The oxen are harnessed in the same way as horses except, as they "chew the cud", they did not have a bridle with a "bit" in their mouths. A bridle with a hinge over the nose and a chain under the jaw was sufficient to control the ox.

An ox, it is said, was of a more placid nature than a horse and certainly this pair seem to be peacefully plodding on in a determined fashion. They are not being led and are making a first class job as can be seen from the straight furrows. As was often the case in former times, this field has been manured with "waur" (seaweed) taken from the low shore on the right. The soil dried by the northerly wind has given a silver sheen to the plough "board". The side or pulling chains are attached to two pieces of shaped hardwood (haimes). The collar made from straw covered with sacking or canvas was soft against the animal's skin and prevented the haimes chaffing. The reins are being held at the stilts by Arthur while the side chains attached to the ammels bear the full strain.

I reckon, this harness being carefully maintained would have been well over a hundred years old when this photo was taken. Such methods of cultivation are now but a memory of the past.

(Earlier on a fine summer's day the sheriff, procurator fiscal and the chief constable visited Swona. It was normal practice to name calves after visitors, so these oxen were called "The Sheriff" and "The Fiscal" and a cow was "Chief Constable Tulloch"!)

Swona Carts

The Swona people used four wheeled carts. They were pulled by two oxen using side chains and ammels, and as they did not have shafts it meant there was no weight on the ox back. The iron-shod wheels were about two feet in diameter and looked like two barrel lids bolted together with the wood running opposite ways. The bushes were made of cast iron in the Wick foundry. There is a ridge of very good smooth blue slate which runs through Stroma, through Swona and the Barth Head and many is the time James Rosie would take a heavy load of these slate down to the Haven for folk in South Ronaldsay.

James Rosie at the helm.

This photo was taken in the "Falcon" at a regatta, and he is on the point of changing course to the port side without easing speed. You can see too, the outstanding integrity of the man, the firmness of resolve and the complete confidence in his own ability to carry out the task he had undertaken. James hated swearing and although he only saw with one eye, was King of the Pentland Firth.

Landmark

The round pillar at the North End was built as a landmark and navigational point by the survey ship "Triton". It is about six feet in diameter and seven feet high. (Mention of a pillar by George Low in Orkney and Schetland in 1774.)

The "Gunnaren"

The "Gunnaren" ran ashore near the Selki Skerry on the west side of Swona in dense fog on 20th August, 1935. An officer with some crew members who came ashore in their own lifeboat were met by James Rosie who could tell them that they were not ashore on Stroma, that they had no chance of leaving with the next high tide, and that they had to get all the men off at once. James had already sent for the Longhope Lifeboat which then took off the crew and the mails. Waves 20 feet high broke over the vessel with the first of the flood and apples, oranges, packets of cigarettes, timber and wreckage were floating everywhere. There were no lives lost. I was with Orkney, Swona and Stroma boatmen who assisted tugs to salvage most of the cargo.

In the top picture the Swedish motor vessel lies forlorn, a "dead" ship, rhythmic heart beat of engine forever stilled. No sparkling wave spreads outwards from bows that once ploughed through their natural element, motionless she rests awaiting an inevitable fate. Only five years before, cheers of wellwishers had rung out as the vessel slid smoothly down the "ways" at Gotaverken shipyard in 1930. One can imagine the sadness felt by her personnel, when, after safely crossing the Atlantic from New York with a full general cargo, their homeward voyage ended abruptly on Swona with but a few days to reach the home port, Gothenburg.

Time had been too short to arrest headway using anchors or engine movements, now, too late the fog has cleared leaving M.V. "Gunnaren" hard and fast, listing slightly to starboard with derricks "topped" for discharge of cargo in a vain attempt to lighten ship. A tug close by, optimistically hopes to free the stranded vessel while reasonably favourable weather conditions prevail.

"Metal Industries of Lyness" cut the vessel into two parts using oxy-acetylene burners which just took about four hours. The aim had been to tow each section clear but an increasing westerly swell put paid to their efforts and the freed stern-half drifted half a mile further east before grounding yet again. We see, captured by the camera, this portion being buffeted by "land sea" from the west though the flying spray indicates wind from a south east direction. The rudder and propeller have been removed but the blue-topped, buff funnel of Rederi Transatlantik remains, as does the main mast with derricks lowered for the last time.

The "Gunnaren"

Stern section of "Gunnaren"

Swona Threshing Mill

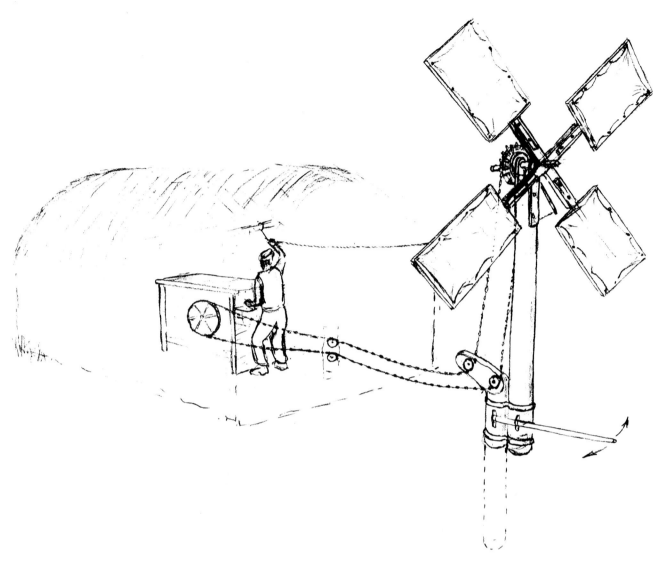

The threshing mills in South Ronaldsay and Swona were made by Wm. Petrie, joiner and millwright from Quindry, near Roeberry, S.R. The Petries were a very clever family who made spinning wheels and furniture besides threshing mills, carts and cartwheels, etc.

The Swona mill was really an improvement on the usual handmill and there was no iron foundry in Orkney. The castings came from either Bruce in Wick or McKidd in Thurso.

The directional windmill consisted of four canvas sails which could be reefed to suit the strength of the wind. The mast was fixed to the stump with iron bands by means of an iron rod. The mast could be rotated to match the direction of the wind. The threshing mill was driven by a chain through two sets of idling pulleys as shown. A hinged brake band on the centre solid pulley could be applied by the man feeding the mill, to stop the windmill when required.

When I was a boy at the end of the First War, I've seen and heard as many as 12 wind threshing mills working on a breezy morning in Sandwick.

An Islander's Dirge
(with warm thoughts of Eva)

Leave me alone in my island home
It's the place where I want to stay
I've no mountains to climb, no cities to see
The swirling tides and the song of the wind
Are more than enough for me.

Alex T. Annal, Myers, South Ronaldsay.

SWONA MINOR LIGHT

"Detailed on-site examination showed that the existing tower was occasionally struck by large boulders washed off the beach and it was decided that the E.R.P. tower would not be sufficiently rigid to withstand such action.

A change of plan was therefore required and a concrete column has now been erected with a reinforced platform on top. This platform will be used to mount the new electrical light with its associated battery boxes."

Courtesy, Northern Lighthouse Journal, 1983.

SWONA

There were 21 people on the island c.1900 and the younger men built good houses before they left. There was one two-storey house and another two very good houses with steadings. There were five crofts with fair good ground. They were given to the sowing of bere and the making of strong ale.

They were very kind to the Stroma people and when they visited them about New Year a favourite drink was the ale mixed with whisky. The women sometimes hid the rudder of the boat to delay them getting home, and all were so delighted with the company. They were a worthy class of people and full of antics.

They were grand cod fishers and so well up to the handlines at Aithe Hope (few places you could know so well up to the handlines as Aithe Hope). If they fell in with a spot of fish they had a practice of waving the other boat over. They tied the two boats, one a penter-length ahead of the other, and with little wind one man with oars could hold the two boats. The more fish they hauled, the more fish vomiting gathered more fish, so that move showed a friendly mind to work together.

They were an inventive people of great genius and I tell you it took some planning and contrivances for three men and one woman to launch and haul their largest boat. The "Hood" was a four ton cargo boat.

They never used horses on Swona but trained oxen. They fed and sold them and trained again. They have a tractor now and it is not for a shortage of money if they do not have any appliance that they need.

The island has had a long spell without wrecks. About 60 years ago (1900) the "Croma" Leith took the tide at the North Tails of Stroma, and either the steering gear jammed or broke, because her bow was fixed on course and she took the tide and went straight across to Swona at the patch west of the Clett and became a total wreck. She was gutted out, helping the islanders to all the good things to be got in labour boating.

The "Johanna Thorden" went on close to the Lighthouse on this side of the Tarf and sadly many of the crew were lost. If the ship went on at full speed there would have been an awful impact, but the Swona men did not know she was there. It looked as if the launching of the boats was done immediately and they got launched alright but did not know what to do. The wind was from the south east and after a gale the Swona men might have encouraged them to anchor in the lee of the ship until the flood eased and they could get round the Tarf. The pressure of the tide might have forced them to leave at once and it is a common rule for seamen, when launched in safety to take to sea and head out clear of land if no landing is seen to be available. This they did and nobody can tell if they went to the north of the Skerries or south of the Little Skerry but in either case heavy seas would be encountered.

The Captain's boat was first to leave and would chance to be further out in more grip of the tide. The mate had an injured seaman with him who was acquaint with sailing ships and boats. He took charge and set the sail and they ran before it north. This helped them to come in sight of the Orkney land and when the visibility got better they watched for a sand creek and then ran the boat high and dry ashore and saved the crew. The Captain's boat came ashore away north of this but there were no survivors.

From "History of the Island in the Pentland Firth", by Donald Banks, Bard of Stroma.

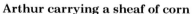

Arthur carrying a sheaf of corn

The Swona School

CANISBAY

Canisbay School 1921

Photo, Mary Sinclair, Hillside, Gills. – Names from Dan MacLeod, Mary Sinclair and Nancy Meiklejohn.
Teachers:– Mr Frank Taylor and Miss Elsie Shearer. Back Row, left to right:– Elsie Shearer, Lower Warse; Mary Gibson, Hillside, Gills; Lil Stewart, Braes of Gills; Ivy Lee, Huna; Joe Smith, Huna; Andrew Sinclair, Huna; Alex MacDonald, Upper Warse; Will Banks, Lower Gills; Jimmy Rosie, Upper Warse; Dan McLeod, Warse Farm; Nell Ann Stewart, Braes of Gills; Frank Taylor, Post Office. Second Back Row:– Marybelle Mackay, Hillside, Gills; Alex Rosie, Upper Warse; Alex Gibson, Hillside, Gills; Will Dunnet, Huna; John Sutherland, Huna; David Dunnet, The Cottage, Canisbay; Will Gibson, Hillside, Gills; Jim Sutherland, Huna; Jack Ross, Albyn, Gills. Third Row:– Julia Taylor, Post Office; Isobel MacDonald, Upper Warse; Nancy Gibson, Hillside, Gills; Winnie Dunnet, The Cottage; Mina Kennedy, Tresdale; Jamesina Miller, Seater; Teeta Dunnet, West Canisbay; Mary Sinclair, Huna; Sheila Ross, "Albyn". Front Row:– Lena Rosie, Upper Warse; Edna Sinclair, Upper Gills; Nell Sinclair, Huna; John Banks, Lower Gills; Jamsie Dunnett, Lower Gills; Jess Mackay, Hillside Gills; Nellie Ross, Albyn, John Rosie, Upper Warse.

Canisbay School

Photo, Mary Sinclair, Hillside, Gills.

LEST WE FORGET

Canisbay School 1926

Photo, Charlie Manson, Canisbay Post Office.

Back Row, left to right:– Willie Leith, Warse; Harry Dunnett, Lower Gills; Jimmy Johnstone, Upper Gills; James Dunnett, Lower Gills; James Rosie, Upper Warse; Alex John McDonald, Upper Warse; Jack Ross, Upper Warse; John Banks, Lower Gills; Sandy Rosie, Upper Warse; Dan McLeod, Warse Farm. Front Row:– Lena Rosie, Upper Warse; Nellie Sinclair, Huna; Bertha Fermor, Huna; Nellie Stewart, Lower Gills; Mary Mackay, Hillside; Isobel McDonald, Upper Warse; Jessie Mackay, Hillside; Julia Taylor, Post Office.

Canisbay School 1936

Photo, Laurence Brown, The North House, John O'Groats.

Back Row, left to right:– Mr Hugh McColl; Clair Leith, Lower Warse; David Shearer, Upper Gills; Jim Shearer, Seater; David Nicolson, Seater; John Nicolson, Seater; Billy Stewart, Lower Gills; Laurence Brown, New Houses; Donnie MacLeod, Huna. Third Row:– Nancy Douglas, Huna House; Betty Dunnett, Victoria Villa; Margaret Lee, Huna; Bina Geddes, Upper Gills; Joey Leith, Lower Warse; Nellie Mackay, Kirkstyle. Second Row:– Nellie Mathieson, Gills; Stella Geddes, Gills; Ruby Douglas, Huna House; Aldie Mathieson, Gills; Ella Henderson, Shepherd's Cottage; Violet Shearer, Seater; Irene Sinclair, Upper Gills; Jessie Mackay, Kirkstyle. Front Row:– Jack Dunnett, Victoria Villa; Walter Rosie, Huna; Peter Douglas, Huna House; Nancy MacLeod, Huna; Jennie Bremner, Canisbay; Betty Geddes, Gills; Hamish Manson, Tresdale; Billy Dunnett, Gills.

CANISBAY

Canisbay School 1947

Teachers:– Miss Mollie Simpson, Miss Beth Shearer. Back Row, left to right:– Sandy Banks, Back Road; John McIntyre, Newton (minister's son); Christina Shearer, Seater; Winnie Mowat, The Shop, Canisbay; Annie Alexander, West Canisbay; Nellie Dunnett, Lower Gills; Peggy Shearer, Seater; Nancy Robertson, Huna; Nellie McGregor, Newton; Jenny Sinclair, Hillside, Gills; Margaret Dunnet, St Clair Cottage, Huna; Hamish Donn, Orcadia; Willie Mathieson, Lower Gills. Middle Row:– Gordon Gill, Pentland View; Frank McGregor, Newton; Davie Shearer, Seater; Charlie Manson, Canisbay; Percy Fermor, Huna; Colin Mackay, Lower Gills; Danny Banks, New Houses; James Dunnett, Hillside, Gills; Willie Dunnet, St Clair Cottage, Huna; Jack Sinclair, Hillside, Gills; Ian Banks, Back Road; Hamish McLeod, Warse; Angus Banks, New Houses. Front Row:– Betty Spence, New Houses; Catherine Banks, New Houses; Christine Banks, New Houses; Dinah Manson, Lower Gills; Anne Banks, Back Road; Helen McLaren, Smiddy House.

Canisbay School 1954

Teachers:– Miss Molly Simpson, Miss Elsie Houston. Back Row, left to right:– Sheena Johnstone, Newton; Elizabeth Sinclair, Braes of Gills; Billy Cormack, Huna House; Alexander MacGregor, Newton; Alistair Cormack, Post Office, Huna; James Magee, New Houses; Hugh Ross, Upper Gills; Isobel Cormack, Kirkstyle; Nellie Cormack, Huna House. Third Row:– Anne Fraser, Church Hall House, Sheena Green, Roadside Gills; Isobel Sinclair, Hillside, Gills; Joyce Dunnet, Quoys; Isobel Mathieson, Lower Gills; Jean Short, New Houses; Margaret Fraser Church Hall House; Ethel Banks, Back Road, Gills; Valerie Bremner, Seater. Second Row:– David Kennedy, Tresdale; David Green, Roadside, Gills; John Gill, Pentland View; John Green, Roadside, Gills; Miss Elsie Houston, The Ha', John O'Groats; Miss Molly Simpson, Schoolhouse; William Manson, Lower Gills; David Dunnett, West Canisbay; Ian Fraser, Church Hall House; John Cormack, Huna House. Front Row:– James Cormack, Huna House; Gordon Shearer, Seater; Elizabeth Sinclair, Hillside, Gills; Alistair Manson, Lower Gills; Clara Fraser, Church Hall House; Ian Magee, New Houses; Michael Rosie, New Houses.

Canisbay School (The Big Room) 1962

Photo, Sutherland Manson, 6 Bower Court, Thurso.

Back Row, left to right:- Ian Fraser, Cairnlee; William Manson, Lower Gills; David Dunnet, Quoys; William Magee, New Houses; Sandy Cormack, Huna; John Gill, Pentland View; David Kennedy, Tresdale. Front Row:- Isobel Sinclair, Hillside; Elna Banks, New Houses; Flora Johnstone, Newton; Isobel Shearer, Seater; Sally Rosie, New Houses; Miss Molly Simpson, Schoolhouse; Dinah Manson, Lower Gills; Anne Banks, Back Road; Isobel Mathieson, Lower Gills; Joyce Dunnet Quoys, Margaret Fraser, Cairnlee.

Canisbay School (The Peedie Room) 1962

Photo, Janet Gunn, Emohruo, Mey.

Back Row, left to right:- Margaret Cormack, Huna House; John MacDonald, New Houses; Tommy Magee, New Houses; Donnie Cormack, Huna House; Marjory Dundas, Warse; Sandra Moar, Quoyawa, Huna. Middle Row:- James Dunnett, Hillside, Gills; Clarence Fraser, Cairnlee; Mrs Janet Gunn; Jimmy Moar, Quoyawa; David MacDonald, New Houses, Donnie Dundas, Warse. Front Row:- George Gulloch, Stemster; Edward MacDonald, New Houses, Alan MacLeod, Gills.

The Big Room Canisbay School 1972

Photo, Janet Gunn, Emohruo, Mey.

Back Row, left to right:– Michael Ross, Upper Gills; James Dunnet, Seater; Denver Banks, Sea Crest; Ricky Banks; Sea Crest; Stephen Ross, New Houses; Alistair Gunn, West Canisbay; Mrs Janet Gunn. Middle Row:– James Gulloch, Seater; John Shearer, Upper Gills; Christopher Keay, Huna; Richard Keay, Huna; Hamish Bremner, Victoria Villa; John Farquhar, Croft Road; George Shearer, Brabster. Front Row:– Elizabeth Dundas, Stroma View; Kathleen Mathieson, Lower Gills; Marion Magee, Lower Gills; Ruth Cormack, Huna House; Violet Leitch, East Canisbay; Alison Dunnett, Lower Gills; Louisa MacDonald, New Houses.

The Peedie Room Canisbay School 1972

Photo, Janet Gunn, Emohruo, Mey.

Back Row, left to right:– Mrs Elsie Cowe, The Ha'; Alan Dundas, Warse; Lesley Ross, Upper Gills; John L. Cormack, New Houses; William Cormack, New Houses; John Dunnet, Lower Warse; John Wm. Cormack, Huna; David Keay, Huna; John Keay, Huna. Middle Row:– Sandy Shearer, Brabster; William Magee, Lower Gills; Helen Mathieson, Lower Gills; Lorna Shearer, Brabster; Caroline Gulloch, Seater; Christine Simpson, Burnside; Alan Green, Burnside; Matthew Dundas, Stroma View. Front Row:– Carol Magee, Lower Gills; Irene Ross, Upper Gills; Anne Dunnet, Seater; Fiona Bremner, Victoria Villa; Margo Gunn, West Canisbay; Isobel Farquhar Hillside House; Kirsten Shearer, Brabster.

Canisbay School September 1979

Photo, Sina Houston, The Mill, John O'Groats.

Back Row, left to right:– Steven Mowat, Victoria House; William Dunnett, Lower Gills; Calum Kennedy, Tresdale; Marsaili MacLeod, John O'Groats House Hotel; J.O.G.; Barbara Mathieson, Lower Gills; Campbell Drummond, (District Nurses's son); Margo Gunn, West Canisbay; Eric Green, Heatherbell Cottages, J.O.G.; Fiona Bremner, Victoria Villa; Iain Smith, Lighthouse; Wilma Green, Huna; Shirley Magee, Lower Gills; Jennifer Cormack, J.O.G.; Stefan Ward, Brabster. Fourth Row:– Alan Dundas, Warse; John Pyle, St Ronans; Janet Houston, Mill House; David Shearer, Brabster; John Dunnet, Lower Warse; Catherine Green, Upper Gills; Ellie Cormack, Huna; Laura Steven, St Rowan, J.O.G.. Third Row:– Mrs B. Brown, Newton, J.O.G.; Isobel Simpson, Freswick; Marie Shearer, Seater; Anne Steven, St Rowan, J.O.G.; Alison Cormack, Huna; Anne Shearer, Seater; Susan Flockhart, Croft Road, Huna; Kenneth Miller, Mansefield Cottages; Bruce Cormack, Huna; Anne-Shirley Mowat, Roadside, J.O.G. David Dunnett, Lower Warse; Dawn Cormack, Huna; Mary Ritchie, Huna. Second Row:– William Steven, St Rowan, J.O.G.; Anne-Louise Drummond, Halkirk; Graeme Dundas, Huna; Kevin Shearer, Upper Gills; Sandra Manson, J.O.G. Post Office; James Cormack, Huna; Lynda Angus, Freswick; Calum Green, Heatherbell Cottages, J.O.G.; Sandy Bremner, Freswick; Karen Miller, Mansefield Cottages; Sandy Cormack, Huna; Ann-Marie Dunnett, Lower Warse; Gary Sinclair, Gills. Front Row:– Donald Shearer, Seater; Andy Flockhart, Croft Road, Huna; Wilma Banks, Gills; Bronwyn Drummond, Mrs C. Shearer, Brabster; Mrs E. Cowe (and "Sporran"), The Ha, J.O.G.; Alan Cormack, Huna; Aileen Smith, Lighthouse; Joe Ward, Brabster; William Miller, Mansefield Cottages, Sandy Mowat, Roadside, J.O.G.

Canisbay School 1986

Photo, Sina Houston, Mill House, John O'Groats.

Back Row:- Mrs Morna Wilson; Mrs Christine Shearer, Brabster; Mrs Elsie Cowe, The Ha; Andrew Mowat, Balquholly; Maree Steven, Caberfeidh; Anne Houston, Mill House; John Banks, The Broo; Gavin Mowat, Heatherbell Cottages; James Mathieson, Lower Gills; Dave Kennedy, Tresdale, Susan Munro, Harley; Lindsay Inglis, Skirza; Graham Muir, The Manse; Miss Jessie Coghill, Keiss (cook); Mrs Dot Cormack, Huna. Third Row:- Tanya Banks, Rowena; Michael Green, Burnside, Gills; Maureen Bruce, Bellevue; Derek Munro, Roadside, Huna; Melanie Harper, Heatherbell Cottages; Alexander Manson, J.O.G. Post Office; Alex Ross, White Broo; Paula Honeyman, Schoolhouse, J.O.G.; Alan Campbell, Heatherbell Cottages; Donna Flockhart, Croft Road, George Green, Roadside, Gills; Marie Ross, White Broo. Second Row:- Janet Honeyman, Schoolhouse, J.O.G.; William Ross, White Broo; Catherine Mowat, Balquholly; Danny Miller, Mansefield Cottages; Robert Inglis, Skirza; Alex Rosie, The Broo; Gary Munro, Roadside Huna; Michelle Harper, Heatherbell Cottages; Liam Simpson, Larkway; Fiona MacKenzie, Quarryside, J.O.G.; Front Row:- James Banks, The Broo; Holly Robinson, Skirza House; Toby Renouf, Skirza; Andrea Sinclair, Pentland View, J.O.G.; Tracy Banks, Rowena; Bryony Robinson, Skirza House; John Banks, Back Road; Kevin Banks, Back Road; Caroline Connor, Lighthouse; Kirsten Brown, Swartigill; Susan MacKenzie, Quarryside; Jodie Bremner, Heatherbell Cottages; Ruth Flockhart, Croft Road; Lorraine Fraser, Heatherbell Cottages; Debbie Fraser, Heatherbell Cottages.

Canisbay School September 1990

Photo, Christine Shearer, Brabster.

Back Row:– Mrs Linda Brown, Swartigill, J.O.G.; Helen Inglis, The Shop, Skirza; Stuart Sinclair, Pentland View, J.O.G.; Susan MacKenzie, Quarryside, J.O.G.; Michael James Green, Burnside Cottage, Gills; Catherine Mowat, Balquholly, J.O.G.; Derek Munro, Roadside Huna; Tanya Banks, Rowena, J.O.G.; George Green, Roadside, Gills; Tracy Banks, Rowena, J.O.G.; Robert Inglis, The Shop, Skirza; Fiona MacKenzie, Quarryside, J.O.G.; Liam Simpson, Larkway, Gills; Janet Honeyman, Schoolhouse, J.O.G.; Mrs Lena Simpson, Burnside, Gills. Second Row:– Mark Munro, Roadside, Huna; Jodie Bremner, Heatherbell Cottages; Nicola Muir, Newton, J.O.G.; Kevin Banks, Gills; Kirsten Brown, Swartigill, J.O.G.; William Ross, White Broo; Karen Green, Roadside, Gills; Gary Munro, Roadside, Huna; Holly Robinson, Skirza House, John Banks, Gills; Ruth Flockhart, Sunray Cottage, Croft Road; Andrea Sinclair, Pentland View, J.O.G.; Christopher Green, Roadside Gills. Third Row:– Mrs Christine Shearer, Brabster; Laura Brown, Swartigill, J.O.G.; Brian Fraser, Heatherbell Cottages; Nicola Coghill, Croft Road, Huna; Andrew Manson, Gills; Sarah Ross, White Broo; Alistair Muir, The Manse; Jenna Banks, Rowena, J.O.G.; Iain Rosie, Heatherbell Cottages; Kerry Shearer, Mansefield Cottages; David Mowat, Balquholly, J.O.G.; Lorraine Fraser, Heatherbell Cottages; Shane Harper, Heatherbell Cottages; Leanne Simpson, Larkway, Gills; Callum Shearer, Mansefield Cottages; Mrs Elsie Cowe, The Ha, J.O.G. Front Row:– Julie Anne Mowat, Heatherbell Cottages, J.O.G.; John MacLeod, Mansefield Cottages; Lindsay Henderson, Upper Gills; William Fraser, St Leonards; Debbie Fraser, Heatherbell Cottages; Greg Muir, Newton, J.O.G.; Susan Mackay, Ceol-na-Mara, J.O.G.; Marie Anne Fraser, St Leonards; Sandy Ham, Sonsiquoy; Dawn Rosie, Heatherbell Cottages; Bobby Manson, Gills; Kara Sutherland, Sunray, J.O.G.; Bryden Mackay, Ceol-na-Mara, J.O.G.. Absent:– Bryony Robinson, Skirza House.

Childrens Game:

Throwing and Catching Ball
Against a Wall

1. Plainy: Throw ball catch with both hands.

2. Clappy: Throw ball, clap hands at front, catch ball.

3. Roll a Boll: Throw ball, roll hands round one another at front, catch ball.

4. 'T Backy: Throw ball, clap hands at back, catch ball.

5. Right Hand: Throw and catch ball with right hand only.

6. Left Hand: Throw and catch ball with left hand only.

7. Through It Goes: Throw ball through raised right leg, catch ball.

8. Through It Goes: Throw ball through raised left leg, catch ball.

9. Heely: Throw ball touch right heel, catch ball.

10. Toey: Throw ball, touch right toe, catch ball.

11. Heely: Throw ball, touch left heel, catch ball.

12. Toey: Throw ball, touch left toe, catch ball.

13. Double Clap: Throw ball, clap above, below and above raised right knee, catch ball.

14. Double Clap: Throw ball, clap above, below and above raised left knee, catch ball.

15. Touch the Ground: Throw ball, touch ground, catch ball.

16. Turn Around: Throw ball, turn right round, catch ball.

Elizabeth Gates, Hillside, Gills.

Mrs Bells' Version:–

Plainy, clappy, rolly, backy,
Under-leggy, Whalesmouth,
Eskatoosh – Dab! Dab! Dab!

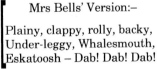

Canisbay WRI Picnic c.1927

Daniel Mowatt's photo from John Dunnet, Seater.

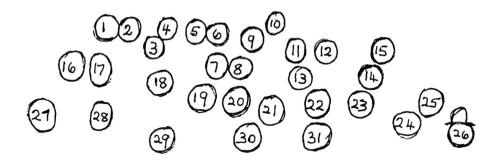

1, Bella Dunnet, Seater (Mrs Wm. Cummings); 2, William Dunnett, Seater; 3, Mrs Ross, Albyn; 4, Jesssie Kennedy, Tresdale (Mrs Wm. Dunnett); 5, William MacRae, Broo, J.O.G.; 6, Jessie Sutherland, Huna Post Office; 7, John Gunn, Brabster; 8, Mackie Dunnet, Ha of Gills; 9, Maggie Kennedy, Tresdale; 10, Jack Manson, Seater (home on holiday); 11, Mary Dunnet, Quoys (Mrs G. Green); 12, Cathie Manson, Seater (Mrs J. Shearer); 13, Jimmy Miller, Seater (Mrs B. Gualt); 14, Mina Kennedy, Tresdale (Mrs N. Campbell); 15, Donald Dunnet, Quoys; 16, Alex Kennedy,Tresdale; 17, Lil Stewart, Lower Gills (Mrs Wm. Banks); 18, Marybelle Mackay, Hillside (Mrs G. Sinclair); 19 Jessie Mackay, Hillside (Mrs I. Gray); 20, Jessie Banks, Lower Gills; 21, Katie Banks, Lower Gills (Mrs Wm. Allan); 22, Maggie Dunnet, Quoys; 23, Liz Calder, Teacher (Mrs Mackie); 24, George Manson, Post Office; 25, Davie Shearer, Upper Warse; 26, Peter Banks, Lower Gills; 27, Willie Banks, Gills; 28, Bob Lyall, Brabster; 29, Sandy Lyall, Brabster; 30, Hugh Lyall, Brabster; 31, Danny Banks, Gills.

CANISBAY WRI 1918-1972

The Canisbay WRI really started as a working party during the First World War. They knitted socks, balaclavas, gloves etc., and sent them to the boys serving in the forces.

After the war finished, these ladies started the first Canisbay WRI in November 1918. The first office bearers were as follows:– President: Mrs Slater; vice-president, Mrs Forbes; secretary, Miss J. Sutherland; treasurer, Miss J. Kennedy. Committee: Misses V. Houston, B. Nicolson, L. Dunnett, J. Shearer, C. Banks and M. Dunnett. The annual subscription was two shillings (10 pence!). There were certain rules which they had to promise to carry out, and one of these was to attend the meetings regularly.

Of course, there were no cars in those days, and many of the members had to walk or cycle over three miles to the meetings. At the first meeting they made a syllabus for December to May. The December meeting was a Soiree and Christmas Tree for the children, and the motto was "The World Marches Forward on the Feet of Little Children".

All the meetings and social events were held in the Canisbay school, which at that time contained a "Big Room" for the senior pupils and a "Peedie Room" for the infants. The big room was where they held the concerts and dances. Many a good night was had dancing to a fiddler or a "boxie" (accordion). There was a Burns night every year, when the local artistes put on a splendid programme and the ladies of the WRI served up a grand supper, all cooked on the black stove in the peedie room.

During the Second World War the WRI again rallied round by knitting for the troops. I remember one night during the war, when we came out from our meeting, the first we heard was the zoom of a jerry plane. That was the night they tried to bomb the defenceless harbours in the Pentland Firth. My friend and I jumped on our bikes, and I am sure we set up a new record for the distance from Canisbay to Hillside, Gills, as we pedalled along even up and down the Gills braes and arrived home with our breath on our lips.

The WRI always had a tent at the local Agricultural Show. There was great competition in the baking and handicrafts, which were of a very high standard, and they even won prizes in the handicraft section at the Royal Highland Show. There were many more classes and entries in the produce section than there are now at the County Show. Of course in those days, every croft had its own milking cow, and kept hens and ducks. No doubt the Butter Making class held in July 1922 in the Canisbay School helped to produce the lovely butter and cheese for the show. The lecturer at that class was Mrs Penny, and it was run by the North of Scotland College of Agriculture.

The WRI celebrated their Golden Jubilee in the Seaview Hotel, John O'Groats, and I am sure that for all who attended that special occasion it was a night they would always remember.

I still have the photograph of two founder members, Mrs J. Dunnett and Nurse Cook, cutting the Birthday Cake which was donated by Mrs Dunnett.

Once the Canisbay Public Hall was opened, all social functions were held there, but the WRI continued to hold their meetings in the school until the membership declined to such a low number that it was an embarrassment to ask a speaker or demonstrator to come to address us, and sadly we decided to finish up this long-standing organisation.

Mrs Mary Sinclair, Hillside, Gills.

RECOLLECTIONS OF CANISBAY AND GILLS

My very early life was dominated by the black-out and food rationing brought on by the Second World War. We watched "tracer" flares going up over Scapa Flow when there was a fear of German bombers. I remember running to the house for cover when occasionally, enemy planes flew overhead and then searching in the field and finding a spent shell. We watched the "Ships of War" going through the Firth and also one of the "Queens".

On the croft, food was not the problem it was in towns, because there were eggs, milk, butter and vegetables. There were plenty of rabbits, the occasional hen and, although against the law, some times a sheep got killed! There were no deliveries of milk by the Milk Marketing Board. The crofters used to sell milk to people who did not have a cow and the price was two old pence for a whisky bottleful. A shilling was paid on Saturday morning and Sunday's milk was always given free. Skimmed milk was known as baking milk – it was also given away free.

There were no school dinners either. A big black kettle was set on the stand on the open fire to boil. We got a tin mug of cocoa and brought our own pieces. After the war, school dinners were cooked in Keiss and delivered to Canisbay. They were two course meals and cost five pence, four pence or three pence in old money.

The new government after the war thought that bairns would be run down after food rationing and shortages, so each child got a free third of a pint of milk and also one free tablespoon of cod liver oil daily . . . ugh!

The morning break or peedie play lasted about 20 minutes and we usually went to Taylor's shop (Charlie's now) for a cookie. The games we played were football, dogs and rabbits and rounders. War games were frowned upon and woe betide you if you were caught at that.

Starting school at Canisbay meant a three mile walk, each way every day, rain, hail or shine (no school transport). There used to be a big hole of water at the end of the school, and on days of rain we used to walk through it to get our feet wet in the hope of being sent home. – No such luck! The teacher used to haul the big armchair to the front of the roaring fire and we had to sit there until we got our feet dried!

"Sand Lorries" carting lime sand from John O'Groats shore for spreading on the fields were steady on the roads, and as many as a dozen lorries could be seen leaving the sand plant near the "Ness". It was every schoolboy's dream to drive one of these tipping lorries. We aye marvelled at the speed they went at on the return journeys.

After the war the new road was constructed

through the braes of Gills. It was the first track laying digger that had been seen in Canisbay and all were fascinated by the weird and wonderful assortment of wire ropes and pulleys that worked the digging bucket.

More grocery vans began to appear on the roads and they carried a wide range of goods other than foodstuffs. A 45 gallon drum of lamp-oil on the front – roof-rack laden with egg boxes – bags of feeding stuff on the mudguards. They also collected wireless batteries (two volt accumulators) for charging at a cost of two pence old money, took them away one week and back the next. It was fortunate for van owners that there was no MOT! More and more mobile shops appeared and spelled

the death knell of small local shops. One shopkeeper called them "Damn trawlers poaching our trade". At one time a dozen vans could be counted on the road over the week but now like the small shops, they too have fallen victim of the big chain stores in town.

The Firth has changed too. We used to see Stroma boats at their creels in summer and at the line fishing in winter. They would also be crossing to Huna for mails and supplies. In winter they often called at Gills when landings were impossible at Huna. In very stormy weather the Wick or Thurso lifeboat could be called out to take the doctor to Stroma in an emergency. Morse signals were used before they had wireless or telephone.

Anon.

Coxswain's Collection

A bonnie lassie and a good peat stack at Tresdale

Betty Dunnett, Victoria Villa.

Setting up Peats on the Freswick side of the Shepherds c.1932

Back: David Cummings, Maggie Muir née Dunnet.
Front: Jessie Dunnett, Bella Cummings née Dunnet.

Feeding the Calves

Arthur Marshall and Jimmy Miller behind the girl with pail.

Heading the Screw

Dannie Nicolson on the screw with Beel Bremner, forking.
Photos, John Dunnet, Seater.

SEATER

Everyone has a favourite place for remembering and at Seater we stand at the end of the house and have the wide view over Gills, Huna, the Firth, Stroma and beyond. We stand there on a fine night and there is time for listening and going over old yarns and remembering the folk before us who had done the very same things.

So many memories flood in of the pier, lifeboat, smiddy and especially the folk. The fishermen considered it unlucky to go down to the "slip" between the smiddy and the lifeboat shed – one had to go round the north end of the lifeboat shed to get a good "tide of fish". It was really to check the "weather glass" or barometer (screwed on to the north wall) that took the men round that way, now the barometer is gone but that is still the way to go.

Fishermen did not like meeting certain people on their way to the sea and if they met someone who was a "bad feet" some would turn and go home, so convinced were they that they wouldn't catch a thing. The minister was considered an especially bad foot and if he was standing on the brae it wasn't worth hauling creels! It was bad luck to see a hare, cat or pig on their way to the sea, and if one saw a crow or a raven it was ominous. "Cold iron" covered words like salmon, silkies, pigs and ham and there were other words that never should be said in a boat – above all, no whistling or dire trouble could be expected. No Canisbay fisherman, would turn his boat against the sun.

The moon too was important and they took good care when they first saw the new moon, not to see it through glass and at the same time had money in their pocket to turn over. Planting potatoes, starting the harvest and killing the pig were best done with a waxing moon. Spitting on money brought luck. People spat on their hands before shaking them to clinch an agreement. I am not sure if it is for luck, or to give a better grip that one spits on the hands before starting a difficult manipulative job.

The end kitchen window was the stance to take when it was cold and wet, and much of what was going on at Huna could be fathomed out – whose carts were at the smiddy – smoke signals to Stroma from the "rickan hillag". The glass (telescope) was aye kept handy to pick out the names of the boats smoking through the "Soon". (Smoke belching from coal fired boilers could be seen long before the boats.)

Earlier than this, my grandfather Hugh Green

John Dunnet (Coxswain) and John Nicolson

Isabella Miller (Coxswain's wife) c.1933

The water tank is a ventilator (off a steamer) which has had the end cemented up and is laid on its side.

Sleeves rolled up for washday action

Margaret and John Dunnet, Greenock.

from the Biel used to remark on the vast amount of "spunks and tobacco" he saw going through the Firth on a Monday morning when he was at "The Rock". This was in the days when there would be many big ferthies going through, each with maybe nine of a crew.

It should be remembered too there was no Sunday fishing. Creels were not put out until about May, when the ploughing and sowing was done and they were lifted again about September when the harvest had to be secured.

There was so much weather-lore too:

"St Swithin's Day if it be fair
For forty days it will rain nae mair

But if St Swithin's Day be wet
For forty days it raineth yet."
(St Swithin's day – July 15.)

"A misty May and a dripping June
Never left Canisbay teem."
(Good growing weather.)

"A silken Sunday makes a canvas week."
(A sunny Sunday means a wet week.)

"What Friday gets she keeps."
(Weather remains same all day.)

"A kep (cap) on Hoy is a sure sign of rain."
John Dunnet, Seater.

"HIM WI' THE CURLY TAIL"

Mzuri Sana

Photo, Dundas, Warse.
Donnie and Alan Dundas.

When William Banks from Stroma lived here this was two houses. John Dunnet (Tailor John) lived in the one at the west end and Will Banks stayed with his sister-in-law Betty Sinclair in the other one. Will (nephew of Dan Banks, boatbuilder) was a good hand at repairing boats. He had the "Mizpah", a boat he had bought from Donald Mowat, John O'Groats, which had been built for Donald by his cousin Donald Muir, Leith when he was working at the construction of Duncansby Head Lighthouse.

Will had the "Mizpah" at the back of the house to get some repairs done when Will Cormack's old sow and grices got out. Now there is nothing a pig loves better than a right good "claw" and she clawed herself on Will Bank's boat. Pigs and boats do NOT go together and when afloat a pig was referred to as "him with the curly tail". What could be more vexing than a "her wi' the curly tail" and a whole lot of peedie curly tails clawing and scraping themselves on his boat? Many would sympathise with him to this day when he lost heart and gave up on the repairs because he knew he could never risk putting her in the water again.

Will sold the boat to Col. William Gulloch, Freswick, who renamed her Mzuri Sana which means new life.

The next owner was Donnie Dundas, Warse, who got her renovated by Johnnie Moar, Huna.

Some might reckon she is still not entirely trustworthy after what happened at the back end of 1983 to Billy Magee.

There was a heavy westerly running at the old Gills pier, and after Billy had tied extra tyres as fenders on his own boat he thought he would fix one on the "Mzuri Sana" to prevent her scraping on the quay. He had less than two feet to jump down on to the deck (which was gloss painted) and she threw him "heels-a-been" right over her and into the sea with the tyre still over his shoulder and I can tell you he had a narrow escape before he got clear of the tyre and ropes and swam ashore and all this in a heavy swell. Never say "touch wood" in a boat, always "touch cold iron" and never whistle because it raises the wind. Rabbits are "furry feet". I don't think there are any pigs in the parish now, but if you must refer to them say 'clivvie feet' when afloat.

Johnny Green, Havengore, Huna.

Footnote:– My father William Gulloch was an engineering student in Glasgow when he joined the Scottish Rifles (Cameronians) in 1914 and was wounded on the Somme in 1917. After he had recovered he was transferred to the Gold Coast Regiment and when the war ended he joined the Colonial Police. He was commissioner of Police (Colonel) in Gibraltar, Cyprus and Kenya and adviser to Haile Selassie in Abyssinia before he retired to Freswick in 1950.

Margaret Harris, Poet's Croft, Freswick.

Circle round the moon – its going to rain.
The bigger the circle – the nearer the storm.
Gap in circle shows the direction of the storm.
Magnus Houston.

Sundogs – sign of bad weather to come.
(Round sort of spiky reflection of the sun
seen over a bit from the sun.)
Robbie Dundas, Huna.

FRANCIE DUNDAS

Canisbay Post Office

Photo, Joey Bremner, St Clair, John O'Groats.

Post Office and Hall

Photo, Katie Henderson, Upper Gills.
Alex Taylor and his wife at the door. Alex Nicolson was the first man in the parish to have a motorbike.

The Dundas families in this parish are all closely related and said to be descended from four Dundas brothers who came up from the Midlothian area and settled here. The Canisbay Baptismal Records show they were in a position of some standing because in 1659 Sir Wm. Sinclair and John Sinclair of Brabster witnessed the baptism of Margaret, daughter of James Dundas, and his son Gilbert's baptism in 1664 was witnessed by Donald Groat of Warse and Robert Sinclair.

It was Francis Dundas, master mason, who built the three large houses c.1888 near the school and started the village. He built Victoria Villa for John Sutherland, the retired schoolmaster, Pentland View for the doctor and the "shop" as a business and family home for himself. The three houses were supplied by piped water from a strong spring at the reservoir in the field below Tresdale.

Masons selected the best ideas from houses they had constructed and incorporated them in the plans for their own homes. The excellent stonework and the fancy ridging above the Welsh slated roof shows to this day that this was a master mason's home. The iron rhones, rainwater heads and down pipes are all the originals. The glass roof and the triangular top section of the porch have been replaced. Charlie Manson has the cast iron thistle and perhaps one day it will be back in place. The attractive windows with intricate panes of coloured glass and the cast-iron work look good for another 100 years.

Francie and his family moved to Dumfries where they set up a knackery business and did very well indeed. It is the same family "Dundas Brothers" who have the same very extensive knackery business in Kintore and Turriff. George Dundas (son of Francie) was Provost of Kintore for some years.

Dundas Family, Warse.

Lots of birds fennan in one field –
Sign of bad weather.
Mary Sinclair, Hillside, Gills.

Them that get the name of "early risers"
Can lie to the top of the day!

CANISBAY IN MY YOUNG DAYS

I well remember the first day in my life I ever met or had contact with anybody from Canisbay. I was a young lad of 15, staying at my uncle's at Shore of Rattar, Scarfskerry. It was March Fair Day, a feeing market at Georgemas, Halkirk, My cousin who had recently married had a push bike (I had none). He was going to the feeing market to try and get a job for himself as the croft could not support two families, so he promised he would scout around for me too. When he came home in the afternoon he had fee'd with Charlie MacPherson, Shorelands, as foreman, and he told me there was a farmer from Canisbay coming to see me.

It was a typical Caithness March day, strong winds and heavy showers. Later on, Mr Donnie Dundas arrived in his small gig and a little shalt. He had another old man with him, Mr Tom Campbell, cattleman on West Canisbay, whose two sons were horsemen on the farm. They were looking for a move but they never got one. My aunt took them both in for a cup of tea, and my uncle did the negotiating for me. I had to help with the animals and do whatever I was told, for the magnificent sum of seven pounds for six months. (My second six months I only got six pounds to myself, by then I had become eligible to pay National Health Insurance.) Between then and the summer term 28th May, my cousin used to tease me that I would have to get my stomach pumped to enlarge it, as I would have to eat all my breakfast in one go. At my uncles we had our porridge at nine o'clock and our afters at 12 o'clock, but I found after spreading dung in the drills for four hours I managed!

Twenty-eighth May, 1926 I went to work at Warse and I quickly met two things I had never seen before. I came off the bus at Isey Moad's shoppie. Walking down the farm road, I was struck by the beautiful smell from the whin bushes which grew in profusion in the field on my left. There were no whins in Wick, there were no whins in Scarfskerry, and I loved it. I learnt later on, it was about the first food in Caithness for honey bees. The other thing I met for the first time was a water tank made from sawn-edged Caithness flag stone.

Transport has changed greatly since those days, in type and time. I remember John S. Banks calling at Warse one day in his car at breakfast time. Everybody sat at the same table. Donnie Dundas was chaffing him about being well off travelling around in his car. John S. said he believed he would live to see the day everybody would have a car or at least a car in every home. Time wise, you could leave Warse today and be in Edinburgh as quick as we could go to Wick with a cart and many days it was as difficult to find stable accommodation as it is now to find space for a car in Edinburgh. It used to take us five hours to go to Wick and that was keeping scutching her up. Our trip was usually to the mart with sheep and Shearer and Millers for feeding stuff, oilcake, bran and at times manure, or just Shearer and Miller itself. If we got in to the stable at Shearer and Millers we were lucky, but if the stable was full, we would be allowed to put the horses in one of the sheds, but not before Bartlett the storeman was satisfied that the horses had made their water, (there was no drainage on the shed floors, and it could spread among the different goods in the shed) so sometimes we had to whistle to them for some time, before they complied.

Putting down turnips has changed dramatically since those days, and there were various methods then in use, dunging on the face, single drilling or double drilling with the manure sown in the drill right under the turnip seed, and double drilled, no dung just manure. Warse had a manure sower for sowing in drills, not broadcast. It was sown broadcast on the grain by the foreman (Sanny Rosie). In the harvest in those days, roads were cut round the field by scythe, usually by the foreman. Nearly everybody had a piece under bere, Warse would have one to one and a half acres and although they had a binder, the bere was cut with the back-delivery. I never knew the reason for it. I used to wonder, too, why the grain was not of a regular crop right up to the fence. I got the answer the following spring when I was giving manure in two pails to the foreman. I noticed then that he sowed no manure round the edges of the field.

Round about that time there came into farming, the greatest innovation in agriculture since the beginning of the root crop _ wild white clover. Farmers and crofters that never had grass, now found they had good grass and in the cultivation for tatties and turnips, great reduction in the amount of weeds to be gathered. Before the root crop was established as part of the farmer's rotation, farmers were still doing what they were doing in Bible times. After two, sometimes three crops of grain, the ground got infested with weeds, so the farmer had to plough the field but sow no crop in it, but spend all his spare time during the growing season in dressing the ground and gathering the weeds, hence it derived its name, fallow break. (Jer. 4.3. Break up your fallow ground.) Before the advent of the disc and the rotovator, farms with strong clay ground used to have a hard job getting a meal for their turnip seeds to germinate in.

Agriculture has made big strides the last 70 years, farmers and crofters have a tremendous range of grass seeds from which to choose and no doubt the introduction of wild white clover which not only gave better bottom of grass but in its actual growing aerated the soil with the result you got a bumper crop after grass. Up till 60 years ago perennial ryegrass and broad leaved red clover helped to give bulk to the hay crop, but to calves and stirks its stalk was indigestable and was most often left at their heads like short lengths of wire. Cows ate it all. Quite a number of crofters used to sow an area in the sowing out with just perennial ryegrass which they used to cut and harvest, build in a small screw (or stack) and then in the spring it was threshed with the flail.

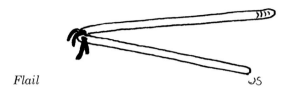

Flail

This was two lengths of wood roughly four feet in length (each piece) with a hand grip formed on one end of one piece, and a one inch hole drilled in the other end. A similar hole was drilled in one end of the other section through which was inserted a short length of rope or leather through both holes. The rope or leather thong was then knotted on the two outsides, but left slack enough in between to allow free movement of the flail section to be directed at whatever target the wielder desired. There was a frame (five feet by three feet) of latticed woodwork having square openings formed in the lattice work one and a half inch by one and a half inch.This was laid on the floor and the sheaf of ryegrass was spread on it and threshed with the flail, the seeds fell through the openings and were swept up periodically and gathered up to leave room for more. An expert on the flail could make it land whereever he wanted. Before the advent of the static steam engine came into prominence, all the horsemen on a farm had to thresh oats with the flail to get straw for his horses, this was all done in his own time.

The last brick chimney stack from such steam engines, I can remember, was at Quoys of Reiss, but I can't pinpoint when it was demolished. I have no knowledge of when a corn bruiser came into being or what they did before then.

Crofters used to use a hand mill. It was merely an iron frame on an iron stand about 18 inches wide, with two rollers (not smooth) which were rotated by a handle at each side. Later on in years when the mobile mill came round it was perhaps used in emergency. It was looked upon more as a thing of entertainment rather than a thing of torture. There was also the horse driven mill, either single, double and sometimes three horses. The one horse mill was usually quite a simple affair. On the outside it was the same as the others. It had the same built-up piece of ground, which the horses walked round in an endless circle. They were hitched to a wooden shaft which reached from the outside of the circle to the centre where it revolved quite a large size solid cast iron cog wheel. This in turn rotated a transverse cog wheel fixed on the end of a long, three inch thick, solid iron shaft which reached right into the barn. On the end of this was another iron cog which drove an iron cog on a shaft with a pulley at the other end and all the organs of the mill were then driven by pulleys and belts. The one horse mill just separated the entire grain from the straw, the grain having to be separated from the chaff by the act of winnowing. This was accomplished with the aid of a sieve which was formed by a circular frame of wood approximately two inches deep and 20 inches diameter. Its bottom was lined with a pig skin with holes bored in to let the grain pass through, while the chaff was blown aside by the draught between the two open doors. It was usually done on a breezy

Horse Mill Kirkstyle

Photo, Margaret Cormack, Kirkstyle.
George Grant beside a tidy screw tied down with straw simmons with Prince and Beda pulling mill. Note 'Whoa-hole'
in barn wall.

day (not many non breezy days in Caithness). The two horse mill usually had a fanners which separated the grain from the chaff which saved a great lot of work especially cleaning up. The three horse mill was generally on larger holdings and on farms.

I remember how as a young lad I used to wonder how a farm the size of West Canisbay had no mill. Many a crofter in quite a large area would go to his bed at night having the portable mill in his stack yard ready set up for threshing but in the morning when he rose there was no mill, everybody seemed to know where it went and just took it for granted, he had to attend to his best customers, and that he would make a far bigger day's pay in one stack yard! I found out later on that West Canisbay did used to have a huge three horse mill, until one day something frightened the horses and they scared, putting the mill to pulp.

Before crofters had money to buy nets for their screws and gilts, you were never short of work to do on a rough winter's day, just sit on a stool in the barn and make simmons. They were used to tie down the screws and, done well, they made a far bonnier picture than a net.

Flagstone Quarries

There have also been radical changes in the building construction, but sad to say, unlike agriculture, not always for the best. Canisbay played perhaps a minor part in the slate and flagstone industry in its day, but nevertheless it was a great asset to the locality. The Sinclair's of Caithness were very prominent in the slate and flagstone industry, and of course there were Sinclairs in the Mey Castle. Phillip's Harbour at Harrow figured prominently in the export of flagstones. There used to be a cutting and dressing shed in the Harrow Gill which leads to the harbour. There were different quarries dotted over the district. There was a quarry at Rigafa, which didn't seem to be worked to the same extent as the rest, nevertheless it yielded a good quality of stone. There were also quarries at Skirza, again not being used to a great extent; local houses were built and slated with Skirza material. Brabster quarries seem to have been the most used. They were heavier than any of the other Canisbay slate, but after a while on a roof, exposed to sun and weather were inclined to split, sometimes in three layers. With the modern guillotine, this could have been done at the quarry and supplied more slates, and lighter beams could have been used in the roof. Now the roofs are all synthetic, and doors and windows are plastic, wood has become so inferior.

As has been mentioned before, water tanks were made from flagstones cut to the required size, and grooved by the saw for jointing together in putty and white lead. Two light iron rods were bolted near the top of each to hold it all together. There was also a hole jumpered in one end for a tap to be grouted in with putty and lead.

I don't think it would be fair to speak of a bygone Canisbay without mentioning the Red Road, known far and wide as the road leading to John O'Groats. It started at Everly's Corner and went to the shore. If one took a trip in a boat from Groats round the head towards Freswick, one can see the straight line of demarcation between the red stone and the blue stone from the turf right down into the sea. The traveller would also be amazed by the amount of wildlife in, on, and over the sea there. I think it is only right that one should be reminded of the great amount of money that has been spent along the coast. The harbour at John O'Groats may not be exactly what each individual local would have liked, but it certainly makes a bonnie picture on a summer's evening to see the Ferry and a good number of boats tied up, and even in the winter, lobster fishing is still being prosecuted.

I don't know what Jimmy Donn and James William Shearer would have said if they were told that millions of pounds were to be spent on Gills – for what? Maybe if they were still with us they would have been able to advise. On land, what a transformation in housing, outside and inside, all possible through the great upsurge in wages. In 1952 we got electricity, and then later on we got piped water, and from then onwards the countryside was transformed with bathrooms in every home.

During the war, I was in Brighton on a Driv/Mech course. On Sunday at the Baptist Church, there were some other soldiers present too and we were invited to dinner in the Manse, so we went along. I happened to be first in the queue to be greeted by the minister's wife, and, as we shook hands, she asked me if I would like to wash my hands? Well at that time I had a smattering of the English language, but I knew nothing of bathroom language. I just looked at my hands and said they were fine! I sometimes wonder what accent will be prominent in Canisbay in another 50 years, or how long it takes to become a local.

There are tremendous changes in the area of the hotel, compared to the days when the local boys used to sell beads made from Groatie buckies and postcards. In summer there is quite a traffic between buses and cars. It was really congested before the last car park was formed near the Industrial Estate. Long ago there were no toilets except in the hotel. I don't know if the public toilets had an adverse effect on the hotel trade or not! I for one will be very sad to see any of the present hotel being demolished, it is all stone structure, and the last extension only went up in 1938-39. The stones all came from Brabster, as also did the stones used in the building of culverts, and re-arranged farm dykes on the Thurso-John O'Groats road, which was being re-routed at different corners. The new bridges at Gills were constructed, the bridge at the mill was widened, but then at Christmas 1939 all work was stopped until a few years after the war. In fact some of the buildings have only recently been completed.

There are no heaps of metal (stones broken for patching and renewing sections of the road). You never see the water cart on the roads now either, nor do you get the smell of coal smoke, (which was usual in those days) from the roller mens van. The breaking of stones gave many a farm servant an extra pound or two.

The old kirk at Canisbay was a church of great renown long before the Queen Mother began to worship in it. It was the burial place of that famous man, John de Groot. It also stood as a reminder to them who worshipped within its walls, of the days when it was a symbol of terror, tyranny and oppression in the Dark Ages and reminding us of the men and women whose lives were cheap, that we their successors might be free to worship God according to his word. There have been some great men in the Canisbay Manse, but what a contrast today when we meet the old kirk minister on the road compared to 100-150 years ago, when men had to remove their cap, touch their forelock, and bend the leg till the knee touched the ground. I don't know if it is a progressive step, or a retrograde step, that a great many young couples live outside the rule and authority of the church. Less than 100 years ago, couples were never considered really married until they were kirked; that is to attend church as early as possible after the wedding.

There was another church up in Canisbay which was originally the Free Church of Scotland and they did in Canisbay what they did in many other places of Scotland. They set up a place of learning where boys and girls could receive education, long before there was a State school, with a non obligatory attendance, which in my time became compulsory. This was brought into force to compel the wandering folks to put their children to school, and so eventually they gave up their nomadic way of life to live permanently in homes in the towns and villages, and to take their place in society. In its later years, it was very affectionately known as Russell's Kirk. He was a minister in it for 30 years and ended his days there. There is a beautiful stone on his grave in Canisbay churchyard subscribed to by congregation and friends. The church is now used as a store for food for different sheep from Russells flock!

In 1932, the people of Huna especially, but Canisbay as a whole, saw the fruition of an elderly couples dream, Mr and Mrs Wm. Simpson of Huna House. They were both of Stroma descent. She was Barbara Allan and he had been a policeman in London – whether City or Met., I don't know. He could have qualified for either. They had both been concerned for quite some time before that, about the conditions for itinerant preachers in the parish. They were commonly referred to as the Brethren and didn't seem to be so hard hit as others. They usually had a tent, that they used as living quarters and as a place of worship to preach in. Quite a few Brethren names spring to mind, George Bond, Charlie Reid, Walter Anderson, who used to come with their tents and go all over Caithness. Other preachers had often great difficulty. Public halls were not free every night of the week, and for older people, the only transport

was to walk, so when they moved from place to place they tried to make their new venue as relatively close to the old one as possible, so that if any were won by the gospel it was still possible to attend. There used to be a wooden shed beside the lifeboat shed at Huna. It was the Stroma fishermens' shed for storing their fish for transport to Wick. It was not very pleasant to gather in, but it was closed in and had a roof. Now this was right on Mr and Mrs Simpson's doorstep, so they conjured up the wonderful idea of building a hall for meetings, and also providing accommodation for the preachers. They didn't day dream for long. They already had plenty of ground to build on, and there was an unlimited supply of stones on the shore. All that had to be done was transport them. I have no doubt they could have thought of many who were more able, but there was certainly nobody more willing than they were. They had no horse and cart but they had a car. They removed the body from the back and put a platform on it. They must have reminded themselves many times as they handled these stones that a burden shared was a burden halved. He employed masons from Dunnet to build the hall, then employed two local Christian joiners to do the wood work and it was opened in 1932. The Faith Mission was represented. Jock Troup (Wick) was there, but poor Mr Simpson himself was wheeled in, in his wheel chair. There still continued some Brethren preachers for quite a number of years, but now there are none and they are missed, for they were all good expositors of the Word.

In that same year there was another building erected at Canisbay, now often referred to as the Tin Kirk. In spite of its unpretentious appearance, it has continued to herald forth the truth throughout the years. Splits are never really beneficial in a spiritual body, but if a person has ideals of truth that they want to hold onto, and if there is a point in dispute, it is better to live apart in peace than to abide together in contention.

In 1929, it seems that a great percentage of U.F. Church members were in favour of Union with Church of Scotland, but many abstained and worshipped on their own under the title of the Continuing U.F. Church. After a number of years they reverted to the original title, U.F. Church of Scotland. The then Laird of the Mey Estate, an Englishman, Captain Imbert Terry gave permission to them to erect a place of worship on the croft occupied by Wm. Dunnet. This ground was marked off on his title deeds, and those of his successor Wm. Leitch, as no longer belonging to the croft. But after many years, numbers had declined considerably and the U.F. felt that it was a burden they were no longer prepared to bear. When they went to put the church up for sale they found they had no title deeds to the ground. It had seemingly been gifted by the then laird, but he was now dead, all the original recipients were also dead and the transaction had never been legalised. The factor for the new owners wanted £600 for it. The church didn't have that amount of money so they had to accept less. The U.F. headquarters were very gracious and gave the building for a mere nominal sum to make it legal. The new regime has a different church basis and structure than the old, and it seems to be working quite effectively. There have been some men of note in the wee church, such as Rev. Iain Paisley who was two Sundays in the pulpit, then Mr Jackie Ritchie, Evangelist,

Highland Ministries, is often there, and any visiting preacher is always given the invitation to speak so the congregation get a very comprehensive view of the Scriptures. There is quite a strong Sunday School attached to it, in the region of 30, when they are all present.

Alexander S. MacGregor, John O'Groats Post Office.

After Mid-week Service at the Free Evangelical Church 1955

Photo, Sutherland Manson, Thurso.

Back Row:- Dannie Gulloch, Sandy MacGregor, Sandy Cormack, Jean Gulloch. Front Row:- Donald Gulloch, Andrew Phillip, Mrs Simpson, Molly Simpson, Nancy MacLeod, Anne Cormack, Sandy Cormack, Nancy Robertson, Jimmy Cormack, Nellie MacGregor, Barrie MacGregor, Margaret Cormack, Mrs Nellie Cormack, Nellie Cormack, Barrie Cormack, Jessie Cormack.

DAVID SHEARER – MINISTER IN PERTH, WESTERN AUSTRALIA

David Shearer M.A. was born at Warse, Canisbay on 17th July, 1832 fourth son of John Shearer and Elizabeth Banks.

David's brother Donald was the father of Donald (Danny) Shearer who founded the Grocer's business, St John's Square and Robert Shearer, Butcher, Thurso. Donald was the grandfather of Donald Shearer, Seater and Willie Shearer, John O'Groats.

David's brother James was the father of James William Shearer, Lower Warse who died in 1985.

David Shearer was a very intelligent scholar, who at the age of 15, was engaged as a tutor to take charge of a school of 30 pupils, some older than himself. As a result, to improve their instruction, he was compelled to study himself to impart higher education to them. Following his experiences in teaching at Canisbay and Fordyce, and his own self-study, he gained a scholarship for himself. He received a certificate from the Free Church Training College in Edinburgh and then entered Edinburgh University in 1863 for four years in the faculty of Arts and four years in the faculty of Divinity. He received extraordinary help and

encouragement from his mother, who in fact died only a year or so before he himself died. In 1866/67 he was University Prizeman in maths and obtained Certificates of Honour in Natural Philosophy, Moral Philosophy, in Rhetoric and in English Literature.

He was licensed to preach in 1871 and was appointed pastor at Elliston Street Presbyterian Church, Gateshead, on 2nd July, 1872. He had been a close friend of David Livingstone and one son was christened David Livingstone Shearer and the other John. Arising from his association and friendship with Livingstone, he was interested in spreading the gospel overseas and in 1879 was given the task of going to Western Australia to establish, in that colony, the first Presbyterian Church. He sailed with his wife and children on the barque "Charlotte Padbury" and after a three months' voyage arrived on 2nd October, 1879.

The first Presbyterian Church was set up in St George's Hall, Perth, as a temporary arrangement until the foundations were laid on 25th October, 1881 of the church in Pier Street. By the end of 1883, the full cost had been paid off and he then proceeded to set up churches in Freemantle and Albany and a mission church in Jassadale.

He was held in great respect and was ahead of his generation, and his own faith in his great tolerance of other Christian churches not Presbyterian and in his belief that all Christians should be united by their common faith irrespective of their form of worship or of their allegiance to Rome, Canterbury or Edinburgh. This was given evidence at his funeral in November 1891 where the pall-bearers were ministers of the Wesleyan, Congregational,

Anglican and Presbyterian Churches – the R.C. priest in those days was precluded from attending a non-conformist service.

The Queen's representative, the Premier and the Colonian Secretary, were among those who attended the large funeral.

A plaque was placed in the church by members of the congregation and a memorial was erected in the town square, Perth, Australia, by public subscription.

Lorna S. MacKinnon, 5 Greenbank Gardens, Edinburgh.
– (A great grand-daughter of Danny Shearer, Thurso.)

Crow Stepped Gable, Quoys

Photo, Joey Bremner, St Clair, John O'Groats.
Left to Right:– Lee Dunnet, Ella Dunnet, George Green, Mary Green, William Dunnet (Lee and William home on holday from British Columbia.)

The Quoys Well

Photo, John Dunnet, Seater.
Flagstones shelter this roadside well between Quoys and the Old Kirk which was used by the Seater, Quoys and Kirkstyle familes, and many used the tin mug to quench their thirst on the way home from church. It used to have a wooden door to prevent stoor and chips off the road dirtying the water.

A BUSY DAY AT WARSE

The day they killed the pig at Warse was a big day and a lot of things had to be got ready beforehand.

It was Jamie Shearer, Upper Warse who came to kill the pig and he was extra particular, and every thing had to be just right. The big boiler in the wash-house had to be scrubbed and all traces of soap and soda, which were used when boiling towels and sheets, had to be thoroughly rinsed off, as this would not improve the pork! The fire had to be all set ready the day before, ready to be lit at the crack of dawn so that there would be plenty of boiling water.

Jamie took the "swine's box" (a long trunk-shaped wooden box) with him. The scalding water was filled into the swine's box and there was always a pail of cold water set handy to get it all to the right temperature. Jamie was always particular about the temperature and tested it by drawing his finger through the "cooled-a-bit" water. A pail of water was then taken from the box for a final temperature check. If a drop of blood congealed when added to the pail it was too hot and had to be adjusted. This was so important because if the water was too hot it spoilt the appearance of the pork and if too cold it would not remove the bristles.

Long ago the loons would have been waiting impatiently to get the bladder! It made a grand football when blown up. The women took over the puddings (large intestine) which first had to be washed very thoroughly at the stroup in the ditch. Second wash was in pail after pail of clean water from the well. They were left to soak in salt water and were ready to be rinsed and used the next day. Black Puddings:– beremeal, blood, chopped onions, and seasoning were gathered on the kitchen table and the suet was melted in the big iron pan. Oatmeal, more onions etc., for the white puddings – another long day!

Thinning Neeps

The drills were long and you had to be careful that you didn't knock out the whole lot of neeps and leave a "scolag". I never could keep up with the thinning or the crack! Warse always had a good squad of six to nine at the thinning and the yarns, banter and laughing that went on the whole time is something I'll never forget. – Ta-Ta.

Cathie McLeod, Lochend.

Doctor Gill

Photo, Margaret Magee, Lower Gills.
This photo was taken at his son John's wedding.

The 1955 Snowstorm

Photo, John Dunnet, Seater.
Will Rosie, Willie Nicolson, Jimmy Rosie, Gordon and John Gill pose with Beda who had drawn a sledge with coal from Bella Cummings for Dr Gill.

CAUGHT IN A BLIZZARD

It was a mild and sunny February morning in 1953 when my brother David and I set off for Sunday School which was held in Canisbay school and conducted by Mr Bill Johnston and Mr Danny Gulloch affectionately known to us all as Uncle Bill and Uncle Danny. I was clad in my Sunday best with matching coat and hat and David in his dress suit – knee length trousers and knee length socks in accordance with the fashion of the day.

While happily singing our choruses, we noticed with excitement that it had started snowing heavily but left the school with the impression it was only a heavy shower and it would soon pass. By this time, the wind had increased to perhaps gale-force causing drifting and while passing "Hikes", visibility was down to a few yards. Knowing the road so well we were able to determine various landmarks such as the entrance to Beil Bremner's and a part of the dam further down, but by this time the severe cold had a numbing effect and the whirling drift made breathing very difficult and we were like to choke. One side of our heads and clothing was thick and heavy with snow and in the main, our slow progress was made by a sixth sense, because the telegraph poles and fences were very difficult to see.

Eventually, after tumbling into a ditch and being absolutely petrified before we got out of it, we struggled on with David tightly holding my hand until we reached the welcome green door of Charlotte Dunnet's and we were safe. Charlotte, Constie and David were so good to us and shook off the snow and rubbed and dried us in front of the open fire. Before long the kettle on the swey was boiling for tea and to this day, David has never tasted gingerbread that was half as good as Charlotte's.

Dad had taken the car to collect us when he saw the weather worsening and got stuck coming up the manse road and then raised the alarm. Dad, Wm. Dunnett, Victoria Villa, Rev Nigel Johnstone, Will Rosie and others, made up a search party and I can remember Will Dunnett with a shawl over his head and covered in snow opening Charlotte's door, saying a few words and then turning and going back out into the blizzard to call off the search.

Hamish Donn, William and Dinah Manson were among the Gills pupils who stayed at Victoria Villa, the Doctor's or the Post Office, until the storm abated and their parents collected them.

Dad arrived with our rubber boots when the weather moderated and we walked home to Quoys, crossing over "fans" that were mountains high.

(A combined effort from David and myself).

Joyce Reid, 56 High Street, Thurso.

At a Dunnet Marymas, a Canisbay Crofter approached Jenny Ronaldson – a well known horse dealer from Wick – asking if she had a good, strong, healthy horse about five years old, that was quiet and tractable. My dear friend, she says "the man with a horse like that is no selling him."

M.H.

Footnote:– David Dunnet now has his home in Milltimber and is captain of the North Sea oil supply vessel "Sovereign".

A.H.

THE AUTHOR'S YARN

The Last Cruise of "The Dwarf"

"The Dwarf", a small boat of about 10 feet keel, was the property of several partners, one of whom was represented by Finlay MacLeod, a youth of about 17 years of age. A larger boat had been purchased by the "Company" and "The Dwarf" was sold to be employed as a "lighter" at Wick. A few days previous to the departure of "The Dwarf" from Canisbay, I accepted the invitation of Finlay MacLeod to have a farewell sail in the little boat. Caught by a sudden squall, we ran before it, as described, with unshortened sail, and it was the opinion of Mr John Gibson, my nautical "guide, philosopher and friend", that we had been in imminent danger of running our tiny craft to the bottom of the sea.

It was Saturday, the nineteenth day
  Of the pleasant month of June,
And the sun o'er the Kirk of Canisbay
  Proclaimed it the hour of noon'
A gentle breeze from the south-sou'west
  Invited us out to sail;
So gentle it was that we never dreamt
  Of its bursting a tearing gale;
When we launched "The Dwarf" at the "Old Distil",[1]
  And west away stood we,
With a wind that bellied our single sail,
  But barely ruffled the sea.
Finlay MacLeod took rudder in hand,
  And I got charge of the sail –
I, who had never, in seaman's phrase,
  Been a mile from a brown cow's tail!
The Red Rock passed, and the Black Hole passed,
  And scouring across the Bay,
Right speedily fleeted the little "Dwarf"
  Till we reached the Men of Mey.
Then the wind it veered, and a black cloud peered
  On the brow of the western height;
Cried Finlay MacLeod – "Look out for the squalls"
  And Finlay MacLeod was right.
For scarce had we put "The Dwarf" about,
  On the homeward tack to stand,
When over the Bay, like a thunder-clap,
  The black squall blew from the land.

"Sheet home! Sheet home!" cried Finlay MacLeod,
  "Hard home it is!" shouted I;
As through the waves, like a winged thing,
  Our vessel began to fly.
"Ho, here she goes!" cried Finlay MacLeod,
  "But it's all that "The Dwarf" can do."
I looked a-head, and the roaring sea
  Was terrible to my view.
"No fear! No fear!" cried Finlay MacLeod;
  "But I wish that we could reeve!"
I looked abaft, and the bubbling brine
  Was wetting Finlay's sleeve.
And the sky grew blacker overhead,
  And stiffer the tempest blew,
But through the foaming waters "The Dwarf",
  With her sail unshortened, flew.
She cut the waves as her prow had been
  Not of timber, but burnished steel;
She dashed them off like a man-of-war,
  Though only of ten feet keel.
"Well done, brave "Dwarf!" cried Finlay MacLeod,
  "Let the tempests rage their fill;
We'll soon be out of their fury's reach,
  For yonder's the "Old Distil"![1]
But the black clouds burst, and the big drop gushed
  From the fountains of the sky;
And before "The Dwarf" had touched the shore
  Not a stitch of our clothes was dry.
Yet we drew her high on the pebbled beach –
  For we've neither pier nor wharf –
And thus had Finlay MacLeod and I
  Our last cruise in "The Dwarf"!
For the men of Wick have heard of her,
  And thither she's bound to go,
To ply 'midst the billows of their Bay,
  When the wild nor'easters blow.
For the Wickians know that the gallant "Dwarf"
  O'er the crested waves will spin,
When even the life-boat can't put out,
  And the steamer can't put in.
        From "Yarns of the Pentland Firth"
                by David Grant.

[1] Distillery, See page 345.

David Grant, author of "Yarns of the Pentland Firth" was born in 1823 at Banchory and was schoolmaster in this same school at Canisbay 1857-1861, by which time the whisky venture had failed. He wrote several poems in the Huna Inn Visitors' Book [1] and one can be sure it was there that he listened to the fishermen/pilots recounting their experiences and thrilling exploits and where he caught the spirit of Canisbay. He wrote "I have endeavoured to retain, as nearly as possible, the particulars as I received them."

A.H.

[1] See page 146.

Ruins of Parochial School

Sandy Cormack c.1950 removing Caithness slate from the roof of the old school which is on the sea side of the church yard dyke. The building had three chimneys, flag floors and it is thought the schoolroom was at the west end.

Margaret Cormack, Kirkstyle

James Trail Calder, the Historian of Caithness, was born in 1794 at Stanergill near Castletown and was schoolmaster in Canisbay Parochial School 1815-1856. Salary in 1840, including what he received as Session Clerk, was £45 per year. There is a tall granite obelisk memorial to him beside the tower of the church, a stone's throw from where he lived for 40 years. He was there when the distillery was being built c.1826 and John Gibson, who it is said helped him with the "History of Caithness", was given as his next door neighbour in the 1841 census.

L.O.B.

Calder's Tombstone Shapinsay

Photo, James Sinclair, Lucknow, Shapinsay. Sacred to the memory of Marcus Calder who died 3rd July, 1881 and his brother J.T. Calder who died 17th January, 1864. Erected in loving remembrance by their brother and niece.

Singing Games – Action Songs

"In and Out the Dusty Bluebells"

Standing in a circle, hands joined one girl dances in and out under outstretched arms, others sing:

"In and out the dusty bluebells
In and out the dusty bluebells
In and out the dusty bluebells
I am your master."

The girl then chooses someone, goes behind them and gently! taps them on alternate shoulders in time to the music.

"Pit-a-Pit-a-Patty on your shoulder
Pit-a-Pit-a-Patty on your shoulder
Pit-a-Pit-a-Patty on your shoulder
I am your master."

Both then go in and out the "ring". Choose next person and so on until conga-type line is in progress.

"In and out the window
In and out the window
In and out the window
As we have done before

Stand and face your partner
Stand and face your partner
Stand and face your partner
As you have done before.

Shake hands before you leave her
Shake hands before you leave her
Shake hands before you leave her
As you have done before."

Elizabeth Gates, Marlbank, Gills.

HISTORY OF CANISBAY PARISH CHURCH

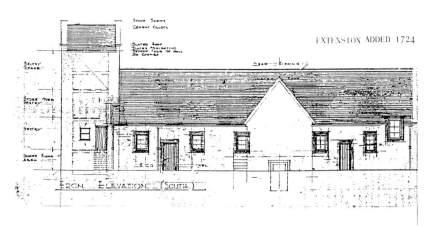

EXTENSION ADDED 1724

FRONT ELEVATION (SOUTH)

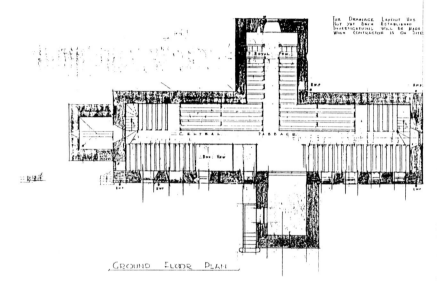

GROUND FLOOR PLAN

When the church was erected in 1720, the standard design at that time was a "T" shaped building with the pulpit on the long wall or north wall. This was a development of the small rectangular buildings erected after the Reformation of which there are still several in service throughout the country.

The usual custom was the Heritor would decide to erect a Laird's Loft on the North wall which in turn became the accepted design.

In 1720, a "T" shaped church was erected with a tower at the west gable as shown on sketch with small windows and two doors to the front elevation. Later the window on the centre line was built up. I assume the pulpit was on the centre line and that it was moved westwards to allow the wall to be opened up when, in 1724 the Brabster Aisle (now the main entrance to the church) was constructed. The moulded stone lintel over this doorway is still visible. The floor of the aisle was about 1000 mm above the church floor. There were stone steps up to a platt at the door. When the roughcast was removed from the front elevation, the stone surround of a doorway was exposed indicating that a vault existed under the floor of the aisle. On investigation I found that the area

South half of vault with partition at left and part of built up doorway showing.

Photos, Laurence Brown, North House, John O'Groats.
Built up doorway into church with partition wall to north side.

below the present floor had been infilled when the aisle was converted into the main entrance to the Church.

The vestry which is located in the tower at a high level had an open stone staircase from the ground outside to the vestry floor, the door being where the present press is. I was interested in the area under the vestry and requested the contractor to open up the floor where I found a light timber floor superimposed on top of a stone floor. Later when the roughcast had been removed from the tower, I examined the small air vent below the vestry floor and decided if I removed a large stone forming the north jamb it would be possible to wriggle through and so gain access. After several attempts I was eventually pushed through by the workmen.

I then realised that I was in the vault. It was formed of rough stone with a barrel vaulted roof and had a thick partition wall from east to west dividing the vault into two compartments. On the west wall a door opening had been built up which opened into the church. The built up door cannot be seen from the inside of the church as it was hidden from view when the west gallery was erected. When I had taken all my notes, I realised that I had had difficulty in squeezing through the opening and had only achieved access with much pushing by some of the workmen and unfortunately there were no workers in the vault to push me out. Then I remembered the young workman who helped to push me in and, on the pretext of requiring more dimensions, I requested the foreman to push the young lad through to hold the end of the tape. He in turn pushed me out through the opening to the fresh air.

I understand the vault was constructed for the Earl of Caithness and that the vault on the north elevation was owned by the Heritor from the now castle of Mey.

Reading through the Heritors papers I found a letter complaining that it was impossible to read the Bible in the new south aisle as there were no windows. It was agreed to install a window and so the pointed arch window at the front was installed.

John S. Craig, Edinburgh.
(Architect in charge of 1991 renovations)

Canisbay Church

Photo, Ian Aitchison

THE CANISBAY KIRK

The present church stands on top of a prehistoric mound, the site of an earlier Celtic church dedicated to St Drostan. Drostan headed a mission to Pictland in the sixth century. There is mention of the church in an ecclesiastic document of 1222.

Tradition says that the present steeple was erected on the site of a previous round tower. This tower would have been separate from the small rectangular church of that time and could have been the burial vault of the Sinclairs of Mey.

The Sinclairs of Freswick had a burial vault under the chapel on the site of St Moddans near Freswick House. The Kennedys of Stroma had a fine mausoleum, and it would have been surprising if the Sinclairs of Mey did not have an impressive burial vault.

318

Corinthian Pillars

Photo, Bet Brown, North House, John O'Groats.

The paired fluted Corinthian Pillars, now against the north wall of the Mey aisle, might have been removed from the doorway of the vault and placed there when the church was extended westwards to the doorway of the vault. This doorway was blocked off by the stair to the Mey loft when the church was heightened.

The entrance to the Mey aisle is framed by giant reeded pilasters supporting the corniced lintel. The base of the weathered Corinthian pillars is level with the original flagstone floor under the present wooden one which has a rising incline of about 18 inches from north to south. There is a worn 17th century mural monument or headstone set on the raised floor between the pillars.

In 1660 permission was granted to the Laird of Kermuck to "plant" a seat on the south side under the west-most window between the door and the wall that divides the congregation from the choir. This west-most area is still called the Stroma Aisle.

The Freswick loft is on the east. The present doorway was originally the door to the Brabster aisle with the family burial vault underneath. 1724 is on the date stone and it seems the pointed window was adjusted to fit rather than made to measure.

Some time after the Laird of Brabster gifted land for the Free Church i.e. post 1851, and at least eight years after the Disruption, this aisle was converted to the vestibule. There is still an outside door to the Mey aisle and the 1720 sketch shows two doors to the front. The lofts and aisles got their

names from the lairds who naturally entered by their own doors so that no precedence was shown. One can wonder if John de Groot [or perhaps John Morison] got the idea for an eight sided house from Canisbay Kirk where the different lairds met on an equal footing.

"1572. Rent of Groats' land to be paid in the Kirk of Canisbay upon a "fixed" day twixt the sun rising and down passing of same." Some 50 feet south of the east end of the church is a flat stone with a plain latin cross. Above the cross is a heraldic shield with three open crowns between initials F.G. Around the stone the following inscription in relief: Here lies Finlay Grot in Duncansbay who departed 18th May, 1601. D.G. and E.G. 1789. Finlay might have witnessed the scattered ships of the Spanish Armada fleeing northwards in 1588. He lived at a time when there was a Scottish King in Holyrood and a Scottish Parliament in Edinburgh.

The Session Records 1652 are the second oldest in the county and according to Craven "Fuller and more interesting than the others". Andro Ogstone (son of the minister) was the session clerk and he made it clear that he would only put complaints to the session which were given to him in writing. Funds were raised by imposing fines on wrong-doers and since there would be no wish to close this source of revenue, it can be assumed that there were plenty who could read and write in the different districts. It is not surprising that they had difficulty in getting "elders", because the church had taken on responsibilities for a lot more than religion and attendance at church every Sunday.

Scotland was a lawless country and some historians would have us believe it was even more so on this side of the Ord! The stern firm rule of Puritanism was taking hold, and the church had become a powerful agency in aid of law and order and had assumed powers of inquisitorship into the domestic lives of the people, with the discipline of the General Assembly demanding that superstitious practices, popish and pagan rites should be put down.

The Scots having sided with the King, Cromwell's soldiers were billetted in the houses and their horses stabled in the kirk. Perhaps it was due to session efforts that the soldiers were removed to the Warth Hill where they set up camp. Having masking plays for the Englishmen and being forced to brew ale on the Sabbath were well worn excuses as late as December 1655. It was Donald Beaton who said "Cromwell would have been as scandalised as the session", and concluded, "there were few Puritans in the Cromwellian garrison or the famous Canisbay air had had a civilising effect on the Ironsides!"

The session appointed the teachers and had problems enforcing parents to send their children to school, and more problems when parents took them away before they had reached a suitable standard. Canisbay was ahead of the times because although Parliament had passed a few acts decreeing that there should be a school in every parish there were still parishes in Caithness without schools as late as 1773. (30th May, 1653. "Hew Groat is ordained to write Thomas Taillour that he come to teach the school in Cannasbay according to his ingagement without longer delay.")

The session helped the sick and the poor. (9th August, 1652. Ordained that £10 be distributed amongst the poor being 20 in number. 27th December 1652. 30/- given to two distressed soldiers.) The average collection on a Sunday was about five to six shillings.

Morals, language, Sunday observance were zealously scrutinised and censored as were fights, squabbles and even arguments. Old customs are hard to break and the session dared not show sympathy to those who held to popish rites, firelighting ceremonies, charms or witchcraft. One need not wonder what their reaction would be to all the horoscopes and games of chance so widely advertised on teletext and in magazines.

Interior showing Freswick Loft.

Ministers of Canisbay

1574 John Watsoun.

1577-1581 John Donat – rector and reader.

1601-1610 Alexander Ogston – from Turriff. Ogston was a contemporary of Timothy Pont, minister at Dunnet, who was the first to compile an atlas of Scotland which was published by Blaue, Amsterdam in 1662. It is said he surveyed all the counties and islands of Scotland.

1610-1649 Andro Ogston – teacher from Turriff. The Mowats of Buchollie had the patronage of the church in 1610. (Balquholly now called Hatton was near Turriff.) Ogston adopted original methods to encourage church attendance. He is credited with engaging pipers from the extremities of the parish to play on the way to church so gathering a good congregation. It was said he allowed them a game of knotty on the way home. In the Viking Society "Old Lore 1909", M.A. writes "If Gibb's Craig fa's te'e lan Dungasby 'ill sink for sin" was attributed to Andro Ogston. It was supposed to have been uttered as a warning to the people of Duncansby

who, at that time, are credited with lax views on the question of Sabbath – keeping. Anyone observing the slender "neck" by which the stack is supported and the ominous angle at which it leans towards the land, can understand how effective the warning would be to Sabbath breakers taking their ease at "The Rock". Canisbay tradition says that in 1638, when Presbyterianism took over from Episcopalianism, for want of something better to mark this occasion, they had a bonfire and burnt the church books. Andro is said to have severely rebuked a woman for her irreverence in grazing her cow in the hallowed acre. The woman, resenting this, told him he needn't make such a "carrieshang" because one day the grass would grow over his own grave. "Woman" replied the minister "the grass shall never grow on my grave", and neither it did for 250 years. About 1900 John Nicolson cleaned and renovated the stone and for better preservation fixed it against the south wall of the church yard and now the woman's prediction is true.

1652-1666 William Davidson – To improve Sunday observance and church attendance absentees were to be fined 40 pence and also Stroma boatmen should not charge passengers going to church. Cromwell's soldiers were creating many problems.

1667-1704 James Innes – His son the Hon. Col. James Innes of Cape Fear, North Carolina donated 100 pounds to build a steeple to the church and instal a bell "of which he would not be ashamed" on condition the work would start immediately.

1705-1746 Alexander Gibson – married to Margaret, widow of Alexander Sinclair, Brabster. George Gibson, brother of the minister was schoolmaster in Stroma and married Katharine Rorison who had been engaged to John Gow. Pirate Gow visited Stroma with the intention of carrying her off, or having his revenge, but left again without doing any mischief (Henderson's Family History).

1747-1780 James Brodie – Thomas Pennant in his tour of Scotland in 1769 had a meal with the minister of Canisbay after passing through the bogs of the Warth Hill.

1780-1798 John Morison – born at the farm of Whitehill, Cairney, Aberdeenshire in 1746. Donald Beaton wrote "Like so many other Scottish lads who have risen to fame, Morison, after leaving school, was called to tend the cattle on the farm. He was, however, a much better scholar than a herd, and sometimes, as will happen with boys, his eyes closed in sleep, and his charges wandered at sweet will in forbidden pastures. On one of these occasions he dreamt that someone presented him with a beautiful volume entitled "Goschen". The lad was enraptured with the visionary gift, but on coming back to the world of reality, he was confronted with his father, who upbraided him for negligence. His mother, however, on hearing the dream, with a mother's partiality and a woman's quickness of perception, encouraged her boy by saying to him "you'll get your book: for you will be sent back to school and herd no more."

Morison studied at King's College, Aberdeen, gained his degree in 1771 and became Master of Thurso School about 1773. Mr Sinclair of Freswick presented him to the church of Canisbay. James T. Calder wrote "Freswick was so interested in him that after his settlement he ploughed his glebe, and sowed it with seed taken from his own barn; cut and drove home his peats, and cut and stacked the whole of his crop."

Dr John Morison made a name for himself as joint author with Dr Logan of the 27th and 28th Paraphrases and as sole author of the 19th, 21st, 29th, 30th and 35th. It was said he got his inspiration for the 30th from the view out of the end window of the manse, over the widely changing moods of the Pentland Firth. . . "His voice commands the tempest forth, and stills the stormy wave."

This was the old manse (called Al-Hasa now) where in 1791 "the minister was extremely well accommodated with new office houses". Dr Morison wrote the "Number IX, Parish of Canisbay" contribution to the First Statistical Account of Scotland 1793 and proposed that a lighthouse be built on Duncansby Head and the Pentland Skerries. His words ". . . there is not, around the island of Britain, a station where a lighthouse is more requisite than in the mouth of the Pentland Firth" [The Northern (i.e. Scottish) Lighthouse Board was established in 1786 and the Pentland Skerries light was built in 1794 but incomprehensibly, the light at the pivotal point, Duncansby Head, was not lit until 1924.]

1799-1826 James Smith.

1827-1832 William Milne.

1833-1845 Peter Jolly – Minister at time of Disruption. It is thought that the whole parish worked and supported the building of the Free Church because they thought that Peter Jolly was going to "come out" with them. It was said that he changed his mind at the last minute and stayed with the Established Church. It was because he was such a well loved and respected minister that 50 per cent stayed with him and we owe them thanks for preserving the church.

1845-1866 Alexander Whyte.

1867-1902 James MacPherson – He encouraged and supported the Stroma people in their desire for a church and performed the opening ceremony in December 1878. He accepted, on behalf of the Canisbay Church, the Communion Silver from Sir Oliver Mowat.

1902-1924 John R. Forbes – Loved and esteemed as a minister, friend and physician by the whole parish. He had given ungrudging service by day and night to the sick and suffering in the parish, at a time when there was no resident doctor and their medical adviser had three large parishes to attend to. This is reported in the John O'Groat Journal, 31st December, 1915 and it is worth noting that at the presentation to J. Forbes, the main speakers were staunch adherents of the U.F. Church.

1925-1926 Robert W. Merry.

1928-1949 William Fulton.

1951-1957 Nigel Johnston (Union with U.F. church).

1958-1979 George Bell (U.F. Church sold).

1982-1992 Alex Muir (Canisbay linked with Keiss).

1992-1996 Alex Robertson.

Ministers of U.F. or South Church

1845-1889 Roderick MacGregor.

1890-1897 Donald Davidson.

1898-1915 James Iverach Munro – (The Canisbay U.F. congregation were not dispossessed of their church or manse when the Continuing Free Church was formed.

1915-1949 James Russell.

GROUP TAKEN AT QUINQUENNIAL VISITATION OF CANISBAY SOUTH CHURCH—OCTOBER, 1932.

Behind (left to right)—Rev. A. Aitken, Lybster; Rev. Wm. Fulton, North Church, Canisbay· Rev. G. Gray, M.A., West Church, Wick; Rev. Jas. Russell, M.A., Canisbay South. I, front—Mrs Russell, Mrs Fulton. (Mr Russell celebrated the semi-jubilee of his ordination to the ministry about the same time.)

Quinquennial Visitation of Canisbay South Church 1932

Photo, Marjory Morrison, Glenearn, Mey.

Back Row:– Rev. A. Aitken, Lybster; Rev. W. Fulton, Canisbay; Rev. G. Gray, Wick; Rev J. Russell, Canisbay. Front Row:– Mrs Russell, Mrs Fulton.

Furnishings

The beautiful Communion Silver which is decorated with vine and grape ornamentation is inscribed thus:– "Presented by the Hon. Sir Oliver Mowat, K.C.M.G., Premier and Attorney-General of Ontario, to the Parish Church of Canisbay, as a memorial of his ancestors connected with Canisbay, on the occasion of the semi-jubilee of the Rev J. MacPherson, Minister of the Parish 1892."

(The session clerk has the receipt from Brook & Son, Goldsmiths to her Majesty the Queen, 87 George Street, Edinburgh, for the communion silver, £20, which was sent to the Rev. J. MacPherson.)

The Communion Silver

Bust of **John Morison** presented by John Nicolson, Nybster who made this sculpture from a miniature painting of John Morison.

The **Brass Baptismal Font** fixed by a bracket to the pulpit is said to be of Dutch origin.

The **beautiful organ** was presented in 1902 by Peter Murray, Springfield, USA. He was a Murray from Brabster and a grand uncle of the Angus and Geddes families and also a near relative of the Ross family.

The **Oak Offering Stand** in the vestibule was presented by Dora and William Gulloch, Poet's Croft, Freswick in memory of their son and is inscribed thus: In memory of William Duncan Gulloch, The Black Watch. Born 22nd May, 1924.

Killed in Burma 13th February, 1944.

The **Pulpit Fall** was presented by the family in memory of their parents Jessie Kennedy and William Dunnet, St Leonards. William was senior elder and session clerk for many years.

The **Praise Board** was presented in 1976 by Her Majesty, Queen Elizabeth, The Queen Mother.

The **Lectern** was presented in 1982 in memory of the Rev. George Bell.

The **Communion Table** presented in 1984 by Barbara Mowat, Viewfirth, John O'Groats who was our first lady elder.

The **"Rest for the Weary"** garden seat at the door of the church was presented in loving memory of their dear brother John Thomas Fell (1899-1984) by David and Edith, Mansefield Cottages.

Sources:– A History of the Episcopal Church in the Diocese of Caithness – J.B. Craven.

Ecclesiastical History of Caithness – Rev. Donald Beaton.

Session Records of Canisbay.

Mostly from my mother's notes.
Anne Houston, "St Magnus".

THE MOWAT FONT

This beautiful wooden font was gifted to Finnieston (later Kelvingrove) church in 1956 by John Mowat, Freswick in memory of his wife Georgina Dunnet. When Kelvingrove church closed the font was transferred to Canisbay and now stands in the vestibule.

On 4th June, 1982 four generations were linked through the Mowat Font. The Rev. John Mowat baptised his grand-daughter Kate Mowat Bewick using the memorial font to the great-grandmother of the baby.

The Rev. John Mowat who used to be clerk to the Presbytery of Aberdeen retired with his wife to the old family home at Freswick. They modernised Skirza House and landscaped the area round it very fittingly. The locals got to know and love Jack Mowat well because he was locum minister in Keiss and did a lot of pulpit supply in Canisbay before the Rev. Alex Muir was inducted to the charge.

Lizzie Cook, Skirza.

CANISBAY KIRK

At the top of Britain there you stand –
The most northerly kirk in all the land –
  In a hallowed place;
Where many centuries you have spanned
  With righteous face.

Immune to every vain glorious faction,
Your fabric face a benediction
  In joy and tears;
Aye steadfast in your consecration
  Through the years.

The loved ones now at rest around you,
Knew well they could depend upon you
  To light the way;
Both old and young paid homage to you
  In their day.

Guard them well those in your keeping,
Beloved kinsfolk peacefully sleeping
  In your embrace;
Sheltered so safely in the blessing
  Of divine grace.

John Geddes, "Highlands",
Minchinhampton, Glos.

A CANISBAY MINISTER

There was a very fine minister in Canisbay at the beginning of the 19th Century. He was kind, warm-hearted and had never been heard to raise his voice in anger – not even at any of the pranks the boys played. He had a pony of which he was very fond and the boys thought they would sure rouse him if they did something to the pony. They cut all the hair off the pony's tail and waited for the minister's response which was – "Hallelujah amen, Donald's tail will grow again."

Lizbeth and Lexi, Inglewood,
31 Fauldshead Road, Renfrew.

THE GROAT TOMBSTONE

MEMORIAL STONE AT JOHN O' GROATS

Donald Grot, son to John Grot, laid me here April 13th day of 1568. M.D.L. Likewise and Donald Grot and his Donald lad and the forebears of Donald. Hence God called me the 13th day of April T.D. M.D.L. 1568.

"Amoriale" carved under cross.

(Read from bottom left corner.)

JOHN O'GROATS TOMBSTONE

The tombstone of the original John O'Groats, or Jan de Groot, is currently situated inside the church at Canisbay, and is a major attraction to the thousands of tourists who visit us in the far north. The bare facts of the curious history of this stone are well documented: it was lain on the tomb of Jan de Groot in 1568, in the east end of the church. It was covered over at some point, and lay hidden until unearthed in 1893, when it was removed by John Nicolson to his workshop in Nybster. It was then returned after extensive "renovation" and mounted in the outside wall of the south aisle, until 1982 when, to protect it from erosion, it was again re-sited to its present berth within the church. So much is undisputed fact; but to understand why the stone was ever disturbed in the first place, we must look a little deeper into a curious tale that interweaves the stories of two of the parish's most illustrious denizens – John de Groat and John Nicolson.

Legend has it that the original John O'Groats came to Caithness from Holland, and ran the first ferry over the short sea crossing to Orkney – in those days a much more important cultural and trading centre than it is now. He charged a fare of fourpence, and the ancient Scottish fourpenny piece became known as a Groat in his honour. His ferry service flourished, and he soon became a wealthy man; but his family squabbled continually over precedence, so the story goes, and Jan eventually built an octagonal house, with eight doors, and an octagonal table so that each of the eight contending branches could enter and leave the house, and take their seat at the table, without any quarrel over precedence.

What the popular legend does not reveal is what happened after the old ferryman's day, and what became of his great wealth. One might have expected him to buy extensive lands throughout Caithness and Orkney, and become founder of a dynasty of rich and powerful Groats; but clearly this did not happen. Certainly today there are Groats, both in Caithness and Orkney, who can trace their ancestry back to the original Jan de Groat – but their name is all they inherited.

Jan de Groot was of course a Dutchman; a foreigner, in a strange land. Although he prospered in Caithness, and showed no desire to return permanently to the land of his birth, he never really felt secure in his position. He enjoyed the patronage of the Earl of Caithness, who granted him land by charter in 1496; but in those uncertain times, he knew full well that an Earl could fall just as swiftly as a claymore, and in any time of turmoil, an uppity foreigner lording it over rich estates would be the first against the wall. So, he wisely decided to keep a low profile, live frugally, and avoid antagonising the natives by being seen to accumulate wealth at their expense. But what, then, did he do with his money?

The truth of the matter was discovered by none other than John Nicolson, over 300 years after Jan de Groot was laid to rest in Canisbay Church on 13th April, 1568.

Nicolson was of course a brilliant scholar, a genuine renaissance man, whose interests covered almost every sphere of human knowledge. In the course of his researches, he discovered that Jan de Groot took off every year, just at the end of the busy summer season – a tradition which incidentally persists among ferrymen to this day – and went back to his home port of Amsterdam. In those days, Amsterdam was just establishing itself as the world centre of the diamond trade; and Nicolson put two and two together, and deduced that de Groot steadily turned his wealth into diamonds. In the absence of a Swiss bank account, what better way to protect your wealth in a foreign land in uncertain times? Diamonds – tiny, glittering, brilliantly perfect, the most precious of jewels; easily hidden, easily distributed – pure crystallised wealth.

But what, then, became of the diamonds after the old de Groot passed on? Where had he hidden them? Clearly, whatever de Groot may have intended, they did not pass to his quarrelsome descendants; and for centuries their very existence was unsuspected.

Then fortune played its hand. In 1893, routine renovations inside the church at Canisbay uncovered the tombstone, beneath the flooring at the east end of the church with one of the pillars supporting the gallery resting on it. By pure co-incidence, Nicolson had at that time been researching the history of Jan de Groot, and amongst other papers he found a bill of sale from the quarry at Freswick for one plain sandstone block, purchased in 1560 – eight years before his death – by one Jhone de Grotte. Appended to the bill of sale was a scrap of parchment that bore the legend: "Waarneemen juillie hier ligt in dize schuilplatts alles dat ik gelaten heb" and beneath, in a different hand was a translation: "Behold hiere in thys reffuge lyes my erthly remayningess."

Nicolson was a meticulous man, and several questions arose in his mind. Why did de Groot buy his own headstone – even in those days, it was most unusual. Even more curious was his choice of stone: Nicolson, expert in such matters, would have found the choice of the soft red friable sandstone of Freswick most curious for a memorial. He copied out the original Old Dutch from the old record, and sent it to an acquaintance of his at Oxford. Imagine his excitement when he received the more accurate literal translation in reply: "Look ye; here lies in this hiding place all that I have left."

Nicolson immediately realised the significance of the inscription: This was no idle comment on the future use of the stone as a memorial on his tomb, it was a clear instruction to his Dutch speaking descendants to search inside the stone to find what he had left, not under the stone to find what was left of him!

The rest, as they say, is history.

Keith Muir, Newton, John O'Groats.

Pull the other leg!. . .Ed.

QUEEN ELIZABETH THE QUEEN MOTHER

Queen Elizabeth, the Queen Mother and the Rev. George Bell going into Canisbay Church c.1975.

Photo, J. McDonald, Shore Lane, Wick.
Left to Right:- Miss Elphinstone, Sir Ralph Anstruther (Treasurer to the Queen Mother), Lady Fermoy (grandmother of the Princess of Wales).

For over 30 years now our church at Canisbay has been honoured and happy to have Her Majesty Queen Elizabeth, The Queen Mother, worshipping there with us when on holiday at the Castle of Mey. She has always shown a keen interest in the church, as have her household and her guests. In 1990, which was a very important one for Her Majesty, and for all of us, being her 90th birthday, the congregation and the children of the Sunday School suitably marked the occasion by presenting her with gifts[1] as a token of our love and affection for her, and our joy at having her in our midst.

During those years since Queen Elizabeth took up residence at the Castle, Canisbay Kirk was greatly honoured by one of its ministers[2] being invited to preach at Crathie Church to the Royal family and to be the guest of the Queen at Balmoral. Imagine the minister's surprise when he discovered the church officer had been in charge at Achvarasdale Eventide Home and they were well known to each other!

The Queen Mother meets many people at church from home and abroad and greatly delights everyone with her warmth and friendliness. We pray that she may long be spared to join us in worship in Canisbay Kirk.

[1] The congregation gifted a fine carved walnut tray with the initials E.R. positioned in the centre of the design. The tray was made by Ben and John Calder, The Clett, Castletown and was done in a similar fashion to the McIvor and Allan type of carving. The Sunday School pupils gifted a table lamp whose base was decorated with shells by the children themselves.

[2] The Rev. George Bell.

WORLD SERVICE BROADCAST FROM CANISBAY CHURCH

On 8th August, 1971 the BBC did a World Service Broadcast from Canisbay Church, which some people may well remember. I know that we had it recorded and the minister took it with him on his visits to those unable to attend church at the time and it was much appreciated. What you may not know about, is that he received letters from all over the world from people who had heard the service. I'm sure you may be interested in one or two excerpts from the said letters.

From Rev. Dr J.E. Parry, Livingstone, Zambia.

"Whilst on holiday 800 miles from Livingstone and unable to go to church, we listened to the evening service on the BBC and much appreciated your ministry of the Word and the Hymns – not forgetting Handel's Largo at the end.

With Thanks, J.E. Parry,
(Associate minister of United Church of Zambia)"

Our organist at that time was Marjory Dundas from the farm of Warse who always played with great willingness and we were so pleased that she got a special mention.

This one came from Salisbury Rhodesia and the writer may be known to some people. He went on "Some time ago on a Sunday evening I tuned into the BBC and was deeply moved to find myself listening to a service from Canisbay, where as a young man I sometimes played soccer, playing at outside left for the Castletown boys. In the Canisbay team was a young fellow named MacKenzie. I think that his father ran the hotel." (Would that be John MacKenzie, now of Greenvale?) "At that time my father was minister of Olrig and Dugald MacEchern was in Bower and an uncle Dugald Carmichael was minister in Reay, the parish in which my mother, a MacAuley had been born.

With such a background at any time a Church Service from so near home would have had impact, but at the time I was beset by worry and ill health so that your service came to me as if the answer to a prayer which I had omitted to make and the strangest thing about it was that your organist had chosen as a voluntary Handel's Largo, one of my favourite pieces of music, into which is so beautifully blended the wind and the waves of the sea.

I drop you a line at this time to thank you and the good people of your parish for coming to me across the world at a time when I needed the comfort of warm memories and home." The letter went on at some length but I only want you to have the relevant details and I must not forget to tell you that it was signed N.M. MacLean.

Another letter came from Jerusalem, Israel, which said "Your broadcast over the BBC brought blessing." It went on to say "In the days of mutilated translations your use of the Authorised version gave weight to the message." This gentleman was retired from the US Government and had been living in Israel for over 10 years. He was 84 years old.

These were just a few of the more interesting letters but it was so good to know that the service had actually been heard by so many and also been of some help and blessing.

THE LAST SUPPER

This beautifully framed tapestry was gifted to Canisbay Church by a lady from Grantown-on-Spey. She was Mrs McKail, a good friend of Mrs Bell, whose husband had been minister of Canisbay for over 21 years, more than half of his entire ministry.

This tapestry was the work of Mrs McKail's grandmother, a lady called Jane Elizabeth Wray, whose maiden name was Elcote. She carried out the work on the tapestry from the age of 16 to 23, from 1869-1876. It was embroidered at Woodham North Farm, Aycliffe, County Durham and won first prize at the Durham Show. The frame is the original one, made by the estate joiner and seven different woods were incorporated in its frame, all from trees grown on the estate. The story goes that Jane Elcote was very friendly with the joiner as long as he was engaged in making this very special frame but lost interest in him after it was completed!!!

The estate belonged to Sir William Eden, who was Sir Anthony Eden's father.

Mrs McKail must have inherited her grandmother's flair for knitting and embroidery because she was constantly involved in works for charity and before she died she was invited to one of the Speyside Houses, where she met Her Majesty Queen Elizabeth, The Queen Mother, who came to inspect all the beautifully knitted goods that had been made for one of her special charities. This tapestry is a Berlin Canvas. We are glad that the Kirk Session have had the tapestry hung in the church for the pleasure of our own congregation and the many visitors to our ancient and historic church in Canisbay.

CANISBAY CHURCH

Canisbay Kirk has always been popular with visitors from near and far and in recent years with the increase in tourist buses and in tourists from abroad its popularity has soared. We are delighted to now have a visitors book so that we'll have a record of some of those passing through. In our day, from the old manse we could see buses drawing up at the church and the minister, if he was working in the garden, would down tools, and dressed in his casual clothes, no clerical collar of course, would jump into the car and go down to the kirk to talk to the party. On one such occasion he quietly opened the inside door and was confronted by this captive audience sitting on either side of

the central aisle. In the pulpit was the bus driver telling his party some really wonderful tales, which the minister did enjoy! "Finally", said the preacher, "I want you all to turn round and see the pink glass in that back window because it's there for a purpose. Every night someone comes down here when darkness is falling and that centre light is switched on and all the ships are safely guided through the Firth." I don't know what all the seven or eight lighthouses were doing that we could see from the church! Anyway it was a good story. Maybe the bus driver wasn't so far wrong because not more than a couple of days later we were in the church again when a middle-aged couple came in and the man said, "My wife and I are on holiday and I just telt her that she was to come and see this braw Kirk because ye see I'm a fisherman fae Fraserburgh and this stretch o' water is very familiar tae me and this Kirk is one o'ma landmarks when I'm coming through the Pentland Firth." So whether the bus driver had a point or not, one thing is really sure and that is the light of the gospel has shone from Canisbay Kirk for a very long time, shining forth to guide us all through the sea of life in its storms and in its calm.

Mrs Christian Bell, The Cottage, Mey.

NOTES TAKEN FROM CANISBAY KIRK SESSION RECORDS DATED 1867

Fees for wedding banns – 2/6.

Session clerk paid £2 per year.

John Sutherland head teacher Canisbay (Mrs Duffus's father) was Session Clerk until he died in 1892. Canisbay school teacher Andrew Munro took over and he was also the Precentor. He was followed by George Mackenzie, and after that Arthur Brown, both school teachers in John O'Groats. (They sat in the Precentor's box or seat beneath the pulpit).

1913 the Rev. J. Forbes and the session discussed the building of a Church Hall for the Parish Church. War broke out in 1914 and nothing more was done regarding a hall

Notes taken by Barbara S. Mowat, Viewfirth, John O'Groats.

MY FIRST DAY AT CHURCH

First Recollections of a Canisbay Schoolboy

I would like very well to give in detail
What happened this day, but my memory does fail,
Yet I still remember excitement ran high
As they led me through the church for a seat to try.

Every stroke of the bell was like breaking my heart
I thought quietness was better especially at the start
And the way to the gallery seemed so very long
I thought they were off with me to sing The New Song.

Between my dear parents I then settled doon
And began to look round just as it struck noon
When I spied the parson climbing up the nice stair
With his robes o'er his shoulder, I thought it was rare.

I can't give his text nor a word that he spoke
It was all down on paper and of that a big stock
He kept us but short, and of that I was glad
For I long'd to be free like every else lad.

We always carry something from a service like this
So here is the thing I do not want to miss
The elders went round just nearing the close
With a long handled box and held to my nose.

So I doled out my mite along with the rest
And as proud as the Pharisee that I had done my best
But the thing that tickled me most was when
The women they glower'd at me and also the men.

About the same time I went to the school
My father escorting me for that was the rule
But on entering in and looking around
I felt so shy I could have crept underground.

The master was there with a tawse to his toes
The scholars were staring at me like crows
But it chang'd my thoughts when he laid aside
His ugly weapon which seem'd his pride.

He patted me gently on the head so kind
And told my father, all was right he would find
Then he plac'd a coin in the palm of my hand
An act which still in my memory does stand.

Though many changeful scenes have gone and come
And death has called this dear teacher home
These acts though but trivial do leave their impress
And a teacher like this should be honour'd none the less.

Daniel Dunnett, 15 Bridge Street, Wick.
28th October, 1911.

Footnote:– Daniel Dunnett born 1859 was the son of Alexander Dunnett, stone mason and Jane Banks, Mey. (Her family were highly skilled carpenters of boat building stock.) Alexander lived in Upper Gills and it would have been down the Captain's Road that Daniel would have walked with his father to the church and to the Canisbay Public School, opened in 1864. Daniel married Anne Geddes, Mill of Mey and c.1890 his charge for building a three roomed house was £20. William Dunnett provost of Wick was his son and Daniel (research engineer with Shell), William (retired plumber, Wick), James (with Grover Clyne) and Anne (solicitor) are his grandchildren.

A.H.

Time

Outstretched hand horizontal on horizon
Four fingers = one hour.
Calculate after sunrise and before sunset.
Eric McKay, "Shenaghan".

An hour lost in the morning has to be run after all day.
Magnus MacLean, Duart

Rise when the day daw's
Bed when the nicht fa's

Alan Green.

THE MANSE STEADING AND OUTHOUSES

Established Church Manse c.1900

Photo, Sheila Moir, Scarfskerry.

Bee Skeps 1993

Photo, Rogni Brown, Swartigill, J.O'G.

Winnowing door in barn with round kiln end 1993

Photo, Rogni Brown, Swartigill, J.O'G.

The Statutory List Supplement states "The manse received extensive repairs in 1832". The building is said to be mid to late 18th Century with early 19th Century alterations and additions.

The milk-house or cold-store lean-to at the back of the house with its window in the north wall has a flagstone floor and two feet deep flagstone shelves forming a work surface round three walls. The large iron hooks in the ceiling now carrying strings of onions likely held legs of ham, reested mutton and dried salt fish in days gone by.

Before there was mains water the manse was supplied from the stone built fountain on the Seater Road near Jack Malcolm's, where there was a strong and very good spring. This iron-ever water was piped into a flag-lined, rectangular shaped filtration bed reservoir in the manse garden. This filtration bed had to be cleaned out regularly and the bottom filled with fresh shell sand. [The roadside pump in the corner of Bill Bremner's (Don Wares' now) field was also supplied from this spring.]

"In 1791 the minister was extremely well accommodated with new office houses" and one wonders if the remains of a doo-cot against the garden wall with the pigeon entrance on the west side dates from this time. The bee-skeps in the adjoining wall also face west. It is thought that caisies, usually made here from bulliwans (dockan stalks), straw and heather all woven together were fitted into the recesses as sort of bykes or hives for honey bees.

An 1835 map shows that Peter Jolly had more ground than many of the neighbouring crofters. The 1841 census shows he was there with his wife and two young children and that they had James Shearer (aged 25 to 30), Thomas Dunnet (aged 12) and three female servants living there.

The small courtyard at the back of the house is flanked on

Nest boxes 1993

Manger

Stable Stall

Byre

Photos, Rogni Brown, Swartigill, J.O'G.

the north by the stables, byres and coach house and on the south by the servants' house, barn and kiln. It is worth noting the 14 inches wide by four inches deep drainage channels running along the outer edge of the pavements. The bottom and sides are lined with flag and the tops are still level with the pavement, showing the skill and care of the mason who laid them. The winnowing doors in the north and south walls of the barn which has been extended into the round kiln, would indicate that this is the oldest part of the steading. Between the barn and the servants' house is the hen house with its ten nest boxes recessed into the back of the chimney wall at either side of the fireplace column to provide warmth and thus encourage laying. The cows' and stirks' byres with flagstone floors have troughs and "hallan" stones set one third in the ground. Both byres have a 40 inch wide strand (with drainage channels at each side and a 14 inch wide raised footwalk down the centre) which slopes towards a drainage grid under the window which also acted as the muck hole.

The close-sarked, fine, wood-lined coach house was for the Laird of Mey's coach and the stable next to it was for his driving horses when the Laird's party were at the church. There is also a fine wooden ceiling in the tack or grooms' room which has had a fireplace. It is likely that the minister also used this part for his pony and gig and perhaps those of visiting dignitaries. The second stable was for the working horses. The photo shows the shaped trevis which separates the two stalls with the heel-post at the end which is set in the stone which raised the bottom of the post and prevented urine rotting it.

The horse wore a stall-collar in the stable which had about four feet of rope attached to it. This rope passed through the ring in the front of the manger and had a four inch wooden sinker block attached to it which prevented it tangling and the rope gave the horse more freedom to move up and down in the stall. The close-up photo shows the glazed fireclay feed-box set in the manger which has a strip of metal along the front as has the trevis to prevent the horse chewing it. The pigs' and ducks' houses are positioned a bit away from the steading but are within sheltering dry-stone dykes. The extensive out-houses and steading have been heightened, improved and altered over the years and are still being sympathetically repaired and maintained.

Margaret Blacklock, 'Al Hasa'.

ROUND KILNS

Ground Floor

Floor of Kiln

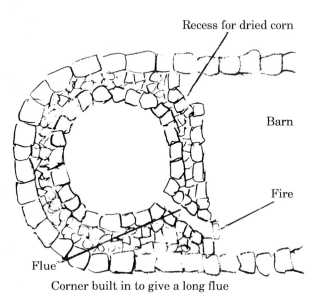

Recess for dried corn

Barn

Fire

Flue

Corner built in to give a long flue

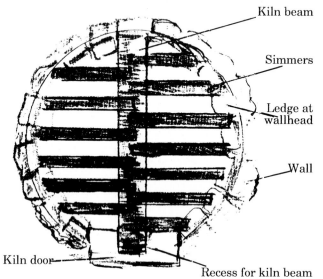

Kiln beam

Simmers

Ledge at wallhead

Wall

Kiln door

Recess for kiln beam

These kilns were higher than the barn and were built egg-shaped to increase the draught and also give more even distribution of heat. The four foot thick walls were perpendicular on the outside and on the inside they curved out gradually as they rose about five feet or so to the floor of the kiln which was laid on a ledge five inches wide running round on the wall heads. The walls then curved in gradually all round leaving a round chimney hole in the centre two to three feet across, and in the parish often the top two or three courses were built of fails (divots). The sornie (kiln fireplace) was in the barn usually at the left hand side, with its vent going through the gable and opening at ground level in the kiln. This long flue helped reduce the risk of fire. There was a recess or small peat neuk above or near the sornie for keeping small black peats dry for starting and stoking the fire. Only the best peats are used for drying because wet or foggy ones would smoke and taint the meal. The door to the kiln was in the centre of the gable between the kiln and the barn and was reached by three or four stone steps projecting in this wall.

Kiln floors were made easily demountable, so that in case of fire, one end of the kiln-beam could be lifted, which collapsed the floor to the bottom of the kiln where the flames were smothered. The kiln-beam – a heavy four inch by four inch plank of wood – was laid across the centre with one end set in a sneck at the kiln door and the other end in a sneck or recess in the wall head. Short pieces of fencing posts, simmers, were set three inches apart resting on the kiln-beam alternately and the wall heads to give a level floor.

Selected unbroken straw (gloy) was carefully laid over the slats and sometimes a pleated straw mat (flet) was put over that. The corn was spread over to a depth of about three inches. The kiln-door was closed or the opening was stuffed with two winlins of straw to increase the draught and keep in the heat. The time for drying varied with the heat, draught, quality and kind of grain. I understand that when the corn was dried the simmers were parted and the grain fell on to the floor.

Magnus Houston.

RODERICK MACGREGOR – CANISBAY'S FREE CHURCH PIONEER

People in Canisbay still call it "the south kirk", or even "Russell's kirk", after the highly respected Rev. James Russell who was minister there from 1915 until 1949. Now, like the kirk of Barrock seven miles to the west, it has become a farm shed. At one time it knew of other harvests.

Some say that D.L. Moody, the Billy Graham of last century, preached from its pulpit. This would have been during the evangelist's second visit to Caithness in December 1891. He and the gospel singer, Ira D. Sankey, whose Sacred Songs and Solos used to be a best-seller in Scotland, stayed at Mackay's Hotel – in those days Bruce's Temperance Hotel.

Moody preached to thousands in Wick and Thurso but he also held services elsewhere. The story goes that in the parish of Canisbay the people, unable to do much on their crofts because of the weather, came across the snow to hear him. Years later, George Green, father of retired schoolmaster Ben Green of John O'Groats, often spoke of "the fervent preaching of D.L. Moody" and of the good work he had done.

But church history shows that religious awakenings are not brought about by evangelists, however eloquent or gifted. Before the harvest there has to be ploughing and sowing, rain and sunshine – the labour of faithful ministers and dedicated Christians with, of course, the blessing of Heaven. In the final analysis, revival is a divine work.

Roderick MacGregor was a faithful minister. He was ordained and inducted as the first minister of Canisbay Free Church on 19th February, 1851 and died on 25th August, 1889. Canisbay was his only charge.

The reason for the Disruption of 1843 was the failure of attempts to do away with the Law of Patronage which gave Scottish landowners the right to appoint ministers to parish churches against the wishes of congregations. The minister who suited the laird was not, necessarily, the best pastor for the people – or for the laird!

About one third of the ministers and members of the National Church left to form the Free Church of Scotland. In the Highlands and in Caithness, the percentage was much higher, possibly 80 per cent or more, which gave rise to the rhyme:

"The Auld kirk, the cauld kirk,
The kirk that has the steeple;
The wee kirk the free kirk
The kirk wi' a' the people."

Of the 12 ministers in the Presbytery of Caithness, only three adhered to the "auld kirk"; the Rev. Peter Jolly of Canisbay was one of them. He was a popular man, so well-liked that parents called their children after him. Even in a later generation such names could be found as Peter Jolly Gunn of John O'Groats and John Jolly Sinclair of Stroma. Because he did not "come out", the defection in his parish was only in the region of 50 per cent.

However, by 1845, the new congregation had completed the building of a church, school and manse on land provided by one of their members, G. Sinclair Sutherland esq, of Brabster. The school and schoolhouse are now the home of Mrs Nan Fraser. Some of the hooks on which the bairns used to hang their coats are still to be seen in the porch.

Their first minister was born in Inverness in 1818. Three years later, he went with his family to Prince Edward Island in Canada where he spent his boyhood. At the age of 16, he returned to

Free Church and Manse c.1900

Photo, Jonty Willis, Old Elm House, Redmire, Leyburn, North Yorkshire.
(Great, great grandson of Rev. Roderick MacGregor).

LEST WE FORGET

U.F. Church c.1920

Photo, William Dunnet, Quoys.

Envelope found in "aise" walls of "St Leonards" formerly the Free Church Manse. Courtesy, Dr Moray E. Fraser.

Scotland and after some time, studied for the ministry of the Free Church at the University of Aberdeen and New College, Edinburgh.

On being licensed, he was appointed to Canisbay, then only a preaching station. He got on well with the congregation and, when the church was given full status, they were happy to call him as their minister.

Shortly afterwards, he married Elizabeth, youngest daughter of the Laird of Brabster. They had a family of three boys, George David and Alex. George became a doctor in Bradford. Alex also studied medicine and became the Canisbay GP. David – a medical student collapsed and died on the stage coach near Duncansby in 1899.

As the years passed, Elizabeth was a great support to him in his work. She knew the people well and took an interest in the young, possibly helping with the Young Women's Class which met after the 10 a.m. Sabbath School and before worship at 12 noon. She also used to visit the poor and the sick. What kind of man was her husband?

In appearance, Roderick MacGregor was tall and well-built; but what most impressed those who met him was his kindly face and his gracious personality. As late as the period after the First World War, almost every house in Freswick had his picture on the wall. However, there was a political side to this.

In those days, the Evangelicals – and all Free Kirk ministers were Evangelicals – were the "left wingers" of the Church. The Disruption was more than a demonstration of religious conviction. It was about democracy. Freswick folk had suffered at the hands of their laird who was a patron of the parish church.

On one occasion, when they did not have enough money to pay for their rents, he took eggs from them instead. There were too many to eat, so he mixed what was left into mortar to repair the walls of Freswick House.

But if MacGregor was looked

332

upon as a champion of the crofters, he was also appreciated as a loving pastor and an exemplary Christian.

As a token of respect, some parents named their children after him too. For example, in 1868, a Freswick couple called their baby son Roderick MacGregor Matheson.

Two tributes, one by the Rev. James MacPherson, his colleague in the parish church, appeared in the Northern Ensign of 3rd September, 1889. The first describes him as "charitable to all who differed from him" and, although "vehement against evil and error", an "exceedingly gentle person."

MacPherson delivered a pulpit tribute: "The deep affection of his family, and all who knew him, testifies to the sweetness and amiability of his character. . . It was not possible to be brought into contact with such a sunny, guileless nature as his without being drawn to him. His piety was of an attractive type, cheerful and trustful, as became one whose feet were firmly planted on the Rock of Ages."

These last words were carefully chosen. Roderick MacGregor's favourite hymn was "Rock of Ages, cleft for me".

Strangely enough he was not what might be termed a popular preacher. His sermons were long and scholarly and, in winter, daylight would be fading as the congregation made their way homeward. But there were flashes of illumination and power in his preaching, and deep pathos in his appeals to the unconverted.

The Rev. Archibald Auld, in his book "Memorials of Caithness Ministers", writes of "one or more revival movements" during his ministry. There were, in fact, several.

In 1859 he visited Ireland to see the great work of revival in progress there and he longed for the same in his own land and parish. By the following year, Scotland, too, was in the grip of a nationwide awakening.

The social benefits were immense as thousands of lives were transformed by the power of the Gospel, and the churches had an accession of 300,000 new members when the Scottish population was only three million. A feature of the movement was the preaching of lay evangelists.

One of these was an Englishman called Brownlow North. He came to Caithness as a guest of Sir George Sinclair and stayed at Thurso Castle. From this centre, he went on an evangelistic tour of the county.

His most memorable meeting took place at the Hill of Barrock. The church was not large enough to hold the hundreds who came, most of them on foot, some in carts and the gentry in their carriages. North preached with great effect on the story of Phillip and the Ethiopian in Acts chapter eight.

According to J.M. Baikie of Bower, Canisbay was also "greatly blessed" by North's preaching. So the parish shared in the general awakening and there is no doubt that Roderick would have been involved, even if no record of what happened has yet been discovered.

But the great spiritual event in the parish last century was in the year 1886. A column of local news appears in the Northern Ensign of 3rd March, that year. An early lambing for those days is mentioned: "On 15th February, a ewe belonging to Mr Dunnet of Quoys dropped twin lambs." There is also a detailed account of a soirée, organised by the John O'Groats Temperance Society, held in the Free Church school.

Among those who took part were Charlotte Manson of Seater, who recited the poem "O man give up the drink"; Ina Matheson who sang "The Four Maries"; and Joseph Smith, better known as Josie, who recited "The Death of Napoleon".

Josie was a local worthy who lost one of his hands as a result of a Hallowe'en prank at a threshimg mill belonging to William Banks of Midtown, John O'Groats. Later in life, with one hand and a hook, he was able to climb the Muckle Stack at Duncansby in the company of fellow-Groater John Green of Roadside. He was also an amateur poet.

The late Sandy Bremner of Everly, Freswick, recalled hearing that "The Death of Napoleon" was one of Josie's party pieces. Maybe he wrote it himself. But hidden away among all the news is a simple but very significant sentence: "A series of evangelical meetings were held here last week by Alex Harper, Wick."

Alex Harper was born in Wick in 1852. A plasterer to trade, he was converted to Christ while plastering the walls of the John O'Groats Hotel in 1875.

Ten years later, he was appointed agent for the North East Coast Mission in Wick and in January 1886, he addressed a Temperance meeting in the Canisbay Free Church school. 18 signed the pledge and Harper was invited to conduct a two-week mission in the church in the following month.

From the start, the meetings were crowded and, as time went on, the interest deepened. Many were converted. Revival being God's work, recognises no denominational boundaries and encouraging numbers joined both churches.

This extract from MacGregor's diary expresses his deep joy and fulfilment:

"Communion Sabbath – 20th June, 1886. I believe that this has been one of the most remarkable and blessed days that ever occurred in the history of Canisbay. No less a number than that of 60 sat down for the first time at the Lord's Table – and were it not that many of the people were away at the coast fishing, the number would, I have no doubt, been 70, if not upward. O my God, "Keep them as the apple of the eye"!"

The quotation is from Psalm 17, and part of the text of his communion sermon. The Rev. John Sinclair[1] a native of Canisbay, came up from Bowden in Roxburghshire to assist at the services. Here is his description of the occasion:

"As young and old came slowly forward to the front pews and took their seats, each bowing his head the moment he sat down, the impression made on us who looked on was such that it was with difficulty that anyone could offer prayer."

Another harvest had been gathered in. Three years later, the much-loved pastor of Canisbay Free Church passed away. He had cared for his people like a father, he had preached the Word faithfully; he had by God's grace, fought the good fight and finished the course.

The parish is not what it was a century ago. Two world wars have come and gone; lifestyles and certain values have changed greatly. The fellowship meetings which used to be held in Gills, Brabster and John O'Groats are long forgotten and worshippers no longer flock to church on the Lord's day.

Canisbay can never have another Roderick MacGregor, but Roderick MacGregor's God is still with us. He still has the power to fill churches with people and to fill people with his grace and love.

[1] John Sinclair seems to have been the brother of the gentle and kindly Alex Sinclair of Brabster, at one time a precentor in the South Kirk and a well-known figure in the parish until his death in 1954. Their grandmother, Ann Sinclair, famous for her piety, and their uncle, the Rev. John Sinclair of Bruan, feature in Alexander Auld's "Ministers and men in the Far North".

Rev. Alex Muir, Clachan, Lochmaddy, North Uist.

SKIPPING DOWN MEMORY LANE

Rev. Roderick MacGregor and Family c.1888

Photo, Mrs Helen Willis, Kevock, Aysgarth, Leyburn Nr. Yorks.
Back Row, left to right:– David MacGregor, Edward Sutherland (cousin of Mrs R. MacGregor), Maggie Fraser, Mrs Alick MacGregor, Dr Alick MacGregor, Dr George MacGregor, Mrs George MacGregor, Lizzie Kennedy. Front Row:– Rev. Roderick MacGregor, Mrs Elizabeth MacGregor née Sutherland with Elsie on her knee (sister of Helen Dove).

Many are the holidays that I have spent in Caithness. The first one I remember was in the late 1890's when I was about six years old. I came with my father and mother from Bingley, Yorkshire, to visit my grandmother the widow of Rev. Roderick MacGregor, late of Canisbay Free Church.

My grandfather, Roderick MacGregor, was a man with a mind of his own and "came out" in the Disruption of 1843 which split the Church of Scotland from top to bottom. Thereafter, he became the first minister in the Free Church, which was officially opened in Canisbay in 1845 on land donated by his father-in-law, Captain George Sinclair Sutherland of Brabster.

Grandfather loved the far north and retained the living until his death in 1889. His eldest son, my uncle Alick, shared his love of the district and the people and settled down happily as the first resident local doctor, after serving as ship's surgeon on a ship to India and then in a partnership practice with my father in Bradford. My father then settled in a practice in Bingley.

Thus I and my two elder sisters were born and brought up in Bingley in the West Riding of Yorkshire. However, with a name like MacGregor we could never forget our Scottish origins, even if we had wanted to. And needless to say, my father was constantly longing for the land of his birth.

I must have made some 40 and more "pilgrimages" back home, last year with my grand-daughter and great-grand-daughter, but no journey stands out as clearly in my mind as that trip at the age of nine. My uncle Alick's invitation to the whole family to go and stay with him and his hospitable wife sparked off great preparations for the long journey and holiday.

True, we could go by train as far as Wick – but what a journey lay ahead of us. Something like 24 hours with no sleeping berths, dining cars or even buffets.

We eventually steamed into the terminus at Wick

and we must have looked a sorry crew to my uncle Alick who was there on the platform to meet us. He had cycled the 16 miles from Canisbay to give us a real Scottish welcome. Soon he was helping to load us and all our paraphernalia into the mail coach, which bore the name "Barrogill" in honour of Barrogill Castle (now owned by the Queen Mother and renamed the Castle of Mey). Our next stop was at Wick Post Office, where we had to wait while the mail was sorted into individual bags for dropping at the villages en route to John O'Groats.

Two horses pulled our long covered coach which was reserved for passengers inside and mail, luggage and assorted parcels heaped on top within a guard rail which encircled the roof.

Our coachman/driver was the famous Archie McLeod, who had held that proud office for many years. He left John O'Groats every morning with a few passengers and collected more passengers or parcels, mail or shopping requests at many call houses and crossroads on his way. He would take boots and shoes to mend, hats for new ribbons or even chickens to market and would drop similar assorted wares at odd points all the way home – irrespective of whether the recipients were waiting for him at the appointed spot. He would just throw the goods on to the grass at the roadside. He had had one holiday in 20 years, he said, and then only because his leg was broken when the coach overturned on a snowbound road. Dr Alick, he told us, had put his leg into "stuck-go" (plaster).

On approaching Keiss an extra horse was attached to help up the hill. Auckengill was the next village – here were the roadside stables where the two weary horses were changed. After passing through Freswick, the road forks to the left, the direct road to John O'Groats was not completed. At this time it was known as the Red Road, I suppose because of the red sandstone surface.

On to what is known as "Maggie's Corner". Many years ago there was a public house here kept by the Cruickshanks. A daughter, Camilla, married Walter Ross who farmed the glebe for the Free Church minister and drove the conveyance for him. (Mrs Walter Ross lived to a great age and has many descendants in the district.)

At "Maggie's Corner" there is a bridle or cart track which was known as the "Captain's Road". It was said to be made by my great-grandfather, Captain S. Sutherland of Brabster House and later of West Canisbay. It was made of imported stone so that a wheeled vehicle could go for peats instead of them being carried on the people's backs.

At this corner, the road straight on goes to Thurso but the coach turns right down the hill for Canisbay, Huna and John O'Groats. Here we alight for Pentland View to spend our holiday with our uncle and aunt, Dr and Mrs MacGregor.

Nothing can ever erase from my memory the pure joy of arriving at Canisbay. As we entered the house there was the unmistakable fragrance of a peat fire, the welcoming sight of a table set for a meal and the beaming smiles of dear Jessie and Maggie. They were old family helpers, the latter having served my grandparents for many years previously at the Manse. Jessie, I recall, was then engaged to marry "Postie" (Willie Dunnet) and was perhaps especially cheerful for that reason. With our arrival, the house must have been bursting at the seams, but nothing flustered my aunt and everything went off very smoothly.

Housekeeping must have been difficult as all drinking water had to be carried from a well in the manse grounds, some distance away. The white enamel buckets were kept cool outside the back door. Rainwater was collected in large barrels. There was an inside toilet, but only to be used in emergencies as it was served with rainwater. The old-fashioned earth closet was outside, round the side of the house. On washdays, Ina, Jessie's teenage sister, used to come to help. I would talk to her as she "tramped" the washing in the low tub with her bare feet. Round and round she would go, holding her skirts with both hands to keep them clear of the water.

Cover of Well at Manse

Jack Dunnet enclosed the square stone built, six to seven foot deep well in a lean-to greenhouse at the front of the manse. The large round cover stone (unfortunately broken) shows the iron lid which allowed a pail to be dropped to lift water.

On Saturday a great deal of time was spent on preparations for the Sabbath, which in those days was truly a day of rest when no menial work could be done. All Sunday's food had to be prepared the day before, shoes cleaned and clothes brushed and laid out.

The service started at noon with the Rev. Mr Munro as minister. There was no organ, but there was a choir of six who sat under the pulpit and faced the congregation. My uncle was their "precentor". He gave them a note on his tuning fork and then led them with great solemnity, despite an occasional tendency to use his fork as a baton. (Later, the people were persuaded to acquire an American organ which was played by my aunt.)

The congregation was a large one and most folk came on foot, many from several miles away. Others came in two-wheeled traps, unyoked their horses on arrival and left them tethered outside the church. Of the services, my own special memory is the odd way that the Psalms were sung by the choir so that the old people at the back (who presumably couldn't follow their lead) were apt to get a verse behind.

A few years ago I was in the church again with one of the early elders who told me that his father had built the roof and pews as a voluntary offering. Another had sold his gold watch to help with the cost. The pews were all hand-hewn and the timber was floated by sea from Wick to the beach, and then drawn to the site on sledges. Now that fine old church, built by so many loving hands is used as a hay shed. It was built to the design of the General Assembly Rooms, Edinburgh. Central heating was installed, but it was very expensive to run and was never really a success.

We young girls used to play on the beach at Huna. I could not walk, having had polio, but a wheel-chair was borrowed so I did not miss the fun. One day there was a lifeboat practice, the sirens sounded and the men were soon on the scene. I think Mr John Dunnet of Seater was coxswain, Willie Dunnett, known as "Postie", and probably Sandy Gunn of John O'Groats were members of the crew. It was a great thrill as the lifeboat went down the slipway, making a huge splash as it entered the sea. Three Misses Davidson lived in a cottage still standing near the boathouse. They sold sweets and chocolate. We often went to speak to Kitty the one who was an invalid, always in bed, and who did such beautiful embroidery.

The mail boat crossed from Huna to Stroma twice a week taking goods of every description. Miss Ina Sutherland was the Huna postmistress for over 50 years. Her brothers and their sons worked at the blacksmiths nearby.

On our way from Canisbay to Huna I remember seeing Mr William Kennedy in his garden with a net over his straw hat as he attended to his bees. We did enjoy the honey in the comb that he gave us. Many are the dear friends now gone, whose descendants I like to think of as my friends. As a very small girl, I remember visiting old Mrs Kennedy in her cottage near the sea at Newton – her four dear daughters were close friends of all my people and myself. For many years I have enjoyed the warm hospitality of my kind friend Mrs McKenzie at John O'Groats Hotel and later of her daughter at Seaview.

In the summer of 1925, after an interval of 22 years, I was able to visit Caithness again. We arrived in Wick on a fine sunny evening. As we came out of the station, I enquired for the "Barrogill Coach" for John O'Groats. The man to whom I spoke told me that he was the driver of the motor mail car which had replaced the horse-drawn "Barrogill" in 1908 and showed us where it was waiting. We asked if we could sit beside him, and climbed aboard.

As we drove along, I asked him if he remembered the MacGregors of Canisbay. He said "Yes" – he had attended "old Rory's" Sunday School at the Free Church. He remembered Dr Alick MacGregor, the eldest son, and he said that there was another son – also a doctor – who had gone south to Yorkshire, but he did not know anything about him. He was most surprised when I told him that I was Dr George's youngest daughter. The driver's name was Daniel Mowatt and he had taken over from Archie McLeod when the new motor coach was brought into service.

Eventually we reached Maggie's Corner and the turn to Canisbay. There was Tresdale Farm on the right and West Canisbay House on the left, where my grandmother Elizabeth MacGregor, née Sinclair-Sutherland, had been brought up. There also was the Free Church. Then we reached Canisbay – we were received with a warm welcome from our dear friends, Postie Willie and Jessie Dunnett and their family. We stayed for several days there, but did so wish it could have been longer.

Mrs Helen Dove, Morecambe.

HILL O'KIRSAN HIGHWAYMAN

Donald Cruickshanks, Andrew's brother, came from Mey to rent Claypotts, now part of West Canisbay Farm. He also drove the gig for the Rev. R. MacGregor, Minister at U.F. or South Church.

His daughter Camilla (Mrs Walter Ross) Rose Cottage, Huna was born at Claypotts in 1852. Donald returned to Mey in the late 1860s. A "boor tree" in Claypotts garden still grows beside the roadway near the brig.

Donald's sister Maggie owned the Prince of Wales Inn at Maggies' Corner, better known now as Canisbay Corner.

Another Cruickshank was a highwayman, who probably worked hand in glove with the Sinclairs of Mey (Barrogill Castle) known rogues who no doubt supplied the horse and shared the loot. Cruickshank operated from the Hill O'Kirsan – some say that is how it got its name.

The Freswick people say it means Hill of Christening – they conveyed their children over the hill to be christened in Canisbay Kirk.

Emma MacLeod, Upper Gills.

When April blows her horn
Its good for both hay and corn.
John Dunnet, Heatherbell Cottages.

A misty May and a dripping June
Is a good hay crop and harvest soon.
Kathleen Ross.

CANISBAY AGRICULTURE SHOW

The Canisbay Show held in Tower Park, West Canisbay and followed by a grand assembly in the public hall, was an exciting day in the parish. With a keen participation in all events, the livestock section alone attracted almost 200 entries. Prizes of 10 shillings were on offer in the sports and competitions, events which included one and two mile cycle races, driving round the ring, and an "exhibition gallop" which I'm sure by the end of the proceedings someone would have performed, on a charger called "Barley Corn".

About eight o'clock in the evening preceding the 1924 show, an additional excitement was generated in the district by the grounding on the Ness of Quoys of the steamer Kentucky. She was later refloated (next day, I believe) after local men jettisoned her cargo of cement and part of her bunkers. An underwater mound, thought to be the cement, can still be seen on the seabed in the locality of the grounding, and small lumps of coal may occasionally be found washed up on the beach.

Billy Magee, Lower Gills.

Looking over the Tower Park to Canisbay and Huna c.1920

Photo, Charlie Manson, Canisbay Post Office.

Canisbay and Huna 1992 (from Memorial Dyke)

Photo, Billy Magee, Lower Gills.

337

'E CANISBAY SHOW

One o' 'e highlights o' wur year
Fan bairnies long ago
Wis a special day in summer
Fan they held 'e Canisbay Show.

We spoke aboot hid weeks 'efore
'E time passed awful slow
We thocht 'e day wid never come
O' 'e Canisbay Show.

We hed nae need o' buses
'Ey werna on 'e go
We never thocht 'e distance far
Till 'e Canisbay Show.

Wi' pennies in wur pockads
An' faces all aglow
Along 'e rod by Outertoon
Till 'e Canisbay Show.

We didna need a strict kerb drill
We all walked in a row
For cars were few an' far between
Fan Canisbay hed hids show.

Then we passed 'e Hill O'Kirshan
Ere wis Stroma doon below
Along till Maggie's corner
An' doon ere wis 'e show.

Past tents an then 'e swingboats
Soarin' high and skimman low
My fat magic all aroond ye
At 'e Canisbay Show.

An machines 'at telt yer fortune
Hoopla stalls till hev a' go
An ye'd mebbey win a coconut
At 'e Canisbay Show.

For we aye got lots o' pennies
Fan we met fowk 'at we know
We sometimes cam' hom' richer
Than we set off for 'e show.

We'd watch 'e animals parade
Roond an roond 'e ring they'd go
Horses pownies coos an' stirks
At 'e Canisbay Show.

Horses wi' their manes tied up
Wi' ribbons in a bow
Their harness gleamin' in 'e sun
At 'e Canisbay Show.

'E sheep wi' bonnie yellow dip
Their fleeces seemed till glow
An' sometimes too a muckle sow
At 'e Canisbay Show.

'E cycle race we aye enjoyed
Till watch them puff an' blow
While their legs went roond lek Jehu
At 'e Canisbay Show

An J.T. Sinclair wi his gig
My could he mak hid go

The powny galloped roond an roond
At 'e Canisbay Show.

Bit a think 'e bit we lek'ed best
If 'e truth ye'd want till know
Wis fan Charlie Hercher took his bow
At 'e Canisbay Show.

Wi' his face all brightly painted
His nose did fairly glow
We wished 'at we were half as swack
As he wis at 'e show.

He'd trip an rise then fa' again
Four, five times in a row
Then somersault an kick his hat
Aboot half way oot 'e show.

Bit all good things come til an end
An' hom' at last we'd go
Till tell hid over all again
Each highlight o' 'e show.

'E bairnies noo hev' treats galore
Bit yet they'll never know
'E magic moments we enjoyed
At 'e Canisbay Show.

'Ere's galas, an' 'ere's County Shows
An' 'e Highland, but although
They try their best they're nothing lek
Wur Good Ould Canisbay Show.

If I could turn 'e clock hours back
A'll tell ye far I'd go
Over 'e hill till Canisbay
Till 'e Canisbay Show.

Clara Clyne, Strathesk Grove, Penicuik.

Photo, Katherine Ross, Upper Warse.
John Ross and his son Jamie with a fine mare and foal at the Canisbay Show.

Wind up of Canisbay Landholders' Show

About the mid 1960s a public meeting was held in the Canisbay Hall to settle up the affairs of the now defunct Canisbay Landholders' Show. The last surviving members of the committee were present being: Magnus Houston, John O'Groats, Alex Kennedy, Tresdale and Walter Gunn, Brabster, these being the only people who could dispose of the assets. It was agreed that the Cup donated by Admiral Sinclair of Dunbeath should be gifted to the Mey Sheepdog Trials. William Leitch accepted the cup and expressed thanks on behalf of the Association. The sum of money in the bank was shared between the hall committees of Auckengill, Freswick, John O'Groats, Canisbay and Mey.

The Canisbay Show started again on 2nd July, 1988 and is going from strength to strength.

Colin Mackay, John O'Groats.

"Oor Stove"

Now I'm just a poor cook
In a ministry shed
Yes I'm cook bottlewasher
And head kitchenmaid
From morning to night
I never get through
And the boys' come expecting
A nice cup of brew
Yes a nice cup of brew
They shall have just the same
Though faith it ain't easy
Shure's Barney's my name.

For the stove is too big
And the fire is too sma'
And the bally old chimney
Refuses to draw
The sticks are too wet
And the coal full of stones
I aint got a bellows
Or neither a tongs
And nothing to start
But a drop of burnt oil
So how in the hell
Can the old kettle boil.

Now we had a wee gratie
That sat on a block
A trusty old servant
That never would smock
No doubt a bit shakey
But we propped it all round
And for boiling the kettle
It ne'er let us down
Till someone condemned it
"A perfect disgrace"
And this dirty old divil
Was stuck in its place.

Now I've cooked on the ocean
And I've cooked on the lan'
And I've boiled my bit ration
In an old billy can
There's one thing I'm finding
Where ever I rove
It's the fire boils the kettle
And not the big stove.

So give me a gun
Of a two three inch bore
And help me to place it
Just outside the door
And help me to load it
With a good going shell
And I'll soon blow the . . .
Well – Ye ken yersel?!

John Fraser, Halkirk.
(Father-in-law of Nan Fraser, Cairnlee, Canisbay.)

THE THRESHING MILL

One o' 'e beeg days on 'e croft was 'e threshing when 'e steam engine came in. Hid wis a beeg day especially, if id wis a Setterday. Supplies were taken in till feed 'em all.

They pulled in at night time an' slept in a kind o' caravan wi' a fire in hid. Us bairns wis fair delighted when efter denner we gaithered roon 'e fire and they telt their tales o' where they hed been. They must have thrown paraffin on 'e fire, – 'e flames stood oot 'e chimney lek 'e Flotta Flame! Hid wis jist great till see.

Next day they went till 'e peat stack and filled up wi' peats and got 'e steam engine started. When they got plenty o' steam up they pulled a cord – hid wis a whistle and 'at wis 'e sign READY FOR ACTION. All 'e neighbours came and gave a han' at 'e threshing o' 'e corn. Our job wis up on 'e top o' 'e mill lousin 'e sheaves and handing 'em till 'e millman and he fed 'em in till 'e mill. There wis a man doon below tending till 'e corn and watchan 'e bags. Anither man wis forking 'e sheaves from 'e screw on till 'e top o' 'e mill. Another wis cairting in till 'e barn, either wi' a barrow or wi' a horse and cairt. Sometimes 'e horse wid get a bit frichtened wi' all 'e noise, so hid wis a bit risky – he micht bolt corn an' all!

Extract from a tape made by
Murray Ross, Mansfield Cottages, Canisbay

Threshing at West Canisbay c.1938

Photo, Lena Simpson, Burnside, Gills.
Beel Bremner, Seater; Jimmy Forrester (jnr), West Canisbay; Bob Lyall, Brabster; Jimmy Ross, Gills; Donald Gunn, engineman; Jocky MacKenzie, millman; Sandy Lyall, Brabster on spanker; Jock Ross, Gills; Donald MacLeod, East Mey; James Forrester (sen).

JOHNNIE'S PEEDIE FIREY

For weeks an' weeks storms niver slackid
  an' rod an' dutch wi' fans wis packid,
'En April's thaw made sich a scutter
  'en weeks o' drocht dried a' 'e gutter,
Till, though yer sock was sharpid new,
  'e steyn-hard grun wid hardly ploo.
"We've been 'at hard on peyts" says Jock,
  "Thirs little left bit fowgie trock,
A'll tirr wir banks an redd 'e tails
  an' maybe thrown doon twa-three fails".
Jock geed an' said "hid's weekid here
  wi' heathercoos as teoch as weer,
A think a'll licht a peedie firey,
  A ken hid canna cross 'e mirey".
He geed his ither bank till redd
  an' took no thocht 'e fire micht spread,
Till he looked up an' saw 'e lowe
  wis roaran halfway up 'e knowe.
Jock said wan beeg bad word
  an' ran till slock 'e muirburn, spade in hand
Bit a' 'at he could dae wis watch her,
  Jock an' his spade wid niver catch her.
"She's at 'e pint o' no return,
  A howp she disna cross 'e burn".
'E keeper cam till save 'e heather
  wi' every man 'at he could gether.
His words till Jock wis no polite,
  'E best o' them a dursna write.
A gamekeeper ye canna please
  unless he's heather till 'e knees,
Though weel he kens 'at fresh young heather
  suits grouse an' deer an' cheviot wether.
'E only fire 'at he can thole
  smoors in his pipe o' bowgie roll.

" 'E burnie is wur only howp an' she's no wide,
  'e lowes may lowp.
We're lucky! at 'e burn she bides
  tho' still she's spreadan till 'e sides.
Hing in noo boys an' do yer bit
  an' work yer brooms for a' yer fit."
Bit 'fore they slockid a' 'e blaze
  three hunder acre lay in aise.
Hid drokid every sowl wi' sweyt,
  scammed boots an' troosers wi' 'e heyt.
Hid burnt 'e roos 'at Duncan's Tom,
  'e canny sowl, hed noor taen hom',
An' Ben's peyt spade in heather deep,
  he thocht 'at Ack took hom' till keep,
An' far Jock's jaikad hed been thrown
  Bit fower black buttons a' wis gone.
'E laird's new fence 'tween Beel an' Rab.
  'e weer wis left bit no one stab.
An' even then hed wisna done
  hid burnt for weeks ablow 'e grun,
An' made sick hols in Daun's peyt roddie
  A doobt if he'll cairt oot a cloddie.
'E keeper treatid Jock lek vermin,
  'e laird geed him a stingan sermon,
Said "Since you set this fearful fire,
  no slate will I put on your byre."
Bit Jock wis reesed by Rab an' Beel,
  their lambs hed never done as well.
On 'e burnt grun peyts dried lek scraes
  and fowks thanked Johnnie for 'e blaze
But though teoch tirren gives him pain,
  Jock niver burnt his bank again.

Willie Alexander, West Canisbay.

The Canisbay Parish Church

Photo, Sina Houston.

BRABSTER

Brabster School 1937
(With the Big House and a good stackyard.)

Photo, Robert Banks, Ardenlea, Castletown.

Teacher: Miss Margaret Hendry. Back Row, left to right:- John Dunnett; Cathie MacDonald; Barbara Banks, Upper Gills; Robert Banks, Upper Gills; John Johnstone, Upper Gills. Front Row:- Frank Dunnett; Cathie Johnstone, Upper Gills; Nan Dunnett; Ann Bain, Brabster; Fanny Johnstone, Upper Gills.

Brabster School c.1948

Photo, Janet Gunn, Emohruo, Mey.

Teacher: Miss Janet Leitch. Back Row, left to right:- Shona Gunn, Brabster; Stella Farquhar, Brabster House; Ann Cormack, Slickly; Margaret Cormack, Slickly; George Johnstone, Upper Gills; Charlie Lyall, Brabster. Front Row:- Jimmy Cormack, Slickly; Nellie Cormack, Slickly; Margaret Farquhar, Brabster; Ann MacLeod, Slickly; Lottie Banks, Upper Gills; William Farquhar, Brabster.

By Gig to Brabster School from Slickly 1952

Barrie, Jessie and Sandy Cormack. Ann MacLeod.

Photos, Sandy Cormack, Huna.
Barrie, Jessie and Jimmy Cormack with Helen at Sally's head.

Brabster School 1952

Photo, Barrie Cormack, 2 Shore Lane, Wick.

Back Row, left to right:– Alan Bain, Lottie Banks, Jimmy Cormack, Sandy Bain. Front:– Lena MacLeod, Ann MacLeod, Helen Cormack, Barrie Cormack, Jessie Cormack.

Parents and Pupils Plant a Tree at Brabster School Coronation Year 1953

Photo, Helen Cormack, 2 Shore Lane, Wick.

Back Row, left to right:– Sandy Cormack, Slickly; Mrs Bain, Brabster; Fanny Johnstone, Upper Gills; Lottie Banks, Upper Gills; Ann Cormack, Slickly; Mrs Elizabeth MacKay, teacher; Sandy Bain, Brabster. Middle Row:– Jimmy Cormack; Helen Cormack; Ann MacLeod; Sandy Bain. Front Row:– Alan Bain; Jessie Cormack, Ian Bain.

'E SCHOOL

'E first school a went till wis a small school in Brebster wi' seven pupils. I started 'e school fan a wis fowr. I couldna wait till get 'ere. I stuck hid for a week! I started again when I wis five, back at 'e same school. We flitted then to anither croft.

Next I went till 'e Canisbay School. Two teachers, an aboot 40 pupils in 'at day. Ee got no school denners then. Ee got a piece an a bottle a milk, an 'at hed till do 'e whole day. There wis no electric in 'e school – paraffin lamps an a coal fire did fine.

Then there wis 'E STRAP!. When I wis goan till 'e school somebody got 'e strap ivry day. A great prank wis till hide 'e strap if ee could. 'Is day I hed a brilliant idea! They were taking oot 'e stove and hed left a beeg hole where 'e chimney wis. So I popped the strap in 'ere. Somebody wis goan till land in trouble? We wis telt till get 'e strap. – No strap till be found! 'Is went on a whole day till somebody telt 'e techer hid wis in 'e hole. They hed till get a joiner till take 'e whole thing oot, and behold there wis 'e strap.

I'm telling ee he made up for hid!

Extract from a tape made by Murray Ross, Canisbay.

BRABSTER

St Drostan's Chapel, Brabstermyre

The site of the chapel dedicated to St Drostan lies on the west side of the road and to the north west of Brabster House. It was excavated and showed a small building of the chancelled type. The nave was 19 feet by 11 feet and the chancel eight feet by eight feet and it was said that the baptismal font was taken to Brabster House. The ruins are now entirely covered over.

☆★☆★☆★☆

1627 Mowat of Buchollie sold Brabstermyre, Slickly and Schoolery to Sir John Sinclair of Dunbeath his own son-in-law.

1650 Sir John Sinclair of Dunbeath settled the estates of Brabster, Slickly and Schoolery on his nephew and namesake John Sinclair from Latheron.

1660 This John Sinclair married Elizabeth Sinclair of Ulbster on 4th November, 1660 (Canisbay Session Records). It is likely that he had the Big House of Brabster built between 1650 and his marriage. Their son married Margaret Sinclair of Rattar and they had a son George. George Sinclair of Brabster married Janet Sutherland, daughter of Sutherland of Langwell. Janet Sutherland was a shrewd active woman who lived to a great age. In 1787 she purchased West Canisbay – a crofting district, and about this time she had West Canisbay House built, presumably a dower house for herself and unmarried daughters. She was a widow by 1787 and their daughter Anne, the heiress was married to a cousin, Captain Robert Sutherland of Langwell.

1787 Captain Robert Sutherland made the road from Alex Sinclair's shop to the Canisbay Corner. That's the short cut through the hill that all the Brabster people used when walking to the church or school in Canisbay. Alex Sinclair used to keep this road in repair and it is still called the Captain's Road.

George Sinclair Sutherland, son of Anne Sinclair and Robert Sutherland of Langwell married his cousin Margaret, daughter of George Gibson and grand-daughter of Alexander Gibson minister of Canisbay. They had seven sons and five daughters:– 1. Robert, Lieut. Col., East India Co.; 2. James, his successor – Lieut. in Navy; 3. George, died in Wisconsin; 4. Alexander, ship's carpenter and farmer, America; 5. John, Captain in East India Co., killed in India; 6, David, merchant, St Thomas, Ontario; 7, William, doctor in Australia. Janet, Anne, Margaret and Camilla did not marry. Eliz. married Rev. Roderick MacGregor. (Dr Fraser found an envelope in the "aise-walls" of the Free Manse addressed to Miss Elizabeth Sutherland, West Canisbay, Near Huna, Caithness. Franked Elgin JA.30.1845).

☆★☆★☆★☆

1804 George Sinclair Sutherland raised a company of men from his estate (about this time there was a renewal of war with France). They were the Light Infantry Company of the 1st Battalion Caithness Volunteer Infantry commanded by the Earl of Caithness (Laird of Mey). Money was always short among the country folk; even more so since the services to the Laird had been commuted into cash rent; and he himself as Captain of the Company would have painted a rosy picture of life in the army when encouraging the young men among his tenants to take the King's shilling and enlist.

The photocopied Pay List along with the names on page two give the men who were in the Laird of Brabster's Co. in 1804. There are a considerable number of Pay Lists over the following years which show who have joined or left the company.

The following names appeared on page two of the Pay List and Returns;–

William Mackay, Alex Manson, George Manson 1, George Manson 2, James Manson 1, James Manson 2, William Manson, Alex Matheson 1, Alex Matheson 2, David Matheson, James Matheson 1, James Matheson 2, William Matheson, George More, Sutherland Munro, William Munro, Gavin Mowat, John Mowat, Charles Nicolson, David Nicolson, Donald Nicolson, Alexander Reid, Donald Sutherland, George Shearer, David Shearer, James Smith, Neil Williamson.

☆★☆★☆★☆

PAY-LIST and RETURN of Captain George Sutherland's 1 light Infantry Company of the 1st Battn. Caithness Volunteer Infantry commanded by The Earl of Caithness from 14 June to 13 July 1804 both Days inclusive.

No. of each Description.	RANK.	NAMES.	Number of Days for which the respective Persons are entitled to Pay, as having been actually assembled.	Rate of Pay per Diem.	Amount of Pay. £.	s.	d.	Signatures of the Officers, and Remarks referring to the Individuals opposite to whose Names they are placed.
1	Captain	George Sutherland	30	9/5	14	2	6	Geo. Sutherland
2								
1	Lieutenant	Vacant						
2								
1	2nd Lieutenant or Ensign.	Magnus Hogston	30	4/8	7	"	"	Magnus Hogston Ensign
2								
	Total Amount of Pay for Commissioned and Warrant Officers £				21	2	6	

No. of each Description.	RANK and NAMES.	PAY: Number of Days for which the respective Persons are entitled to Pay as having been actually assembled.	Rate per Diem.	Amount issued. £.	s.	d.	Increased Rates paid to Innkeepers, &c. No. of Days for which Payment has been made. For Non-Comd. Offrs. Drumrs. Fifrs. Gunrs. & Privts. Billeted on Innkeepers, &c. In Stationary Quarters	On a March.	Permitted to find their own Lodgings, having Orders to be quartered.	In lieu of Beer.	Station where quartered, or encamped, and No. of the Route by which the March was made.	REMARKS.
1												
2												
	Serjeants											
1	James Geddes	30	1/6¾	2	6	10½	~~30~~ 28	2		30	Thurso 1	
2	James Manson	30	1/6¾	2	6	10½	30	2		30	do	
3	Donald Mowat	30	1/6¾	2	6	10½	30	2		30	do	
4												
5												
6												
	Corporals											
1	William Manson	30	1/2¼	1	15	7½	30	2		30	Thurso 1	
2	Robert Murray	30	1/2¼	1	15	7½	30	2		30	do	
3												
4												
5												
6												
	Drummers or Fifers											
1	Alex. Rosie	30	1/1¾	1	14	4½	30	2		30	Thurso No. 1	
2	Donald Robison	30	1/1¾	1	14	4½	30	2		30	do	
	Gunners or Privates											
1	Alexander Begg	30	1/	1	10	"	30	2		30	do	
2	Arthur Cruickshanks	30	1/	1	10	"	30	2		30	do	
3	Wm. Cruickshanks	30	1/	1	10		30	2		30	do	
4	Wm. Cogle	30	1/	1	10		30	2		30	do	
5	James Dunnet 1	30	1/	1	10		30	2		30	do	
6	James Dunnet 2	30	1/	1	10		30	2		30	do	
7	John Dunnet	30	1/	1	10		30	2		30	do	
8	Simon Dunnet	30	1/	1	10		30	2		30	do	
9	Thomas Dunnet	30	1/	1	10		30	2		30	do	
10	William Dunnett	30	1/	1	10		30	2		30	do	
11	William Dunnet	30	1/	1	10		30	2		30	do	
12	George Dunnet	30	1/	1	10		30	2		30	do	
13	John Falconer	30	1/	1	10		30	2		30	do	
14	George Gibbons	30	1/	1	10		30	2		30	do	
15	James Green	30	1/	1	10		30	2		30	do	
16	William Geddes 1	30	1/	1	10		30	2		30	do	
17	William Geddes 2	30	1/	1	10		30	2		30	do	
18	John Hogston	30	1/	1	10		30	2		30	do	
19	James Hogston	30	1/	1	10		30	2		30	do	
20	Willm. Hogston	30	1/	1	10		30	2		30	do	
21	John Harper	30	1/	1	10		30	2		30	do	
22	John Innes	30	1/	1	10		30	2		30	do	
23	Thomas Innes	2	1/	"	2		1	1		2	do	Discharged 16 June
24	Peter Kennedy	30	1/	1	10		30	2		30	do	
25	Alexr. Leetch	30	1/	1	10		30	2		30	do	
26	Sinclair Leetch	30	1/	1	10		30	2		30	do	
	Carried forward .... £			51	12	7½	~~962~~	65	—	962		

Printed by H. Teape, Tower-hill, for His Majesty's Stationary-Office.

897

Courtesy of Public Record Office, Kew, Richmond, Surrey.

Distillery at Kirkstyle

c.1826 George S. Sutherland built a distillery on the east side of the burn mouth at Kirkstyle to make work in the area for his tenants and also his sons. He incurred much expense in erecting a malting kiln, a corn kiln and the distilling plant. In a letter to a son he laments that he had spent over £800 and never got a single dram out of it. Like many of his tenants he too would have been missing his sons who all joined the armed forces or emigrated in order to make a living. Now a bit of wall, red tiles from a collapsed roof and some bricks scattered about are all that remains of the distillery. (The marriage records 25th December, 1828, show that John Swanson, mashman, John O'Groats Distillery married Mary Thomson, Thurso). George S. Sutherland modernised and extended West Canisbay House and lived there with his wife and family. He died in 1840 in their town house at No.2 Janet Street, Thurso.

1849 His son James Sinclair Sutherland married H. Frances. A. Medley, daughter of deceased Lieut. Edward Medley, late Coastguard Inspector and Commander of Coastguard residing at Elzy House, Staxigoe. They had two sons – James Sinclair and George Edward both born in Wisconsin. The census records show that Lieut. E. Medley R.N. – Coastguard born in England (son of solicitor, Westminster) was living with his family at Skirza in 1841. There were five more coastguards with their families living very near – the local ones were Wm. Bruce, Wm. Bremner and Donald Wares. These are the only coastguards mentioned in the parish in the 1841 census. The Coastguard station was closed after Lieut E. Medley was moved to Elzy some time after 1841.

☆★☆★☆★☆

Skirza Coastguard House

The 1828 sketch of the half acre laid off at Freswick for the accommodation of the coastguard stationed there shows the 181½ feet by 120 feet building was 12 feet from the shore line, 93 yards from the well and 172 yards east of the landing place and fish houses (Skirza Pier). It is thought that the building was roofed with slate because so many bits of broken slate are turned up when ploughing in that area. William Bain, Midtown, Freswick, says it was known locally as the Customs House and that this part of the shore is known as the "Slates" because of the big flat shelving rocks which would make it easy for the launching and hauling of customs boats. Local history says that the Laird of Freswick refused absolutely to pay the Coastguard Commissioners any compensation for this rather splendid coastguard house which was no longer required and told them they could take it away.

Imagine his disbelief and wrath when they did just that! Local history also says that a builder from Wick took the house down and that he carted the two fine free-stone pillars to Wick and incorporated them into the house he built for himself at 17 Sinclair Terrace (Duncan Robertson checked the title deed and found that Ebenezer Miller, fischurer bought this site in 1846). The very smooth, 10 feet high sandstone pillars are set in an impressive frontage which is built with stones dressed to a uniform size and one wonders if they also came from Skirza?

There was a surplus of battleship grey paint in Wick during the last war which was freely used and sadly was impossible to remove. Because of the paint, Andrew Sinclair could not tell if the pillars and stones were from the same quarry, but reckoned from the quality and style of the building that this was a master mason's house. He explained that when the herring fishing was in full swing local tradesmen set themselves up in related industries which could explain Ebenezer being a curer in 1846. It is thought his son Ebenezer Miller born 1847 was the architect for the Temperance Hotel (Mackays) built in 1883 and it was from him that the shortest street in Wick got its name.

James S. Sutherland

Photo of oil painting, Anne Houston.

1865 James S. Sutherland sold the estate of Brabster, Slickly, Schoolery and West Canisbay for £16,500 to the Earl of Caithness, Mey. The crofting tenants were removed, a few were given crofts on the estate and others were given some land along the High Road, Upper Gills or the White Broo. The ground was then drained, ditched and parts enclosed with dry stone dykes to make the farms of West Canisbay and the Ha of Brabster.

The new road connecting Gills and Lyth was constructed and the Brabster and Mey quarries were developed after the purchase of this estate.

The memorial stone to the Brabster Family in the vestibule of the church is inscribed thus: Sacred to the memory of James S. Sutherland, late of Brabster, who departed this life 8th November, 1865 aged 71 and also to the other members of the

Brabster Family who along with him are interred within this vault.

Sources:– Henderson's Caithness Family History, Caithness in the 18th Century by John E. Donaldson, letters from Mrs Dove and my mother's notes.

Anne Houston, St. Magnus.

David Dunnett, late of Brabster, (Fire Chief in Winnipeg) said that his brother William had been round Cape Horn many times in charge of ships under sail and steam.

ROMANCE AND TRAGEDY

At the time of the Napoleonic Wars, a young Caithness soldier who became Sergeant William MacKay, my great-great grandfather, was going the rounds of his friends and neighbours to say goodbye prior to going overseas. In one house there was a family of MacKenzies in which there was a young child named Elizabeth. When he saw the child he thought she was so lovely that he asked the family to keep her for him. He survived the war, came home and in due course claimed his Elizabeth and married her. They had several children, but her life ended tragically.

She had walked to Scarfskerry from her home in Slickly to buy fish to tide the family over the New Year. On the return journey she called briefly at a house in Barrock, but then continued on her way as the weather was showing signs of deteriorating. A heavy snowstorm came on and she never reached home. The next morning neighbours first realised that something was wrong when they saw her children outside the house looking for their mother. She had obviously lost her way in the snowstorm and was found drowned in Loch Syster at Caithstone.

This anecdote was told to me by mother, Barbara MacKay Simpson, née Thomson (1893-1967) who was born in Scarfskerry. The details had been given to her by her maternal grandmother Jessie Brotchie, née MacKay (1826-1910) one of the children of the unfortunate Elizabeth.

Loch Syster no longer exists, it was apparently drained many years ago.

William Simpson, Oberer Rebbergweg 90, 4153 Reinach B.L., Switzerland.

Footnote:– Her tombstone stands about half way between the east end of the church and the wall on the sea side. "Erected by George MacKay, Farmer, Slickly in Memory of his mother Elizabeth MacKenzie who died January 10, 1836 aged 50 also his father William MacKay, Sergt. 95th Highlanders who died 8th May, 1860 aged 86." William's grandfather and my grandfather were brothers. They would still have been celebrating Old New Year's Day in 1836. (1752 – Alteration of calendar and adoption of the new style.)

James Simpson, Stroma.

SERGEANT WILLIAM GEDDES, BRABSTER (21.10.1821 - 17.3.1885)

1814 Silver Medal – Sgt. W. Geddes 78th Foot, for Long Service and Good Conduct

Photo, Ian Aitchison.

Sgt. William Geddes (my great grandfather) who was awarded this medal was the son of James Geddes and his wife Isabella Manson, Brabster. Family memories told that he had fought in the Crimean War in 1854 and that he had been wounded at the relief of Lucknow, 1857, during the Indian Mutiny.

John G. Whittier's poem "The Pipes at Lucknow" stirred me as a boy and I always wanted to find out more about the medal winner.

We wondered if he had wanted to go to war and fight for Queen and Country or if the Laird of Brabster had encouraged him to enlist. Captain George S. Sutherland died in 1840 and his heir Robert was a Lieut. Col. in the East India Company. (The immediate cause of the Indian Mutiny was the revolt of the native soldiers in this company.)

Earlier this year my daughter Margaret and her husband David Hunter did some research and found the following information in the Public Records Office, Kew – Sgt. William Geddes enlisted 2.7.1841 joining the 72nd Highlanders and transferred to the 78th on 1.4.1842. His regimental number was 1814. He sailed to India with the 78th in April, 1842, on the "Morley" which took 105 days. He was presented with this large silver long service and good conduct medal and £10 on 24.7.1861.

He was discharged unfit 12.10.1861 and shortly afterwards married Elizabeth Cormack, Freswick. I'm sure the yarns told round their fireside would have been of thrilling exploits in foreign lands and names like Balaklava, Sebastopol, Delhi and Cawnpore would have rolled off his tongue. (It was for her work during the Crimean War that Florence Nightingale earned the gratitude of the nation and the blessings of thousands of wounded men.)

William Geddes died in 1885 at Auckengill and is given as Chelsea Pensioner on his death certificate.
Murdo Sinclair, Main Street Keiss.

ROUND KILN, HA OF BRABSTER

Photo, Jonty Willis, Old Elm House, Redmire, Leyburn, North Yorks. (Grandson of Mrs Dove).

At the time tenants paid their rent in kind to the Laird of Brabster, it was stored here. It is said that the old Brabster House was incorporated in this barn when the Big House of Brabster, seen at right of photo, was built c.1655. When this old barn fell into disuse, a "stop" was made to the removal of stones (for building steadings) because the Freswick fishermen used this kiln as a meeze. The kiln is still standing, as seen opposite.

Photos, Bet Brown.

GILLS

EXPLOITS AND SAYINGS IN THE LIFE OF ALEX MATHIESON, BETTER KNOWN AS "SHEDS"

Alex Mathieson

Photo, Emma MacLeod.
Note pearl studded tie pin on bow tie.

Alex was a life long member of the Labour Party and a well known heckler at opposition meetings. Once he attended a Labour conference in Scarborough, and lost his return railway ticket. Harold Wilson and Barbara Castle had a whip round and raised cash to help him on his way – needless to say the National Press had a field day to his great delight. He was going to another conference and asked his neighbour Murray Ross to drive him to the station. On the morning of departure, Murray arrived to find "Sheds" running late as usual, and asked if he had a case or holdall. Alex said "Ah ha, no no, I'm travelling light." "Sheds" shoved on his rubber boots, socks in pocket, and on arrival at the station, rushed to put on his socks and found he had forgotten his shoes! He made a dash to board the train, one boot on, the other boot and sock under his arm – bought shoes on arrival at his destination.

One of his oft' repeated sayings:– "In Upper Gills they never hed the gless far fae their eyes and in Lower Gills the gless wis never far fae their mooths."

During the Suez Crisis two of his neighbours had a verbal battle regarding a bordering ditch connected to the burn. On hearing this he immediately named the burn the Suez Canal and his neighbours Nasser and Eden. His only experience with the arm of the law occurred during a return motorbike trip from Glasgow, Edinburgh and Aberdeen. Passing through Keiss he was stopped by the police and was "astounded" to discover he had no licence or insurance. He told them as he had gone and come all that distance, it wasn't worth charging him! He got off with a warning.

He had mirrors placed at intervals on the walls facing the windows and also a master mirror enabling him to see the various roads, so he didn't have to move from the table when writing letters. He wrote until he could see the postie coming and then made a last minute dash with his mail. He fixed a weight to the kettle on the old sway, so as the kettle boiled and got lighter, it rose from the fire so wouldn't boil dry.

In the early 30s when his house was being renovated, he and his mother Bawbie aged 85 resided in the barn. The chaff house being warm was his mother's bedroom. One day he decided to thresh and completely forgot she was in bed. After a time he heard a banging. The fan had blown the chaff into her abode and on investigating, he could hardly see her for the swirling mass of chaff and fumes from the engine. She was gasping and choking but he managed to get her outside where she recuperated.

Always in a rush, he had the inside corners of his porch rounded, so could save time when making a "dash" to catch the local bus driven by Peter Gunn, Midtown, John O'Groats. "Sheds" was a man of outstanding wit, sometimes a bit harsh – to outwit him would be quite an achievement.

Alex Mathieson loved classical music, he never swore, smoked or drank and no doubt the man we all knew as "Sheds" will be remembered for many years to come.

Emma MacLeod, Upper Gills
and Wattie Ross, St Clair Cottage, Huna.

Alex Mathieson – "Sheds"

Because of time zones and international date lines the New Year begins somewhere in the Pacific Ocean, but the late Alex Mathieson, "Sheds", strongly disputed this, claiming it was a well known fact that the New Year started and finished in Gills at the foot of the Back Road!

Now and again Alex's sarcastic wit was focused on the local clergy; on one such occasion he declared that if the minister had to please an earthly father instead of a heavenly one he'd be working more than one day a week!

Alex, who was well versed on electricity, was once asked to explain the difference between amps and volts. He replied: "Haw haw, you know wans lek a skelp wae a hammer an theithers lek a prowg wae a peen" (pin prick).

Billy Magee, Lower Gills.

Footnote:– Billy Magee's grandfather James Dunnet (roadman) used to go out with his gun at midnight on Hogmanay and fire three shots in the air to kill off the old year.

D.S.

George Mathieson (brother of Alex) – worked for the Marconi Company and while employed there, invented what came to be known as the Direction Finder – an aid to navigation – it worked in conjunction with radio beacons scattered around the coast. The Direction Finder was much more accurate in deciding the exact position of a ship at sea.

Mr Mathieson, as a result of a dispute with the Marconi Company, left and set up in business on his own behalf in Aberdeen. He was soon able to get his Direction Finders into most of the Aberdeen fleet of fishing trawlers, and so far as I know was able to make a good living from the annual rentals of the Direction Finders in the trawlers.

Ben Green, Roadside, John O'Groats.

Jimmy Ross carting home peats with Cherry between the shafts c.1933

John Ross (son) on a Ford Dexta with a cole on the buckrake c.1960

When folk got buckrakes in the 1950s it was considered a great step forward in haymaking. It was used for sweeping the hay in for coles and for transporting coles to the stackyard.

Kathleen Ross, Upper Warse.

John Williamson, Roadside, Gills, a noted horse and cattle dealer, met a neighbour walking on the road early one morning. The neighbour said he was just going off to the market to buy a half-worn horse. Williamson said "Well watch you don't buy a full worn horse" – and "Man" he said "that's just what he did!"

M.H.

PENTLAND FIRTH

I've lived by the sea
Since I was ever so wee
And often went walks to the pier
I stood by the door
And studied the Boar
What a beautiful view from right here.

I've studied the Firth
Since the days of my birth
Watching boats sailing eastward and west
When the stormy winds blow
It's the fisherman's foe
The dryland for me is the best.

The waves lash the coast
They are seeming to boast
What a dangerous firth I can be
On a grey winter's night
They will give you a fright
It's the stormiest thing you can see.

But on a clear summer's day
This words I must say
It's the loveliest sight ever seen

Viewed from the hill
So calm and so still
It's a mixture of blue and of green.

There's Stroma and Skerries
And now Orkney Ferries
All part of our beautiful Firth
So admire it I will
Whether stormy or still
As this is my homeland since birth.

So if you are passing this way
Please stop at Gills Bay
And study the Firth at its best
The view is so clear
You can see far and near
And the boats sailing out to the west.

I'm sure you'll agree
It's a beautiful sea
Whether studied by night or by day
I hope to stay here for many a year
Overlooking this beautiful bay.

Anne Ross, Haven Fiord, Gills.

WUR GREYHOUND

I mind when 'e travelling fowk came roond and they aye hed their dowgs wi 'em. My brither and me jist hed 'e collie dowg. This tinkler mannie came and wanted till sell his hound for 10/-, I think. Nothing doing at all – no money then ye see. Wattie and me started till think 'is ower. We'd lek till hev hed a hound too. Nearest we could get till 'is wis we thocht till clip 'e collie.

I mind we got 'e dowg in till 'e barn and we clipped him poor owld dog. We clipped a lot, tail legs and all. He looked terrible, but we thocht he wis lovely! We then took and tried him oot till see fit lek he wis. We thocht he wis a good bit faster! We thocht we hed a lovely hound, until 'e auld man came home at nicht. . . Then we copped hid.

Say no more!!!

Extract from a tape made by Murray Ross, Canisbay.

A THATCHED COTTAGE (CONSTRUCTION)

Bella Banks's Cottage
(now Phil Ward's)

tree and walls. The rafters (sma' wood) were laid on loose and the divots were set on them.

The hole in the roof was never made right over the hearth and thus avoided the rain "slocking" (putting out) the fire. The "lum head" was often an open ended herring barrel fixed in the hole to increase draught. Rashes and bent were cut sheaved and stooked for thatch and also straw was used. "Kimpals" (trusses) were secured in overlapping layers on the divots. Heather simmons (ropes) over the roof were weighed down by passing "benlins" (long stones) through the loops of simmons and this secured the roof. The benlins were placed about a foot above the aise-walls and were long enough to take a few simmons and these were checked and tightened when necessary.

From Notes by John Mowat, Skirza, Glasgow.

Heelan couples – several pieces of timber were chacked together and nailed with baaks (collars) to form an arch. Boat timbers were often used in the parish because they were more easily obtained than tree trunks. The couples were recessed in the walls, with the feet of the couples a bit above floor level and "pans" (long thin stones) were laid on the wall head and along the back of the couples to take the roof out beyond the walls. The "aise-waas" were the inside spaces on the wall heads on the top of the "tabling", between the couple-feet and they were very handy storage spaces. On top of the couples was the roof tree under the rigging (ridge). Birks were fixed on the couples parallel to the roof-

Footnote:– The aise-hole (ash-pit) in some cottages was emptied from outside the house. This pit was sloped away from the house for drainage and was covered by a flagstone. As it filled up often a pail or two of water was poured over the ashes to pack them and then it was emptied once or twice a year using a horse and cart.

H.D.

GILLS IN DAYS OF YORE

Gills was the Norse name for the land of two burns; Big and Little Ribigill. The Head of Crees is on the west side of the bay and on it is the Red Hoosie and the lambing pen which were used when the Mey and Gills pastures belonged to Barrogill Mains. There are also the graves of foreign seamen on the braehead, but it is not known when this ship was wrecked. Another schooner with a cargo

of bricks on passage to Harrow was wrecked here and some bricks can still be found on the shore. Horses and a pulley were used to haul freestone from the shore to the braehead. This was done by fixing one end of a long rope at the braehead and the other end in the ebb, and pulling up the selected stones. These were then dressed into door and window lintels, hearth-stones, bree-stones for chimney breasts and turlags (small stone field rollers), which were in use on all the crofts. The Slate Road (east side of Jimmy Mathieson's croft) was used by crofters to cart "ware" (seaweed) from the shore which was used as manure.

A sailing schooner had her bow burst in when she was struck by a heavy sea in the "Men of Mey". The crew along with the help of Gills and Mey fishermen succeeded in patching over the hole with a sail and tar. They managed to get the schooner into the east side of Scotland's Haven where she remained for the winter and then left in the spring.

When the whole of Stroma belonged to the Mey estate they cut their peats in what is now called the Gill's Pasture and the remains of the peat banks can still be seen. After the Mey estate sold part of Stroma to the estate of Freswick and Dunbeath (to provide duck shooting for their guests) the tenants on this side of the island cut their peats in Crog-o-dale at John O'Groats. The Stroma people on the westside were given peat cutting rights in the hill above Sandy Green's. The Mey Estate put in the "Branch Road" for the convenience of the Stroma people when carting their peats to Gill's pier. The Strowmas usually hired local crofters to cart their peats at 6d (2½p) a load, but sometimes brought a horse and cart over from the island. The peats were tipped out on the high-water line and then it was essential to get them home as soon as possible because there was always the risk of losing the lot with a heavy land sea. The Sand Road at Upper Warse, on the west side of James Ross's croft was also used for peat carting. The Strowmas always tried to get their peats cut during the first week of May, before they went off to the herring fishing.

Many years ago a sheep dipper was installed at the burn further up than the brig of Fulltail, and there was also a small quarry thereabouts for the use of tenants on the estate.

The pier at Gills was extended and improved by a Glasgow firm in 1910. There were seven boats there when the work on the pier started and only two at the finish. This prompted a local wag to say "As Pier appeared – boats disappeared". Gills Bay and Pier were surveyed about 1912 and plans were drawn up for the St Ola Pier. A railway line was also mapped out but this was thought unnecessary as road transport was improving. The plan was to run the St Ola from Gills to Scapa and the argument to back up the plan was "If you can cross the Firth you can always land at Gills". The authorities at Thurso and Scrabster were very much against this Gills project because they realised they would lose the Orkney traffic and also, that a lot of fishing boats would leave and berth at Gills. The plans were scrapped at the outbreak of the 1914-18 war. The winch at Harrow was too light for hauling the "big boats" as the Ferthies were called locally and so it was transferred to Gills. The Stroma big boats were wintered in Pan Bay, Flotta, and it was only on an odd occasion that a Ferthie would be beached at Gills for maintenance. A barometer was installed at Gills by the navy before the First World War. There used to be six ousts at Gills, all with stone built sides and flagstone floors. Sadly they were all bulldozed away to make room for the road to the short sea dream crossing. They had stood there for more than 100 years defying the ravages of time and bad weather. The sail shed was rebuilt in 1910 with extra stone left by the contractors as a kind of luck penny when they built the pier. Some of the old road with its notorious Braes of Gills is still there alongside the new.

The east burn of Gills contained some small trout which made grand fishing for school boys. The ruins of a click-mill and a millstone lie further up the burn. A unique feature was that the water-wheel ran on its side because there was a limited fall of water. The mill-house, now improved and extended, is called Hopeland.

The undersea telephone cable to Stroma started at the Haven of Warse and came ashore at Sandgoe in Stroma. It was in operation for a few years but was always breaking and being flung ashore by heavy seas and strong tides. Parts of the cable were salvaged by locals and perhaps are still in use.

The Haven of Warse used to be the home of several small creel boats. The "ousts" there were just cut out of the brae and traces of them can still be seen. The old wooden framed winch came from Gills when they got the one from Harrow. After the pier was built at Gills, the boats left Warse because they could be berthed there without the trouble of hauling them every time. Salmon fishing was carried on at the Haven of Warse before the First World War, mainly by Angus and Will Manson from Mey, and the remains of the Salmon bothy is still there.

In the olden days there used to be a cattle market in the hill parks at the Mains of Warse. The Captain's Road at Lower Warse to the shore was supposed to have been built on the orders of a retired sea captain who had the tenancy of the Mains of Warse. There are the ruins of a smiddy at Upper Warse which used to have a half sized forge and a small bellows.

A fault in the rock ended the life of the old quarry at Brabster. The first council houses in Canisbay were built with stones from a new quarry opened at Brabster. Flags were taken from Brabster by horse drawn lorry to be cut and dressed at Harrow.

The Claypot's burn (behind the council houses) was diverted from Kirkstyle by Mr Purves then tenant of West Canisbay. This was done to supply water to adjoining fields and is now known as the Canisbay Canal.

There were also the trades – three brothers Simpson lived opposite Briar Rose – two were shoemakers and the other worked the croft. Two grocers on the High Road, Cuthbertson, the beadle of the South Church was a tailor and there was another tailor at Kirkstyle. There were the two boat builders, one of them was Mathieson to name. That was the yesteryear and now we look forward to all the industry, bustle and excitement there will be when the Short Sea Dream Crossing gets going. On the other hand you could view the prospects from the Gills Man's Walk, from the pier to the Head of Crees, where one can look west to America and east to Scandinavia. There is an old saying "If one does that walk and stands on the Head of Crees he will never leave Gills!"

Anon

THE PENTLAND FIRTH AND ORKNEYS FROM NEAR JOHN O' GROATS   A 3490

**The Braes of Gills
Showing Stewart's House**

The date stone is set very low down on the sea-side of the bridge nearest "Stewarts". On the other bridge it's on the southside and can be seen from the parapet. The date is 1755 and one wonders what the letters SIS and DMS stand for.

Alistair Manson.

EXILE'S DREAM

It's the far north of Scotland I dream of today
Its headlands its harbours, its islands and bays
With white lobster boats putting out to the sea
In the far north of Scotland, how happy I'd be.

To stand in a storm on that wild Pentland shore
Feel the spray on my face, hear the billow's loud roar
Taste the salt on my lips, hear the seagull's wild cry
I still see it all with a tear in my eye.

Just to walk on the braes where I once used to play
Hear the lark's merry song on a still summer day

See the crofter at work busy cutting the hay
I still see it all though I'm far, far away.

In my doorway I stand it's a crisp winter's night
See the lighthouses flashing their message so bright
The north star shines down with a wink from above
In my heart I've returned to the land that I love.

To the far north of Scotland I dream to return
To that bonnie wee hoose, by the swift flowing burn
To sit on the brae, and look out oe'r the sea
Contented at last, in my homeland I'll be.

Billy Magee, Lower Gills, Canisbay.

GILLS "BREEGS"

Anyone interested in arched bridges should visit the two in the Braes O'Gills spanning "Johnnie's Burn" and "Stewart Burn" officially referred to on survey maps as the east and west burns of Gills. A first glance gives the impression of two fairly wide, not very old bridges similar to many throughout the country, but a more detailed look proves this not to be so.

From underneath it can be seen that extensions have been added to what was originally much narrower structures. This was achieved by building a new archway alongside, but not connected to the original arch. Both bridges contain datestones displaying the date 1755 and two groups of letters SIS and DMS. The datestone in the east bridge would appear to have been removed from its original position and rebuilt into the extension. Both bridges, especially the west one, are in need of attention if they are to remain intact.

As a considerable amount of the water flowing under these bridges comes from Nature Conservancy Council SSSIs, perhaps they could adopt and conserve two bridges built just nine years after Culloden.

Billy Magee, Lower Gills..

A CROFTER'S LOT

The following are some interesting extracts from the title deed of a crofter in the parish purchasing his croft in 1925 from Sir Edwyn Sinclair Alexander-Sinclair of Freswick at the price of £42 for nine acres, one rood and 36 poles.

Certain privileges run with the title such as the right and privilege of being able to cut peats but only when and where directed and subject to him contributing his just share of the upkeep of the roads leading to the peat mosses. The crofter also had the right and privilege of grazing stock on the common grazings also regulated by the rules of souming which determine the number of animals to be grazed per acre. The crofter also was given the free right and privilege of quarrying for stone in any of the quarries on the Lands and Estate of Wares (Warse) but only for the purpose of erecting buildings on the croft.

The croft was at that time also burdened with certain obligations such as four pounds 15 shillings and four pence three farthings Scots for Old Valued Rent; nine pence sterling of Land Tax; and a stipend payable to the minister of the parish of Canisbay of a certain proportion of the total estate stipend of 34 bolls, three stones and seven and one-tenth pounds of meal, 32 quarters, one bushel, two pecks no gallons and three and five-tenth quarts of bere, and 35 pounds 14 shillings and seven pence sterling of money. The crofter's proportion of this obligation was 12 pounds of meal, two pecks, one gallon and one quart of bere and one shilling and 10 pence sterling of money.

I hope the ministers of Canisbay were fond of their porridge, bere meal, brose and gruel.

Anne Dunnett, Clydesdale Bank Buildings, Bridge Street, Wick.

HEAD O'CREES

To stonemasons and local crofters, the Head of Crees was a valuable source of good quality freestone varying in colour from a light grey-brown, to a dark rusty red. Due to the distance apart of its natural seams, the stone quarried out in very thick slabs, which would not accidentally board into thinner slices. This made it ideal for stonemasons fashioning into decorative stonework for buildings and gravestones. Some of the older gravestones in Canisbay Churchyard came from the Head of Crees as did many of the stone rollers and pig troughs in the Gills, East Mey area. A pulley which ran on a rope stretched between the beach and braehead, was used to get the stone within reach of a horse and cart. The rope's anchoring ring can still be seen in the rock about half ebb mark.

When the Queen Mother decided to renovate Barrogill Castle, stonemasons returned to the Head of Crees. Once again the ring of hammer on wedge and "jumper" could be heard, this time a tractor and winch was used to haul the stone to the top of the brae. It was not always necessary to quarry the rock as massive boulders were available, provided they could be reduced to a manageable size.

The Head of Crees can therefore boast to have provided stone not only for a humble pig's house but also for a Royal Castle.

Billy Magee, Lower Gills.

GILLS BAY PIER

The "Girl Marjory" at Gills Pier c.1895

Photo, Hamish Donn, Orcadia, Lower Warse.

William Ham, John Geddes, Peter Green, Will Swanson in the boat and James Donn at the helm (grandfather of Hamish). The "Girl Marjory". a Stroma built yole had 17 feet of keel and cost 16 pounds.

If ye dinna see the bottom, dinna wade (do not be reckless).
David Dunnett.

Gills Bay Pier 1905

Photo, Hamish Donn.
The 1905 date stone with the Sinclair Crest and the initials AL HS has been incorporated in the new harbour.

The Opening 1905

Monday last was observed by the whole population of Gills, and many from the surrounding districts, as a general holiday, the occasion being the formal opening of the Gills Bay Pier. The ceremony was very gracefully performed by Mrs Heathcote Sinclair of Mey. Fortunately for the success of the day's proceedings, the weather proved favourable, and as the committee had forward a splendid programme of events, a very enjoyable day was spent by all who were present.

The sports which were begun at one o'clock, opened with an eight mile cycle race. This event was taken part in by a good many competitors, and a keen contest was the result. When little over a mile from the finish, A. Adamson, Quoys, who was leading, had a nasty spill in taking a corner, but still able to come in a good second. A. Dunnet, Seater, who was first, also had some trouble with his machine, which also delayed him some time.

After the cycle race was finished, other games were proceeded with until three o'clock, at which hour Mr and Mrs Heathcote-Sinclair and party arrived from Barrogill Castle. Proceeding to the end of the pier, which was gaily decorated with bunting, they were there met by the local committee and a large number of spectators.

The Opening Ceremony

Mr James Shearer, Warse chairman of committee, in introducing Mrs Sinclair, referred at some length, to the various plans which had been formed in the past to erect a harbour at Gills Bay so as to connect it with the Orkneys, it being always considered by men of experience as the quickest and safest route across the Pentland Firth.

Mrs Sinclair in a neat and charming speech amid much applause declared the pier open, thanking the committee for asking her to perform the ceremony. Mr Charles Dunnet, Brabster, in name of the committee then presented Mrs Sinclair with a gold bangle and silver scissors, as a memento of the occasion.

Mr Heathcote-Sinclair in thanking the committee on behalf of Mrs Sinclair, also expressed the pleasure it gave him to see the work so satisfactorily finished and hoped that not only would it prove a boon to the local fishermen, but also to the Stroma men who had to boat their peats from that place.

Mr John Nicolson, Nybster, who was present, gave some interesting reminiscences of the time when John O'Groat was ferryman between Caithness and Orkney. This over, Mr John Geddes, Gills proposed "Success to Gills Bay Pier" to which Mr John Nicolson replied.

Mr David Dunnet, Quoys, proposed a vote of thanks to the Gills Pier Committee, and he, too, expressed the hope that the time would come when the Orkney mails would be landed at Gills Bay, and as a consequence the making of a light railway between Wick and Thurso, thus completing the circuit.

Mr Munro, Canisbay, secretary, replied thanking Mr Dunnet for his vote of thanks, and saying that the Pier Committee felt that they were amply rewarded by the Gills Bay Pier being now an accomplished fact, thanks to the many kind friends at home and abroad and specially to their popular proprietor for his handsome donation of £100 and for his granting the foreshore free.

A vote of thanks to the Congested District Board was moved by Mr David Dunnet, East Mey, and Mr Cheyne replied. Mr Donald Banks proposed a vote of thanks to the engineer, the contractor and the inspector for the efficient manner in which they severally did their part of the work. The last item on the programme was a vote of thanks to the chairman. This was done by Mr Peter Keith, factor for the Mey Estates, who eulogised Mr Shearer's many good qualities as a public man.

Three hearty cheers for Mr and Mrs Sinclair and party, from Barrogill Castle, brought the interesting proceedings to a close.

Courtesy, John O'Groat Journal, 15th September, 1905.

PROPOSED PIER AT GILLS 1909

Report from the "Orcadian" 15th May, 1909. Notes supplied by Councillor Dunnet, Quoys, (apparently the local representative for the Gills Bay area) on the advantages of a pier at Gills Bay.

With regard to the Orkney traffic and the conveyance of mails, a saving of at least one and a half hours on the trip to and from the mainland would be effected. Some 50 years ago the Orkney mail service was conducted by a Huna yawl with a regularity equal to what now rules under a steamboat service, and this because, by adopting the route between South Ronaldsay and Huna, the stormy seas off Dunnet Head and Duncansby Head were avoided.

A steamboat service by this route could make the passage to Scapa in all weathers, thus removing the inconvenience suffered by Orkney people from not receiving the mails daily in the winter season.

The many advantages that would accrue from the erection of the proposed pier must be obvious to anyone who has given the subject consideration.

Captain Sinclair, Wick, who was on the committee of inspection says, the route being across the east end of the Pentland Firth, can be crossed in three quarters of an hour in comparatively smooth water, and in any weather comfortably. Numerous passengers would pass and repass by this route who would not at present attempt it.

Courtesy of the Orcadian Newspaper.

Footnote:– Sir Arthur Bignold MP addressed a meeting in Kirkwall and asked support for the scheme.

W.S. Mowatt, Smithy, St Margarets Hope, Orkney.

OASTS OR NOUSTS

An oast or noust is a place where boats were hauled up into for protection, especially on a rocky shore or very exposed landing stage. The outlines of the nousts at the Haven of Seater and at Robbie's Haven can still be seen. They were simply a sort of "V" or boatshaped trench or nest cut out of the sandy brae and the boats were pulled into them and secured by ropes and with a large stone or two at the stern.

It is considered that the nousts at Gills were the best in the parish. They were close together and cut back about eight feet into the brae and then the sides were built up with stones to prevent land slides and the floors were laid with flagstones to ease hauling. Originally there were about seven nousts but over the years some got filled by landslides and it is thought there were several there before the new pier in 1905.

Once when there was a severe storm, James Dunnet (roadman) and his father were down holding on to their boat, the "Daisy" for all they were worth to prevent it being carried out as she was afloat. Another boat was taken from a neighbouring noust and later washed ashore at the burn some distance east. James Wm. Shearer's boat the "Lark" later known as the "Ida" was once damaged by a landslide when it was in his noust.

James Donn (Hamish's grandfather) built the

Two Oasts at Gills c.1989

noust slightly east of the original slipway. It had a flagstone floor and was stone built into the brae with a recess at the point to hold the stem of the boat snugly. It also had a recessed cupboard on the east side about 18 inches square and eight inches deep (called a window) to hold paint etc., when the boat was being done up. The boats were always hauled on Saturday nights and launched again on Monday mornings.

Sadly the nousts were all blasted away c.1989 during the construction of the harbour.

Alistair Manson, "Gorse Bud", Gills.

CATCHING ARSONISTS, SEALS AND VIOLINS

During my lifetime, I have often observed otherwise nice, likeable people, turn different if I mentioned salmon. . . Political undercurrents, envy suspicion and sometimes a germinating ambition would change their eyes. . . (eyes are the windows of one's soul. . .). I can assure all readers, that catching wild salmon, legally, using bag-nets, is no easy way to get rich quickly! It is certainly the most happy adventurous way of working very hard and developing patience, discipline and of learning to make many sacrifices as regards any normal family life.

In 1930 two very hardy men and a hardy youth commenced salmon bag-net fishing at Gills, Canisbay. The "Station" was/is owned by the Crown Estate Commissioners but rented out on nine-year leases. The three hardy fellows had been officially permitted to fish the station on a tentative basis, in between leases. They were Jock Simpson – a huge, kind but tough and far-travelled Merchant Navy man – a really colourful legendary character and Harry Crowden senior, another far-travelled Merchant Navy man, a skilled craftsman and a well-built human dynamo of energy, together with 16-year old George Crowden (a future war-hero and perhaps more challenging – my future husband!?).

Salmon Fishers

Photo, George Crowden, Cedar End, Castletown.
c.1952 – left to right: Donnie Crowden, George Crowden and Harry Crowden.

The Simpson and Crowden Salmon Fishing Company reached Gills. . . having transported much of their gear by horse and cart, the rest in their rowing boat (coble) from Harrow. There were six very ingenious and well made ousts there at Gills to reassure any fisherman contemplating leaving any vessel for the winter. . . Kind and hospitable lodgings had been acquired for young George at Mansons, Lower Gills.

The first set-back for these three worthies came in a very dramatic form – that of ARSON ! Salmon nets are totally negative and ineffective without a "Leader" – 50 to 60 fathoms long and two fathoms deep with corks on top. This fence-like leader, is either anchored close to the rocks or tied to a bolt in the rocks – and it is essential.

One evening a "mannie" asked the "loon" for two matches which the "loon" quite naturally, gave him. Next thing, smoke and flames from a salmon leader which had been stowed beneath the bilge of an old yawl up in one of those super safe oasts! Such a hue and cry amidst the smoke and flames – mainly from the crofter owner of the endangered boat. Always an excitable person and somewhat suspicious and wary of strangers. . . he impulsively shouted to the police "That's one of the culprits, there, that one!!" He rushed up to my young husband-to-be, grabbed a tin out of his hand, triumphantly sniffed it, then murmured his apologies in the form of "no, no-o – its just TAR." A fact to which, his nose bore visible witness!

Anyway the police got their man in the Wick Mart – he confessed and I don't really know what happened to him – it couldn't be worse than what the seals and the strong tides of the Pentland Firth did to our three hardy men of honesty and worth. They were all above average men, all highly motivated men but they gave up the struggle to catch salmon at Gills.

Seals were the main cause – they the men, never once got a whole, intact, unmutilated salmon. Needless to say they never once rowed out to "fish" a whole, intact, unmutilated net, either. Worst, was wondering how many live, beautiful, marketable salmon swam out through the seal entry holes in those huge, laboriously home-made nets? (Nowadays they would be very expensive manufactured nets!)

Now folks, I don't want this well-meant story to degenerate into the controversial. . . Och, Robbie help me! If yon moose had chewed up your manuscripts wid ye have written yon poem!

Anyway, folks, Jock Simpson and Harry Crowden senior, simply gave up the futile struggle to catch salmon at Gills (they were lucky because some years later at Brough – on a fully committed nine year lease. . . twice, a despatch rider came with a telegram signalling the departure to the war of two of Harry Crowden's sons who were by then full crew members. The Crown Estate Commissioners insisted that Harry Crowden senior paid the full rent for the following crew-less years!) Yes they gave up the futile struggle to catch salmon at Gills – retreating from it – like from a war waged by seals or like some scenario in Alfred Hitchcock's "Birds"!

Their retreat was assisted by another of Harry Crowden's sons – also named Harry who was to become an officer in the Royal Navy during the Second World War. (He later settled happily in Australia – well, happily until an Aussie farmer requested he build a wall for him round his farm. The wall was to go round 40 square miles!

Young Harry Crowden joined the retreat from Gills with a violin!? He, aged 19, and George, aged 16, rowed the three-ton salmon coble back to Harrow. As they rowed westwards with some of the very heavy gear, Jock Simpson drove westwards on his horse and cart with some of the more brutally heavy salmon gear back to Harrow. Since a strong ebb tide was virtually carrying the two Crowden brothers westwards and home – they sometimes rested on the oars, and sadly reflected on that failure of a mission. . .

They had both thought that Gills Bay was (apart from having great potential for salmon fishing) quite the most beautiful, picturesque and inspiring coastal area they had ever worked in or even gazed upon. . .

Their reflections were set aside by a shared awareness that the westerly breeze was freshening rapidly. With their shared awareness was the knowledge that the strong west flowing ebb meeting a strong westerly wind always turned the Merry Men O'Mey into menacing Men O'Mey. Their coble with its cargo predictably began plunging down and rearing up and plunging down and rearing up like a demented horse at a rodeo! Suddenly, the violin, encased safely in the bow, hurtled through the air scuffing the heads of the rowers. Each tried to catch it – using one rowing hand each and two pairs of supple and stalwart legs – but to no avail. The violin landed overboard and descended into the depths of the Pentland Firth. Perhaps, long after, when the case disintegrated, the fins of salmon or the flippers of seals have played upon the strings? Perhaps played a symphonic rhapsody to freedom from any human marauders.

Patricia Crowden, Cedar End, Castletown.

S.S. MALIN HEAD 1910

S.S. Malin Head

The steam ship "Malin Head" owned by Ulster Steamship Co., Belfast, loaded at Middlesbrough with a cargo of pig-iron for Montreal, ran aground at the Ness of Quoys on 21st October, 1910 while on passage through the Pentland Firth. The Huna lifeboat was launched and rendered assistance. Later some of the cargo was jettisoned. She was refloated and they attempted to tow her to sheltered water in Orkney for repairs but this had to be abandoned because she was so badly damaged. She was beached at Gills Bay and became a total loss. Much of the cargo was salvaged and divers were employed to recover cargo after she sank. It was

Photo, Alistair Ham, Harrow.

reputed that they encountered conger eels of immense size when they were working on the wreck. I do not know how much cargo was salvaged but I do remember when I was at the Canisbay School during the war years (1939-1945) there was great excitement when a vessel appeared in Gills Bay and put marker buoys on the wreck of the "Malin Head", but nothing more took place and the buoys eventually disappeared.

A piece of the "Malin Head" has been driven ashore by recent storms and can be seen at low water. In 1984 the Thurso Lifeboat received a 500 pound legacy from the Underwriters as a token for the assistance given to the vessel and the Salvage Association Surveyors by the Huna Lifeboat.

The "Malin Head" wore the "Severed Hand of Ulster with three drops of blood" on her funnel, and perhaps there are still some pieces of carpet and dishes with the design in some Canisbay houses.

Colin MacKay, Heatherbell Cottages, John O'Groats.

KITTEN WITHOUT A TAIL – BEDTIME STORY

One fine morning "Thief" the poachers cat, went down to the seashore in search of a fish for breakfast. Rounding a ledge, he spotted something unusual washed up by the tide. "Ah Ah! What's this?" said Thief, stopping in his tracks. "Something to eat perhaps", so off he went to investigate. Imagine his surprise, to discover it was a small kitten!

"Dear me, dear me," said Thief poking around the wet little kitten. "I wonder what's happened here." Suddenly the kitten gave a loud sneeze and opening one eye looked slowly around. "Oh, oh hello!" stammered Thief. "Where have you come from?" "I fell off a ship!" replied the kitten shyly. "You fell off a ship!" said Thief, "Well you've left your tail behind." "No, No!" said the kitten, "I never had a tail." Thief looked puzzled, "You never had a tail, that's impossible! All cats have tails". "But I'm a Manx cat" explained the little kitten, "And Manx cats don't have tails." "Well you had better come along with me," said Thief, "Perhaps one of my friends will take you back home."

But alas none of his friends knew the way to the land of the tail-less cats. They asked "Cinders" the Tinker's cat, who had travelled all over the land, but he did not know the way. They asked "Bosun" the sea captain's cat; he had travelled all over the sea but he did not know the way. They asked "Nick" the policeman's cat but even he did not know the way. "Our only hope," said Thief "Is to go and see "Darkie" the witch's cat. He knows everything."

So off they all went to see "Darkie" who lived over the hill. "Darkie" knew the way to the land of the tail-less cats but said, "It's far too long a journey for such a small kitten, perhaps if I ask the witch she might fly you home on her broomstick." The witch was very kind and agreed to take the kitten home. So that night after the sun had set, and the moon had risen, the witch and the kitten climbed on to the broomstick and flew up into the sky, away to the land of the tail-less cats.

Footnote:– In 1871, the schooner "William Mitchell" from America with a cargo of wood, went ashore at the Ness of Duncansby. One member of her crew, a Manx cat, was adopted by the Steven's of Fernhill, John O'Groats. An offspring of this sea faring cat emigrated to Gills (wise cat) and took up residence with the Manson family, relations of the above mentioned Stevens.

Later generations, although direct descendants of the original cat, began losing their Manx characteristics and taking on the appearance of the local "Heinz" variety. Nevertheless from time to time a litter would be produced containing a throwback of the original breed. That's 122 years ago, and sadly "Smokey" died at Alistair Manson's on 3rd June, 1991 and it is thought that he was the last of that strain.

Billy Magee, Lower Gills, Canisbay.

SHOES MADE FOR WALKING

Fashion-wise 1845

These beautifully preserved, size three shoes are hand-stitched round the uppers which are made from a single piece of leather and still carry the original leather laces. The tiny horse-shoe like heel-shods are smithy made, as are the nails securing them but the "nails" seen in the centre of the heel are really wooden pegs which would have been cheaper to make and less likely to come through the sole. George Dunnett, shoemaker, had them on display in his window in Bridge Street, Wick and a big Glasgow shoe company were very keen to buy the shoes because they were a unique example of skilled craftsmanship from an early era.

The shoes were made by the Simpson family who were shoemakers for generations at the Back Road; their name can still be seen carved on a red corner stone on their house (now steading) opposite Briar Rose. My grandfather Walter Ross, Huna, was born in 1845 and the shoes were made for his granny McDonald. She lived in East Mey and got them specially made for walking over to see her first grandson. George MacDonald (great-great-granny's husband) was descended from the McDonalds of Glencoe and they wanted their descendants to remember the nurse who escaped with a child to Ross-shire. This bairn who escaped the massacre was the ancestor of George who settled in Lower Gills and later Mey.

Walter Ross, St Clair, Huna.

A TIDY CROFT HOUSE

Lower Gills

Photo, Nan Fraser, Cairnlee, Canisbay.

John Mathieson and his wife Alexina Mackay with their son Willie in the cart.

The long house was typical of the parish c.1900 onwards. It was usually the case that when a son who was to carry on the croft or business got married, he built a large room on to the but and ben croft house.

GILLS LOGIC

Some Gills men, including Willie Mathieson and Johnnag Innes, were at the cod in the "Soon" when Willie accidentally dropped Johnnag's knife overboard. Now Willie knew he would have to come up with something good if he was to escape a severe telling off. After a moment's thought, Willie turned to his crewmate and asked, "Johnnag is something lost if you know where it is?" Johnnag made it plain he was in no mood for stupid questions and demanded to know how something could possibly be lost if you knew where it was. That was exactly the answer Willie wanted, and pointing over the side, he said, "Well, Johnnag your knife's down there."

Billy Magee, Lower Gills.

ALEX BEGG'S FAMILY

Alex Begg who married Elizabeth Wares from Rigifa had three sons and five daughters. Robert and Alex are in the photo and George was the one who went to Brisbane and later Johannesburg. Katie also went to Australia and sailed on the "Cloncurry" which left Glasgow on 18th June, 1886 and arrived 14th August, 1886 at Brisbane which was then a developing town. She married Malcolm McDonald, a workmate of George's who hailed from Stornoway.

They had seven of a family and started off with twin boys, one of which was Alexander Roderick MacGregor McDonald named after her father and the minister who had baptised her. Christina married Wm. Lowden, General Merchant, Govan. Lizzie married John Gray, boiler erector with B. & W. Ltd., Renfrew. Margaret married David Dunnet, Huna, flour miller Glasgow. Isabella married George Sinclair, estate mason, Gills.

George Begg was well known as a builder in the early development of Johannesburg. He was a Lieutenant in the Transvaal Scottish Volunteer Regiment and a keen rifleman and crack shot. In 1912 he won the Transvaal Bisley.

It was when George Begg was home on holiday in 1901 that he presented a beautiful silver cup standing on three crossed rifles to the Mey Company 1st Caithness Volunteer Army. This 14 inch high trophy is engraved thus:— Presented to the Mey Coy 1st C.V.A. by George Begg Johannesburg.

The Begg Cup

W. Banks (thrice), J. Duncan, R. Sinclair, W. Smith (twice) and A. Swanson were the volunteers who won the cup and their names are inscribed on it. The company was disbanded in 1908 when G.T. MacKenzie was the C.O. The cup was passed to the Pentland Rifle Club in 1910 and the different branches of the club compete for this trophy at the Summer Shoot or Wapinschaw (weapon show). This outdoor shoot is usually held at Sannick and the Begg Cup goes to the person with the highest aggregate over the 25, 50 and 100 yard targets and always remains in the parish.

Lisbeth, Lexie and Clara.

Family and Friends at Alex Begg's "The Back Road Shop" (now Ancala) Gills 1905

Photo, Lexie Paterson, "Inglewood", 31 Fauldshead Road, Renfrew.

Back Row, left to right:– John S. Banks, John O'Groats, Robert Begg, merchant, Rattar; Maggie Mowat, John O'Groats (sister of Daniel); Donald Banks, Back Road (uncle of Peter Banks). Third Row: John Manson, Edinburgh; Helen Shearer (Mrs Robert Begg); Mrs J. Manson; Lizzie Begg (Mrs Gray); Alex Begg, merchant. Second Row:– George Begg, Rattar; Eliz. Gray (Mrs Rice); Lexie Gray (Mrs Paterson). Front Row: John Gray; Willie Shearer, Thurso; Alex Begg, Rattar; Donald Shearer, Thurso; Alex Gray; Bob the dog.

ROAD ROLLER

Road Roller 1947

Photo, Philip Henderson, Upper Gills. Back Row:– Sandy Henderson, Castletown, Colin Mackay, Mindy Mathieson. Middle Row:– Wullie Mathieson. Front Row:– William Manson, Isobel Mathieson, Dinah Manson and Jimmy Mathieson.

Green's road roller, weighing 10 tons and powered by a Perkin's Diesel P.6 engine, taken on a Sunday in the Braes of Gills cutting on what was then Malcolm Geddes' croft. George Wimpey completed the improvements to the John O'Groats to Thurso road 1947-48 which had been started by Baxters in the late 1930s and stopped with the outbreak of war.

By that time the bridges were completed and excavation of the cuttings had begun and most of the work was done manually with wheel barrows. After the war David Steven of Caberfeidh played a major part in the excavation of the cuttings in the Braes of Gills driving the excavator (19 RB). Several other local men worked on the contract.

Colin Mackay.

THE BACK ROAD SHOP

A glance in the window shows the choice is limited:– A packet of A.1, or Hudsons powders for washing day, a cake of Monkey brand for scouring pans, a quarter Good as Gold tea, card of pot menders. As soon as you go in at the door you notice the different smells – is it gingerbread or currants? Two customers in front of you, means there is plenty of time to look around before it is your turn.

On a low chair is a two hundred-weight bag of sugar, rolled down neatly at the top, and the scoop in readiness for weighing the two pounds the customer will ask for. Why always two pounds of sugar and only one pound of barley or lentils? They are taken from brown paper bags sitting on the counter which hold one stone. Two nicks cut out of the inside of the counter puzzles but only for a minute. The grocer pulls a coil of Bogie Roll out of the counter drawer, unwinds it and measures the strip between the two nicks before twisting it off. The tobacco is set on the scales and weighs one ounce exactly. A couple of candles and a box of matches and then the drawer is closed. A pair of leather laces for working boots is taken from a card hanging on a nail. A gallon of paraffin taken from

the store and that's all.

The next customer wants six fathoms of rope for a cow's tether. Up snakes the thick rope from under the counter and it is stretched across the grocer's out-flung arms, once, twice, three times maybe more – I've lost count! Next five fathoms of rein rope – its thinner and does not cost so much and it also is weighed on the scales. Meanwhile all the local gossip is exchanged between the customer and the shopkeeper before it's my turn at last.

Half a stone rough salt, a half loaf (i.e. one loaf) is pulled from a batch all stuck together, a cake of blacklead and a sheet of emery paper. I explain that I'll be back for another half stone of salt as we are going to kill the pig, and I remind the grocer to keep the sugar bag when it's empty for my mother, because she wants to make a new rag mat.

Dan McLeod, Lochend.

GILLS STANDING STONE

A few hundred yards west of Sinclair Innes's old house, in Hillside, Gills, stands an unusual freestone measuring roughly three feet high, three feet wide and one foot thick, slightly fan shaped with vertical rounded grooves Whilst probably not from the pre-historic past, this stone nevertheless has an air of mystery about it.

Why should this gravestone shaped slab rest here in the middle of the hill? Does it mark the last resting place of some long-gone human or animal, Tam O'Shanter's Meg perhaps, or maybe it just dropped from the sky? Few people know of its existence let alone why it's there.

One evening, whilst walking home through the hill, I decided to have yet another look at this curious stone. My dog "Rocky" was running around chasing anything that moved and lifting his leg on everything that didn't. When about 20 yards away, he suddenly became aware of the stone, his burse went up and he began snarling viciously. This lasted for about five to 10 seconds, he then returned to normal and set off running to and fro. It took slightly longer for the hair to go down on the back of my neck.

P.S. The stone measurements are from memory. I didn't chance going back.

Billy Magee, Lower Gills.

Photo, Ian Sargent, Tourist Board.

Footnote:–I remember as a child being warned not to go near the standing stone which was on the way up to the hill from Alex Begg's croft in the Back Road. This would have been in the early 20s and we always regarded the stone with respect and a certain apprehension.

C.C.

DUNKIRK AND BACK

I, James Dunnett, my brothers Tom and Donnie and my brother-in-law James Forrester and William Magee who later married my sister Peggy volunteered or were called up at the beginning of the war, and surprisingly, were all in the 119 Company Royal Engineers.

We were in Belgium when the Belgian army surrendered and were part of the Allied army which retreated to Dunkirk. We set out to march to

Calais but were turned back and then had to tramp mile after weary mile over fields, roads, ditches, mires and added to that there were enemy planes overhead and also the risk of attack and ambush from German tanks and artillery. We marched for hours and then were allowed a 10 minute stop for hard biscuits and bully beef and it was after one of these rests that we noticed Tom was missing. We had to get permission from our

Back Row:– Jimmy Forrester, Hillside, Gills; George Dunnet, Brough; James Dunnett. Front Row:– Tom and Donnie Dunnett and Peter Manson, Barrock.

rails before exploding in the sea. After all this commotion died down and Tom had had a sleep, he started wondering how the rest of us had fared. He could not believe it when a mate told him he had seen me on deck but there were so many tired wet men aboard, packed like herring in a barrel that we didn't see each other until we reached Chester.

We both hoped the captain[1] of the "Icarus" got a medal because he did an outstanding job when we were attacked by an enemy plane and certainly distinguished himself that night by zig-zagging so skilfully and he got clear of the enemy by steaming under a smoke screen he put up. We were landed at Dover where we boarded a troop train for Salisbury Plain. I remember feeling a bit of consternation when I wakened in a thick fog and could see no one – the hot packed compartment was so full of steam from our wet clothes you could cut it with a knife! Dinner that day was stewed prunes and custard and what a night we spent with so many soldiers trying to get near the dug-out latrines. We were all granted 48 hours home leave and decided to interpret this as 48 hours in Gills! When we returned to Chester we were all put on charge but this was later dropped.

The sea was calm that night at Dunkirk but we must never forget the men who defended our rear and made escape possible, and the crews of the little ships, and the big ships who carried out this tremendous evacuation.

A combined effort from Donnie, Tom and James Dunnett, Lower Gills.

Commanding Officer before being allowed to go back. Thankfully we found him lying sound asleep in the open at our last stop and it was some job to get him wakened and going. It was after that, that a piper volunteered to play, and the skirl of the pipes fairly wakened us and we marched with renewed vigour.

The beaches at Dunkirk were swarming with men and there was a flotilla of little boats working tirelessly and undauntedly under an incessant pounding from enemy planes and artillery. It was a navy rowing boat that picked up Jimmy and Donnie and this for Donnie (who wasn't tall) was after quite a few had used his head as a spring board when trying to get aboard and he was up and down under the water like a yo-yo. They were put aboard a coaster which landed them at Dover. Tom said his job of "lining up" the men in three columns in preparation for, and during the wading or swimming out to the little boats was the worst job he ever had because he had to threaten any who queue-jumped. None did.

We didn't want to test our luck by all going on the same boat because with the heavy casualties all around us and the continuous bombardment the outlook was bleak and grim. About 10 of us waded out and were hauled aboard a small rowing boat which took us to a coal boat and I remember when I tumbled aboard, that I couldn't get to my feet because of the weight of water in my clothes, especially my great-coat. This boat was attacked and after heavy bombing, sank and the next I knew I was aboard the destroyer "Icarus". Tom too, was picked up by one of the little boats and placed aboard the "Icarus". He was below when there was an almighty crash which rocked the boat and put out all the lights and they thought they were done for. Tom decided that since he couldn't swim he would be just as well to stay where he was and let the others run for the deck. The violent crash was a heavy bomb hitting the steel deck but fortunately it slid across the deck and went out through the

Margaret Cormack, 35 Finians Close, Honey Hill, Uxbridge, Middlesex, who is Honorary Secretary "Dunkirk Little Ships" has strong Back Road connections. Her great-great-grandmother Christina Dunnet who married Alex Begg was the sister of Thomas Dunnet, James's great-great-grandfather.

A.H.

[1] Lieut-Commander Edward Gregson Roper RN. Captain of the "Icarus" and Lieut. Derek P. Willan RN were awarded the D.S.C. Four more of this gallant grew got the D.S.M. and six were mentioned in Dispatches.

29th May, 1940. The "Icarus" coming through the crowded Channel, was attacked by 10 aircraft, one of which came in persistently at low level, but by using smoke and zig-zagging violently, got clear.

From "Dunkirk" by A. David Divine by permission of David Higham Associates.

JOHN O'GROATS

Land of my fathers! None but you
Holds me by any tie
With you my heart shall aye remain
Beneath your northern sky.

Tell me not in phrases fine
The world is free to me
Nor that I'd love some other land
Far, far across the sea.

The bridegroom may forsake his bride,
The maid her lover, too
But Caithness! Who can e'er forget
Love's pledge once vowed to you.

The king has got his palace great
The prince his mansion hall
Yet all the glory of their state
Would never me enthral.

My life's great aim is to secure
A cottage by the shore
Far North somewhere near John O'Groats
Where billows break and roar.

Near Pentland Firth I'd build that cot
Where Stroma stems the stream
And Bor'as stirs the racing tide
'Neath bright Aurora's gleam.

There shall I scan the ocean wide
From headlands rising high
While on the studded Orkney Isles
I'd gaze with pensive eye.

Ye booming caves in rocky shores
Ye Merry men of Mey
Ye pebbled strands and braes o' Gills
Ah, near ye all I'll stay.

And landward I will praise the charms
While distant hills I'll view
The babbling burns and warbling birds
Will days of youth renew.

I'll rise betimes and hasten on
At Braemore I will dine
And then I'll take the road again
To Morven towering fine.

But oh! I'll miss the old folks gone
The grandmas from their chair
The fathers, kindly good and grave
Whose bounty I did share.

Land of the North! These are my dreams
Of you I loved so well
Some day I'll realise my hopes
And in your bosom dwell.

Till I go hence and pass away
And join the fleeting throng
I'll daily tender thanks to those
Who guard your shores from wrong.

George Gibson, Edinburgh.

GIBSON FAMILY NOTE

Betty was the wife of James Gibson who was a mason at the Castle of Mey and built the house "Granny Gibson's" with its tremendous view over Gills Bay. (The house on the left after passing Peter Gate's house Marlbank.)

It is claimed the Gibsons were descended from Alexander Gibson, Minister in Canisbay 1705-1745. George Gibson who wrote the nostalgic poem John O'Groats was the son of James and Betty Gibson. George and others went back to Canisbay School in 1880 to learn Greek and Latin.

He had five of a family: George – a doctor (was one of the team who discovered that the source of the tetanus which killed so many babies in St Kilda came from the oil the women rubbed on the umbilical cord. This was fulmars and other seabird oil which they kept in store). Templeton was a dentist, James a lawyer, Robert taught in Stroma, Margaret was a pharmacist.

Nancy Meiklejohn, 73 Princes Street, Thurso.

Mrs Betty Gibson and grandson Andrew

Mrs Betty Gibson is using a hoop to carry a fraught of water from the Marl Well and the photo shows the Pasture Dyke (flagstone) is well maintained.

ALEXANDER GIBSON – MINISTER OF CANISBAY

Alexander Gibson was born in 1674 the son of Alexander Gibson, minister of Bower and Archdeacon of Caithness, and Katharine Sinclair of Assery. He was licensed by the presbytery of Orkney on 7th September 1704, and ordained on 29th August, 1705. In 1709 he married Margaret Sinclair of Rattar, widow of Alexander Sinclair of Brabster.

They had six sons and a daughter, of whom John, the eldest, became Sheriff Substitute of Caithness, and George became a Merchant in Thurso. As well as his duties as minister, Alexander was a tacksman to James Sinclair of Mey, and was involved in the export of grain from Caithness. Considerable correspondence between Alexander and Sinclair of Mey survives, and these letters throw much light on the culture of the early 18th century. They are also evidence of the difficulty ministers had in obtaining their stipend from heritors.

In 1727 Sir James Sinclair presented Alexander Gibson to Wick, but Alexander refused, giving as his reason:–

"The power of lay patrons in pretending to impose ministers upon paroches without their consent and approbation has always been considered contrary to our constitution since our first Reformation from Popery and complained of as a yoke and burden upon the Church of Scotland, and an undue encroachment upon the natural rights which the people claim of choosing their own pastors."

He died on 1st May, 1745 aged 71 years, in the 40th year of his ministry, and was buried at Canisbay.

Sources:– Beaton, Rev. D.: Ecclesiastical History of Caithness and Annals of Caithness Parishes. Published W. Rae, Wick, 1909.

Donaldson, John E.: The Mey Letters. Published J.P.H. Donaldson, Sydney, 1984.

Fasti Ecclesiae Scoticanae, Vol. VII. Published Oliver and Boyd 1928.

Henderson, John W.S.: Caithness Family History. Published David Douglas, Edinburgh, 1884.

Gordon J. Gibson, 4 Elizabeth Crescent, Dornoch.

THE MARL WELL

Andrew Manson, studies Marl Well, 1992

The Marl Well is reputed to have been built by Cromwell's men c.1652 and it was used by the Lower Gills folk as their main supply of drinking water until the mains water supply was installed.

The tap for drawing the water was low down at the foot of the steps and it was still there in the 60s. Before this, a "bung" fixed in the centre of a solid block of wood had to be removed. The steps are an unusual feature and appear as old as the well, and the complete round stone cover, although now broken, does not appear to have had a round or square opening in the top.

The metal grating near the top on the south east side is more recent, and would be for ventilation and to keep the water sweet (iron-ever water). The well is in the Gills pasture and you cannot miss it if you use the small gate opposite "Marlbank".

Alistair Manson, Gorse Bud, Gills.

You're born but not buried.

You can't put auld heids on young shoulders.

A narrow glenning, sometimes gets a wide scaling.

You'll live long after you're laughed at.

Keep your breath to cool your own porridge.

Mary Sinclair, Hillside.

The late Alex Mathieson (Sheds) is reputed to have said:

The rich the poor
The meek the lowly
They're all the same
When they reach the Moley.

J.D.

DONALD MACKAY (THE MOLEY)

Donald cycled all over Caithness catching moles on the various farms. He made all his own traps and as seen in the photograph, had his own special spade.

As he took the dead moles out of the traps, he cut off their tails as he had to hand these over to the farmers when they paid him. He skinned the moles, and each skin was stretched out and tacked on to long boards. Once dried, they were parcelled up and sent away to a furrier.

Donald Mackay followed John Ross as grave digger at Canisbay Church.

Mary Sinclair, Hillside, Gills.

Donald Mackay – Mole Catcher

Bikes without mud-guards are back in fashion.

MY FAVOURITE CAITHNESS VIEW

My favourite view in Caithness is certainly that of the Pentland Firth but there are so many vantage points from which to enjoy its soul-stirring panoramic grandeur, that after half a century I've given up trying to decide which one I prefer.

From the age of five until I was 22, I enjoyed the privilege of living and working on a small croft between Gills and Huna, commanding a view of Hoy, South Ronaldsay, the Skerries, Swona – with perhaps the main feature being that of Stroma, its shape reminding my youthful eyes and imagination of that of a gigantic duck-billed platypus!

Standing at the braehead in Canisbay, gazing at the view, was a constant childhood pleasure. When I was big enough to gain access to a coveted telescope, that pleasure of Firth-watching through the years, the seasons and variable weather, was further enhanced.

Sometimes I had to lean the telescope on a stone, such was the suspense and physical effort of waiting for a questing, urgent, Stroma yawl to reappear out of some deep trough whilst setting or hauling creels in water the colour of lead, with Hoy snow-capped.

Likewise for trawlers and seine-netters, plunging and rearing and sometimes apparently floundering their way through the tumultuous "Men O'Mey". . .

It was nearly always a blue, playful sea that supported the recreational mini-convoys of Stroma yawls crossing to "E Groats" on summer Sundays. Once, from John O'Groats, I observed a courting couple crossing back to Stroma in the moonlight – their yawl, and they themselves, mere silhouettes on the smooth, silvery water. I thought of Debussy's classic "Clair de Lune".

When I wasn't viewing the Pentland Firth from braehead level, it was from the flat and easy southern shore below as I walked from "Blackhol" (a small but picturesque waterfall) eastwards to the "Ness O' Quoys" – passing en route the "Black Rocks" and the "Red Rocks" (picturesque mini-cliffs) and "Seabank" (a little sandy bay where I had learned to swim and where one could catch "sellags" by the hundredweight).

Other walks were westwards past "Captain's Road" and The Haven of Warse, where "my" seal-colony was. Then, further westwards past Gills Harbour, and descending to my favourite route – that of a sheep's path; fast and inspired, unerring even when it was wet and slippery and eroded, but inevitably lured down into Scotland's Haven – that tranquil, so private, so unexploited sandy bay, with heather-clad cliffs and caves on its western side.

Then again, lured down to the more austere, slightly daunting "Bocht", a working little harbour but easily left behind to its raucous colonies of screeching, neurotic fulmars. . . Onwards – after dallying to drop a small boulder through a treacherous narrow fissure and listening as it struck the rocky walls and shelves again and again – to finish its descent with a deep, liquidy ploomph – onwards. . . To St John's Point, traversing a virtual trampoline of moss and heather. . .

Whin-blooms added their scent and radiance to the intoxicating beauty all around; such beauty, from the grandeur and aloofness of Dunnet Head and of Hoy, to Stroma's less familiar western cliffs, with their mixture of free-stone and blue-stone looking somewhat disarranged and tired out by all the centuries of receiving more poundings than caresses from the indefatigable Atlantic. . .

Patricia Crowden, Cedar End, Castletown.

MEY

Mey Public School 1931-1932

Teachers: Mr Donald McAlpine, Miss Lily Bnaks, Sunnybrae. Back Row, left to right:– Jimmy Harris, Lowland Cottage, Mill of Mey; A. George Moir, Mey; Jack Shearer, Scarfskerry; Henry Sutherland, Harrow; Angus Manson, East Mey; William Gunn, Police Station; John Geddes, East Mey. Second Row:– Ellen Geddes, East Mey; Dorothy Banks, St John's, East Mey; Kathleen Manson, East Mey; Margaret McKenzie, Barrogill Mains; Mary Henderson, Mey; Marjory Geddes, East Mey; Nettie Coghill, East Mey. Third Row:– Irene Sinclair, Burn of Rattar; Cathie Cormack, Phillips Mains; Jean Banks, East Mey; Marcia Swanson, Phillips; Tina Begg, Rattar; Margaret Banks, East Mey; Irene Miller, Harrow; Sheila Miller, Harrow; Mary Mowat, Phillips Mains; Dora McKenzie, Mey. Front Row:– Andrew Moir, Mey; Charlie Geddes, East Mey; Jimmy Miller, Harrow; Billy Manson, East Mey; James Mowat, Phillips Mains; Willie Sinclar, Burn of Rattar; Tommy Dunnet, East Mey; James McKenzie, Barrogill Mains; Robert Begg, Rattar, Robert Sutherland, Mey.

Mey School 1936

Teachers: Mr McAlpine, Miss Margaret Robertson (Stroma). Back Row, left to right:– George Cormack, Phillips Mains; Robert Sutherland, Mey; Jimmy Miller, Harrow; Charlie Geddes, East Mey; Tommy Dunnet, East Mey; Billy Manson, East Mey; James MacKenzie, Barrogill Mains; Robert Begg, Rattar; Davie Geddes, East Mey. Middle Row:– Alice Miller, Harrow; Irene Miller, Harrow; Dora MacKenzie, Mey; Jean MacLeod, East Mey; Kathleen Manson, East Mey; Tina Begg, Rattar; Margaret Banks, East Mey; Nessie Ainslie, East Mey; Cathie Cormack, Phillips Mains; Ethel Allan, Roadside. Front Row:– John Swanson, Phillips; Duncan Cameron, West Lodge; Sandy Allan, Roadside; Irene Sinclair, Burn of Rattar; Don Moir, Mey; Willie Ham, Harrow; Ben MacGregor, East Mey.

Mey School c.1952

Photo, Donald MacKay, Smithy, Mey.

Teacher: Mrs McPherson. Back Row, left to right:– Alex Grant, Hillcrest; George King, Lowland Cottage; George Miller, West Mey; John Ross, Rose Cottage; Robert Begg, Clovelly. Middle Row:– Donald MacKay, Smithy; Christine Grant, Hillcrest; Jean Ham, Harrow; Hazel Miller, West Mey; Peggy Malcolm, Rose Cottage, Burn Road; David Oag, Hillhead. Front Row:– Donnie Morrison, Glenairn; Elicia Barret, Police Station; Sandra Manson, Viewfirth; Elizabeth Oag, Hillhead; Wilma Geddes, Rose Cottage; Sheila Geddes, Island View; Chrissie Geddes, Island View; Jean King, Lowland Cottage; Ian Grant, Hillcrest.

Mey Public School 1960-61

Photo, Mrs Ethel Jack

Teacher: Mrs Ethel Jack. Back Row, left to right:– Hugh Grant, Royal Crescent, Mey; Jennifer Tait, Schoolhouse; Sandy Swanson, Long-goe Farm; Charles Tait, Schoolhouse; Keith Sutherland, Quoys; Valerie Grant, East Mey. Middle Row:– Manson Grant, Royal Crescent; Ramsay Grant, East Mey; Jean Ross, Mey; Michael Anderson, Royal Crescent; Thomas Geddes, East Mey; John Ferguson, Royal Crescent. Front Row: Brian Sutherland, Quoys; Duncan Ferguson, Royal Crescent; Elaine Tait, Schoolhouse; Elspeth Anderson, Royal Crescent; Esther Anderson, Royal Crescent; Pattie Simpson, on holiday from Thurso; Charles Ferguson, Royal Crescent; George Harper, Police Station.

Mey Sunday School at Sunnybrae 1934

Photo, Lottie Sinclair, Sunnybrae, East Mey.

Back Row, left to right:– Alistair McDonald, c/o Long-Goe; Magnus Banks, Sunnybrae; Angus Manson, Morven View; David Banks (sen), Sunnybrae; William Banks, St Johns; David Banks (jnr), Sunnybrae; Mrs David Banks (née Cormack), Sunnybrae; Billy Manson, Pasture Dyke; Mrs William Banks (née Jess Dunnet), St Johns; Eric Banks (from Stroma); John Geddes, Glenearn. Middle Row:– Kathleen Manson, Morven View; Jean Banks (from Stroma), Glenyra; Nellie Geddes, Glenearn; Barbara McLeod, Heatherbell; Dorothy Banks, St Johns; Elsie McKenzie, Barrogill; Marjory Geddes, Glenearn; John Allan, Hill View; Mrs Annie Bella Allan (née Forsyth), Hill View; Lily Banks, local teacher, White House; Lottie Banks, teacher, Sunnybrae. Front Row:– Charles Geddes, Glenearn; Ben MacGregor, Island View; Ian McDonald, c/o Long-Goe; Jean MacLeod, Heather Bell; ? McDonald, c/o Long-Goe; Nessie Ainslie, Clovelly; Margaret Banks, Sunnybrae; Catherine McDonald, c/o Long-Goe; David Geddes, Glenearn.

Coronation Day at Barrogill Castle 1953

Mey and Canisbay Schools joined for the Celebration.

Photo, Nan Fraser, Cairnlea, Canisbay.

Front Row:– Donald Dunnet, Quoys; William Bremner, (Norseman), Freswick; William Allan, Roadside, Mey.

THE NORSEMAN

Most of the inhabitants of the northern shores of Caithness are of Norse origin, but in no part of Scotland are the natives more strongly attached to their birthplace. Point St. John, from which our Norseman is supposed to have taken his survey, overlooks the Pentland Firth, Orkney Islands, and Skerry Lighthouses, from the Caithness side.

On Point St. John the Norseman stands alone,
With Phoebus' setting glories round him thrown,
And as he turns his gaze on either hand,
He sees the great, the terrible, the grand –
The dreaded Pentland's rough and rapid flow,
The wide Atlantic lit with evening's glow,
High Dunnet Head, the Pentland's towering lights,
The Orkney Islands, mountains, capes and bights,
A lengthened stretch of bay-indented coast,
Whose cliffs arise, a bold defiant host,
From which the shattered might of Ocean reels,
Like phalanx broken on a thousand steels.

These meet the pensive Norseman's gaze by turns,
Warm in his breast the love of country burns;
He weaves his patriot thoughts in rugged verse,
Which thus to winds and waves he did rehearse:–

"My Northern Clime! my Northern Clime!
  Though cold thy breezes be;
Though round my home the fleecy foam
  Is wafted from the sea;
Though late thy vernal flowers appear,
  Thy winters early come,
I would not for a milder clime
  Exchange my northern home.

"I would not give the Orcadian hills,
  The home of fog and breeze,
The battered cliffs that rear their crests
  Above the stormy seas,
The winding creeks, the elfin caves
  Along thy rugged coast,
For all the art-engendered grace
  That softer climes can boast.

"Let Southern prize his fatter field,
  His sunny slopes and vales,
His leafy groves, whose rich perfumes
  O'erload the languid gales;
His sluggish streams and level meads,
  His plains unmarked and tame,
His crowded towns, where all is art,
  And nature but a name:

"Give me the bold and beetling crags,
  Where whitening breakers roar;
The bleak, untrodden mountain steep,
  Where eagles proudly soar;
Give me the beauties sternly grand
  Which Nature's hand doth trace,
Which daring men can never smooth,
  Nor daring art efface.

"And where's the clime can match the charms
  That now before me lie?–
The charm of mountain-head and isle,
  Of blending sea and sky;
Those scenes supremely beautiful,
  When winds and waters sleep;
Those scenes tremendously sublime
  When storms bestride the deep!

"My Northern Clime! my Northern Clime!
  He is not son of thine
Who does not love the white sea-mew
  And the sparkle of the brine.
The man who fears to brave the breeze,
  Or breast the billow's foam,
Can not be sprung from northern sires
  Nor reared in Northman's home."

Thus spoke the Norseman on his rugged shore,
Where tempests howl and waves incessant roar,
Where wide morass and treeless wastes appear,
And winter's reign is lengthened, and severe.
On that bare soil, beneath that cloudy sky,
Few beauties meet the southern traveller's eye,
Yet there the Norseman builds the cherished home
To which he turns where'er his feet may roam,
Nor ever finds in any fairer zone
A land so dear, so beauteous, as his own.
From Yarns of The Pentland Firth,
By David Grant.

THE HEAD OF MEY

In the First Statistical Account (1793), the Rev. John Morison wrote "Near to St. John's Head is one of the pleasantest spots in the whole parish. . . . . but whether it has been the residence of saints or heroes, it affords ample proof, that neither taste nor judgement were wanting in the choice of it as a habitation."

Scotland's Haven

Scotland's Haven is still the pleasantest spot in the parish and impossible to beat on a fine summer's day with the sea and shore, sun and sand, seals and seabirds, and all the more touching when one remembers that our ancestors two to three hundred or even four to five thousand years ago would have enjoyed the same beauty, and tranquility. There are few places left where one can stand and look north, south, east or west and everything (creel-markers excluded) is the same yesterday today and tomorrow. The Scottish bluebell grows well on the braes and there are quite a few unusual plants on the Head of Crees, locally called the Red Head (red sandstone) which provides shelter from the east. A depth of boulder clay with a mix of shells makes up the south facing brae, and its Caithness flagstone on the west. Not so long ago people went specially to the mineral well at the west corner of the beach for iron water, thought to be good for anyone with anaemia. The site of the well is easily distinguished by the red

Scotland's Haven

Photo, Lottie Sinclair, Sunnybrae, Mey.

The Fort Dyke

St John's Chapelstone

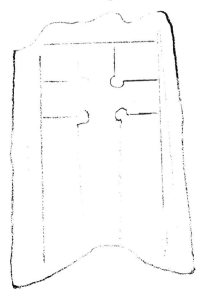

rusty looking stones and if these are cleared away the water will have settled and cleared in half an hour and you can enjoy a healthful and lovely drink. The caves on the west side are handy if you get caught in the rain. Tinklers used to live in the biggest cave in the summer but never stayed there in the winter as the caves are washed out by the sea. There is tremendous variety in the stones on the shore and there is a large colony of seals who are barely distinguishable from the rocks.

The Fort Dyke

In 1793 there were just vestiges of a ditch and drawbridge remaining, so it hasn't changed much in 200 years. The Fort Dyke runs from Boat Geo on the west to the Bocht on the east and encloses about six acres of the promontory at St. John's Point. (This can be clearly seen as one goes east on the Longoe to Maligoe Road). The moat must have been about 30 feet wide and had a low "fail" dyke on its landward side and it is said that the rampart on the other side was originally 10 feet high.

There were Pict's houses on both sides of the promontory dyke – the biggest on the landward side at the bottom left of photo. The site of St. John's chapel is the grassy knoll over the dyke from that and a bit further back and nearer to the Bocht.

In 1919 John Nicolson uncovered the west gable of the chapel which measured 11 feet internally and part of the lateral wall for 22 feet. He found a cross-slab forming the head of a slab-lined grave inside the doorway in the gable. The yellow sandstone cross-slab measured 76 x 58 cms at its widest parts and was decorated with a plain incised cross with hollows at the intersections of the arms and the shaft. The shaft tapered slightly towards its base. The slab was removed to Barrogill Castle for preservation and is now in the Northlands Viking Centre.

The Graveyard is to the north of the dyke and most years mushrooms grow here in profusion filling large circles about 30 to 50 feet across. c.1910, my father came across a cist-like grave when they were digging in the face of the brae near the church-yard and close to the Bocht. Archaeologists made a search and removed the bones for examination and dating. It is thought that the unnatural looking grassy mound is a cairn.

The photo shows the ruins of a "recent" drystone dyke which was in fair good repair until 1938-39. The St. John's Common

Grazing Committee saw to this, to prevent horses getting out on to the Point of the Men. The entrance through the rampart was built up like a low doorway and had a heavy wooden lintel on top. The sheep got through here to the grazing on the point which was too dangerous for horses. This could be at the original entrance, where there were remains of an ancient wall on top of the rampart about 25 yards from Boat Geo.

The fail dyke at the point dividing the Geo of the Men from Poordirt has lasted well and would have been built to provide shelter for sheep on the head. The cultivated part of the head was south of the Fort Dyke and lay towards the Bocht. It shows clearly that it was ploughed in the rig and furrow system. (One rig is five spaces or yards.)

The croft steading just 200 yards back from the Bocht was where Tom Rosie lived. He was the great-great-grandfather of Tom Rosie, Hunster, Jean who was Head of Tabeetha School, Jaffa, Israel, Willie in Pontypool and Nana in Australia.

The Bocht got its name when sheep on the pasture were collected for clipping and were "bochted" down the slope and round the corner on to the flat grassy piece which is only about 50 yards long. Improvements were made to the pier about 1938-39 and to make it easier to get cement-mixers etc., down, the steps were removed, otherwise the Bocht is as bonnie today as it was lang syne.

Standing on St. John's Point in a westerly gale when the Men are at their merriest, or on a fine night when all is quiet are unforgettable experiences which tug at the heart strings all the more when one's thoughts turn to those who over the centuries have lived and loved, worked and played on the Head of Mey.

Mackie Banks, Ancala, Gills.

Footnote:– James Dunnett, Lower Gills (Roadman) told that the Rosies were a clever, well-handed family and that they had shown him a small tablecloth which had been spun and woven by their family from bog cotton plucked on the Head of Mey.

B.M.

PROPOSED HARBOUR AT THE BOCHT

The Bocht c.1930

The need for harbours to connect the shortest, safest and easiest route for shipping between Orkney and the mainland of Scotland has long been recognised.

James Purves, tenant of Barrogill Mains has a long article in the Orcadian, 16th November, 1869 entitled "Orkney and Shetland attached to Scotland by a Caithness Harbour" and has also included plans of suggested routes. The herring fishing was at its height, and he extols the tremendous benefits the coastal places, as well as Orkney and Shetland, would derive from a railway connecting Wick to Thurso via Gills. . . . the present total average yearly value of all the sea fisheries of Scotland, exclusive of salmon, is only £1,500,000 and that the century before the Shetland fisheries alone were worth £2,000,000 to the Dutch. . .

. . . The required site for this crossing exists in the proper place, on the east sheltered side of St. John's Head, directly opposite the entrance to Longhope. The passage of eight and a half miles across the Pentland Firth is sheltered from the north by the Orkney Islands and the storm waves are run down in the tides of the Firth. The tides, whether it is flood or ebb, instead of being an obstruction, can be taken west or east of Stroma so

The Bught and Stroma, Mey.

Photo, Robert Begg, Rattar.

as to facilitate the passage; within Cantick Head is a calm inland sea, with harbours of refuge, in which each of the South Isles can be called at, as well as Kirkwall and Stromness.

The site of the harbour is in the right place at the northern extremity of Great Britain, and in a situation which a local railway can and should approach. It is perfectly sheltered, has ample sea room, and a depth of water sufficient for the largest ship in the navy. It is the only site of a low-water harbour on the north-east coast of Scotland. All engineering skill has failed in erecting harbours on this coast, because the laws of nature are against them. Wick's breakwater is a notable example of such failures. The perfect natural breakwaters at St. John's Head makes it a wild looking place, the appearance of which would frighten the highest authorities in engineering. But even with the roughest storms the pilots of the Pentland Firth take and leave the Bocht in their yawls with perfect safety. . .

It is unnecessary to discuss the restriction on the investment of capital in the improvement of the soil of Great Britain. In the Dominion of Canada there are no such restrictions and she opens her arms to receive any number of the strong, muscular energetic, healthy and intelligent sons of our small crofters who would a thousand times rather remain at home. . .

. . . following paragraph from the John O'Groat Journal a few weeks back.

. . . "It is touching, week after week to witness the parting scenes at Scrabster and Wick, as the steamers leave our shores. Fathers and mothers bid farewell to sons and daughters and the last fond look and waving of handkerchiefs parts them probably for ever. These occur as regularly as the steamers sail and have been going on to an extent that would waken a feeling of intensity but for its regularity."

He points out the advantages and benefits of ". . . one or two training ships of war stationed in these northern seas, where there would be no fear of losing ships as there are harbours of refuge in each quarter, afforded perfect shelter from every storm that can blow. There is no leashore in the Pentland Firth and the pilots of the Pentland Firth are the bravest of men and the best of sailors who would teach the naval officers to keep their ships afloat. . ."

Courtesy of the Orcadian Newspaper.
William S. Mowatt, Smiddy, South Ronaldsay.

SIR OLIVER MOWAT

Oliver Mowat was born in Kingston, Ontario in 1820. His father, John Mowat came from the croft in East Mey, now known as Island View where Nancy and Davie Geddes live. John Mowat took the King's shilling when he was 16 and enlisted, probably in the regiment raised by the Earl of Caithness, then the Laird of Mey, but the family refused consent and his father bought his discharge. Two years later he joined the Third Buffs and served under Wellington in the Peninsular Wars and later in Lower Canada. The Buffs were ordered to Flanders but Sergeant Mowat's term of service had expired, and he was granted his discharge and 200 acres of land near Kingston. Helen, daughter of George Levack, factor to the Trails of Castlehill and Rattar, was his childhood sweetheart and a lass with courage. She left family and friends and crossed 3000 miles of sea to marry John Mowat on the 16th June,

1819, the day she arrived in Montreal.

Their eldest son Oliver, studied and qualified as a lawyer in Kingston under Sir John A. Macdonald – the man who built Canada into a Dominion. In 1840 Oliver Mowat moved to Toronto and established a flourishing law practice. Later he entered politics and served in the Cabinet of Sir John A. Macdonald, first Prime Minister of Canada (Sir John's father was born at Dalmore, Rogart).

In 1872 Oliver Mowat was elected Prime Minister and Attorney-General of the Province of Ontario and his regime lasted for nearly 24 years. He resigned in 1896 to accept an appointment as Lieutenant Governor of the Province of Ontario – a position he retained until his death in 1903.

Canada's impressive monument to Sir Oliver stands in a place of honour at the main entrance to the magnificent red sandstone Parliament Buildings in Toronto. Oliver is looking south towards Ontario, down a busy six lane boulevard and his statue is still a place of pilgrimage for Toronto-Caithnessians and friends from the homeland. He married Jane Ewart in 1846 and they had a family of three sons and four daughters.

Sir Oliver Mowat's Statue

Sir Oliver Mowat

In recognition of his outstanding public services to Ontario, he was in 1892 created a Knight Commander of the Most Distinguished Order of St Michael and St George, by Queen Victoria. This was further augmented in 1897 by his promotion to Knight Grand Cross of the same Order. In 1962 a historical plaque was unveiled in the Court House, Kingston to commemorate Sir Oliver Mowat.

First day of sale for the Mowat stamp was the 12th August, 1970. Sir Oliver Mowat visited Mey, Canisbay and Buchollie in July 1892.

He was made a Burgess of Wick by Mr Paterson Smith, Provost, and the Town Council.

In his reply Sir Oliver said: "It had always seemed to him that there was evidence of greater and more exceptional attachment on the part of those who had left this county compared with other counties. One illustration that had oft occurred to him was that Caithness Associations could be found everywhere and that he did not find the like for many other counties of Scotland.

He had been honoured to be the President of the Toronto Caithness Society.

Caithnessians had proved themselves to be industrious, resolute, thrifty, successful, law-abiding and he was proud to be a Caithnessian."

*Notes, Annie Houston, The Mill House,
John O'Groats.*

Fiona Bremner, "Victoria Villa", now working in Deep River, Ontario felt very much at home in the Algonquin Provincial Park beside Lake Canisbay, so named by Sir Oliver Mowat.

S.M.

THROUGH MARGIE'S EYES

What is a croft? If you came from the Bullring in Birmingham for a summer holiday it would spell Utopia. Ask my younger sister who, on leaving school, spent several harrowing years coping with the seemingly endless chores when my parents were each incapacitated and she would say "I never want to see a croft again." "You learn to compromise" was the reply a student gave when asked by a professor at Oxford if there were any benefits in coming from a croft. To me it meant home, in the best sense of the word: not that it would have been my chosen lifestyle, but think of the friends, the freedom, the fresh air.

Glenearn, which is still the home I share with my husband, was the dilapidated croft with a thatched roof where my parents started off their married life. My father, who was a mason, restored the stonework and made a roof of Caithness slate procured from the Brabster Quarries. Freestanding at the back of the house, were a stable, a barn and a hen house, all needing to be re-roofed.

Inside the house were three rooms the "but", the "ben" and the closet. The "but" was the hub of the household where we cooked, ate and gathered around the fireside on a winter's night. Furnishings were basic. There was a table, a cupboard for food, a dresser stacked with bowls, cups and plates and a few ornaments. A simple armchair was at each side of the fireplace and half a dozen plainer ones were scattered around. This room also contained a bed where my parents slept. The open fireplace had iron slats enabling the peat ash to fall down into the ash hole which had to be emptied weekly causing a lot of dust. At each side there was symmetrical slab of freestone quarried from nearby Scotland's Haven and that formed the hearth. The iron "swey" held a variety of "crooks" on which to hang the cooking pots, while the sides of the chimney were whitened and the hearth stones and metal slats blackleaded daily. The floor in this room was of Caithness flagstones and when we were older my sister and I made various colourful rag rugs, one of which was laid in front of the fire and the other in front of the bed.

The "ben" had a fire "grate" with pretty green tiles at the side and linoleum on the floor. There was a double bed, a wardrobe and a chest of drawers, all made by the local joiner, Davie Banks of Sunnybrae. My sister Nellie and I shared this room and in winter it was nice and cosy with the peat fire in the grate. My four brothers shared the two double beds in the closet where there was room for little else except for two wooden kists.

My father, who had worked as a builder in Toronto, was now the mason for the Mey Estate and, as such, was considered to be well off in crofting circles! Dishonesty and ostentation were his pet hates. He had a big strong frame as befitted a hewer of stone and he worked hard at his trade, demanding the same dedication from his employees. His day started at around half-past six with feeding the horse and the two cows. Five minutes later, having fortified himself with a bowl of oatmeal brose, a home baked oatcake and tea, he would be on his bicycle, perhaps to Barrogill Castle where he would be paid a few extra coppers for going up in the bosun's chair to coat the outside walls of the building with a protective oil paint. No sooner would he have consumed his dinner of tatties and herring on returning home at six o'clock, than he would have yoked the horse and be out in the field ploughing or harrowing. Uncle Johnnie, renowned for his expressive, if sometimes unguarded expletives, made it quite plain that ploughing or harrowing until late at night was in no way conducive to an active sex life!

My mother was kindness personified: she was generous to a fault and no tinker ever went away empty handed. She worked exceedingly hard, looking on it all as a labour of love. As well as caring for a family of six, there was her Aunt Maggie who lived only a couple of hundred yards away – too near! Having no children herself, she was the complete authority when it came to sorting out our lives. I remember well the day I was blackleading the fireplace and mother saw her coming up the road: "Hurry and put on your "coorse brat" (an apron made from sacking) before she gets here," Mother said. With reluctance I complied, knowing that otherwise there would be instant criticism from Aunt Maggie.

Life was hard on the croft: the cows had to be milked three times a day and in summer they had to be taken to the nearby quarry to quench their thirst, while in winter the problem was in keeping the lantern lit until you reached the byre when the snow would be drifting around the doors. Our drinking water came from "Angus' well" some distance from the house. This meant a daily trip with two pails and a wooden "hoop" which kept the water from spilling. In a very dry summer we had to go to the "fountain", a reservoir near Donald MacKay's, the blacksmith's, which supplied water to the castle. My father built two large flagstone tanks to hold rainwater for such purposes as washing clothes. Because of the young children, mother often had to take the washing tub into the house and, if the child was old enough to stand, he or she was placed in a wooden chair turned on its side, this made a playpen! I've known mother to get up at four o'clock in the morning to wash. The white clothes were all bleached on the green and sometimes on the heather and then "washed up" with a "blue bag" in the water. The men's white collars were all starched. Eventually mother's relation Ena Banks came once a week and spent the whole day at the wash tub in the barn where my father installed a boiler which not only heated the water but also provided warmth. As well as the milking, mother had to "flit" the cows to a new patch of grass several times a day; there were no fences in those days. When the cattle were indoors there was hay and straw to be brought in as well as turnips. The hay "gilt" in particular had been so well trampled and compacted by us kids in order to keep out the rain, that it was a terrible struggle trying to extract even a small amount by hand. She also had to keep an eye on the half dozen sheep in lambing time, while all the small potatoes had to be washed and boiled up daily to provide one warm feed for the hens. In spring there would be a "clocker" (a broody hen) hatching out chickens and she would have to be guarded to make sure she went back on the eggs.

The men folks had quite an arduous job fitting in the peat cutting in their spare time; admittedly the women were often involved with the "scaling", which meant carrying out the top layer of peat so as to leave space for the bottom layer. "Sheds", a well known local worthy said. "Ye lose a lok a' sweit 'efore ye get any heit 'fae a peit."

He himself managed heit with little sweit!!!

The crofters in those days must have welcomed the Sabbath as a day of rest. On Sunday my father would lie back in his chair at the table after dinner.

He would close his eyes and would often sing "What a friend we have in Jesus" or another favourite hymn until sleep took over. On one such Sunday, his mouth wide open; there was a solitary cold "tattie" on the table. It was too much for my brother to resist. He popped the "tattie" in my father's mouth. Some things you only try once!

Schooldays were happy days; with a teacher like Lily Banks in the infant room it couldn't be otherwise. She lived next door to her joiner brother at Sunnybrae. I thought she looked very posh when she wore her spats to keep her legs dry as she cycled to school. "If you're good I'll read you a story from my new book of Fairy Tales" she would say. We sat enthralled longing for the next instalment. Mr McAlpine, the headmaster, who stayed in the Mey Hotel, came from Kinlochleven. He was a man far ahead of his time. The boys loved him for his interest in sport and gardening. He kept perfect discipline without ever raising his voice. What a debt we owe to those two teachers! In winter we went up to the old school, adjoining the schoolhouse, where Mrs Dunnet prepared us bowls of steaming hot cocoa. How tempting were those chocolate bars in Di Laing's shop window. If only I had had a penny!

No less deserving of praise, were Mr and Mrs David Banks of Sunnybrae who gave of their time and talent in forming a Sunday School which all the local children attended. Sunday afternoon saw their living room transformed with rows of forms brought in to seat everyone. There would be huge coloured pictures relating to the particular bible story. Mrs Banks played the organ and their son Magnus, the fiddle, while all the family were singers. Every summer we had a picnic in their lovely garden at Sunnybrae and at Christmas time, the whole house was thrown open and I used to help set the table and spread the home-baked scones with Davie Banks' own heather honey. Later there would be lots of home-made coconut tablet and we would play at charades.

In those days Sundays meant a very strict routine. Every other week, Geordie Begg's bus from Rattar was hired to take us to Russells' United Free Church in Canisbay (now a barn, alas!). Several times a year, Mr Russell would hold an evening service in the Mey Hall. His son James brought over his organ which he played and we sang from the Revival Hymn Book. A great favourite of mine was "There were 90 and nine that safely lay in the shelter of a fold." Mr Russell and Christianity walked hand in hand and his sincerity when he preached could never be doubted. He was greatly loved and respected by all his flock. Mrs Russell seemed synonomous with Sloan's liniment which she appeared to use as a talisman! She too could preach and once, in the Mey Hall, I remember her giving a lively discourse entitled "Hitherto and Henceforth."

There were no paid cars for ministers in those days! At their own expense, they hired Geordie Begg's car to visit the parishioners. The first occasion on which they had breakfast with us,

(11 a.m. was the breakfast time on the croft), Mrs Russell said to my mother "I never place less than two boiled eggs before the minister" – mother was happy to conform. In those days we were given only half an egg! As children, the religious service which appealed most to us was conducted by Jock Troop when he pitched his tent at Sandy Manson's, in Gills. It was standing room only as the singing soared heavenwards. Nevertheless, there was added appeal in going to church, in that my younger sister Nellie and I were given new hats and shoes. I can still see those lovely brown shoes, sitting on a shelf till they were too small, because my father wouldn't allow us to wear such posh footwear to school; besides, when it was weather fit for shoes, it was fit for bare feet! You cringed a bit for the first few days walking on the rough metal roads! We were never allowed to play outside on Sundays: hide and seek among the stooks of corn was forbidden, although when father and mother were at the kirk, we couldn't resist gathering those lovely red poppies which grew in the corn. Every Sunday night we sat around the peat fire and took turns in reading a passage from our Bibles.

As my brothers grew older, they each in turn worked for Alex Forsyth, the farmer next door, or some other local farmer, at the same time continuing to help at home especially cutting peat, lifting potatoes and fetching in the turnips. John liked taking the mare and foal and the cows to Canisbay Show and more than once he came home with a first prize. By the time John was 15 he worked the horse and cart. He loved the horse. First there was the white ex-army horse called Jamie and later it was Maggie the mare. I remember well the day that our six-year-old brother Tommy was already in the cart. John started yoking Maggie but she was having none of it. She bolted, cart and all, catapulting Tommy over the garden dyke landing him among the kale while she ended up the wrong way around in the cart! On another occasion a neighbour borrowed her to drill for potatoes. He forgot that Maggie couldn't stand the smell of manure. She took off, drill plough in tow, never stopping till she reached Sandy Manson's in Gills, her legs cut and bleeding. No vet was needed. Hemp, the collie dog who always slept beside her, licked her wounds till they healed. Since two horses were often required, lots of land work had to be shared with a neighbour. In our case, the neighbour was Donald MacKay, the blacksmith, who lived opposite the joiner shop at Sunnybrae. We loved Granny MacKay and her family and we were always visiting each other for Sunday tea after an outing to the beach at Scotland's Haven or the nearby sanny braes. Together we harvested the corn and potatoes, which meant that the work became much less of a chore.

Across the field was Camilla MacKenzie's little shop. We were daily customers but on Saturday night we took the eggs to pay for the weekly messages and father's "Bogie Roll" tobacco. Tuppence worth of Scotch Mixture sweets was our weekend treat and we never looked for more. Geordie Begg and Di Laing also came around with travelling grocery vans as did Wildy Rosie with his horse drawn vehicle and Jamie Henderson with his "spring kert". We loved Jamie's Co-op gingerbread and he would buy our butter if we happened to have any surplus. One Saturday Jamie knocked at the door: my brother John answered, "You want butter Jamie?" "Butter, I'll gie ye butter, far's yer mither?" Well did John know that Jamie's kert wheel had disappeared in the Barrogill dam on Halloween's night!

The big shopping day came when mother and I boarded Peter Gunn's bus to go to Wick. David Robertson's shop was the usual venue but if we wanted a special coat and hat we went to Fred Shearer's, the "select" shop! Mr Shearer, clad in a dark suit complete with red carnation, simply walked around greeting the customers. While in Wick we always visited our cousin and dear friend Mrs Annie Budge whose husband was a coal merchant. Mother would have a freshly killed chicken for her and I would fall heir to a coat and hat which one of her girls, Meta or Chattie, had outgrown. They always had lovely clothes so I was thrilled. Tea at Bowles bakery in High Street was a must – the hygiene might have been below par but that did nothing to impair the taste of those lovely currant jelly pies! I remember being told of a particular trip which Uncle Johnnie made to Wick on Peter Gunn's bus in wartime. A neighbour sitting next to him remarked, "Things are looking bad, the Japanese are about to invade Australia." "Ochanee," replied Uncle Johnnie, "I'm more concerned aboot' getting a collar for 'e horse." On another occasion, when he called at David Robertson's shop, a traveller arrived. With an attempt at diplomacy, the traveller greeted Uncle Johnnie with, "nice weather for the ploughing, you'll be getting on with the land work", only to have Johnnie retort, "Ochanee, the grun's fair in a myarter hid's joost lek marmalade!"

Holidays for me meant visiting Granny Banks and Aunt Bella in Gills, a few miles away. Their white washed cottage with its tidy thatched roof and rose scented garden, conjured up a vision of pure delight. The garden path was bordered with red daisies; there were paeony roses and honeysuckle. The white net curtains with ribbon bows were a perfect foil for the petunias in the window. A blazing peat fire said welcome as you walked in at the ever open door, while by the end window, Granny would be sitting at her well-worn Singer sewing machine stitching one more quilt, perhaps for one of our beds! Aunt Bella would be stirring the porridge pot over the open fire since that was the time that I would arrive with Peter Gunn's bus. Three small bowls of milk would be on the dresser – I knew I would get the rose painted one for my porridge. I had to eat it all till the black cat appeared on the bottom of the plate, only then would I get that lovely green duck egg. What a cosy house they had! Rag rugs on the stone floor, cushions on the chairs, shining brasses on the mantleshelf, and a "wag-at-the-wa'" clock that sounded so restful. I'd never seen so many ornaments; Aunt Bella loved her ornaments. The spotless white counterpane on the bed had a deep crochet border which she had made and on the table was a pretty waxcloth cover strewn with flowers. Ours was always so old and worn!

Aunt Bella's Crochet

My aunt kept busy tending her cow, making butter and crowdie, baking scones and pancakes and making no end of rhubarb jam, mostly for us. There were hens to be fed and there were the ducks who had such an idyllic time in the burn across the road that it was a problem getting them in at night. The burn had a fascination for me too, especially since lovely Forget-Me-Nots and Lady's Thimbles grew along the edge.

The highlight was the day I walked with my aunt the three miles to Taylor's shop and Post Office in Canisbay where she lifted her pension. There were such mouthwatering cakes and sweets on the counter and she always bought some for me, particularly Fry's chocolate cream. We would cross the road to "Wildy Post" who would have her shoes mended and ready to be picked up. Between collecting and delivering the mail on his bicycle, Wildy Dunnet was also the local cobbler. We would set out for home, sampling the sweets as we went. Next stop was Isa Mowat's shop; it would have been unkind not to give her some custom. Donald Shearer also had a shop, but there was no need to call there since he would be along with his horse-drawn van on Saturday.

Back home, Granny would have the kettle boiling for our half-yoking. Sometimes there would be yearned milk, with cream floating on the top. That day it was pancakes with lashings of butter and rhubarb jam, followed by one of the cakes we bought from Taylor's shop.

I loved hearing about my grand-uncle Peter Murray who had a draper's shop in Springfield, Massachusetts, and of the lovely dresses trimmed with ribbons and lace which he sent home to mother and my aunt. They did lose a bit of their charm worn with their heavy every-day boots! If only he had sent shoes! But who would complain when the following year two brand new bicycles arrived? Indeed many were the luxury items which crossed the Atlantic, courtesy of Peter Murray. It was he who also gifted an organ to the Canisbay Church.

The red letter day was when my Aunt Bella decided to take me into Wick to have my photo taken. It would have been my sixth birthday. Will I ever forget Barbara Bain's shop on the corner of Market Square? The collection of beads and bangles mesmerised me – I came out looking like a Christmas tree! My aunt bought me a string of red beads, a red bangle with shiny stones, a red ring, a blue brooch and a fancy clasp for my hair. All this was to tone in with a blue dress which a neighbour, Mrs William Banks from Stroma, had made me and had ornamented with red feather stitch. Now I was ready to make my debut in Johnstones in Market Square! I was even more mesmerised when the photographer covered his head with a black curtain type cloth. I clutched my dress, he clicked the camera – the result – a solemn, sulky face that said "I'll be happy when I get out of this place." I discovered later that I'd made a good job of showing off my white cotton drawers with their fancy crochet edging!

Holidays had to come to an end. Aunt Bella would say "You will have to go home and help your mam." Armed with a big bag of her home-made toffee, she would walk with me to the bridge at the main road and see me on Peter Gunn's bus. The return fare was sixpence which he seldom took!

There were so many jobs to do at home. At an early age I learned to scrub the wooden chairs, clean the brasses and wash the stone floor. I wanted to iron as soon as I could reach the table, (would that I had the same enthusiasm today)! Every little treat that mother could think of, she gave us. My sister Nellie always had at least one doll. I preferred our real live cat and I used to play with her, taking her up in my lap. In winter evenings we would play at Snakes and Ladders and my father would play at board games with the boys when he wasn't cobbling – he was a dab hand at repairing boots and shoes. The sure recurrence of chilblains never deterred us from building one more snowman. In summer time we looked on working in the hay as a picnic since we always had lemonade and biscuits and the weather was so good that it was great fun just frolicking around in the hay.

Granny Geddes lived with Uncle Maikie in Lower Gills. Their home was a solid stone building complete with a roof of Caithness slate and some fancy stonework around the door, but the inside was rather stark and bare with few ornaments although granny did have a marvellous picture of a Gospel ship with a text on every section of the sails – I never did get them all read. Some Saturdays I would walk over and polish the candlesticks, the brass rod and the door knob and I would wash the stone floor. I really enjoyed it; it looked so good when it was done. On one occasion, Uncle Maikie went through to the closet, opened his kist and gave me half-a-crown. I nearly had the edges worn smooth taking it out and in my pocket as I walked home up the Mey brae. That was a lot of money for a seven-year-old! Uncle Maikie used to go to the fishing but now he had only his croft from which to scrape a living. His main source of cash was when he sold a stirk in the mart at Thurso, so the price was very important. When his stirk was in the ring and the bidding started he would say to the auctioneer, "Keep her "goan" Sanny boy, keep her "goan", plenty room for it a'."

At the age of eight, I suddenly found myself in the role of home-help to my grand-aunt Maggie who lived next door. She was unwell and suggested that "Margie" as she called me, could come and sleep with her in the box bed. Margie was not exactly enamoured at the idea but saw no escape. At 20 minutes past seven every morning, an elbow would be nudging me telling me to get up and light the peat fire with sticks and paraffin. While the kettle was boiling, the hens had to be fed. I would go into the small closet and put "euveca" from one kist in a tin and corn from another. I then took the lot over to my aunt to scrutinise the quantities. Maybe if she had lived long enough I would have got it to her satisfaction eventually! Her morning tea consisted of a slice of white bread spread with butter and real strawberry jam – I was only allowed to use the mixed fruit! Will I ever forget the guilt I felt at pinching a small strawberry from her jar? Every morning her chamber pot had to be emptied. One day the pavement was very icy; the pot and I ended up in a heap; the blood was pouring from my wrist –

how was I going to explain my bandaged wrist to the other schoolchildren? I can trace the cut yet!

One night I was awakened by a loud crashing noise. I was petrified. I lay panting and quietly sobbing, feeling sure that some ogre of a man was going to appear. Daylight revealed "Uncle Rory" lying on the floor in the "ben end", the picture frame and the glass in pieces! Once a week I had to collect the "News of the World" from Janet Swanson's. How I hated passing the quarries on either side in the darkness. No sooner would my aunt get the paper, than she would start reading aloud all the gruesome murders. I would be through in the front porch where I washed the dinner dishes. Wondering what was keeping me, she would call "Margie, are you not finished yet?" Little did she know that Margie was standing, a finger tight in each ear, wondering when the last murder would end! But there were compensations. When the English friend of the 15th Earl of Caithness rouped out of Barrogill Castle, (now the Castle of Mey), my father yoked the horse and cart and took Aunt Maggie and me down to the roup. She bought two carpets which my father laid on the stone floors of her croft. This made her house look and feel cosy. Also I had a comfortable armchair with cushions all to myself and there were only the two of us to share the peat fire. One Christmas she gave me a pair of brown rubber boots bought from J.D. Williams' catalogue. That was a super present! When our cow wasn't milking, we went either to Mrs Donald Banks or to Mrs Angus Manson to collect milk before going to school. Since it was winter time and the rubber boots could be worn by three of us there was no lack of a volunteer to plod through the snowy fields to fetch the milk!

My aunt died when I was 10 years-old. I was happy just to be back home where I belonged.

Such were the relatively carefree, halcyon days of my early youth on the croft that for me still spells home.

Marjory Morrison, Glenearn, Mey.

THE WHITE HORSE, JAMIE

My father, Charles Geddes, mason, East Mey owned a white horse called Jamie. He had been branded with the initials N T with an arrow underneath on his left rearquarters and the initial C under his mane. He was known in Mey as "the War Horse".

My uncle lived in Edinburgh when the horses pertaining to the Scots Greys were disbanded at Jock's Lodge, nearby in 1920, the very year my father would be looking for a horse. Perhaps Jamie was one of the number?

He was such a placid horse and, as well as doing the usual croft work, he used to take us in the cart to Dunnet Marymas and also to our school picnics. My older sister, Marjory, recalls him taking us to a picnic at the then Barrogill Castle where we all received a gift from the bran tub at the castle door, courtesy of the owner, Mrs Geraldine Sinclair. In

later years she remembers her father yoking Jamie in the cart and taking herself and her grand-aunt to the castle roup.

David Banks, the local carpenter, always borrowed Jamie to transport the wood from Wick to his shop in Mey, a round trip of 43 miles and, when carting home the Sunnybrae peats, the new apprentices trusted this white horse to lead the way to the right peat bank, stepping only where the heather was firm under foot.

Jamie was my pride and joy; he had no vices whatsoever. Many a time in the stable I would speak to him, clap him and crawl under him. He didn't mind in the least; however, if he was treated at all unkindly, his reactions were quite different. He loved being between the shafts of a cart but if he was tipped with the rein that meant a fruitless day for the handler. The result was the same if he was shouted at when ploughing. Since my father was busy at his trade, various people would be handling Jamie without taking these things into account. I well remember the results!!

Since he was getting old and uncontrollable in some people's eyes, he had to go. That was the saddest day of my life but when I saw that the horse dealer had brought stirrups I felt a little cheer at the thought of Jamie still enjoying a canter.

John Geddes, 84 Newburgh Crescent, Bridge of Don, Aberdeen.

BANKS THE JOINERS

Some Sunday School Pupils c.1938

Back Row:– David Banks, John Allan. Middle Row:– Magnus Banks, Davie Geddes. Front Row:– Donald Cameron, Sandy Allan, Tommy Geddes, Duncan Cameron, Mackie Banks.

David Banks, born 1808, was a younger son of the Harrow boat building family and trained as a joiner in Thurso. He married Jean Innes, Gills and set up business in Mey as estate joiner, croft-house builder and repairer, furniture maker and undertaker. Two sons, David and John, emigrated to Australia. Magnus returned after trying out life in America, married Margaret Jack, Scarfskerry and carried on the family business at Sunnybrae.

The Joiner shop was just across the road from the Smithy which was an ideal arrangement for both, because the woodwork and metalfittings were individually made and checked out for accuracy. Cart wheels made with oak spokes, beech hub and elm fillets, were taken across the road to be ringed at the smithy. This was done by heating the shods or hoops until red hot over a fire of wood and peats – lifted on to the wooden wheel using tongs and then quickly and deftly hammered into position and sloshed with pails of water to prevent the wood burning and to contract the iron shod to fit the wood tightly – a very skilled job. Dunlop wheels complete with axles came in in the middle 30s, so after that we just repaired carts.

Bee-keeping was a special interest of my father's. He made all his own hives.

David Banks, Sunnybrae

GREAT GRANNIE'S

Thrift was a virtue when I was young, and because money was short, families made sure that nothing whatsoever was wasted.

My great-granny Manson was an enterprising hardworking woman with an eye to business. About 1820 the going rate for making a herring net was 10/- (50p), so great-granny got going and made a net. She walked barefoot to Wick from East Mey, carrying this heavy net on her back. She was paid the money, walked home the 20 miles and her twins were born the same night.

My granny, Kirsty MacLeod from Eilean nan Ron, met and married William Manson when she was working in the John O'Groats Hotel. They lived in a thatched cottage beside the Pasture Dyke and my grandfather and Jocky Mackay from "Glenearn" used to fish from the Bocht. They went out on a lovely summer's day when they were older men, and the wind suddenly rose. Their small boat capsized and they were both drowned. Tragedy struck again when granny was an old woman. In these days the houses all had box-beds, and it was said they were made with tops or ceilings to prevent slaters or other creepie-crawlies out of the thatch, falling down on the heads of the sleepers. A good layer of straw was laid under the mattress to prevent the slatted wood wearing or tearing the ticking of the caff-seck. Kirsty took matches or a lighted paper to look for something under the bed and some wisps of straw caught and then the chaff mattress and the whole house was burnt. She had good neighbours and they got a book going and collected £20 for her, which was a lot of money about 1918. Everyone helped and they got the new roof on and the house trimmed and snug for her in no time at all.

I don't know what great-granny would have made of this throw-away age when everything is disposable but I'm sure she would have adapted. I'm a great-granny now and because it's so easy to forget, I've been writing down a patchwork of memories for the two Jameses, Brian, John, Emma and Janice.

Kathleen Ross, Upper Warse.

BEFORE T.V.!

I am often asked by a girl of nine
Just what I did to pass the time
Long years ago when I was wee
Before bingo, hi-fi or TV.
So before my memory gets any worse
I'll just relate it all in verse
A list of all the jobs and errands
We did to help our hard-pressed parents
Meit eh chickens, lift eh eiggs
"Mind eh clocker'll pick yer leigs."
Feed eh caffie, sort his tether
Bonfires we' dowed gress or heather
Butch eh peggie, makan' puddings
Sweep eh lum, fishin' cuddings
Kertan peits for weeks and weeks
Plantan tatties, thinnan neeps
Turn eh sheepies off eh heid
"Keel eh toop make sure it's reid."
Till eh toorists' busses wavan
Then a dip in Scotland's Haven
Catchan rabbits in eh dick
Twietan snare pins oot a stick
At eh handline or eh creels
Reetan in eh stack hill meals
Watch eh Merry Men o' Mey
Lift eh tatties, cole eh hey
Take eh stotties oot in spring
Watch 'em, do eh Highland Fling
Weed eh floories side eh walkie
Flit eh coos, pit doon eh backie
Watch eh Spring-time lammies leap
Take in peits, then dip eh sheep
At eh table mind yer manners
In eh barn pit roon eh fanners
Till eh Sabbath school on Sunday
Till eh Public school on Monday
The steam mill comes, eh barn is full
Take eh quiag till eh bull
Tirran and shiellan in eh moss
Hear eh Sporties lattan blost
Dressed in plus-fours eh silly mutts
Scookin in their bourag butts
Yer uncle comes tay visit yee
He'll tak ye up upon his knee

Yer reward ye hope when he pits ye doon
A word o' praise – a half a croon
Eh chicken's oot "Now dinna chace 'em"
Come in and learn yer Catachism
On Sunday ye'd be on yer way
Till a moosty kirk in Canisbay
This duty we just dare-na shirk
It's Russell preachan in eh kirk
Spartan doung, eh yerd till dell
A fraght o' water fay eh well
Take in neeps, muck oot eh byre
Twa weet piets tay rest eh fire
Bit sometimes there wis time for play
Especially on a summer's day
Football, rounders, seek and hide
And when it's weet ye went inside
When what brought oot eh loudest chuckles
Wis a swing high in eh stable couples
When ye wis aboot fifteen
And Week and Thursa ye hed seen
Ye'd follow roond eh ploo we' dad
Praying he'd offer ye a hadd
Or build a scroo, or yok a kert
Or pit a biestie till eh mert
Tae eh shoppie on yer leigs
Eh shopping it wis payed wi' eigs
And if there wis some change in lieu
Perhaps a cake o' Highland Coo
It seemed to last far ower a week
Yet wis never known to make ye seek
When nights were dark we' storms and snows
Ye'd play at cerds or dominoes
Rowe some worsad we' yer mither
Or listen till eh wireless shither
O' TV then there wis no mention
But eh Tilley wis a great invention
Slung fae eh reef on a winter's night
It gave off scades o' heit and light
Pumped fill o' win' and paraffin oil
Ye'd see it beam for half a mile
But it's gettan late, ma clothes I'll shed
So goodnight all 'am off till bed
Now ye'll understand Maree
Just how time passed without TV

Tommy Geddes, Sen., 3 Houston Terrace, Thurso.

The Head of Mey

Remains of moat divides off Point of the Men. Maligoe at right and some of the Queen Mother's Aberdeen Angus cattle in foreground.

Photo, Magnus Houston.

Mr Donald Dundass, Farmer, East Mey, Thurso

To William Mackay,

❧ GENERAL BLACKSMITH, ❧
MEY, THURSO.

1923

						£	s	d
Apr	9	To	32 new bolts & washers for harrows @ 4½					.12
			40 new harrow tines 40 lbs @ 10½ 33/4			1	13	4
			2 new drawers and bolts 6½ lbs @ 1				6	6
			2 new swedish eyes for hinges of harrows 10d					10
	20		2 new shoes 3/6				5	6
						£3	4	4
May	18		Paid by Cash			3	4	4

← Donald Mackays, The Old Smithy and Estate Poorhouse, end on to the road. Sunnybrae and David Banks Joiner Shop (note slatted windows for seasoning wood).

The Dundas croft was next occupied by Willie Allan, bus driver.

Wm. Mackay beside Back Delivery at Smithy.

Account and photos, Donald Mackay, Smithy, East Mey.

WALTER STEVEN – CAPTAIN OF THE "ROWENA"

Walter Steven was born in 1876, the elder son of John Steven and Elizabeth Banks, Snowflake, John O'Groats, and no doubt as a boy would have been fascinated by the ships under full sail going through the Firth. He went to sea when a young lad, started at the bottom and with hard work, perseverance and dedication became master of the "Rowena". His knowledge of navigation, seamanship and managerial qualities must have been put to the test when in command of the "Rowena" and taking her round Cape Horn.

This painting shows the four masted barque sailing briskly in a moderate sea with a breeze strong enough to keep her single topgallant and royal sails furled, while signal flags J.1.P.K. streaming out from the jigger mast halliard, were a customary means of specific vessel identification before the days of wireless at sea. Barclay, Curle & Co., built the barque on the Clyde in 1883 for Donald Currie, London as the "Cluny Castle" to be engaged initially in the Australian emigrant traffic.

Her owner founded the Union Castle Line whose well known liners later maintained a regular passenger and mail service between the UK and South Africa.

The immaculate appearance of the vessel, as depicted by the artist, is in sharp contrast to the photograph where she has a more realistic, weary and weather-beaten look, possibly taken during the later years of her life. Her starboard anchor is "catted" so that its cable can be used as a trustworthy mooring while the port anchor is "hung off" ready for instantaneous dropping at a berth where calm conditions may be the exception rather than the norm.

In 1905 the "Rowena" was sold to R. Ferguson of Greenock and in 1909 W. Thomas & Co., Liverpool became her owners. Power driven ships inevitably ousted the windjammers in this country so that in 1915 we find this vessel flying the Finnish flag until 1925 when she ended her days in a shipbreaker's yard after 32 years of world-wide trading. Her figurehead, a person wearing a crown, is presumably the original adornment, having some connection with "Cluny Castle" whereas the name "Rowen" is no doubt taken from Scott's novel, where the heroine of that name, in love with Cedric the Saxon's son and despite murderous threats from his rival De Bracey, finally marries her Ivanhoe and presumably all lived happily ever after.

The camera captures the "Rowena", her hull rust-streaked and bereft of paint which could be the result of a long voyage, and having discharged, now awaits another cargo and probably a new crew.

The "Rowena"

"Rowena"

Photo of painting

Photo, courtesy of "Sea Breezes".

Furled sails would seem to indicate that she is not yet laid up awaiting an end to her seagoing days.

Walter Steven took an extra master's ticket and after that was captain of the S.S. "Ashbourne", "Auckland" and "Montrose", Trinder Anderson Line ships. (They carried a live bear as mascot on the "Montrose".)

He married Barbara Mowat (a close relative of Sir Oliver Mowat) from Longoe and called their home in East Mey "Rowena". It was in 1940 that his two sons qualified as master mariners at Glasgow. His elder son Walter John went to sea when he was 17 with the Australind Steamship Co., London. A few days after receiving his master's ticket he sailed as chief officer on one of the company's vessels to Australia and on his arrival was transferred as captain of the "Australind", a ship his father and brother had both sailed on. Walter John, as captain of his ship, left Adelaide on 8th July, 1941 for Balboa (Pacific end of Panama Canal), thence to the UK. They were intercepted by the German raider "Komet"[1] on 14th August and the "Australind" was sunk by gunfire.

Captain Walter John Steven was 31 when he was killed. His brother (my father), Donald Mowat Steven, was only 29 when he gained his master mariner's certificate. He was commended for brave conduct in 1942 when sailing as chief officer on the S.S. "Toward", a convoy rescue ship employed on war service in the Atlantic.

Walter Steven, 19 Old Road, Llanelli, Dyfed, North Wales.

[1] The "Komet", a very fast vessel, was built in 1937 for North German Lloyd as the "Ems" and the German admiralty decided she would make an excellent commerce raider. She left Bergen on 9th July, 1940 and went round the north of Russia aided by three Russian icebreakers, arriving in the Pacific on 10th September 1940. She sank eight merchant ships, five of which were British and returned safely to Hamburg on 30th November 1941. She left on her next raiding voyage on 8th October, 1942, was intercepted by five of our destroyers and several

M.V. "Australind"

The "Australind" was built in 1929 by W. Denny and Bros., Dumbarton for the Australind Steamship Co. Of 5020 tons her dimensions were 410 feet x 54 feet x 26 feet. The Australian black swan was in the centre of the Co. flag and also on the funnel of their ships.

torpedo boats on 14th October when she blew up and sank in a few minutes.

S.M.

Footnote:– The value of tobacco in Captain Steven's time could have been similar to this description taken from "Voyage in the Rowena" 1909 by J.H. Wood.

The "Rowena", like all ships, carried a large stock of duty free tobacco, very important commodity, and, when at sea, weather permitting, the hands would "lay aft" in the second dog watch of a Saturday evening and, the captain and steward officiating, the slop chest would be open, and the crew would draw their tobacco and other things against their signature or mark.

In addition to smoking, a much indulged in pastime, tobacco was also used for chewing, particularly at the wheel, where smoking, of course, was not allowed, and a spitoon or bucket was secured nearby for the chewer's convenience, (emptied daily by the junior boy of the watch). Tobacco was also used as currency and for barter of every description, ready money seldom being available. Lastly, but not least, it was used for gambling.

Courtesy of "Sea Breezes", C.H. Milsom, editor.

When rain comes before wind,
Halyards, sheets and braces mind;
When wind comes before rain,
Soon you may make sail again.
Clair Calder.

ROUND CAPE HORN

Quite a number from this parish sailed round Cape Horn, and thanks are due C.H. Milsom, Editor of Sea Breezes, for this account of a voyage in the "Dynomene" describing what conditions could have been like for those from Canisbay who sailed before the mast. Sutherland Manson drew the diagram to help explain the fascination sail has for those with their roots on the shores of the firth.

A VOYAGE ROUND THE HORN

The "Dynomene" was a three-masted barque with 28 of a crew – Captain Procter, chief and second officers, four apprentices besides myself, berthed in a half deck under the starboard side of the break of the poop. Fifteen men were accommodated in the forecastle, a large house on deck and as was usual on British ships, they were a mixed lot representing 10 different nationalities.

The "Dynomene" sailed from South Shields for San Francisco on 7th February, 1907, towed by the Antwerp tug "Vulcan", setting sail off Beachy Head five days later. We met with very bad weather in the Channel, and it was soon found that our cargo of coke, pig-iron and bricks, sometimes known as "a Shields general", gave her a very quick and violent roll, the decks being continually full of water.

On the night of the 20th, the ship had a narrow escape from being blown on to the Casquets, a lee shore, but a few days later the weather moderated and an uneventful passage followed until 28th April, when we had our first gale off Magellan Straits. Staten Island was passed the following day, and the weather soon became very cold, the masts and rigging being coated with ice and snow. On 7th May, in the early morning, while all hands were making the foresail fast, a big four-masted barque loomed up ahead in a snow squall, but just cleared us in time. For the next 12 days we were beating against a succession of heavy westerly gales, being driven down as far south as 59 degrees.

The bad weather and our subsequent misfortunes, were attributed by some of the crew to the presence of a solitary bird, of the species known as a "booby", which disconsolately hovered over the ship, much in the same way that the black albatross accompanied Shelvocke, when he was off the Horn in the privateer "Speedwell" in October, 1719, the well-known incident that is said to have inspired Coleridge in "The Rime of the Ancient Mariner". Shelvocke states that the albatross "from his colour" was considered an "ill omen", and that it was shot by Hatley, his second captain, in the hope "that we should have a fair wind." In our case, too, the bird's colour, which was brown, made it unpopular, and when on 10th May, it flew on board and was caught by two of the watch on deck, who let it go again, this was looked upon as a fatal mistake and occasioned gloomy forebodings. It was considered unlucky by the old school of seamen to kill a white albatross.

By Whit-Sunday, 19th May, we were more than 500 miles to the westward of the Horn and were hoping that before long there would be a good slant to the northward. At four p.m., the barometer reading was 29.60 inches, and the glass then commenced falling rapidly with a strong gale from the north-west, so that by eight o'clock, we were reduced to foresail, three lower-topsails and fore top mast staysail, the ship being on the port tack. At 9.15 p.m. all hands were called to haul the foresail up, and while on the yard furling the sail, the gale suddenly increased to hurricane force, blowing the fore-lower-topsail clean out of the bolt-ropes, followed almost immediately by the other two lower-topsails.

The man next to me at the weather yard-arm, a Swede, when passing a gasket up, had his hand smashed by the chain lower-topsail sheet flying through the lead, and the force of the wind was so great that it was much as we could do to avoid being blown bodily over the yard, but at last all managed to get down on deck safely, leaving the sail half fast. The fore-topmast-staysail went next, and the crossjack lifts carried away, but we could not do very much, the wind being estimated at 100 miles an hour. Soon afterwards, the fore-brace carried away, and while trying to make it fast to the windless barrel, she shipped a very heavy sea over the forecastle head, which resulted in two men being knocked down and badly injured by pieces of a heavy harness cask weighing over a ton, which had broken adrift and taken charge.

At midnight the barometer reading was 27.90 inches, a fall of 1.70 inches in eight hours, and it was then impossible to distinguish sea from sky, the night being pitch dark and only lit up by the sparks caused by chains and gear flying about aloft and banging against the iron lower-masts. In the middle watch, the spike boom snapped off short through plunging into the heavy seas, thus causing the fore-topmast to break off above the cap and fall aft, and when daylight came the old ship looked a sorry sight. The topmast had crashed down through the starboard lifeboat, the fore-yard was up on end, and the topsail-yards were partly over the side, all swinging against the fore-stay at every roll and threatening to bring down the lower-mast; the fore-topgallant-yard was sticking down through the top of the forecastle into an empty bunk, but although the injured Swede was lying close by and there were other men in the forecastle, no one was hurt. The main-topgallant and royal masts had been pulled down by the falling topmast, and with their yards were hanging in the gear and flying about in pieces, and all the sails that were fast (except the mizen-topgallant-sail and royal) had been blown out of the gaskets and were in strips.

Our first job was to get the wounded men aft, where the "old man" set their broken bones and made them as comfortable as possible in his own quarters. The smashed lifeboat was dumped overboard, and the after-one provisioned in case it became necessary to abandon ship. All hands then set to clearing away the spars and gear, which meant cutting through the wire rigging lanyards with nothing better than cold-chisels and mauls, no very easy task with the ship rolling heavily and shipping water, but before dark we had succeeded in getting rid of the topmast and topsail-yards and lashing the fore-yard to the rail in its cockbilled condition. The helm was lashed down and all hands spent the night aft in the cabin (or saloon) with no watch kept, except a look-out on the poop.

On Tuesday she rolled so heavily that the pig-iron could be heard being tossed about in the 'tween decks, and a trysail was set abaft the mainmast and a royal hoisted in the mizen rigging in an effort to steady the ship and keep her up to the wind. On the following day the "old man" obtained an observation by which he estimated that she had drifted 227 miles due east since Sunday; two rockets were fired in the evening as a distress signal, but we were just out of the track of steamers. Thursday was a very bad day, but we did as much work as possible and were able to get some fresh water from the pump, a wet job in bad weather as the main deck was always awash. All this time there was a mountainous sea running with very heavy snow blizzards and hail squalls.

On Friday the weather moderated a little and we squared up the fore-yard on which was bent a main topsail, and cut away the main topgallant mast and yard. When the "old man" was up aloft on the main giving us a hand, he was badly injured in the back by a flying clew-iron, from the effects of which he never altogether recovered. On Saturday we bent a couple of main-topsails and sighted a vessel a long way off. On the following day, 26th May, we bent a foresail, and setting it with a main-topsail and main-topmast-staysail, got steerage way on the ship for the first time since she had been dismasted. Our luck was out, though, as in the first watch it came on to blow again and at midnight all hands were called to reef the foresail. Whilst hauling up the sail, a young Dane jumping on the rail to go aloft, was knocked overboard and lost. Nothing could be done for him, and a few hours later, at seven a.m., she shipped a sea which washed away the two after-boats, skids, booby hatch and fore and aft bridge, making a clean sweep of everything except the port davits, which were bent double. The bridge was left on deck in a 'thwartship position, washing from side to side with every roll, and before it could be secured, several rivets had been shaken out of the starboard bulwarks, which were so weakened that they could be moved by hand. The "old man" had all hands aft again that night, and at one a.m., the spanker and main-topsail blew away, and not long afterwards the poop was swept by a very heavy sea which carried away the port rail, smashed the wheel, and washed the compass overboard. Fortunately, no one was on the poop at the time, the helm being lashed down. The tarpaulins were also washed off No.3 hatch, but by crawling along on top of the cargo we managed to screw grummets on to the wooden hatch covers and then lash them to

battens placed under the coamings.

In the morning we rigged a steering compass by up-ending and lashing the steward's sea-chest to the deck, slinging a spare compass in a hole cut in the top, while a hurricane lamp made fast to a broomstick alongside served as a binnacle light. That afternoon, a man going aloft on the mizen, reported land to leeward on the starboard bow, towards which the ship was fast drifting. We ran forward to set our only available sail, the foresail, to make her pay off before the wind, but while doing so it blew away. It then looked as if it was all up, but by a miracle she paid off just the same; Captain Procter said it was the closest shave he had had since he had been to sea, and that we owed our escape to a favourable current. The land, composed of high, precipitous rocks covered with snow, proved to be the Ildefonso Islands. We kept running all that night under the few scraps that were left of the foresail and main-topsail, and the next day sighted False Cape Horn. On Thursday, 30th May, we were in finer weather, and bending a topsail on the fore-yard, set all available sail. The ship "Deccan" passed, outward bound, and asked if we needed any assistance, but the offer was declined as were now making for Port Stanley, though the "old man" afterwards changed his mind and steered for Monte Video, as being a better port for refitting. The pumps had to be kept going night and day, but considering the hammering the ship had gone through, she was not making very much water.

A few days later we were off the River Plate, and at daybreak on the 17th, when close in under the land at Punta Negra, the ship became unmanageable and refused to steer, the compass being apparently affected by the magnetic attraction which is said to exist in the locality. Having been reported by the S.S. "Galicia", two tugs came out in the evening and towed us up to Monte Video, where we arrived early the following morning. Here we remained for more than three months, being joined later on by two more "lame ducks", the British ship "Langdale" and German barque "Undine", both dismasted off the Horn. Captain Procter, who had worked like a Trojan after the ship was dismasted, had to be invalided home, and was succeeded by Captain John Barr, who had been with Wright, Graham & Co. Under the superintendence of Captain Pearce of the Liverpool Salvage Association, the ship was re-rigged by the five apprentices and five remaining men of the crew, the rest having deserted or been shanghaied. By the time the "Dynomene" was ready for sea, she had an entirely new crew, of which only about six could be called seamen.

We sailed on 25th September and had a good run to the Horn, which was rounded on 12th October under full sail, with dry decks, bright sunshine, and the sea as smooth as a mill-pond. After an uneventful run up the Pacific, the "Dynomene" arrived at 'Frisco on 26th December, 92 days from Monte Video, and 322 from the Tyne, during which time, some of us had not set foot on dry land. The newspapers made much of our experience, and one appeared with the head-line: "Bird brings bad luck

After discharging, we loaded wheat at Port Costa, 30 miles from 'Frisco, and on 25th February, 1908 sailed, for Queenstown for orders. Captain Barr believed in cracking on, and we made a smart passage of 17 days to the Line. On 11th April, the port side of the forecastle house was smashed in by a sea when approaching the Horn, which we rounded three days later under royals. A couple of small icebergs were passed and at dusk one evening, a craft which was believed to be a derelict. We had strong south-east and north-east trades with no doldrums, and on 28th May, sighted Flores in the Western Islands, 93 days out. A head wind now set in, and although on 2nd June we overhauled and passed the four-masted barque "Glenogil", homeward bound from Tacoma, it was not until the 10th that we reached Queenstown, 106 days out from 'Frisco, a very good passage for a ship with no pretensions as a clipper. After lying at anchor off Monkstown for three months, orders were at last received for Fleetwood, where we ended our voyage on 11th September.

J.W. Damer Powell, Courtesy of Sea Breezes.

UNDER SAIL

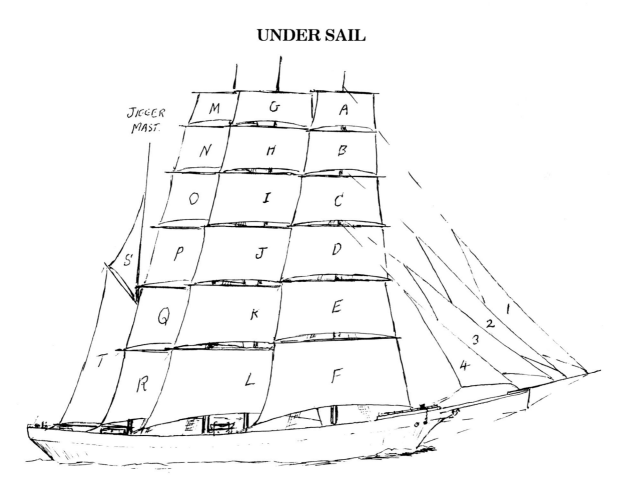

P Mizen Upper Topsail	**K** Main Lower Topsail	**F** Fore Course or Fore-sail	**A** Fore Royal	**1** Flying Jib
Q Mizen Lower Topsail	**L** Main Course or Main Sail	**G** Main Royal	**B** Fore Upper Topgallant	**2** Gutter Jib
R Mizen Course or Cro' Jack	**M** Mizen Royal	**H** Main Upper Topgallant	**C** Fore Lower Topgallant	**3** Inner Jib
S Jigger Topsail	**N** Mizen Upper Topgallant	**I** Main Lower Topgallant	**D** Fore Upper Topsail	**4** Fore Topmast Staysail
T Spanker	**O** Mizen Lower Topgallant	**J** Main Upper Topsail	**E** Lower Topsail	

In early vessels topgallant sails were single but divided later into two (upper and lower) for ease of handling.

Sutherland Manson.

CAPTAIN ALAN WALLACE

Born in Scarfskerry in 1858, Alan Wallace was one of a family of 11 – three boys and eight girls. Their home is still known as Dollies – first left down the harbour road and now a byre. His mother, following the death of her first born, went to Edinburgh where she trained as a nurse/midwife and then returned to provide the local nursing service.

Something of this enterprising attitude and quality must have been passed on to her children _ two of her sons became captains and another a bosun/ship's carpenter. A number of her daughters emigrated to New Zealand as also did her son Captain Alexander Wallace.

Alan Wallace, having been taught his navigation initially at school in Scarfskerry, left home at the age of 14 and went to sea in sailing ships. At an age when most young men were only beginning to think about passing examinations, Alan Wallace had gained his Master's Certificate and had his own command.

Captain Wallace married Annie Paterson and later had Seaview House built. He chose this site so as to get the best view of ships sailing through the Firth and always declared he had a better view than they had from the Castle. We now use his telescope in the manse to study ships going through the Firth of Tay. I also have a handsome barometer presented to him in recognition of the brave rescue of the crew of a pilot cutter during a storm in the Bristol Channel in 1886. He would have been 28 and that was young to have his own command.

Captain and Mrs Wallace had five of a family and was followed to sea by his son Alex who enjoyed the distinction of not only being a tanker captain but was also a Royal Navy Commander. As a result of bravery during the Second World War, he was twice mentioned in dispatches and also received the OBE. Post war, he became principal examiner to the Extra Masters Ticket with the Board of Trade, thus ensuring that the highest standards of seamanship were maintained. One daughter married Captain James Campbell, another Mr James Laurie and the youngest Mr Willie Finlayson. Despite the strong seafaring background, none of the succeeding generations have followed the call of the sea.

Captain Wallace retired from the Sutherland Line of Newcastle as Commodore Captain, having initially sailed as a young man with the Glen Line of Leith. Retiring in 1913 when only 55 must have been quite unusual but by then he had completed 41 years of service and his health had been impaired by years spent in tropical climate.

I spent many happy holidays at Seaview.

Nan Fraser, South Manse, Monifieth.

CAPTAIN WALLACE, SEAVIEW HOUSE

It was said that Captain Wallace was one of the best and truest men that ever trod the deck of a ship. He had Seaview House built, with its tremendous view over the Pentland Firth, for his retirement and then lived a life he loved. He got a small boat and fished for pleasure from below the house, and had his own capstan for hauling the boat up the beach in the summer. He had a special bay dug into the brae which was roofed over and the boat was wintered in this small boathouse with the mast, sails and a pair of oars stored in the roof. One winter during a severe storm the boat was split from stem to stern in the boathouse. John Simpson, Fassberry got the capstan which he took over to Harrow Harbour.

David Banks.

NOTED NAVIGATOR – EDWARD PATERSON 1814-1886

It is a well known fact that there came more sea captains per head of population out of Dunnet and Scarfskerry than any other part of Caithness and far beyond. The credit must go to Edward Paterson who held a navigation school at the Breck. The Rattar Assembly School is still standing and lies in the first field south west of the Rattar Smiddy and 300 yards from the main road. The school was built in 1839, teacher Ed. Paterson, and closed in 1879 when Crossroads School was built (see Caithness Book).

The herring fishing was flourishing then and there was employment for every able-bodied man. In the winter months when the boats were tied up, the younger men went to Edward's navigation school at night. He was a clever man with an inspiring personality, and one can understand the young men in the area hanging on to his every word as they learned seamanship, to box the compass, read charts and above all navigation. It was said he was the foremost navigator north of Aberdeen. His nephew William Paterson, harbour master at Wick, became a captain at the age of 18.

Edward was born in Scarfskerry and married Janet Taylor in 1840 and they had nine of a family. He was my great granny's brother.

Willie Jack, Scarfskerry.

May Gobbs – storm about the middle of May.
Kevin Mackay.

Ne'er cast a cloot until the month of May is oot.
Paul Begg.

HAIVERING ABOUT HORSES AND OTHER CANISBAY DELIGHTS

Today we may complain about the petrol tax but, some 200 years ago, our ancestors were vexed about the Horse Tax of the late 1790s. It caused a Lowland minister (from Strathaven in Lanark) to lament in Sir John Sinclair's "Statistical Account of Scotland" that: "The grievance the farmers here most complain of, is the tax upon saddle horses. Few can afford to keep a horse for the purpose of riding; yet, if they mount a labouring horse on Sunday to go to church they are fined. The rigorous execution of this Act has done more towards souring their minds against the Government than all the seditious pamphlets that have been published."

In Canisbay, Dr John Morison, the parish minister, had sent in his entry for the parish to "The Statistical Account" before the Horse Tax Assessment was made in Caithness in 1797/8. . . So we do not know whether any of his congregation were equally "soured". Presumably, there were some criteria concerning horses' age and size before they became eligible for assessment so not everyone in Canisbay was affected.

In fact, apart from Dr Morison himself, who was taxed on three of his five horses, only six other horse owners were listed in the assessment records for Canisbay. Three of these were sizeable land owners:– the Earl of Caithness at Mey, with 12 horses, of which six were taxed, Captain Sutherland of Brabster with seven, of which three were taxed, and Captain Innes of Freswick with six, of which two were taxed. John Manson in Warse and Donald Coghill in Long Goe each had four horses of which two were taxed. Mrs Sinclair in West Canisbay, who was the mother-in-law of Captain Sutherland in Brabster, had two horses, one of which was taxed.

Discovering Long Goe in this list diverted me for a time because the name prompted memories of childhood holidays in the 1920s and 1930s, when Long Goe meant many delectable things:– exciting cliffs, enticing rock pools, clover-scented fields, peat fires, freshly baked scones and all the fascinations of the farm steading. But, most important of all to me, it meant horses.

Long Goe was then an ordinary small farm struggling to survive in the lean inter-war years. (To anticipate for a moment: during the Second World War my grandfather, Henry Finlayson, died, so my father, Donald Finlayson, ran it from a distance, with George Allan as manager. My father later sold it to George Allan, who in turn sold it to the Queen Mother.)

In the 1920s it might have seemed an unlikely place to keep a top quality horse. But my grandfather had a passion for horses and the stable, in fact, held a fine display of red First Class Show Awards, won for jumping by a splendid black horse called Dickie. In his prime and ridden by my uncle Willie, he was only beaten once, in 1920, when my father, just out of war service with a M.C. from the Lovat Scouts, borrowed Daisy, a dapple-grey mare of equal calibre, from Nancy Harrold in Wick, and won. Dickie was felt to be almost too good for pulling the gig but was needed to take us to Canisbay Kirk on Sundays.

In his later years I was allowed to ride Dickie myself and would sometimes go two miles west along the shore road below Barrogill Castle, as we called the Castle of Mey, to where my aunt lived, just beyond the Mill of Mey, at "Rose Cottage" (later "The Moorings"). Aunt Mary was married to Captain George Sutherland[1] (later to be Harbour master at Wick), but at that time widely acclaimed among seamen for having, in 1924, pioneered a passage through the hazardous Magnetic Channel of the Great Barrier Reef, thereby cutting 600 miles off his route to save a perishable cargo.

At Aunt Mary's, Dickie would be stabled in the byre end of the old thick-walled house referred to as "The Camp". It stood across the road from "The Moorings", right on the edge of the cliff, and held a fascinating collection of mementoes from their far eastern travels, including a mermaid carved into a ship's prow. The gate to "The Moorings" had the ship's wheel from the Linkmoor built into it, a very suitable symbol for Captain George. He also had a flagstaff just beside the house and, when he was at home, he would exchange signals with passing ships. Long Goe was just in sight and the flagstaff could also conveniently be used for signalling to my grandmother, for instance to say that I was on my

Long Goe with Dunnet Head in background

way back. At other times, my grandmother would herself communicate with her daughter by covering the west side of Long Goe's peatstack with a plain sheet meaning "someone is coming over" or a patterned tablecloth meaning "come over yourselves", if I remember the code correctly.

Reverting to horses at the time of "The Statistical Account", I found Dr Morison writing: "In the summer season, there is almost a continued communication between Caithness and Orkney, in the traffic of horses. Colts from the Highlands of Caithness, from Sutherland and Strathnaver are sold to Orkney; and these very colts, when past their prime, are again brought from Orkney, and re-imported into Caithness. By far the greatest number of these cross to and from the shores of Canisbay, on account of the shortness of passage. Large boats are made for transporting them; and the freight of each colt is 1/-, and a full grown colt 1/8 to the nearest land."

At Long Goe we always thought our view across to Orkney was better than that from the castle. The farm buildings stretched, as they still do, in a continuous line from the stable at the west end, through the long byre, to what was then in the east end a little two-roomed house where my grandmother's two elder sisters lived. My great aunt Meyna was generally accorded her full title of "Miss Sutherland", in recognition of her status as a former Queen's Scholar, who had retired from teaching at Greenland School in the early 1920s. Aunt Meg, a former dressmaker, kept house for her sister, as she had done at Greenland. They had a little trap drawn by a very fat pony called Rosie, which was described as "loitering furiously" when left behind by Dickie and on annual family picnic outings.

Rosie used to graze beside Dickie and the other horses and sheep in the "parks" (fields) to the east of my aunts' house and I could wander there towards St. John's Head. Sometimes I would climb over the flagstone dyke on to the cliff top, where there was a tiny headland just large enough for me to lie on, which I thought of as a secret place, being out of sight from the farm. But I knew well enough not to venture by myself too near to the Geo from which the farm takes its name. Sometimes, if there were visitors, as was often the case, my grandmother would lead us carefully, with due warnings, down the Geo after tea.

Perhaps only a hundred yards from the end of the steading, the Geo entrance, overgrown with thistles and long grass, was (and still is) invisible – and unsafe, unless you know the way. Then, a narrow, steeply dropping track, over slippery stones, leads westward down the great cleft in the rock. It is so narrow that, for most of the way, you can stretch out your arms and touch both sides at the same time. About one-third of the way down, I was always alarmed, when looking up to see above our heads a huge cube-shaped boulder, which straddled the edges of the cliff and, being apparently held only by its corners, looked ready enough to fall in on us; that great boulder is still there. For most of the way, however, it is wiser to keep your eyes on your feet

than to look up, until, at last, the cliff meets again overhead, as the track turns northward and widens out to a small stony beach into which the sea roars. There is no safe way in at this level.

My father, when on army leave during the war, had explored the sea end of the Geo with Willie. They had found a crack in the southern face of the cliff, amounting almost, they thought, to an extremely narrow cave running at right angles inland, roughly southward, (which would lead it under the steading). They had pushed their way through for several yards until the air became foul, when they retreated, thereafter piling stones into the opening until it was hidden. They said that it would have been unsafe to leave it open but I was somewhat disappointed about that, having had visions of smugglers and buried treasure. However, even without the cave, the Geo was a fascinating, if frightening place.

It only occurred to me in later life to wonder why it was Kate, my grandmother, rather than my grandfather, who headed these expeditions so surefootedly. She was born a Sutherland, brought up near Corbiegeo in Thrumster, and was accustomed to precipitous cliffs and the power of the sea. In the summer of 1931, arriving at Long Geo in the early hours of the morning, we were mystified to see a long line of seamens' clothing drying in the garden. Then we found my grandmother feeding 14 crew members from the "Akranes", which had run aground, during the foggy night, on the rocks below the western side of the steading.

I had sometimes heard ships sounding their sirens, as they edged their way through the treacherous Men O'Mey, when my grandfather or uncle would take the dinner bell and walk along the cliff tops to warn them off, but this time the ship was on the rocks before anyone had heard a siren. The crew of the homeward bound Grimsby trawler had been rescued by the Thurso Lifeboat with help from the Scarfskerry Coastguards. The trawler was eventually refloated by Stroma fishermen.

While the wreck remained for several days there was more coming and going than usual on the beach where, generally, there was hardly a stranger to be seen. The ground becomes flatter, where the foreshore runs with that below the Castle, and the cattle could safely graze here. I delighted in running over the rocks, which slope like broad staircases that have slipped sideways, and, more restfully, I would lie beside rock pools searching for whelks, limpets and groatie buckies.

Unlike my grandmother, my grandfather, Henry Finlayson, had been brought up further inland, at East Greenland, his great grandfather, Donald Finlayson, having moved there from Auchorn, Bower. This Donald, (who was also the great-great grandfather of my husband, David Finlayson) appeared on the Horse tax assessment as having four horses, of which one was taxed. I suspect that Donald, like my grandfather, kept one more quality horse than he could really afford and that he transmitted a passion for horses down through the generations.

From East Greenland my grandfather had moved first, with his elder brothers to Auchorn, Keiss, and then on marriage in 1888, to Holland Mey. My father was brought up there and always remembered a time when, as a schoolboy, he was sent to sell a mare at Wick. A heavy mist set in, no one was buying, so he set off for home, only to realise that he was completely lost in the mist over treacherous, boggy ground. Sensibly, he abandoned the reins, gave the mare her head and she took him safely back to Holland Mey.

In the First World War, when my father was in France with the Lovat Scouts, his parents moved from Holland Mey to Long Goe. It was thought that the sea air would be better for my grandfather's asthma. The move suited my father's young brother, Willie, who married Captain Wallace's daughter, Annie, from Seaview House just above Long Goe. It was Willie's riding breeches which were altered for me and his bowler hat, that I rather reluctantly had to wear for riding in the late 1920s and early 1930s.

It was also Willie who showed me how to make simmens for holding the hay screws. As well as Dickie, he also let me help with the four big work horses. One, named Mey, was branded as bad-tempered, reputedly having had a previous bad owner, and I was told to avoid her. However, when I once rashly hitched a lift on a hay "coalie" and fell over the top, landing at her hind feet, she waited patiently until I scrambled out, aware as I did so of alarm changing to relief on the adult faces above me. It occurs to me now that Mey and the others could be descendants, or at least distant relatives, of those undersized, hard-worked garrons described in "The Statistical Account". Perhaps it is worth reflecting that it is not only people who have ancestors and who make history.

Footnote:– About Dr Morison's dates, I found discrepancies. Beaton and Calder both quote the date on his gravestone as 1796. Horne, however, gives his death as 1798 and this must be more nearly accurate as he was certainly listed in the Caithness Horse Tax assessment lists of 1797/8.
Angela Finlayson, Greenloaning, Kingsbarns, St Andrews.

[1] **Captain George Sutherland** in command of the steamer "Madawasha" after crossing 6000 miles of sea successfully negotiated the Magnetic Channel, a canyon in the Great Barrier Reef 32 miles long with a minimum depth of 23 fathoms. The chairman of the Townsville Harbour Board said it was one of the best things done in the Pacific since the days of Captain Cook.

Captain Sutherland was under 30 years of age at the time and was accompanied on that eventful voyage by his wife. George was the only son of the late Captain and Mrs Sutherland, Mill of Mey.
Courtesy of John O'Groat Journal, 29.11.1924.

Donald McCarthy, manager for the Queen Mother at Long Goe, has it on the very best authority that a goe extends underground from here right to Phillips Mains.

LORRIES AND BUSES

James MacKenzie c.1928 with Model T Ford Mail Bus

Photo, Sheila Moir, Scarfskerry.

Photo, Robert Begg, Rattar.

I started driving for George Begg, in May, 1928. He had two Ford Model T Lorries at that time. I had the one lorry, and that first year I was the whole summer carting "metal" (stones) for the road from the Birkle Hill to Pulhoy where they were improving the road. I carted just about everything – livestock of all kinds, supplies for the farms, coal, etc. – you name it I carried it. The other lorry had a joiner

Ack Gunn with Dual Purpose Vehicle

Photo, Sheila Moir Scarfskerry.

Robert Begg 1931 with Ford Bus used for School, Service and Picnic Runs

Photo, Robert Begg, Rattar.

made square body fitted on, which converted it to a van or bus. George Banks, Rattar, was the joiner who made it. Behind the cab, the "body" was split at the front and joined behind the driver's seat. When a lorry was wanted, the back part was taken off and a lorry platform fitted on. When the square body was on, it made a grand bus with the seats facing each other and the door at the back.

It was a bus on Sundays for the Kirk, Thurso sale day (Wednesday then), picnics, and the Simpsons when they were home on holiday from Edinburgh always hired it for a family outing to John O'Groats (parents of Mrs Munro, Brough). It was a van on Fridays and Saturdays. Friday run was East Mey to John O'Groats. Saturday run – Barrock, Dunnet, Brough. Boxes full of every kind of groceries were set out on the seats and the parcel rack held the

little things like Andrew's Liver Salts, Brasso, Rennet, Oxo, aspirins, laces and so on. There was a divided box with oranges and apples. A box for eggs (the eggs paid for most of the groceries). The women brought out washed flour bags to carry in the half or quartern loaves which were not wrapped. Paraffin was also carried and they brought out jars, jugs, tins, or any kind of receptacle for that.

After the Road Traffic Act of 1931, a bus had to be a bus so George Begg bought a Ford Model A bus with the seats facing the front as is usual now. It was used in the same way as the first. The old van-lorry was still going strong and was used temporarily if there was a breakdown or when they were busy in the summer.

I enjoyed my five years with George Begg. Once when I was taking men to a funeral, I went over the hump-back bridge at Lyth too fast and Charlie Geddes' head hit the roof. His head was OK but his hard hat was right down over his loogs, and it was about torn in two before he got it off.

The next four or five years went in very quickly too, when I worked for Jimmy Reid, Builders Merchant, Thurso. He sold all building supplies – slate, chimney cans, lime, cement, etc. and coal. I then got George Sinclair's job of driving Wilson's mail bus. (Wilsons had the Station Hotel, Thurso and Willie Wilson who had the garage, and then was with Dunnets Garage is of the same family.)

There was a big space in the back of the bus for goods and a rail on top for wood, bikes and awkward things. We carted just about everything – papers, medicines, calves (tied in a bag with head sticking out), boxes of chickens, the odd clocker and so on. Messages of every kind and description to and from Thurso, and other things equally pressing and important to any house along the road! In between the Thurso to Gills runs, I did the Orkney mail run to and from Scrabster. It was the old St Ola then under Captain Swanson.

Wilson gave up the buses at the beginning of the war (1940) and the Highland took over. J.B. Geddes drove the scholars and I was on the mails. (J.B. Geddes was married to a daughter of Danny Smith who had Smith's bus Lyth). Johnnie Grant started when Geddes was recalled to Thurso. (Johnnie married Isobel Manson from John O'Groats and Manson and Hugh of "Dynamos" fame are their family.)

When the school roll went up it needed a double decker to take the pupils and shop workers to Thurso. The buses ran from Billy Dunnett's at the Back Road, through East Mey, Scarfskerry, Barrock, Brough to Thurso. Donnie MacLeod came on the buses when Dounreay increased. I couldn't have wished for better conductresses than Sheila Moir and Sheila Wares. I really enjoyed all the fun, companionship and good crack on the buses and I made so many true and faithful friends.

I've turned many a corner thinking about this tonight and now. I think I could safely reverse. . . . my age and be 18!

Willie Allan, Castletown, late of East Mey.

THE MEY RIFLE CLUB
Winners of the Bain Shield 1927-28

Photo, John Swanson, Thuster.

Back Row:– Ronnie Mackay, Rattar; Donnie Sutherland, Shore Rattar; Wattie Smith (Stroma man who worked at Alfred Moirs); John Barnetson (police); Alex Wallace, (first place down the Harrow Road). Middle Row:– James Baikie, Tanghead; Tom Sutherland, Blackpeel (Thompsons); Willie Swanson, Phillips; Wildie Finlayson, Longoe; Magnus Swanson, Phillips; Christie Mackay, Rattar; Di Laing, Shop. Front Row:– Alfred Moir, Joiner; Davie Morrison, Burn of Rattar (undertaker, Munro's now).

Wilson's Mail Bus – Model T Ford at Berriedale Arms c.1927

George Sinclair, Driver.

Photo, Robert Begg, Rattar.

The Berriedale Arms was built as a staging inn for the mail coach which came via the coast from Wick. In the 1861 census it is given as the Prince of Wales Inn but by 1871 it was the Berriedale Inn. Originally this was a single storey building and the iron ring for hitching horses to is still beside the front door.

Snowdrift against Schoolhouse and Wm. Allan's c.1902

Photo, Robert Begg, Rattar.

Sanny Allan's, Hotel and Schoolhouse
(Note road and that the "planting" is hedge high.)

Photo, Robert Begg, Rattar.

"EH WAUTHER"

O aa the topics banded roon,
When Gollachs get together,
Politics, sport or ah thing else,
Take hindmost tae eh weather.

"Its cowld bit dry, its weet bit
    warm,
Eh win's got up again,
It wis ower bright early on eh
    day,
It will likely turn to rain."

"There's boaties sheltering in the
    bey,
Eh Ola stuck at Screbster,
Eh Burnies lipping till the brim,
An hids couped twa scroos in
    Brebster."

"Boy wis hid no wrough last
    night,
I was soaked till eh skin,
If it cerries on much more like
    iss,
Eh byce 'ee be coming in."

"Yin wis a piercan win last night,
It wid nearly numb yer brain,
Bit its no as bad as yin frost and
    snow,
Or yin horosontal rain."

If auntie's cycling frae eh Azores,
Her chain hes comin off,
Wis hid no some night estreen,
I am starting wi a cough.

"Man bit hid wis warm last week,
What a scade a heat,
Ah headna coaled twa squarrs, a
    hey,
When an wis in a droke a sweit."

Eh forecast shither hev there
    say,
But I sometimes doot their
    words,
When its turned oot fine in
    Caithness,
An Rain stopped play at Lords."
    Tommy Geddes,
    3 Houston Terrace, Thurso.

ID'LL BE SURE TAE RAIN

At nicht – if 'e sun looks kinda blear,
An' far awa' sounds come loud an' clear;
Fan hills an' mountains a' seem near,
Id's a sign o' rain.
In 'e early morn ye'll be sure tae hear
'E peltan' rain.

Fan 'e corns on yer taes begin tae stoon,
Or ye can see a circle 'roond 'e moon,
Ye can mark ma words 'at very soon
Id'll start tae rain.
An, if 'e midjags start fleean' up an' doon
Id'll rain again.

Fan reflections on 'e loch are bricht,
Lek a painted scene – a bonny sicht'
Mebby ye'll no believe id's richt,
But it foretells rain'
An 'e crawan' cockeral late at nicht
Is a hearald o' rain.

John Geddes "Highlands", Minchinhampton, Glos.

BARROGILL c.1920

Barrogill Mains

East Mey Pump

BARROGILL LODGE, MEY

Photo, Margaret Banks, Ancala.

My father John Allan was under gardener at the Castle and worked seven days a week – rain, hail or snow attending the vineries. One year when there was a heavy fall of snow, he was walking over the top of the dykes because the snow was level with them.

James Johnstone (grandfather of the late Jimmy Johnstone) pumped the water and filled the bath at the Fountain (reservoir just west of Smiddy) and the water then ran down to the castle. When the "sporties" were staying at the castle they came off the hill about four o'clock in the afternoon and then it was a steady job working the hand pump until they all got baths etc. The Barrogill Mains House was originally a lodge for sporties.

I think there were four pair of horses and a staig in training on Barrogill Mains at this time. Jock Gunn, Sandy MacLeod and George Allan were the horsemen. Sandy and George lived near at hand so they went out and home at nights. All took their own "pieces" with them as there was no tea supplied. John Sutherland was cattleman and he stayed in the end house next to the trees. Will Swanson was grieve (father of the late George Swanson, Keiss). A very good grieve he was too and a mini-vet. Neighbours from all round used to get his expert help when animals were ill or bad in calving or lambing.

Heelan Johnnie lived at Barrogill about that time too. He had a steady job pulling neeps all winter and he did all manner of odd jobs in the summer. He was quite houseproud and his home was chock full of lovely ornaments and dishes. Nurse Cook told that when he broke his leg she went over early

to give him a wash etc., before the doctor would get there. There was no sign of Johnnie and then she saw him below the bed! – He explained he was washing the floor "cause you never knew where the beggar might look!"

It was said that the north east corner of Barrogill Mains was the scene of a battle and that parts of human bones are turned up when the field is being ploughed.

Willie Allan, Castletown, late of East Mey.

The Fountain was deepened by blasting in the 1880s and was then walled and roofed. Blasting out a depth of rock lowered the water table and caused some consternation because it dried all the wells round about.

This pump was then installed by the Laird at the roadside near the "Rowena" road end to supply the nearby houses. It is still useable and Wendy Dixon, "Rowena" had it working recently after she primed it with two pails of water.

The bath that James Johnstone filled was a very early cast iron bath (bathroom style but before the days of enamel) and this head of water was enough to supply upstairs in the castle. The fountain supplied the ground floor directly. The castle water supplied Barrogill Mains House or the cottage as it was called in the days it was used by shooting tenants. Later on a motor pump was fixed up at the castle.

David Banks.

DRILL HALL MEY C.1900

Drill Hall, Mey.

Photo, Marjory Morrison, Glenearn, East Mey.

P.C. sent to Miss Banks, Roadside, Gills.

Dear Bella,

Just a P.C. to say if the day is good we will be over tomorrow or Thursday. Hoping you are all well and with kindest regards to all.

M.K.S.

(Margaret K. Sutherland, Newton, John O'Groats).

It was c.1900 that the wooden beam supporting the roof of the Drill Hall was replaced by a heavy metal beam. All the available blacksmiths with their "prents" gathered at the Harrow Smiddy where there was a flagstone or an iron-door at the back of the furnace (common in all smiddies) which opened so that long lengths could be handled. This massive long beam was successfully welded and can be seen holding up the roof of the Mey hall.

THE CASTLE OF MEY – THE SINCLAIRS OF MEY, LATER EARLS OF CAITHNESS

West View of Castle of Mey

Photo, John Adams.

Located six miles west of John O'Groats near the road leading from that place to Castletown and Thurso (the A836), stands the Castle of Mey, the Scottish home of Her Majesty Queen Elizabeth the Queen Mother. Although originally known by its present name, it was nevertheless throughout the greater part of its long history, called Barrogill Castle, and the home farm, the fields of which surround the castle, is still known as Barrogill Mains. The transactions of few estates are better documented, for the Sinclair lairds kept voluminous records of all their main managements and agricultural projects which were the basis of the late J.E. Donaldson's very interesting book "Caithness in the Eighteenth Century".

The Mey Papers

These Mey papers, now in Register House in Edinburgh, tell us that at Barrogill there was lack of nothing needed to rejoice the human heart. This was a golden age for Caithness and Barrogill was at the heart of it. Exports of bere and barley by the shipload – imports of sugar, teas of all sorts, oranges, lemons, spices, nutmeg, walnuts, raisins, candy soaps of the rarest and the best, gold lace, coloured satins and silks, stiff taffetas, muslins, ruffles and cravats, scarlet nightgowns and white waistcoats.

The name Mey is believed to be from the Norse – meaning "middle" "Township at the middle of the Pentland Firth", Barrogill could also be from the Norse – Bor-gil although Christina Keith gives it a Gaelic root meaning "cille" or cell of St. Bar.

The traveller on the A836 will first see the profusion of towers and turrets which adorn, with striking effect, the outline of the castle above its sheltering screen of trees which almost hide it from the main public road. From there one gets the impression that the castle stands much nearer the sea than it actually does. There is a tradition that a tunnel once connected the castle to the sea and a story has been told that during the Second World War, an army truck sank into what was believed to be a part of an underground passage. However, the distance from the sea - a good quarter-mile – and the very rocky nature of the fore-shore make the possibility of a tunnel highly unlikely.

It seems incredible now that this ancient and historic place was faced with abandonment and even demolition, being only saved from this dire fate by the timely intervention by the Queen Mother who became enamoured with it while visiting the nearby House of the Northern Gate.

Originally Church Lands

The lands of Mey, styled a barony, were previous to 1566 held by the church, and in that year the Bishop of Caithness granted the property to George Sinclair fourth Earl of Caithness, who proceeded almost immediately with the erection of the castle. The site had previously been built upon by the Bishops of

Caithness as a fortified storehouse where the tiends, in the form of meal and the other produce of the land, due to the church were kept. A few years later, in 1572 a charter dated March of that year was granted by the Earl in favour of his second son William Sinclair who thus became the first Laird of Mey. William did not survive long to enjoy his heritage. He was unmarried, although he left two illegitimate sons, one of whom became the ancestor of the Sinclairs of Ulbster. Mey, with its by then partially built castle, was passed by special gift to the Earl's next and youngest son, George, who held the office of Chancellor of the diocese of Caithness.

The Early Lairds

To this son the fourth Earl left all his considerable fortune in cash but not the estates of the Earldom which passed to the next Earl, his grandson by his eldest son John, Master of Caithness who predeceased his father. George of Mey died about 1610, being followed in the lairdship by his eldest son, afterwards Sir William Sinclair (Knighted 1631). He it was as a young boy attending the Royal High School of Edinburgh, who shot and killed Bailie John MacMoran a wealthy merchant of the city. Some boys including young Sinclair, all the sons of gentlemen, had barricaded themselves in the school as a protest against curtailment of their holiday period and the Bailie was leading the magistrates in breaking down the door when the unfortunate episode occurred. Although taken to court, the boy was eventually pardoned as well as all his accomplices.

In later life Sir William was the subject of a complaint by the minister of Canisbay to the General Assembly in 1639. (It was in 1637 that Jenny Geddes threw her stool at the minister in St. Giles, and in 1638 the National Covenant was signed.) Proprietors were uneasy in case that, along with the change of religion, the church would repossess its lands, and this left Sir William feeling

Front View of Castle

Photo, John Adams.

395

very vulnerable because he was an underholder and would have had to pay considerable tithes to the church. Mr Andrew Ogstone, then parish minister who had about that time changed from being an Episcopalian to a Presbyterian, complained that only nine or 10 of his congregation entered the church on a specially appointed Sunday to fast and supplicate a blessing on the work of the Assembly. The people had congregated in the church yard and, after sending his sexton out repeatedly to bring them in, Mr Ogstone went out himself only to be told that Sir William Sinclair had commanded that no one should enter the kirk that day. Sir William gave protection to all sorts of delinquents in the parish and he also kept his tenants from satisfying church discipline.

On one occasion when a servant of Sir William had been cited to appear before the Presbytery, the laird himself took the summons from the bearer, beat him, and put him in prison for two nights. The minister concluded his complaint by entreating their "Godly wisdomes to seriously consider the case that he might henceforth be enabled to discharge the sacred duties of his office."

Unfortunately no record exists of how the Assembly dealt with the matter. Mr Ogstone's descendants afterwards changed their surname to Houston and became the well known Caithness family of millers, a branch of which still operates the only meal mill in the north.

The Baronets of Mey

Sir William Sinclair of Mey had two brothers, one of whom was Sir John Sinclair of Dunbeath (Caithness Field Club Bulletin, April 1979) and the other Alexander Sinclair of Latheron who was ancestor of both the Barrock and Brabster lines. Sir William is often styled of Cadboll (Ross-shire) which he also owned. His title was a knighthood only, and it was his eldest son Sir James who became the first Baronet of Mey created as such in 1631 with remainder to male line only. His son and successor Sir William, found himself so heavily in debt that his estates, including the castle, were judicially sold to pay them. The second Baronet's brother, Robert Sinclair, became laird of Durran and ancestor of the present Earl of Caithness. A sister Anne Sinclair married the Earl of Cromarty and her son, Lord Tarbat, purchased the Mey estates from the creditors and placed them in trust for the benefit of the next heir, his cousin the third Baronet Sir James. This laird was succeeded by his son, another Sir James, fourth Baronet, who in turn was followed by yet another Sir James, fifth Baronet. His son the sixth Baronet Sir John, was yet another laird who became insolvent but this time the estates which included Snottergill (now known as Shielton) in the parish of Watten, were protected from seizure by a strict entail. However, his son and heir Sir James, was a man of great energy and resource, and not only restored the estates to solvency but eventually carried out great improvements both to the lands and the castle.

The Earldom Comes to Mey

He it was who in 1789 succeeded his distant cousin as 12th Earl of Caithness. No other estates but his own came to him with the title as the previous Earl's lands of Rattar and Greenland passed to a sister whose husband James Trail purchased them, thus founding the family who later became so well known in Caithness.

Barrogill Castle thus became the seat of the Earldom, a position it held for the next hundred years through the reigns of four successive Earls in line, the 13th Earl, Alexander, the 14th James, and the 15th George. Of these the 14th was a man who distinguished himself as an inventor and scientist. He was a Fellow of the Royal Society, a Lord in Waiting to Queen Victoria, and his inventions included a steam carriage (in which he and Lady Caithness travelled from London to Mey over the primitive roads of that time) a loom and a gravitating compass. He was twice married, the second time to a Spanish Duchess. The connection between the Sinclair family and the castle ended with the death of the young 15th Earl unmarried. He was a strange youth in life – in death he was also strange, for he left Mey and all its landed heritage to a stranger – a college friend named Heathcote, who on inheriting added the name Sinclair with a hyphen to his own. The next and 16th Earl, for the first time in the long history of the ancient title, had no land in Caithness. So it remained until the father of the present Earl bought back Girnigoe just before the last war.

No marriages and no births ever again brought joy to Barrogill and after being owned for a number of years by a member of the Terry family it passed by purchase to the Queen Mother.

Distinguished Guests

Of the distinguished travellers who during the centuries have visited the Castle of Mey, there was Lithgow who stayed there on his way to Orkney in 1629. So hospitably was he entertained by Sir James the first Baronet, that he left us the following grand description in verse:–

"Yet with good lucke, in Februar, Saturnes prey
Have I not sought, and found out Fruitfull May,
Flanked with the Marine Coast, prospective stands,
Right opposite to the Orcade Isles and Lands;
Where I for floures, ingorg'd strong grapes of Spaine
And liquor'd French, both Red and White amaine:
Which pallace doth containe, two foure-squaréd courts,
Graft with brave Works, where th' Art-drawn pensile sports
On hals, high Chambers,Galleries, office Bowres
Cells, Roomes and Turrets, Platforms, sately Towres."

MacFarlane:– In the "Geographical Collections" 1726 the castle is described as "a good building with a tower. . . built by the Earle of Caithness 120 years ago, but is going to ruin." This corresponds with one of the periods of strict economy owing to the petitions of creditors.

Pennant writes in 1769 – "A beautiful strong castle belonging to Sir John Sinclair".

In the Statistical Account of 1793, the Rev. John Morison relates that Barrogill Castle is an old aristocratic pile, but renewing its age under the additions and embellishments it is daily receiving from its noble owner.

Bishop Forbes visited the castle in 1762. It delighted him for he wrote – "One of the best houses in all Caithness with 18 fire-rooms, two of which being large dining rooms and hall". And of the gardens he wrote "I went into the gardens of Mey where I saw apples, strawberries, and some cherries".

Then that indefatigable artist Daniell strolled along to Mey in 1821 or so and this time the impression of the traveller are not in words but in pictures – and a bare place it looked then.

But Barrogill really came into its own on that day in 1876 when the Prince and Princess of Wales (later King Edward VII and Queen Alexandra) stayed there as the guests of the 14th Earl and Countess of Caithness. They had come to Caithness to open the new bridge over the river at Wick and to open an Exhibition in Thurso. Both royal guests planted a tree in the grounds to commemorate their visit, and it is said his tree has grown better than hers!

The Gardens of Mey

The gardens of the Castle of Mey have long been famous as we have already seen. In a booklet entitled the "Castle of Mey" published shortly after its purchase by the Queen Mother, the late Christina Keith M.A. (Oxon) describes in full detail and in vivid language the beauty of the gardens of old Barrogill.

The Castle Today

An excellent ground plan of the Castle is shown in the Inventory of Ancient Monuments of Caithness (1911). It shows in lighter shade the modern additions as well. In form it is a very typical example of the Scottish Z plan castle of the 16th century. The original doorway faced the sea and on that side of the house there is a large courtyard measuring 67 feet by 42 feet, also original with a round arched entrance. The ground floor of the main block comprises two cellars and the kitchen, all of which are vaulted. The kitchen has a massive

The Divided Staircase

Photo courtesy of John O'Groat Journal.

fire-place measuring 12 feet six inches wide and six feet in depth.

As always, the great hall is on the first floor above the two cellars and extends to 40 feet by 18 feet. A private room opens off it which is over the kitchen. The upper floors are devoted to bedrooms. Of the two tower "jambs" of the Z plan, one on the north west corner contains the spiral stairway which is a large and roomy one with vaulting at the top. The south east tower begins at ground level as a vaulted cellar with rooms thereafter as it rises upward. It is in the north west tower at the foot of the spiral stair that the original entrance was. A porch now shelters this entrance, and another large porch on the south front of the castle now contains the main entrance and hall. All the original windows have been enlarged.

References

Curle – Inventory of Ancient Monuments of Caithness – HMSO 1911.

Calder – History of Caithness – Rae 1887.

MacGibbon & Ross – The Castellated and Domestic Architecture of Scotland – Douglas 1889.

Anderson – The Scottish Nation (3 Vols.) – Methuen 1867.

Innes – Tartans of the Clans and Families of Scotland – Johnston 1938.

Ross – The Castles of Scotland – Letts & Co. 1973.

Munro – Kinsmen and Clansmen – Johnston & Brown 1971.

Donaldson – Caithness in the Eighteenth Century – Moray Press 1938.

Henderson – Caithness Family History – Douglas 1884.

David B. Miller, Old Stirkoke, Wick.

Earls of Caithness

The 15th Earl died in 1889 and James Augustus Sinclair, a chartered accountant in Aberdeen, was judged to be the nearest male heir and became the 16th Earl. He was descended from Robert Sinclair, Durran, the third son of Sir James Sinclair of Canisbay and Mey. James Augustus had three sons. John the 17th Earl who was unmarried. Norman the 18th Earl who had four daughters and Charles who was father of Roderick the 19th Earl and grandfather of Malcolm the present Earl.

Captain D.W.S. Buchan,
of Auchmacoy House, Ellon (grandson of Norman 18th Earl).

THE CASTLE OF MEY

Mey Castle 1821

Daniell's Print.

The Earl's Steam Car at the Portland Arms Hotel

Photo of painting, Bert Mowat, Lybster.

It was George Sinclair fourth Earl of Caithness who brought brothers by the name of Banks [1] over from Orkney in 1567 as the main masons in charge of building the Castle of Mey. The walls of the main tower (south east) are over six feet thick at the base and there were narrow slits in it and in the other rooms on the ground floor for shooting arrows through. The slits or gun loops are still there but they have been built up on the inside. There was a small cellar under this tower which I understand was always just a wine cellar. The front door was in the north west tower and one of the steps in the circular stair had an opening where burning cloots, molten lead or pitch or anything handy could be rained down on unwelcome visitors. This "firing hole" (or spout), later reduced to an eye-hole, was in the bottom of the projecting turret above the door. There was another in the south turret of the main tower.

The Sinclair arms carved on the red sandstone block set above the arched doorway into the large quadrangle bear the initials J.S.S. and C.S.S. joined with a heart and the date 1762. Sir John Sinclair Sinclair married Charlotte Duffus and their son James (10th of Mey) succeeded to the dignity, and in 1789 became the 12th Earl of Caithness. He was the Lieut. Col. James Earl of Caithness who in 1794 helped Col. Sir John Sinclair of Ulbster raise the Rothesay and Caithness Fencibles. He was Commander of the

Caithness Volunteer Infantry by 1804 and would have built the Battery at Mey.

It can be seen from Daniell's print that by 1821 the main entrance was at first floor level on the south side. The ground floor rooms had vaulted ceilings and it is not surprising they were called cellars with the only natural light coming from arrow slits. It is certain there was never an escape tunnel to the sea. (During the last war an army truck sank into a mason built drain and not into an underground passage as some believed.)

The 12th Earl died in 1823 and his son Alexander the 13th Earl of Caithness was Laird of Mey in 1836 when the first John O'Groat Journal was published. It was about this time that tenants started paying their rent in cash rather than in kind. At the time rent was paid in grain or other farm produce. The crofters carted it to the stable, now garages, at the north east of the castle where it was stored in the loft. When the tide was right and the seas were calm, small boats could come into the goe below the castle to collect the grain, but most of the trading was done from Harrow. The 13th Earl died in 1855 – the year that the Registration of Births, Marriages and Deaths became compulsory.

James the 14th Earl, still known locally as the Old Earl, was born in 1821 and on inheriting in 1855, started straight away to improve the estate and create employment. He had Phillips Harbour built (named in honour of his wife Louisa Georgiana Phillips) and started the flagstone industry there. Phillip's Mains was "broken in", Barrogill Mains improved and the castle extended and renovated.

It could have been about this time that the huge iron fireplace with a kind of oven at the side was installed. There was a turning mechanism above the fire which would have spit-roasted a whole sheep, pig or small side of beef. There was a sink in the scullery made from a solid block of red sandstone. The large porch, front hall and grand staircase were added in 1866. David Banks, my great-grandfather, was in charge of the carpenter work. It was his son, David, who made the heavy studded front door and it was my grandfather, Alexander Cormack, Freswick, an apprentice at the

time, who helped to hang the doors which are sound to this day. The fine corner stones and lintels are red sandstone from the Head of Creese and about a hundred years later the Queen Mother used stone from the same quarry when she had repairs done to the Castle.

David Banks (who made the castle door) was in charge of the Earl's yacht "Francesca", which he kept moored on the Thames most of the year. David did a lot of work on the yacht, got on well

James 14th Earl of Caithness
Lord Lieutenant and Vice-Admiral of Caithness

Photo, James P. Campbell, Rose Cottage, Halkirk.
This large painting of the 14th Earl set against a background of Dunnet Head and the setting sun beaming across the firth, is hanging in the front hall of the Castle.

Her Majesty Queen Elizabeth the Queen Mother has graciously allowed us to include this photograph of her painting.

with the earl and no doubt helped him sail her up to Harrow. (David, John and a sister emigrated to Australia.)

The 14th Earl had his own steam car[2] and he is credited with inventing the mechanism for reverse gear for steam trains. He had medals to show he exhibited at the Great Exhibition 1851 in Crystal Palace and that later on he was a judge at top engineering exhibitions in London and Paris. (The

Family at Front Door c.1863

Photo, Jonty Willis, Old Elm House, Redmire, Leyburn, Yorks.
Countess Louisa in light dress beside 14th Earl (bare headed) in doorway. James
S. Sutherland, Brabster (black armband) at right.

Mey Memorabilia

Photo, John Adams.
David Banks, my father showing the "Cock of the North" on the Castle flags, and the photo above is of James 14th Earl. At the left, Lady Fanny's silk parasol with the hand painted panels trimmed with swansdown and the carved ivory handle. The Banks family photos are at right of picture.

glass house in the east border was a miniature of the Crystal Palace. This greenhouse was always called the Crystal Palace and it was mostly flowers that were grown here while the vines and figs were in greenhouses at the west side.)

The Earl was very knowledgeable about electricity and was also interested in experimenting, so much so that he had a science room fitted out in the castle with special science room sink where he worked on his investigations. The Earl's bathroom had a cold shower made from a ring of pipe nine inches in diameter with holes to allow the water to spray out. It was adjacent to the Eagle room at the west end of the lower bedroom floor. This room had a big four poster bed with an elaborate canopy and there was an enormous eagle embroidered on the upholstered back-rest (headboard) of this impressive bed.

My granny, Charlotte Cormack, worked in the castle kitchen as a young girl and used to tell many upstairs and downstairs stories. In that day (c.1860) the staff lined up in the morning and the housekeeper doled each one their allowance of oatmeal for the day. Belle, the laundry-maid, gripped up the bottom of her white apron to make a "poke" to hold the meal and it was the housekeeper's fault that some was spilt. When Belle, who was over six feet tall, was refused more meal, she marched to the dining room in high dudgeon, pushed the butler, who tried to restrain her, aside and went straight up to the table and asked "How would your ladyship like to do a day's laundry on this pickle of meal?" The Earl enjoyed the interruption and told Belle she would have meal in plenty for the rest of her days. He kept his promise and he also gave her the life rent of the gate-house which is still called Belle's Lodge.

It was the 14th Earl who tutored Prince Edward and his brothers in engineering and who entertained the

Princess of Wales in 1876 when the Prince (later King Edward) opened the John O'Groats House Hotel and the Mill Bridge at John O'Groats.

Lady Fanny, daughter of the 14th Earl, was a lovely young woman and because she was so well liked and admired, several parents called their babies Frances after her.

This was a time of progress, success and celebrations at Barrogill, but there was sadness too. Countess Louisa Phillips died in 1870 aged 43. The 14th Earl died in 1881 aged 60 and both are buried in the ancestral vault in the Chapel royal, Holyrood. Lady Fanny died in 1883 aged 28 and her brother George Phillips Alexander Sinclair the 15th Earl, died in 1889 aged 31. There was a feeling of sympathy among the tenants because every family knew the scourge of T.B. and it was well known that Lady Fanny and Lord Berriedale were not strong. James the 14th Earl married twice – the second time in 1872 to a Spanish Duchess who inherited their London home. The "Groat" records that in 1891, Lady Caithness who was always known as the Duchess de Pomar, was apparently making all of Paris talk about the extravagant refurbishment of a house there.

George the 15th Earl of Caithness and last of Mey willed the estates in Scotland to his Cambridge University friend Frederick Granville Heathcote (who had been engaged to Lady Fanny) on condition he took the name Sinclair and lived three months of the year in Mey Castle.

Frederick Heathcote was born in 1857 and studied mechanics, chemistry and biology at Trinity College. The 15th Earl would have known of his friend's interest in embryology and they had no doubt discussed the wonderful and natural opportunities at Barrogill for his research in animal breeding, which would have been impossible to achieve in the Cambridge area. Heathcote married Miss Barnes, Richmond, Surrey in 1888 and was a good estate manager, a capable yachtsman and a keen canoeist. He was a crack shot, and at this time the Mey Estate was famous for its stock of birds and also for the fact that they were one of the few remaining moors which were shot over dogs during the whole of the season.

He started his research by breeding a small flock of sheep from a Rocky ram and two ewes from Duncansby Head. He also experimented with deer and established the deer park in front of the castle. Some time after he died (1914) his widow married a man, Gerald, who also took the name Sinclair. No sweeping changes were made until 1929 when it was sold to Captain Imbert Terry. There was a big sale in the courtyard at the back of the castle and most of the contents were auctioned. A few pictures and valuables were sold at Christies.

Mrs Fitton (Mrs Terry's widowed sister) spent a lot of time at the castle and it was she who financed the installation of the gas lighting. This petrol gas came in ordinary black two gallon petrol tins. The gas was rich in butane, very volatile and used with incandescent mantles. It was operated by a mechanism worked by wires and heavy

Her Majesty at the Back Gate to the Castle

Photo, John Adams.

This fine iron gate with the unusual arrowheads was made in 1955 at the Smithy by Donald MacKay and assistant William Banks of St. John's Mey.

weights which were hung outside the castle and were wound up by hand. A lift was installed to the east of the main door about 1930.

When the castle was taken over by the army at the beginning of World War Two, valuables were packed along with the wine in the cellar and in the cutlery store at the old front door and the wall was built up and sealed. There were other valuables stored in a room with the door taped and sealed with sealing wax. Ted Sinclair, the gardener, regularly checked that those seals were not broken. I still regret I didn't accept the Rolls or Humber which Captain Terry offered to sell me for £40. They were stored for the war years in the John O'Groats Hotel garage.

Queen Elizabeth the Queen Mother bought the Castle in 1952 and it was a red letter day for us when she visited Sunnybrae. She was pleased to accept the flags and my father always thought that it was due a little to his influence that she reverted to the old name for the Castle. We wish her many happy holidays at the Castle of Mey in the years to come.

[1] **Widow Banks** and her three sons Magnus, Donald and Gilbert came from Orkney and settled in Mey about 1655. And it was said that Donald her husband was of Norwegian origin. This Banks family built boats at Harrow for over 200 years and earned a reputation for building fast inshore boats with a good cut. The ferthies were built at the west side of the Gill at Harrow and were strong enough to transport flagstones to the growing towns around the coast of Scotland.

It was considered unlucky to damage a boat, even an old boat so they were given an out-of-the-way berth and not broken up for firewood when their sea days were over.

[2] See "Times Gone By" Vol I P11, December, 1926.

David Banks, Sunnybrae, Mey.

In 1762 **Bishop Forbes** wrote "Left Mey Castle... and as we still had to pass from moss to moss, John Banks, Sir James' principal servant became our guide."

A.H.

A FLOCK OF BLACKSHEEP

F.G. Heathcote Sinclair wrote ". . . One day when I took some of my friends to Duncansby Head to see the stacks, a fog came down. . . The fog suddenly lifted and there stood a small flock of little black sheep close by, looking at us with startled eyes. They were called Rocky sheep, and there were a good many of them on the headland, the little group I had seen being one of similar flocks. . .There was also a tradition that there were at one time several flocks of similar black sheep on other headlands in the county. I further gathered that this particular flock had been on this headland for a long time and that no one knew when they had first come there.

F.G. Heathcote Sinclair with his flock of Rockies

Note flagstone dyke.

The information that I gathered interested me so much that I determined to see whether I could not get a male and female and start breeding them. I found no difficulty in this and in the year 1890 became the possessor of a Rocky ram and a pair of ewes from Duncansby Head. They bred and I soon had a small flock of them.

Rocky Ram

The Rocky sheep are very intelligent animals and the brain case of the Rocky is much bigger than that of others in proportion to their size. They are exceedingly agile and active and it is very difficult to devise a fence to keep them within bounds. Their constitution is strong and they suffer very little from the usual sheep ailments.

The fleece is rather short compared with that of a domesticated sheep and is mostly composed of hair, the short fibres next the skin alone showing the characteristic appearance of wool. The wool makes good cloth when woven, the natural colour renders dyeing unnecessary and the colour of the undyed cloth is a chocolate brown.The cloth has good water resisting qualities. In spite of these excellencies, however, the wool fetches a very low price.

Both sexes have horns, the males invariably, the females usually. The Rocky ram has fine horns, thick at the base and sweeping down in a grand spiral. The horns of the ewe are not as strongly formed as those of the ram, and they do not form a complete spiral. Comparing the Rocky with any of the cultivated breeds, the head of the former gives one a strong impression of superior alertness and of intelligence, it also has much more of the shy look which is so marked a characteristic of all wild animals."

From, "A Flock of Black Sheep" and other Essays,
By Frederick Granville Heathcote Sinclair, Adlard & Sons and West Newman Ltd.

BARROGILL BOULDER AND CASTLE POOL

The Cairn Cross

The cross was erected over the cairn in 1840 in honour of the Great "Charles John" Earl Canning the statesman, born 1812, died 1862, who was a particular friend of old Lord Caithness (12th Earl) and who used to visit Castle of Mey before he became Governor General of India.

CAIRN CROSS OF MEY, CAITHNESS   *Copyright J. Adams*

There is a large roundish freestone boulder on the shore near the mouth of the Barrogill burn and there are two smaller ones lying further east. These must have been carried thousands of years ago by ice or sea from Dunnet Head as there is no similar stone near here and it is amazing that they have not been smashed to pieces by the heavy seas. A few feet from the Barrogill Boulder there is a fine little swimming pool measuring some 20 by 30 feet which has been cut out of the shelving rock.

It is supposed it was the 14th Earl who had this made for George his son and heir and his daughter Lady Fanny. It is a tidal pool with a sandy bottom which warms up quickly on a nice afternoon. One can see the ruins of a stone built changing-hut at the foot of the brae with steps leading up to it. Also here about the mouth of the Barrogill burn there used to be a vein of bituminous shale which shone like jet and burnt with a bright flame.

THE CAIRN OF MEY

The Cairn is now just a low mound some 20 feet or so in diameter but the way that the ground slopes away from it in all directions suggests that this is the remains of a very large construction which has been levelled down and cultivated. It lies west of the castle in one of the biggest fields on Barrogill Mains.

It was near to this cairn that in 1700 David Sinclair of Broynach married Janet Ewing (his housekeeper). Proof of the marriage became important as Broynach was brother of the Earl and the descendants came into the line of succession. (See page 191 "Diocese of Caithness" by J.B. Craven.)

It is thought that Barrogill took its name from the gill beside the barrow or burial cairn and the land on this farm is said to be the best in Caithness.

Alistair Ham, Harrow.

LADY FANNY'S LOVER

The Cruickshanks came from Aberdeenshire as grooms to the Earl of Caithness at Barrogill Castle. Andrew Cruickshanks, a tall handsome man, usually accompanied Lady Fanny, the Earl's daughter when out riding. Being the groom he had to ride so many paces behind her. However when out of sight of the castle she would draw rein and wait for him to come alongside. Their love affair blossomed. Someone on the estate reported the young lovers to the Earl, and Andrew was banished to London to attend to the horses at one of the railway stations and told if he looked at or spoke to Lady Fanny he would never work again.

Lady Fanny followed him to London, traced him to the station and on seeing him, called his name and spoke, to no avail. She returned to Mey broken hearted, went into a decline, developed T.B., or consumption as it was called in those days, and died. This is contrary to the belief that she committed suicide. Andrew never returned to Caithness.

Emma MacLeod, Upper Gills.

MEY BATTERY

Harrow and Dunnet Head in background

It is thought that the Battery was built about the time of the Napoleonic Wars. It is sited on a snib of the brae head between the castle and Harrow with a commanding view over the bay. The stone-built, five feet high revetment wall has been left untouched and is in good condition.

On the east side, little remains of a shelter room for the volunteers, but at the west, down a few steps, the kiosk-shaped ammunition store just wants a door. The area was flagged over, but few of the heavy flagstones are still in position. (A sheep dipper was made on the site c.1920 and used by Barrogill Mains and nearby farms.) On the sea side, large five inch thick flagstones are angled out from the two embrasures like a "V" which gave added protection to the soldiers, and allowed the guns a perfect firing arc over the Western Haven and the Castle Goe. The ground was banked upon the outside to the top of this defensive wall with the flagstones and the embrasures bolted back into the grassed over build up of stones and earth which gave perfect camouflage and looked like the braehead. Volleys from ships of war would have had little effect against this battery unless they

achieved a direct hit through an embrasure but thankfully Mey was never under attack.

The original two cannons used at the Battery are now in front of the Castle. They were made at the Carron Foundry and dated 1820 and also have the letters C.V.A. (Caithness Volunteer Artillery) and G.R. (Georgius Rex). The cannons measure eight feet 10 inches overall, firing barrel seven feet two inches, the bore is six and three-eighth inches and they have a sighting mechanism on the side.

It was said it took four horses in front with two behind (to hold back) to move a cannon down to the battery and it took four men using long levers (hand spikes) to man-handle it round corners and into position. After being fired the cannons ran back on recoil and were then pushed forward to the embrasure, tipped up and reloaded. On one occasion during a rapid fire practice the ram-rod was not removed in time and went sailing out into the Firth.

My grandfather, Magnus Banks, was one of the last corporals to fire these cannons c.1890 by which time they were becoming obsolete. James the 14th Earl built the Drill Hall and also three small houses for the resident sergeants in 1875. The 1881 census shows Alex Marshall, Edinburgh was the Drill Instructor of Volunteers. The new cannon was likely bought about this time. It was breech loading and much lighter in weight than the old cannons. A section of the floor in the new hall was made of very hard green heart wood for the gun drill. The Volunteers wore their uniform for drill – a smart black jacket with stand-up collar and a neat pill-box hat with a band and chin strap. The Volunteers were disbanded in 1908 and the "new" cannon was taken to Thurso.

David Banks, Sunnybrae, Mey.

THE CANNONS AT THE CASTLE

The above description suggests that the guns are almost certainly 32-pounders of the pattern designed by General Sir Thomas Blomefield in 1787. Guns are measured technically rather than by overall length, but from the lengths given, they are probably the eight foot pattern weighing 48 cwt – ie. roughly two and a half tons. The bore diameter of a 32-pr was 6.41 inches, and it fired a solid iron shot (weighing approximately 32 pounds) of 6.2 inches diameter. The slight difference

(known as "windage") allowed the shot to be muzzle-loaded without sticking! They were a fairly common pattern for coast defence.

They were used both on land and at sea, but only the bigger warships could mount 32-prs – most would not mount guns larger than 24-prs. These "Men of War" would also have carried many other sizes of guns.

The "proof" or test charge for this gun was 21.5 pounds of large grain gunpowder but the service charge (ie. the normal charge) was eight pounds. It would probably only ever have been proof-fired once, immediately after manufacture. The gunpowder was already weighed out and assembled into a charge bag, usually made of cotton. It was this bag – shaped like a long canister – which was pushed down the bore of the gun. The cannon ball was then rammed down on top of the powder bag and was held in place by a wad made of coarse felt material, to prevent it rolling out.

To fire the gun, a long metal spike would first be pushed down the vent hole (on top of the gun at the breech end), to make a hole in the charge bag and to get some of the gunpowder accessible to the flame of firing. There were then various ways of getting the flame to the powder. One method was to put some loose gunpowder down the vent hole, and to light that with a "portfire" – basically, a length of "slow match".

Gunpowder doesn't "explode", but burns, producing large quantities of gas. Because there's nowhere for the gas to get out except past the cannonball (and there's very little room around the ball!), pressure starts to build up very quickly. Since the powder burns faster when the pressure is high, the pressure mounts very quickly indeed – the whole charge burns in about a hundredth of a second! The pressure is of the order of several tons per square inch, which is why the cannonball comes out at high speed – the velocity at the muzzle is about 1500 feet per second, though of course it falls off as the ball meets air resistance during its flight.

The range of these guns, of course, depends on the elevation given them; fired horizontally, range was 330 yards, increasing to 1740 yards – effectively a mile – at five degrees of elevation. Extreme range would be approximately double that.

Everything required for the gun, including ammunition, was provided from central stores. By the 19th Century, the iron shot would have been made centrally rather than locally – probably at Carron's foundry at Falkirk. As the guns were emplaced in a coast defence battery, any shot fired seawards would not have been retrievable, but it is true that, in land battles, it was common practice to collect up cannonballs for re-use – they were virtually indestructible! (I wonder if this was the origin of the cry, "Can we have our ball back, mister?"!!)

There were a number of designs of 32-pr gun subsequent to this pattern, but the gun was not obsolescent until the introduction of the rifled breech loading gun in 1859, and certainly not obsolete until much later; the occasional similar piece was still in England in 1920 and in the colonies in 1937.

The Caithness Artillery volunteers were raised in the early 1860s. 4th Corps (later No.5 Battery) was raised at Mey on 1st December 1866.

Brigadier K. A. Timbers, Historical Secretary, Royal Artillery Institution, Woolwich, SE18 4DN.

THE BROCH AT HARROW

Harrow could mean the landlord's place (N. harri = a lord) and being the piece of land that the chief kept for his own use, would have been the best land in the neighbourhood.

Archaeologists tell that brochs were built c.100 BC – 100 AD and that they were all similar in design, and usually built where there was good arable land, near to the sea and that they incorporated a well. The walls of these drystone built circular towers were about 20 feet wide at the base and enclosed a courtyard about 30 feet in diameter. The entrance was a low passageway opening on the sea side and brochs were built up to 50 feet high to resist attack against battering rams and scaling-ladders. It is worth noting that brochs are only found in areas of Scotland which were not conquered by the Romans.

The Harrow broch lay behind the steading on the point of the brae overlooking the harbour and the circular remains are best seen in the spring before the grass and weeds are growing. The remnants of the outside wall stand about two to three feet high in places showing that the broch had been built right on the very edge of the brae and measured about 50 feet in diameter. My father never used weedkiller on the nettles here, but I'm thinking that it must have taken more than long, tough nettle roots to hold the brae together under what is said to have been a massive tower. There are so many wells around Harrow that it could be said with certainty that one would have been enclosed in the broch.

Alistair Ham, Harrow.

Footnote:– In the First Statistical Account (1793) John Morison writes "The ruins of three ancient towers or castles are still to be seen, one in Mey another south of the present mansion house of Freswick and a third situated on the west side of Stroma." Is it reasonable to suggest that these ruins could have been the tower at Harrow and the castle ruins at Buchollie and Nestag? Easy access at Harrow (unlike Buchollie and Nestag) made removal of stones easy.

A.H.

When April blows her horn
It's good for both hay and corn.
Danny Hughes.

April Weather –
Rain and sunshine, both together.
Marie Ham.

Last Steam Engine in Caithness Marshall SK 457 – 1951

Photo, Ethel Jack.

Beelie Manson, Ethel Jack, Wm. and Lilla Allan. Sandy Allan at Wheel.

Steam Engine – Ploughing

Photo, Sheila Moir, Scarfskerry.

Steam Engine – Sawing Wood

Photo, Ethel Jack.

STEAM PLOUGH

It was a local man, Duncan Munro, who worked the steam plough for the Laird of Mey and it was used for breaking in land on crofts as well as on Phillips' Mains and Brabster.

The steam engine sat on the head-rig and there was an anchor fixed at the opposite end. The plough was reversible (ie. ploughed in one face). The winch on the steam engine pulled the wire rope attached to the plough one way and then the other way. A flagman followed the plough and if it struck an obstacle, up went the flag and the man stopped the winch. On Phillips, because of the shallow ground and shelving rock, the ploughing was done one way.

M.H.

DIV YE MIND?

A bakery behind the shop at the Berriedale Arms when Laings were the owners.

A Debating Society in Mey, Mey Drama Club in 1930s.

Swimming Club formed early 1930s at Phillips Harbour[1]. Climax of the year was Swimming Gala when they held races across the harbour, dived for plates thrown into the water and had pillow fights on a greasy pole etc.

George S. Begg's Ford-Model A bus ran in middle 30s on school[2] contract to Castletown, and to Thurso on sale days. With a full load of pigs and calves in bran-bags and farmers celebrating the sale thereof, egg boxes (30 dozen size) and school bairns, the bus would maybe go as fast as 15 m.p.h., although fitted with low speed and overdrive gearing. Around this time a new Ford V8 bus was acquired which ran until Highland Transport took over. Wattie Wares, J. B. Geddes and James Johnstone, Gills were among the first drivers. James

Johnstone drove an old Albion bus which was notoriously bad to start in the mornings – the comment was "chip o' roost in carburettor".
Willie Jack, Sunfield, Scarfskerry.

[1] Mackie Banks remembers the kists of lobsters and hampers of dead rabbits on the scholar's bus.

[2] Sandy Cormack, Huna has the Grade A certificate his father got from the Mey branch of the Northern Swimming Association in 1930.

Stackyard at Roadside

Photo, Jessie Cormack, Shore Lane.
Sandy Cormack building the screw, Wildie Allan forking from the cart with Beauty between the shafts, Sandy with hurley. Nessie Ainslie, East Mey, Lilla and Ethel Allan. Note the neep chapper and the screw stadle steethe at right.

MEY SHEEPDOG TRIALS ASSOCIATION

In 1945, just after the Second World War, three Mey stalwarts, James Cameron, James Geddes and Donald Gunn met to discuss ways of raising money to boost the funds for a Welcome Home to local servicemen. They decided, among other things, to hold a local Sheep Dog Trials. This proved successful and aroused considerable local interest.

The following year they held a meeting in the Old School, Mey, which was well attended and a committee was formed and rules drawn up. James Cameron was elected president, Alex Kennedy, vice-president, and Sandy Mathieson, secretary and treasurer, and the Trials were to be for the parishes of Canisbay and Dunnet. That was in 1946, and they have been going strong ever since. In a few years the Trials were opened to the county, later to the Northern Counties, then open to Scotland and about 1954 were open to Britain.

During all these years the Association has been fortunate in getting the use of a field for the Trials from Messrs Angus, Barrogill Mains Farm, a gesture which is very much appreciated.

In October, 1954, Sandy Mathieson resigned as

The Queen Mother presenting her Trophy to Andrew Chapman

Photo, Jack Malcolm, Seater.

secretary and treasurer, and Willie Leitch agreed to take on the job for one year, but continued to hold that post till 1975, when Donnie Cormack, the present secretary and treasurer, was appointed.

At the AGM in 1962, Alex Kennedy became the new president and Willie Allan, vice-president. In 1967, Mr Kennedy resigned for health reasons, and Willie Allan was elected president and Keith Malcolm, vice-president. Willie Allan resigned in 1970 and the new president was James Sinclair, who resigned in 1979 and Mackie Banks was appointed president, a post he still holds with Sandy Green, the vice-president.

Over the years the Association has been presented with a good selection of trophies to be competed for annually.

In 1968, Her Majesty, Queen Elizabeth, the Queen Mother, who graces the Trials with her presence each year, presented the Association with a perpetual trophy for the competitor with the most points in the open section. This cup was first won by Andrew Chapman, Dunbar, and has gone the rounds ever since. Three Caithness men have been successful in winning the much-coveted Queen Mother's Cup. – Wm. Cormack in 1974 (June), Sandy Campbell in 1977 (Hemp), Sandy Campbell in 1985 (Bill) and Donnie Cormack in 1992 (Coon).

In 1990, the year of her 90th birthday, the Queen Mother expressed a wish to meet all the men who had won her cup in the intervening years. 12 of those were able to be present. Afterwards, Robert Banks, a founder member of the Association presented Her Majesty with an engraved Caithness Glass bowl. It is noteworthy that the design of a sheepdog, engraved on the bowl, was drawn by a Canisbay Schoolboy, Alex Ross.

Janet Gunn, "Emohruo", Mey.

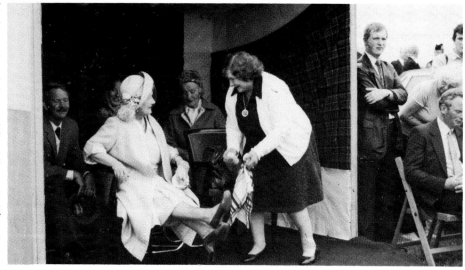

Top Right:
The Queen Mother with Mrs Bell wielding midge spray

Photo courtesy of J. McDonald, Wick.
The Commander and his wife from the American Base and Lady Fermoy.

Centre Right:
Her Majesty receives engraved bowl from Robert Banks

Photo courtesy of Northern Studios, Wick.
Left to Right:– David McTeir, Hamish MacLean, Jack Campbell, John Bathgate and Pat MacGettigan.

Bottom Right:
The Queen Mother's 90th Birthday Reception in British Legion Hall

Photo courtesy of J. McDonald, Wick.
Left to Right:– ?, Willie Jack, Ian Malcolm, Ethel Jack, Janet Gunn and Christian Bell.

HEATHER BURNING AND GROUSE

Butts were situated all along the back road from Phillips Mains Farm. Also butts at Brabster, remains of which can still be seen. Squares of turf were put in the bases of the butts for standing on. The Laird of the Barrogill Castle entertained small shooting parties, keeper was Mr Dunnett who lived in East Lodge and who was called "Moolhill" from the place where he was born. Methodical heather burning preceded the grouse shooting and was very carefully monitored, with local lads at hand to beat out anything that got out of control. Local lads were also brought in as beaters of the grouse. They raised the birds out of the heather and drove them towards the butts where the shooters were ready for them. Gun dogs retrieved the grouse and brought them to the keepers. Pay for a day was six shillings.

When Her Majesty Queen Elizabeth, the Queen Mother bought a renovated Barrogill Castle, it reverted to its former name Castle of Mey. Mr Jim Cameron was employed as Her Majesty's keeper and served her for many years with great acceptance. It was a great source of joy to the whole community when Her Majesty the Queen, conferred on him a personal honour for services to her mother, Queen Elizabeth the Queen Mother, so revered and greatly loved by the people of Caithness. Like the Queen Mother, Jim has also celebrated his 90th birthday and maintains a keen interest in his garden and in snooker and sport on his television. Long may both of them be spared to inspire us with their enthusiasm and their love of Caithness in all its changing scenes.

Mrs C. Bell, The Cottage, Mey.

THE SAGA OF SANNY MANSON

The Caithness-Norse family of Magnuson (corrupted into Manson) as well as their near kindred, the Gunns and Hendersons, inherited to a remarkable degree, many of the distinctive traits of their Viking ancestors. In the Manson family this hereditary inheritance took the form of a restless, tireless, indomitable energy. A member of the family, named Sanny Manson, had his humble home near the shore in the district of Mey. His surplus energy found plenty of scope in wresting a living for his young family from the turbulent and treacherous waters of the Pentland Firth. He was the owner and skipper of a large, finely modelled, Orkney-type yawl and in the course of time his daring as a successful fisherman and fine seaman became widely known. At this period, probably about 1740, cattle dealers from the south used to visit Orkney every year and make large purchases of young cattle and horses. These had to be ferried across the Pentland Firth in open or undecked yawls. For this purpose, Manson's services were in great demand and many a cargo of live beasts did he and his crew in the yawl, successfully ferry from Orkney to the Mey landing place.

But disaster at last overtook the daring crew. It happened thus – dealer had purchased a large

number of young horses in Orkney and Manson had successfully ferried most of them across to the mainland. Owing to fine weather and light winds, the trip across with the last of the horses was unduly protracted. At last as the boat drew near the Mey shore the "staigs" grew restive. At the seeming near approach of the land, the excitement of the animals got more intense and when within a few hundred yards of the shore, they upset the boat. In that maelstrom of terrified horses, the crew perished quickly. Manson managed to get clear and scrambled up on to the keel of the overturned boat and drifted seawards. His Viking ancestors, if denied a glorious death in battle and feeling the near approach of death, elected to meet the last dread adversary alone on the sea so that they would not be thought contemptuously as having died in their beds. In like manner, in sight of and in almost hailing distance of his home and loved ones, Manson drifted out to the Atlantic towards the setting sun on the "Aul Ebbs".

When the people of Mey were rebuked by the minister for not going to Manson's assistance they excused themselves by saying "It wisna lucky to save a droonan man forby nae doot his time had come."

From "Efter Dayset Yarns in Memory of the Poet" by Simon Bremner, Midtown, Freswick.

THE HARROW ICEHOUSE

The walls of the icehouse are about two and a half feet thick and are backed by the brae. They rise about 14 feet to the top of the brae and the vaulted roof rises about six feet above that. Great credit must go to the masons, because after all these years, there is not a stone out of place. The roof was then covered over with flagstones and there is three feet of soil on top of that. There was a three

by three feet opening built into the back gable (ground level at top of brae) and this was closed by a heavy flagstone. Large stones kept this in position and then divots were built over to give protection and insulation.

The porch was nine by eight feet and 11 at its apex. With all this insulation, it is not surprising that the ice lasted all summer.

Harrow Icehouse

The icehouse consisted of an inner and outer chamber, each 10 feet long by 12 feet wide and 20 feet high. A double six inch brick wall with a two and a half by five foot door at one end, separated the two chambers. The floors were flagged and there was a drain (with a grating over) near the door in the inner chamber which removed water as the ice melted.

The ice was carted from the Mey Loch during the winter months to fill the inner chambers. The large flagstone was removed from the ice-door, the horse and cart carefully backed up and the ice tipped in. Snow was shovelled in to fill spaces between the chunks of ice or if they were short of ice to fill it brim full. It was left all tightly sealed until the salmon fishing started about April/May and finished the last Tuesday in August.

The salmon were kept on ice in the outer chamber, possibly overnight, or until they were packed with ice in the special salmon boxes which had a steel band round them. They were then carted to the station and thence by rail to Billingsgate.

Harry Crowden, Dunnet and John Simpson, Brough, took over the salmon fishing about 1932-33 and Donnie, George and young Harry Crowden got their sea legs then. Donnie said that Alex Begg (Ackers) Auckengill, and John Banks, East Mey carted ice for a year or two when they started at Harrow, but then after that it was easier to get the ice from Wick.

The salmon fishing at Harrow ceased about 1938-1939.

Footnote:– During the Second World War, RAF in Wick had a mobile beacon which was set up three nights at Clyth, three in the Keiss quarry behind the Baptist Church and three nights in Mey. It was parked beside the ice house and flashed a coded light skywards at certain times. Harry Bowles, Barclay Bremner, George Stewart and a man Townsend shared their N.A.A.F.I. cake and biscuits with me and I remember them well.

William Ham, Hoy View, Scarfskerry.

Salmon Fishers 1936

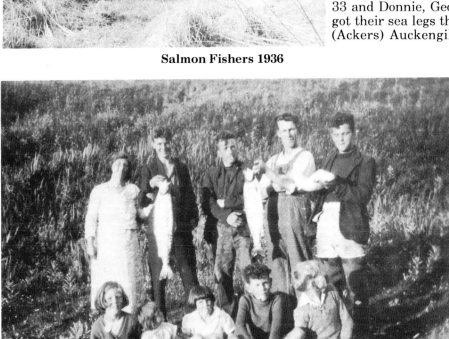

Photo, Elsie Anderson, Scarfskerry.
Back Row:– Mrs Lottie Miller, Henry Sutherland, George Crowden, James Miller and Watt Sutherland. Seated:– Alice Miller, Jenny Miller, Elsie Miller, James Miller and Robert Sutherland.

This and better may do, but this and woar winna.

It's not what you hae, but what you do wi' what you hae.

Wilful waste may become woeful want.

When the auld cock craws, the young cock learns.
Mary Sinclair.

THE "PRODUCE" C.1905

This early photo shows the herring boat "Produce" lying starboard side to the quay in Harrow Harbour with obviously peaceful sea conditions, as an unused fender lies on deck beside the fore yard. James Donn (second left) is slacking away the heavily tarred head rope, so presumably, nets made up in bundles are being taken on board prior to the start of the summer fishing. John Angus, on the extreme right, is lowering a made-up net into the fish hold by means of a rope running through a block on the fore mast. George Rosie (third left), at the coaming, guides the net which is suspended by a bridle having a hook at each end and normally used when discharging a catch, the hooks then being attached to fish basket hand grips. William Ham, on the extreme left, holds on to a steadying rope. It is noticeable that none of the men of that era wore gloves. The vertical steering wheel, apparently locally made or possibly adapted from a farm implement, is entirely of metal with a projecting pin on the rim for quick movement and also to indicate when the rudder was amidships. Forward of the steering gear, still protected from the elements by a canvas cover since the end of the previous fishing season, stands the "Iron Man", a type of hand operated winch dating from about 1890-95 until superseded by the steam capstan. No doubt this first form of mechanisation eased the hard labour of hoisting yards, sails and hauling nets. The boat, level with the quay and the appearance of the beach opposite, suggests high water, a convenient time for the task in hand.

In those days the only aid to navigation on the "Produce" would have been the compass. I have my grandfather's dry compass, simple yet robust and in its original hardwood box, it continues to indicate magnetic north with unfailing accuracy.

William Ham, Hoy View, Scarfskerry.

William Ham, Harrow; James Donn, Warse; George Rosie, Freswick and John Angus, Brabster

Meeze for Sailing Ships

The Castle of Mey a handspike high.
The Main Skerry Rock you'll n'er come nigh.

A handspike = spike about 21 inches long which went into a hole provided in the rigging to tie the end of the rope to, or the rope was secured by twisting figure of eight style round it.

Big Skerry Rock

Big rock seen at Men of Mey when the ebb is out. On a still day the silkies can be heard quarrelling on this rock from "Glenyra".

Meeze for Rowing Boat going West

Look out and get the third chimney of Harrow clear of the land. It is then safe to turn west.

George Banks, Glenyra, East Mey.

PHILLIPS HARBOUR

James Sinclair 14th Earl of Caithness married Louisa G. Phillips and it was in her honour that Phillips Harbour and Phillips Mains were so named. This postcard shows the ideal harbourage and the homes of the Banks family, who were famous boatbuilders in the parish and far beyond. The ferthie at the foot of the brae had likely been hauled up by Allan's steam engine. The pavilion gabled salmon house is there, the green where they dried their nets, and to the right the bothy. John Simpson, Fassberry who had the "Celtic" (now at John O'Groats Post Office), used to stay occasionally in the bothy as late as 1926, when he wanted to get very early to his creels. John emigrated to Australia and did well there. His son John visited Harrow in 1991 and was happy to keep up his connection with Mey and very proud and humble to tread the road to the harbour which

Phillips Harbour c.1900

Picture, Robert Begg, Rattar.

his father had done so often before.

One always hopes someone will turn up to tell if James Bremner, Wreck Raiser, built this harbour. It is certainly constructed in a similar way to the harbour at Ham which was built under his supervision, and could be about the same age. It was James Bremner, Wreck Raiser, who hit on the idea of setting the stones on end so that the seas would "run up" the stones without bursting them apart as happened when they were laid horizontally. The west side of the pier is very skilfully "dished" so that the heavy westerly seas would run up and then roll back instead of going over the harbour wall.

A Job Creation team, mostly locals, made a first class job of renovating the harbour about 1979. Derry Ross calculated that some of the enormous stones (flag) on the west side must have weighed six to seven tons each. They were wedged securely and the ingenuity and skill of the original builders commanded all their respect. It was Derry too, who carved the trawler and seine-netter out of standard shuttering. Then as each 16 feet shutter was shifted for the next pour-in of cement, he repeated them along the harbour wall and the boats came out as from a mould.

The big slabs of stone which stand perpendicularly in the harbour, were quarried from the ebb below the Castle of Mey. They were loaded on wooden rafts which were floated at high water and then were towed by rowing boats over to the harbour.

David Mathieson, The Breck, John O'Groats, said that to burst off the big slabs of stone from the face, a line of holes was drilled perpendicularly at the desired width, maybe 10 inches apart and six

to eight inches deep. Pegs made from dried wood were then driven into the holes, and as the tide came in, the wood expanded with the water and burst off the stones. To drill the holes, one man held the "jumper" (one inch steel rod three feet long) with pincers and turned the "jumper" a fraction between blows which were struck "time about" by two men with hammers.

It can be seen that the outside point of the harbour has been damaged by a storm and this has occurred several times. Also in the photo are two sets of well-dressed, wide, stone steps with an easy-rise which would likely have been dressed locally. Not in the photo but there just the same, half way down the brae, was a well with good drinking water. There was also a very deep stone-built well in the square. The water was drawn by a hand pump, which had to be primed with two skelladfuls (half pail) of water while a second person pumped hard. This water was not used for drinking but pumped for cattle and horses when the wade ran dry. There were several wells in the Gill – the best water was got from the well on the upper side of the flagstone complex.

William Ham, Hoyview, Scarfskerry.

Footnotes:– One of the blue stones which had been dislodged from the harbour wall during a westerly storm and landed in the basin, was lifted out by Charlie Brims' digger. The stone measured 16 feet by three feet three inches by 16 inches and after finding out the density of the stone, we calculated that it weighed about six to seven tons. It was James Bremner, Wreck Raiser's, idea to cassie the stones and so reduce resistance to the driving forces of winter storms. The air, in the spray and spindrift of these whipped up seas, has a powerful raising action when pounded into harbour walls. Stones set on their end allows the upward escape of air through joins and cracks, whereas stones set on their flat, offers a wide bed with no escape cracks for the air, thus the pressure and lifting power is increased.

Derry Ross.

A straight lift is very heavy but large stones could be man-handled more easily using systems of block and tackle.

I.B.

THE MEY FLAGSTONE INDUSTRY

The Flagstone Works at Harrow

Photo, Hettie Munro Collection.

The main quarries on the estate were at East Mey, Rigifa and Brabster. The best of the flagstones would have been carted to the cutting plant at Harrow. The ones used in the Pasture Dyke and thereabouts, would just have been hammer dressed at the quarry.

The flagbeds were almost horizontal and every eight or so feet there is a main seam. Steel wedges were driven into this seam to raise it enough to get crowbars inserted, and by moving them up and down, the bed or layer was loosened. It was then moved away from the face a short distance and steel wedges were again driven in at the smaller seams to lift off the separate layers of flagstones ranging from one and a half inches to three inches depending on the seam. The flagstones were then roughly squared and loaded on carts to be taken to Harrow.

Slates were also cut at the quarries and this was done with a slate knife at the face and they were never sawn. There was a small dam up the gill which supplied water for the flagstone plant. This was not used to power the plant, but for the steam boiler and to help in the cutting process.

The Flagstone Plant was set in a fine sheltered position, beside a good harbour and near the main road, which in that day ran along the coast from Scarfskerry past the Castle of Mey.

This photo was taken before the shed for storing the coal for the castle was built at the upper end of the flagstone complex. There was also a shed at the lower end which was a lime store. The draining tiles, which were imported at the same time, were stacked against the brae and many bits of red tile still litter the gill. A covered built drain ran down the front of the plant to the shore which got rid of the "swashing" of water that was used to aid the cutting process and keep down the "stoor".

The building on the left with pavilion gables, housed a small smiddy for sharpening the tools and also the furnace and steam engine for driving the saws. The chimney was built very high to get draught on the fire and also to keep the smoke away from the workmen on days of dead heavy weather. The chimney is very wide at the base and the stone-built part has steps on the inside going right to the top, and these can still be seen.

There were five cutting beds at Harrow and the flagstone saw consisted of a long iron blade maybe 14 feet long with no teeth which was drawn backwards and forwards. Fine sharp sand and water was applied during the whole process and the flagstone was cut a half inch deep and then snapped off. The scrap bits were then knocked off by a small hammer. At Spittal quarries, sand from Levad near Rangag was used. It was fine and sharp and much superior to fine sand from the shore. Where the sand used at Harrow came from is unknown. It used to take roughly 40 minutes to saw through the flagstones. The saw was never sharpened but just discarded when worn.

It is thought that at Harrow the flagstones for cutting were pushed under the saw on a trolley contraption on rails. If polished flags were required this was achieved by covering the surface with sand and rubbing this down in a circular motion with a weighted wooden plate.

If the man with the hard hat and light trousers was Baird Carswell, the foreman who lived in the house at the top of the Gill, then this photo must have been taken c.1870. "B.C. 1871 Mey" can still be seen carved on a stone in the doorway. Baird Carswell was given as engineer and blacksmith in the 1861 census and was at Harrow until he died in 1892 aged 75. The 1871 census returns show that Donald Fraser, who was superintendent of the pavement works in 1861, is no longer there.

The dressed flag set across from the plant are ready for transporting to the harbour. The low built retaining wall can be seen at the east side of the road and it was alongside this, that there was a narrow gauge bogie track. It is not thought that a horse was used because it's a short distance and it would not be difficult to push the loaded bogies downhill to the harbour.

The flag was then "walked" along the harbour. "Walking" a flag was done by one man, holding it upright on one corner and twisting it forward on to the other in a zig zag manner. Once the "swing" got into rhythm, this was not difficult.

Great care had to be taken loading the flag on to the schooner. They were slid down on two planks and then very carefully stowed on end. It was a very skilled job stowing flagstones on a schooner because in heavy seas, they would be inclined to slide and shift. On their return journeys, the schooners brought back coal, lime, wood and draining tiles. This was the time of great improvement in agriculture. (The "Groat" reported that the schooner "Lark" was in Phillips Harbour in 1898, 1899 and 1902).

Special thanks to Archie Sinclair, Spittal for all his help.

Willie Ham, Hoy View, Scarfskerry.

Flagstone Tanks

Harrow Flagstone Tank at Sunnybrae, Mey

A lot of water tanks were made at Harrow and often the flags used were from the Rigifa quarries. Steam power was used when trimming the flagstones. For the joints, two grooves were cut two inches apart using copper ribbon with grit and then the centre piece was chiselled out. The flagstones were then bedded in white lead putty to prevent leakage and the iron bars, as seen in the photo, firmed up the sides. The baptismal font in the Scarfskerry Baptist Church was made at Harrow and still holds good. It was a big step forward when roofs were slated and rhones collected and channelled the rain water into tanks or barrels. Drinking water was always drawn from a well and the soft rain water used for washing.

Grooves

David Banks.

MOSTLY TANGHEAD

Chrissie Simpson with learner milker

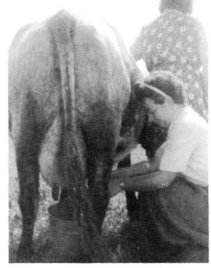

No milk for Jim's tea!

Sandy Cormack harrowing with Beauty, Miss and a staig in training at Roadside

Photo, Sandy Cormack, Huna.

Magnus, Georgina and George Baikie thinning neeps at Tanghead

Photo, Sheila Moir, Scarfskerry.

Jim Baikie cutting corn with Bisset binder c.1940

Half yoking in hayfield, Jim Baikie on back delivery c.1940

Photo, Jean Sutherland, Durban.
Dunnet Head in background.

Photo, Jackie Ham, Ord Terrace, Invergordon.
Alexia Cairns, Margaret Baikie, Magnus Waters and Lorna the dog.

It is contracted Agreed and finally concluded between the parties following viz: that James Bremner Shipbuilder in Pulteneytown On the one part and James Geddes residing in Wick son of John Geddes Miller in Lybster with the special advice and consent of the said John Geddes and the said John Geddes for himself and advocatioe and surety for the said James Geddes and otherwise bound in manner underwritten On the other part in manner following that is to say the said James Geddes with consent pursuant hereby becomes bound Apprentice to the said James Bremner in the art and profession of a Shipbuilder and that for the full space of seven years from and after the first day of March Eighteen Hundred and thirty seven years at which period the said Apprenticeship is hereby declared to have commenced notwithstanding the date hereof during which space the said James Geddes binds and obliges himself to serve his said Master honestly and faithfully by night and by day holy day and work day small things faithful and honest and that he shall not absent himself from his said Masters service without leave first asked and obtained and shall not waste the tools, timber or other utensils committed to his charge but to the utmost of his Masters business and shall not see or hear his Master the done giving him damage inform... tion thereof and preventing the same to the utmost of his power and in case he shall to otherwise be Bonds and Obliges himself to serve two days for each days absence after the expiration of these Indentures and to pay every loss and damage which his said Master shall sustain through his neglect or default and the said Apprentice becomes bound to conduct himself with propriety towards his said master, the other Apprentices and others in his employment, and he further binds and obliges himself to shun all evil and profane company and abstain from drunkenness and all other vicious habits and the said John Geddes hereby binds and obliges himself conjunctly and severally with the said Apprentice for his lawful and obedient service during the space and in the terms aforesaid and for his fulfilling the whole obligations incumbent on him under this Indenture for which cause and on the other hand the said James Bremner Binds and obliges himself to learn and instruct or cause to be taught and instructed the said James Geddes his Apprentice in the art and profession of a Shipbuilder insofar as he has capacity to conceive the same or the foreman employed by the said James Bremner finds or has occasion to practice and to make payment to his said Apprentice at the rate of three shillings per week for the first three years and six months of his said apprenticeship and at the rate of five shillings per week for the remainder of his Apprenticeship

JAMES GEDDES

James Geddes (1820-1885) of Mill of Mey – the subject of the apprenticement contract drawn up in 1837 with James Bremner, Shipbuilder, Pulteneytown (Wreck Raiser), was a son of John Geddes (1789-1866) Miller, Mill of Mey and his wife, Jean Ham.

Later in life, James went to sea and became the captain of a schooner, believed to have been the "Barrogill Castle", a vessel of 73 tons built in Garmouth in 1858 which traded mainly as a collier between Newcastle, S. Shields, Stromness and Scrabster.

The schooner is known to have been owned by George Geddes (brother of James) of Thurso from 1880 till 1892, but James was captain of the schooner for some time before it was taken over by his brother George in 1880.

Thanks are due to Mr Harry S.M. Taylor of Edinburgh for the information about the "Barrogill Castle".

John Geddes, "Highlands", Minchinhampton.

Family Note:- James Geddes married Helen Banks in 1857 and their daughter Margaret married James Geddes (unrelated), Rosebank Farm, Mey.

The Mill of Mey c.1918

Nellie Sutherland with bike, Alex Geddes (Sgt. and brother of Wm.), William Geddes, the miller in light dusty clothes and behind him and to the left is Sandy Swanson, kilnman.

(The adverts on the wall:– Lactifer – calfmeal, Thorleys Food – minerals, Ovum – for hens).

A MEMORY O' SMELLS

Clearly dae A mind id still,
Waftan' fae 'e owld water mill
   Yinder at 'e shore;
'E rare warm smell o' dryan' grain –
Could I but smell id noo again!
   But alas 'e mill's no more.

Burnan' heather A still can smell;
Roaran' sparkan' peit fires as well
   Wi' blue reek curlan' high.
An' 'e smell o' tar 'ave noor forgotten,
Fan heited for 'e owld boat's bottom
   Tae keep her dry.

'E fresh air smell fae aff 'e sea,
Is lek a breath o' life tae me
   Fan A can get id!

But 'e heap o' seaweed decomposed,
Ochanee – 'at's still in ma nose!
   A canna' get rid o'd.

'E smell o' fish spread oot tae dry,
Attracted ilka blue blow-fly
   Their eigs tae lay.
An' 'e ither thing A near forgot,
Wis 'e smell o' 'e boilan' porridge pot
   'At began 'e day.

Anither livener for warsie stamags,
'E hamely smell o' new baked bannags!
   Fat can beit id?
Wi' a divad o' butter an' crowdie spread,
Ye'll bless 'e wife for hame-baked bread
   Fan ye eite id.

John Geddes.

JOHN SIMPSON BORN FASSBERRY, MEY 1875 – DIED AUSTRALIA 1969

John Simpson arrived at North Entrance Australia with his wife and daughter in 1929 where he built his own store and church. During his time at the Entrance, he proved to be a very capable businessman. John and his family were highly respected in the community where he was also a nondenominational lay preacher.

John used to collect his bread from a bakery in the Entrance where he had to cross a bridge – he used a wheelbarrow to do the job. On one occasion, he held up all vehicular traffic on the bridge with his load of bread – cars were tooting behind him – but he had the right of way and showed his disdain for all of them by pretending he was a horse. When he reached the by-pass, he bowed to each vehicle as it passed! John Simpson died in 1969 at the age of 94. He was survived by three daughters and three sons – Maggie, Bella, Jean, Johnny, George and Bob.

One of John Simpson's sons, Robbie, was given the name of "The Piper from Over the Way" by many people living in the Entrance, as the skirl of his bagpipes could be heard far and wide.

Margaret Simpson, one of John's daughters better known amongst the family as "The Maggie" and in Australia as "Matron", arrived at the Entrance in 1931 after completing her studies and practice as a nursing sister in Glasgow, where she attained the highest nursing degree as gold medallist of the Nursing Profession of Scotland. She practiced as a nursing sister at the Entrance for 11 years and in 1942, she opened Bowenfals Hospital at the Entrance North. In 1958, after the closure of Bowenfals, she became, by popular choice, matron-in-charge of the Long Jetty Community Hospital and supervised it until 1972. Matron Simpson then retired and she will always be remembered for her 41 years faithful service to the Entrance community.

John Simpson's son, Johnny, was well known to the people of Caithness as he often paid a visit to his old homeland – he died in April 1992.

John Simpson's three daughters are still alive but, alas, his three sons have passed on.

North Entrance is situated north of Sydney.
Helen Sinclair, 17 High Street, Keiss.

HARROW HARBOUR 1994

Photo, Jackie Ham, Ord Terrace, Invergordon.
Scarfskerry and Dunnet Head in background.

418

MISCELLANY

"Ohio" 1897

Photo, Donnie Robertson, Auckengill

S.S. "Thyra" 1913

Photo, Hugh Simpson, Freswick.

"Stellatus"

John Sinclair, Scartan on the left.

Photo, Wick Society.

"Salvage King"

British Columbia Maritime Museum.

SAVED FROM THE SEA

The Essex car belonging to Andrew Dunnet, Keiss, salvaged off the "Pennsylvania". Magnus Bain assisted his father to assemble this car.

These and many more "treasures" are in use in and around the parish.

Writing desk/chest of drawers – "Pennsylvania".
Damask tablecloth – "Thyra".
Plates on top of chest – "Ohio".

Gasket; part of clapper valve – "Malin Head".
Brass ashtrays – "Ben Barvas".
Bell – "Chimœra".
Plates on pull out shelf – "Thyra".
Ladle – "Stellatus".
Fine lawn hankie – "Thyra".
Silver fork – "Pennsylvania".
Plate – scene of Phoenix Park Dublin – "Ohio".
Captain's Chair – "Salvage King".
Meat and soup plates – "Salvage King".
Chart cupboard – "Pennsylvania".
Glass dishes on cupboard – "Ohio".
Keiller's marmalade jar – "Croma".
Liqueur glass – "Gunnaren".
Beautiful brass lamp which fits snugly into bowl shaped holder screwed to wall – "Pennsylvania".
Copper and brass stern light lantern.
Brass candlesticks, Dry compass, Octant.
Captain's chair – "Empire Parsons".
Malcolm Dunnet's telescope.
Chart of the Pentland Firth.

Footnote:– It was said that the rubber boots on the "Pennsylvania" were not packed in pairs but the left boots were together in boxes and the rights in other boxes. Islanders are reputed to have had some job matching them up. It was also said that there were typewriters under every bed on the island.

The Stranding of the "Ohio"

The "Ohio" was on passage from Rotterdam to Baltimore, USA, when she grounded in fog on the 28th May, 1897 at 3.10 a.m. The vessel, under the command of Captain Robert Parker Ovens, had 1050 tons of general cargo, a crew of 24 and two passengers [the captain's wife and child]. After bunkering in Sunderland she left at 11 a.m. on the 26th May. A course was set up the east coast of Scotland, the weather was fine but hazy. By the 27th the fog got thicker and the ship was going at reduced speed. At this time the master decided he was clear of Rattray Head, as his log showed 165 miles. Still going at reduced speed, he laid a north-west course to clear Duncansby Head. This course would have cleared him of all danger. He did continue on that course until 11 p.m. on the 27th May, the log showing 240 miles now.

At midnight a cast of the lead was taken showing 35 fathoms, hard bottom. As the master decided he was close up to Duncansby Head, he altered course to south by east until 2 a.m. when the vessel was turned round again on a north west heading. A cast showed 19 fathoms this course and he continued going dead slow. At 3.10 a.m. breakers were heard but before the way could be stopped she grounded on the "Ruff of Auckengill". Bad weather held up salvage but after some of the cargo was jettisoned she was refloated early in June, beached in Sinclair Bay by three tugs, made seaworthy and taken to Sunderland, arriving on the 29th of June.

At the Court of Enquiry in Sunderland, into the circumstances surrounding the casualty, it was found that the stranding was caused by the neglect of the master to turn the ship's head off the land, when she got into 19 fathoms at 3 a.m. on 28th May. His Master's Certificate was suspended for three months but he was granted a Chief Mate's Certificate. The vessel and navigation equipment were found to be in good order.

The "Ohio" was built of steel in 1888 at Sunderland – 2389 GRT and almost 300 feet in length, powered by a triple expansion steam engine. The vessel was also schooner rigged.

At least part of the cargo was made up of various types of dishes, ranging from ashets to bon-bon baskets – highly decorated. To this day, in some of the older croft houses in the area, these are to be seen, proudly displayed in china cabinets and brought out on special occasions. As can be imagined, when the host and hostess explain the history behind the dishes, it makes for a most interesting conversation piece, especially if their guests are visitors from the south, who have no knowledge of the hazards faced by shipping in the treacherous Pentland Firth.

Donnie Robertson.

The S.S. "Thyra"

The S.S. "Thyra" of Tonsberg ran aground in fog near the Stacks of Duncansby in 1913. Her general cargo was salvaged by Danish tugs but the ship became a total loss. Fortunately her crew all survived.

Colin Mackay.

The "Thyra" boilers are lying southerd of the Stacks.

Hugh Simpson.

Amongst the many bits and pieces salvaged from the wreck of the "Thyra" were barrels of lime and the lime was used for building houses and steadings throughout the district. I know for a fact that the house at "Roadside" renovated between 1916-18 was built with lime from the "Thyra".

Ben Green.

My father James Rosie, Burnside carried up rolls of packsheet from the "Thyra" and used this when he re-roofed the house.

Jim Rosie.

The "Stellatus"

The "Stellatus" was a Swedish tramp of 1827 GRT which grounded at Auckengill on 4th March 1959 about half a mile south of Buchollie Castle. Her cargo was paper pulp. The cargo was mostly salvaged overland, as the vessel was close up to the cliff face, and taken south. The vessel was broken up not long after the stranding by heavy seas.

Donnie Robertson.

"Salvage King" 1925-1940

The "Salvage King" was ordered and built for the Pacific Salvage Company of Victoria, British Columbia, Canada in 1925 at Bow McLachlan Co. Ltd., Paisley, Scotland with its Port of Registry Victoria, B.C. under the British Flag. Registered with Lloyds of London Book No.33941, its official number was 150909. She was one of the finest craft of her type in the world. A single decked vessel of steel construction, 1164 tons gross weight, and with dimensions of 186.3 x 36.2 x 16.2, she was driven by an oil fired 3000-horsepower reciprocating steam engine, having a cruising range of 15,000 miles, and a top speed of 14 knots. She was fitted with equipment to distil sea water at a rate of a ton an hour, wireless, radio telephones, walkie talkies for communication with barges or ships in tow, a fully equipped machine shop, air compressors, decompression chamber for divers and a battery of portable pumps with a capacity of 50 tons of water per minute. She was skippered by an Orkney man, Captain J.M. Hewison, a veteran British Columbia Salvage Master who served the Pacific Northwest well, both in salvage work, and also carried out some of the longest tows on record from the Pacific Northwest while under his command.

During the early part of the war the "Salvage King" went to the Orkney Islands in the service of the Royal Navy, and ended its career in 1941 in a storm on the Ness of Duncansby.

Captain Hewison passed away in March of 1940 while engaged in work for the British Navy as Salvage master in the Orkney Islands.

All that remains of the "Salvage King" are the boilers of the ship lying on the rocks at the Ness of Duncansby.

Information from record books, and the picture came through the courtesy of the B.C. Maritime Museum, Victoria.

Gilbert Brown, Victoria, B.C.

PENTLAND FIRTH PILOTS

As named in census returns. (The age of the person is given after his name.)

1841

Stroma

William Sinclair 50
William Sinclair 20
Andrew Sinclair 45
his son, John Sinclair 20
John Sinclair 45

Freswick

Alex. Bremner 25
Arch. Bremner 35
David Henderson 45
George Bremner 35
John Bain 45
Donald Cook 50
James Bremner 25
Simon Bremner 20
Andrew Bremner 45
Andrew Bain 30

Staxigoe

Donald Gunn 55

Papigoe

William Steven 55
John Anderson 40
Peter Anderson 35
Alex Hossack 58

Crosskirk

Nicol Robertson 46
Hugh Morrison 45
Joseph Smith 25
Sinclair Robertson 25
William MacKenzie 35

(The Crosskirk men give their occupations as fishermen but we know that they did pilotage also.)

1851

Stroma

William Simpson 41
Malcolm Simpson 37
Walter Smith 21
? Sinclair 68
Donald Banks 30
George Banks 26
Andrew Sinclair 48
John Sinclair 56
his son, Alex Sinclair 23
James Sinclair 30
John Manson 24
John Robertson 36
William Robertson 43
John Bremner 41

Freswick

Archibald Bremner 47
George Bremner 45
John Bain 58
his son, Robert 31
Andrew Bremner 77
Donald Henderson 59
John Mowat 49
Donald Cook 63 (Uncle Dan)
his son, William 35
Robert Bain 37
James Wares 29
Andrew Bain 40
Wm. Cook 32
David Henderson 55
James Mowat 36
Gavin Mowat 42

(men born in Canisbay parish)*

Staxigoe

*Donald Bruce 54
? Gunn 39
*Robert Bruce 63
Peter Gunn 42

Papigoe

*Wm. Steven 66
*Wm. Manson 51
*Wm. Manson 58
George Manson 25
*John Anderson 52
Peter Anderson 47
Alex Hossack 68

Crosskirk

*? Robertson 37
*George Smith 43
*Wm. MacKenzie 47
*Joseph (?) Smith 36
*? Smith 47
*Nichol Robertson 55

(born on Stroma)

1861

Stroma

Wm. Simpson 17
James Sinclair 24
George Banks 37
Walter Smith 31
James Simpson 32
Wm. Laird 40
James Moodie 42
John Robertson 19
Donald Wares 20

John Robertson 23
Wm. Sinclair 31
his brother, Charles 29
John Sinclair 26
John Sinclair 43
James Sinclair 40
John Sinclair 65
his son, Alex 33
his son, Eric 21
Wm. Sinclair 32
John Bremner 22
his brother, William 17

Papigoe

Wm. Manson 68
John Anderson 61
George Manson 33
George Bain 45

Crosskirk

*Wm. Manson 26
*George Smith 53
*Wm. MacKenzie 58

(occupations given as fishermen)

1871

Stroma

John Bremner 38
John Robertson 33
David Simpson 36
James Simpson 42

Freswick

John Bain 78
John Mowat 72

Papigoe

Wm. Manson 80
George Manson 47

Staxigoe

Robert Bruce 63

1881

Stroma

Walter Smith 51
James Simpson 52
James Jolly Sinclair 45
William Sinclair 43
William Sinclair 51

Papigoe

John Anderson 83
Peter Gunn 73
Robert Bruce 72

SOME PILOTS AND PILOT CREWS LOST AT SEA

(This list is almost certainly incomplete)

19.10.1838 Papigoe: Wm. Thomson, Wm. Anderson, Wm. Sandison, John Anderson, Wm. Bain. The pilots went out from Broadhaven to a brig and were never seen again. The brig knew nothing of their fate and it was surmised that they were lost while returning to the shore in a gale.

23.4.1840 Nybster: James and Samuel Geddes, Peter Henderson. The pilots took a vessel to Longhope. On the passage home in the evening in their own yole, in a strong west-south-west wind, they shipped a sea off Burwick and capsized. They were seen hanging on to the hull but the gale prevented rescuers putting out from Burwick. James left a widow and five bairns; Peter a widow and two bairns; Samuel was 19 and unmarried. The boat had been bought only two weeks before. Another Geddes brother was in Burwick at the time and saw the death of his brothers.

31.3 or 1.4.1843 Duncansby: Two sons of Malcolm Ross, John Geddes. Missing – Andrew Bremner and ? Bain. The pilots' yole drifted ashore at Nybster, part flooded and with the mast hanging in the halyards. The men were lost at night – exact details unknown.

16.3.1846 Duncansby: ? Robertson at Armadale. Robertson went on board the barque "Belfast" off Duncansby at midday on 16th to guide her west. In the afternoon the wind changed suddenly from west-south-west to north-east and blew up like a hurricane. At midnight the "Belfast" was driven ashore at Armadale. The mainmast broke and fell overboard. The ship lay in the breakers until dawn. The survivors, rallied by Robertson, tried to struggle ashore at low tide and while doing this a wave caught Robertson and washed him to his death.

21.4.1848 Duncansby: George Green and his son Andrew, Hugh and William Manson brothers, James Simpson (survivor Malcolm Dunnet). The pilots went out to a north-bound ship, the "William Gouland" of Sunderland which had hoisted colours for a pilot.

To quote from the John O'Groat Journal 28th April, 1848: "It was unsettled weather – pretty smart breeze from north-east and a good deal of sea, but not enough to occasion any alarm in the minds of the pilots and their friends. Six men manned the boat and as is the practice one was put on board – the remainder of the crew keeping to their own boat was taken in tow by the vessel. The rope which attached the boat to the vessel broke and the same force dragged the boat violently towards the vessel which was pitching heavily, and in a moment the little boat was under the vessel's quarter. The vessel lurched, the boat capsized and the five poor men were in an instant engulfed in the water. All was anxiety aboard the vessel and every desperate effort was made to save the drowning pilots but one by one they sank."

[Since the above was set in type the following has been received from the lips of the sole survivor.]

"The master, the mate and indeed all on board did all they could and exhibited the utmost concern. The mate, secured by a rope, dived in with a boat hook and managed to grab one man but his jacket came off in the mate's hand and he fell back to his death. The survivor Malcolm Dunnet who was pilot aboard the ship had to witness all this, and while he had to lift his eyes in heartfelt gratitude to the preserver of his own life he had to endure the unspeakable anguish of returning home alone and to be the first to communicate the sad intelligence to the bereaved families, friends and neighbours."

12.6.1853 Staxigoe: Alex Bain, Hugh Mowat, Donald Barry, John MacLeod. In a heavy south-east sea, the pilots' boat capsized. Most of the community was at the kirk at the time (it was Sunday) but a few managed to set off to sea in a rescue attempt but failed to reach the pilots in time in the heavy sea. Bain left a widow and child – the others were unmarried.

James Miller, Inchmore, Inverness, (ex-Keiss).

SOME FISHING MEEZES

Meeze – Land marks on shore which pin-point a particular spot at sea. This is actually cross bearings and marks the position of the boat exactly and accurately. The meezes were remembered and handed down in families from generation to generation, and of course the same meezes will remain forever.

To fish halibut, go out until you get the Summerbank Road open (i.e. seeing straight up the road) and then get the Knee off the land.
Hugh Simpson, Freswick.

Freswick Bay – Keiss old kirk on the old castle of Keiss. Freswick House clear of the Greyhead and then as the tide ran to slack you can run off, always keeping the kirk on the castle and you can take the Stacks clear of Skirza.

The Tippet on Ackers Begg's with the Duncansby lighthouse just clear of the Skerries is a good place for halibut.

Mary's at the Head (Sonsiquoy) and Barth Head in Orkney just clear of Duncansby is good for a blockie (small cod three to four pounds). Again just run off when the tide is done keeping Mary's clear Orphir, Langhill and Wideford Hill (Orkney).

Rona – Steam off Skirza keeping Mary's clear of Skirza until you get the tip of Rona (Swona) – you will nearly always get a fish and it's fine for a halibut.

Stacks – about a mile off the Stacks there is a spot for cod which lies between the flood tide and the Nor-birth. That state of tide lasts about a couple of hours and then dies.

Firth – David Dunnett's, Hillhead, on the face of Sannick. Cantick Head lighthouse on the second step of Swona.

Greyhead is some 300 yards south of Freswick House.

John Dunnett, Heatherbell Cottages, John O'Groats.

The breast mark was taken from the sea looking in to the Caithness land at right angles if possible. The height mark was the distance from the land and was taken for example Duncansby Head on certain places on Orkney or Rona (fishermen's name for Swona).

Summerbank road open (breast mark). Tip of the Muckle Stack (height mark).

House of Freswick up to Greyhead (breast) the point of Rona (Swona) (height).

House of Brabster in on Greyhead (breast). The half of Langhill, Orkney (height).

Mary Bremner's (Sonsiquoy) at point of Skirza Head and point of Rona.

Louther to the Skerry (height) and Mary Bremner's at Skirza Head. That was called a "Far Sea" on a good day.

We fished for lobsters in a deep trench we called the Hole. House of Freswick up on the point of

Greyhead and half of Langhill. Shoot creels north east with slack ebb tide and finish the shooting with Rona just coming out.

[The volcanic eruption which formed the island of Surtsey off the south of Iceland in 1963 sent tremendous shoals of cod down round the Caithness coast and some boats were fishing 40 boxes of cod.]

Jimmy Nicolson, Croft House, Auckengill.

The Barth off and Wife Geo dutch, ye'll aye get a little, it mayna' be much.

John Bremner – The Poet.

Maggie's Hole for cod in the Pentland Firth. It lies halfway between South Ronaldsay and Duncansby Head and is not far from the Skerries.

Walter Mowat.

The Haven Road, Stroma, open and the second hump on Dunnet Head.

Owld Robbies on the Stroma beacon and the second hump of Dunnet Head on the Men of Mey – both good places for cod.

Peter Sinclair, Keiss.

A great mark in Brough Bay when setting up for fishing cod is the stalk of Ratter on the kirk of Barrock.

Willie Ham, Harrow.

WEATHER HEADS

A straight strip of cloud standing out clearly and stretching a long way across the sky was called a weather head. It was not always easy to tell which way the head was running and this was critical and needed careful interpretation. A weather head stretching north-east by south-west was a good one with dry quiet weather. A north-west by south-east was a very bad one with atrocious weather and severe gales, but a south-east by north-west indicates changeable showery weather and it may be windy. North by south means a change soon and this may be for better or worse. (Gale and calm within 24 hours is another version.) East by west

warns of bad weather with wind and rain immediately. Occasional showers during which the force of the wind is increased is called a wind feed.

Robert Hughson, Uyeasound, Unst.

Weather Mouth

When clouds form lines radiating from an open space or "mouth" on the horizon the gale will come from that direction. If they converged to a "receiver" or similar opening on the otherside it was a sign of a very severe gale.

M.H.

SHIPPING INTELLIGENCE OF PAST DAYS

In 1851 morse code became recognised internationally as a rapid and effective form of communication. Signalling by prescribed flag hoists was considered by the Board of Trade in 1857 but several years passed before a final format was agreed. However, according to reports in the "Northern Ensign" for 1855 a method of contacting passing vessels and obtaining information was being used successfully by the "ship-agent" at Huna augmented by despatches from Skirza Head.

Huna at this time was strongly linked with Stroma and continued thus for as long as the island remained inhabited. Here was the embarkation point for island visitors whose arrival on occasion gave little cause for rejoicing. Nine days before Christmas 1855, certain officials put a damper on planned seasonal celebrations. Messrs Helm, McKay and McDougald came all the way from Helmsdale to pay a visit to the famed smuggling Isle of Stroma where, after a laborious search, they found nine and a half bushels of green malt artfully concealed on a small island at the south end of Stroma (could this locality be the Stack of Flenic1ett, just north of the cemetery?).

The gleeful gaugers consigned their exciting discovery to Pulteney Distillery.

On 25th March the Huna agent reported that the full rigged ship "Dunrobin Castle" belonging to Aberdeen was taking advantage of a south east breeze. She had come from Callao, then a well known Chilean guano port. Her cargo destined for Invergordon would no doubt enrich Ross-shire farm lands. The day previous, there had been a stiff east north east wind when the whalers "Pacific" and "St Andrews" were sighted off Freswick Bay bound for the Davis Strait.

A month elapsed before the next report appears for 23rd April. The Dundee brig "Ruthenia", commanded by Captain Scott, is proceeding eastwards with a cargo of coal for the Baltic Fleet stationed at Elsinore.

Another gap occurs until 19th July when the Liverpool brig "Herald" is heading west from Hamburg to St John N.B. Six days at sea, she made the signal that all was well on board. Three days later, four ships under canvas proceeding through the Firth would be a normal event. Today the vision of two barques, a full-rigged ship and a schooner in one day would arouse intense interest. The barques were the "Paragon" on her way from Quebec to South Shields and the "Wild Irish Girl" bound east to Sunderland from America while the full rigged ship "William Dawson" of Alloa had loaded at Quebec for Leith. The Anstruther schooner "Java" was homeward bound from Liverpool.

The barque "Brothers" was heading out into the Atlantic on 24th July having sailed from her home port London to load at Quebec.

No reason is given for another lapse of nautical news only resumed on 16th September when it is

stated that the brig "Hannah" of Shields passed east from Liverpool to the Baltic and the Newport brig "Minerva" signalled she was bound to Dublin from Newcastle. The barque "Retriever" of and from Dundee informed Huna that she was on passage to St John N.B.

Two days later, for reasons not stated, the barque "Indian Queen" belonging to and bound for St John N.B. had put in to Stromness.

Next day three barques gave their names, home ports and destinations. The "Caroline" was heading home to Newcastle having left Quebec 27 days previously. Owned in Prince Edward Is. the "Venus" had loaded there and was on an easterly course. The Leith registered "Larne", after 27 days voyage from St. John N.B., was heading for the Firth of Forth.

19th September saw the Newcastle brig "Richard Reynolds", 30 days out of Quebec, passing through the Firth on her way to Newcastle. The barque "Brutus" on passage to Sunderland had taken the same time, sailing from the same port. She had "spoken" the ship "Vale of Vienna" in 40°15'N 58°03'W. All was well on board the latter vessel, then bound from Malta to Quebec. On that date another barque, the "Stark" of Dundee, proceeded east from Liverpool towards Memel.

Local pilots must have been busy, every sail on the horizon a welcome sight for hopeful fishermen maintaining large families on meagre incomes.

On 7th April of 1856 five full rigged ships and three barques passed on vital information to their owners via the ship agent at Huna. If the ship-agent lived in Henny Davidson's house he must have had a good telescope to make out flags of ships passing through the Firth. Some smaller ships might have come through the Sound but the bigger vessels would keep to the Firth. Perhaps Huna was chosen because there was a direct road to Wick from there before a road was made to John O'Groats. Some old maps show this to be the case.

Sutherland Manson.

ADMIRAL SINCLAIR LAIRD OF FRESWICK AND DUNBEATH

Sir Edwyn Sinclair Alexander-Sinclair (1865-1945) born in Malta, was son of Captain Alexander and his wife Isabella Hume, Halifax, Nova Scotia. Isabella's mother was the daughter and heiress of William Sinclair of Freswick and Dunbeath, and Edwyn adopted the additional surname of Sinclair when he succeeded as 12th Laird to the estates.

He entered the Royal Navy as a cadet in 1879 and with dedication worked his way steadily up through the ranks. He started his service on the armour-plated "Iron Duke" followed by service on the "Active", "Fearless", "Ramillies" and in 1902 commanded the destroyer "Albatross", and in 1904 the dispatch vessel "Surprise".

From 1909 until 1910 he commanded the second destroyer flotilla in home waters; was flag captain to Sir Arthur Moore from 1911 to 1913 when he

returned to sea as captain of the "Temeraire" in the Home Fleet and was still in command of her at the outbreak of war in 1914.

As a part of the extensive reorganisation of the Grand Fleet which followed the battle of the Dogger Bank in January 1915, Alexander-Sinclair became Commodore commanding first light cruiser squadron with his broad pennant in the "Galatea". On 31st May, 1916 the "Galatea" was part of the screen of the battle cruiser fleet under Sir David (later Earl) Beatty when she altered course to examine a neutral merchant vessel. As Alexander-Sinclair closed this ship he sighted two enemy destroyers approaching from the opposite direction. His "enemy in sight" signal brought the battle cruiser fleet, and subsequently the whole Grand Fleet, into the action known as the Battle of Jutland.

Alexander-Sinclair was appointed C.B. in 1916. In 1917, when he reached flag rank at the age of 51, he was appointed Rear-Admiral commanding sixth light cruiser squadron with his flag in the "Cardiff" and in November 1917 played a prominent part in the action with the German second scouting group in the "Heligoland Bight". Twelve months later he had the great honour of leading the surrendered German High Sea Fleet with the British Grand Fleet in columns on either beam into the Forth (off Rosyth) and later to its anchorage in Scapa Flow.

In 1920 he was appointed Admiral Superintendent, Portsmouth. 1920, Vice-Admiral commanding first battle Squadron. 1925, Commander-in-chief, "China Station". 1926 promoted to full rank of Admiral. 1927, Commander-in-Chief, "Nore". 1930 Principal Aide-de-camp to King George V. During his distinguished naval career of more than 50 years he had received foreign decorations, including American D.S.M, the French Croix de Guerre and had been appointed a Commander in the Legion of Honour.

Alexander-Sinclair married twice: first in 1892 Julie Hamilton of Netherplace, Ayrshire. By this marriage he had two sons and one daughter. Secondly he married Maud, widow of Major Campbell of the 14th Hussars.

He died in 1945 after a short illness in his home, Dunbeath Castle. Stroma, his daughter, used to visit the parish frequently before she and her husband emigrated and ran a Roadhouse on the Alaskan Highway. The sons, Commander Mervyn, and Lieut. Commander Roderick Alexander-Sinclair also helped maintain this country's mastery of the sea. Mervyn's son, Major General David Boyd Alexander-Sinclair of Freswick C.B., is mentioned in "Who's Who 1993".

Family Footnote:– William Sinclair of Rattar bought the Freswick Estate in 1661 from Magnus Mowat of Buchollie and was the first Sinclair of Freswick. William Sinclair, eighth of Freswick, died in 1838 aged 90. He was a doctor of medicine and known locally as the Black Doctor because he had black hair and a swarthy complexion. He was succeeded by his son William (ninth) who died unmarried in 1855. Barbara succeeded her brother and was the 10th of Freswick. She married William Thomson and they had an only child William Sinclair Thomson-Sinclair 11th of

Freswick who was born in 1844 and married Isabella Henderson of Bilbster in 1872. He

Admiral Sinclair R.N. K.C.B., M.V.O. of Freswick

Photo, Dunbeath Preservation Trust.

Royal Naval College, Osborne, Isle of Wight 1908

Photo, Dunbeath Preservation Trust.
Sir Edwin was captain of this naval college from 1905-1908. Middle Row:– middle (with beard) Prince of Wales – later King George V. Front Row, left to right:– ?, Prince Edward aged 13, his mother Princess of Wales later Queen Mary, Admiral Edwin Sinclair Alexander-Sinclair – commander of the college, Lady Julia née Hamilton-Campbell (his wife).

succeeded to the estates in 1876 and lived at Dunbeath Castle from 1894-1899 and it was during this time that they built the House of the Northern Gate. They had no issue.

Edwin Sinclair Alexander-Sinclair's maternal grandmother (sister of Barbara) married Thomas Hume and their daughter Isabella married Captain John H. I. Alexander.

Sources:– J. H. Lloyd-Owen, 1941-1950 Dictionary of National Biography by permission of "Oxford University Press". Dunbeath Preservation Trust, John O'Groat Journal, Hendersons Family History. Special thanks to Allison Duffield in the Imperial War Museum and D.B. Miller, Old Stirkoke.

Anne Houston, St Magnus.

May 1909 – **Commander Sinclair** of H.M. cruiser "Sapphire" and eight torpedo boats anchored in Dunnet Bay and the commander went ashore to see what progress was being made in the building of his mansion. (House of the Northern Gate). Sometime after this event when staying at Dunnet Hotel he was motoring to Thurso and a horse and cart appeared ahead so he held up his hand for farmer Donald Gunn to stop. The latter took no heed and his cart load of timber broke some glass in the commander's vehicle. At the subsequent court case the farmer never stood a chance and was fined. During the proceedings he was asked why he did not halt when the Commander held up his hand. Farmer Gunn said "he thought it was someone waving who knew him so he just waved back".

Courtesy of Caithness Courier.

CAMMELL LAIRD, SHIPBUILDERS

It was well known in the John O'Groat's area that the "Cammell Lairds" hailed from the parish and it's a great pity that the Cammell Lairds didn't know this! Daniel Mowatt said they were the Stroma Lairds – Sandy Manson is certain that they were from Duncansby and the "authorities" here say that both could be right.

The story goes that two clever, well handed Laird brothers went as young men to Clydeside and got a start in a sail and rope-making business. One of the brothers became a co-partner in the business which went from strength to strength. He kept an open door and his success is remembered because with his marine connections he helped many young men from this area to find employment.

The Shipbuilding Lairds claim to be descended from Alexander Laird who married c.1750 a Janet Robertson or Janet Bain – good Canisbay names. It was Alexander's grandson William (1780-1841) who moved to Liverpool and set up the boiler-making business. A few years later he was able to buy land on the Birkenhead side of the river Mersey where he established his shipbuilding and engineering yard and started building the town of Birkenhead for his workers. William's son John Laird (1805-1874) became one of Merseyside's most celebrated industrialists and was the first M.P. for Birkenhead. There is a fine statue of him standing in Hamilton Square, Birkenhead.

To begin with, the Laird's built wooden ships and

then they amalgamated with Cammells of Sheffield, a steel firm, and went on to pioneer the building of iron ships. It is claimed they built one of the first, possibly the very first, iron vessel on Merseyside.

Taines "Notes on England" page 282 states that: "We visited several workshops, among others the establishment of Messrs. Laird, the Builders of iron ships at Birkenhead. It is said that within the last 30 years they have built 250. They employ 1500 work people and have gigantic furnaces and machines".

Business efficiency and initiatives teamed with superb design and craftsmanship guaranteed the success of this family firm which was employing 17,000 people at its peak. The battleships "Rodney" and "Prince of Wales", both "Ark Royals", the passenger liners "Mauritania" and "Windsor Castle" and the nuclear submarine "Conqueror" were among the ships they built.

"Builders of Great Ships" published by Cammel Laird in 1959 tells their story. Sadly the yard closed at the beginning of 1993.

Information from Gordon Howell, Managing Director, Cammell Lairds. Anne McGrail, Bridge Cottage, Chilmark, Salisbury. (Great-great-grand-daughter of John Laird who founded the firm of Cammel Laird) and from local hearsay.

Magnus Houston, Mill House.

Robbie Cowe bought in some ewes from the Highlands, and being used to the freedom of the wild open spaces, they were inclined to show scant respect for Robbie's fences. One in particular was forever breaking out, and in exasperation Robbie fitted a very large wooden triangle round her neck to stop her boring through the fence wires. This sheep was spotted by passengers in a Wallace Arnold touring bus and such was the concern for

the sheep that they stopped the bus. The driver and some agitated tourists shouted to Robbie, stressing the urgency of getting this strangely adorned animal out of its predicament. Puffing gently on his pipe, Robbie eyed the miscreant sheep, and explained. "Well now did you ever see such a fine looking ewe in all your days? She has such a bonnie face on her, I just had to frame it!"

Keith Muir.

YOUNG ACHIEVERS

Sky-Divers

Ronnie was a Royal Marine Commando, at the Brandenburg Gate when the Berlin Wall came down. He saw action in the Falklands and has travelled the world but still thinks there is no place half as fine as Stroma.

Katrina Beesley (née Green, Roadside, J.O.G.) receiving the degree of Doctor of Philosophy from the Princess Royal at a ceremony in the New Connaught Rooms, London, 1992.

Ronnie Dunnett in the Marine Free Fall Parachute team which broke the world record in 1992.

Photos, Isobel Sinclair, Cerdon, Bayview, Wick.

Davina Cowe, The Ha, in the Londoner Hotel with the Henry Williamson Trophy and her prize winning dish – John O'Groats Haddie Karaté. Davina was 15 when she won the United Kingdom Fish Cookery Competition in 1973.

The Violet Leitch School of Dancing 1992

Back Row, left to right:– Catherine Mowat, Donna Flockhart, Marie Ross, Fiona MacKenzie, Julie Gates, Tanya Banks, Susie Gates. Middle:– Sarah Ross, Nicola Muir, Ruth Flockhart, Kirsten Brown, Joanna MacKay, Lynsey Miller, Jenna Banks. Front:– Leanne Simpson, Fiona Topping, Dawn Rosie, Yvonne Shearer, Laura Brown, Lyn Farquhar.

Photo, Northern Studios.
Wilma Banks, Ancala, Gills with Kim at the Mey Sheep Dog Trials 1988. She won the Parish Championship Cup, the Ladies' and the International Shields.

Nine-year-old **Anne Houston**, Mill House, J.O.G. with Nerys Hughes and Bill McCue when she won the championship and was United Kingdom Junior Cook of the Year. 1984. She cooked her chosen meal in the Savoy Hotel and was the youngest ever winner of the competition.

HOMEWARD BOUND

Using my Camcorder as I journey on

Away up in Caithness in Scotland's far north
There's a place that I love on the shores of the Firth.
As I look ower the Pentland I see Orkney's Isles
From my home the nearest is only six miles,
And Stroma the Isle in the midst of the sea
Is no distance away in miles only three.

I've been off on holiday and I'm heading home
Where I'll walk ower the fields and around the shore roam.
My heart sings for joy when I'm homeward bound
I'll have friends, relations and neighbours all round.
At night time I'll sit by my ain fireside
Looking ower at the lassie who came here as my bride.

We've travelled through Wick, Keiss and round the Dogs Nose
He's been there a long time. He must be comatose.
Then down by the shore three cairns stand out clear
They were built to remind us the Picts once lived here.
Close by them the remains of a Broch can be seen
There's a path from the harbour to keep your feet clean.

Here by the roadside we can see Summerbank
For its fine sculptured figures we've Old John to thank.
On the left the old school which is now a museum
Where local artifacts are there to be seen.
So up and ower Harley we now wend our way
Then into our vision appears Freswick Bay.

From its little harbour in days long gone by
Went brave men of Freswick when sailing vessels drew nigh.
The tides they knew well and as Pilots were the best
To bring ships through the Pentland as they journeyed out west.
Freswick House you can see close by to the sand
And the old fashioned Doo Cot, it stands close at hand.

So we travel onward and it gives us a thrill
As a bit further on we come to the Warth Hill.
I'll walk up to the top and what do I find
The Orkneys in front and Morven far behind
Away to the west Ben Loyal we see
And out to the east fishing boats in the sea.

And so I move onward and down the road go
And I come to the bend that I very well know
I'll reach for the camera the first that I'll do
For all John O'Groats is now clearly in view
Then I'll swing round the camera just to let you see
The part of the country that's homeland to me.

The first place on the left is the Novelty Shop
You'll be welcomed by Walter and Jess if you stop
And if you are tired I'm sure you'll be gled

When they feed you your supper and give you a bed
Elsie and John have their farm over here
Where thousands of tatties they lift every year.

On the left you will find the Post Office and store
Selling petrol and postcards and sweeties galore
Then here is the house where I've lived all my life
Where 50 years back I brought my young wife.
As time has gone by we've brought up bairnies three
Who've had nine of their own we did rock on our knee.

Now I'll take you a journey going towards Duncansby
Past the house where Billy and Clara do stay
On our left is the hall on our right is the school
Where long time ago I learned the golden rule.
The Sinclair Contractors we now have in sight
Then there's William who sells planes you can put in flight.

So we're getting nearer to the East End
And here is where Frank his retirement does spend
Past Snowflake and Davies down to Sannick Bay
Higher up is the Lighthouse that's called Duncansby
We'll stop and we'll have a look at the Long Goe
And at rocks where the seabirds when nesting do go.

Looking south from up top what's this that we see
The Stacks standing high in full majesty
The Muckle Stack here is largest of all
But the Peedie Stack it is nearly as tall
But down at the bottom taking up little room
Is a peedie wee stack that we all call Tam Thoom.

In on the cliffs we can see the Thirl Door
Where in winter time storms the seas fairly roar
Out on this reef you can sometimes see seals
With all round about them the fishermen's creels
It was here the "George Robb" was driven ashore
All twelve of her crew gone for evermore.

Now here we see Gibbs Craig close in to the cliff
Just like a Scots Guard standing up straight and stiff
Then as we look down standing there in the sea
Is a square lump of rock that we all call the Knee
At the mouth of the Goe we find Humlies Hole
Where mountainous seas sometimes roar and roll.

Further out is the Skerries with Lighthouse and Foghorn
Where hundreds of seals on the rocks there are born
There in fifty six "Dovrefjell" went ashore
A Norwegian Tanker and carrier of ore
Helicopters rescued her crew of two score
(41 actually)
And landed them safe quite near to our door.

I'm glad that we're getting a very good day
As it gives us a chance to see Copinsay
South Ronaldsay Island is plain to be seen

With the wild boars of Duncansby here in between
Next the Island of Swona and then the Oil Base
Where the big flare on Flotta lights up the whole
place.

The Lighthouse on Cantick sends out its bright
light
To warn off the ships which sail by at night
South Walls and Longhope are all close together
And the lifeboat stands ready in all kinds of
weather
Hoy hills to the west you can see reaching high
The Old Man you can't see but he's still standing
by.

Away at the back you can see the Ward Hill
And a bit further east Wideford near Kirkwill
Then right in the centre you can see Scapa Flow
Where in wartime the navy to safety did go
Ships passing by may be stemming the tide.
On through Pentland Firth as they travel
worldwide.

Then so near at hand is Stroma's fair Isle
From the harbour at Groats it is only three mile
The houses are empty, there's nobody there
Only cattle and sheep to keep the grass bare.
Its people are scattered and afar they did roam
But their thoughts aye return to the Isle they call
home.

So its back to Post Office I am wending my way
Going down past Seaview and also Caberfeidh
Down at the end if you care to turn right
You find Billy and Clara and their Caravan Site
At the Last House in Scotland you surely must
stop
It is now a museum and there's also a shop.

Nearby the Wool Shop with Sandra and Ann
And from Sheila you'll get lovely soup from a pan
At the end of the road you'll find Groats Hotel
All over the world it is known right well
Then close at hand is the First and Last
You'll land in the harbour if you carry on past.

Here we see in the harbour Thomas's Ferry Boat
Far larger than the one plied by Old John De Groat
Four times a day Pentland Venture sails o'er
To reach Burwick Pier on Orkney's south shore
There you'll step on a bus and you'll travel for
miles
And you'll never forget your visit to those Isles.

The fishermen's boats are tied up at the quay
It's lobsters and partans they fish for at sea
At times when they've finished lifting their creels
They will take you to Stroma to see all the seals
Or if tide is right up round Duncansby Head
Where if you get sick the fish get well fed.

But time's going on so we will turn west
Just to show you some more of this place I love
best
Here as you can see is the Lifesaving Store
Where the crew quickly gather when boats go
ashore
Then it's on past the Ha we have no time to wait
To see Robbie or Elsie or Andrew or Kate.

Now here on our left can be seen the Mill House
Where Magnus the Miller lives with Sina his
spouse
And then the old mill standing nearer the shore
Still grinding the oats as in days of yore
Yes this is the only mill in the north
Still grinding away for all that it's worth.

I look back in time with nostalgic heart
When I yoked the horse into the old cart
I heaved in bags of oats and also of bere
And brought them to Magnus for grinding down
here
He dropped down a chain, a thing he did oft
And he hoisted those bags up and into his loft.

Over this Waide the water did flow
To turn the big wheel to make the mill go
Then see the Old Brig it really looks fine
Built by Cromwell's soldiers in sixteen forty nine.
A much larger bridge has been built further up
But comparing its age it is only a pup.

A bit further on live the Broons and Frankie
But nearer the road we find our good friend Nancy.
Who spent most of her life teaching young folk to
cook
Now she's put together the Groats Cookery Book
Her garden is lovely with flowers galore
And a welcome awaits as you step in her door.

So we journey on the eight three six road
To where Jackie and Nancy have their nice abode
As an oldtime Gospel Preacher Jackie loves to tell
Of Jesus his Saviour whom he loves so well
He travels o'er Scotland, England, Ireland and
Wales
To tell of his Saviour whose love never fails.

Then here is the Mission Hall the place that I love
It was here I met the Saviour who came from above
In the year thirty nine I asked him in my heart
And I prayed that I never from him would depart
I've failed him so often my Saviour and friend
But he promised he'd keep me right on to the end.

Passing Robbie's we soon time come to Havengore
Where Johnnie and Margaret keep an open door
To tourists who come from both far and near
They will get bed and breakfast if they step in here
Johnnie Cormack he lives just over the road
He sells tractors and implements by the lorry load.

At Huna we saw the old Lifeboat Shed
And the rails to the sea down where the boat sped
And also the harbour so recently made
With the help of some cash by local folk paid
A bit further o'er is the Old Huna Inn
Where travellers of old got a welcome within.

Here the Old Church of Scotland a long time has
stood
Inside is the tombstone of old Jan De Groot
When Queen Mother comes north to Mey for a trip
It is here on a Sunday she comes to worship
Here you'll get a welcome if you care to come in
From the Parson you'll hear there's a pardon from
sin.

432

The Church Yard and tombstones are here all around
Where friends and relations last resting place found
I think when time comes of that great wondrous day
When the graves will be opened and they'll fly away
To be with their Saviour to dwell evermore
Cause they opened their hearts and asked Him in the door.

Now I'll turn up the road and a little time spend
To show you the Tin Kirk I always attend
Here you'll be welcome. Come in and sit doon
The service begins here on Sunday at noon
The preacher will tell you from sin you can flee
To the Saviour who died on Calvary's tree.

Maybe you say for that tripe you've no time
Just think of your friends cut off in their prime
Old Satan will tell you there's no hurry at all
Take a look in the churchyard they're there old and small
Get rid of your sin, give Jesus your love
Then one day we will meet in His home up above.

We journey on and come to Gills Bay
To the harbour wherein the linkspan wouldn't stay
And the Ferry Boat "Varagen" it had to flee

When the harbour got battered with mountainous sea
Here there is still lots of work to be done
While seals lie on the rocks and bask in the sun.

Onward we go, we have no time to stay
The next stopping place is the Castle of Mey
It's the Queen Mother's home up here in the North
With its view of the Orkneys across Pentland Firth.
The Queen and her family sometimes come for tea
Giving us all a chance just to see Royalty.

I have showed you the harbours as we have come past
So now we'll turn right and make the next one the last
From Harrow Farm up above we'll be able to show
Phillips lovely wee harbour nestling down below.
A bit further on is the Old Meal Mill,
Its wheels turn no longer, it's silent and still.

I have showed you some bits of the place I love best
So I'll turn back and go home just to have a good rest.
I'll sit in my chair and switch on our TV
And look at the places you all now can see
If you've friends and relations tell them to come north
For a visit to GROATS the place of my birth.

George M. Steven, Seaview, John O'Groats.

KELP

It is a known fact that Canisbay produced a lot of kelp c.1800. It seemed too good a chance to miss when I read how it was made in Eday and Faray c.1920 in "Don't Tell Bab" by Annie Harcus (Hamish Donn's aunt). We are indebted to her for the following article.

Kelp Making

During the winter time my father and brothers used to gather tangles on the shore. If the beach was accessible a horse and cart was used, otherwise they were carried up manually on a hand-barrow. They were built in a pile two feet high and four or more yards long. The tangles were left to dry until summer and then burnt in a kiln. The kiln was a hole in the ground five feet in diameter and 15 inches deep. It was completely lined bottom and sides with Caithness type stones (flag). These were carefully placed to prevent earth contaminating the kelp. Each family had their own kiln, usually at the foot of a shore field. A winlin (small bundle) of straw was used to start a fire in the bottom, then the dried ware was added. When the fire was well under way the dried tangles were piled on gradually.

This process usually took a whole day and towards the end of the burning the tangles had to be raked through to get all the bits burnt up. The kelp by this time was almost liquid and resembled thick porridge. Sometimes two of us youngsters would hold a sack over the kiln to speed up the burning down process.

We loved making kelp, as it was like a holiday to us bairns. When all the tangles were burnt up, the kelp was left in the kiln to cool and harden overnight. The kelp, now solid had to be broken into manageable pieces so that it could be put in the cart. There was always a quantity of crumbled bits which had to be swept up and put in sacks. It was taken to the kelp store at the pier where it was weighed and stored ready for shipping.

Annie Harcus, Dawnvale, Willow Road, Kirkwall.

OWLD BANGERS

My husband and I share a belief that modern cars and drivers are much more dangerous to themselves and others — because of their capabilities of great speed and power which encourage the delusion of drivers that just such a car is indestructible, and that they, the drivers, are infallible. Indeed, some male drivers even angle back their heads like supercilious Border Leicester tups (when they are chewing the cud).

All cars are so streamlined and immaculate and boringly uniform there's no such thing as the individuality, charm or personality that could cause such fun and games long ago. I can mind back before this need for an M.O.T. – what fun and adventure with owld bangers!

There was very little danger because one never drove them anywhere fast, in case they fell apart! All other road users could hear them, smell them, see them – well in advance, which let them get oot o' 'e road in plenty of time. I've seen Sandy Green's horse-drawn binder come doon 'e "back-brench" at Gill's faster than some old bangers I've driven.

The pleasure of the very first one I owned (while living in Canisbay) has never been equalled. "IT" was a bottle-green ex-Post Office van that cost me a fiver in Castletown. A charming but dubious admirer (of mine, not of the vans!) said I could get it "fixed up" in Wick. I confess I was as happy and thrilled as a young child at a Circus as I drove that vehicle with its wobbly wheels, slack steering, dirty windscreen and either ineffective or non existent wipers! My heart thumped with joy, louder than the big-end thumped with protest, as I drove all the way to Wick singing "The Dead-Wood Stage" ("is a-comin' on over the hill"?).

No potential or established mechanic would touch it – so back to Castletown, somewhat less euphoric, than before. Then a P.C. Rhodes, shouted "Miss Allman, take that THING out of my sight and BURN IT!!" (he must have been working-class English – cos they can be ever so rude and tactless). My cheeks burned with indignation!

A few years later when I had become as stained and hurt by the world as anyone else – I was ambitious, acquisitive and sought a real status symbol. It was on a garage forecourt, in Halkirk. A light blue Ford Popular – a prestigious 45 pounds worth of status symbol, although I didn't know it at the time, it was going to keep two of my more persistent admirers in occupational therapy, for years to come! (One of them in a last bid to impress me and present a macho-image, had me as a passenger, in his much "superior" car, sort of driving cross-country from Upper Gills to Brabster. Talk about eye-to-hand co-ordination in trainee pilots? Talk about a combination of a good jockey and horse, taking Beechers, in their stride!)

First, they had to teach me to give "her" oil and water, stick a spring clothes peg on 'e choke, place a stone on the throttle, watch the starting handle didna kick and mind and hev her oot o' gear! Ah, that Ford Popular became such a focal point on our lives. We all appeared to have fallen in love with "her"!

Gradually, I built up faith in her, and in my own ability to cope with her minor problems, so much so, that I invited my fiancé to go a run with me to Duncansby Head on a night of a full moon. Being a romantic at heart and fond of all types of music I am very moon-conscious as it were – and to match the sea-scape up there at Duncansby Head – Debussy's "Claire de Lune" and Rachmaninov's

"Moonlight Sonata" drifted gently through my mind. Wonder why I forgot Respighi's "Cavalleria Rusticana". . .? cos Rustic Chivalry was certainly going to be needed.

When we stopped and got out and stood, both spellbound by the moon and stars and spellbound by each other, some embarrassing distraction crept in. Whose stomach was rumbling and gurgling? Och, ye've guessed folks? Yes, it was the car radiator and it was boiling!

Always so proud of my dependable and quietly chivalrous fiancé – he wrapped a cloth around his hand and slowly unscrewed the cap off the radiator, and we were soon enveloped in steam and not silhouetted by romantic moonlight at all! So, tactfully, on the way home, he told me of some comical experiences he'd had, with his owld bangers, as it were.

Once he and his crew members were driving from Sandside to Castletown with a heavy load of crabs – on a Royal visit occasion – well, yon boatie was moored off Scrabster. Crowds were lining the pavements waiting. Policemen, worrying about trouser creases, lumbago and dandruff, mums worrying if the bairns got fretful. At last – in the distance a vehicle was spotted, expectant murmurs from the crowd – but the happy murmurs became shaded with anxiety and bewilderment because of sudden, alarming, explosive sounds! Och only fishermen, in a violently back-firing van (ssh-ma chiel's!).

Another time, he and some pals were driving home from Kinlochbervie when the exhaust pipe actually fell off! They asked a fellow, called Billy (one of their number) to crawl underneath and hold it in position. George (my husband of 25 years) fixed it, but for a laugh, organised the manual moving of the van, further along the road. Billy, still lay back there, his hands still raised as if still holding that exhaust pipe! Mind you he'd had "a drammie" – as one euphemistically puts it. (Reckon he was catatonic.)

Best yarn, coming up – going doon, 'e Scrabster Brae, with another load of crabs, and old Harry Crowden and another fellow, squashed in the cab. A front wheel came off, and rolled ahead with utter dignity (like a riderless horse can do!). "My George" knew fine, but had said nothing and tenaciously tried to keep control, without causing any panic. His father, yawningly and unsuspectingly, asked "Phit'n a wheel is 'at Geordie?" He replied, through clenched teeth "wur wheel".

Prior to the advent of indicators on cars, when drivers had to use hand-signals, an old man who once lived here at this very spot (before re-construction) once remarked to George (my future husband): "D'ye ken iss Geordie? Ah dinna ken half 'e fowk passing in their cars that wave to me noo-a-days!"

Patricia Crowden, Castletown.

Winter weather and women's thoughts often change.
Willie Ham, Lochend.

1901 CHARGED WITH SPEEDING!

George Dower (son of Gordon Dower, Louisburgh and Eliz née Houston, East End, John O'Groats), painter, Wick, was charged that on the Wick to Castletown road he did exceed 14 m.p.h. in his motor car. The Chief Constable and a friend in a wagonette were passed by the car. The friend with his stopwatch said the car passed between two milestones in three minutes. The owner said his car was not built to do more than 10 m.p.h. Witnesses agreed with his statement and the charge was found not proven.

Courtesy of Caithness Courier

Footnote:– 1966 – The grandson of a Wick fishcurer developed a new instrument that appeared to be twice as accurate as the standard electrocardiograph in detecting heart damage. Vancouver scientist Dr Gordon Dower claimed that, with the new device, any family doctor could quickly become more skilful at diagnosing heart attacks than the most highly trained cardiologist. Dr Dower was a grandson of the late Mr Gordon Dower, Girnigoe Street, Wick.

Courtesy of John O'Groat Journal.

THE WAY IT WAS IN THE DEVONIAN PERIOD IN THE PARISH OF CANISBAY

Long before the first tourist sent a picture post card of the Last House to envious friends, long before John O'Groats built his house at Duncansby, long before the dinosaurs, before the coal forests even, the whole of the parish of Canisbay was in the middle of a huge lake and the lake itself was in the middle of an enormous arid desert. The earth spun faster than it does now, and the sun was younger and hotter. There were droughts lasting thousands of years, followed by cooler, wetter spells and the evidence for this can be seen in the rocks of the parish if you can read what those ancient pages have to say.

We can't put an actual date on things but, give and take a year or two, it was about 370 million years ago. If we look at the rocks around the Castle of Mey we will see that they are largely grey in colour. When these rocks were being formed by the deposition of layer upon layer of sediment the lake was full of strange fish with tongue-twisting names. There was **Thursius** (which really means the fish from Thurso), **Dipterus** (which means "two wings" referring to its long fins) and **Millerosteus** (which means "Hugh Miller's bone" because he first described it). As time went by the lake began to silt up and shrink in size and the parish was now a river system feeding a shrinking lake towards the north. If we take a walk along the shore from Gills to the Parish Church or along the shore from John O'Groats to the Bay of Sannick we will see that the rocks here are red in colour, quite unlike those at Mey. These are the rocks laid down in the this fast-flowing river. But we are not yet done with the lake. On at least two occasions, the lake once more covered the parish and the evidence for this is two bands of grey rock in the brick-red sandstones of John O'Groats.

Again this lake teemed with fish with even more unpronounceable names. There was **Tristichopterus**, **Pentlandia** (because it was first found on the shores of the Pentland Firth), **Microbrachius** (which means "tiny arms", referring to its pectoral fins) and **Watsonosteus** (meaning "D. M. S. Watson's bone" since he was the first to describe it). But, eventually, drought won out over the lake and the rest of the rocks of the parish revert to the typical red colour of the John O'Groats sandstones.

Fossil Fishes

Thursius pholidotus is similar to *Th. macrolepidotus* but is rather larger, about 220 mm in length. It is found in the Mey beds and possibly also in the Spittal Beds and their equivalents.

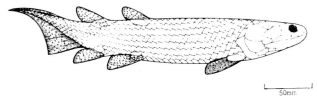

Reconstruction of Thursius pholidotus Traquair (after E. Jarvik).

Tristichopterus alatus is confined to the John O'Groat Sandstones and their equivalents. It is a large fish of the order of 600 mm in length. The ephichordal lobe is roughly the same size as the hypochordal lobe and, in its symmetry, much more resembles the caudal fin of modern fish than does *Gyroptychius*.

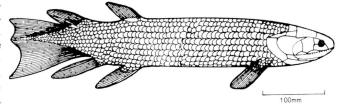

Reconstruction of Tristichopterus alatus Egerton (after D. M. S. Watson).

Dipterus probably appears in the Wick Beds, as fragmentary remains seem to indicate, and persist to the top of the Mey Beds. Its size is very variable, mature specimens range from 70 mm to 600 mm.

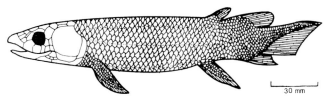

Reconstruction of Dipterus valenciennesi (after Forster-Cooper).

Pentlandia macroptera is similar to *Dipterus* but is a little plumper. It is confined to the John O'Groats Sandstones and their equivalents. *Pentlandia* rarely exceeds 170 mm in length.

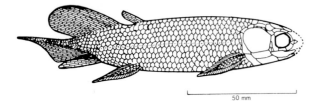

Reconstruction of Pentlandia macroptera (Traquair) after D. M. S. Watson.

Watsonosteus fletti is again similar to *Coccosteus* but is very much larger, probably 700 mm in length. It is again easily distinguished by the shape of its median dorsal plate.

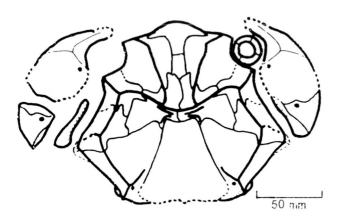

Skull of Watsonosteus fletti (Watson) (after R. S. Miles and T. S. Westoll).

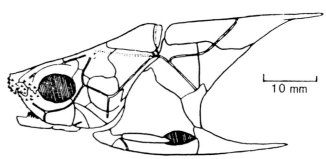

Reconstruction of head and thoras of Millerosteus minor (Miller) (after A. Desmond).

Microbrachius dicki is a tiny antiarch about 30 mm in length. It is found in the John O'Groats sandstones and their equivalents.

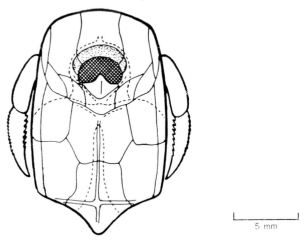

Reconstruction of the inner surface of the dorsal head and body armour of Microbrachius dicki Traquair.

And so these fishes remained locked in the rocks waiting for Robert Dick to be born and for Hugh Miller of Cromarty to come to visit him in his bakehouse in Thurso and discuss the wonders of creation as they split the rocks open with their hammers and gazed for the first time with wonder on the strange fishes which had not seen the light

of day since they died some 370 million years ago.

Acknowledgement:– The drawings of the fossil fishes are from "The Fossil Fishes of the North of Scotland", by J. Saxon, Caithness Books, 1978.
John Saxon, 9 Rockwell Terrace, Thurso.

The **John O'Groats Gala** was for many years the highlight of the summer; and the parade of floats would have done credit to a much larger community. The locals turned out in force to support the event, and of course the bemused tourists greatly swelled the ranks of spectators. One year, a genteel lady was watching spell-bound when she was accosted with a collecting tin by the brave figure of one J. Green Esquire, all 16 hairy stone of him exposed to the summer sun, bar for a large nappy swaddling his nether regions, a baby bonnet crowning his golden locks, and a baby-bottle of suspiciously amber-coloured milk gurgling happily down his throat. Smiling graciously, she handed over her small change, and asked: "Tell me my good man, what is the big occasion?" Removing

the bottle, Johnny gave her a toothy smile and replied: "It's Saturday, Jeck!"

The resurrection of the **Canisbay Show** has proved a great success, and has attracted its fair share of Press attention. One brave journalist, who shall remain nameless, despatched to cover the event, decided to seek shelter from the cutting east wind, and maintained a watching brief from the security of the Beer Tent, where he set about boosting the Show's profits with almost missionary zeal. On the Monday, he phoned a local resident – and fellow imbiber – and casually worked the conversation round to Canisbay's Big Day. "I don't suppose you caught the name of the Gala Queen..."
Keith Muir, Houston Drive, Canisbay.

JOURNEYS WITH THE 51ST HIGHLAND DIVISION

Much of what is written here was the work of various officers and other ranks of the battalion, most of whom are no longer with us.

They wrote for the battalion scrap book which is housed in the Seaforth Museum at Fort George. Prominent at the start, were writings by the late Colonel then Captain H. A. C. MacKenzie; the late Major J. H. Davidson and the late Corporal Parkinson of his company. Later Sir P. D. Nairn, then Captain, wrote volubly and with graphic illustrations but there were many others whose accounts told of the battalion's doings in foreign fields.

"Sans Peur" by Alastair Borthwick, was published after the war and a revised edition "Battalion" was published in 1994. For obvious reasons these travels mention few, if any, battles or individuals. The heading "Travels with the 51st Highland Division" concentrates on the long journeys of those who were lucky enough not to have them cut short by the fortunes of war. The travels of course did not end in Sicily.

I am referring to the Highland Division that was reconstituted after the original had become prisoners of war in Germany. It consisted for the most part of duplicate battalions or units that had spent the first years of war guarding vulnerable places in Scotland. After considerable training, mostly in Aberdeenshire, it proceeded to the Aldershot area and later embarked at Gourock in June 1942. It included our own county battalion, the 5th Battalion Seaforth Highlanders, and, as I served continuously with them until I was demobbed in October 1945, I had fully five years travelling at H.M.'s expense with an H.D. on my shoulder.

We boarded the "Bergensfjord", a Norwegian troopship at Gourock. She was no beauty. Built before the First World War, she stood high out of the water, gaunt, grey and ungainly. In peace time her cabin accommodation might have been comfortable but when there were tens then, there were hundreds now. We slept four in a small cabin though two was a crowd in the floor space and the morning ablutions were performed in strict rotation. The food and service were excellent however. How we admired the stewards manipulating a dozen plates of soup with dexterous ease while we, poor land lubbers, could scarcely carry it from plate to mouth, but we did somehow for we had a healthy appetite and great interest in our food and drink.

And that brings me to the bar. Viewed before opening time, it seemed a peaceful spot where one might imbibe in silent and satisfied reverie, but it belied its appearance. Even on the first night it proved a veritable Black Hole of Calcutta. Arid tobacco smoke, mixed with heavy perspiration from hundreds of overheated bodies rose to the ceiling in a thick pall and, finding no way of escape stayed and thickened to a pea soup density. It was invariably over-crowded and the queue waiting to

Major George H. Green 1943

Photo, George Green, "Tjaldur", Gerston, Halkirk.

be served extended through the doorway, down the stairs and half way along the corridor below. Excuse the non nautical language! Yet it was the pulse of the ship. Here we talked, laughed, played cards, drank and shouted to our hearts' content. And for us it was not one long stag party. We had 80 sisters of the 92nd General Hospital on board and their company enlived the long hours of black-out and intolerable heat.

On the second day rain fell, the sea was choppy and the "Bergensfjord" began to roll a little. And now we had to learn the routine of a troopship – ships rounds, troop deck inspections and boat drill to start the day. Then a little training to keep us from getting bored, Bren guns, rifles, mortars etc. emerged from the bowels of the ship. It became a veritable hive of industry. Mess orderlies toiled below decks. Hammocks had to be rolled, tables scrubbed and utensils polished. Overhead there were lectures. Bren gun instruction, compass lessons and P.T. struggled for space and hearing. The afternoons passed more quickly with boxing and Highland dancing. So we sailed on.

The weather grew warmer and a week out from Gourock we changed into K. D. Soon Freetown came in sight. We welcomed the distant view of cool, dark greenery and laughed at the native bum boys diving for pennies. The twinkling shorelights and the undimmed port holes of ships lying in the harbour were refreshing after the years of blackout. But there was little else at Freetown to enjoy. The atmosphere was damp and oppressive. The heat was great and unrelieved by the normal sea breeze. There was danger of malaria and precautions had to be taken. Shirts were buttoned up, slacks worn, sleeves rolled down and our evil smelling mosquito ointment used for the first time. At night the heat in cabins and troop decks was such that our clothes were continually damp with perspiration. Nearly everyone carried a towel instead of a handkerchief. As the danger of malaria forced all and sundry to sleep below decks, B.O. was so strong that even your best friend would tell you. So we were glad to get to sea again and have our deck breeze and sleeping under the stars.

And now we were approaching the equator and lively plans were formulated for "crossing the line". I won't linger over the wild ceremony that went on for nearly 10 hours. Sufficient to say that it was certainly wild and less restrained than would normally happen on a more formal voyage. At the end of the day nearly all of us were bruised, battered and half drowned and the ship's captain stopped it when he found that constant hosing might eventually sink the ship!

On the third week of July we turned east to round the Cape. Here we touched the fringes of the Roaring Forties but fortunately it was not too stormy. The ship, however, was light in fuel and water and inclined to roll. At meals, chairs slid from the tables and then crashed back into them. We berthed at Cape Town on the morning of the 18th July. We found our geography books had indeed described it accurately as nestling at the foot of Table Mountain. For this reason its greatest breadth is somewhat less than a mile but it is almost 20 miles long including the suburbs. Seen at night from the ship the myriads of lights cast a multi-coloured twinkling quilt round the mountain's great bulk.

How we had looked forward to visiting Cape Town but the anticipation fell far short of the real thing. As we trooped off the ship, a fleet of cars and welfare workers descended on us. We were whisked off to private houses, hustled into hotels, invited to dances and parties, fêted and treated wherever we went. No words can describe the real warmth of Cape Town's welcome. Even years later all ranks tell of it and even correspond with friends they met there. We stayed in port for three days and the welcome increased each day so it was with great regret that we eventually prepared to continue our voyage. A parting gift of three lorry loads of oranges arrived as we were slipping our moorings too late to load in normal quayside manner. But our newly found friends arose to the occasion. A quayside party tossed them all on board in record time. No time was lost in consumption either but the ship smelt of oranges for days.

Our next lap was Aden. Time dragged a little now. The highlight of our voyage had passed, but we did our best to relieve the monotony. Our pipe band played regularly on all decks. We had, too, a good instrumental band. The night was beautiful as we neared the equator again and a new moon encouraged us to arrange dances in spite of the enforced black out. These met with varying success for space was limited and various tastes struggled for expression above decks. Our stay at Aden was far from pleasant. Shore leave was banned, though this evoked little disappointment for there was small promise of fun or gaiety ashore. The welcome sea breeze was stilled and we sweltered under a burning sun. We studied the shore life through our glasses but there was little to see except a few camels toiling wearily against a red dusty background of barren rock.

How slowly these days passed here compared to Cape Town and how we welcomed the sea breeze after our first experience of a Rhamseen. It came suddenly one night before sunset, blowing up at an hour least expected. No natural breeze but like the blast from a furnace, dust laden and breathing fire. It came from the west and filled us with a vague disquiet for it smelt of sand and the heat of the desert. So up the Red Sea and now we were the last ship in the convoy. Land on both sides and blazing heat. Sweat oozed from every pore, handkerchiefs soaked, towels soaked. Drops trickled down your neck, gathering volume as they by-passed your tummy and raced over your knees to saturate your hose tops.

On the 14th of August, we dropped anchor at Fort Fufic. The sun came up over the hills of Suez to find the "Bergenfjord" already astir. We were glad and sorry to be at the end of our eight weeks' voyage. Slowly some peculiar steam lighters appeared alongside manned by villainous looking natives. We transhipped and made for the hot dry dustiness of the quayside. So much for our long journey.

You will notice there has been no mention of the dangers of wartime voyages. Well we saw none. We were a huge convoy and occasionally we saw a destroyer racing backwards and forwards as we zigzagged on our course. But if there was danger we were not told and the only casualty we knew of was in one of the other ships when someone rolled fast asleep from the decks into the water. It was monotonous and yet it was fun. I can remember a tiny flying fish fall on deck and someone pointing out an albatross as we neared South Africa but I remember most the long dark nights with the decks blacked out and far below the scintillating sparkle of phosphorescence as we steamed on and on. In most ways an uneventful voyage but one that we were to look back on for long months as an oasis of peace.

After a wait of about three hours, the train duly appeared and we bundled on board and were off without further delay. The first few miles were occupied in throwing overboard all undesirables. They stowed away during the hubbub of entraining. Our way lay along an irrigated area and the novelty of it all had not worn off when we reached Quassassin Station where we detrained and then embussed and eventually arrived at a base camp – El Tahag. There I am afraid a reaction set in.

El Tahag was a grim place. It was still light enough to see a bare, bleak, flat, barren bit of gritty desert broken only by the dim outline of scattered tents. Eventually everyone was fed. Unlike our country, darkness falls very suddenly in Egypt and many of us had our first experience of being lost around our own camp. No one liked Tahag. Dysentery i.e. gippy tummy, began the night we arrived and stayed with us for many months in greater or less degree, according to the individual constitutional power to withstand it. We grew used to strange vegetables of the water melon type in all colours varying from bright green to dark purple. Ants crawled about our beds and myriads of flies swarmed everywhere. These made life almost unbearable at times. Meat arriving at the camp would be literally black with them. It was often impossible to eat a piece of bread with jam on it and manipulate a cup of tea at the same time. Lesser insect evils were the scorpions, of which we had heard dread reports. They were like tiny lobsters, some black, some yellow. Occasionally we found one among our bedding in the sand. Their bite is said to be very serious but I was never bitten by one and never heard of anyone who suffered seriously from them.

By this time our transport had arrived and shortly after, we left Tahag and went by road through Cairo to Mena. It was an established military camp but still growing and we were given a piece of virgin desert on the outskirts of it. By this time we had begun to realise what it meant to have a water ration. Actually it was a liberal one to break us in – about two gallons per head per day – but we did not think it liberal at that time. Later it was reduced to half a gallon. This had to do for everything – cooking, washing faces and clothes, brewing up to satisfy a constant thirst and even filling our vehicle radiators. To say that it was inadequate was an understatement. After we had done everything we could with it, we used to try amateurish methods of filtering and re-using it.

We were at Mena as part of a force defending Cairo in case Rommel would break through the Alamein line. One platoon was dug in just beside the Sphinx. The Cairo scare died however and we left Mena and trundled northwards on the main Alexandria road en route for El Hamman on the railway running west from Alexandria. We left the main road just north of Alexandria and launched out on a desert track for about 30 miles. As it happened, we timed this desert run to coincide with a dust storm. The track was about nine inches deep in dust so fine that it would pour like water. It penetrated everything and we never quite got clear of it again until we left Africa. Even when there is no dust storm there is a continual sand-laden breeze blowing in the desert. We ate dust, we drank dust. Our faces were always covered with it but, like the flies, we grew used to it and scarcely noticed.

But we were learning what might be called desert craft. We had discarded our sun helmets and our shirts when not on duty. We slept always in the open usually in a trench, not forced to yet by hostile action but to gain the extra warmth at night when the desert becomes bitterly cold. Cooking was no longer done centrally but each section of men did their own. Nearly everything they cooked came out of a tin but the culinary art made all the difference to the result. We began to realise the importance of sanitation. Bigger and bigger latrines were invented. Later when we became operational, we were forced to abandon them, but we soon realised the necessity for cleanliness and no one ever went out to relieve himself without a spade in his hand.

We were now in the main defences in depth facing Rommel. His last armoured threat had petered out where we were. Minefields abounded on all sides and out in No Man's Land we could see burned out trucks, crashed planes and all the aftermath of battle. The Hun was well back beyond the Alamein line but now and then an odd plane came along to machine gun us. We stayed here for about a fortnight. There was a continual sand-laden breeze that blew through the valley levelling our doovres and permeating everything with its gritty breath. Only at night did the breeze die down and we crept to an early bed for there was little encouragement to do anything else. Once the light had faded I used to lie and watch the wonderful starlit sky of the western desert. The Scorpion coiled its huge length over the southern sky and the Great Bear and its lesser brother blazed in the north.

As night wore on the cold grew intense. Stand to in the grey dawn with life at its lowest ebb was a nightmare. Then the agony of shaving in cold water before the sun got up. How quickly it rose and with it came the flies – a little timid and lazy at first then fiercer, pestilential and determined as the sun blazed out with a blinding white heat. With the slow rising day came the breeze that sent the sand swirling about us again.

So far we had had no actual contact with the enemy although we had lost some men from bombing raids. Now began a series of attachments to an Australian battalion in the line, quickly followed by a spell of duty in the line itself as a preliminary to our taking part in the Battle of Alamein. The battle itself I am not going to dwell on for plenty has been said and written about it already.

On 4th November when the Africa Corps was racing westwards along the scarred coast road, we were wearied, unshaven, stiff and bruised from squatting for 10 days under heavy fire in narrow, jagged slit trenches. The noise of shelling was replaced by the unceasing and stimulating roar of 10th Corps transport launched in head to tail pursuit of Rommel. We were out of the main drive but followed on foot to El Daba, rounded up German prisoners beyond Tuka, marched for three days to Sidi Haneish, endured torrents of rain above the escarpments of Tuka, trickled slowly westwards to Acroma and then began a 500 mile drive to Agedabia. This was our first operational move in desert formation.

When deployed in such, the brigade of three battalion (ourselves, the 2nd Seaforths and 5th Camerons) covered an area of about two square miles – guns, three tonners, 15 cwts. wireless trucks all ploughing the sand like a gigantic convoy at sea. As darkness fell, the intervals between vehicles were shortened and the closing in developed into a mad rush for fear of getting lost and losing the one guiding light of the navigator's truck.

The desert seemed to be limitless, mile after mile of sandy shingle, flat and trackless and the monotony broken only by an occasional salt pan or a patch of scrub. During the heat of the day the inevitable mirage glimmers on the skyline and represents anything from a lake of blue water to a forest upside down. Desert formation – maybe five or six hundred vehicles in station moving on – each one blazing its own track and raising its own dust collectively making a noise utterly peculiar to itself. As one vehicle stops little figures appear, the sun glints on food tins and little columns of smoke appear beside each truck. Tea is made, bully is eaten. The figures disappear and the fires go out. As one the formation moves on. Dinner has been cooked and eaten and the time required is 30 minutes but by this time we were expert at living in the desert. The really skilled specialist can brew tea for a truckload in about 10 minutes and his home made Benghazi stove is a cherished article of equipment. Imagine a five gallon square petrol can with the top removed; imagine a lattice platform of wire half way down the inside; imagine a draught hole cut in the side near the bottom. A little petrol-soaked sand is the fuel. This is a Benghazi.

Night comes on and the formation has closed up. On we go as it is not good policy to be observed halting. The roar of engines, the billowing clouds of dust all seem to be intermingled. Speed is reduced and there is someone on each vehicle looking out for the ubiquitous slit trench. Finally a halt for the night. There is no thought of eating as fires are out of the question. All that remains to be done is to dig in, lay out defences and sleep. Alas! All too short as we have filled in our bedrooms for the night, embussed and moved on before first light. The first halt for the day is for breakfast and so it goes on. We found ourselves now facing the Axis forces at Mersa Brega, one of the most strongly defended wired and mined fortresses on the great coast road. A battle seemed imminent but the Axis flank was turned and they withdrew.

We spent a few days in the area among the sand dunes bordering the Mediterranean. I remember clearly how brilliant white the sand was here and how beautifully it contrasted with the deep blue of the sea. It was December now and the day temperature was about what we get in Scotland on an average summer day. There were periodic bursts of heavy rain, and curiously enough this did not drain away among the sand as one might expect. Often there were great stretches of what one might term sandy marsh land. All along the coast the sea seemed held back by undulating sand dunes not unlike those at the beach between Castletown and Dunnet. Behind these dunes the desert seemed to be often under sea level, hence the marshy effect. In the rainy season the desert becomes quite green superficially but, of course there was no thickness of vegetation – only a few shrubby growths at irregular intervals. Occasionally, near the sea there was an odd palm tree. Somehow it was great to find one and it would even induce the troops to go for a walk to see it for normally there was little incentive to take a walk in the desert as there were no landmarks to strike out for and no novelty further than nearer.

One day the C.O. came back from such a stroll with a cupful of mushrooms found among a heap of camel droppings at the seaside. Another day he came back with a flower whose botanical name I know not but which he said was generally called the desert rose. There was always some animal, flower and bird life, however scanty. A little beetle used to provide endless amusement by rolling over and over camel droppings about 10 times its own size. In a land of such scarcity I suppose it stored them up for a winter larder. One day we raised a hare. It looked like a cross between a hare and a rabbit. It was thin and couldn't run fast but its chase and capture provided the troops with an unaccustomed thrill.

There was an occasional desert fox, a red scraggy beast about half the size of our red fox. God knows how it made a living. I didn't see one myself but its appearance was reported once or twice. There was an occasional small tortoise, common now in pet shops. When found, someone invariably painted an H.D. on its scaly back and set it off on a propaganda tour. These and a few lizards satisfied the normal soldiers yearning for pets. Ah no! I have forgotten. Each company carried a few scraggy hens, begged, borrowed or stolen from the Bedouins. Some companies had quite a collection of them. They were normally housed in the cooks' truck. If they ever laid, it was kept a dark secret among the cooks. We saw few Bedouins. They wisely kept well off the army's beaten tracks.

At one or two places near the sea I saw an occasional strip among the sand that might, by a long stretch of imagination, be called ploughing. The resultant green crop would scarcely seem worth harvesting. The green stalks were many inches apart and only four of five inches high. Later in Tripolitania there were more wandering tribesmen. Occasionally a sheep of sorts would change hands with the troops for a pound of tea. At this time an ounce of tea seemed to have a monetary value of many shillings. As the exchange racket increased however, the Arabs became wise to the soldiers' prodigality and an egg became valued at about a tablespoonful of tea. Throughout the Highland Division, although we were well fed, a fresh egg was a great luxury and both races understood the familiar cry "Eggis for Shy". This was the nearest approach to trading in Arabic .

We spent Christmas Day on the borderland between Libya and Tripolitania among the sand dunes. Amazing what efforts were made to provide Christmas festivities. The NAAFI supplied pork, turkey and beer but how to set a Christmas table without tables and dishes of any kind? The table problem was solved by building a flat surface of sand and digging a trench all the way round to accommodate the sitters' feet. Petrol cans were cut up to provide serving dishes and the impromptu tables were garnished with desert shrubs garnished with cotton wool from the doctor's truck and ornamented with a gigantic Sans Peur cut in the sand and girt with white shells. And we had the pipes and little luxuries saved up from the rations for weeks ahead. Perhaps that Christmas dinner was more enjoyed than a more formal one arranged with less difficulty.

Two or three days after Christmas we moved to Ras El Ali. It was a broad sand beach separated from the main road two miles away by the sort of cliff we had learned to call an escarpment. The view from the rocky white road as it came over the escarpment showed a broken down jetty which had attracted round it, like a magnet, tank landing craft, battered R.A.S.C. trucks, and selection of Bofors guns and convoys of staff officers. We lived on the escarpment and unloaded supplies at the jetty. The soldiers had to work by shifts, sometimes stripped in the water, sometimes nauseated by fumes in the holds. We were soldiers but Montgomery had to have supplies if he were to reach Tripoli and an enemy raid had destroyed much of what he had accumulated at Benghazi.

Tripolitania fascinated the desert army much as the Promised Land must have fascinated the Children of Israel. It possessed all the glamour of the land of milk and honey. It was where the Intelligence summaries stated that eggs, date palms and tunny fishing flourished, where the pleasure steamers used to dally in peacetime. To get to Tripoli necessitated for us, another wild drive by day and night to reach the enemy and prevent him from taking up any organised defensive position.

By this time the country had changed radically. The shrubby growths were thicker, sometimes like long heather on a Scottish hillside. There were flowers, sometimes in profusion and, in the cool of the evening when we had time to notice, the air was sweet with the perfume of wild flowers that resembled night scented stock. But the most cheerful differences were the signs of human habitation. I remember what a thrill it gave me to pass a house in the moonlight with a dog barking about the steading and an open door flooding out a friendly human light. We drove till dawn and before our eyes lay fields of tall green asphodel, trim white villas, high water towers and small green trees. Scarcely two miles away stood Misurata gleaming white, romantic and seductive through the black olive trees. Next night we spent in empty Italian farm houses – the first house I had slept in for more than seven months. There was water in abundance although Mussolini's colonists had fled taking everything except the walls with them. We wandered through the houses, deliriously happy to be in some sort of human abode, sniffing the warm friendly smell of the empty stables and byres. Next night however, we were fighting a grim battle for Tripoli which cost the battalion some of its best in all ranks.

Wearily we watched by the roadside while other troops marched into the Tripoli we had dreamed of. When we eventually reached it ourselves, much of the anticipated glamour had vanished and anticlimax came fast. It was dirty. The wealthier citizens had gone taking their valuables with them. Only those who had nothing to lose remained. The 5th Seaforths company you saw in Churchill's march past with the caption "Style and Air" were unloading ships at the docks two hours later. Nights were disturbed by heavy bombing. Few of us were sorry to shake clear of the dust, faded splendour and hosts of dirty villainous looking "wogs" for a three days' march to the Mareth Line.

Here we spent five weeks moving from place to place as the tactical situation determined. The vegetation had changed again. We had left behind the irrigation area around Tripoli and were once more in desert country but with a difference. It was the desert spring now. There were flowers and greenery in profusion, occasionally charming in a sheltered spot but mostly churned and filmed with dust as the 8th Army prepared for its last great battle in North Africa. The Mareth was a vast succession of wadis. Generally a wadi is simply a crack in the general flatness of the desert in the dry season. At other times an occasional one was quite pleasant and with running water and shrub-covered banks, but mostly they were boggy, slime-encrusted, stagnant and infested with a most vicious species of midges.

In one of them we found a sort of small turtle, almost as if the land tortoise had accommodated itself to the wonder of water. The desert here was stony and full of cracks or wadis branching like little tributaries from the mains ones. At places, such as where the battle of Wadi Akarit was fought, the flatness disappeared and heights of considerable proportions appeared, cracked, scarred, rocky and barren like the plains below.

Early in May, when the Mareth fighting was almost over, we went by troop-carrying transport for three days by Kairouan, Sbitla, Kasserine and Setif to a small French village in Algiers called Cavallo. The scenery en route was magnificent and varied – endless, rolling, pastoral hills with numerous flocks of sheep, pine forests just like those of Scotland, grand, bold, rocky, mountains and rugged ravines with cool streams, traversed by narrow roadways hewn out of perpendicular rock. The lovely blue Mediterranean was flanked by cool vineyards and cork forests. You can imagine how we felt after the hundreds and hundreds of war strewn, desert miles we had covered.

We lived at Cavallo, perched high on a grassy ridge overlooking the sea. The funny but genial French farmer beside us was friendly and hospitable. His cattle and goats browsed daily among our bivvies. The sound of cattle plucking the fresh, green grass at five o'clock in the morning brought a pang of home-sickness to many. The sea, only 500 yards away was as good as it looked. Here we trained for the invasion of Sicily but life was pleasant. We bathed and swam. There was fresh fruit and plenty of common red wine of the country. There was some leave too. I went to Algiers for a couple of days. I remember little about it and didn't particularly enjoy my short stay. Much more vividly I remember a boar hunt. Some of us spent a whole day hunting for the wary boars which our French farmer friend assured us lurked in the wooded hills behind us. It was a pleasant day, but I saw no boars. The C.O. saw one, but the adjutant was in his line of fire. He nearly shot him in a combination of excitement and thwarted missed chance.

But all good things come to and end and soon we were thickly massed in disembarkation camps at Sousse waiting for the invasion of Sicily.

On the 5th of July, we sailed for Malta and, after a pleasant and uneventful voyage, landed at Valetta harbour next day. We moved inland to open fields where we lived and slept for three days beside the dry stone dykes that border nearly every field in Malta. The country people we saw were dark skinned and pleasant looking. The dry stone dykes everywhere testified to the struggle to wrest a living from the soil of Malta. I saw no bird life anywhere. We were told that the Maltese ate all birds however small, that they lured them to their guns by some strange whistling and that they stole incredible quantities of army ammunition to convert somehow into powder and shot for this humble purpose.

On the early morning of 10th July, we formed up in a rising wind and choppy sea for the invasion. Most of us had secretly dreaded this moment for weeks for at this time heavy resistance was expected but as we sailed in that great convoy towards the enemy shores our anxieties were mercifully dulled by the trifling discomfort of acute seasickness and the final anticlimax was as peaceful as many of our rehearsals on the shores of Algeria.

The fighting in Sicily lasted for 39 days. We were there for fully three months. Our first few days were too busy to notice much. We came up against the Herman Goering paratroopers at Francoforte and had heavy losses. A week after we landed, we found ourselves in a typical Sicilian farm surrounded by barley fields ready for harvesting. Someone thoughtlessly lit a fire among the barley and a light breeze fanned it into an enormous blaze. All our efforts were needed to save the fire engulfing our vehicles. This was our first experience of such fires but, in spite of this warning, we lost a motor cycle a few days later. Perforce we had to abandon our methods of camouflaging our vehicles by heaping sheaves of barley around them. Intermittent shelling continually started fires among the barley, devastating large areas and leaving smouldering piles of straw burning day and night. Smoke from these fires combined with a dust-clouded atmosphere and a scorching sun, caused us acute discomfort and a burning thirst. Unlike the desert however, there was no lack of water when movement was possible, for every farm had its own large, circular, sunken well where the water was cool and refreshing, if of doubtful purity. Once it was transferred to our water bottles it became so hot that even the most avid thirst was somewhat daunted.

The scorching heat and constant fires remain my strongest impression at this time – that and the dust. Everywhere in Sicily there is dust – powdery, sooty dust that films everything. It is only to be expected in a country that is said to owe its birth to a volcano. The volcano dominates the island from shore to shore. Many of us climbed it later. I went with a party that climbed all through the night to stand on the brink of the crater as the sun rose. I would hate to climb it by day. The last few hundred yards were utterly exhausting and the suffocating smell of sulphur was most unpleasant. Once our eyes had become accustomed to the fumes, we peered into the great pit below us. The big crater is not a bottomless pit penetrating into the bowels of the earth as some of us had expected. It was however, a good 300 or 400 feet deep with a diameter of at least 400 yards and the angry looking puffs of white smoke springing at irregular intervals all round its sides, makes its appearance far from inviting. The active crater which is much smaller and which is just over the northern ledge of the big one, was out of view but its position was unmistakably marked by dense volumes of sulphur smoke rising into the sky.

I should have mentioned the cactus hedges before I left Africa, for it is perhaps the most characteristic plant of Tunisia and Algeria as well as Sicily. Everyone has seen the little cactus plants where each fat, fleshy leaf seems to have been glued by a lunatic on to its neighbour. Well, the Mediterranean variety is its larger brother. It surely makes the ugliest hedge ever known and perhaps the most effective. It is about the height of an ordinary cattle fence and of a tired green colour wherever the green shows through the dust. Its equally ugly yellow flowers mysteriously appear at the side of its bulbous leaves and later they develop into what is commonly called a prickly pear. Its name suggests everything there is to know about it, except that the seeds are harder than a date palm. These and its prickly skin, handicap an otherwise delectable fruit. In the poor quarters, native vendors peel and offer them for sale on the streets and at this time they seemed the main item of diet with many.

Once we moved north from the dusty, sun-scorched plain of Catania, we entered a country almost entirely devoted to vineyards. I can remember with what wild abandon we ate the grapes at first and some continued to eat them for weeks in spite of the ravages of gippy tummy, for they were filmed with dust and the filth of flies. Every available inch of space in places were plastered with vines. We were obliged to pitch our bivouacs in the vineyards. It sounds marvellous to reach up for a cluster of delicious black grapes as you lie in bed. We could do this almost anywhere but there were disadvantages too, for the dust beneath them permeated everything like the finest of coal dust and as greasy.

We spent our last six weeks in Sicily in a little town near Biancavilla in the north. The little town was most unattractive. Many of the people were half starved and in rags. Once the troops good-natured generosity became known, our areas were infested with beggars of all kinds. The one main street stank from end to end. There seemed to be no sanitary conveniences whatever. Lanes leading off the main streets were used as public lavatories and dumping places for every form of filth. This was common everywhere in Sicily even in the larger towns. The people generally took great pride in keeping their own houses clean but no corporate spirit existed and municipal sanitation was completely lacking.

The grape harvest was now in full swing, grapes of every variety and hue – red, blue, purple and green. From dawn to sunset, barefooted women worked in the fields, trooping in succession to and from the wine presses, erect of carriage with continual carrying of heavy baskets on their heads. Their dark skin and jet black hair contrasted with the gaiety of their brightly coloured and spotlessly laundered dresses. They were generally shy, even to the extent of avoiding our approach by taking another route, very different from their good-natured and somewhat garrulous menfolk. The latter took no hand in gathering the harvest but they trampled the grapes in the less than hygienic presses. This idea may sound somewhat nauseating but some of our own small bakeries once had somewhat the same method. Only it seems the Sicilian peasant saw no need to wash his feet at reasonable intervals for his swarthy legs had tide marks of bright crimson deepening to the dark purple of the previous week's immersions. Should a wayward sheep or goat claim his attention, his journey might lead through half a dozen manure heaps straight to the vat again. Certainly our taste for vino was not what it had been.

One day General Monty visited us. The whole brigade paraded to hear his words. He had said he would never leave the H.D. behind and he had meant it. He had decided not to use us at the start of the Italian campaign. Where should he send us now. Maybe to the Far East (suppressed groans). Maybe to England, even Scotland. Yes, he was sending the H.D. back home, once arrangements could be made. Our wild dreams had come true. We were going home.

It is difficult to describe the reaction. Not even the casual mention of further operations directed from Britain could still our wild applause. How we cheered him! Never was applause more real or more heartfelt. To see Scotland again. To know that the fate that had left hundreds of our friends dead in foreign lands had passed us by, and, whatever her final decision, she was to let us see our homes and our families once again!

George H. Green.

DUNCANSBY HEAD

Come stand on Scotland's farthest edge
To view the scene with me,
In the teeth of a gale, when the wild waves flail
Crashing mercilessly.
Watch the surging tide on every side
Feel the sting of the salty spray
And remember the lives of the men it has claimed
When you stand on Duncansby.

Come stand again on a summer's morn
When the sea is a shimmer at dawn
Watch the lapping waves round the darkened caves
'Neath the cliffs glowing russet and warm.

From their ledges high the fledglings fly
Or perch precariously
While their guardian parents screech and swoop
As you stand on Duncansby.

Come stand upon this rugged land
View the panoramic scene,
From John O'Groats to the Orkney coast
With Stroma – Isle in the stream.
'Gainst the western sky Dunnet Head stands high.
Far beyond Loyal's peaks rise grey
No better vantage point you'll find
Than to stand on Duncansby.

Elsie Cowe, The Ha, John O'Groats.

THE PARISH IN 18th AND 19th CENTURIES

Occupying as it does the north-east corner of the county of Caithness the Parish of Canisbay can boast a unique location. Its form is roughly triangular though its coastline is warped by many a cape and bay. The northern coast picturesquely faces the Orkney Islands with beyond them the cold Arctic climes and, in consequence, is unceasingly pounded by the wild waters of the Pentland Firth. The eastern coast lies fully open to the fierce storms of the North Sea towards which it presents a strong bulwark. To the south-west Canisbay borders with the parishes of Wick, Bower and Dunnet and this wavy parish boundary completes the third side of the triangle. About two miles off the northern shore lies the tight little island of Stroma, sadly now no longer inhabited, but part of the parish none the less. Geographically then, the Parish of Canisbay is one of the most exposed parts of mainland Scotland but we like to think that within these rugged shores there dwelt, and dwells, a kindly, alert, intelligent people whose physical and mental characteristics have been moulded by their environment and who in turn have battled with their rather unfavourable situation to keep their parish abreast of the times. Since the parish has never had any of the mineral resources which brought the Industrial Revolution to the Central Lowlands of Scotland, throughout the 18th and 19th centuries the people had to depend mainly on agriculture supplemented by fishing for a livelihood.

At the beginning of the 18th century agriculture in Caithness, as in the rest of Scotland, was on a feudal basis and the tenants held their strips of land in the runrig or rig and rennal system. With the exception of the lands of the Brabster Estate, the cultivated land lay, as indeed it does yet, round the coast in blocks of varying size, enlarged from time to time by the addition of outbreaks or patches of moorland broken in by the tenants. These lands were divided among the tenants in octos, farthinglands, half-pennylands and pennylands; one octo being equal to one and a half acres, two octos equalling one farthingland, two farthinglands equalling one half-pennyland and two half-pennylands equalling one pennyland. These measurements of land continued till the time of the Old Statistical Account in the last decade of the 18th century but would seem to have passed out of use soon after that.

The tenants rented from the landlords so many octos, farthinglands, half-pennylands or pennylands as the case might be. Unlike those in the rest of Scotland the tenants of the Sinclairs of Mey, Freswick and Brabster, who were the three landlords in the parish of Canisbay, held their lands directly from the laird and not through a tacksman. Moreover these tenants differed from those in the rest of Scotland in that they did not work their crofts communally, each crofter having his own plough team. Since, according to the rentals of the estates, the average size of the crofts in the parish would be about six acres it would hardly seem possible for each croft to support a plough team. However it is believed that the tenants held more land than that for which the rent was actually paid. For example John Brand writing in 1700 tells us that only arable land was accounted for and Robert Maxwell of Arkland writes, "Indeed if the tenants had not as much land besides their arable as is sufficient to pay their rent they would never be able to carry on their husbandry in the way they do." Taking these statements into consideration it is possible that most of the crofters were able to keep their own plough teams. Those who did not were able to work in partnership with a neighbour or were able to hire an ox from the laird to tide them over the busy season. No doubt there was some communal work in the parish at this time but it was certainly not carried on to the extent to which it was practised further south.

With regard to conditions of tenure at this time, the rent was paid mostly in victual (grain) and services, and to a lesser extent in money. In the victual line the largest part of the rent was paid in bere; bere-firm, miln multure, the yule bannock, the halk hen, the meat goose, and the meat lamb comprised the rest of the victual rent. Then, one of the laird's cattle had to be wintered and some people had to pay peats to the smiddy. All this was rounded off by the payment of horn tows, hair sithrops, fathoms of simmons, winlins of straw, and eggs of which each tenant paid two dozen. As for services, Sir James Sinclair of Mey, writing to his legal agent in Edinburgh stated, ". . . . . and you will observe that the services of the tenants of this country are not defined, but in the will of the possessor to call them when he pleases, and if he pleases, call the whole family every day of the week and oblige them to do any work he thinks proper at the time." If this right of the proprietor had been rigidly exercised, it coupled with the rents, would have imposed a crippling burden on the people of the parish. It is obvious however from the state of agriculture at this time that the tenants did not find the system too onerous. Indeed it was not till payments in kind had been converted into money that the tenants found themselves hard put to make ends meet. Most sources seem agreed that during the 18th century Canisbay was comparatively prosperous and did not feel the pinch of hunger to anything like the extent to which it was felt in the rest of Scotland at periodic intervals. We are told that it abounded in good beef, mutton and fowl. Significantly, in a tavern, no money was asked for victuals consumed: only what one drank was put on the account. It is probably worth mention that the parish and Caithness as a whole had a reputation as a grain producing country. Concentration was laid on the cultivation of the bere crop and it received all the manure of the croft as well as the sea ware and shell sand used as a supplement. After the bere a crop of oats was raised without giving the land any further fertiliser. The sole rotation seemed to have been bere, oats, lea with the bere always getting the manure and the oat crop grown on the principle, "I have planted, Apollos watered, but God gave the increase." Backward though this system may seem the results were quite good, in fact they were good judged by the standards of the day, drawing favourable comment from many writers of the time. John Brand, for example, in his "Brief Description of Orkney, Shetland and the Pentland Firth" says, ". . . . . the land is very fertile exporting much grain and stock, grain being from three to five shillings a boll, while good cattle sell at three or four shillings. This is the cheapest market in the world; a thousand merks here being worth more than four thousand in the south."

The plough in common use in Caithness at this time was the old thrapple plough of wooden construction which required four horses and perhaps two oxen to pull it and three men to handle it. In Canisbay however, owing to the constant application of ware and shell sand, the earth was so loose that a lighter plough for two horses could be used. At the beginning of the century many crofters did not use a plough at all and in the year 1724 there was not a single plough in the island of Stroma where all cultivation was done by the spade. Other implements on the farm were few and those that existed were very simple; a pair of wooden harrows and a "huik" for mowing the crops often formed the sum total of a Canisbay crofter's farm implements. As for transport, carts at this time being non existent, recourse had to be made to pack horses when bulky items required conveyance. One such regular, if seasonal, trade was the transport of grain from the parish to Staxigoe whence it was exported from the county. The grain was carried in crubbans or panniers hung from wooden clibbers or saddles across the backs of the horses. For loads not needing a horse's strength the folk became their own beasts of burden using a home-made back pack – a keysie. There are as many spellings of it as there are people who know the meaning of the word. As the main human means of porterage it was often used along with the crubbans to carry the manure to the rigs.

Such, then, was the state of agriculture in Canisbay Parish at the beginning of the 18th century and so it existed without much change till the middle of the century when the improving movement started.

The "Improving Movement", though it began about the middle of the 18th century and continued right through to the end of the 19th century and beyond, made little progress at first and it was not till the time of the Old Statistical Account in the 1790s that the movement really got into its stride. The rise in the price of produce between the years 1750 and 1790 and the much quicker rise between the years 1790 and 1798 bear this out. Scrutiny of relative prices for the years in question show that prices rose about eight times as quickly over the eight years from 1790 to 1798 as they had done in the preceding 40 years between 1750 and 1790, indicating a much slower rate of development in the earlier period. The reason for this apparent sluggishness in the agricultural scene probably lay in the fact that although improvements were introduced it took some time for them to gain impetus. For example potatoes were introduced in 1754 but for a long time they were grown only as a garden crop on the policies of the lairds. When the tenantry did begin to grow them about the 1840's, they planted only a few of them in lazy-bed fashion. The underlying reason for this was the perceived importance of grain, and to a certain extent straw, in the parish. The crofters did not want to plant large areas with potatoes for fear of losing these two basic products. The result was that the 19th century had well begun before potatoes were planted to anything like the extent their value merited. When dug up the potatoes were kept over winter in "pits" of straw covered with turves and earth to protect them from the frost. This is seldom done now though there are still plenty of people around who will remember the tattie lifting and storing as a labour intensive exercise. Turnips when introduced in the 1780s were not widely grown but by the end of the century they were a general crop.

In many ways though the parish was still backward. In 1769 there were neither barns nor granaries. The corn or bere was thrashed outside and preserved in chaff bikes thatched round with straw. The first really satisfactory cart did not appear till 1780. Servants wages were lower in Caithness than in the rest of Scotland – about mid century Sir John Sinclair of Mey paid his men servants 25 shillings per year. By 1775 annual wages had risen to 30 shillings. This was little enough but such was the cost of living and the frugality of the servants that many managed to save out of their wages enough to start them up in a croft of their own after they had been working for some years. When a young man wanted to follow this road he went out "thigging"; that is, he took a big bag and went round all the more prosperous, and generous, farmers who would give him some grain for his first sowing.

Throughout the most of the 18th century servants and services existed side by side on the Canisbay estates but towards the end of the century nearly all the services had been commuted into money payments – only two days being exacted in the spring and harvest. This proved to be a doubtful blessing to the people, for hitherto the services, though they seem burdensome to us today, were taken as matter of course. Crofters could always find time to do a day's work: finding money for rent could prove more difficult. Their services were converted into money at the current rate of wages and as wages rose the tenants found it harder and harder to meet the cost. To make matters worse, they had an increasing money rent to pay as well. To quote two examples; two tenants in Harrow, Mey, paid in 1786 16 shillings and sixpence, and one pound two shillings and sixpence respectively while their respective service money was eight shillings and four pence; and 13 shillings and fourpence. Their victual had remained the same but the price of it had increased and so the landlord had benefited more than the tenants.

Though it may seem that it was the landowners who took most advantage from the advancing state of agriculture the people also were undoubtedly better off. The Reverend John Morison writing in the First Statistical Account in 1793 attributes the increase in the population of the parish from **1480** in 1775 to **1950** in 1793 to the advancement of civilisation, the free enjoyment of property, (the tenants certainly felt free-born citizens when the services were done away with), better cultivation and the multiplicity of small farms, and the extensive employment in fishing.

As yet, however, although the proprietors were beginning to use implements and to enclose their land and to cultivate green crops, the common people had not adopted the more liberal scale of agriculture. No leases had been granted and this certainly militated against the progress of the improving movement. Bere and oats with a little flax and potatoes were still the sole objects of cultivation while the bere still received all the manure. The chief manure was still sea ware though the crofters now made better use of it by mixing it with earth and allowing it to stand for six to 12 months to decompose before applying it to the land. This, along with the widely used shell sand, made the earth very free with the result that the light plough was now universally used. Dung was the only other fertiliser used and it was thought it gave best results when mixed with peat mould before being applied to the soil. This was said to be three times as good as ordinary dung and was especially good if allowed to stand over the winter.

This husbandry raised good crops as witness the fact that on average five returns were achieved from oats and seven from bere, while on occasions as high as 11 returns of bere were gathered. Taking into consideration the farming methods then practised these returns were very good and enabled the parish to export annually from 1200 to 1500 bolls of victual (grain).

Oats were begun to be sown about the first week of April and bere was sown from the 12th of May to 21st of June. Grey and black oats were better thought of than white oats; partly because they were better suited to the climate and partly because they could flourish on less rich soil and did not leave the patch where they were grown as impoverished of its nutrients. The harvest began about the beginning of September and was generally finished in the course of a month, after which great merrymaking took place.

As a result of the all importance of the grain crop Canisbay was not a cattle parish. Apart from bog, and such land as it would not be remunerative to cultivate, little ground was left for pasture and the parish reared only about one third of the cattle and horses used in cultivation. An interesting trade developed between John O'Groats, Huna and South Ronaldsay as an outfall of this. Young, immature horses were shipped over the Firth to where the pasture and feeding was good and returned when they had reached adulthood and were ready for work. Interestingly too, the Ha, a much bigger farm then, had the reputation of being the one really good "dairy" farm in the parish, capable of supporting 30 cows and famous throughout the county for its butter and cheese.

Sheep also were neglected. When the First (Old) Statistical Account was written there were 2000 in the parish. Poor pasture, dogs and foxes had cut down the number to one third of what it had been formerly. The "Rockies" though, still ranged the cliffs up at The Stacks and their place in the economy of the local crofters is well put elsewhere in the book. Pigs however were plentiful and nearly every croft had one along with a flock of geese and of hens.

The size of the crofts had not changed much during the 18th century and at the end of it the average croft rented about nine pounds at 21 to 30 shillings an acre. There were few large farms apart from those of the landowners which were valued at a hundred pounds yearly rent.

In the 50 years of so between the First (Old) and Second (New) Statistical Accounts, roughly between 1790 and 1840, we are told that the general aspect of the parish did not change much. However by 1840 the lairds, of whom Sinclair of Brabster was the only one permanently resident in the Parish, had instituted many improvements on their farms. By 1812 they had introduced iron ploughs, rollers, harrows, threshing machines, turnip sowers, wheelbarrows, grapes (four tined forks), and mattocks. Also, they now worked a five year rotation of turnips, bere with grass seeds, hay, pasture, and oats. They were now tending to sow and reap their crops earlier and this was conducive to a better yield. The grain however was still measured by volume, as weighing machines had not reached the scene. The livestock also had been upgraded. Larger horses were brought in for the iron ploughs, Galloway cattle were stocked and

crossed with the local breed to improve them as hitherto they had never been thought much of in the south. Highland cattle too were put on the rough pastures which were being enclosed. Cheviot sheep were largely replacing the native horned breed.

Prices had all risen; bere which before 1800 seldom cost more than 13 shillings and fourpence per boll of 134 pounds, at the end of the first decade of the 19th century, varied from 16 to 30 shillings a boll and in 1808 after a bad year it was as high as 40 shillings a boll. Other necessities had become dearer also – for example a pair of boots and a suit of clothes, made in 1770 by the itinerant shoemaker and tailor, together cost 10 shillings but by 1812 a pair of boots to follow the plough, alone cost 25 shillings. The travelling tailor and shoemaker disappeared soon after 1770 as did the practice of home making "rillings" for use instead of boots at ploughing time. Rillings were pieces of untanned hide, cut to fit the foot and bound on, hair inside, with thongs of the same material. They are said to have been very comfortable and lasted a season.

Annual wages had also risen from about 25 or 30 shillings in 1770 to six or seven pounds in the second decade of the 19th century. Lads got from 40 to 50 shillings plus three bolls meal cost and women got 20 to 24 shillings plus two bolls meal cost. The rate for day labourers was one shilling and sixpence for men and one shilling for women. This was the state of labour at the time of the Second (New) Statistical Account.

Although the lairds had improved the husbandry on their own farms the state of agriculture among the peasantry did not change much in the years between the two Accounts. In 1843 not more than 10 per cent of the parish was cultivated. Bere, oats and potatoes were still the only crops and they were still grown in the same way. Moreover there was still no improvement in the stock on the crofts.

It was in reality the lairds who were the cause of this backwardness – though they improved their own lands they gave little encouragement to improvements among the tenantry. They seldom granted leases and still sustained the rig and rennal system with the result that, though the occupants of the crofts saw the advantages of turnips and grasses, the practice of turning loose the animals after the harvest deterred them from growing these crops. The undivided state of the commons was an inhibiting consideration for anyone who might wish to break in an extra piece of land, as everyone sent their animals to the common pasture in the spring and autumn. But brighter times lay ahead as the Earl of Caithness instituted a scheme for the division of all the common in the parish. For the moment however the country folk were as badly off as they had ever been. The rent of arable land was high, around two pounds per acre. On top of this the victual rent had recently been changed into money at a rate of one pound per boll of victual (grain). This was really equivalent to an increase in rent for the tenants seldom got more than 12 to 18 shillings for their victual, at the market. And so this state of affairs might be summed up by saying: "The landlords had progressed, the rents had risen, but the tenants, at least in the short term, got little out of progress apart from their pride as freemen."

In the 20 years following this however the parish made rapid progress. Leases were granted, run-rig (rig and rennel) and all its attendant evils were abolished, and the new five year rotation was adopted by the crofters. The appearance of the parish changed completely. Draining and enclosing went on apace. The fields were usually enclosed by whin or hawthorn hedges backed by flagstone or drystone dykes which afforded some shelter from the all too prevalent Caithness winds. Along the hedges there usually ran a ditch for draining the field and vestiges of this hedge and ditch system can still be seen in some parts of the parish. From this time forward, despite its disadvantages of climate and remoteness, the parish succeeded in keeping itself abreast of the times. The crofters, now that they had been granted the security of leases, saw that it was worth their while to carry out improvements and brought their natural shrewdness and intelligence into play in an attempt to better their lot. They became most quick to perceive and avail themselves of the advantages of the most improved agricultural implements so that by 1887 it was the exception to find a farm of any size that had not its reaping machine and threshing mill – the shearing hook and flail having been done away with on all but the smaller crofts.

The Crofters' Act of 1886 proved a great benefit. With security of tenure, fair rents, and compensation for improvements a large number of previously high-rented crofters set energetically about making changes on their holdings and homes and by the end of the century signs of improvement were obvious. Great attention was paid to the breed and rearing of stock. The super importance of the grain crop had passed away and now, though it still remained an important factor in Caithness husbandry, cattle and sheep from the parish could fetch high prices at the local markets and further south. By the end of the century the condition of servants, though they would have our sympathy today, had also improved and their number had increased with the increased size of the crofts. Now they got better wages, food and housing, while the formation of the Farm Servants' Benefit Society raised the social condition of the farm servants as a class by means of a periodic payment by the members as a source of income in sickness, want and old age.

Though agriculture in Canisbay, and Caithness as a whole, made great strides in the last 40 years of the 19th century the climate did not suit the parish to any particular branch of husbandry and farming remained mixed. Lack of capital and accessible markets may have prevented ventures like dairying and poultry keeping from developing commensurably with other branches of agriculture. Lack of capital was by no means peculiar to the farming scene in Caithness. It was part of the rural distress prevalent throughout Scotland in the closing years of the 19th century. Such was the severity of the problem that tenants entering crofts often did so at a reduced rent; while in 1887, the striken crofters lodged an application with the Crofters' Commission for reduced rents. On top of this, larger crofts meant fewer crofts being available for tenancy and many Canisbay sons and daughters had to go south to seek employment. Those who remained at home always had to work hard to take a living from the soil.

Such then was the state of agriculture in Canisbay Parish at the end of the 19th century, and as its soil has been the main provider for most of our families it is their story too. Before we leave the land to look at that other great provider we need to remember that though life could be hard and hunger might stalk sometimes, Canisbay Parish never denied her children warmth. The peat harvest was as important a part of the annual calendar as the sowing and the reaping and when the peat stack was built the family knew they need have no worry about the fuel bill.

Apart from agriculture the only other major occupation of the people in the parish was fishing and this was never a full time job from the Canisbay shore, even in Stroma. It was always prosecuted along with crofting. It was none the less very important as it helped many of our folk to make a tolerable living, who would have found it hard to take all their sustenance from the soil alone.

The early writers make comparatively little mention of fishing but we do know that by the beginning of the 18th century there were no piers or landing places constructed in the parish and that fishers had to put to sea from the beach and manhandle their boats back up on the beach when they came ashore again. At Mey there was "a tolerable haven where ships on occasion could be loaded." The haven at Mey was important as affording shelter for the grain ships which came north periodically to take away this one export of the parish. Stroma, lying right in the track of the merciless Pentland currents and being particularly dependent on the sea for its food and livelihood, had no ports but there were two places where boats could be hauled up on the beach. The best haven was on the south side of the island but even it was dangerous in the calmest of weather. Today even those of us from island and seafaring stock find it difficult to imagine how the 150 inhabitants of Stroma contrived to live under such conditions. Many a stormy day they must have wondered where their next meal was to come from. They present to us an admirable lesson in self sufficiency and tenacity in the face of adversity. Stroma was fertile enough but as if fate felt that it had provided for them too well, surrounding them with bounteous seas and rich soil, it decided that it must add to the travail of their lives by giving them no peat moss. We can try to imagine the effort involved in securing a fire of peats on the mainland and after that transporting it to Stroma and thence home to the croft. These hardy folk survived however and remained in the island till the second half of the 20th century a strong, daring group of expert mariners. For the whole of the 18th and the greater part of the 19th centuries they crossed the Firth to church in Canisbay every Sunday that the weather was favourable. Their faith must have sustained them well! They were the tenants of the Sinclairs of Freswick to whom they paid in the first quarter of the 18th century 1300 merks in money and victual.

To return to the mainland; right round the coast of Canisbay there could be found shingly or sandy beaches with fishing boats drawn up on them. At this time John O'Groats was particularly important as it was from here that the ferry operated to Burwick in the Orkney island of South Ronaldsay. In 1725 the freight was 40 pence, but to hire a boat for a crossing cost double this amount, or four pounds Scots. It is round the first ferryman that the legend of John O'Groats House is centred.

The sea-faring state of the parish had changed little in the ages before the First Statistical Account. All crofters, except those from inland districts like Brabster, engaged in the fishing to a greater or lesser extent and there were about 60 boats in the parish. Boats were owned communally between two or three families and the fish caught were divided according to the shares held in the boat. The fishing was prosecuted on a subsistence basis which is to say that the sole object of the fishing was to provide food for the families engaged and it was a thing unknown – for a man to SELL fish to his neighbour. By this time however a few boats at Mey were beginning to fish lobsters "for the behoof of Messrs Selby & Co. of London" and Morison tells us that "the bays of Mey, Gills and Duncansby abound in lobsters to a great degree." How the times have changed! The aforesaid notwithstanding, the main fish caught were cod and ling, though inshore and off the rocks sellags and cuddens, young saithe or coal-fish, were caught in abundance. It was not to be long before fishmongers began to buy and retail fish.

When he contributed to the First Statistical Account the Rev John Morison tells us that the ferry to South Ronaldsay had been transferred from John O'Groats to Huna whence it operated once a week carrying the mails to Orkney. To cross with the mail boat cost one shilling but it cost seven shillings to hire the boat. The cost of shipping stock in a larger boat was one shilling for a colt and one shilling and eightpence for a grown horse. Previous mention has been made of the transport of horses to and fro across the Firth.

When the New Statistical Account was written by the Rev. Peter Jolly in 1840 the character of the fishing industry had changed. It was no longer on a subsistence basis, though much fishing for the household still continued; as it did throughout the century. It was now prosecuted with a view to taking more money into the households and into the parish. The transition was gradual but by the 1840s several boats were employed in fishing lobsters for the London market and at three pence per lobster this brought about 50 pounds into the

parish every year. In addition to this there were about 30 boats of 10 tons each engaged in the herring fishing. They left for Wick and the neighbouring fishing stations in July and operated from there till the end of the season. They sold their catches to the various curers and the average annual income to each crew of five was from £50 to £60. Despite the large number of boats in the parish the fishers were still without a harbour.

While this transition was taking place in the fishing industry the sailings of the ferry between Huna and South Ronaldsay were increased, first, to three times a week and later to six times. By 1812 it cost nine shillings by ferry and the freight on cattle was 11 shillings per head. Despite the treacherous currents and violent storms of the Pentland Firth few accidents happened while crossing it and no greater tribute can be paid to the ferrymen than to quote the fact that though the ferry had been operating for over a century only one boat had been lost by 1843.

Fishing continued to develop along the above lines after the New Statistical Account had been published. Lobster fishing gradually became more and more important and the herring fishing continued to flourish. About 20 years before the end of the century however the herring fishing began to decline and by the beginning of the present century few people from Canisbay Parish were involved in it. The wider scale of agriculture absorbed people's energies that previously had gone on fishing, both herring and line. In Stroma though, the cod fishing remained an important part of the economy for many years yet. That said, by 1900 though fishing was a useful supplementary source of food and income it was not the essential factor in the life of the Canisbay crofter that it had been 50 years before.

It may seem something of a paradox that the decline of the fishing should coincide with a decline in the population of the parish due to a southward drift but when we remember that the fishing by itself had rarely been sufficient to support a family, we can understand how people had to go south to earn a living.

Throughout the ages fishing was a hazardous business and though Canisbay seamen were among the most skilful in the country many a life was lost in the thundering waves of the Boars of Duncansby and the Men o' Mey. And along the rugged coast one heard all too often:

> "The noise of seaward storm that mocks,
> With roaring laughter from reverberate rocks,
> The cry of ships near shipwreck."

The good people of Canisbay, however, always accepted such calamities stoically. Indeed a shipwreck was looked upon as a god-send in the more barbarous days of the 18th and 19th centuries for it offered a chance of plunder not to be missed. As minister of this sea-girt parish John Morison could not condone such on-goings but it is surely not without significance that he chose a vivid and appropriate maritime picture to illustrate the second verse of his 30th paraphrase:–

His voice commands the tempest forth
and stills the stormy wave;
And though his arm be strong to smite
'tis also strong to save.

As early as 1794 he was one of those who recognised that the number of shipwrecks on the shores of the Pentland Firth would justify the building of a lighthouse somewhere at the eastern and more dangerous entrance to this hazardous waterway – "Hell's Mouth", as the seafarers called it in the sailing ship days. It was not long after this, around 1801, that a light or rather two lights were provided on the Pentland Skerry but it was 1899 before a really adequate light shone out from Stroma and the 1914/18 War had ended before Duncansby Head got its light. It is worth mention that it was with the erection of the lighthouse that Stroma got its first pier, a construction 170 feet in length costing £800, towards which the government gave a grant of £600. Stroma now received its mails once a week from Huna on whichever day was suitable for crossing.

Many of the Canisbay people regarded the building of lighthouses with considerable disfavour and the following story is told which might typify at least some attitudes. – One of the Stevensons of lighthouse building fame had on one occasion to hire a local boat on an errand of coastal inspection. As they sailed along Mr Stevenson said to the boatman in a tone of sympathy and interest, "Your sails are pretty ragged and tattered. You must have a rough time of it."

To which the reply came, "Yea 'at o' 'id! If hid hed been Goad's wull 'at 'ee hedna beelt sae mony lichthooses, a wid hev gotten new sails last wunter an' a lock else besides."

Apart from fishing and the plunder of shipwrecks the sea from time to time has provided the parish with various subsidiary sources of income. Up to the middle of the 18th century smuggling formed a lucrative by-employment to many of the fishers, especially those of Stroma. In the 1840s however, better organisation of the Customs and Excise curtailed this though they never managed to stamp it out.

Then of course the Pilots of the Pentland Firth have a history all of their own which lasted from the dawn of shipping in the Firth well through the days of steam. Many of the fishermen were pilots too and got ample trade from captains who feared to undertake the treacherous passage without a guide. There were dangers here for pilots, who might be shanghaid by unscrupulous masters or carried abroad because the weather turned too stormy for them to be transferred back to their own boats.

Kelp too provided employment and income and up to 1790 the parish produced 100 tons of kelp annually which was more than double that produced by the rest of Caithness. The restless sea cast up more than shipwrecks. Apart from the kelp, we have mentioned earlier the ware for the land, and, when the storms blew huge waves washed fish on to the beach where the people collected them.

It is justly reckoned that it was the sea which enabled many of the parishioners to save themselves from the indignity of accepting "Poor Relief". The number of persons getting Poor Relief was never high and the result was that not much attention was paid to the organisation of Poor Rates. There is no reference to the state of Poor Relief before the First Statistical Account. In 1794 Morison says that though there were many poor people in the parish there were no strolling beggars and throughout the 11 years that he had been in the parish he had been asked for only about half a dozen certificates for indigence. Ten or 12 pounds were distributed annually among the poor from the Session Fund. Reference to prosperity in the parish before this seems to imply that at no time in the 18th century would there have been need for a larger poor fund.

When the Second Statistical Account was written however, the number of persons in receipt of parochial aid had increased to 90. This increase in the number of poor can be directly connected with the rising rents and other agricultural developments mentioned above. The Parochial Fund now totalled £38 and consisted of church collections averaging £14 yearly plus the interest from several legacies. From this the poor received, every year, from six to 10 shillings each. As yet there were no Poor Rates.

By the end of the century there was little change in the situation. Only a very small proportion of the Parish were in receipt of Poor Relief and the Parish was without public institutions or Poor Houses of any sort. Throughout the two centuries, then, the majority of the people managed to keep body and soul together and to maintain a home without external assistance.

The homestead was always of simple construction and by the end of our period usually consisted of no more than "A but, a ben and a closet". Throughout the 18th century the houses were built of turf and stone with a divot roof. They were usually divided into two apartments, the fire-house or kitchen, and the cellar or better room. The fire-house, as the name suggests, was the place where the cooking was done on a fire in the middle of the floor and it was here also that the inmates took their food and here that the housewife went through her daily duties and probably where the parent couple slept. The cellar on the other hand, had no fire and apart from the fact that it was slept in, it was seldom used. The byre was also part of the main dwelling, the cattle entering by the house door. When in the byre, the cattle were separated from the people only by vertical flagstone or two overhung from the roof by a crude partition of straw mat, a stray fleet. The barn and the kiln were usually at the upper end of the house, while the midden was at the front and the kail-yard, well supplied with cabbages but little else, was at the back. Some people who were a little better off than the general run had an additional room – the chaumer – probably used only on special occasions.

The furniture was the same as that used in

crofting districts in the rest of Scotland at this time, but it is interesting to note that a piece of bogwood, lit and stuck in a hole in the floor, was used when a light was needed in addition to that given by the fire – cheaper and more readily available than candles or a goose-neb lamp!

The food of the parish in the 18th century was essentially simple though as a rule there was no shortage. Indeed the population figures show that the parish did not suffer from the famines that were so prevalent in Scotland at the beginning of the century. Naturally, round the coast much fish was consumed. Meat however, apart from pork, was rare, though most families killed a pig in the back end of the year, to tide them over the winter. Before the introduction of potatoes in 1754, breakfast consisted of brose or porridge, dinner of cabbage boiled with oatmeal while supper was bere bread and brochan.

As regards dress during this period home-spun woollens were worn by all. Men wore coats, vests and breeches of black or hodden grey with wooden buttons or "knobbies". On Sunday they wore finer manky, generally dyed blue. Women wore drugget gowns and since silk and straw hats were unknown, the younger women went to kirk bare headed with only a narrow strip of ribbon round the brow and a kepping-comb at the back of the head. The headgear of a married woman was a plain toy-mutch while a matron in full dress wore a box-pleat mutch or cap puffed out at the top and encircled with a flashy ribbon. Elderly women wore scarlet plaids over short blue gowns with red sleeves. The chief finery of the female sex was a string of glass beads.

By the end of the 18th century domestic life was beginning to change. In the first place the construction of the cottages was improving; they were built more solidly of stone and thatching with straw was becoming more common. Also the fire was moved to the gable of the house. The older type of cottage was still much more common however and was to remain so for a considerable time yet. The goose-neb lamp and the candle were now the usual means of lighting and before long, most houses had their own candle moulds for making candles. The home made candle was used right up to the end of the 19th century when it was displaced by the paraffin lamp.

We find little change in the popular diet right up to the end of the 19th century though the extension of the railway to Wick in 1874 introduced many little luxuries that had not been available before.

With the beginning of the 19th century the Canisbay people began to pay more attention to their dress for though everyday wear was of home manufacture special occasion clothes of better quality were sometimes taken from the south. They seem to have had a distinct penchant for fine clothes and from this time forward they were always abreast of the times as far as clothing was concerned. But it was still usual to go barefoot and, apart from in winter, boots were worn only in the ploughing and harvesting seasons and to church and market.

We hear that with the introduction of linen wear about the end of the 18th century consumption (tuberculosis), colds and rheumatism became much more prevalent. In spite of this however Canisbay was always a healthy Parish and the inhabitants as a rule lived to a good old age: many nonagenarians and centenarians dying without recollecting a day of illness. Apart from colds and rheumatism, diseases were rare – the only scourge being tuberculosis or consumption as it was called. At the end of the 18th century inoculation was not practised but smallpox though it occurred quite frequently, seldom proved fatal. At this time there were only two doctors in the whole of Caithness. The health of the parish showed little change throughout our period and it was nearly the end of the 19th century before the Canisbay people thought they needed a doctor of their own.

The absence of proper medical knowledge and skill gave rise to many superstitions in trying to cure man and beast. As in the rest of Scotland, superstition played a prominent part in the every day life of the parishioners till the rise of education banished some of the ill-founded beliefs.

Apart from superstition, the Canisbay folk had many characteristics in common. In the first place, a high proportion of them had a high percentage of Norse blood in their veins. Gaelic was unknown among them and they tended to scorn anything "heilan". They were, on the whole, an alert and industrious people whose chief trait was, perhaps, a love of getting together. Every possible opportunity was taken to get together at some house or other for discussion or merrymaking. Great festivities were held at the contract of marriage while funerals were made an occasion for drinking. In this, of course, they were no different from their Hielan' cousins. The spread of roads and communications however, introduced external influences and by the middle of the 19th century many of the old customs were dying out while the typical "Persian" (that is one from the parish) was becoming harder to find. Also with the invasion by these external influences and the increased facilities for travel, the drift southward, already general in the Highlands, began to affect Canisbay. In 1861 it had reached its maximum population of 2730 and from then on, the population of the parish declined steadily till it was only in the region of 2000 by the end of the century. There had been a certain amount of emigration from the parish before, but it was only after the 1861 census that the population started to decline. Many went south to seek employment but none were driven by the lairds and there were no "clearances" as happened in the Highland glens.

Their love of company led the Canisbay people to do much visiting. In the early days when there were no roads this was no easy business. The horse was the only means of transport and was often ridden for long distances over roadless moors. This meant that visits lasted, not for the afternoons, but for two or three days.

Up until the 1770s Canisbay had no roads apart

from the footpaths which led from all quarters to the church. The church was situated where it still stands, on the north shore midway between East and West ends of the parish. By 1790 a road of sorts had been constructed from Wick to Huna where the mails for Orkney and Stroma were deposited. This road had not been completed when the First Statistical Account was written and in winter it was all but impassable. Another road from Mey to Thurso, also incomplete, was in an even worse state. Turnpike roads were not established in Canisbay till the 1830s and the road from Huna to Wick and Thurso, when built, was maintained by statute labour.

By 1840 however 12 miles of good turnpike had been constructed on the Wick route and two Post Offices had been established, one at Mey and one at Huna. Mails were brought every day to Huna from Wick in a gig and from Thurso to Mey by a runner. There was no connection between Mey and Huna Post Offices.

In 1874 tolls on the roads were abolished and the roads were maintained by an assessment of about ninepence in the pound. This system of financing the roads remained till the end of the century. It was well nigh the end of the century before a branch road was taken from the Huna to Thurso road to the inland district of Brabster and these were the only roads existing in the parish at the end of our period (1900).

The social leanings of the parishioners of Canisbay, especially their habit of congregating to drink, was not without its effect on the religious life of the parish. The contributors to the two Statistical Accounts both indicate anything but a high code of sanctity among the people, pointing to cases of fornication, drinking, swearing on the Lord's Day and other backslidings like belief in witchcraft. It must be acknowledged however that most contributions across Scotland were written in the same vein. Yet! when the weather was favourable the church was well attended though in winter the condition of the paths, where they existed, must have been a deterrent to walking long distances.

At the beginning of the 18th century the minister's stipend was four score merks and four chalders of meal to which was added the small tiends. An attempt was made early in the century to get the stipend raised to 300 merks and six chalders of victual but it failed, being opposed by the patron, Sinclair of Freswick. By the time of the First Statistical Account the stipend had risen to 200

merks and six chalders of victual, to which was added the small tithes giving 200 merks more. The glebe however was small and there was little or no grass with it. Also although the church had been recently repaired the manse was rather dilapidated.

Throughout the 18th century the entire Parish of Canisbay was of the Established Church. A few Anabaptists came to the Parish after 1780 but they did not persist.

By 1840 the manse had been repaired and the church had been given another overhaul in 1832; this time in connection with the seating. Before this the parishioners had seats of their own which they claimed as private property but when the new seats were put in the heritors divided them according to their value and rented them annually. This innovation was not at all popular in the parish and was for some time regarded as an imposition.

At this stage the stipend was 120 bolls of oat meal and 87 quarters, three bushels of barley at a conversion of six shillings and 11 pence per boll, that being the universal rate in the sale of land. The minister also got £10 for Communion Elements while the glebe of four and a half Scotch acres was valued at £8 per year.

The Reverend Peter Jolly in the second Statistical Account tells us that a government church had been established in Keiss, in the Parish of Wick, to which was attached a contiguous district of Canisbay, making the quoad sacra parish smaller by some 160 souls than the actual parish.

There were no dissenters in the parish, but about 70 baptists met in a room in the west side. The parishioners of Canisbay were mostly firm supporters of the Established Church and it was 1851 before a Free Church was set up. It lasted until 1900 when it joined with other United Presbyterian Churches to form the United Free Church. Ultimately, in 1929, the Free Church and the Church of Scotland united to form what has become regarded as Scotland's national church under the latter title and, in Canisbay, under the latter roof.

As this was the end of an auld sang it is perhaps a fitting point at which to conclude our voyage through the economic and social development of the Parish of Canisbay in the 18th and 19th centuries. Education remains unexplored but that is the subject of a separate cruise.
Laurence Ollason Brown, The North House, J.O'G.

KAILYARD OR KELP-KILN

The enclosure known as the Quoys Kailyard was a plant-cot and is said to have produced good, disease-free plants because of its exposed and isolated position (see page 16). The yard was approximately 21 x 10 yards with an opening in the east side. The walls, built of shore "bools" are three feet thick and four to five feet high.

Experts have suggested this originally could have been a kelp-kiln. It was an ideal situation near a

low flat beach where great piles of tangles still come ashore.
Joyce Reid, High Street, Thurso.

Long ago couples liked to get married with a growing moon and a flowing tide so that their family would grow and prosper.
Willam S. Mowatt, South Ronaldsay.

David Houston

Photo, Janet Pabian (née Swanson), formerly of Phillips Mains.

David Houston author of 'e Silkie Man was born at the Mill House, John O'Groats in 1860, and it was John Dunnet of the Burn, Huna (Aal Seaman) who told him the story of the Silkie Man. It is told in the Canisbay dialect of the early to middle part of the 19th century. David Houston wrote, ". . . the generations who sang sea-songs or sagas and told yarns round the kiln fire, did so in a simple effective fashion recording the events for future generations."

In those days the crofters brought their own peats to the mill and helped with the drying of their grain, and as the miller's son he heard many stirring tales extolling the exploits and dangers of seafaring men. He wrote: "These days are gone but often in my waking dreams I can hear the long drawn, reverberating roar of the billows breaking on the shore of the Firth and the echoes of the old kiln days come back all the clearer and dearer for the time and space between."

'E Silkie Man by The Rev David Houston M.A., published by John Humphries is still on sale.

THE SILKIE MAN – A STORY OF THE PENTLAND FIRTH
(A translation from the Canisbay Dialect)

It was Old Seaman, as I remember, who told us boys the story of "the seal man" as we sat round him in the ingle nook of the kiln. The glow of the peat fire split the surrounding darkness like a great wedge. It lit up also, the kindly face of the old man, and made visible the sculpturings which time and weather had engraven on it. The only sound that broke the stillness of that calm, frosty night was the sound of the breakers that rise and roar for ever on the shores of the Firth.

"Well boys" began Old Seaman, "This is the tale of "the silkie man" as I had it out of Andrew Corner's mouth, and he knew, (so he told me) one of the two men who went through it. They've all given in their account, and it's not for me, an old man, to add to it or take from it. The Most High is my witness! Well it was a bonnie morning at barley-time. For in those days the weather was worth calling weather and not like what it is now with the wind cutting in your face like a knife till well on "Johnsmas" [1]. It was a fine morning, as I was saying, and Donald Rugg rose and looked out about the house. His brother, Peter, was out before him lighting his pipe at the lee side of the peat stack. Donald went over to him and they both stood there a while, looking out over the back of the Ness, but saying nothing. The flood tide was wearing off and the ebb had begun to make. Then Donald said to his brother: "Boy, there might be a chance today for some fishing in the Sound (the channel between Canisbay and Stroma) if we had two or three limpets" "Oh, yes" says Peter, "that may be, but there'll be no ebb nor Sound for us today, we must finish the barley rig, Donald – if we don't finish it this week, we'll be the talk of the parish. Other folk are all finished a week ago."

Now just as the men were speaking, a woman came out to put the cattle to the grass and Kirsty, their sister, was standing in front of the byre door,

with her arms round the neck of the red stirk, trying to put the branks over its head, and she heard the men speaking about the bait (limpets) and she said "Boys, you go to the barley rig and I'll go to the ebb when I put this "miracle" (the cow) to the grass." Now, Kirsty was a well-built lass coming up towards 20. The Ruggs were all folk good to look on, and Kirsty was not less than any of them as far as looks went; and more than that, she was a good hearted lass, with a kind word and smile for everybody. There was no-one to match her in the district, so everybody said.

Well then, when Kirsty had tethered the stirk she came back to the house, and she took off her soiled clothes, put on her blue coat and short dress, and she took off her shoes and stockings and she put her bare feet on the ground (in these days the lasses all went bare-footed to the ebb) and she lifted the bait basket off the wall and went off over the rigs with the basket on her arm. The new grass was coming up all over the links and the morning sun was shining on the white buckies and making them like the driven snow, and where will you see a finer sight than the Ness of Duncansby on a lovely May morning. The neighbours were all at the rig as Kirsty went down with her bare feet skipping over the grass and her coat swinging between her ankles and her knees. There she went singing like a lark and the folk all said long afterwards that the lass was fey (possessed) that day. She'd been no time in the ebb when the day changed. Following the warm morning there came down a thick fog that you could have cut with a knife, but people didn't give a thought about the lass as she was well acquainted with the ebb. But now, an hour goes by, and then two hours and there's no sign or sight of the lassie coming back, and now the breakfast time comes and the men are in from the rig and still there's no word of her. And Donald asks Sarah: "Isn't Kirsty back from the ebb yet?" and Sarah says, "No, she's not back yet." And now it is three hours since she left the house and the folk are beginning to doubt that something has happened to her.

So Donald and Peter put on their caps and went off over the links as hard as they could go, to see what has happened to her. They parted at the point of the Ness, and Donald, he went east till he came to Sannick and Peter, he went west almost till he came to Robbie's Haven. They searched every hole and corner. They cried and they whistled, but there's no sight or sign of Kirsty. And now as they came back to where they had parted, and there the fog lifts, and the shore's clear before them but it's the same tale. They thought perhaps she'd gone to chase the rockies off the breether [2], and then they thought that perhaps she'd gone to Stroma for a laugh. The Stroma people had been at the peats on the east hill, and many's the time the Stroma folk had tried to get Kirsty to sail over with them. Their young lads were daft about her, and many's the night that they had gone round her father's house, trying to get their eyes on her, when they were at the mill here getting their corn milled.

Well, they searched here and there. They sent word around, but it was all the same. Weeks and months went past but not a vestige was seen or heard of her. There was but one thing for it, poor Kirsty must have slipped with her feet in the seaweed, groping after the limpets, and been carried off with the tide. God save us all. What chance had a human who fell in yonder with the tide going like a mill-steam.

☆★☆★☆★☆

And now the time passes by. Three years had gone by, it might be more. It was about the same time of the year, and the weather was holding fine and settled, so one morning Donald and Peter put off to catch the end of the ebb tide. They reached out with a fine grey of wind from the south-east, and they set themselves up on the back of the Boars (Boars of Duncansby). They had come upon a fine lot of fish and they were casting and pulling in for all they were worth when, lo and behold! – before they could say, Jack Robinson, here down came the fog as thick as gruel. Here they were bearing west in the middle of it, on the tail of the west-going tide! What were they to do now in the middle of this mishap? When the fog comes down on you in the Sound, what can you do? If it's the ebb-tide you are out beyond Dunnet Head before you know where you are! If it is the flood-tide you are out past the Pentland Skerries. One way or the other it doesn't make much odds. It is death or starvation staring you in the face, whichever way you take it.

Peter was the first to speak and he says: "Donald we must pull up and get out of this, for we are now on a risky course with this fog about us." But Donald was eager on the fishing, and he says: "Boy, what good would that do us? If we lift the oars in the middle of this, we're as like as not to take a straight road to Norway. No boy, we'll hold on, and before we're down on Stroma the fog may have cleared and we'll see better where we are."

So with this Peter was somewhat pacified, and they turned to the handline fishing again. They lay-to for more than two hours but the fog was as thick as ever. But they couldn't lie "laid-to" much longer because the ebb-tide was almost past, and they knew that "the young man" as they named the start of the flood-tide, would be on them before they could look round again, and if the flood grips you during a fog, God help you! So now Donald himself began to get a bit anxious, and he said, "Boy, we must get out of this wherever we go, I am seeing the guillemots flying past and taking to the wing, and that is a sure sign that the slack is over and the flood-tide will be on us very soon. By my consideration of reckoning, we can't be far off the east side of Stroma, and with God's help we must try to make there till we see.

So they pulled up their lines and took to the oars. They pulled and they pulled till they were blind with sweat, but they had no idea where they were pulling to. Donald is always pulling and looking over his shoulder, in the hope that something familiar might come into his sight, and at long last there's a great black bulk towering above them higher than the mast of a ship! At the sight of this Donald says nothing, but Peter lifts his arm off the oar and rubs the cold sweat off his brow.

When Donald got his breath he speaks up and says "Hi! Peter there's land anyway as far as I can make out, so boy with the help of the Lord we'll creep in till we see." So they rowed slowly in, and when they reached the length of the rocks they saw that they were at the mouth of a geo, narrowing as it went in. They rowed in through the narrow passage as far as they could work the oars and then they shipped the oars and took to their hands. They shoved the boat in and in, but the further in the darker it became. The geo had narrowed so much that the boat would barely push through and now they see that the geo is covered on the top as well. Above them it was as black as tar and there's nothing beneath them but the growl and grumble of salt water. They kept shoving and shoving and Donald says nothing, but Peter is always wiping the cold sweat from his brow. They pushed through this murk of darkness for something like 300 or 400 yards, when they saw a lightening at the land end of the passage, and before they knew where they were, they are floating in a wide basin of water in the heart of the land! All round them the high rocks are looming down and the swell of the sea is heaving them up and down, and the long brown tangles were twisting about them like adders in the peat-moors. They draw in and at long last they see a shelf of rock where they can land, and as their keel touched the shingle Donald lifts his cap and says "Thanks to the Almighty, it's land anyway."

So now, they came out of the boat and drew her up on the shingle and off they set through the boulders to see where they were, and as they were turning the point of the rock they came to a kind of dark mouth, and Peter peering in through it, turns rounded with his hands above his head and cries out "Lord be here, Donald. As sure as I'm a living sinner, there's a woman in here rocking a cradle."

Donald hearing this thinks that Peter has gone out of his mind with all they'd gone through, so to put him off his delusion he says out loud, "What's that you're saying, you foolish creature?" But Peter's not to be put off with that, and he says: "Donald, the Most High is my witness! Use your own eyes. Look in here!" When Donald got the sight of his eyes, there before him, sure as anything, is a woman sitting on a flat ledge with her feet on a cradle, and her eyes resting on something in her hands. "Well" says Donald after he had the witness of his own eyes, "Many is the poor house where I've seen a cradle rocking but this beats everything! However, if she's human I'll talk to her. She'll surely know where she is, and maybe she'll know where we are."

So with this they went in through, Donald first and Peter after him. They looked about them and really the place wasn't too untidy. There was sand all over the floor, same as you've seen in any other house. Here and there were shells and bits wreck wood, and dented brass and ships kettles battered out of all shape and use.

The woman all this time, had never lifted her eyes, and Donald was just going to hail her when lo; they heard a sort of disturbance, as though a stirk had fallen into a peat bank. They looked around and there they see a large seal coming up out of the sea. There he is before their eyes walking with difficulty among the stones in the ebb, making straight for the mouth of the cave. They thought the creature gave them an uncanny look out of his watery eyes as he struggled up over, but he took no more notice. He hobbled up and down among the boulders till he came right up in front of the woman, and now they looked at the creature more astonished than ever. What is it they see round his neck but a string of great big codlings! And as soon as he managed up before the ledge, he took the string of codlings off his neck and laid them down at the woman's feet. This done he shuffles away round the corner where their eyes couldn't follow him. Donald and his brother were so overcome that they couldn't open their mouths, and before they could gather their senses, what do they see coming out round the corner where the seal had disappeared, but a well set up like man! He had on a cloth jacket and trousers, with brass buttons up and down, and one of these cheese-cutter caps on his head, and a napkin round his neck. He wasn't what you would call a tall man, a bit low set and bent in the legs as though he'd been used to heavy lifts, but not all that bad-looking in the face.

So out he comes and goes up to the men. He turns out a civil speaking man, and passes the time of the day, and hears their story – who they are and how they came there. All this time the woman keeps rocking the cradle but never says a word, and the man, he looks first at the woman, then at the brothers, and then says with a laugh on his face "Men", he says "you'll not be recognising who this woman is who is rocking the cradle?" "No", says Donald "that's what we don't know, and it's not our fault for we haven't exchanged a word with her." Well, to make a long story short, says the man: "That's your sister Kirsty that you all thought was

drowned at the Ness of Duncansby four years ago, about this same time of the year. And more than that I'm her husband, no less, and that's our child she is rocking in the cradle!"

The brothers, hearing this, looked at one another but whatever they thought they said nothing, for the less said the soonest mended, but it was beginning to dawn on them now what had happened to Kirsty. "Yes", says the seal man, going on with his tale, "we're married here right enough, but I got no dowry with her same as other men get with their women."

Donald hearing this is rather irritated, and he says with a sneer "Well, man! it was difficult for us to give her a dowry considering the way you took her away from us, but the dowry is waiting for you, says Donald, a fine red cow, five years old, and not its match in the parish. She's a cow now but was a stirk, when Kirsty went from us, as we know to our sorrow."

"Oh! it's all right" says the seal man. "It's just my way of speaking, so don't let it bother you. I'm not thinking all that much about the cow. Cow or no cow, I've got a woman that any man might be proud of, and don't you think that I'm rueing my bargain, but for all that our own's our own and if the cow is to be had, I'll come for her when you cross the Sound. But, to change the subject, have you any idea of where you are?" "No", says Donald, "we haven't." "Well", says the seal man, "You're on the west side of Stroma, and this is what they call the Devil's Punch Bowl, and not a bad name for it. Many's the wild sea that is here on a winter's day, but for the like of us that can live beneath the water as well as above, we are none the worse. Your sister here has the same power now as I have, and so has the child. Many's the humbling sight we see – wrecked ships and drowning men that we have no power to help. All this rubbish that's lying about is from wrecked ships, and we've plenty more of it we needn't speak of."

Well, they stayed with the seal man all that day for the fog was still down. They stayed with him the next day as well, the fog wouldn't let them go. But, they couldn't say that they felt themselves at home. The seal man went out and in and to and from on his own errands, now in his natural shape as they had seen him first and then in the shape of a human! They only saw glimpses of Kirsty. The seal man kept her out of the way. They didn't care to look at the child, for they thought it might be uncanny. So now the third day comes and the fog lifts and glad they are to see an open sky above their heads. They were more than glad to get away, and the seal man tells them that he's ready when they are. So they pushed out on the first of the flood-tide, the wind from the south-west and Donald steering. It was no time till they were down on the back of the "Boars", but by this time the "Boars" were getting up, and as Donald thought it would not be wise to cross them, he kept away and steered up to the back of the Ness. But, now the flood is stronger on the Ness that they expected and Donald tried her this way and that, but the Devil be in it if he could edge the boat round the Ness, try as he could. So the seal man he says "Let me try it Donald," and gripping the helm out of Donald's hand, goodness! they're round the Ness before you could say "Jack Robinson".

And now they are in over the tide and in still water, and coming up by Robby's Haven when all at once they hear a splash, as though you had thrown a lobster creel over the boat, and there when Donald and Peter looked round there's no seal man to be seen! Donald jumps aft and grips the helm not knowing very well if his head or his heels are above him. They are well in to the haven now, and Peter is looking up over the brae and what does he see but his sister, Sarah, running over the links like a woman out of her mind. She was at the water's edge as the boat landed on the sand, and before they could speak to her she calls out, with her hands above her head "Oh, bairns, bairns, am I not glad to see your two faces, but what a day I've had. He alone knows who made us all! When Sarah got her breath back this was the story she had to tell. "Bairns, bairns", says she "When I was up on the head moving the cattle, I saw a boat approaching the Ness, and I was standing with the red cow's tether in my hands, looking at the boat, and just as it got beyond the Ness the red cow sprang from my side, and before I could bless myself she took a jump and went clean over the rock." "Lord, save us," cried Peter. "The Devil must have been in the cow." "No, no," says Donald, in his ear. "It's the seal man that's off and taken Kirsty's dowry with him and let him be off." Then stepping out of the boat, he says to Sarah, "Thank God, woman, we've got home out of that fog, I'm sorry about the red cow, but we must put up with our loss the best way we can. We've not had much luck with the beast anyway since Kirsty went from us."

[1] Johnsmas = 23rd June, Midsummer.

[2] Breether = The first green shoots of oats and bere as it starts to grow.

A translation from the Dialect by **Clara Cormack,**
Great grand-daughter of Aul Seaman
– John Dunnet o' the Burn

"The Rockies". The "rockies" were small wild sheep which lived outside the fence at the stacks along to Skirza Head. The East End folk were pestered by them coming in and eating their grass and crops especially in the spring.

The "rockies" belonged to the crofters and twice a year there was a big round-up with a lot of "shouting and shooing" until they got them all gathered. They were chased down the cliffs and along the shore to the Bocht. The first gathering was at the end of June for clipping and marking, and then in October a percentage of the adults were taken home for killing and some smaller ones were fattened. The "rockies" were very frightened when they were tethered at home and took a long time to settle.

It was through eating the "rockies" that the Duncansby folk were called the "Mutton Eaters".
M.H.

JOHN O'GROATS

Hail to thy bleak and stormy strand!
Though kindlier nature cheers thee not,
Thy fame is known in every land,
Thou celebrated spot!

Pilgrims from many a clime afar –
From lands that lie beyond the sea –
Led by thy glowing polar star,
Have come and gazed on thee.

Thou hast no classic dome to show,
No hallowed fane, or sainted shrine;
But ocean's wildest waves that flow,
And rudest rocks are thine.

Thy music is the Pentland's roar,
Loud bursting over rocks and sands,
Yon headland frowning on the shore,
Thy dome "not made with hands".

On thee no flaunting flowers appear,
Nor fragrant shrubs of southern sky;
The lowly daisy blooming near
Is all that meets the eye.

But thou hast beauties of thine own;
When wintry storms have ceased to rave,

How glorious doth the sun go down
Within thy burning wave.

Then comes, with all its balmy power,
Thy summer twilight, long and bright;
A holy stillness marks the hour,
That's breathless with delight.

Alas! since first in life's young day
I saw thy bare and billowy shore,
Years, like a dream, have passed away,
And friends I see no more.

And early hopes that once were bright,
And fancies brighter still than they,
Like fleeting meteors of the night,
Have faded, too, away.

Yet though thou wak'st oft times a sigh,
Though cold and bleak thou dost appear,
With all thy gloom of sea and sky,
Thou still to me art dear.

Yes! in thy darkest wintry hour,
When storms sweep o'er thee from the pole,
Thy wild waves, thundering in their power,
Give pleasure to the soul.

Poems from John O'Groats, by **James T. Calder.**

WORDS AND EXPRESSIONS OF YESTERYEAR

Something a friend said the other day made me think of some phrases and sayings used regularly in the seemingly distant past.

Perhaps they are not all confined to Caithness and no doubt they vary from district to district but they were colourful and expressive and now seldom, if ever, used so I thought it might be interesting to see what I could remember. "God" was seldom mentioned, that is the word itself. He was spoken of as "The Most High", "Yir Maker" and by children as "The Good Man". Likewise prayers were called "Good Words" and the devil was called "The Bad Man", Devil being counted a bad word, hell was the "Worst Place".

When someone was ill he was "laid up", if seriously ill was "badly" and then "far through". When someone died he was "away" or "gone an given in his account". This last expression was specially used when quoting some saying or action a deceased person had said or done to verify the statement for none would willingly speak ill of the dead.

Swearing was frowned on, at least in front of the bairns and a favourite way to get round this was to substitute a milder word instead followed by the explanation "But he used the broad name". For example, "He telt them he hed a good mind till kick their tail ends", by the "broad name", leaving us in no doubt what the original word had been. If someone was working very hard or was ill and perspiring freely – he was said to be, "In a droke o' sweit". Anyone who took offence at something said or done was said "To hev dorted' on me" and if deeply hurt was "Cut till 'e quick".

Best clothes were kept for Sundays and special occasion but the men always had a "Scodgan jaikad" for second best. This was usually worn over a "gansey" with a "gravad" in place of a tie. The womenfolk wore cross-over styled aprons most of the time, but for scrubbing floors, etc., a sacking apron was tied round the waist and this was called a "brat".

If someone "kent ye unca", he realised you were a stranger. Someone who had a receding lower jaw was "shuttle moothed" and "shandigabbed" was the opposite and a long thin face was "lantern jawed". This was used to refer to animals as well. I once heard an old man speak of a friend of his who had a hernia as being "rumbursted" and if someone had a very florid complexion it might be said "Ye could hev bled him wi' a straw."

All socks and some underwear were hand knitted and if a lady had time on her hands you could be sure she would be "Pittan a roond on her stocking". A lot of wool was hand spun but if bought it was made up in hanks not balls as today. A hank was, I think, a "Hunder o' worsad" that being equal to a "cut of wool" which in time became two ounces and now so many grammes. This hank you, of course, wound into a "clew" or ball. You can imagine the blank stares if you asked in the wool shop today for so many "clews o' worsad". Oversocks worn inside Wellington boots were called "futags" or "moogans".

A young cat was a "kettling" and a puppy a "folp" and a dog given to wandering outwith his own territory was called a "scuddler". Water was carried from the well and two pails were a "fracht" of water. If you carried something heavy for any distance it might be said "ye hed some fang". Bundles of straw were "winlanes" and a smaller bundle was a "turse". This was also applied to one who was rather plump.

To praise someone was to "reese" them and someone who was clear thinking and a trifle deep he was "far drachted". A doctor was referred to as "skeely". An only child was an "oakie" and a mischievous child was "ill tricked". If one threw a tantrum he "took a richt tirrymirry". An old lady used to say of a child she considered cheeky, "he hed ower much of what a cat licked her tail wi". And someone who was a bit sharp tongued and had plenty to say "hed a tongue 'at wid hev clipped cloots."

A bit of gossip was something heard on the "clashmarket". A nasty cough wis a "fearful hoast" and a touch of laryngitis wis a "rooped throt". When visiting in the evening you went "oot for 'e efterdayset". The twilight was " 'e darkening". Someone losing his or her temper was "wild as a plucker". To squeeze was to "birze", a forefinger was a "borrag". Freckles were "ferny tickles" and to plead was to "preeg". Tinklers and tramps were "goan aboot shither" and someone feckless "couldna mak salt for his brose."

If you were at a complete loss you were "clean strapped". This was a favourite expression if a piece of machinery broke down and the job couldn't be completed until this was mended. A withered plant was "dowed" and an itch wis a "humour". A "kenning" was a very small amount and to go all out at something was "till work till 'e bleed spring". "Scammed" was scorched, "hirple" was to limp and when a friend was advised by his wife to put on a clean boiler suit he insisted "bit they're no dirty chist "castened" wi 'e sun" meaning faded or bleached.

I have just jotted these few examples down as I remembered them and spelt them as I heard them pronounced. There will be many variations, I have no doubt beautifully descriptive words and phrases that were in everyday use at one time, now forgotten until someone says something that jogs the memory.

Clara Clyne, Strathesk Grove, Kirkhill,
Penicuik.

Packman clouds or Packies (peedie cloudies like balls) – sign of rain and bad weather.

Robbie Dundas.

If there is ice in November that will hold a duck,
There will be naething efter but mire and muck.

Elizabeth Munro.

ECHOES OF THE PAST

The smell of the kiln and the moon rising over the Skerries and the Firth tugged forever at my mother's heartstrings and she hauled us all to John O'Groats each summer. Our accents were different but it was the call-words that caused the problems.

The dogs, Flora and Toby were called by name – but for the rest!

Tick tick	– hens
Teuchie teuchie	– ducks
Tehue tehue (sucking sound)	– pigs
Caddie caddie	– sheep
Pet pet	– lamb
Howks howks	– cow
Toch toch	– calf
Shook shook	– horse

There was a special "click" sound made when pressing tongue against roof of mouth which got the horses to go, or move on and "whoa" halted the horse. We didn't miss high-tech talking toys because we were busy learning the skills to get sounds out of everyday things at hand.

Skirlag – a thin leaf about half inch wide was stretched between thumbs and when blown on made a skirling sound.

Peepag – a stripped strong quarter inch thick stalk of oats about three to four inches long, flattened with your teeth for about quarter an inch at one end. Blow through to make a whistle.

Snorag – made from button and string. By twirling and then pulling out and in on the band of string, the button spins round, backwards and forward making a snoring sound.

The sea and the shore had a great fascination, yielding new treasures every day and I can tell you it's much easier to hearken to the noise of the waves in a big buckie than to get a snorag to snore.

Magnus MacLean, Duart, Auckengill.

SOME LOCAL WORDS

Acerspired	– Mildewed		Fire	– Throw
Aikles	– Molars		Flech	– Flea
Aise	– Peat ashes		Fleep	– Lazy character; dolt
Antle	– Nag		Flype	– Turn socks partially inside out
Backie	– Iron peg on end of tether		Flyte	– Scold
Beest	– First milk after a cow calves		Forfochen	– Tired out
Beilan	– Festering		Fusoum	– Dirty
Birse	– Temper. As in "his birse was up"		Futrat	– Weasel
Birse	– Crush		Gaikan	– Looking all around
Bletherskate	– One who talks too much		Gaillan	– A burning pain
Blost	– Boast		Galoot	– Stupid person
Boak	– Retch		Gant	– Stammer
Boorag	– Rough piece of turf used as a peat		Gapus	– Stupid person
Bowel-knot	– Appendicitis		Gaun	– Young
Bracht	– Rift or belch		Geecher	– Grandfather
Brander	– To darn		Gey	– Very, e.g. gey cold
Branks	– Halter with wooden side pieces		Gilt	– Stack of hay or straw
Breenge	– Lunge forward		Gizzaned	– Barrel tub etc. dried out and leaking
Brochan	– Gruel		Gobbag	– Kiss
Bruffle	– Untidy person		Gosk	– Chickweed
Caff	– Chaff		Gouff	– Smell
Carvey	– Caraway seeds		Grooshan	– Fringe of hair on forehead
Carfuffle	– Disorder, mess		Gushel	– Handless person
Chaird	– Dirty Tramp		Heathercow	– Strong stem of heather
Clype	– Tell tales		Heelser	– Bad fall, esp. off a bike
Corrag	– Pinkie		Heuky	– Itchy
Coup	– Overturn or fall		Hirple	– Walk with a limp
Cutty	– Short clay pipe		Hunkers	– Squatting, as in sitting on your hunkers
Deugen	– Stubborn		Keb	– Sheep tick
Dirler	– Chamber-pot		Kep	– Cap with a peak
Dottled	– Forgetful		Kep	– Ward off and catch
Doud	– A lump, eg. of clay or earth		Kithan	– Rascal
Dunt	– Thump or knock		Kittlan	– Tickling
Fantoush	– Posh		Leepid	– Pampered
Farley	– Strange sight		Liv	– Open hand
Faup	– Curlew			

Meef	– Damp sultry day	Swite	– Sweat
Miraclous	– Awkward or untidy	Swither	– Hesitate
Nev	– Fist	Thraw-crook	– Tool used to make a simman
Ondach	– A feeble, weak person	Trauchled	– Bedraggled
Ondach	– A weak and sad looking sight	Trippery work	– Daily household chores
Pech	– Breathe fast, pant	Trock	– Trash
Peeping	– Crying	Trosk	– Slow-witted person
Pooshan	– Poison	Trump	– Jew's harp
Purler	– A fall	Trushel	– Untidily dressed
Randar	– A form of darning	Tyauve	– Knead dough
Rax	– Stretch, over-strain	Vratch	– Nuisance
Reddar	– Comb, esp. fine-tooth	Warsie	– Faint from lack of food
Scart	– Scratch	Wazzan	– Windpipe
Shift	– Move, change eg. clothes	Whaup	– Curlew
Shilp	– Sharp voice	Wheech	– Exclamation of disgust
Shooing	– Sewing	Wheech around	– Quick tidy up
Shouks	– Jaws	Wime	– Belly
Sitten	– Rotten, eg. egg	Wrack	– Search your brain
Skleeteran	– Walking clumsily	Wrunkled	– Creased, crumpled
Skollag	– Weed resembling a young turnip	Wumple	– A tangle
Slaister	– A messy worker	Yap	– Bark
Slocher	– Drink noisily	Yirned milk	– Curds junket
Slock	– Quench		
Sochan	– Breathless		
Sneether	– Giggle		
Snib	– Lock the door		
Snotter	– Running nose		
Soorag	– Type of sorrel		
Sore hand	– A thick sandwich		
Sornan	– Searching		
Spartan	– Spreading (dung)		
Spounkans	– Sandshoes		
Spew	– Vomit		
Stooshie	– A panic		
Stooter	– Ungainly shuffling person		
Stroup	– Spout of kettle etc.		
Swadge	– Sit back and let a good meal digest		

Some of Mum's Sayings

If ye canna help – Dinna hinder.

Wir ain fish guts for wir ain sea maws.

There's aye a drap o' water where the stirkie drooned.

Sticks and stanes will break ma bones – but names will never hurt me.

There's aye a muckle slippery stane at ilka buddy's door.

Powder and paint fills many a rent.

Ye canna mak' a silk purse oot o' a soo's loog.

Mary Sinclair, Hillside, Gills.

YOUR HERITAGE

Climb upon my knee my lovely
I will tell you old, old stories,
About box socials that were held
In the twenties and thirties.
The girls they brought a box for supper
With a ticket in it,
The MC called a number out
A handsome lad would win it.
You had a partner for the dance
Maybe one for life,
For many a lad at the box social
Was where he found a wife.
They would walk in the evening under the moon,
No cars in those far off days,
No machines to do the work
Life was different in many ways,
There were horses, pigs, cattle and hens,
Ploughing to be done,
Thinning neeps and heaping tatties
Come wind or rain, or sun.
We always worked in fours or fives

A very merry mix.
Half yoking was a welcome call
With bannocks and tea, enough for all,
Then salt herring and tatties at six.
They stooked the corn, coled the hay,
Cut the peats and tilled the land.
At harvest time neighbours came all day
To give a helping hand.
There's been a revolution
In village croft and farm,
From clearances to "White Settlers",
Is a mighty span.
So tell your children all you read
Within the pages of this book,
For in twenty years I'm sure this land
Will have a different look.
Pass down your culture of which you read,
Pass on your customs by word and deed.
Make your decendants proud to say,
I have my roots in Canisbay.

Rosemary Laird, 1 Heatherbell Cottages, John O'Groats.

THE ROCKS REMAIN

The **Canisbay Stone** stands nearly eight feet high on land belonging to the farm of West Canisbay and can be seen from the Manse Road – opposite the entry to the old and new manses – if one looks in the direction of St. John's Point. It is a stone pillar about 15 inches wide and five inches thick with no carving to be seen, and set so that the sun would strike its face at the winter solstice. No one seems to know how long it has stood there or for what purpose – or indeed whether it has always been solitary or was once part of a group of stones. . . . **A mystery?**

M.E.B.

A Canisbay Toast

May the best you've ever seen
Be the worst you'll ever see
May a moose n'er leave yer girnal
Wi' a teardrop in its e'e
May yer lum keep blithely reeking
Till you're old enough tae dee
May you all be fit and happy
As I'd like you aye to be.

The Standing Stone of Canisbay

West Canisbay Farm in background.

The Stacks of Duncansby

Photo, John Adams.

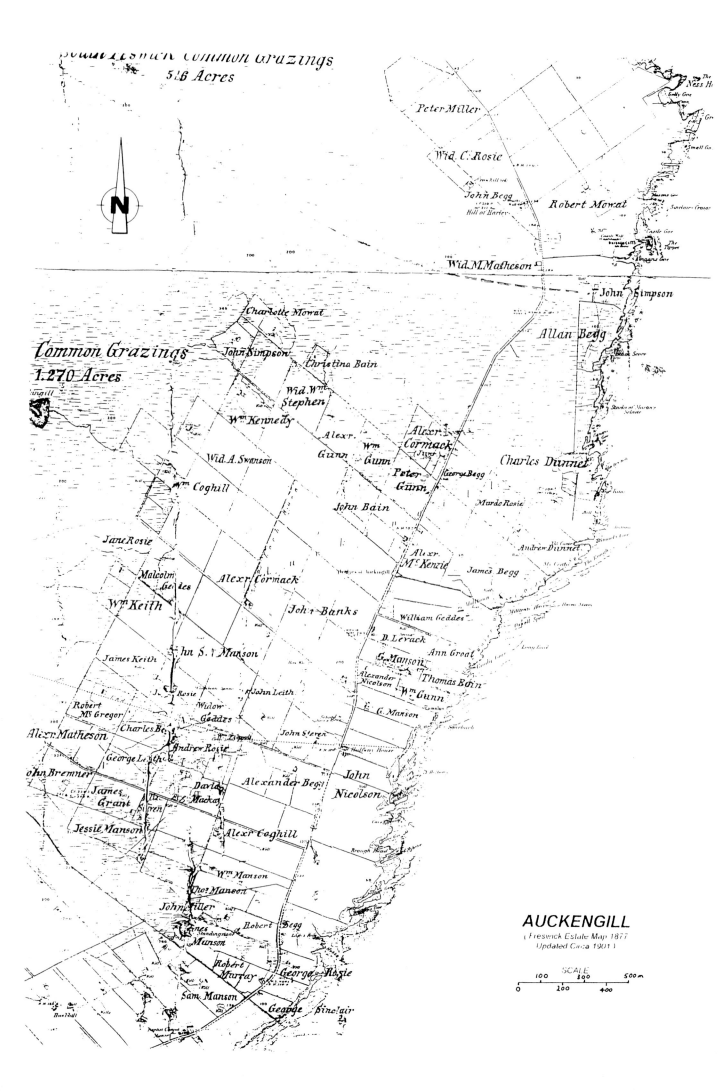

South Freswick Common Grazings
5 6 Acres

N

Common Grazings
1.270 Acres

Peter Miller

Wid. C. Rosie

John Begg
Hill of Harley

Robert Mowat

Wid. M. Matheson

John Simpson

Allan Begg

Charlotte Mowat

John Simpson

Christina Bain

Wid. Wm.
Stephen

Wm. Kennedy

Alexr.
Gunn

Wm.
Gunn

Alexr.
Cormack
Junr.

Charles Dunnet

Wid. A. Swanson

Peter
Gunn

George Begg

Wm. Coghill

John Bain

Murdo Rosie

Jane Rosie

Alexr.
McKenzie

James Begg

Andrew Dunnet

Malcolm
Geddes

Alexr. Cormack

Wm. Keith

John Banks

William Geddes

James Keith

John S. Manson

D. Levack

G. Manson

Ann Groat

Alexander
Nicolson

Thomas Bain

Wm. Gunn

J. Rosie

John Leith

Widow
Geddes

C. Manson

Robert
McGregor

John Steven

Alexr. Matheson

Charles Be...

Andrew Rosie

Hudson House

George Leith

John Bremner

James
Grant

David
Mackay

Alexander Begg

John
Nicolson

Jessie Manson

Alexr Coghill

Brough Head

Wm. Manson

Thos. Manson

John Miller

Manson

Robert Begg

Robert
Murray

George Rosie

Sam Manson

George Sinclair

AUCKENGILL

(Freswick Estate Map 1877
Updated Circa 1901)

SCALE

100   300   500 m

0   200   400

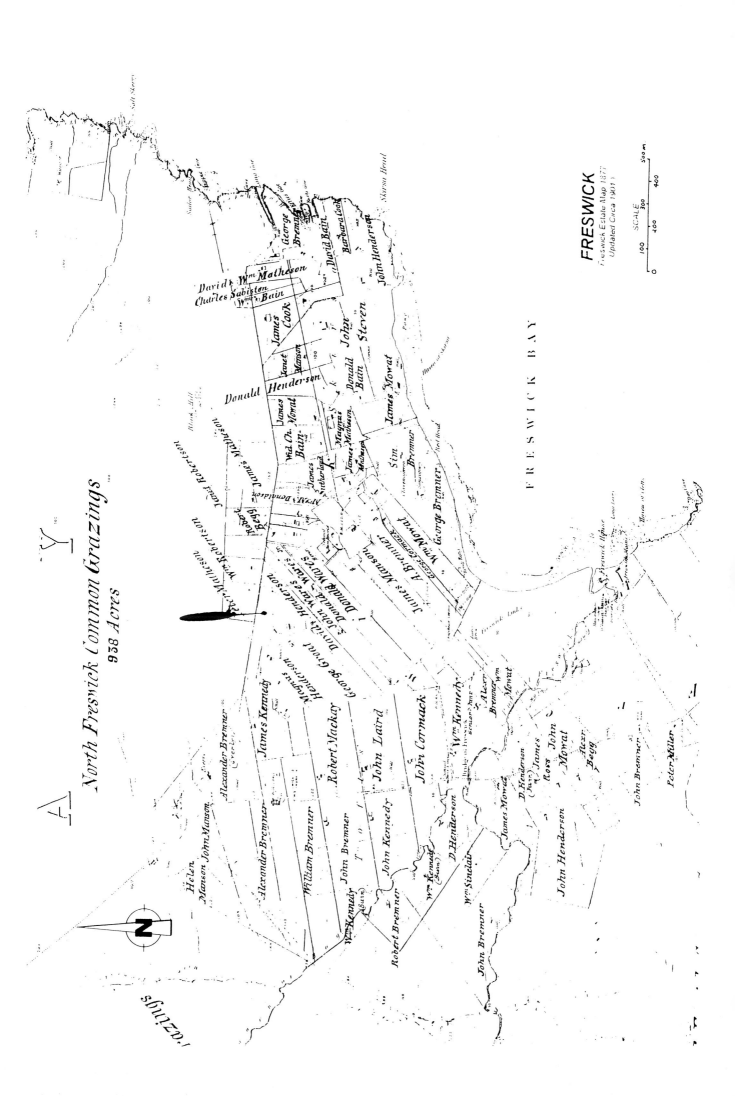

FRESWICK

Freswick Estate Map 1877
Updated Circa 1901

SCALE

North Freswick Common Grazings
958 Acres

FRESWICK BAY

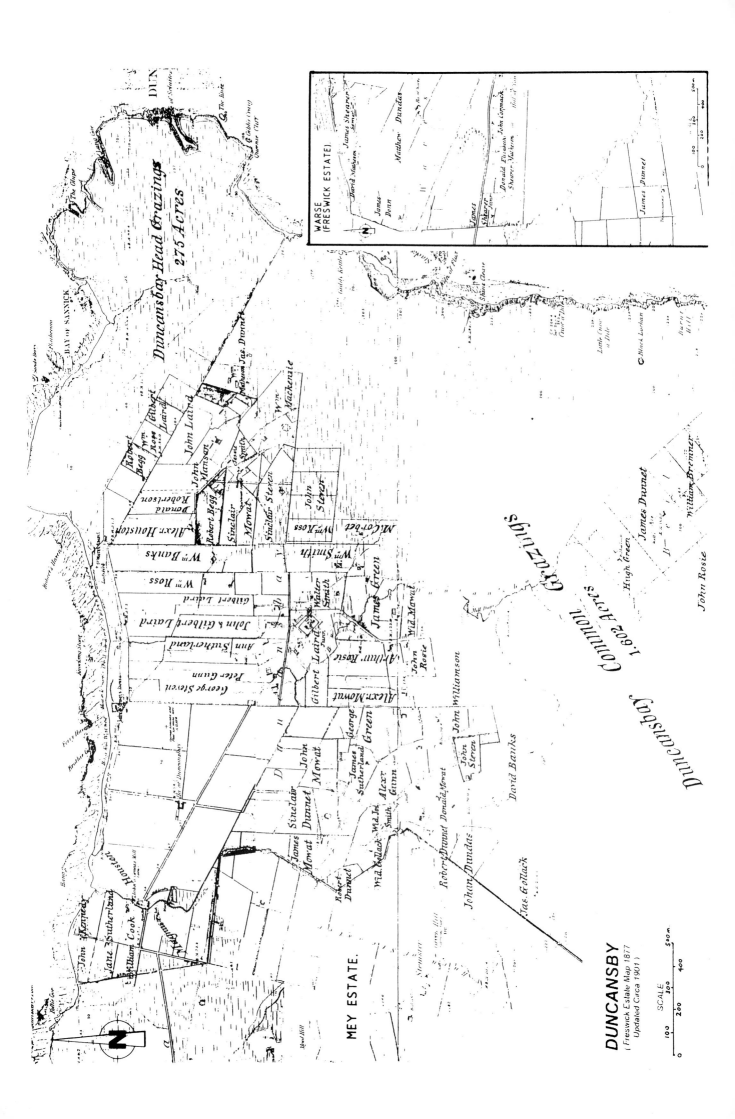

DUNCANSBY

(Freswick Estate Map 1877
Updated Circa 1901)

SCALE

MEY ESTATE.

WARSE
(FRESWICK ESTATE).

Duncansbay Head Grazings
275 Acres

Common
1,602 Acres

Grazings

Duncansbay

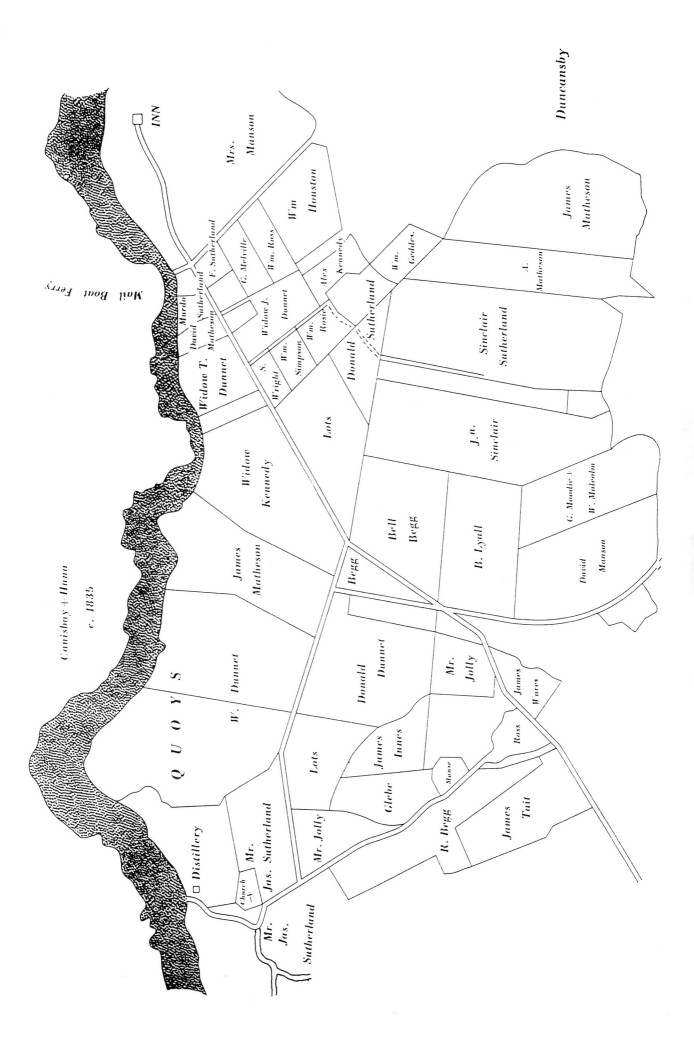

Canisbay + Huna
c. 1835

Duncansby

Mail Boat Ferry

INN

Mrs. Manson

Wm Houston

F. Sutherland

G. Melville

Wm. Ross

Murdo Matheson

David Sutherland

Widow J. Dunnet

Alex Kennedy

Wm. Geddes

James Matheson

A. Matheson

Widow T. Dunnet

S. Wright

Wm. Simpson

Wm. Rosie

Donald Sutherland

Sinclair Sutherland

Lots

Widow Kennedy

Jᵃ. Sinclair

James Matheson

Bell Begg

B. Lyall

G. Moodie + W. Malcolm

David Manson

Begg

QUOYS

W. Dunnet

Donald Dunnet

Mr. Jolly

James Wares

□ Distillery

Mr. Jas. Sutherland

Lots

James Innes

Ross

Mr. Jolly

Glebe

Manor

Church

R. Begg

James Tait

Mr. Jas. Sutherland

STROMA

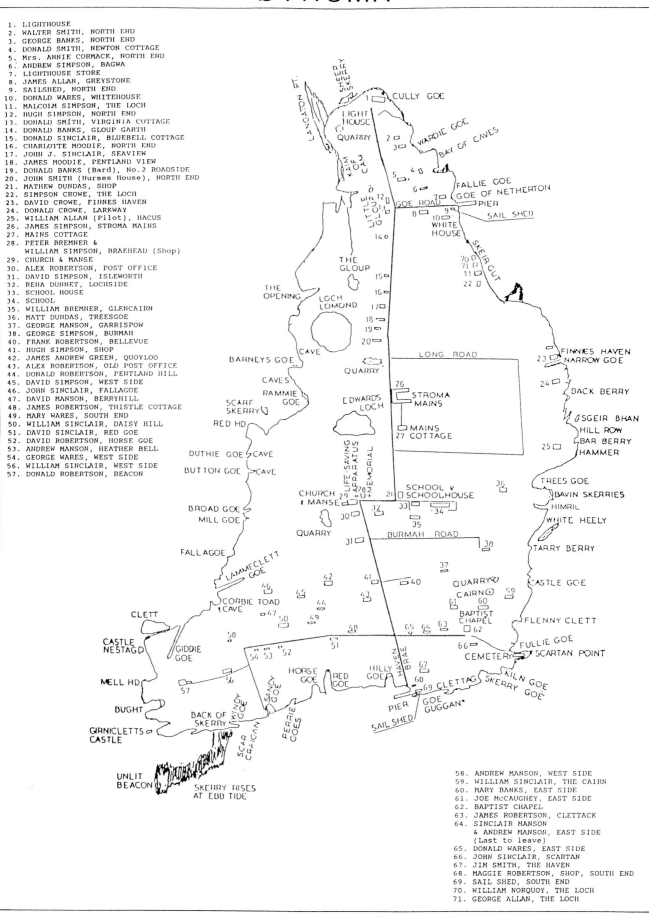

1. LIGHTHOUSE
2. WALTER SMITH, NORTH END
3. GEORGE BANKS, NORTH END
4. DONALD SMITH, NEWTON COTTAGE
5. Mrs. ANNIE CORMACK, NORTH END
6. ANDREW SIMPSON, BAGWA
7. LIGHTHOUSE STORE
8. JAMES ALLAN, GREYSTONE
9. SAILSHED, NORTH END
10. DONALD WARES, WHITEHOUSE
11. MALCOLM SIMPSON, THE LOCH
12. HUGH SIMPSON, NORTH END
13. DONALD SMITH, VIRGINIA COTTAGE
14. DONALD BANKS, GLOUP GARTH
15. DONALD SINCLAIR, BLUEBELL COTTAGE
16. CHARLOTTE MOODIE, NORTH END
17. JOHN J. SINCLAIR, SEAVIEW
18. JAMES MOODIE, PENTLAND VIEW
19. DONALD BANKS (Bard), No.2 ROADSIDE
20. JOHN SMITH (Nurses House), NORTH END
21. MATHEW DUNDAS, SHOP
22. SIMPSON CROWE, THE LOCH
23. DAVID CROWE, FINNES HAVEN
24. DONALD CROWE, LARKWAY
25. WILLIAM ALLAN (Pilot), HACUS
26. JAMES SIMPSON, STROMA MAINS
27. MAINS COTTAGE
28. PETER BREMNER &
    WILLIAM SIMPSON, BRAEHEAD (Shop)
29. CHURCH & MANSE
30. ALEX ROBERTSON, POST OFFICE
31. DAVID SIMPSON, ISLEWORTH
32. RENA DUNNET, LOCHSIDE
33. SCHOOL HOUSE
34. SCHOOL
35. WILLIAM BREMNER, GLENCAIRN
36. MATT DUNDAS, TREESGOE
37. GEORGE MANSON, GARRISPOW
38. GEORGE SIMPSON, BURMAH
40. FRANK ROBERTSON, BELLEVUE
41. HUGH SIMPSON, SHOP
42. JAMES ANDREW GREEN, QUOYLOO
43. ALEX ROBERTSON, OLD POST OFFICE
44. DONALD ROBERTSON, PENTLAND HILL
45. DAVID SIMPSON, WEST SIDE
46. JOHN SINCLAIR, FALLAGOE
47. DAVID MANSON, BERRYHILL
48. JAMES ROBERTSON, THISTLE COTTAGE
49. MARY WARES, SOUTH END
50. WILLIAM SINCLAIR, DAISY HILL
51. DAVID SINCLAIR, RED GOE
52. DAVID ROBERTSON, HORSE GOE
53. ANDREW MANSON, HEATHER BELL
54. GEORGE WARES, WEST SIDE
56. WILLIAM SINCLAIR, WEST SIDE
57. DONALD ROBERTSON, BEACON

58. ANDREW MANSON, WEST SIDE
59. WILLIAM SINCLAIR, THE CAIRN
60. MARY BANKS, EAST SIDE
61. JOE McCAUGHEY, EAST SIDE
62. BAPTIST CHAPEL
63. JAMES ROBERTSON, CLETTACK
64. SINCLAIR MANSON
    & ANDREW MANSON, EAST SIDE
    (Last to leave)
65. DONALD WARES, EAST SIDE
66. JOHN SINCLAIR, SCARTAN
67. JIM SMITH, THE HAVEN
68. MAGGIE ROBERTSON, SHOP, SOUTH END
69. SAIL SHED, SOUTH END
70. WILLIAM NORQUOY, THE LOCH
71. GEORGE ALLAN, THE LOCH

REPRODUCED FROM A MAP DRAWN BY WM. J. SINCLAIR, WEST SIDE, STROMA
THE LAST CROFT HOLDERS AND OTHER NUMBERED NAMES (c.1950) SUPPLIED BY THE LATE PAT SIMPSON OF CANISBAY
AND ADDRESSES BY ELIZABETH BRUCE, BELLEVUE, HUNA.

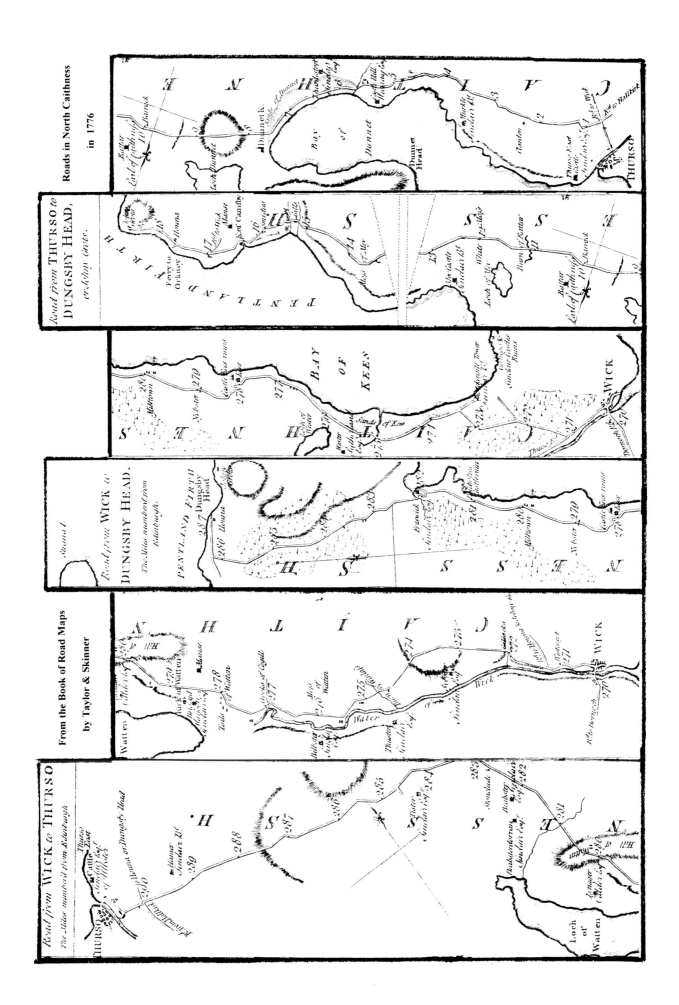

Roads in North Caithness
in 1776

Road from THURSO to
DUNGSBY HEAD,
or John Grots.

Road from WICK to
DUNGSBY HEAD.
The Miles numbered from
Edinburgh.

From the Book of Road Maps

by Taylor & Skinner

Road from WICK to THURSO
The Miles numbered from Edinburgh.

INDEX OF AUTHORS